T0297594

JOE CELKO'S
SQL FOR SMARTIES

JOE CELKO'S SQL FOR SMARTIES ADVANCED SQL PROGRAMMING

FIFTH EDITION

Joe Celko

Executive Editor: Steven Elliot
Development Editor: Kaitlin Herbert
Project Manager: Punithavathy Govindaradjane
Designer: Mark Rogers

Morgan Kaufmann is an imprint of Elsevier
225 Wyman Street, Waltham, MA 02451, USA

ISBN: 978-0-12-800761-7

British Library Cataloguing-in-Publication Data
A catalogue record for this book is available from the British Library

Library of Congress Cataloging-in-Publication Data
A catalogue record for this book is available from the Library of Congress

For information on all MK publications
visit our web site at www.mkp.com

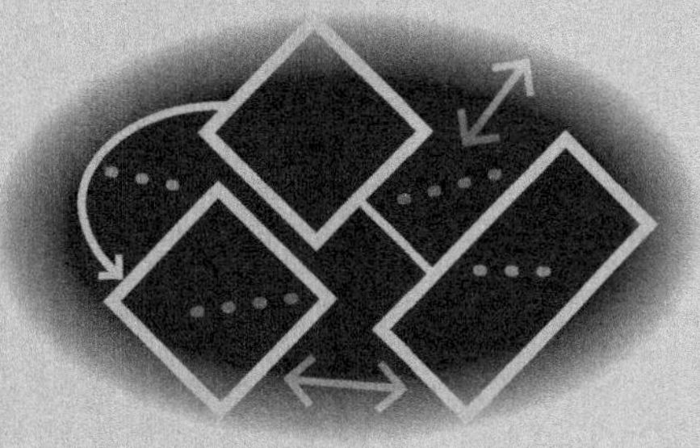

To Ann and Jackers

C O N T E N T S

INTRODUCTION TO THE FIFTH EDITION

This is not an introductory book. This book, like the editions before it, is for the working SQL programmer who wants to pick up some advanced SQL techniques and programming idioms. I put programming tips for newbies into their own book (*SQL Programming Style*, Morgan-Kaufmann, 2005, ISBN: 978-0120887972) because this book is an advanced programmer's book and I assume that the reader is now writing real SQL, not some dialect or his native programming language in a thin disguise. I also assume that he or she can translate Standard SQL into their local dialect without much effort.

I have tried to provide comments with the solutions, to explain why they work. I hope this will help the reader see underlying principles that can be used in other situations.

The first edition was published in 1995 and became a minor classic among working SQL programmers. I have seen copies of this book on the desks of real programmers in real programming shops almost everywhere I have been. The true compliment is the Post-it notes sticking out of the top. People really use it often enough to put stickies in it! Wow!

What is New in this Edition

The ANSI/ISO Standard is revised every 5 years. The prior standards were SQL-86, SQL-89, SQL-92, SQL:1999, SQL:2003, SQL:2008, and SQL:2011. The SQL-86 Standard was a crude effort to lock down the language, so it would not drift into dialects like BASIC did. The SQL-92 and SQL-99 were the first "workable" standards for production work. The vendors had joined the ANSI X3H2 Committee (now INCIT H2) and agreed to align with the standards. This made SQL one of the easiest languages to port from product to product. The standards that followed kept the tradition. However, like COBOL, committees tend to add lots of features over time. Sometimes, it is "feature bloat" to no good purpose (to parody an old television advertisement for a kitchen gizmo, "It slices, dices, rapes, and pillages!"), but most of them have come from actual user needs. Declarative languages like SQL tend to evolve by looking for common patterns in procedural code and then putting them into a construct. For example, 80-90% of the actual procedural code in TRIGGERs was used to reenforce the data integrity constraints that we do with "ON [DELETE | UPDATE] CASCADE" clauses today. The difference is that the declarative code can be optimized and implemented anyway that works.

I have edited old solutions that can now be done with new features. I have added new idioms and solutions.

Hierarchical and network databases still run vital legacy systems in major corporations. SQL people do not like to admit it. The new NoSQL flavors are now more than a fad for big data on the web (see *Joe Celko's Complete Guide to NoSQL: What Every SQL Professional Needs to Know About Non-Relational Databases*, Morgan Kaufmann, 2013, ISBN: 978-0124071926). SQL people do not like to admit this either!

The SQL programmer's revenge is that SQL has become the COBOL of database, and the Relational Model is the basis for the way that we think of data. It is everywhere and we still write a lot of it. In fact, the Relational Model is such a dominant model of data and SQL the language of data, the NoSQL products keep adding SQL-like front ends! The victory of SELECT-FROM-WHERE!

Corrections and Additions

Please send any corrections, additions, suggestions, improvements, or alternative solutions to me or to the publisher. I am easy to find on the internet. Especially if you have a better way of doing something.

Data Declaration Features

Databases Versus File Systems

It ain't so much the things we don't know that get us in trouble. It's the things we know that ain't so.—Artemus Ward (William Graham Sumner), American Writer and Humorist, 1834-1867

Perfecting oneself is as much unlearning as it is learning—Edsgar Dijkstra

If you already have a background in data processing with traditional file systems, the first things to unlearn are

(0) Databases are not file sets.

(1) Tables are not files.

(2) Rows are not records.

(3) Columns are not fields.

(4) Values in RDBMS are scalar, not structured (arrays, lists, meta-data).

Do not feel ashamed of getting stuck in a conceptual rut; every new technology has this problem.

The US standard railroad gauge (distance between the rails) is 4 ft, 8.5 in. This gauge is used because the English built railroads to that gauge and US railroads were built by English expatriates.

Why did the English build railroads to that gauge? Because the first rail lines were built by the same people who built the pre-railroad tramways, and

that's the gauge they used. Why did those wheelwrights use that gauge then? Because the people who built the horse-drawn trams used the same jigs and tools that they used for building wagons, which used that wheel spacing.

Why did the wagons use that odd wheel spacing? For the practical reason that any other spacing would break an axle on some of the old, long distance roads, because this is the measure of the old wheel ruts.

So who built these old rutted roads? The first long distance roads in Europe were built by Imperial Rome for their legions and used ever since. The initial ruts were first made by Roman war chariots, which were of uniform military issue. The Imperial Roman chariots were made to be just wide enough to accommodate the back-ends of two war horses (this example is originally due to Professor Tom O'Hare, Germanic Languages, University of Texas at Austin; email: tohare@mail.utexas.edu).

This story does not end there, however. Look at a NASA Space Shuttle and the two big booster rockets attached to the sides of the main fuel tank. These are solid rocket boosters or SRBs. The SRBs are made by Thiokol at their factory at Utah. The engineers who designed the SRBs might have preferred to make them a bit fatter, but the SRBs had to be shipped by train from the factory to the launch site in Florida. The railroad line from the factory runs through a tunnel in the mountains and the SRBs have to fit through that tunnel. The tunnel is slightly wider than the railroad track. So, the major design feature of what is arguably the world's most advanced transportation system was determined by the width of a horse's ass.

In a similar fashion, modern data processing began with punch cards (Hollerith cards if you are *really* old) used by the Bureau of the Census. Their original size was that of a US dollar bill. This was set by their inventor, Herman Hollerith, because he could get furniture to store the cards from the US Treasury Department, just across the street. Likewise, physical constraints limited each card to 80 columns of holes in which to record a symbol.

The influence of the punch card lingered on long after the invention of magnetic tapes and disk for data storage. This is why early video display terminals were 80 columns across. Even today, files which were migrated from cards to magnetic tape files or disk storage still use 80 column physical records.

But the influence was not just on the physical side of data processing. The methods for handling data from the prior media were imitated in the new media.

Data processing first consisted of sorting and merging decks of punch cards (later, sequential magnetic tape files) in a series of distinct steps. The result of each step feed into the next step in the process. Think of the assembly line in a factory.

Databases and RDBMS in particular are nothing like the file systems that came with COBOL, FORTRAN, C, BASIC, PL/I, Java, or any of the procedural and OO programming languages. We used to say that SQL means "Scarcely Qualifies as a Language" because it has no I/O of its own. SQL depends on a host language to get and receive data to and from end users.

1.1 The Schema Statement

Programming languages are usually based on some underlying model; if you understand the model, the language makes much more sense. For example, FORTRAN is based on algebra. This does not mean that FORTRAN is exactly like algebra. But if you know algebra, FORTRAN does not look all that strange to you the way that LISP or APL would. You can write an expression in an assignment statement or make a good guess as to the names of library functions you have never seen before.

Likewise, COBOL is based on English narratives of business processes. The design of COBOL files (and almost every other early programming language) was derived from paper forms. The most primitive form of a file is a sequence of records that are ordered within the file and referenced by physical position.

You open a file (think file folder or in-basket on your desk) and then read a first record (think of the first paper form on the stack), followed by a series of next records (process the stack of paperwork, one paper form at a time) until you come to the last record to raise the end-of-file condition (put the file folder in the out-basket). Notice the work flow:

1. The records (paper forms) have to *physically exist* to be processed. Files are not virtual by nature. In fact, this mindset is best expressed by a quote from Samuel Goldwyn "a verbal contract ain't worth the paper it is written on!"

2. You navigate among these records and perform actions, one record at a time. You can go backward or forward in the stack but nowhere else.

3. The actions you take on one file (think of a clerk with rubber stamps) have no effect on other files that are not in the same program. The files are like file folders in another in-basket.

4. Only programs (the clerk processing the paperwork) can change files. The in-basket will not pick up a rubber stamp and mark the papers by itself.

The model for SQL is data kept in abstract sets, not in physical files. The "unit of work" in SQL is the *whole schema*, not individual tables. This is a *totally different* model of work! Sets are those mathematical abstractions you studied in school. Sets are not ordered and the members of a set are all of the same type. When you do an operation on a set, the action happens "all at once" to the *entire membership*. That is, if I ask for the subset of odd numbers from the set of positive integers, I get *all them* back as a single set. I do not build the set of odd numbers by sequentially inspecting one element at a time. I define odd numbers with a rule—"If the remainder is ±1 when you divide the number by 2, it is odd"—that could test any integer and classify it. Parallel processing is one of many, many advantages of having a set-oriented model. In RDBMS, everything happens all at once.

The Data Declaration Language (DDL) in SQL is what defines and controls access to the database content and maintains the integrity of that data for *all* programs that access the database. Data in a file is passive. It has no meaning until a program reads it. In COBOL, *each* program has a `DATA DIVISION;` in FORTRAN, each program has the `FORMAT/READ` statements; in Pascal, there is a RECORD declaration that serves the same purpose. Pick your non-SQL language.

These constructs provide a template or parsing rules to overlay upon the records in the file, split them into fields and get the data into the host program. Each program can split up the sequence of characters in a record anyway it wishes name and name the fields as it wished. This can lead to "job security" programming; I worked in a shop in the 1970's where one programmer would pick a theme (nations of the world, flowers, etc.) and name his fields "Afghanistan" or "Chrysanthemum" or worse. Nobody could read his code, so we could not fire him.

Likewise, the Data Control Language (DCL) controls access to the schema objects that a user can create. Standard SQL divides the database users into USER and ADMIN roles. These schema objects require ADMIN privileges to be created, altered, or dropped (CREATE, ALTER, DROP, etc.). Those with USER privileges can invoke the schema objects with UPDATE, DELETE,

INSERT, SELECT, and other statements that work with the *data* but not the *structure* of the schema.

I do not spend much time on DCL in this book, since I deal with the USER (programmer), but the basic model is that the ADMIN level can grant or revoke privileges on schema objects to USERs. This USER can also grant or revoke his privileges to other users at lower levels, if his admin allowed it. If this chain of privileges is broken at any level, the users at lower levels no longer have those privileges. The principle is that access privileges flow downhill.

There is no such access model in a file system. Traditionally, access control is external to a file system at the operating system level. Neither SQL nor file systems can be concerned with security; encryption, elaborate passwords, etc. are all external to the data.

There is a CREATE SCHEMA statement defined in the standards which brings an entire schema into existence all at once. In practice, each product has very different utility programs to allocate physical storage and define a schema. Much of the proprietary syntax is concerned with physical storage allocations.

A schema must have a name and a default character set, usually ASCII or a simple Latin alphabet as defined in the ISO Standards. There is an optional AUTHORIZATION clause that holds a <schema authorization identifier> for security. After that the schema is a list of schema elements:

```
<schema element> ::=
 <domain definition> | <table definition> | <view definition>
 | <grant statement> | <assertion definition>
 | <character set definition>
 | <collation definition> | <translation definition>
```

A schema is the skeleton of an SQL database; it defines the structures of the schema objects and the rules under which they operate. The data is the meat on that skeleton.

The only data structure in SQL is the table. Tables can be persistent (base tables), used for working storage (temporary tables), or virtual (VIEWs, common table expressions, and derived tables). The differences among these types are in implementation, not performance. One advantage of having only one data structure is that the results of all operations are also tables—you never have to convert structures, write special operators, or deal with any irregularity in the language.

The <grant statement> has to do with limiting access by users to only certain schema elements. The <assertion definition> is still not widely implemented yet, but it is like a constraint that applies to the schema as a whole. Finally, the <character set definition>, <collation definition>, and <translation definition> deal with the display of data. We are not really concerned with any of these schema objects; they are usually set in place by the DBA (Database Administrator) for the users and we mere programmers do not get to change them.

Conceptually, a table is a set of zero or more rows, and a row is a set of one or more columns. This hierarchy is important; actions apply at the schema, table, row, or column level. For example, the DELETE FROM statement removes rows, not columns, and leaves the base table in the schema. You cannot delete a column from a row.

Each column has a specific data type and constraints that make up an implementation of an abstract domain. The way a table is physically implemented does not matter, because you access it only with SQL. The database engine handles all the details for you and you never worry about the internals as you would with a physical file. In fact, almost no two SQL products use the same internal structures.

There are two common conceptual errors made by programmers who are accustomed to file systems or PCs. The first is thinking that a table is a file; the second is thinking that a table is a spreadsheet. Tables do not behave like either one of these, and you will get surprises if you do not understand the basic concepts.

It is easy to imagine that a table is a file, a row is a record, and a column is a field. This is familiar and when data moves from SQL to the host language, it has to be converted into host language data types and data structures to be displayed and used. The host languages have file systems built into them.

The big differences between working with a file system and working with SQL are in the way SQL fits into a host program. Using a file system, your programs must open and close files individually. In SQL, the *whole* schema is connected to or disconnected from the program as a single unit. The host program might not be authorized to see or manipulate all of the tables and other schema objects, but that is established as part of the connection.

The program defines fields within a file, whereas SQL defines its columns in the schema. FORTRAN uses the FORMAT and READ statements to get data from a file. Likewise, a COBOL program uses a Data Division to define the fields and a READ to fetch it. And so on for every 3GL's programming, the concept is the same, though the syntax and options vary.

A file system lets you reference the same data by a different name in each program. If a file's layout changes, you must rewrite all the programs that use that file. When a file is empty, it looks exactly like all other empty files. When you try to read an empty file, the EOF (end of file) flag pops up and the program takes some action. Column names and data types in a table are defined within the database schema. Within reasonable limits, the tables can be changed without the knowledge of the host program.

The host program only worries about transferring the values to its own variables from the database. Remember the empty set from your high school math class? It is still a valid set. When a table is empty, it still has columns but has zero rows. There is no EOF flag to signal an exception, because there is no final record.

Another major difference is that tables and columns can have constraints attached to them. A constraint is a rule that defines what must be true about the database after each transaction. In this sense, a database is more like a collection of objects than a traditional passive file system.

A table is not a spreadsheet, even though they look very much alike when you view them on a screen or in a printout. In a spreadsheet you can access a row, a column, a cell, or a collection of cells by navigating with a cursor. A table has no concept of navigation. Cells in a spreadsheet can store instructions and not just data. There is no real difference between a row and a column in a spreadsheet; you could flip them around completely and still get valid results. This is not true for an SQL table.

The only underlying commonality is that a spreadsheet is also a declarative programming language. It just happens to be a nonlinear language.

The schema model is that the data is separate from the programs using it. The database system maintains the integrity of that data. This has a lot of implications. There must be universal names for data elements; a uniform set of data element rules enforced by the "active storage management" system are part of the database.

Data in files has no integrity constraints, default values, or relationships among other files or even in the same file.

Another conceptual difference is that a file is usually data that deals with a whole business process. A file has to have enough data in itself to support *applications for that one business process*. Files tend to be "mixed" data which can be described by the name of the business process, such as "The Payroll

file" or something like that. Tables can be either entities or relationships within a business process. This means that the data which was held in one file is often put into several tables. Tables tend to be "pure" data which can be described by single words. The payroll would now have separate tables for Personnel, Projects, and the relationship between those two things, timecards.

1.2 Tables as Entities

An entity is a physical or conceptual "thing" which has meaning by itself. A person, a sale, or a product would be an example. In a relational database, an entity is defined by its attributes, which are shown as values in columns in rows in a table.

To remind users that tables are sets of entities, ISO-11179 Standard likes to use collective or plural nouns that describe the set of those entities for the names of tables. Thus "Employee" is a bad name because it is singular; "Employees" is a better name because it is plural; "Personnel" is best because it is collective. Imagine the characters of DILBERT!

If you have tables with exactly the same structure, then they are sets of the same kind of elements. But you should have only one set for each kind of data element! Files, on the other hand, were *physically* separate units of storage which could be alike—each tape or disk file represents a step in the `PROCEDURE`, such as moving from raw data, to edited data, and finally to archived data. In SQL, this should be a status flag in a table.

1.3 Tables as Relationships

A relationship is shown in a table by columns which reference one or more entity tables. It can include attributes of the relationships.

Without the entities, the relationship has no meaning, but the relationship can have attributes of its own. For example, a show business contract might have an agent, an employer, and a talent. The method of payment (percentage of sales, foreign royalties, etc.) is an attribute of the contract itself and not of any of the three parties. This means that a column can have a REFERENCE to other tables. Files and fields do not do that.

1.3.1 E-R Diagrams

Peter Chen's 1976 paper in *ACM Transactions on Database Systems* introduced the most popular variant of the idea of Entity-Relationship modeling and diagramming. The advantage of the *simple version* of this diagramming technique is that it is fast, easy, and can be read without special training. This makes it a good mind tool for explaining an RDBMS schema to users … or yourself.

The symbols are rectangles for entities, diamonds for relationships, and lines to connect them. The rules are easy to understand; each relationship connects to its entities; no two entities connect directly to each other; and no two relationships directly connect to each other.

The connectors explain the relationship. Initially, we use straight lines just to show something is there. After that, we can add terminator symbols to the lines. This is easier to show with a diagram than with a narrative.

Cardinality constraints are expressed with graphic symbols for the minimal and maximal elements.

- A vertical line means one member of the entity set has to be involved (think one).
- A circle means no member of the entity set has to be involved (think zero).
- A "crow's foot" means many members of the entity set have to be involved (think of a small child holding up bunch of finger, saying "many!"). This is used in Barker's Notation, SSADM, and Information Engineering.

This diagram says that "at least one or more authors write zero or more books" in the data model. And yes, you can be listed as an author without doing anything on a particular book. In the book business, "Gloria Glamor's True Story" as told to Ghenta Ghostwriter will list both Gloria and Ghenta as authors.

This diagram says "one or more authors must write *exactly one book, no more no less*" in the notation.

There are many E-R diagramming tools with different graphic conventions, free and commercial, but my point is that even a simple "pen and paper" tool helps. The "slash-circle-crows-foot" maps easily into SQL's REFERENCES clauses declarative referential integrity (DRI) constraints.

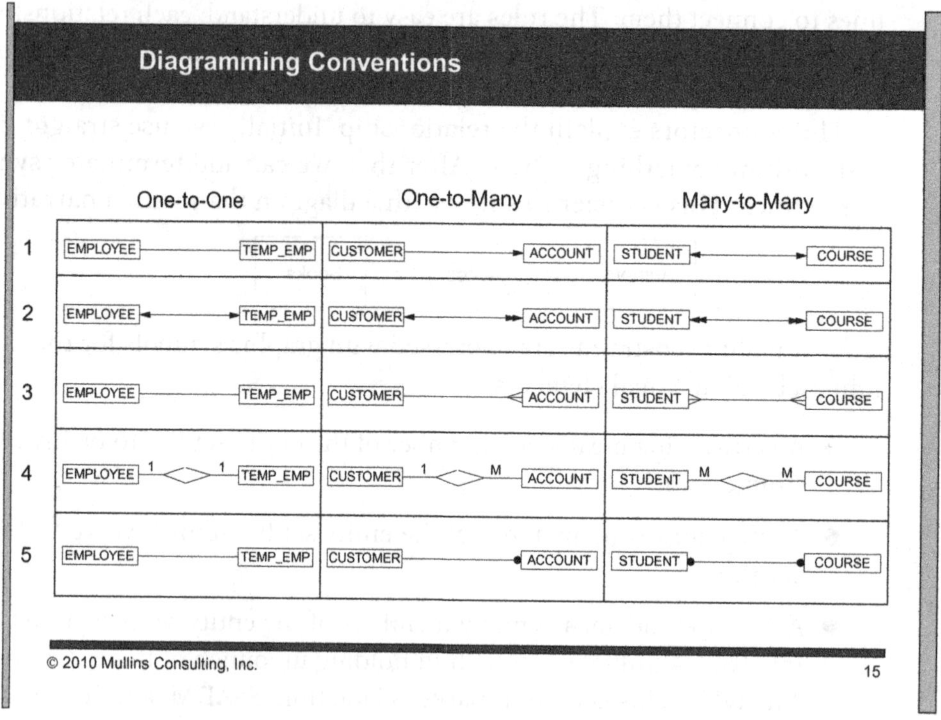

Chen proposed the following "rules of thumb" for mapping natural language descriptions into ER diagrams:

Proper noun	Entity
Transitive verb	Relationship
Intransitive verb	Attribute
Adjective	Attribute for entity
Adverb	Attribute for relationship

1.4 Rows Versus Records

To reiterate, rows are not records. A record is defined in the application program which reads it; a row is named and defined in the DDL of the database schema and not by a program at all. The names of the fields are in the READ or INPUT statements of the application. Likewise, the PHYSICAL order of the fields in the READ statement is vital ("READ a,b,c;" is not the same as "READ c, a, b;"; but "SELECT a,b,c FROM Foobar;" is the same data as "SELECT c, a, b FROM Foobar;" in SQL).

All empty files look alike; they are a directory entry in the operating system with a name and a length of zero bytes of storage. But empty tables still have columns, constraints, security privileges, and other structures, even though they have no rows.

This is in keeping with the set theoretical model, in which the empty set is a perfectly good set. The difference between SQL's set model and standard mathematical set theory is that set theory has only one empty set, but in SQL each table has a different structure, so they cannot be used in places where nonempty versions of themselves could not be used.

Another characteristic of rows in a table is that they are all alike in structure and they are all the "same kind of thing" in the model. In a file system, records can vary in size, data types, and structure by having flags in the data stream that tell the program reading the data how to interpret it. The most common examples are Pascal's variant record, C's struct syntax, and COBOL's OCCURS clause.

The OCCURS keyword in COBOL and the VARIANT records in Pascal have a number which tells the program how many time a subrecord structure is to be repeated in the current record.

Unions in "C" are not variant records but variant mappings for the same physical memory. For example:

```
union x {int ival; char j[4];} mystuff;
```

defines mystuff to be either an integer (which are 4 bytes on most C compilers, but this code is nonportable) or an array of 4 bytes, depending on whether you say mystuff.ival or mystuff.j[0];

But even more than that, files often contained records which were summaries of subsets of the other records—so-called control break reports. There is no requirement that the records in a file be related in any way—they are literally a stream of binary data whose meaning is assigned by the program reading them.

1.5 Columns Versus Fields

A field within a record is defined by the application program that reads it. A column in a row in a table is defined by the database schema. The data types in a column are always scalar.

The order of the application program variables in the READ or INPUT statements is important because the values are read into the program variables in that order. In SQL, columns are referenced only by their names. Yes, there are shorthands like the SELECT * clause and INSERT INTO <table name> statements which expand into a list of column names in the physical order in which the column names appear within their table declaration, but these are shorthands which resolve to named lists.

The use of NULLs in SQL is also unique to the language. Fields do not support a missing data marker as part of the field, record, or file itself. Nor do fields have constraints which can be added to them in the record, like the DEFAULT and CHECK() clauses in SQL.

Files are pretty passive creatures and will take whatever an application program throws at them without much objection. Files are also independent of each other simply because they are connected to one application program at a time and therefore have no idea what other files look like.

A database actively seeks to maintain the correctness of all its data. The methods used are triggers, constraints, and DRI.

DRI says, in effect, that data in one table has a particular relationship with data in a second (possibly the same) table. It is also possible to have the database change itself via referential actions associated with the DRI.

For example, a business rule might be that we do not sell products which are not in inventory.

This rule would be enforced by a REFERENCES clause on the Orders table which references the Inventory table and a referential action of ON DELETE CASCADE. Triggers are a more general way of doing much the same thing as DRI. A trigger is a block of procedural code which is executed before, after, or instead of an INSERT INTO or UPDATE statement. You can do anything with a trigger that you can do with DRI and more.

However, there are problems with triggers. While there is a standard syntax for them since the SQL-92 standard, most vendors have not implemented it. What they have is very proprietary syntax instead. Secondly, a trigger cannot pass information to the optimizer like DRI. In the example in this section, I know that for every product number in the Orders table,

I have that same product number in the Inventory table. The optimizer can use that information in setting up EXISTS() predicates and JOINs in the queries. There is no reasonable way to parse procedural trigger code to determine this relationship.

The CREATE ASSERTION statement in SQL-92 will allow the database to enforce conditions on the entire database as a whole. An ASSERTION is like a CHECK() clause, but the difference is subtle. A CHECK() clause is executed when there are rows in the table to which it is attached.

If the table is empty, then all CHECK() clauses are effectively TRUE. Thus, if we wanted to be sure that the Inventory table is never empty, and we wrote:

```
CREATE TABLE Inventory
( . . .
 CONSTRAINT inventory_not_empty
 CHECK ((SELECT COUNT(*) FROM Inventory) > 0),
 . . . );
```

it would not work. However, we could write:

```
CREATE ASSERTION Inventory_not_empty
CHECK ((SELECT COUNT(*) FROM Inventory) > 0);
```

and we would get the desired results. The assertion is checked at the schema level and not at the table level.

I tell students that most of the work in SQL is in the DDL and not the DML. Unlike a field, a column can have all of these constraints on your data and keep them in one place, one way, and one time.

Transactions and Concurrency Control

IN THE OLD days when we lived in caves and used steam-powered mainframe computers with batch file systems, transaction processing was easy. You batched up the transactions to be made against the master file into a transaction file. The transaction file was sorted, edited, and ready to go when you ran it against the master file from a tape drive. The output of this process became the new master file, and the old master file and the transaction file tapes went into a huge closet in the basement of the company.

Scheduling batch jobs was an external activity. You submitted a job, it went into a queue, and a scheduler decided when it would be run. The system told an operator (yes, this is a separate job!) which tapes to hang on, what paper forms to load into a printer, and all the physical details. When a job is finished, the scheduler has to release the resources so that following jobs can use them.

A simple queue will always finish, but we want to change the sequence of jobs to reflect the higher priority of some jobs. Getting the payroll out is more important than running a company sports team calendar.

A job might not finish if other jobs are constantly assigned a more immediate, lower priority number in the queue. This is called a "live lock" problem. Think of the runt of a litter of pigs always being pushed away from its mother by the other piglets. He never gets to be piglet #1. One solution is to decrease the priority number of a job when it has been waiting for (n)

seconds in queue until it eventually gets to the first position at the front to be processed.

If two jobs, J1 and J2, both want to use resources A and B, we can get a dead lock situation. Job J1 grabs resource A and waits for resource B; Job J2 grabs resource B and waits for resource A. They sit and wait forever, unless one or both of the jobs releases its resource or we can find another copy of one of the resources.

2.1 Sessions

The concept of a user session involves the user first connecting to the database. This is like dialing a phone number, but with a password, to get to the database. The Standard SQL syntax for this statement is:

```
CONNECT TO <connection target>
<connection target> ::=
 <SQL-server name>
 [AS <connection name>]
 [USER <user name>]
 | DEFAULT
```

but you will find many differences in vendor SQL products and perhaps operating system level log on procedures that have to be followed.

Once the connection is established, the user has access to all the parts of the database to which he has been granted privileges in the DCL. During this session, he can execute zero or more transactions. As one user inserts, updates, and deletes rows in the database, these changes are not made a permanent part of the database until that user or the system issues a COMMIT [WORK] statement for that transaction.

However, if the user does not want to make the changes permanent, then he can issue a ROLLBACK [WORK] statement and the database stays as it was before the transaction.

2.2 Transactions and ACID

The late Jim Grey invented modern transaction processing in the 1970s and put it in the classic paper "The Transaction Concept: Virtues and Limitations" in June 1981. This is where the ACID acronym started. Grey's paper discussed the terms Atomicity, Consistency, and Durability;

Isolation was added later. Bruce Lindsay et al.[1] wrote the paper "Notes on Distributed Databases" in 1979 that built upon Grey's work, laying down the fundamentals for achieving consistency and the primary standards for database replication. In 1983, Andreas Reuter and Theo Härder published the paper "Principles of Transaction-Oriented Database Recovery" and coined the term ACID. There is a handy mnemonic for the four characteristics we want in a transaction: the ACID properties. The initials are short for four properties we have to have in a transaction processing system.

(1) Atomicity: This means that the whole transaction becomes persistent in the database or nothing in the transaction becomes persistent. The data becomes persistent in Standard SQL when a COMMIT statement is successfully executed. A ROLLBACK statement removes the transaction and the database restored to its prior (consistent) state before the transaction began.

The COMMIT or ROLLBACK statement can be explicitly executed by the user or by the database engine when it finds an error. Most SQL engines default to a ROLLBACK, unless it is configured to do otherwise.

Atomicity means that if I were to try to insert one million rows into a table and one row of that million violated a referential constraint, then the whole set of one million rows would be rejected and the database would do an automatic ROLLBACK.

Here is the trade-off. If you do one long transaction, then you are in danger of being halted by just one tiny little error. However, if you do several short transactions in a session, then other users can have access to the database between your transactions and they might change things much to your surprise.

The solution has been to implement SAVEPOINT or CHECKPOINT option that acts much like a bookmark. The CHECKPOINT is a local COMMIT, while the SAVEPOINT is a bookmark. This model comes from IMS systems. A transaction sets savepoints during its execution and lets the transaction to perform a local rollback to the checkpoint. In our example, we might have been doing savepoints every 1000 rows. When the 999,999th row inserted has an error that would have caused a ROLLBACK, the database engine removes only the work done after the last savepoint was set and the transaction is restored to the state of uncommitted work (i.e., rows 1 through 999,000) that existed before the savepoint.

---

[1] Bruce Lindsay et al., "Notes on Distributed Databases," Research Report RJ2571(33471), IBM Research, July 1979.

You will need to look at your particular SQL product to see if it has something like this. The usual alternatives are to break the work into chunks that are run as transactions with a host program or to use an ETL tool that scrubs the data completely before loading it into the database.

(2) Consistency: When the transaction starts, the database is in a consistent state and when it becomes persistent in the database, the database is in a consistent state. The phrase "consistent state" means that all of the data integrity constraints, relational integrity constraints, and any other constraints are true.

However, this does not mean that the database might not go through an inconsistent state during the transaction. Standard SQL has the ability to declare a constraint to be DEFERRABLE or NOT DEFERRABLE for finer control of a transaction. *But the rule is that all constraints have to be true at the end of session.* This can be tricky when the transaction has multiple statements or fires triggers that affect other tables.

(3) Isolation: One transaction is isolated from all other transactions. Isolation is also called serializability because it means that transactions act as if they were executed in isolation of each other in a queue. One way to guarantee isolation is to use serial execution like we had in batch systems. In practice, this might not be a good idea, so the system has to decide how to interleave the transactions to get the same effect.

This actually becomes more complicated in practice because one transaction may or may not actually see the data inserted, updated, or deleted by another transaction. This will be dealt with in detail in the section on isolation levels.

(4) Durability: The database is stored on a durable media so that if the database program is destroyed, the database itself persists. Furthermore, the database can be restored to a consistent state when the database system is restored. Log files and backup procedure figure into this property, as well as disk writes are done during processing.

This is all well and good if you have just one user accessing the database at a time. But one of the reasons you have a database system is that you also have multiple users who want to access it at the same time in their own sessions. This leads us to concurrency control.

2.3 Concurrency Control

Concurrency control is the part of transaction handling which deals with how multiple users access the shared database without running into each other—like a traffic light system. One way to avoid any problems is to allow only one user in the database at a time. The only problem with that solution is that the other users are going to get lousy response time. Can you seriously imagine doing that with a bank teller machine system or an airline reservation system where tens of thousands of users are waiting to get into the system at the same time in a queue?

2.3.1 The Transaction Phenomena

If all you do is execute queries against the database, then the ACID properties hold. The trouble occurs when two or more transactions want to change the database at the same time. In the SQL model, there are several ways that one transaction can affect another.

P0 (Dirty Write): Transaction T1 modifies a data item. Another transaction T2 then further modifies that data item before T1 performs a COMMIT or ROLLBACK. If T1 or T2 then performs a ROLLBACK, it is unclear what the correct data value should be. One reason why Dirty Writes are bad is that they can violate database consistency. Assume there is a constraint between x and y (e.g., $x = y$), and T1 and T2 each maintain the consistency of the constraint if run alone. However, the constraint can easily be violated if the two transactions write x and y in different orders, which can only happen if there are Dirty Writes.

P1 (Dirty read): Transaction T1 modifies a row. Transaction T2 then reads that row before T1 performs a COMMIT. If T1 then performs a ROLLBACK, T2 will have read a row that was never committed and that may thus be considered to have never existed.

P2 (Nonrepeatable read): Transaction T1 reads a row. Transaction T2 then modifies or deletes that row and performs a COMMIT. If T1 then attempts to reread the row, it may receive the modified value or discover that the row has been deleted.

P3 (Phantom): Transaction T1 reads the set of rows N that satisfies some <search condition>. Transaction T2 then executes statements that generate one or more rows that satisfy the <search condition> used by transaction T1. If transaction T1 then repeats the initial read with the same <search condition>, it obtains a different collection of rows.

P4 (Lost Update): The lost update anomaly occurs when transaction T1 reads a data item and then T2 updates the data item (possibly based on a previous read), then T1 (based on its earlier read value) updates the data item and COMMITs.

These phenomena are not always bad things. If the database is being used only for queries, without any changes being made during the workday, then none of these problems will occur. The database system will run much faster if you do not have to try to protect yourself from them. They are also acceptable when changes are being made under certain circumstances.

Imagine that I have a table of all the cars in the world. I want to execute a query to find the average age of drivers of red sport cars. This query will take some time to run and during that time, cars will be crashed, bought and sold, new cars will be built, and so forth. But if I accept a situation with the transaction phenomena because the *average* age will not change that much from the time the query starts to the time it finishes. Changes to the data set after the second decimal place of the average really don't matter.

However, you don't want any of these phenomena to occur in a database where the husband makes a deposit to a joint account and his wife makes a withdrawal. This leads us to the transaction isolation levels.

The original ANSI model included only P1, P2, and P3. The other definitions first appeared in Microsoft Research Technical Report: MSR-TR-95-51 "A Critique of ANSI SQL Isolation Levels" by Hal Berenson, Phil Bernstein, Jim Gray, Jim Melton, Elizabeth O'Neil, and Patrick O'Neil (1995).

2.4 The Isolation Levels

In Standard SQL, the user gets to set the isolation level of the transactions in this session. The basic isolation level avoids some of the phenomena we just talked about and gives other information to the database. The syntax for the <set transaction statement>

```
SET TRANSACTION <transaction mode list>

<transaction mode> ::=
 <isolation level>
```

```
 | <transaction access mode>
 | <diagnostics size>

<diagnostics size> ::= DIAGNOSTICS SIZE <number of conditions>

<transaction access mode> ::= READ ONLY | READ WRITE

<isolation level> ::= ISOLATION LEVEL <level of isolation>

<level of isolation> ::=
  READ UNCOMMITTED
  | READ COMMITTED
  | REPEATABLE READ
  | SERIALIZABLE
```

The optional <diagnostics size> clause tells the database to set up a list for error messages of a given size. The reason is that a single statement can have several errors in it and the engine is supposed to find them all and report them in the diagnostics area via a GET DIAGNOSTICS statement in the host program.

The <transaction access mode> explains itself. The READ ONLY option means that this is a query and lets the SQL engine know that it can relax a bit. The READ WRITE option lets the SQL engine know that rows might be changed and that it has to watch out for the three phenomena.

The important clause, which is implemented in most current SQL products, is the <isolation level> clause. The isolation level of a transaction defines the degree to which the operations of one transaction are affected by concurrent transactions. The isolation level of a transaction is SERIALIZABLE by default, but the user can explicitly set it in the <set transaction statement>.

The isolation levels each guarantee that each transaction will be executed completely or not at all, and that no updates will be lost. The SQL engine, when it detects the inability to guarantee the serializability of two or more concurrent transactions or when it detects unrecoverable errors, may initiate a ROLLBACK statement on its own.

Let's take a look at a table of the isolation levels and the three phenomena. A "Yes" means that the phenomena are possible under than isolation level:

Isolation Levels and Three Phenomena

Isolation level	P1	P2	P3
SERIALIZABLE	No	No	No
REPEATABLE READ	No	No	Yes
READ COMMITTED	No	Yes	Yes
READ UNCOMMITTED	Yes	Yes	Yes

The SERIALIZABLE isolation level is guaranteed to produce the same results as the concurrent transactions would have had if they had been done in some serial order. A serial execution is one in which each transaction executes to completion before the next transaction begins. The users act as if they are standing in a line waiting to get complete access to the database.

A REPEATABLE READ isolation level is guaranteed to maintain the same image of the database to the user during this session.

A READ COMMITTED isolation level will let transactions in this session see rows that other transactions commit while this session is running.

A READ UNCOMMITTED isolation level will let transactions in this session see rows that other transactions create without necessarily committing while this session is running.

Regardless of the isolation level of the transaction, phenomena P1, P2, and P3 shall not occur during the implied reading of schema definitions performed on behalf of executing a statement, the checking of integrity constraints, and the execution of referential actions associated with referential constraints. We do not want the schema itself changing on users.

Vendors add more levels to this basic one. IBM has a CURSOR STABILITY isolation level, extends READ COMMITTED locking behavior for SQL cursors by adding a new read action for FETCH from a cursor and requiring that a lock be held on the current item of the cursor. The lock is held until the cursor moves or is closed, possibly by a COMMIT. Naturally, the fetching transaction can update the row, and in that case a write lock will be held on the row until the transaction COMMITs, even after the cursor moves on with a subsequent FETCH. This makes CURSOR STABILITY stronger than READ COMMITTED and weaker than REPEATABLE READ.

CURSOR STABILITY is widely implemented by SQL systems to prevent lost updates for rows read via a cursor. READ COMMITTED, in some systems, is actually the stronger CURSOR STABILITY. The ANSI standard allows this.

The SQL standards do not say *how* you are to achieve these results. However, there are two basic classes of concurrency control methods—optimistic and pessimistic. Within those two classes, each vendor will have his own implementation.

2.5 Pessimistic Concurrency Control

Pessimistic concurrency control is based on the idea that transactions are expected to conflict with each other, so we need to design a system to avoid the problems before they start.

All pessimistic concurrency control schemes use locks. A lock is a flag placed in the database that gives exclusive access to a schema object to one user. Imagine an airplane toilet door, with its "occupied" sign.

The differences are the level of locking they use; setting those flags on and off costs time and resources. If you lock the whole database, then you have a serial batch processing system since only one transaction at a time is active. In practice you would do this only for system maintenance work on the whole database. If you lock at the table level, then performance can suffer because users must wait for the most common tables to become available. However, there are transactions which do involve the whole table and this will use only one flag.

If you lock the table at the row level, then other users can get to the rest of the table and you will have the best possible shared access. You will also have a huge number of flags to process and performance will suffer. This approach is generally not practical.

Page locking is in between table and row locking. This approach puts a lock on subsets of rows within the table, which include the desired values. The name comes from the fact that this is usually implemented with pages of physical disk storage. Performance depends on the statistical distribution of data in physical storage, but it is generally a good compromise.

2.6 SNAPSHOT Isolation Optimistic Concurrency

Optimistic concurrency control is based on the idea that transactions are not very likely to conflict with each other, so we need to design a system to handle the problems as exceptions after they actually occur.

In Snapshot Isolation, each transaction reads data from a snapshot of the (committed) data as of the time the transaction started, called its Start_Timestamp. This time may be any time before the transaction's first read.

A transaction running in Snapshot Isolation is never blocked attempting a read because it is working on its private copy of the data. But this means that at any time, each data item might have multiple versions, created by active and committed transactions.

When the transaction T1 is ready to commit, it gets a Commit-Timestamp, which is later than any existing start_timestamp or commit_timestamp. The transaction successfully COMMITs only if no other transaction T2 with a commit_timestamp in T1's execution interval [start_timestamp, commit_timestamp] wrote data that T1 also wrote. Otherwise, T1 will ROLLBACK. This "first committer wins" strategy prevents lost updates (phenomenon P4). When T1 COMMITs, its changes become visible to all transactions whose start_timestamps are larger than T1's commit-timestamp.

Snapshot isolation is nonserializable because a transaction's reads come at one instant and the writes at another. We assume we have several transactions working on the same data and a constraint that $(x+y)$ should be positive. Each transaction that writes a new value for x and y is expected to maintain the constraint. While T1 and T2 both act properly in isolation, the constraint fails to hold when you put them together. The possible problems are

A5 (Data Item Constraint Violation): Suppose constraint C is a database constraint between two data items x and y in the database. Here are two anomalies arising from constraint violation.

A5A Read Skew: Suppose transaction T1 reads x, and then a second transaction 2 updates x and y to new values and COMMITs. If now T1 reads y, it may see an inconsistent state, and therefore produce an inconsistent state as output.

A5B Write Skew: Suppose T1 reads x and y, which are consistent with constraint C, and then a T2 reads x and y, writes x, and COMMITs. Then T1 writes y. If there were a constraint between x and y, it might be violated.

Fuzzy Reads (P2): A degenerate form of Read Skew where $x=y$. More typically, a transaction reads two different but related items (e.g., referential integrity).

Write Skew (A5B): Could arise from a constraint at a bank, where account balances are allowed to go negative as long as the sum of commonly held balances remains nonnegative, with an anomaly arising as in history H5.

Clearly neither A5A nor A5B could arise in histories where P2 is precluded, since both A5A and A5B have T2 write a data item that has been previously read by an uncommitted T1. Thus, phenomena A5A and A5B are only useful for distinguishing isolation levels below REPEATABLE READ in strength.

The ANSI SQL definition of REPEATABLE READ, in its strict interpretation, captures a degenerate form of row constraints, but misses the general concept. To be specific, Locking REPEATABLE READ of Table 2.2 provides protection from Row Constraint Violations but the ANSI SQL definition of Table 2.1, forbidding anomalies A1 and A2, does not.

Returning now to Snapshot Isolation, it is surprisingly strong, even stronger than READ COMMITTED.

Table 2.1 ANSI SQL Isolation Levels Defined in Terms of the Three Original Phenomena

Isolation level	P0 (or A0) Dirty Write	P1 (or A1) Dirty Read	P2 (or A2) Fuzzy Read	P3 (or A3) Phantom
READ UNCOMMITTED	Not possible	Possible	Possible	Possible
READ COMMITTED	Not possible	Not possible	Possible	Possible
REPEATABLE READ	Not possible	Not possible	Not possible	Possible
SERIALIZABLE	Not possible	Not possible	Not possible	Not possible

Table 2.2 Degrees of Consistency and Locking Isolation Levels Defined in Terms of Locks

Consistency Level = locking Isolation Level	Read Locks on Data Items and Predicates (the same unless noted)	Write Locks on Data Items and Predicates (always the same)
Degree 0	None required	Well-formed writes
Degree 1 = locking Read uncommitted	None required	Well-formed writes Long duration Write locks
Degree 2 = locking Read committed	Well-formed reads short duration read locks (both)	Well-formed writes, long duration write locks
CURSOR STABILITY	Well-formed reads Read locks held on current of cursor Short duration read predicate locks	Well-formed writes Long duration write locks
Locking Repeatable read	Well-formed reads Long duration data item Read locks Short duration read Predicate locks	Well-formed writes Long duration Write locks
Degree 3 = locking serializable	Well-formed reads Long duration Read locks (both)	Well-formed writes Long duration Write locks

This approach predates databases by decades. It was implemented manually in the central records department of companies when they started storing data on microfilm. You do not get the microfilm, but instead they make a timestamped photocopy for you. You take the copy to your desk, mark it up, and return it to the central records department. The Central Records clerk timestamps your updated document, photographs it, and adds it to the end of the roll of microfilm.

But what if user number two also went to the central records department and got a timestamped photocopy of the same document? The Central Records clerk has to look at both timestamps and make a decision. If the first user attempts to put his updates into the database while the second user is still working on his copy, then the clerk has to either hold the first copy or wait for the second copy to show up or to return it to the first user. When both copies are in hand, the clerk stacks the copies on top of each other, holds them up to the light, and looks to see if there are any conflicts. If both updates can be made to the database, he does so. If there are conflicts, he must either have rules for resolving the problems or he has to reject both transactions. This is a kind of row level locking, done after the fact.

2.7 Logical Concurrency Control

Logical concurrency control is based on the idea that the machine can analyze the predicates in the queue of waiting queries and processes on a purely logical level and then determine which of the statements can be allowed to operate on the database at the same time.

Clearly, all SELECT statements can operate at the same time since they do not change the data. After that, it is tricky to determine which statement conflicts with the others. For example, one pair of UPDATE statements on two separate tables might be allowed only in a certain order because of PRIMARY KEY and FOREIGN KEY constraints. Another pair of UPDATE statements on the same tables might be disallowed because they modify the same rows and leave different final states in them.

However, a third pair of UPDATE statements on the same tables might be allowed because they modify different rows and have no conflicts with each other.

There is also the problem of having statements waiting in the queue to be executed too long. This is a version of livelock, which we discuss in the next section. The usual solution is to assign a priority number to each waiting transaction and then decrement that priority number when they have been waiting for a certain length of time. Eventually, every transaction will arrive at priority one and be able to go ahead of any other transaction.

This approach also allows you to enter transactions at a higher priority than the transactions in the queue. While it is possible to create a livelock this way, it is not a problem and it lets you bump less important jobs in favor of more important jobs, such as payroll checks.

2.8 CAP Theorem

In 2000, Eric Brewer presented his keynote speech at the ACM Symposium on the Principles of Distributed Computing and introduced the CAP or Brewer's Theorem. It was later revised and altered through the work of Seth Gilbert and Nancy Lynch of MIT in 2002, plus many others since.

This theorem is for distributed computing systems while traditional concurrency models assume a central concurrency manager. The Pessimistic model had a traffic cop and the Optimistic model had a head waiter. The letters in the acronym CAP stand for Consistency, Availability, and Partition Tolerance. You can see a diagram of this at http://architects.dzone.com/articles/better-explaining-cap-theorem.

1. Consistency is the same idea as we had in ACID. Does the system reliably follow the established rules for its data content? Do all nodes within a cluster see all the data they are supposed to? Do not think that this is so elementary that no database would violate it. There are security databases that actively lie to certain users! For example, when you and I log on to the Daily Plant database, we are told that Clark Kent is a mild mannered reporter for a great metropolitan newspaper. But if you are Lois Lane, you are told that Clark Kent is Superman, a strange visitor from another planet.

2. Availability means that the service or system is available when requested. Does each request get a response outside of failure or success? Can you log on and attach your session to the database?

3. Partition Tolerance or robustness means that a given system continues to operate even with data loss or system failure. A single node failure should not cause the entire system to collapse. I am looking at my three-legged cat; she is Partition Tolerance. If she was a horse, we would have to shoot her.

Distributed system can only guarantee two of the features, not all three. If you need Availability and Partition Tolerance, you might have to let Consistency slip and forget about ACID collapse. Essentially, the system says "I will get you to a node, but I do not know how good the data you find there will be"; or "I can be available and the data I show will be good, but not complete.," etc. This is like the old joke about software projects: you have it, on time, in budget or correct; pick two.

2.9 BASE

The world is now full of huge distributed computing systems, such as Google's BigTable and Amazon's Dynamo and Facebook's Cassandra. Here is where we get to BASE, deliberately cute acronym that is short for:

1. Basically Available: This means the system guarantees the availability of the data as per the CAP Theorem. But the response can be "failure," "unreliable" because the requested data is in an inconsistent or changing state. Have you ever used the Magic Eight Ball?
2. Soft state: The state of the system could change over time, so even during times without input there may be changes going on due to "eventual consistency," thus the system is always assumed to be "soft" as opposed to "hard," where the data is certain. Part of the system can have hard data, such as a table of constants like geographical locations.
3. Eventual consistency: The system will eventually become consistent once it stops receiving input. This gives us a "window of inconsistency" which is acceptably short. The term "acceptably short window" is a bit vague. A data warehouse doing noncritical computations can wait, but an online order taking system has to respond in time to keep the customers happy (less than 1 min). At the other extreme, real-time control systems must respond instantly. The Domain Name System DNS is the most commonly known system that uses eventual consistency. Update to a domain name is passed around with protocols and time-controlled caches; eventually, all clients will see the update. But it is far from instantiations. This model requires a global timestamp so that each node knows which data item is most recent version.

Like the ACID model, eventual consistency model has variations:

1. Causal consistency: If process A has sent an update to process B, then a subsequent access by process B will return the updated value and a write is guaranteed to supersede the earlier write. Access by process C that has no causal relationship to process A is subject to the normal eventual consistency rules. This was also called a buddy system in early network systems. If a node could not get to the definitive data source, it would ask a buddy if he had gotten the new data and trust his data.
2. Read-your-writes consistency: Process A, after it has updated a data item, always accesses the updated value and will never see an older value. This is a special case of the causal consistency model.
3. Session consistency: This is a practical version of the previous model, where a process accesses the storage system in a session. As long as the session exists, the system guarantees read-your-writes consistency. If the session terminates because of a failure, a new session will be created and processing will resume with a guarantee that it will not overlap the prior sessions.
4. Monotonic read consistency: A process returns only the most recent data values; it never returns any previous values.
5. Monotonic write consistency: In this case, the system guarantees to serialize the writes by the same process. Systems that do not guarantee this level of consistency are notoriously hard to program. Think of it as a local queue at a node in the network.

A number of these properties can be combined. For example, one can get monotonic reads combined with session-level consistency. From a practical point of view, these two properties (monotonic reads and read-your-writes) are most desirable in an eventual consistency system, but not always required. These two properties make it simpler for developers to build applications, while allowing the storage system to relax consistency and provide high availability.

Eventual consistency has been part of the backup systems in RDBMS products and in synchronous and asynchronous replication techniques. In synchronous mode the replica update is part of the transaction. In

asynchronous mode the updates are delayed by log shipping. If the database crashes before the logs are shipped, the backup data can be out of date or inconsistent. Basically, the inconsistency window depends on the frequency of the log shipping.

2.10 Server-Side Consistency

On the server side, we will have the same data in several, not necessarily all, nodes. If all (n) nodes agree on a data value, then we are sure of it. Life is good.

But when we are in the process of establishing a consensus on an update, we need to know how many nodes have acknowledged the receipt of the update so far out of the nodes that are on the mailing list. We are looking for a quorum rule that accounts for node failures and incomplete replication. These rules will vary with the application. Large bank transfers will probably want complete agreement on all nodes. An abandoned Web site shopping cart application can be happy if the customer returns to any node to continue shopping with some version of his cart, even one with some missing items. You just have to be sure that when he hits the "check out" key the other nodes know to delete their local copy of that cart.

What we do not want is sudden emergency restarts of nodes as a default action. This was how early file systems worked. Many decades ago, my wife worked for an insurance company that processed Social Security data. A single bad punch card would abort the entire batch and issue a useless error message.

We want a system designed for graceful degradation. The Sabre airline reservation system expects a *small* number of duplicate reservations. It does not matter if somebody has two conflicting or redundant reservations in the system. Since the passenger cannot be in two places at once or in one place twice, the problem will be resolved by a human being or the physical logic of the problem.

When one node is overloaded, you will tolerate the reduced performance and move some of the load to other nodes until the first system can be repaired. The best example of that is redundant array storage systems. When a disk fails, it is physically removed from the array and new unit is plugged in to replace it. During the reconstruction of the failed disk, performance for accesses will take a hit. The data has to be copied from the alternative array blocks while the system keeps running its usual tasks.

2.11 Error Handling

There are two broad classes of error messages. We can have an anticipated problem, like an invalid password, which can have a standard response or process. We all have gotten an invalid password, and then been locked out if we fail to get right in some number of tries.

The second class of error message tells us what happened, perhaps in painful detail. This invites some action on the part of the user or lets them know why they are stuck.

But users might be uncomfortable with NoSQL's eventual consistency model. Things stop or lock and you have no idea why, what to do, or how long it will take to resolve (if ever). In 2011 August, Foursquare reported 11 hours of downtime because of a failure of MongoDB. In distributed systems, nodes can have stale data and not know it. In short, eventual consistency is not a silver bullet.

2.12 Deadlock and Livelocks

It is possible for a user to fail to complete a transaction for reasons other than the hardware failing. A deadlock is a situation where two or more users hold resources that the others need and neither party will surrender the objects to which they have locks. To make this more concrete, imagine user A and user B need tables X and Y. User A gets a lock on table X, and User B gets a lock on table Y. They both sit and wait for their missing resource to become available; it never happens. The common solution for a deadlock is for the database administrator to kill one or more of the sessions involved and rollback their work, either explicitly or with an eventual consistency.

A livelock involves a user who is waiting for a resource, but never gets it because other users keep grabbing it before he gets a chance. None of the other users hold onto the resource permanently as in a deadlock, but as a group they never free it. To make this more concrete, imagine user A needs all of table X. But table X is always being updated by a hundred other users so that user A cannot find a page without a lock on the table. He sits and waits for all the pages to become available; it never happens in time.

The database administrator can again kill one or more of the sessions involved and rollback their work. In some systems, he can raise the priority of the livelocked session so that it can seize the resources, as they become available.

None of this is trivial and each database system will have its own version of transaction processing and concurrency control. The internal details should not be of great concern to the applications programmer, but should be the responsibility of the database administrator. The user needs to be aware of the high level effects.

Tables

CONCEPTUALLY, A TABLE is a set of *zero* or more rows, and a row is a set of one or more columns. This hierarchy is important; actions apply at either the schema level, table level, row level, or column level. For example, the DELETE FROM statement removes whole rows, not columns, and leaves the base table in the schema. You cannot delete just a single *column* from a row. Likewise, DROP TABLE is a schema level command that removes a table completely.

I am starting with tables because eventually, everything comes back to tables. It is the only data structure in SQL. We do not have files, arrays, lists, pointers, and so forth. This is a set-oriented model of data and is as simple and implementation independent as we could make it.

- The tables have no particular ordering in the schema; they are referenced by table names.
- The rows have no particular ordering in their table; they are referenced by a key. Each row has, for each column, exactly one value or NULL in the data type of that column.
- The columns have no particular ordering in the row; they are referenced by column names. Each column has a name and a data type.

Each column has a specific data type and constraints that make up an implementation of an abstract domain. The way a table is physically

implemented does not matter, because you access it only with SQL. The database engine handles all the details for you and you never worry about the internals as you would with a physical file. In fact, almost no two SQL products use the same internal structures.

There are two common conceptual errors made by programmers who are accustomed to file systems. The first is thinking that a table is a file; the second is thinking that a table is a spreadsheet. Tables do not behave like either one of these, and you will get surprises if you do not understand the basic concepts.

It is easy to make these conceptual errors. When data moves from SQL to a host language, it has to be converted into host language data types and data structures to be displayed and used. The host languages have file systems built into them.

Another major difference is that tables and columns can have constraints attached to them. A constraint is a rule that defines what must be true about the database after each transaction. In this sense, a database is more like a collection of objects than a traditional passive file system.

3.1 CREATE TABLE Statements

The CREATE TABLE statement does all the hard work. The basic syntax for base table declarations looks like this:

```
CREATE TABLE <table name> (<table element list>)
<table element list> ::=
 <table element> | <table element>, <table element list>
<table element> ::=
 <column definition> | <table constraint definition>
```

The table definition includes data in the column definitions and rules for handling that data in the table constraint definitions. This means that a table acts more like an object (with its data and methods) than just a simple, passive file. We will get into the details shortly.

3.1.1 Base Tables

A base table is a table that has an actual physical existence in some kind of persistent storage. Virtual tables eventually are built from the base tables.

3.1.2 [GLOBAL | LOCAL] TEMPORARY Tables

The temporary tables can be used to hold intermediate results rather than requerying or recalculating them over and over. The syntax for creating a TEMPORARY TABLE is

```
CREATE [GLOBAL | LOCAL] TEMP[ORARY] TABLE <table name>
 (<table element list>)
ON COMMIT [PRESERVE | DELETE] ROWS;
```

This is just like the usual CREATE TABLE statement with the addition of two pieces of syntax. The access option to the table is given between the key words. The behavior of the data when a COMMIT is performed is shown at the end of the declaration.

The GLOBAL option in the TEMPORARY means that one copy of the table is available to *all* the modules of the application program in which it appears. The GLOBAL TEMPORARY TABLE is generally used to pass shared data between sessions.

The LOCAL option means that one copy of the table is available to each modules of the application program in which the temporary table appears. The LOCAL TEMPORARY TABLE is generally used as a "scratch table" by the user within a single module. If more than one user accesses the same LOCAL TEMPORARY TABLE, they each get a private copy of the table, initially empty, for their session or within the scope of the module that uses it.

If you have trouble imagining multiple tables in the schema with the same name (a violation of a basic rule of SQL about uniqueness of schema objects), then imagine a single table created as declared, but with an extra phantom column which contains a user identifier. What the users are then seeing is an updatable VIEW on the LOCAL TEMPORARY TABLE which shows them only the rows where this phantom column is equal to their user identifier, but not the phantom column itself. New rows are added to the LOCAL TEMPORARY TABLE with a DEFAULT of CURRENT USER.

Since this is a table in the schema, you can get rid of it with a DROP TABLE <table name> statement and you can change it with the usual INSERT INTO, DELETE FROM, and UPDATE statements. The differences are at the start and end of a session or module.

The ON COMMIT [PRESERVE | DELETE] ROWS clause describes the action taken when a COMMIT statement is executed successfully. The

PRESERVE options means that the next time this table is used, the rows will still be there and will be deleted only at the end of the session. The DELETE options means that the rows will be deleted whenever a COMMIT statement is executed during the session. In both cases, the table will be cleared out at the end of the session or module.

3.2 Column Definitions

Beginning SQL programmers often fail to take full advantage of the options available to them, and they pay for it with errors or extra work in their applications. A column is not like a simple passive field in a file system. It has more than just a data type associated with it.

```
<column definition> ::=
 <column name> <data type>
 [<default clause>]
 [<column constraint>...]

<column constraint> ::= NOT NULL
 | <check constraint definition>
 | <UNIQUE specification>
 | <references specification>
```

The first important thing to notice here is that each column must have a data type, which it keeps unless you ALTER the table. The SQL standard offers many data types, because SQL must work with many different host languages. The data types fall into three major categories: numeric, character, and temporal. We will discuss the data types and their rules of operation in other sections; they are fairly obvious, so not knowing the details will not stop you from reading the examples that follow.

3.2.1 DEFAULT Clause

The default clause is an underused feature, whose syntax is

```
<default clause> ::=
 [CONSTRAINT <constraint name>] DEFAULT <default option>

<default option> ::= <literal> | <system value> | NULL

<system value> ::= CURRENT_DATE | CURRENT_TIME | CURRENT_TIMESTAMP |
SYSTEM_USER | SESSION_USER | CURRENT_USER | NEXT VALUE FOR <sequence name>
```

Whenever the system does not have an explicit value to put into this column, it will look for its DEFAULT clause and use that value. The default option can be a literal value of the relevant data type, or something provided by the system, such as the current timestamp, current date, current user identifier, the e3xt value from a SEQUENCE, and so forth. If you do not provide a DEFAULT clause and the column is NULL-able, the system will provide a NULL as the default. If all that fails, you will get an error message about missing data.

This is a good way to make the database do a lot of work that you would otherwise have to code into all the application programs. The most common tricks are to use a zero in numeric columns, a string to encode a missing value ('{{unknown}}') or a true default ('same address') in character columns, and the system timestamp to mark transactions.

3.2.2 NOT NULL Constraint

The most important column constraint is the NOT NULL, which forbids the use of NULLs in a column. Use this constraint automatically and then remove it only when you have good reason. It will help you avoid the complications of NULL values when you make queries against the data.

The NULL is a special value in SQL that belongs to all data types. SQL is the only language that has such a creature; if you can understand how it works, you will have a good grasp of SQL. In Relational Theory, the NULL has no data type, but in SQL, we have to allocate storage for a column which has a data type. This means we can write "CAST (<expression> AS NULL)" in our code.

A NULL means that we have a missing, unknown, miscellaneous, or inapplicable value in the data.

The problem is that exactly which of these four possibilities the NULL indicates depends on how it is used. To clarify this, imagine that I am looking at a carton of Easter eggs and I want to know their colors. If I see an empty hole, I have a missing egg, which I hope will be provided later. If I see a foil-wrapped egg, I have an unknown color value in my set. If I see a multicolored egg, I have a miscellaneous value in my set. If I see a cue ball, I have an inapplicable value in my set. The way you handle each situation is a little different. The best solution is to design encodings with values that cover as many situations as you can have. Much like clothing catalogs we can have "multicolored," "camouflage," (better: "desert camouflage," "jungle

camouflage," etc.) "animal print" (better: "leopard," "tiger," "zebra," etc.). And "bald" is a perfectly good hair color in my world.

When you use NULLs in math calculations, they propagate in the results so that the answer is another NULL. When you use them in logical expressions or comparisons, they return a logical value of UNKNOWN and give SQL its strange three-valued logic. They sort either always high or always low in the collation sequence. They group together for some operations but not for others. In short, NULLs cause a lot of irregular features in SQL, which we will discuss later. Your best bet is just to memorize the situations and the rules for NULLs when you cannot avoid them.

3.2.3 CHECK() Constraint

The check constraint tests the rows of the table against a logical expression, which SQL calls a search condition, and rejects rows whose search condition returns FALSE. However, the constraint accepts rows when the search condition returns TRUE or UNKNOWN. This is not the same rule as the WHERE clause which rejects rows that test UNKNOWN. The reason for this "benefit-of-the-doubt" feature is so that it will be easy to write constraints on NULL-able columns.

```
<check constraint definition> ::=
 [CONSTRAINT <constraint name>] CHECK (<search condition>)
```

The usual technique is to do simple range checking, such as CHECK (rating BETWEEN 1 AND 10), or to verify that a column's value is in an enumerated set, such as CHECK (sex_code IN (0, 1, 2, 9)), with this constraint. Remember that the sex column could also be set to NULL, unless a NOT NULL constraint is also added to the column's declaration. While it is optional, it is a really good idea to use a constraint name. Without it, most SQL implementations will create a huge, ugly, unreadable random string for the name since they need to have one in the schema tables. If you provide your own, you can drop the constraint more easily and understand the error messages when the constraint is violated.

For example, you can use a single check clause to enforce the rule that a firm does not hire anyone under 21 years of age for a job that requires a liquor-serving license by checking the birth date and their hire date.

However, you cannot put the current system date into the CHECK() clause logic for obvious reasons— it is always changing.

The real power of the CHECK() clause comes from writing complex expressions that verify relationships with other rows, with other tables, or with constants. Before SQL-92, the CHECK() constraint could only reference columns in the table in which it was declared. In Full SQL-92 and beyond, the CHECK() constraint can reference any schema object. However, you will have a hard time finding it in a SQL implementation.

3.2.4 UNIQUE and PRIMARY KEY Constraints

The UNIQUE constraint says that no duplicate values are allowed in the column. It comes in two forms. The syntax is

```
<UNIQUE specification> ::= UNIQUE | PRIMARY KEY
```

There are some subtle differences between UNIQUE and PRIMARY KEY. There can be only one PRIMARY KEY per table but many UNIQUE columns. A PRIMARY KEY is automatically declared to have a NOT NULL constraint on it, but a UNIQUE column can have a NULL in a column unless you explicitly add a NOT NULL constraint. Adding the NOT NULL whenever possible is a good idea, as it makes the column into a proper relational key. I also add NOT NULL to PRIMARY KEY to document the table and to be sure it stays there when the key changes.

File system programmers understand the concept of a PRIMARY KEY, but for the wrong reasons. Their mindset is a sequential file, which can have only one key because that key is used to determine the *physical order of the records* within the file. There is no ordering in a table; the term PRIMARY KEY in SQL has to do with defaults in referential actions, which we will discuss later.

There is also a multiple-column form of the <UNIQUE specification>, which is usually written at the end of the column declarations. It is a list of columns in parentheses after the proper keyword; it means that the combination of those columns is UNIQUE. For example, I might declare PRIMARY KEY (city, department), so I can be sure that though I have offices in many cities and many identical departments in those offices, there is only one personnel department in Chicago.

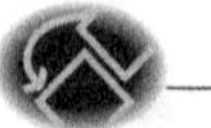

3.2.5 REFERENCES Clause

The <references specification> is the simplest version of a referential constraint definition, which can be quite tricky. For now, let us just consider the simplest case:

```
<references specification> ::=
 [CONSTRAINT <constraint name>]
  REFERENCES <referenced table name>[(<reference column>)]
```

This relates two tables together, so it is different from the other options we have discussed so far. What this says is that the value in this column of the *referencing* table must appear somewhere in the *referenced* table's column that is named in the constraint. Notice the terms *referencing* and *referenced*. This is not the same as the parent and child terms used in network databases. Those terms were based on pointer chains that were traversed in one direction; that is, you cannot find a path back to the parent from a child node in the network. Another difference is that the referencing and referenced tables can be the same table. Self-references can be a useful trick.

Furthermore, the referenced column must have UNIQUE constraint. For example, you can set up a rule that the Orders table will have orders only for goods that appear in the Inventory table.

If no <reference column> is given, then the PRIMARY KEY column of the referenced table is assumed to be the target. This is one of those places where the PRIMARY KEY is important, but you can always play it safe and explicitly name a column. There is no rule to prevent several columns from referencing the same target column. For example, we might have a table of flight crews that has pilot and copilot columns that both reference a table of certified pilots.

A circular reference is a relationship in which one table references a second table, which in turn references the first table. The old gag about "you cannot get a job until you have experience, and you cannot get experience until you have a job!" is the classic version of this.

3.2.6 Referential Actions

The REFERENCES clause can have two subclauses that take actions when a database event changes the referenced table. This feature came with and took awhile to be implemented in most SQL products. The two database events are updates and deletes and the subclauses look like this:

```
<referential triggered action> ::=
  <update rule> [<delete rule>] | <delete rule> [<update rule>]

<update rule> ::= ON UPDATE <referential action>
<delete rule> ::= ON DELETE <referential action>

<referential action> ::= CASCADE | SET NULL | SET DEFAULT | NO ACTION
```

When the referenced table is changed, one of the referential actions is set in motion by the SQL engine.

(1) The CASCADE option will change the values in the referencing table to the new value in the referenced table. This is a very common method of DDL programming that allows you to set up a single table as the trusted source for an identifier. This way the system can propagate changes automatically.

This removes one of the arguments for nonrelational system-generated surrogate keys. In early SQL products that were based on a file system for their physical implementation, the values were repeated both in the referenced and referencing tables. Why? The tables were regarded as separate units, like files.

Later, SQL products regarded the schema as a whole. The referenced values appeared once in the referenced table, and the referencing tables obtained them by following pointer chains to that one occurrence in the schema. The results are much faster update cascades, a physically smaller database, faster joins, and faster aggregations.

(2) The SET NULL option will change the values in the referencing table to a NULL. Obviously, the referencing column needs to be NULL-able.

(3) The SET DEFAULT option will change the values in the referencing table to the default value of that column, NULL. Obviously, the referencing column needs to have some DEFAULT declared for it, but each referencing column can have its own default in its own table.

(4) The NO ACTION option explains itself. Nothing is changed in the referencing table and it is possible that some error message about reference violation will be raised. If a referential constraint does not specify any ON UPDATE or ON DELETE rule, update rule, then NO ACTION is implicit.

You will also see the reserved word RESTRICT in some products. This option can act as a "place holder" during the design phase while you are waiting for final specifications. Full ANSI/ISO Standard SQL has more options about how matching is done between the referenced and referencing tables. Full SQL also has deferrable constraints. This lets the programmer turn a constraint off during a session so that the table can be put into a state that would otherwise be illegal. However, at the end of a session, all the constraints are enforced. Many SQL products have implemented these options, and they can be quite handy, but I will not mention them anymore.

All the constraints can be defined as equivalent to some CHECK constraint, for example:

```
PRIMARY KEY = CHECK (UNIQUE (SELECT <key columns> FROM <table>)
              AND (<key columns>) IS NOT NULL)

 UNIQUE = CHECK (UNIQUE (SELECT <key columns> FROM <table>))

 NOT NULL = CHECK (<column> IS NOT NULL)
```

These predicates can be reworded in terms of other predicates and subquery expressions and then passed on to the optimizer.

3.2.6.1 Nested UNIQUE Constraints

One of the basic tricks in SQL is representing a one-to-one or many-to-many relationship with a table that references the two (or more) entity tables involved by their primary keys. This third table has several popular names such as "junction table," "Associative Entity," or "join table," but we know that it is a relationship. The terms "junction table" is a pointer structure from Network databases, not part of RDBMS. For example given two tables,

```
CREATE TABLE Boys
(boy_name VARCHAR(30) NOT NULL PRIMARY KEY
 ...);

CREATE TABLE Girls
(girl_name VARCHAR(30) NOT NULL PRIMARY KEY,
 ...);
```

Yes, I know using names for a key is a bad practice, but it will make my examples easier to read. There are a lot of different relationships that we can make between these two tables. If you don't believe me, just watch the Jerry Springer Show sometime. The simplest relationship table looks like this:

```
CREATE TABLE Couples
(boy_name INTEGER NOT NULL
        REFERENCES Boys (boy_name)
        ON UPDATE CASCADE
        ON DELETE CASCADE,
 girl_name INTEGER NOT NULL,
        REFERENCES Girls(girl_name)
        ON UPDATE CASCADE
        ON DELETE CASCADE);
```

The Couples table allows us to insert rows like this:

```
INSERT INTO Couples
VALUES
('Joe Celko', 'Miley Cyrus'),
('Joe Celko', 'Lady GaGa'),
('Alec Baldwin', 'Lady GaGa'),
('Joe Celko', 'Miley Cyrus');
```

Opps! I am shown twice with "Miley Cyrus" because the Couples table does not have its own compound key. This is an easy mistake to make, but fixing it is not an obvious thing.

```
CREATE TABLE Orgy
(boy_name INTEGER NOT NULL
        REFERENCES Boys (boy_name)
        ON DELETE CASCADE
        ON UPDATE CASCADE,
 girl_name INTEGER NOT NULL,
        REFERENCES Girls(girl_name)
        ON UPDATE CASCADE
        ON DELETE CASCADE,
 PRIMARY KEY (boy_name, girl_name)); -- compound key
```

The Orgy table gets rid of the duplicated rows and makes this a proper table. The primary key for the table is made up of two or more columns and is called a compound key because of that fact. These are valid rows now.

```
('Joe Celko', 'Miley Cyrus')
('Joe Celko', 'Lady GaGa')
('Alec Baldwin', 'Lady GaGa')
```

But the only restriction on the couples is that they appear only once. Every boy can be paired with every girl, much to the dismay of the traditional marriage advocates. I think I want to make a rule that guys can have as many gals as they want, but the gals have to stick to one guy.

The way I do this is to use a NOT NULL UNIQUE constraint on the girl_name column, which makes it a key. It is a simple key since it is only one column, but it is also a nested key because it appears as a subset of the compound PRIMARY KEY.

```
CREATE TABLE Playboys
(boy_name INTEGER NOT NULL
        REFERENCES Boys (boy_name)
        ON UPDATE CASCADE
        ON DELETE CASCADE,
 girl_name INTEGER NOT NULL UNIQUE, -- nested key
        REFERENCES Girls(girl_name)
        ON UPDATE CASCADE
        ON DELETE CASCADE,
 PRIMARY KEY (boy_name, girl_name)); -- compound key
```

The Playboys is a proper table, without duplicated rows, but it also enforces the condition that I get to play around with one or more ladies, thus.

```
('Joe Celko', 'Miley Cyrus')
('Joe Celko', 'Lady GaGa')
```

The ladies might want to go the other way and keep company with a series of men.

```
CREATE TABLE Playgirls
(boy_name INTEGER NOT NULL UNIQUE -- nested key
        REFERENCES Boys (boy_name)
```

```
        ON UPDATE CASCADE
        ON DELETE CASCADE,
 girl_name INTEGER NOT NULL,
        REFERENCES Girls(girl_name)
        ON UPDATE CASCADE
        ON DELETE CASCADE,
 PRIMARY KEY (boy_name, girl_name)); -- compound key
```

The Playgirls table would permit these rows from our original set.

```
('Joe Celko', 'Lady GaGa')
('Alec Baldwin', 'Lady GaGa')
```

Think about all of these possible keys for a minute. The compound PRIMARY KEY is now redundant. If each boy appears only once in the table or each girl appears only once in the table, then each (boy_name, girl_name) pair can appear only once. However, the redundancy can be useful in searching the table because the SQL engine can use it to optimize queries.

The traditional marriage advocates can model their idea of stable couples. With this code

```
CREATE TABLE Marriages
(boy_name INTEGER NOT NULL UNIQUE -- nested key
        REFERENCES Boys (boy_name)
        ON UPDATE CASCADE
        ON DELETE CASCADE,
 girl_name INTEGER NOT NULL UNIQUE -- nested key,
        REFERENCES Girls(girl_name)
        ON UPDATE CASCADE
        ON DELETE CASCADE,
 PRIMARY KEY(boy_name, girl_name)); -- redundant compound key
```

The Couples table allows us to insert these rows from the original set.

```
('Joe Celko', 'Miley Cyrus')
('Alec Baldwin', 'Lady GaGa')
```

Making special provisions for the primary key in the SQL engine is not a bad assumption because the REFERENCES clause uses the PRIMARY KEY

of the referenced table as the default. Many new SQL programmers are not aware that a FOREIGN KEY constraint can *also* reference any UNIQUE constraint in the same table or in another table. The following nightmare will give you an idea of the possibilities. The multiple column versions follow the same syntax.

```
CREATE TABLE Foo
(foo_key INTEGER NOT NULL PRIMARY KEY,
  ...
 self_ref INTEGER NOT NULL
          REFERENCES Foo(fookey),
 outside_ref_1 INTEGER NOT NULL
             REFERENCES Bar(bar_key),
 outside_ref_2 INTEGER NOT NULL
             REFERENCES Bar(other_key),
 ...);

CREATE TABLE Bar
(bar_key INTEGER NOT NULL PRIMARY KEY,
 other_key INTEGER NOT NULL UNIQUE,
 ...);
```

3.2.6.2 Overlapping Keys

But getting back to the nested keys, just how far can we go with them? My favorite example is a teacher's schedule kept in a table like this (I am leaving off reference clauses and CHECK() constraints):

```
CREATE TABLE Schedule -- skeleton table. WRONG!
(teacher_name VARCHAR(15) NOT NULL,
 class_title CHAR(15) NOT NULL,
 room_nbr INTEGER NOT NULL,
 period_nbr INTEGER NOT NULL,
 PRIMARY KEY (teacher_name, class_title, room_nbr, period_nbr));
```

That choice of a primary key is the most obvious one—use all the columns. Typical rows would look like this:

```
('Mr. Celko', 'Database 101', 222, 6)
```

The rules we want to enforce are

(1) A teacher is in only one room each period.

(2) A teacher teaches only one class each period.

(3) A room has only one class each period.

(4) A room has only one teacher in each period.

Stop reading and see what you come up with for an answer. Okay, now consider using one constraint for each rule in the list, thus.

```
CREATE TABLE Schedule_1 -- version one, WRONG!
(teacher_name VARCHAR(15) NOT NULL,
 class_title CHAR(15) NOT NULL,
 room_nbr INTEGER NOT NULL,
 period_nbr INTEGER NOT NULL,
 UNIQUE (teacher_name, room_nbr, period_nbr), -- rule #1
 UNIQUE (teacher_name, class_title, period_nbr), -- rule #2
 UNIQUE (class_title, room_nbr, period_nbr), -- rule #3
 UNIQUE (teacher_name, room_nbr, period_nbr), -- rule #4
 PRIMARY KEY (teacher_name, class_title, room_nbr, period_nbr));
```

We know that there are four ways to pick three things from a set of four things; it is called a combination.

I could drop the PRIMARY KEY as redundant if I have all four of these constraints in place. But what happens if I drop the PRIMARY KEY and then one of the constraints?

```
CREATE TABLE Schedule_2 -- still wrong
(teacher_name VARCHAR(15) NOT NULL,
 class_title CHAR(15) NOT NULL,
 room_nbr INTEGER NOT NULL,
 period_nbr INTEGER NOT NULL,
 UNIQUE (teacher_name, room_nbr, period_nbr), -- rule #1
 UNIQUE (teacher_name, class_title, period_nbr), -- rule #2
 UNIQUE (class_title, room_nbr, period_nbr)); -- rule #3
```

I can now insert these rows in the second version of the table:

```
('Mr. Celko', 'Database 101', 222, 6)
('Mr. Celko', 'Database 102', 223, 6)
```

This gives me a very tough sixth period teaching load since I have to be in two different rooms at the same time. Things can get even worse when another teacher is added to the schedule:

```
('Mr. Celko', 'Database 101', 222, 6)
('Mr. Celko', 'Database 102', 223, 6)
('Ms. Shields', 'Database 101', 223, 6)
```

Ms. Shields and I are both in room 223, trying to teach different classes at the same time. Matthew Burr looked at the constraints and the rules came up with this analysis.

```
CREATE TABLE Schedule_3 -- corrected version
(teacher_name VARCHAR(15) NOT NULL,
 class_title CHAR(15) NOT NULL,
 room_nbr INTEGER NOT NULL,
 period_nbr INTEGER NOT NULL,
 UNIQUE (teacher_name, period_nbr), -- rules #1 and #2
 UNIQUE (room_nbr, period_nbr)); -- rules #3 and #4
```

If a teacher is in only one room each period, then given a period and a teacher I should be able to determine only one room, i.e., room is functionally dependent upon the combination of teacher and period. Likewise, if a teacher teaches only one class each period, then class is functionally dependent upon the combination of teacher and period. The same thinking holds for the last two rules: class is functionally dependent upon the combination of room and period, and teacher is functionally dependent upon the combination of room and period.

With the constraints that were provided in the first version, you will find that the rules are not enforced. For example, I could enter the following rows:

```
('Mr. Celko', 'Database 101', 222, 6)
('Mr. Celko', 'Database 102', 223, 6)
```

These rows violate rule #1 and rule #2.

However, the UNIQUE constraints first provided in Schedule_2 do not capture this violation and will allow the rows to be entered.

The constraint

```
UNIQUE (teacher_name, room_nbr, period_nbr)
```

is checking the complete combination of teacher, room, and period, and since ('Mr. Celko', 222, 6) is different from ('Mr. Celko', 223, 6), the DDL does not find any problem with both rows being entered, even though that means that Mr. Celko is in more than one room during the same period.

```
UNIQUE (teacher_name, class_title, period_nbr)
```

doesn't catch its associated rule either since ('Mr. Celko', 'Database 101', 6) is different from ('Mr. Celko', 'Database 102', 6), and so, Mr. Celko is able to teach more than one class during the same period, thus violating rule #2. It seems that we'd also be able to add the following row:

```
('Ms. Shields', 'Database 103', 222, 6)
```

which violates rules #3 and #4.

Try to imagine enforcing this with procedural code. This is why I say that most of the work in SQL is done in the DDL.

3.3 Computed Columns

A computed column calculates a value from other columns in the same row. Each vendor has different syntax, but the two options are virtual and persisted. The virtual option is like a local VIEW that puts the expression's value in a new column when the row is invoked. The persistent option actually creates and stores the value in the table. Here is the syntax:

```
<column name> <data type> [GENERATED ALWAYS] AS (<expression>)
[VIRTUAL | PERSISTENT]
```

The column name obeys the same rules as a regular column. It is always best to specify the storage option. As an example, here are the classic order details with a line extension computation.

```
CREATE TABLE Order_Details
(order_nbr CHAR(15) NOT NULL
  REFERENCES Orders(order_nbr),
 gtin CHAR(15) NOT NULL,
 PRIMARY KEY (order_nbr, gtin),
  order_qty INTEGER NOT NULL,
  unit_price DECIMAL(10,2) NOT NULL,
```

```
  line_tot DECIMAL(15,2) GENERATED ALWAYS AS (order_qty * unit_price)
VIRTUAL
);
```

3.4 [NOT] DEFERRABLE Constraints

The one firm rule about constraints is that they are all valid at the *end of a session*. This lets you control what happens during the session. First, you decide if the constraint can be deferred during a session at all. When you start the session, you can decide the initial state of the constraint (initially deferred, initially immediate).

```
CONSTRAINT <constraint name>
 [INITIALLY DEFERRED | INITIALLY IMMEDIATE]
 [[NOT] DEFERRABLE]
 [NOT] ENFORCED
```

Some of these options are obviously contradictory and are disallowed.

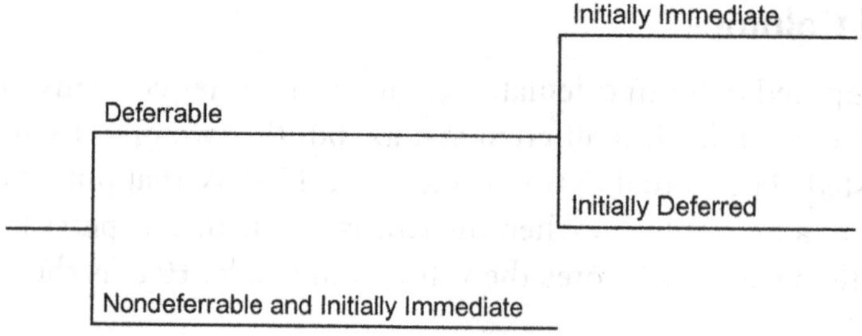

The default is `INITIALLY IMMEDIATE NOT DEFERRABLE ENFORCED.` These options are invoked by the SET CONSTRAINTS statement.

```
SET CONSTRAINTS <constraint name list> {DEFERRED | IMMEDIATE}
<constraint name list> ::= ALL | <constraint name> [{<comma>
<constraint name>}...]
```

The constraints named in the <constraint name list> have to be deferrable. Here is an example of how to use this.

Consider this self-reference trick to prevent gaps in a timeline of events. We have made sure that the starting and ending dates of an event are in the right order and that the previous event is contiguous to this event.

```
CREATE TABLE Events
(event_id CHAR(10) NOT NULL,
 previous_event_end_date DATE NOT NULL
  REFERENCES Events (event_end_date),
 event_start_date DATE NOT NULL,
 event_end_date DATE UNIQUE, -- null means event in progress
 PRIMARY KEY (event_id, event_start_date),
 CONSTRAINT Event_Order_Valid
 CHECK (event_start_date <= event_end_date),
 CONSTRAINT Chained_Dates
 CHECK (previous_event_end_date
       + INTERVAL '1' DAY = event_start_date)
 INITIALLY IMMEDIATE DEFERRABLE
);
```

First we disable the Chained_Dates constraint to be able to start a chain of dates.

```
SET CONSTRAINT Chained_Dates DEFERRED;
```

While the constraint is off, insert a starter row

```
INSERT INTO Events(event_id, previous_event_end_date, event_start_date,
event_end_date)
VALUES ('Foo Fest', '2016-01-01', '2016-01-02', '2016-01-05');
```

Now re-enable the constraint in the table

```
SET CONSTRAINT Chained_Dates IMMEDIATE;

-- this works
INSERT INTO Events(event_id, previous_event_end_date, event_start_date,
event_end_date)
VALUES ('Glob Week', '2016-01-05', '2016-01-06', '2016-01-10');

-- this fails
INSERT INTO Events(event_id, previous_event_end_date, event_start_date,
event_end_date)
VALUES ('Snoob day', '2016-01-09', '2016-01-11', '2016-01-15');
```

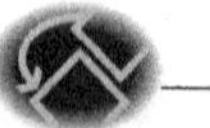

3.5 CREATE DOMAIN and CREATE SEQUENCE

There are two constructs that are used in table which live at the schema level. They are kinds of shorthand that could have been with a hugely expensive stored procedure. They make programming much easier so they are worth learning.

3.5.1 CREATE DOMAIN

A domain schema object is shorthand for a column declaration which can be used in several table declarations. For whatever reason, this never became popular and it is not widely implemented.

```
CREATE DOMAIN <domain name> [AS] <predefined type>
[<default clause>]
[<domain constraint>...]
[<collate clause>]
```

The term <predefined type> is one of the built-in types in SQL; you cannot nest domains. If <constraint characteristics> is specified, then neither ENFORCED nor NOT ENFORCED is specified and the <constraint characteristics> is not specified, then INITIALLY IMMEDIATE NOT DEFERRABLE is implicit.

3.5.2 CREATE SEQUENCE

A sequence schema object is a generator for an ordered list of whole numbers. It is at the schema level and you can have several of them. But there are some subtle things to watch out for.

A series is not a sequence. A series is a mathematical construct that is based on adding the terms. Series can converge to a limit at infinite. We do not need to do that very often in RDBMS.

A Sequence is not an IDENTITY (physical insertion to the disk count), auto-increment (counter attached to a table), a row_id (physical location on a disk). It is a *logical concept, not related to physical storage*. In the case of inserting a set of rows, these proprietary features will use a permutation on the rows, queue, and number them in that order. It is nondeterministic.

Whole numbers are not identifiers; we use them for math. What you want for an identifier is a tag number, a string, usually of fixed length, made up of digits. You keep them in sort order so you can spot gaps, easily sort, and generate them. Think of a serial number on a manufactured product. The most common example is a vehicle identification number (VIN). This is a unique code which is used by the automotive industry to identify individual motor vehicles, as defined in ISO 3833. The positions 12-17 are a sequence prefixed by codes for the Manufacturer Identifier, some vehicle attributes, a check digit, model year, and plant code.

The check digit is a major reason we like tag numbers. This is a topic in itself, but the idea is that we can take each digit in the tag number and run it through a formula as an integer. We get a result, usually another digit, and we attach it to the tag number. For example, the Luhn algorithm is a common method defined by ISO/IEC 7812-1. We like it because it is simple to put in hardware.

1. Compute the sum of the digits.
2. Take the units digit from this total.
3. Subtract it from 10.

It is not a great check digit, but it catches *most* of the common input errors—missing digits, extra digits, wrong digits, and pairwise transposes.

The CREATE SEQUENCE Statement is easier to explain with a physical model. Imagine you are in the butcher store. You walk in and pull a service ticket number from a roll of tickets on the counter. Sequence numbers are generated outside the scope of the current transaction, just like the tickets. The numbers are consumed whether the transaction using the ticket number is actually served (committed) or they walk out (rolled back). Here is the BNF for CREATE SEQUENCE.

```
CREATE SEQUENCE <sequence_name>
 [AS <built_in_integer_type>
 [START WITH <constant>]
 [INCREMENT BY <constant>]
 [{MINVALUE [<constant>]} | {NO MINVALUE}]
 [{MAXVALUE [<constant>]} | {NO MAXVALUE}]
 [CYCLE | {NO CYCLE}]
```

Let's go through the BNF in detail. The <sequence_name> and its qualifiers explain itself. This is pure SQL. Sequence numbers are generated outside the scope of the current transaction. They are consumed whether the

transaction using the sequence number is committed or rolled back. Think about the butcher shop ticket that gets dropped on the floor.

A sequence can be defined as any integer type. That means TINYINT, SMALLINT, INTEGER, and BIGINT. But it also allows DECIMAL (s, 0) and NUMERIC(s, 0) data types. You can also use a user-defined data type that is based on one of the allowed types. Do not do that; it destroys portability.

If no data type is provided, BIGINT is the default. Do not use this unless you really need more numbers than atoms in the Universe. As with most defaults, this is the largest, safest value in the problem space.

```
START WITH <constant>
```

This is the first value returned by the sequence. The START value must be a value between the minimum and maximum values. The default start value for a new sequence is the minimum value for an ascending sequence and the maximum value for a descending sequence. Note this is a constant, no function calls.

```
INCREMENT BY <constant>
```

Value used to increment (or decrement if negative) the value of the sequence for each call to the NEXT VALUE FOR. If the increment is a negative value, the sequence is descending; otherwise, it is ascending. The increment cannot be 0, obviously. The default increment for a new sequence is 1. Again, this is a constant and not a function call.

```
[MINVALUE <constant> | NO MINVALUE]
```

Specifies the bounds for the sequence. The default minimum value for a new sequence is the minimum value of the data type of the sequence. This is zero for the TINYINT data type and a negative number for all other data types. NO MINVALUE is probably a really bad design choice. You probably wanted zero or one.

```
[MAXVALUE <constant> | NO MAXVALUE
```

Specifies the bounds for the sequence. The default maximum value for a new sequence is the maximum value of the data type of the sequence.

NO MAXVALUE is probably another bad design. If you are going to use this to create a tag number, you have to worry about overflowing the length of your string.

If you are casting the numeric data type to strings for tag numbers, you will want to be sure that the numbers do not overflow in the conversion. And you probably do not need the upper limit of a data type.

```
[CYCLE | NO CYCLE]
```

Property that specifies whether the sequence should restart from the minimum value (or maximum for descending sequences) or throw an exception when its minimum or maximum value is exceeded. The default cycle option for new sequences is NO CYCLE. *Note that cycling restarts from the minimum or maximum value, not from the start value.*

3.5.2.1 Using the SEQUENCE

How do you use this feature? You simply call the next value with "NEXT VALUE FOR <sequence name>" wherever a numeric value of the appropriate type would go. This returns one value.

Remember earlier in this article when I mentioned that how IDENTITY and other such features were not deterministic? SEQUENCE has a way to fix this problem; you can queue the set using the sequence with an ORDER BY clause. If another process is accessing the sequence object at the same time, the numbers returned could have gaps.

An OVER clause applied to the NEXT VALUE FOR function does not support the PARTITION BY or the [ROW | RANGE] subclauses for obvious reasons. The following additional rules apply when using the NEXT VALUE FOR function with the OVER clause.

Multiple calls to the NEXT VALUE FOR function for the same sequence generator in a single statement *must* all use the same OVER clause definition. Again, this is obvious.

Multiple calls to the NEXT VALUE FOR function that references different sequence generators in a single statement can have different OVER clause definitions. They are separate schema objects.

If all calls to the NEXT VALUE FOR function in a SELECT statement specify the OVER clause, an ORDER BY clause may be used in the SELECT statement. Again, the SEQUENCE is a separate schema object.

The OVER clause is allowed with the NEXT VALUE FOR function when used in a SELECT statement or INSERT … SELECT … statement. The NEXT VALUE FOR function is not allowed in UPDATE or MERGE statements.

To get a feel for how this works, create a simple sequence and play with it.

```
CREATE SEQUENCE Invoice_Seq
 AS INTEGER
 START WITH 1
 INCREMENT BY 1
 MINVALUE 1
 MAXVALUE 99
 NO CYCLE;
```

Now, just play with it. Just hit "`SELECT NEXT VALUE FOR Invoice:Seq;`" a few times. When you hit 99 and invoke the next value, you will get an error message. When you hit the limit, you can reset things.

```
ALTER SEQUENCE <sequence name> RESTART [WITH <constant>];
```

The WITH option lets you assign the new starting value. If you do not give a specific value, the default is the original starting value. In this example, we can use

```
ALTER SEQUENCE Invoice_Seq RESTART WITH 3;
SELECT NEXT VALUE FOR Invoice_Seq;
```

This will return 3. Most of the situations where you want to restart a sequence can be done with the CYCLE clause.

The use of the ORDER BY clause can let you build groupings. Create sequence groups of 10:

```
CREATE SEQUENCE Ten_Seq
 AS INTEGER
 START WITH 1
 INCREMENT BY 1
 MINVALUE 1
 MAXVALUE 10
 CYCLE;
```

A fun example is using the same sequence in more than one table. Let's go back to the original service ticket example. When you come into the shop, you pull a ticket.

```
CREATE SEQUENCE Service_Ticket_Seq
 AS INTEGER
 START WITH 1
```

```
INCREMENT BY 1
MINVALUE 1
MAXVALUE 100
CYCLE;
```

We have two departments in this delicatessen, meats and fish. If you have been to Kosher market, you know that these two areas are kept separate. A ticket can be used in only one department.

```
CREATE TABLE Meats
(ticket_seq INTEGER NOT NULL PRIMARY KEY,
 meat_type VARCHAR(15) NOT NULL);

CREATE TABLE Fish
(ticket_seq INTEGER NOT NULL PRIMARY KEY,
 fish_type VARCHAR(15) NOT NULL);

CREATE PROCEDURE Ticket_Service
(IN market_code CHAR(1),
 IN product_name VARCHAR(15))
BEGIN
DECLARE local_ticket_seq INTEGER;
SET local_ticket_seq = NEXT VALUE FOR Service_Ticket_Seq;
IF market_code = 'M'
THEN INSERT INTO Meats
      VALUES (local_ticket_seq, product_name);
ELSE IF market_code = 'F'
     THEN INSERT INTO Fish
          VALUES (local_ticket_seq, product_name);
     END IF;
END IF;
END;
```

Now, let's call the procedure a few times:

```
EXEC Ticket_Service 'M', 'Brisket';
EXEC Ticket_Service 'F', 'Lox';
EXEC Ticket_Service 'M', 'Chicken';
EXEC Ticket_Service 'M', 'Brisket';
EXEC Ticket_Service 'F', 'Sturgeon';
EXEC Ticket_Service 'F', 'Haddock';
```

And now let's see how this works.

```
SELECT * FROM Meats;
```

1	Brisket
3	Chicken
4	Brisket

```
SELECT * FROM Fish;
```

2	Lox
5	Sturgeon
6	Haddock

If I UNION ALL the two tables, I get a complete sequence and I am sure their intersection is empty. Doing this without a SEQUENCE is a lot harder. But I did resort to if-then-else flow control because I have two different tables. UGH!

I can put a SEQUENCE in the DEFAULT clause of the DDL for table:

```
CREATE TABLE Service_Tickets
(ticket_nbr INTEGER DEFAULT NEXT VALUE FOR Service_Ticket_Seq,
 department_code CHAR(1) NOT NULL
 CHECK (department_code IN ('M', 'F')));
```

Now play with this code.

```
INSERT INTO Service_Tickets (department_code)
VALUES ('M');
SELECT * FROM Service_Tickets;
```

That is cool! But do not stop here. Let's redo the Meats and Fish tables with this feature:

```
CREATE TABLE Meats
(ticket_seq INTEGER DEFAULT NEXT VALUE FOR Service_Ticket_Seq
 PRIMARY KEY,
 meat_type VARCHAR(15) NOT NULL);
```

```
CREATE TABLE Fish
(ticket_seq INTEGER DEFAULT NEXT VALUE FOR Service_Ticket_Seq
 PRIMARY KEY,
 fish_type VARCHAR(15) NOT NULL);
```

Now to get you started, try these statements. I dropped the Kosher theme:

```
INSERT INTO Meats (meat_type) VALUES ('pig');
INSERT INTO Fish (fish_type) VALUES ('squid');
SELECT * FROM Meats;
SELECT * FROM Fish;
```

There are no guarantees as to how the sequence numbers will be assigned; it is pretty much first-come first-served in the system. Did you notice that the sequences are the PRIMARY KEY?

```
INSERT INTO Meats VALUES (8, 'Cat');
```

will give us an error when the sequence gets to that value.

3.6 Character Set Related Constructs

There are several schema level constructs for handling characters. You can create a named set of characters for various language or special purposes, define one or more collation sequences for them, and translate one set into another.

Today, the Unicode Standards and vendor features are what are really used. Most of the characters actually used have Unicode names and collations defined already. For example, SQL text is written in Latin-1, as defined by ISO 8859-1. This is the set used for HTML and it consists of 191 characters from the Latin alphabet. This is the most commonly used character set in the Americas, Western Europe, Oceania, and Africa and for standard Romanizations of East-Asian languages.

Since 1991, the Unicode Consortium has been working with ISO and IEC to develop the Unicode Standard and ISO/IEC 10646: the Universal Character Set (UCS) in tandem. Unicode and ISO/IEC 10646 currently assign about 100, 000 characters to a code space consisting of over a million code points, and they define several standard encodings that are capable of representing every available code point. The standard encodings of Unicode and the UCS use sequences of one to four 8-bit code values (UTF-8), sequences of one or

two 16-bit code values (UTF-16), or one 32-bit code value (UTF-32 or UCS-4). There is also an older encoding that uses one 16-bit code value (UCS-2), capable of representing one-seventeenth of the available code points. Of these encoding forms, only UTF-8's byte sequences are in a fixed order; the others are subject to platform-dependent byte ordering issues that may be addressed via special codes or indicated via out-of-band means.

3.6.1 CREATE CHARACTER SET

You will not find this syntax in many SQLs. The vendors will default to a system level character set based on the local language settings.

```
<character set definition> ::=
CREATE CHARACTER SET <character set name> [AS]
<character set source> [<collate clause>] <character set source> ::= GET
<character set specification>
```

The <collate clause> is usually defaulted also, but you can use named collations.

3.6.2 CREATE COLLATION

```
<collation definition> ::=
CREATE COLLATION <collation name>
 FOR <character set specification>
 FROM <existing collation name> [<pad characteristic>]

<pad characteristic> ::= NO PAD | PAD SPACE
```

The <pad characteristic> option has to do with how strings will be compared to each other. If the collation for the comparison has the NO PAD characteristic and the shorter value is equal to some prefix of the longer value, then the shorter value is considered less than the longer value. If the collation for the comparison has the PAD SPACE characteristic, for the purposes of the comparison, the shorter value is effectively extended to the length of the longer by concatenation of <space>s on the right. SQL normally pads a shorter string with spaces on the end and then matches them, letter for letter, position by position.

3.6.3 CREATE TRANSLATION

This statement defines how one character set can be mapped into another character set. The important part is that it gives this mapping a name.

```
<transliteration definition> ::=
CREATE TRANSLATION <transliteration name>
 FOR <source character set specification>
 TO <target character set specification>
 FROM <transliteration source>

<source character set specification> ::= <character set specification>

<target character set specification> ::= <character set specification>

<transliteration source> ::= <existing transliteration name> |
<transliteration routine>

<existing transliteration name> ::= <transliteration name>

<transliteration routine> ::= <specific routine designator>
```

Notice that I can use a simple mapping which will behave much like a bunch of nested REPLACE() function calls or use a routine that can do some computations. The reason that having a name for these transliterations is that I can use them in the TRANSLATE() function instead of that bunch of nested REPLACE() function calls. The syntax is simple:

```
TRANSLATE (<character value expression> USING <transliteration name>)
```

DB2 and other implementations generalize TRANSLATE() to allow for target and replacement strings so that you can do a lot of edit work in a single expression. We will get to that when we get to string functions.

Keys, Locators, and Generated Values

KEY IS AN unfortunate term in IT. We have encryption keys, sort keys, access keys, and probably a dozen other uses for the term I cannot think of right now. Unless I explicitly say otherwise, I will mean a relational key in this book. A (relational) key is a subset of one or more columns in a table which are guaranteed unique for all possible rows. If there is more than one column in the subset, this is a compound key. We have seen the UNIQUE and PRIMARY KEY constraints in Chapter 3; now let's discuss how to use them properly.

The concept of a (relational) key is central to RDBMS, but it tactfully goes back to a fundamental law of logic known as the Law of Identity. It is the first of the three classical laws of thought. It states that: "each thing is the same as itself," often stated as "A is A." This means each entity is composed of its own unique set of attributes, which the ancient Greeks called its essence. Consequently, things that have the same essence are the same thing, while things that have different essences are different things.

I like the longer definition: "To be is to be something in particular; to be nothing in particular or everything in general is to be nothing at all" because it makes you focus on a clear definition. The informal logical fallacy of equivocation is using the same term with different meanings. This happens in data modeling when we have vague terms in specifications.

Thanks to Ayn Rand, Aristotle gets credit for this law, but it is not his invention (Google it). Aristotle did "invent" noncontradiction (a predicate

cannot be both true and false at the same time) and the excluded middle (a predicate is either true or false).

A table is made of rows; each row models an entity or a relationship. Each entity has an identity in the logical sense (do not confuse it with the vendor's IDENTITY feature that numbers the physical records on a particular disk drive). We use this key, this logical identity, to find a row in a table in SQL.

This is totally different from magnetic tape file systems which use a record count to locate a physical record on the tape. This pure sequential-only access made having a sort key important for tape files; doing a random access search would take far too long to be practical!

This is totally different from random access disk file systems which use pointers and indexes to locate a physical record on a particular physical disk. These systems depend on searching pointer chains in various structures such as various flavors of tree indexes, junction tables, join tables, linked lists, etc.

We do not care *how* the SQL engine eventually locates the data in persistent storage. We do not care if the data is moved to new locations. One SQL might use B-Tree indexes and another use hashing, but the SQL stays the same. *In fact, we do not care if the data has any actual physical existence at all!* A virtual table, a derived table, CTE, and VIEW are assembled by the SQL engine when the data is needed.

4.1 Key Types

The keys, logical and physical, for a table can be classified by their behavior and their source. Here is a quick table of my classification system.

	Natural Key	Artificial Key	Exposed Physical Locator	Surrogate Key
Constructed from real attributes	Y	N	N	Y
Verifiable in reality	Y	N	N	N
Verifiable in itself	Y	Y	N	N
Visible to the user	Y	Y	Y	N

Now let's define terms in detail.

4.1.1 Natural Keys

A natural key is a subset of attributes that occur in a table and act as a unique identifier. The user sees them. You can go to the external reality and verify them. Example: bar codes on consumer goods (read the package), geographic coordinates (get a GPS), or the VIN on an automobile (read the tag riveted to the dashboard, etched into the windows, and engraved on the engine block).

Newbies worry about a natural compound key becoming very long. Yes, short keys are nice for people. My answer is: So what? Since it is a key, you will have to add a UNIQUE constraint to have a valid schema. I will argue that this is the twenty-first century and we have much better computers than we did in the 1950s when key size was a real physical issue.

Replacing a natural two or three integer compound key with a huge GUID that no human being or other system can possibly understand because they think it will be faster only cripples the system and makes it more error-prone. I know how to verify the (longitude, latitude) pair of a location; how do you verify the GUID assigned to it?

A long key is not always a bad thing for performance. For example, if I use (city, state) as my key, I can get a free index on just (city) in many systems. I can also add extra columns to the key to make it a super-key when such a super-key gives me a covering index (i.e., an index which contains all of the columns required for a query, so that the base table does not have to be accessed at all).

4.1.2 Artificial Keys

An artificial key is an extra attribute added to the table that is seen by the user. It does not exist in the external reality but can be verified for syntax or check digits inside itself. Example: the open codes in the UPC/EAN scheme that a user can assign to his own stuff.

For example, a grocery store not only sells packaged good with preprinted bar codes but also bakes bread in the store and labels them with an open code. The check digits still work, but you have to verify them inside your own enterprise.

Experienced database designers insist on industry standard codes, such as UPC/EAN, VIN, GTIN, ISBN, etc., as keys. They know that they need to verify the data against the reality they are modeling. A trusted external source is a good thing to have. I know why this VIN is associated with this

car, but why is a proprietary vendor autonumber value of 42 on one machine associated with this car? Try to verify the relationship in the reality you are modeling. It makes as much sense as locating a car by its parking space number.

4.1.3 Exposed Physical Locators

An exposed physical locator is not based on attributes in the data model but on the storage used and is exposed to user. There is no way to predict it or verify it. The system obtains a value through some physical process totally unrelated to the logical data model. The user cannot change them without destroying the relationships among the data elements.

Examples would be physical row locations encoded as a number, string, or even a proprietary data type. If hash values were accessible in an SQL product, then they would qualify, but they are usually hidden from the user.

Many programmers object to putting IDENTITY and other autonumbering devices into this category. To convert the number into a physical location requires an index search, but the concept is the same. The hardware gives you a way to go directly to a physical location which has nothing to do with the logical data model, and which cannot be changed in the physical database, or verified externally. Again, this is locating a car by its parking space number in one garage.

Most of the time, exposed physical locators are used for faking a sequential file's positional record number, so I can reference the physical storage location—a 1960s ISAM file in SQL. You lose all the advantages of an abstract data model, SQL set oriented programming, carry extra data, and destroy the portability of code.

The early SQLs were based on preexisting file systems. The data was kept in *physically contiguous* disk pages, in *physically contiguous* rows, made up of *physically contiguous* columns, in short, just like a deck of punch cards or a magnetic tape. Most programmers still carry that mental model, which is why I keep ranting about file versus table, row versus record, and column versus field.

But physically contiguous storage is only one way of building a relational database and it is not the best one. The basic idea of a relational database is that user is not supposed to know how or where things are stored at all, much less write code that depends on the particular physical representation in a particular release of a particular product on particular hardware at a particular time. This is discussed in the section on IDENTITY columns.

Finally, an appeal to authority, with a quote from Dr. Codd: "... Database users may cause the system to generate or delete a surrogate, but they have no control over its value, nor is its value ever displayed to them...."

This means that a surrogate ought to act like an index: created by the user, managed by the system, and NEVER seen by a user. That means never used in code, DRI, or anything else that a user writes.

Codd also wrote the following:

> *There are three difficulties in employing user-controlled keys as permanent surrogates for entities.*
>
> (1) *The actual values of user-controlled keys are determined by users and must therefore be subject to change by them (e.g. if two companies merge, the two employee databases might be combined with the result that some or all of the serial numbers might be changed).*
>
> (2) *Two relations may have user-controlled keys defined on distinct domains (e.g. one uses social security numbers, while the other uses employee serial numbers) and yet the entities denoted are the same.*
>
> (3) *It may be necessary to carry information about an entity either before it has been assigned a user-controlled key value or after it has ceased to have one (e.g. an applicant for a job and a retiree).*
>
> *These difficulties have the important consequence that an equi-join on common key values may not yield the same result as a join on common entities. A solution - proposed in part [4] and more fully in [14] - is to introduce entity domains which contain system-assigned surrogates. Database users may cause the system to generate or delete a surrogate, but they have no control over its value, nor is its value ever displayed to them..... Codd, E. Extending the Database Relational Model to Capture More Meaning, ACM Transactions on Database Systems, 4(4), pp. 397-434, 1979.*

4.2 Practical Hints for Denormalization

The subject of denormalization is a great way to get into religious wars. At one extreme, you will find relational purists who think that the idea of not carrying a database design to at least 5NF is a crime against nature. At the other extreme, you will find people who simply add and move columns all over the database with ALTER statements, never keeping the schema stable.

The reason given for denormalization was performance. A fully normalized database requires a lot of JOINs to construct common VIEWs of data from its components. JOINs used to be very costly in terms of time and computer resources, so by "preconstructing" the JOIN in a denormalized table could save quite a bit of computer time. Today, we have better hardware and software. The VIEWs can be materialized and indexed if they are used frequently by the sessions. Today, only data warehouses should be denormalized and never a production OLTP system. The extra procedural code needed to maintain the data integrity of a denormalized schema is just not worth it.

Today, however, only data warehouses should be denormalized. JOINs are far cheaper than they were and the overhead of handling exceptions with procedural code is far greater than any extra database overhead.

4.2.1 Row Sorting

Back on May 27, 2001, Fred Block posted a problem on the SQL Server Newsgroup. I will change the problem slightly, but the idea was that he had a table with five character string columns that had to be sorted alphabetically within each row. This "flatten table" is a very common denormalization, which might involve months of the year as columns or other things which are acting as repeating groups in violation of First Normal Form.

Let's declare the table to look like this and dive into the problem.

```
CREATE TABLE Foobar
(key_col INTEGER NOT NULL PRIMARY KEY,
 c1 VARCHAR(20) NOT NULL,
 c2 VARCHAR(20) NOT NULL,
 c3 VARCHAR(20) NOT NULL,
 c4 VARCHAR(20) NOT NULL,
 c5 VARCHAR(20) NOT NULL);
```

This means that we want this condition to hold:

```
CHECK ((c1 <= c2) AND (c2 <= c3)
  AND (c3 <= c4) AND (c4 <= c5))
```

Obviously, if he had added this constraint to the table in the first place, we would be fine. Of course, that would have pushed the problem to the front end and I would not have a topic for this section in the book.

What was interesting was how everyone that read this Newsgroup posting immediately envisioned a stored procedure that would take the five values, sort them, and return them to their original row in the table. The only way to make this approach work for the whole table was to write an update cursor and loop through all the rows of the table. Itzik Ben-Gan posted a simple procedure that loaded the values into a temporary table, and then pulled them out in sorted order, starting with the minimum value, using a loop.

Another trick is the Bose-Nelson sort (Bose, R. C., Nelson, R. J. A Sorting Problem Journal of the ACM, 9, 282-296), that I had written about in DR. DOBB'S JOURNAL back in 1985. This is a recursive procedure that takes an integer and then generates swap pairs for a vector of that size. A swap pair is a pair of position numbers from 1 to (*n*) in the vector which need to be exchanged if their contents are out of order. These swap pairs are also related to Sorting Networks in the literature (see Knuth, D. The Art of Computer Programming, vol. 3, ISBN 978-0201896855).

There are other algorithms for producing Sorting Networks which produce swap pairs for various values of (*n*). The algorithms are not always optimal for all values of (*n*). You can generate them at http://jgamble.ripco.net/cgi-bin/nw.cgi?inputs=5&algorithm=best&output=svg

You are probably thinking that this method is a bit weak because the results are only good for sorting a fixed number of items. But a table only has a fixed number of columns, so that is not such a problem in SQL.

You can set up a sorting network that will sort five items (I was thinking of a Poker hand), with the minimal number of exchanges, nine swaps, like this:

```
Swap(c1, c2);
Swap(c4, c5);
Swap(c3, c5);
Swap(c3, c4);
Swap(c1, c4);
Swap(c1, c3);
Swap(c2, c5);
Swap(c2, c4);
Swap(c2, c3);
```

You might want to deal yourself a hand of five playing cards in one suit to see how it works. Put the cards face down in a line on the table and pick up the pairs, swapping them if required, then turn over the row to see that it is in sorted order when you are done.

In theory, the minimum number of swaps needed to sort (*n*) items is CEILING ($\log_2 (n!)$) and as (*n*) increases, this approaches $O(n\log_2(n))$. The Computer Science majors will remember that "Big O" expression as the expected performance of the best sorting algorithms, such as Quicksort. The Bose-Nelson method is very good for small values of (*n*). If ($n<9$) then it is perfect, actually. But as things get bigger, Bose-Nelson approaches O(*n* 1.585). In English, this method is good for a fixed size list of 16 or fewer items and goes to hell after that.

The obvious direct way to write a sorting network in SQL is as a sequence of UPDATE statements. Remember that in SQL, the SET clause assignments happen in parallel, so you can easily write a SET clause that exchanges several pairs of columns in that one statement. Using the above swap chain, we get this block of code:

```
BEGIN ATOMIC
-- Swap(c1, c2);
UPDATE Foobar
   SET c1 = c2, c2 = c1
 WHERE c1 > c2;

-- Swap(c4, c5);
UPDATE Foobar
   SET c4 = c5, c5 = c4
 WHERE c4 > c5;

-- Swap(c3, c5);
UPDATE Foobar
   SET c3 = c5, c5 = c3
 WHERE c3 > c5;

-- Swap(c3, c4);
UPDATE Foobar
   SET c3 = c4, c4 = c3
 WHERE c3 > c4;

-- Swap(c1, c4);
UPDATE Foobar
   SET c1 = c4, c4 = c1
 WHERE c1 > c4;
```

```
-- Swap(c1, c3);
UPDATE Foobar
   SET c1 = c3, c3 = c1
 WHERE c1 > c3;

-- Swap(c2, c5);
UPDATE Foobar
   SET c2 = c5, c5 = c2
 WHERE c2 > c5;

-- Swap(c2, c4);
UPDATE Foobar
   SET c2 = c4, c4 = c2
 WHERE c2 > c4;

-- Swap(c2, c3);
UPDATE Foobar
   SET c2 = c3, c3 = c2
 WHERE c2 > c3;

END;
```

If you look at the first two UPDATE statements, you can see that they do not overlap. This means you could roll them into one statement like this:

```
-- Swap(c1, c2) AND Swap(c4, c5);
UPDATE Foobar
  SET  c1 = CASE WHEN c1 <= c2 THEN c1 ELSE c2 END,
       c2 = CASE WHEN c1 <= c2 THEN c2 ELSE c1 END,
       c4 = CASE WHEN c4 <= c5 THEN c4 ELSE c5 END,
       c5 = CASE WHEN c4 <= c5 THEN c5 ELSE c4 ENDWHERE c4 > c5 OR c1 > c2;
```

The advantage of doing this is that you have to execute only one UPDATE statement and not two. In theory, they will execute in parallel in SQL. Updating a table, even on nonkey columns, usually locks the table and prevents other users from getting to the data. If you could roll the statements into one single UPDATE, you would have the best of all possible worlds, but I doubt that the code would be easy to read.

Here are some Sorting Networks for common numbers of items, such as 12 for months in a year, 10, and 25.

$n = 5$: 9 comparisons in 6 parallel operations.

```
[[0,1],[3,4]]
[[2,4]]
[[2,3],[1,4]]
[[0,3]]
[[0,2],[1,3]]
[[1,2]]
```

$n = 10$: 29 comparisons in 9 parallel operations.

```
[[4,9],[3,8],[2,7],[1,6],[0,5]]
[[1,4],[6,9],[0,3],[5,8]]
[[0,2],[3,6],[7,9]]
[[0,1],[2,4],[5,7],[8,9]]
[[1,2],[4,6],[7,8],[3,5]]
[[2,5],[6,8],[1,3],[4,7]]
[[2,3],[6,7]]
[[3,4],[5,6]]
[[4,5]]
```

$n = 12$: 39 comparisons in 9 parallel operations.

```
[[0,1],[2,3],[4,5],[6,7],[8,9],[10,11]]
[[1,3],[5,7],[9,11],[0,2],[4,6],[8,10]]
[[1,2],[5,6],[9,10],[0,4],[7,11]]
[[1,5],[6,10],[3,7],[4,8]]
[[5,9],[2,6],[0,4],[7,11],[3,8]]
[[1,5],[6,10],[2,3],[8,9]]
[[1,4],[7,10],[3,5],[6,8]]
[[2,4],[7,9],[5,6]]
[[3,4],[7,8]]
```

When (n) gets larger than 16, we do not have proof that a particular sorting network is optimal. Here is a quick table of the number of comparisons for the best networks under ($n = 16$).

Inputs	1	2	3	4	5	6	7	8	9	10	11	12	13	14	15	16
Comparisons	0	1	3	5	9	12	16	19	25	29	35	39	45	51	56	60

Normalization

THE RELATIONAL MODEL and the Normal Forms of the Relational Model were first defined by Dr. E.F. Codd (1970) then extended by other writers after him. He invented the term "normalized relations" by borrowing from the political jargon of the day. A branch of mathematics called relations deals with mappings among sets defined by predicate calculus from formal logic. Just as in an algebraic equation, there are many forms of the same relational statement, but the "normal forms" of relations are certain formally defined desirable constructions. The goal of normal forms is to avoid certain data anomalies that can occur in unnormalized tables. Data anomalies are easier to explain with an example, but first please be patient while I define some terms. A predicate is a statement of the form A(X), which means that X has the property A. For example, "John is from Indiana" is a predicate statement; here "John" is the subject and "is from Indiana" is the predicate. A relation is a predicate with two or more subjects. "John and Bob are brothers" is an example of a relation. The common way of visualizing a set of relational statements is as a table where the columns are attributes of the relation and each row is a specific relational statement.

When Dr. Codd defined the relational model, he gave 0-12 rules for the visualization of the relation as a table:

0. (Yes, there is a rule zero.) For a system to qualify as a relational database management system, that system must use its relational

facilities (exclusively) to manage the database. SQL is not so pure on this rule, since you can often do procedural things to the data.

1. The information rule: this simply requires all information in the database to be represented in one and only one way, namely by values in columns within rows of tables. SQL is good here, but columns are found by their names and not by their positions in a row in a strict RDBMS model. SQL allows the use of a * as shorthand for a list of column names.

2. The guaranteed access rule: This rule is essentially a restatement of the fundamental requirement for primary keys. It states that every individual scalar value in the database must be logically addressable by specifying the name of the containing table, the name of the containing column, and a key value of the containing row. SQL follows this rule for tables that have a key, but SQL does not require a table to have a key at all.

3. Systematic treatment of NULL values: The DBMS is required to support a representation of missing information and inapplicable information that is systematic, distinct from all regular values, and independent of data type. It is also implied that such representations must be manipulated by the DBMS in a systematic way. SQL has a NULL that is used for both missing information and inapplicable information, rather than having two separate tokens as Dr. Codd wished in his second version of the Relational Model (Codd, E.F., The Relational Model for Database Management: Version 2 Hardcover, May 1, 2000; ISBN: 978-0201141924).

4. Active online catalog based on the relational model: The system is required to support an online, inline, relational catalog that is accessible to authorized users by means of their regular query language. SQL does this.

5. The comprehensive data sublanguage rule: The system must support at least one relational language that (a) has a linear syntax, (b) can be used both interactively and within application programs, and (c) supports data definition operations (including view definitions), data manipulation operations (update as well as retrieval), security and integrity constraints, and transaction management operations (begin, commit, and rollback).

SQL is pretty good on this point, since all of the operations Codd defined can be written in the DML (Data Manipulation Language).

6. The VIEW updating rule: All views that are theoretically updatable must be updatable by the system. SQL is weak here and has elected to standardize on the safest case. View updatability is now known to be NP-complete and therefore impossible to enforce in general. INSTEAD OF triggers in SQL allow solutions for particular schemas.
7. High-level insert, update, and delete: The system must support set-at-a-time INSERT, UPDATE, and DELETE operators. SQL does this.
8. Physical data independence: This is self-explanatory; users are never aware of the physical implementation and deal only with a logical model. Any real product is going to have some physical dependence, but SQL is better than most programming languages on this point. In particular, auto-incrementing row identifiers based on physical insertions into a table like the IDENTITY table property in MS SQL Server are in total violation of this rule.
9. Logical data independence: This is self-explanatory. SQL is quite good about this point until you start using vendor extensions.
10. Integrity independence: Integrity constraints must be specified separately from application programs and stored in the catalog. It must be possible to change such constraints as and when appropriate without unnecessarily affecting existing applications. *Standard SQL* has this.
11. Distribution independence: Existing applications should continue to operate successfully (a) when a distributed version of the DBMS is first introduced and (b) when existing distributed data are redistributed around the system. We are just starting to get distributed versions of SQL, so it is a little early to say whether SQL will meet this criterion or not.
12. The nonsubversion rule: If the system provides a low-level (record-at-a-time, bit level) interface, that interface cannot be used to subvert the system (e.g., bypassing a relational security or integrity constraint). SQL is good about this one.

Codd also specified 9 structural features, 3 integrity features, and 18 manipulative features, all of which are required as well. He later extended the list from 12 rules to 333 in the second version of the relational model. This section is getting too long and you can look them up for yourself.

Normal forms are an attempt to make sure that you do not destroy true data or create false data in your database. One of the ways of avoiding errors is to represent a fact only once in the database, since if a fact appears more than once, one of the instances of it is likely to be in error—a man with two watches can never be sure what time it is.

This process of table design is called normalization. It is not mysterious, but it can get complex. You can buy CASE tools to help you do it, but you should know a bit about the theory before you use such a tool.

5.1 Functional and Multivalued Dependencies

A normal form is a way of classifying a table based on the functional dependencies (FDs) in it. A functional dependency means that if I know the value of one attribute, I can always determine the value of another. The notation used in relational theory is an arrow between the two attributes, for example $A \rightarrow B$, which can be read in English as "A determines B." If I know your employee number, I can determine your name; if I know a part number, I can determine the weight and color of the part; and so forth.

A multivalued dependency (MVD) means that if I know the value of one attribute, I can always determine the values of a set of another attribute. The notation used in relational theory is a double-headed arrow between the two attributes, for instance $A \twoheadrightarrow B$, which can be read in English as "A determines many Bs." If I know a teacher's name, I can determine a list of her students; if I know a part number, I can determine the part numbers of its components; and so forth.

5.2 First Normal Form (1NF)

Consider a requirement to maintain data about class schedules at a school. We are required to keep the course_name, class_section, dept_name, time, room_nbr, professor, student, student_major, and student_grade. Suppose that we initially set up a Pascal file with records that look like this:

```
Classes = RECORD
    course_name:  ARRAY [1:7] OF CHAR;
```

```
class_section:  CHAR;
  time_period:  INTEGER;
     room_nbr:  INTEGER;
    room_size:  INTEGER;
    professor:  ARRAY [1:25] OF CHAR;
    dept_name:  ARRAY [1:10] OF CHAR;
     students:  ARRAY [1:class_size]
                OF RECORD
                   student_name ARRAY [1:25] OF CHAR;
                   student_major ARRAY [1:10] OF CHAR;
                   student_grade CHAR;
                   END;
       END;
```

This table is not in the most basic normal form of relational databases. First Normal Form (1NF) means that the table has no repeating groups. That is, every column is a scalar value, not an array or a list or anything with its own structure.

In SQL, it is impossible not to be in 1NF unless the vendor has added array or other extensions to the language. The Pascal record could be "flattened out" in SQL and the field names changed to data element names to look like this:

```
CREATE TABLE Classes
(course_name CHAR(7) NOT NULL,
 class_section CHAR(1) NOT NULL,
 time_period INTEGER NOT NULL,
 room_nbr INTEGER NOT NULL,
 room_size INTEGER NOT NULL,
 professor_name CHAR(25) NOT NULL,
 dept_name CHAR(10) NOT NULL,
 student_name CHAR(25) NOT NULL,
 student_major CHAR(10) NOT NULL,
 student_grade CHAR(1) NOT NULL);
```

This table is acceptable to SQL. In fact, we can locate a row in the table with a combination of (course_name, class_section, student_name), so we have a key. But what we are doing is hiding the Students record array, which has not changed its nature by being flattened.

There are problems.

If Professor 'Jones' of the math department dies, we delete all his rows from the Classes table. This also deletes the information that all his students were taking a math class and maybe not all of them wanted to drop out of school just yet. I am deleting more than one fact from the database. This is called a deletion anomaly.

If student 'Wilson' decides to change one of his math classes, formerly taught by Professor 'Jones,' to English, we will show Professor 'Jones' as an instructor in both the math and the English departments. I could not change a simple fact by itself. This creates false information and is called an update anomaly.

If the school decides to start a new department, which has no students yet, we cannot put in the data about the professor we just hired until we have classroom and student data to fill out a row. I cannot insert a simple fact by itself. This is called an insertion anomaly.

There are more problems in this table, but you see the point. Yes, there are some ways to get around these problems without changing the tables. We could permit NULLs in the table. We could write triggers to check the table for false data. These are tricks that will only get worse as the data and the relationships become more complex. The solution is to break the table up into other tables, each of which represents one relationship or simple fact.

5.2.1 Note on Repeating Groups

The definition of 1NF is that the table has no repeating groups and that all columns are scalar values. This means a column cannot have arrays, linked lists, tables within tables, or record structures, like those you find in other programming languages. This was very easy to avoid in Standard SQL, since the language had no support for them. This is no longer true after SQL-99, which introduces several very nonrelational "features" and since several vendors added their own support for arrays, nested tables, and variant data types.

Aside from relational purity, there are good reasons to avoid these features. They are not widely implemented, and the vendor specific extensions will not port. Furthermore, the optimizers cannot easily use them, so they degrade performance.

Old habits are hard to change, so new SQL programmers often try to force their old model of the world into Standard SQL in several ways.

5.2.1.1 Repeating Columns

One way you "fake it" in SQL is to use a group of columns which all the members of the group have the same semantic value; that is, they represent the same attribute in the table. Consider the table of an employee and his children:

```
CREATE TABLE Personnel
(emp_nbr INTEGER NOT NULL PRIMARY KEY,
 emp_name VARCHAR(30) NOT NULL,
 . . .
 child1 CHAR(30), birthday1 DATE, sex1 CHAR(1),
 child2 CHAR(30), birthday2 DATE, sex2 CHAR(1),
 child3 CHAR(30), birthday3 DATE, sex3 CHAR(1),
 child4 CHAR(30), birthday4 DATE, sex4 CHAR(1));
```

This looks like the layouts of many existing file system records in COBOL and other 3GL languages. The birthday and sex information for each child is part of a repeated group and therefore violates 1NF. This is faking a four-element array in SQL; the index just happens to be part of the column name!

Suppose I have a table with the quantity of a product_name sold in each month of a particular year and I originally built the table to look like this:

```
CREATE TABLE Abnormal
(product_name CHAR(10) NOT NULL PRIMARY KEY,
 month_01 INTEGER, -- null means no data yet
 month_02 INTEGER,
 . . .
 month_12 INTEGER);
```

and I wanted to flatten it out into a more normalized form, like this:

```
CREATE TABLE Normal
(product_name CHAR(10) NOT NULL,
 month_nbr INTEGER NOT NULL,
 product_qty INTEGER NOT NULL,
 PRIMARY KEY (product_name, month_nbr));
```

I can use the statement

```
INSERT INTO Normal (product_name, month_nbr, product_qty)
SELECT product_name, 1, month_01
```

```
  FROM Abnormal
 WHERE month_01 IS NOT NULL
UNION ALL
SELECT product_name, 2, month_02
  FROM Abnormal
 WHERE month_02 IS NOT NULL
. . .

UNION ALL
SELECT product_name, 12, month_12
  FROM Abnormal
 WHERE bin_12 IS NOT NULL;
```

While a UNION ALL expression is usually slow, this has to be run only once to load the normalized table and then the original table can be dropped.

5.2.1.2 Parsing a List in a String

Another popular method is to use a string and fill it with a comma-separated list. The result is a lot of string handling procedures to work around this kludge. Consider this example:

```
CREATE TABLE InputStrings
(key_col CHAR(10) NOT NULL PRIMARY KEY,
 input_string VARCHAR(255) NOT NULL);

INSERT INTO InputStrings VALUES ('first', '12,34,567,896');
INSERT INTO InputStrings VALUES ('second', '312,534,997,896'); . . .
```

This will be the table that gets the outputs, in the form of the original key column and one parameter per row.

```
CREATE TABLE Parmlist
(key_col CHAR(5) NOT NULL PRIMARY KEY,
 parm INTEGER NOT NULL);
```

It makes life easier if the lists in the input strings start and end with a comma. You will also need a table called Series, which is a set of integers from 1 to (n).

```
SELECT key_col,
       CAST (SUBSTRING (',' || I1.input_string || ',', MAX(S1.seq || 1),
                        (S2.seq - MAX(S1.seq || 1)))
```

```
        AS INTEGER),
      COUNT(S2.seq) AS place
 FROM InputStrings AS I1, Series AS S1, Series AS S2
WHERE SUBSTRING (',' || I1.input_string || ',', S1.seq, 1) = ','
  AND SUBSTRING (',' || I1.input_string || ',', S2.seq, 1) = ','
  AND S1.seq  <  S2.seq
  AND S2.seq  <=  DATALENGTH(I1.input_string) + 1
GROUP BY I1.key_col, I1.input_string, S2.seq;
```

The S1 and S2 copies of Series are used to locate bracketing pairs of commas, and the entire set of substrings located between them is extracts and cast as integers in one nonprocedural step.

The trick is to be sure that the left-hand comma of the bracketing pair is the closest one to the second comma. The place column tells you the relative position of the value in the input string.

A very fast version of this trick is due to Ken Henderson. Instead of using a comma to separate the fields within the list, put each value into a fixed length substring and extract them by using a simple multiplication of the length by the desired array index number. This is a direct imitation of how many compilers handle arrays at the hardware level.

Having said all of this, the right way would be to put the list into a single column in a table. This can be done in languages that allow you to pass array elements into SQL parameters, like this:

```
INSERT INTO Parmlist
VALUES (:a[1]), (:a[2]), (:a[3]), ..., (:a[n]);
```

Or if you want to remove NULLs and duplicates

```
INSERT INTO Parmlist
SELECT DISTINCT x
   FROM VALUES (:a[1]), (:a[2]), (:a[3]), ..., (:a[n]) AS List(x)
WHERE x IS NOT NULL;
```

5.3 Second Normal Form (2NF)

A table is in Second Normal Form (2NF) if it is in 1NF and has no partial key dependencies. That is, if X and Y are columns and X is a key, then for any Z that is a proper subset of X, it cannot be the case that $Z \rightarrow Y$. Informally, the table is in 1NF and it has a key that determines all nonkey attributes in the table.

In the Pascal example, our users tell us that knowing the student and course_name is sufficient to determine the class_section (since students cannot sign up for more than one class_section of the same course_name) and the student_grade. This is the same as saying that (student_name, course_name) → (class_section, student_grade).

After more analysis, we also discover from our users that (student_name → student_major)—students have only one student_major. Since student is part of the (student_name, course_name) key, we have a partial key dependency! This leads us to the following decomposition:

```
CREATE TABLE Classes
(course_name CHAR(7) NOT NULL,
 class_section CHAR(1) NOT NULL,
 time_period INTEGER NOT NULL,
 room_nbr INTEGER NOT NULL,
 room_size INTEGER NOT NULL,
 professor_name CHAR(25) NOT NULL,
PRIMARY KEY (course_name, class_section));

CREATE TABLE Enrollment
(student_name CHAR(25) NOT NULL,
 course_name CHAR(7) NOT NULL,
 class_section CHAR(1) NOT NULL,
 student_grade CHAR(1) NOT NULL,
PRIMARY KEY (student_name, course_name));

CREATE TABLE Students
(student_name CHAR(25) NOT NULL PRIMARY KEY,
 student_major CHAR(10) NOT NULL);
```

At this point, we are in 2NF. Every attribute depends on the entire key in its table. Now if a student changes majors, it can be done in one place. Furthermore, a student cannot sign up for different sections of the same class, because we have changed the key of Enrollment. Unfortunately, we still have problems.

Notice that while room_size depends on the entire key of Classes, it also depends on room_nbr. If the room_nbr is changed for a course_name and class_section, we may also have to change the room_size, and if the room_nbr is modified (we knock down a wall), we may have to change room_size in several rows in Classes for that room_nbr.

5.4 Third Normal Form (3NF)

Another normal form can address these problems. A table is in Third Normal Form (3NF) if it is in 2NF and for all X→Y, where X and Y are columns of a table, X is a key or Y is part of a candidate key. (A candidate key is a unique set of columns that identify each row in a table; you cannot remove a column from the candidate key without destroying its uniqueness.) This implies that the table is in 2NF, since a partial key dependency is a type of transitive dependency. Informally, all the nonkey columns are determined by the key, the whole key, and nothing but the key.

The usual way that 3NF is explained is that there are no transitive dependencies, but this is not quite right. A transitive dependency is a situation where we have a table with columns (A, B, C) and (A→B) and (B→C), so we know that (A→C). In our case, the situation is that (course_name, class_section)→room_nbr and room_nbr→room_size. This is not a simple transitive dependency, since only part of a key is involved, but the principle still holds. To get our example into 3NF and fix the problem with the room_size column, we make the following decomposition:

```
CREATE TABLE Rooms
(room_nbr INTEGER NOT NULL PRIMARY KEY,
 room_size INTEGER NOT NULL);

CREATE TABLE Students
(student_name CHAR(25) NOT NULL PRIMARY KEY,
 student_major CHAR(10) NOT NULL);

CREATE TABLE Classes
(course_name CHAR(7) NOT NULL,
 class_section CHAR(1) NOT NULL,
 PRIMARY KEY (course_name, class_section),
 time_period INTEGER NOT NULL,
 room_nbr INTEGER NOT NULL
  REFERENCES Rooms(room_nbr));

CREATE TABLE Enrollment
(student_name CHAR(25) NOT NULL
  REFERENCES Students(student_name),
 course_name CHAR(7) NOT NULL,
 PRIMARY KEY (student_name, course_name),
 class_section CHAR(1) NOT NULL,
```

```
  FOREIGN KEY (course_name, class_section)
   REFERENCES Classes(course_name, class_section),
 student_grade CHAR(1) NOT NULL);
```

A common misunderstanding about relational theory is that 3NF tables have no transitive dependencies. As indicated above, if X→Y, X does not have to be a key if Y is part of a candidate key. We still have a transitive dependency in the example—(room_nbr, time_period)→(course_name, class_section)—but since the right side of the dependency is a key, it is technically in 3NF. The unreasonable behavior that this table structure still has is that several course_names can be assigned to the same room_nbr at the same time.

Another form of transitive dependency is a computed column. For example:

```
CREATE TABLE Boxes
(width INTEGER NOT NULL,
 length INTEGER NOT NULL,
 height INTEGER NOT NULL,
 volume INTEGER NOT NULL
        CHECK (width * length * height = volume),
 PRIMARY KEY (width, length, height));
```

The volume column is determined by the other three columns, so any change to one of the three columns will require a change to the volume column. You can use a computed column in this example which would look like:

```
(volume INTEGER COMPUTED AS (width * length * height) PERSISTENT)
```

5.5 Elementary Key Normal Form (EKNF)

Elementary Key Normal Form (EKNF) is a subtle enhancement on 3NF. By definition, EKNF tables are also in 3NF. This happens when there is more than one unique composite key and they overlap. Such cases can cause redundant information in the overlapping column(s). For example, in the following table, let's assume that a course code is also a unique identifier for a given subject in the following table:

```
CREATE TABLE Enrollment
(student_id INTEGER NOT NULL,
 course_code CHAR(6) NOT NULL,
 course_name VARCHAR(15) NOT NULL,
```

```
 PRIMARY KEY (student_id, course_name)
-- , UNIQUE (student_id, course_code) alternative key
);
Enrollment
student_id course_code course_name
=======================================
   1        'CS-100'      'ER Diagrams'
   1        'CS-114'      'Database Design'
   2        'CS-114'      'Database Design'
```

This table, although it is in 3NF, violates EKNF. The primary key of the above table is the combination of (student_id, course_name). However, we can also see an alternate key (student_id, course_code) as well. The above schema could result in update and deletion anomalies because values of both course_name and course_code tend to be repeated for a given subject.

The following schema is a decomposition of the above table in order to satisfy EKNF:

```
CREATE TABLE Subjects
(course_code CHAR(6) NOT NULL PRIMARY KEY,
 course_name VARCHAR(15) NOT NULL);

CREATE TABLE Enrollment
(student_id INTEGER NOT NULL
  REFERENCES Students(student_id),
 course_code CHAR(6) NOT NULL
   REFERENCES Subjects(course_code),
 PRIMARY KEY (student_id, course_code));
```

For reasons that will become obvious in the following class_section, ensuring that a table is in EKNF is usually skipped, as most designers will move directly on to Boyce-Codd Normal Form after ensuring that a schema is in 3NF. Thus, EKNF is included here only for reasons of historical accuracy and completeness.

5.6 Boyce-Codd Normal Form (BCNF)

A table is in BCNF when for all nontrivial FDs ($X \rightarrow A$), X is a superkey for the whole schema. A superkey is a unique set of columns that identify each row in a table, but you can remove some columns from it and it will still be a key. Informally, a superkey is carrying extra weight.

BCNF is the normal form that actually removes all transitive dependencies. A table is in BCNF if for all (X→Y), X is a key period. We can go to this normal form just by adding another key with UNIQUE (room_nbr, time_period) constraint clause to the table Classes.

There are some other interesting and useful "higher" normal forms, but they are outside of the scope of this discussion. In our example, we have removed all of the important anomalies with BCNF.

Third Normal Form was concerned with the relationship between key and nonkey columns. However, a column can often play both roles. Consider a table for computing each salesman's bonus gifts that has for each salesman his base salary, the number of gift_points he has won in a contest, and the bonus gift awarded for that combination of salary range and gift_points. For example, we might give a fountain pen to a beginning salesman with a base pay rate between $15,000.00 and $20,000.00 and 100 gift_points, but give a car to a master salesman, whose salary is between $30,000.00 and $60,000.00 and who has 200 gift_points. The functional dependencies are, therefore,

```
(pay_step, gift_points) → gift_name
 gift_name → gift_points
```

Let's start with a table that has all the data in it and normalize it.

```
Gifts
salary_amt gift_points gift_name
==================================
15000.00       100        'Pencil'
17000.00       100        'Pen'
30000.00       200        'Car'
31000.00       200        'Car'
32000.00       200        'Car'
```

```
CREATE TABLE Gifts
(salary_amt DECIMAL(8,2) NOT NULL
 gift_points INTEGER NOT NULL,
 PRIMARY KEY (salary_amt, gift_points),
 gift_name VARCHAR(10) NOT NULL);
```

This schema is in 3NF, but it has problems. You cannot insert a new gift into our offerings and points unless we have a salary to go with it. If you remove any sales points, you lose information about the gifts and salaries (e.g., only people in the $30,000.00 to $32,000.00 range can win a car). And, finally, a change in the gifts for a particular point score would have to affect all the rows within the same pay step. This table needs to be broken apart into two tables:

```
PayGifts
salary_amt gift_name
=====================
15000.00      'Pencil'
17000.00      'Pen'
30000.00      'Car'
31000.00      'Car'
32000.00      'Car'

CREATE TABLE Gifts
(salary_amt DECIMAL(8,2) NOT NULL,
 gift_points INTEGER NOT NULL,
 PRIMARY KEY(salary_amt, gift_points),
 gift_name VARCHAR(10) NOT NULL);

GiftsPoints
gift_name gift_points
======================
'Pencil'    100
'Pen'       100
'Car'       200

(salary_amt, gift_points) → gift
 gift → gift_points

CREATE TABLE GiftsPoints
(gift_name VARCHAR(10) NOT NULL PRIMARY KEY,
 gift_points INTEGER NOT NULL));
```

5.7 Fourth Normal Form (4NF)

Fourth Normal Form (4NF) makes use of multivalued dependencies. The problem it solves is that the table has too many of them. For example, consider a table of departments, their projects, and the parts they stock. The MVD's in the table would be:

```
dept_name ↠ jobs

dept_name ↠ parts
```

Assume that dept_name 'd1' works on jobs 'j1,' and 'j2' with parts 'p1' and 'p2'; that dept_name 'd2' works on jobs 'j3,' 'j4,' and 'j5' with parts 'p2' and 'p4'; and that dept_name 'd3' works on job 'j2' only with parts 'p5' and 'p6.' The table would look like this:

dept	job	part
'd1'	'j1'	'p1'
'd1'	'j1'	'p2'
'd1'	'j2'	'p1'
'd1'	'j2'	'p2'
'd2'	'j3'	'p2'
'd2'	'j3'	'p4'
'd2'	'j4'	'p2'
'd2'	'j4'	'p4'
'd2'	'j5'	'p2'
'd2'	'j5'	'p4'
'd3'	'j2'	'p5'
'd3'	'j2'	'p6'

If you want to add a part to a dept_name, you must create more than one new row.

Likewise, to remove a part or a job from a row can destroy information. Updating a part or job name will also require multiple rows to be changed.

The solution is to split this table into two tables, one with (dept_name, jobs) in it and one with (dept_name, parts) in it. The definition of 4NF is that we have no more than one MVD in a table. If a table is in 4NF, it is also in BCNF.

5.8 Fifth Normal Form (5NF)

Fifth Normal Form (5NF), also called the Join-Projection Normal Form or the Projection-Join Normal Form, is based on the idea of a lossless JOIN or the lack of a join-projection anomaly. This problem occurs when you have an n-way relationship, where (n>2). A quick check for 5NF is to see if the table is in 3NF, and all the candidate keys are single columns.

As an example of the problems solved by 5NF, consider a table of house notes that records the buyer, the seller, and the lender:

```
HouseNotes
buyer       seller      lender
-----------------------------------------
'Smith'     'Jones'     'NationalBank'
'Smith'     'Wilson'    'HomeBank'
'Nelson'    'Jones'     'HomeBank'
```

This table is a three-way relationship, but because older CASE tools allow only binary relationships it might have to be expressed in an E-R diagram as three binary relationships, which would generate CREATE TABLE statements leading to these tables:

```
BuyerLender
buyer       lender
------------------------------
'Smith'     'NationalBank'
'Smith'     'HomeBank'
'Nelson'    'HomeBank'

SellerLender
seller      lender
------------------------------
'Jones'     'NationalBank'
'Wilson'    'HomeBank'
'Jones'     'HomeBank'

BuyerSeller
buyer       seller
-----------------------
'Smith'     'Jones'
'Smith'     'Wilson'
'Nelson'    'Jones'
```

The trouble is that when you try to assemble the original information by joining pairs of these three tables together, thus:

```
SELECT BS.buyer, SL.seller, BL.lender
  FROM BuyerLender AS BL,
       SellerLender AS SL,
       BuyerSeller AS BS
 WHERE BL.buyer = BS.buyer
   AND BL.lender = SL.lender
   AND SL.seller = BS.seller;
```

you will recreate all the valid rows in the original table, such as ('Smith,' 'Jones,' 'National Bank'), but there will also be false rows, such as ('Smith,' 'Jones,' 'Home Bank'), which were not part of the original table. This is called a join-projection anomaly.

There are also strong JPNF and overstrong JPNF, which make use of JOIN dependencies (JD). Unfortunately, there is no systematic way to find a JPNF or 4NF schema, because the problem is known to be NP complete. This is a mathematical term that means as the number of elements in a problem increase, the effort to solve it increases so fast and requires so many resources that you cannot find a general answer.

As an aside, Third Normal Form is very popular with CASE tools and most of them can generate a schema where all of the tables are in 3NF. They obtain the FDs from an E-R (entity-relationship) diagram or from a statistical analysis of the existing data, then put them together into tables and check for normal forms.

The bad news is that it is often possible to derive more than one 3NF schema from a set of FDs. Most of CASE tools that produce an E-R diagram will find only one of them, and go no further. However, if you use an ORM (Object Role Model) tool properly, the schema will be in 5NF. I suggest strongly that you get any of the books by Terry Halpin on this technique.

5.9 Domain-Key Normal Form (DKNF)

Ronald Fagin defined Domain/Key Normal Form (DKNF) in 1981 as a schema having all of the domain constraints and functional dependencies enforced. There is not yet a general algorithm that will always generate the DKNF solution given a set of constraints. We can, however, determine DKNF in many special cases, and it is a good guide to writing DDL in the real world.

Let's back up a bit and look at the mathematical model under normalization. A functional dependency has axioms that can be used in normalization problems. These six axioms, known as Armstrong's axioms, are given below:

Reflexive: $X \rightarrow X$

Augmentation: if $X \rightarrow Y$, then $XZ \rightarrow Y$

Union: if ($X \rightarrow Y$ and $X \rightarrow Z$) then $X \rightarrow YZ$

Decomposition: if $X \rightarrow Y$ and Z a subset of Y, then $X \rightarrow Z$
Transitivity: if ($X \rightarrow Y$ and $Y \rightarrow Z$) then $X \rightarrow Z$
Pseudo-transitivity: if ($X \rightarrow Y$ and $YZ \rightarrow W$) then $XZ \rightarrow W$

They make good sense if you just look at them, which is something we like in a set of axioms. In the real world, the FDs are the business rules we are trying to model.

In the normalization algorithm for 3NF (developed by P. A. Berstein, 1976), we use the axioms to get rid of redundant FD's. For example, if we are given:

```
A   → B
A   → C
B   → C
DB  → E
DAF → E
```

$A \rightarrow C$ is redundant because it can be derived from $A \rightarrow B$ and $B \rightarrow C$ with transitivity. Also $DAF \rightarrow E$ is redundant because it can be derived from $DB \rightarrow E$ and $A \rightarrow B$ with transitivity (which gives us $DA \rightarrow E$) and augmentation (which then allows $DAF \rightarrow E$). What we would like to find is the smallest set of FDs from which we can generate all of the given rules. This is called a nonredundant cover. For the FD's above, one cover would be:

```
A  → B
B  → C
DB → E
```

Once we do this Berstein shows that we can just create a table for each of the FD's where A, B, and DB are the respective keys. We have taken it easy so far but now it's time for a challenge.

As an example of a schema with multiple Third Normal Form (3NF) tables, here is a problem that was used in a demonstration by DBStar Corporation (now Evoke Software). The company used it as an example in a demonstration that comes with their CASE tool.

We are given an imaginary and simplified airline that has a database for scheduling flights and pilots. Most of the relationships are obvious things. Flights have only one departure time and one destination. They can get a different pilot and can be assigned to a different gate each day of the week. The functional dependencies for the database are given below:

```
 1) flight → destination
 2) flight → hour
 3) (day, flight) → gate
 4) (day, flight) → pilot
 5) (day, hour, pilot) → gate
 6) (day, hour, pilot) → flight
 7) (day, hour, pilot) → destination
 8) (day, hour, gate) → pilot
 9) (day, hour, gate) → flight
10) (day, hour, gate) → destination
```

A purist will look at this collection of FDs can be bothered by the redundancies in this list. But in the real world, when you interview people, they do not speak to you in a minimal set; they state things that they know to be true in their situation. In fact, they very often leave out relationships that they considered to be too obvious to mention.

Your problem is to find 3NF or stronger database schemas in these FD's. You have to be careful! You have to have all of the columns, obviously, but your answer could be in 3NF and still ignore some of the FD's. For example, this will not work:

```
CREATE TABLE PlannedSchedule
(flight, destination, hour, PRIMARY KEY (flight));

CREATE TABLE ActualSchedule
(day, flight, gate, pilot, PRIMARY KEY (day, flight));
```

If we apply the Union axiom to some of the FD's, we get:

```
(day, hour, gate) → (destination, flight, pilot)
(day, hour, pilot) → (destination, flight, gate)
```

This says that the user has required that if we are given a day, an hour, and a gate, we should be able to determine a unique flight for that day, hour, and gate. We should also be able to determine a unique flight given a day, hour, and pilot.

Given the PlannedSchedule and ActualSchedule tables, you cannot produce views where either of the two constraints we just mentioned is enforced. If the query "What flight does pilot X have on day Y and hour Z?" gives you more than one answer, it violates the FD's and common sense. Here is an example of a schema that is allowable in this proposed schema which is undesirable given our constraints:

PlannedSchedule

flight	00:00	destination
118	05:00	Dallas
123	01:00	Omaha
155	05:00	Los Angeles
171	01:00	New York
666	01:00	Atlanta

ActualSchedule

day	flight	pilot	gate
Wed	118	Tom	12A
Wed	155	Tom	13B
Wed	171	Tom	12A
Thu	123	John	12A
Thu	155	John	12A
Thu	171	John	13B

The constraints mean that we should be able to find a unique answer to each the following questions and not lose any information when inserting and deleting data.

(1) Which flight is leaving form gate 12A on Thursdays at 13:00 Hrs? This looks fine until you realize that you do not know about flight 666, which was not required to have anything about its day or pilot in the ActualSchedule table. And likewise, I can add a flight to the ActualSchedule table that has no information in the PlannedSchedule table.

(2) Which pilot is assigned to the flight that leaves gate 12A on Thursdays at 13:00 Hrs? This has the same problem as before.

(3) What is the destination of the flight in query 1 and 2? This has the same problem as before.

(4) What gate is John leaving from on Thursdays at 13:00 Hrs?

(5) Where is Tom flying to on Wednesdays at 17:00 Hrs?

(6) What flight is assigned to Tom on Wednesdays at 17:00 Hrs?

It might help if we gave an example of how one of the FD's in the problem can be derived using the axioms of FD calculus, just like you would do a geometry proof:
Given:

```
1) (day, hour, gate)→ pilot
2) (day, hour, pilot) → flight

prove that:
(day, hour, gate) → flight.

3) (day, hour) → (day, hour);           Reflexive
4) (day, hour, gate) → (day, hour);     Augmentation on 3
5) (day, hour, gate) → (day, hour, pilot);  Union 1 & 4
6) (day, hour, gate) → flight; Transitive 2 and 5
Q.E.D
```

The answer is to start by attempting to derive each of the functional dependencies from the rest of the set. What we get is several short proofs, each requiring different "given" functional dependencies in order to get to the derived FD.

Here is a list of each of the proofs used to derive the 10 fragmented FD's in the problem. With each derivation, we include every derivation step and the legal FD calculus operation that allows me to make that step. An additional operation that we include here which was not included in the axioms we listed earlier is left reduction. Left reduction says that if XX→Y then X→Y. The reason it was not included is that this is actually a theorem and not one of the basic axioms (side problem: can you derive left reduction?).

```
Prove: (day, hour, pilot) → gate
a) day → day;                     Reflexive
b) (day, hour, pilot) → day;          Augmentation (a)
c) (day, hour, pilot) → (day, flight);   Union (6, b)
d) (day, hour, pilot) → gate;          Transitive (c, 3)
Q.E.D.

Prove: (day, hour, gate) → pilot
a)  day → day;                Reflexive
b)  day, hour, gate → day;       Augmentation (a)
```

```
c)  day, hour, gate → (day, flight);  Union (9, b)
d)  day, hour, gate → pilot;       Transitive (c, 4)
Q.E.D.

Prove: (day, flight) → gate
a) (day, flight, pilot) → gate;   Pseudotransitivity (2, 5)
b) (day, flight, day, flight) → gate; Pseudotransitivity (a, 4)
c) (day, flight) → gate;      Left reduction (b)
Q.E.D.

Prove:  (day, flight) → pilot
a) (day, flight, gate) → pilot;   Pseudotransitivity (2, 8)
b) (day, flight, day, flight) → pilot; Pseudotransitivity (a, 3)
c) (day, flight) → pilot;      Left reduction (b)
Q.E.D.

Prove: (day, hour, gate) → flight
a) (day, hour) → (day, hour);  Reflexivity
b) (day, hour, gate) → (day, hour);    Augmentation (a)
c) (day, hour, gate) → (day, hour, pilot);   Union (b, 8)
d) (day, hour, gate) → flight;        Transitivity (c, 6)
Q.E.D.

Prove: (day, hour, pilot) → flight
a) (day, hour) → (day, hour);  Reflexivity
b) (day, hour, pilot) → (day, hour); Augmentation (a)
c) (day, hour, pilot) → day, hour, gate; Union (b, 5)
d) (day, hour, pilot) → flight;      Transitivity (c, 9)
Q.E.D.

Prove: (day, hour, gate) → destination
a) (day, hour, gate) → destination; Transitivity (9, 1)
Q.E.D.

Prove: (day, hour, pilot) → destination
a) (day, hour, pilot) → destination;    Transitivity (6, 1)
Q.E.D.
```

Now that we've shown you how to derive 8 of the 10 FD's from other FD's, you can try mixing and matching the FD's into sets so that each set meets the following criteria:

(1) Each attribute must be represented on either the left or the right side of at least one FD in the set.

(2) If a given FD is included in the set then all the FD's needed to derive it cannot also be included.

(3) If a given FD is excluded from the set then the FD's used to derive it must be included.

This produces a set of "nonredundant covers," which can be found with trial, error, and common sense. For example, if we excluded (day, hour, gate) → flight, we must then include (day, hour, gate) → pilot and vice versa because each is used in the others derivation. If you want to be sure your search was exhaustive, however, you may want to apply a more mechanical method, which is what the CASE tools do for you.

The algorithm for accomplishing this task is basically to generate all the combinations of sets of the FD's. (flight → destination) and (flight → hour) are excluded in the combination generation because they cannot be derived. This gives us (2^8) or 256 combinations of FD's. Each combination is then tested against the criteria.

Fortunately, a simple spreadsheet does all the tedious work. In this problem, the criteria #1 eliminates only 15 sets. Then a criterion #2 eliminates 152 sets, and a criterion #3 drops another 67. This leaves us with 22 possible covers, five of which are the answers we are looking for (we will explain the other 17 later).

These five nonredundant covers are:

```
Set I:
flight → destination
flight → hour
(day, hour, gate) → flight
(day, hour, gate) → pilot
(day, hour, pilot) → gate

Set II:
flight → destination
flight → hour
(day, hour, gate) → pilot
(day, hour, pilot) → flight
(day, hour, pilot) → gate
```

```
Set III:
flight → destination
flight → hour
(day, flight) → gate
(day, flight) → pilot
(day, hour, gate) → flight

Set IV:
flight → destination
flight → hour
(day, flight) → gate
(day, hour, gate) → pilot
(day, hour, pilot) → flight

Set V:
flight → destination
flight → hour
(day, flight) → pilot
(day, hour, gate) → flight
(day, hour, pilot) → gate
(day, hour, pilot) → flight
```

At this point, we perform unions on FD's with the same left-hand side and make tables for each grouping with the left-hand side as a key. We can also eliminate symmetrical FD's (defined as $X \rightarrow Y$ and $Y \rightarrow X$, and written with a two headed arrow, $X \leftrightarrow Y$) by collapsing them into the same table.

These possible schemas are in at least 3NF. They are given in shorthand SQL DDL (Data Declaration Language) without data type declarations.

```
Solution 1:
CREATE TABLE R1 (flight, destination, hour,
 PRIMARY KEY (flight));
CREATE TABLE R2 (day, hour, gate, flight, pilot,
  PRIMARY KEY (day, hour, gate),
  UNIQUE (day, hour, pilot),
  UNIQUE (day, flight),
  UNIQUE (flight, hour));
```

```
Solution 2:
CREATE TABLE R1 (flight, destination, hour, PRIMARY KEY
(flight));
CREATE TABLE R2 (day, flight, gate, pilot,
  PRIMARY KEY (day, flight));
CREATE TABLE R3 (day, hour, gate, flight,
  PRIMARY KEY (day, hour, gate),
  UNIQUE (day, flight),
  UNIQUE (flights, hour));
CREATE TABLE R4 (day, hour, pilot, flight,
  PRIMARY KEY (day, hour, pilot));

Solution 3:
CREATE TABLE R1 (flight, destination, hour, flight
  PRIMARY KEY (flight));
CREATE TABLE R2 (day, flight, gate, PRIMARY KEY (day, flight));
CREATE TABLE R3 (day, hour, gate, pilot,
  PRIMARY KEY (day, hour, gate),
  UNIQUE (day, hour, pilot),
  UNIQUE (day, hour, gate));
CREATE TABLE R4 (day, hour, pilot, flight
  PRIMARY KEY (day, hour, pilot),
  UNIQUE(day, flight),
  UNIQUE (flight, hour));

Solution 4:
CREATE TABLE R1 (flight, destination, hour, PRIMARY KEY (flight));
CREATE TABLE R2 (day, flight, pilot, PRIMARY KEY (day, flight));
CREATE TABLE R3 (day, hour, gate, flight,
  PRIMARY KEY (day, hour, gate),
  UNIQUE (flight, hour));
CREATE TABLE R4 (day, hour, pilot, gate,
  PRIMARY KEY (day, hour, pilot));
```

Once you look at these solutions, they are a mess, but they are a Third Normal Form mess! Is there a better answer? Here is one in BCNF and only two tables, proposed by Chris Date (RELATIONAL DATABASE WRITINGS 1991-1994; ISBN 0-201-82459-0; pp. 224).

```
CREATE TABLE DailySchedules (flight, destination, hour PRIMARY KEY
(flight));
CREATE TABLE PilotSchedules (day, flight, gate, pilot, PRIMARY KEY (day,
flight));
```

This is a workable schema. But we could expand the constraints to give us better performance and more precise error messages, since schedules are not likely to change:

```
CREATE TABLE DailySchedules
(flight, hour, destination,
 UNIQUE (flight, hour, destination),
 UNIQUE (flight, hour),
 UNIQUE (flight));

CREATE TABLE PilotSchedules
(day, flight, day, hour, gate, pilot,
 UNIQUE (day, flight, gate),
 UNIQUE (day, flight, pilot),
 UNIQUE (day, flight),
 FOREIGN KEY (flight, hour) REFERENCES R1(flight, hour));
```

5.10 Practical Hints for Normalization

CASE tools implement formal methods for doing normalization. In particular, E-R (Entity-Relationship) diagrams are very useful for this. However, a few informal hints can help speed up the process and give you a good start.

Broadly speaking, tables represent either entities, relationships or they are auxiliary tables. This is why E-R diagrams work so well as a design tool. The auxiliary tables do not show up on the diagrams, since they are functions, translations, and look-ups that support a declarative computational model.

The tables that represent entities should have a simple, immediate name suggested by their contents—a table named Students has student data in it, not student data and their bowling scores. It is also a good idea to use plural or collective nouns as the names of such tables to remind you that a table is a *set* of entities; the rows are the single instances of them.

Tables which represent one to many relationships should be named by their contents and should be as minimal as possible. For example, Students are related to Courses by a third (relationship) table for their attendance. These tables might represent a pure relationship or they might contain attributes that exist within the relationship, such as a student_grade for the class attended. Since the only way to get a student_grade is to attend the class, the relationship is going to have a compound key made up of references to the entity keys. We will probably name it "ReportCards," "Grades," or something similar. Avoid naming entities based on M:M relationships by combining the two table names. For example, "Students_Courses" is an easy but really bad name for the "Enrollment" entity.

AvoiNULLs whenever possible. If a table has too many NULL-able columns, it is probably not normalized properly. Try to use a NULL only for a value which is missing now, but which will be resolved later. Even better, put missing values into the encoding schemes for that column. I have a whole book on this topic, SQL PROGRAMMING STYLE (ISBN 978-0120887972) and mention in other books.

As a gross generalization, normalized databases will tend to have a lot of tables with a small number of columns per table. Do not panic when you see that happen. People who first worked with file systems (particularly on computers that used magnetic tape) tend to design one monster file for an application and do all the work against its records. This made sense in the old days, since there was no reasonable way to JOIN a number of small files together without having the computer operator mount and dismount lots of different magnetic tapes. The habit of designing this way carried over to disk systems, since the procedural programming languages were still the same for the databases as they had been for the sequential file systems.

The same nonkey attribute in more than one table is probably a normalization problem. This is not a certainty, just a guideline. The key that determines that attribute should be in only one table, and therefore its attributes should be with it. The key attributes will be referenced by related tables.

As a practical matter, you are apt to see the same attribute under different names and need to make the names uniform in the entire database. The columns "date_of_birth," "birthdate," "birthday," and "dob" are very likely the same attribute of an employee. You now have the ISO-11179 for naming guidelines, as discussed in SQL PROGRAMMING STYLE (Morgan Kaufmann, May 1, 2005; ISBN: 978-0120887972).

5.11 Non-Normal Form Redundancy

Department of Redundancy Department
Monty Python's Flying Circus

The goal of databases, *not just Relational Databases*, was to remove redundancy in the data. When we used punch cards and magnetic tapes, the data were always being sorted and duplicated so that batch jobs for various departments could be done in parallel.

But any error in one of these data silos means that they could not be summarize together, thrown out of balance a single typing error, timing problems, and other things. I summarized the goal of database as "one fact, one way, one time, one place" in one of my famous quotes.

Normalization prevents some redundancy in a table. But not all redundancy is based on Normal Forms. In Section 5.4, we saw how a computed column could be used to replace a base column when the base column is a computation.

5.11.1 Aggregation Level Redundancy

A common example is the "Invoices" and "Invoice_Details" idiom which puts detail summary data in the order header. This is usually a column for "invoice_total" which has to be re-computed when a order item changes. What has happened is a confusion in levels of aggregation.

```
CREATE TABLE Invoices
(invoice_nbr CHAR(15) NOT NULL PRIMARY KEY,
 customer_name VARCHAR(35) NOT NULL,
 invoice_terms CHAR(7) NOT NULL
    CHECK (invoice_terms IN ('cash', 'credit', 'coupon)),
 invoice_amt_tot DECIMAL(12,2) NOT NULL);

CREATE TABLE Invoice_Details
(invoice_nbr CHAR(15) NOT NULL
   REFERENCES Invoices (invoice_nbr)
   ON DELETE CASCADE,
 line_nbr INTEGER NOT NULL
  CHECK (line_nbr > 0),
 item_gtin CHAR(15) NOT NULL,
```

```
-- PRIMARY KEY (invoice_nbr, line_nbr),
-- PRIMARY KEY (invoice_nbr, item_gtin),
 invoice:qty INTEGER NOT NULL
  CHECK (invoice:qty > 0),
 unit_price DECIMAL(12,2) NOT NULL)
```

There is redundancy in line_ nbr and item_gtin as components in a key. The invoice line numbers are physical locations on paper forms or a screen. A line number lets you place one product (item_gtin) in several places on the order form. Line numbers are not part of a logical data model.

But did you notice that Invoices.invoice_amt_tot = SUM (Invoice_Details. invoice_qty * Invoice_Details.unit_price)?

5.11.2 Entire Table Redundancy

Entire tables can be redundant. This often happens when there are two different ways to identify the same entity.

```
CREATE TABLE Map

(location_id CHAR(15) NOT NULL PRIMARY KEY,
 location_name VARCHAR(35) NOT NULL,
 location_longitude DECIMAL(9,5) NOT NULL),
 location_latitude DECIMAL(9,5) NOT NULL);
```

location_id is the key, This might be a HTM (*Hierarchical Triangular Mesh*) number or a SAN (Standard Address Number, used in the Book and other industries). I can use a formula to compute the distance between two locations with this table. But I can also build a table of straight line distances directly:

```
CREATE TABLE Paths
(origin_loc CHAR(15) NOT NULL,
 dest_loc CHAR(15) NOT NULL,
 straight_line_dist DECIMAL(10,3) NOT NULL,
 PRIMARY KEY (origin_loc, dest_loc));
```

This is an actual case from Tom Johnston. The (longitude, latitude) coordinate pairs would get out of alignment with the distance computations because they were maintained by two different people. The solution was VIEW to construct Paths when needed.

5.11.3 Access Path Redundancy

A more subtle redundancy is in the roles an entity plays in a data model. Try this example: A sales team is responsible for every customer that a member of that team (a salesperson) is assigned to and not responsible for any other customer. Here is the ER diagram

Now look at the redundant relationship. We have options.

1. Eliminate the redundancy: remove the is-responsible-for relationship from Sales-Team to Customer. The model is just as expressive as it was before the redundancy was eliminated.
2. Control the redundancy: add DRI actions. Because the two foreign keys that must be kept synchronized are in the same row, only one update is required.

Here is the DDL for the possible solutions:

```
CREATE TABLE Sales_Teams
(sales_team_id INTEGER NOT NULL PRIMARY KEY,
 sales_team_name CHAR(10) NOT NULL);

CREATE TABLE Salespersons
(sales_person_id INTEGER NOT NULL PRIMARY KEY,
 sales_person_name CHAR(15) NOT NULL,
 sales_team_id INTEGER NOT NULL
           REFERENCES Sales_Teams(sales_team_id)
           ON UPDATE CASCADE);

CREATE TABLE Customers
(customer_id INTEGER NOT NULL PRIMARY KEY,
 sales_team_id INTEGER NOT NULL
           REFERENCES SalesPerson(sales_team_id)
           ON UPDATE CASCADE,

 sales_person_id INTEGER
       REFERENCES Salespersons(sales_person_id)
       ON UPDATE CASCADE
       ON DELETE SET NULL);
```

Another possible schema:

```
CREATE TABLE Sales_Teams
(sales_team_id INTEGER NOT NULL PRIMARY KEY,
 sales_team_name CHAR(10) NOT NULL);

CREATE TABLE Salespersons
(sales_person_id INTEGER NOT NULL PRIMARY KEY,
 sales_person_name CHAR(15) NOT NULL,
 sales_team_id INTEGER NOT NULL
             REFERENCES Sales_Teams(sales_team_id)
             ON UPDATE CASCADE,
 UNIQUE (sales_person_id, sales_team_id));

CREATE TABLE Customers
(customer_id INTEGER NOT NULL PRIMARY KEY,
 sales_team_id INTEGER NOT NULL,
 sales_person_id INTEGER
        REFERENCES Salespersons(sales_person_id)
        ON UPDATE CASCADE ON DELETE SET NULL,
 FOREIGN KEY (sales_person_id, sales_team_id)
 REFERENCES Salespersons (sales_person_id, sales_team_id)
             ON UPDATE CASCADE);
```

5.11.4 Attribute Splitting

Would you have a "Female_Personnel" and a "Male_Personnel" table in a schema? No, of course not! We need a "Personnel" table, not two tables constructed by using the values in a "sex_code" column as the splitter for table names. Making a table per calendar year (or month) is very common because it looks like how we did magnetic tapes. Another common split is a physical data source, such as each store in an enterprise.

Chris Date calls it "Orthogonal design" and I call it "Attribute Splitting," but I use this for more general errors than just tables.

This is not disk partitioning! That is a *physical* vendor feature for accessing the data, but the table is still one *logical* unit in the schema.

VIEWs, Derived, and Other Virtual Tables

VIEWs ARE ALSO called virtual tables, to distinguish it from temporary and base tables which are persistent. Views and derived tables are the ways of putting a query into a named schema object. By that, I mean these things hold the *query code* rather than the *results* of the query. The query is executed and the results are effectively materialized as a table with the view name.

The definition of a VIEW in Standard SQL requires that it acts as if an actual physical table is created when its name is invoked. Whether or not the database system *actually* materializes the results or uses other mechanisms to get the same effect is implementation defined. The definition of a VIEW is kept in the schema tables to be invoked by name wherever a table could be used. If the VIEW is updatable, then additional rules apply.

The SQL Standard separates administrative (ADMIN) privileges from user (USER) privileges. Table creation is administrative and query execution is a user privilege, so users cannot create their own VIEWs or TEMPORARY TABLEs without having Administrative privileges granted to them.

6.1 VIEWs in Queries

The Standard SQL syntax for the VIEW definition is

```
CREATE VIEW <table name> AS
[WITH RECURSIVE <table name> (<view column list>)
```

```
AS (<query expression>)]
SELECT <view column list> FROM <table name>
<levels clause> ::= CASCADED | LOCAL
```

We seldom use recursive views. Recursion is expensive, has poor performance and there are better way to do this in the schema design or in the host program. This is basically the same syntax as a recursive query. Here is a VIEW for a table of integers from 1 to 100 done recursively.

```
CREATE VIEW Nums_1_100 (n) AS
WITH RECURSIVE X (n)
AS (VALUES (1)
    UNION ALL
    SELECT n+1 FROM Nums_1_100 WHERE n < 100)
SELECT n FROM X;
```

Now let's worry about the important stuff.

The <levels clause> option in the WITH CHECK OPTION did not exist in SQL-89 and earlier standards. This clause has no effect on queries, but only on UPDATE, INSERT INTO, and DELETE FROM statements. It is tricky and not well-understood, so we will discuss it in detail later in this chapter.

A VIEW is different from a TEMPORARY TABLE, derived table, and base table. You cannot put constraints on a VIEW, as you can with base and TEMPORARY tables. A VIEW has no existence in the database until it is invoked, while a TEMPORARY TABLE is persistent. A derived table exists only in the scope of the query in which it is created.

The name of the VIEW must be unique within the database schema, like a base table name. The VIEW definition cannot reference itself, since it does not exist yet. Nor can the definition reference only other VIEWs; the nesting of VIEWs must eventually resolve to underlying base tables. This only makes sense; if no base tables were involved, what would you be viewing?

6.2 Updatable and Read-Only VIEWs

Unlike base tables, VIEWs are either updatable or read-only, but not both. INSERT, UPDATE, and DELETE operations are allowed on updatable VIEWs and base tables, subject to any other constraints. INSERT, UPDATE, and DELETE are not allowed on read-only VIEWs, but you can change their base tables, as you would expect.

An updatable VIEW is one that can have each of its rows associated with *exactly one row* in an underlying base table. When the VIEW is changed, the changes pass through the VIEW to that underlying base table unambiguously. Updatable VIEWs in Standard SQL are defined only for queries that meet these criteria:

(1) They are built on only one table

(2) No GROUP BY clause

(3) No HAVING clause

(4) No aggregate functions

(5) No calculated columns

(6) No UNION, INTERSECT, or EXCEPT

(7) No SELECT DISTINCT clause

(8) Any columns excluded from the VIEW must be NULL-able or have a DEFAULT in the base table, so that a whole row can be constructed for insertion

By implication, the VIEW must also contain a key of the table. In short, we are absolutely sure that each row in the VIEW maps back to one and only one row in the base table.

Some updating is handled by the CASCADE option in the referential integrity constraints on the base tables, not by the VIEW declaration.

The definition of updatability in Standard SQL is actually pretty limited, but very safe. The database system could look at information it has in the referential integrity constraints to widen the set of allowed updatable VIEWs. You will find that some implementations are now doing just that, but it is not common yet. The SQL standard definition of an updatable VIEW is actually a subset of the possible updatable VIEWs, and a very small subset at that! The major advantage of this definition is that it is based on syntax and not semantics. For example, these VIEW skeletons are logically identical:

```
CREATE VIEW Foo1 -- updatable, has a key!
AS SELECT *
   FROM Foobar
  WHERE x IN (1,2);
```

```
CREATE VIEW Foo2 -- not updatable!
AS SELECT *
   FROM Foobar
  WHERE x = 1
  UNION ALL
  SELECT *
   FROM Foobar
  WHERE x = 2;
```

But Foo1 is updatable and Foo2 is not. While I know of no formal proof, I suspect that determining if a complex query resolves to an updatable query for allowed sets of data values possible in the table is an NP-complete problem.

Without going into details, here is a list of types of queries that can yield updatable VIEWs, as taken from "VIEW Update Is Practical" (Goodman 1990):

1. Projection from a single table (Standard SQL)
2. Restriction/projection from a single table (Standard SQL)
3. UNION VIEWs
4. Set difference views
5. One-to-one joins
6. One-to-one outer joins
7. One-to-many joins
8. One-to-many outer joins
9. Many-to-many joins
10. Translated and coded columns

It is possible for a user to write INSTEAD OF triggers on VIEWs, which catch the changes and route them to the base tables that make up the VIEW. The database designer has complete control over the way VIEWs are handled. But as Spiderman said, "With great power, comes great responsibility," and you have to be very careful. I will discuss triggers in detail later.

6.3 Types of VIEWs

The type of SELECT statement and their purpose can classify VIEWs. The strong advantage of a VIEW is that it will produce the correct results when it is invoked, based on the current data. Trying to do the same sort of things with temporary tables or computed columns within a table can be subject to errors and slower to read form disk.

6.3.1 Single-Table Projection and Restriction

In practice, many VIEWs are projections or restrictions on a single base table. This is a common method for obtaining security control by removing rows or columns that a particular group of users is not allowed to see. These VIEWs are usually implemented as in-line macro expansion, since the optimizer can easily fold their code into the final query plan.

6.3.2 Calculated Columns

One common use for a VIEW is to provide summary data across a row. For example, given a table with measurements in metric units, we can construct a VIEW that hides the calculations to convert them into English units.

It is important to be sure that you have no problems with NULL values when constructing a calculated column. For example, given a Personnel table with columns for both salary and commission, you might construct this VIEW:

```
CREATE VIEW Payroll (emp_nbr, paycheck_amt)
AS
SELECT emp_nbr, (salary + COALESCE(commission), 0.00)
 FROM Personnel;
```

Office workers do not get commissions, so the value of their commission column will be NULL, so we use the COALESCE() function to change the NULLs to zeros.

6.3.3 Translated Columns

Another common use of a VIEW is to translate codes into text or other codes by doing table look ups. This is a special case of a joined VIEW based on a FOREIGN KEY relationship between two tables. For example, an order table might use a part number that we wish to display with a part name on an order entry screen. This is done with a JOIN between the order table and the inventory table, thus:

```
CREATE VIEW Display_Orders (part_nbr, part_name, ...)
AS SELECT Orders.part_nbr, Inventory.part_name, ...
     FROM Inventory, Orders
    WHERE Inventory.part_nbr = Orders.part_nbr;
```

Sometimes the original code is kept and sometimes it is dropped from the VIEW. As a general rule, it is a better idea to keep both values even though they are redundant. The redundancy can be used as a check for users, as well as a hook for nested joins in either of the codes.

The idea of JOIN VIEWs to translate codes can be expanded to show more than just one translated column. The result is often a "star" query with one table in the center, joined by FOREIGN KEY relations to many other tables to produce a result that is more readable than the original central table.

Missing values are a problem. If there is no translation for a given code, no row appears in the VIEW, or if an OUTER JOIN was used, a NULL will appear. The programmer should establish a referential integrity constraint to CASCADE changes between the tables to prevent loss of data.

6.3.4 Grouped VIEWs

A grouped VIEW is based on a query with a GROUP BY clause. Since each of the groups may have more than one row in the base from which it was built, these are necessarily read-only VIEWs. Such VIEWs usually have one or more aggregate functions and they are used for reporting purposes. They are also handy for working around weaknesses in SQL. Consider a VIEW that shows the largest sale in each state. The query is straightforward:

```
CREATE VIEW Big_Sales (state_code, sales_amt_max)
AS SELECT state_code, MAX(sales_amt)
     FROM Sales
   GROUP BY state_code;
```

SQL does not require that the grouping column(s) appear in the select clause, but it is a good idea in this case.

These VIEWs are also useful for "flattening out" one-to-many relationships. For example, consider a Personnel table, keyed on the employee number (emp_nbr), and a table of dependents, keyed on a combination of the employee number for each dependent's parent (emp_nbr) and the dependent's own serial number (dependent_nbr). The goal is to produce a report of the employees by name with the number of dependents each has.

```
CREATE VIEW Dependent_Tally1 (emp_nbr, dependent_cnt)
AS SELECT emp_nbr, COUNT(dependent_nbr)
   FROM Dependents
  GROUP BY emp_nbr;
```

The report is then simply an OUTER JOIN between this VIEW and the Personnel table. The OUTER JOIN is needed to account for employees without dependents with a NULL value, like this.

```
SELECT emp_name, dependent_cnt
 FROM Personnel AS P1
   LEFT OUTER JOIN
   DepTally1 AS D1
   ON P1.emp_nbr = D1.emp_nbr;
```

6.3.5 UNION-ed VIEWs

Until recently, a VIEW based on a UNION or UNION ALL operation was read-only because there is no general way to map a change onto just one row in one of the base tables. The UNION operator will remove duplicate rows from the results. Both the UNION and UNION ALL operators hide which table the rows came from. Such VIEWs must use a <view column list>, because the columns in a UNION [ALL] have no names of their own. In theory, a UNION of two disjoint tables, neither of which has duplicate rows in itself should be updatable.

Using the problem given in Section 6.3.4 on grouped VIEWs, this could also be done with a UNION query that would assign a count of zero to employees without dependents, thus:

```
CREATE VIEW DepTally2 (emp_nbr, dependent_cnt)
AS (SELECT emp_nbr, COUNT(dependent_nbr)
   FROM Dependents
   GROUP BY emp_nbr)
  UNION
  (SELECT emp_nbr, 0
   FROM Personnel AS P2
   WHERE NOT EXISTS (SELECT *
            FROM Dependents AS D2
           WHERE D2.emp_nbr = P2.emp_nbr));
```

The report is now a simple INNER JOIN between this VIEW and the Personnel table. The zero value, instead of a NULL value, will account for employees without dependents. The report query looks like this.

```
SELECT empart_name, dependent_cnt
 FROM Personnel, DepTally2
 WHERE DepTally2.emp_nbr = Personnel.emp_nbr;
```

Some of the major databases, such as Oracle and DB2, support inserts, updates, and delete from such views. Under the covers, each partition is a separate table, with a rule for its contents. One of the most common partitioning is temporal, so each partition might be based on a date range. The goal is to improve query performance by allowing parallel access to each partition member.

The trade-off is a heavy overhead under the covers with the UNION-ed VIEW partitioning, however. For example, DB2 attempts to insert any given row into each of the tables underlying the UNION ALL view. It then counts how many tables accepted the row. It has to process the entire view, one table at a time and collect the results.

(1) If exactly one table accepts the row, the insert is accepted.

(2) If no table accepts the row, a "no target" error is raised.

(3) If more than one table accepts the row, then an "ambiguous target" error is raised.

The use of INSTEAD OF triggers gives the user the effect of a single table, but there can still be surprises. Think about three tables; A, B, and C. Table C is disjoint from the other two. Tables A and B overlap. So I can always insert into C and may or may not be able to insert into A and B if I hit overlapping rows.

Going back to my "Y2K Doomsday" consulting days, I ran into a version of such a partition by calendar periods. Their Table C was set up on Fiscal quarters and got leap year wrong because one of the fiscal quarters ended on the last day of February.

Another approach somewhat like this is to declare explicit partitioning rules in the DDL with a proprietary syntax. The system will handle the housekeeping and the user sees only one table. In the Oracle model, the goal is to put parts of the logical table to different physical table spaces. Using standard data types, the Oracle syntax looks like this:

```
CREATE TABLE Sales
(invoice:nbr INTEGER NOT NULL PRIMARY KEY,
 sale_year INTEGER NOT NULL,
 sale_month INTEGER NOT NULL,
 sale_day INTEGER NOT NULL)
PARTITION BY RANGE (sale_year, sale_month, sale_day)
(PARTITION sales_q1 VALUES LESS THAN (1994, 04, 01) TABLESPACE tsa,
 PARTITION sales_q2 VALUES LESS THAN (1994, 07, 01) TABLESPACE tsb,
 PARTITION sales_q3 VALUES LESS THAN (1994, 10, 01) TABLESPACE tsc,
 PARTITION sales q4 VALUES LESS THAN (1995, 01, 01) TABLESPACE tsd);
```

Again, this will depend on your product, since this has to do with the physical database and not the logical model.

6.3.6 JOINs in VIEWs

A VIEW whose query expression is a joined table is not usually updatable even in theory.

One of the major purposes of a joined view is to "flatten out" a one-to-many or many-to-many relationship. Such relationships cannot map one row in the VIEW back to one row in the underlying tables on the "many" side of the JOIN. Anything said about a JOIN query could be said about a joined view, so they will not be dealt with here, but in a chapter devoted to a full discussion of joins.

6.3.7 Nested VIEWs

A point that is often missed, even by experienced SQL programmers, is that a VIEW can be built on other VIEWs. The only restrictions are that circular references within the query expressions of the VIEWs are illegal and that a VIEW must ultimately be built on base tables. One problem with nested VIEWs is that different updatable VIEWs can reference the same base table at the same time. If these VIEWs then appear in another VIEW, it becomes hard to determine what has happened when the highest-level VIEW is changed. As an example, consider a table with two keys:

```
CREATE TABLE Canada
(english INTEGER NOT NULL UNIQUE,
 french INTEGER NOT NULL UNIQUE,
```

```
 eng_word CHAR(30),
 fren_word CHAR(30));

INSERT INTO Canada
VALUES (1, 2, 'muffins', 'croissants'),
    (2, 1, 'bait', 'escargots');

CREATE VIEW EnglishWords
AS SELECT english, eng_word
   FROM Canada
  WHERE eng_word IS NOT NULL;

CREATE VIEW FrenchWords
AS SELECT french, fren_word
   FROM Canada
  WHERE fren_word IS NOT NULL);
```

We have now tried the escargots and decided that we wish to change our opinion of them:

```
UPDATE EnglishWords
  SET eng_word = 'appetizer'
 WHERE english = 2;
```

Our French user has just tried haggis and decided to insert a new row for his experience:

```
UPDATE FrenchWords
  SET fren_word = 'd''eaux grasses'
 WHERE french = 3;
```

The row that is created is (NULL, 3, NULL, 'd"eaux grasses'), since there is no way for VIEW FrenchWords to get to the VIEW EnglishWords columns. Likewise, the English VIEW user can construct a row to record his translation, (3, NULL, 'Haggis,' NULL). But neither of them can consolidate the two rows into a meaningful piece of data.

To delete a row is also to destroy data; the French-speaker who drops 'croissants' from the table also drops 'muffins' from VIEW EnglishWords.

6.4 How VIEWs are Handled in the Database Engine

Standard SQL requires a system schema table with the text of the VIEW declarations in it. What would be handy, but is not easily done in all SQL

implementations, is to trace the VIEWs down to their base tables by printing out a tree diagram of the nested structure. You should check your user library and see if it has such a utility program (for example, FINDVIEW in the old SPARC library for SQL/DS). There are several ways to handle VIEWs, and systems will often use a mixture of them. The major categories of algorithms are materialization and in-line text expansion.

6.4.1 View Column List

The <view column list> is optional; when it is not given, the VIEW will inherit the column names from the query. The number of column names in the <view column list> has to be the same as the degree of the query expression. If any two columns in the query have the same column name, you must have a <view column list> to resolve the ambiguity. The same column name cannot be specified more than once in the <view column list>.

6.4.2 VIEW Materialization

Materialization means that whenever you use the name of the VIEW, the database engine finds its definition in the schema information tables creates a working table with that name which has the appropriate column names with the appropriate data types. Finally, this new table is filled with the results of the SELECT statement in the body of the VIEW definition.

The decision to materialize a VIEW as an actual physical table is implementation-defined in Standard SQL, but the VIEW must act as if it were a table when accessed for a query. If the VIEW is not updatable, this approach automatically protects the base tables from any improper changes and is guaranteed to be correct. It uses existing internal procedures in the database engine (create table, insert from query), so this is easy for the database to do.

The downside of this approach is that it is not very fast for large VIEWs, uses extra storage space, cannot take advantage of indexes already existing on the base tables, usually cannot create indexes on the new table, and cannot be optimized as easily as other approaches. However, materialization is the best approach for certain VIEWs. A VIEW whose construction has a hidden sort is usually materialized. Queries with SELECT DISTINCT, UNION, GROUP BY, and HAVING clauses are often implemented by sorting to remove duplicate rows or to build groups. As each row of the VIEW is built, it has to be saved to compare it to the other rows, so it makes sense to materialize it.

Some products also give you the option of controlling the materializations yourself. The vendor terms vary. A “snapshot” means materializing a table

that also includes a time stamp. A "result set" is a materialized table that is passed to a front end application program for display. Check you particular product.

6.4.3 In-Line Text Expansion

Another approach is to store the text of the CREATE VIEW statement and work it into the parse tree of the SELECT, INSERT, UPDATE, or DELETE statements that use it. This allows the optimizer to blend the VIEW definition into the final query plan. For example, you can create a VIEW based on a particular department, thus:

```
CREATE VIEW SalesDept (dept_name, city_name, ...)
AS SELECT 'Sales', city_name, ...
  FROM Departments
 WHERE dept_name = 'Sales';
```

and then use it as a query, thus:

```
SELECT *
 FROM SalesDept
 WHERE city_name = 'New York';
```

The parser expands the VIEW into text (or an intermediate tokenized form) within the FROM clause. The query would become, in effect,

```
SELECT *
 FROM (SELECT 'Sales', city_name, ...
     FROM Departments
     WHERE dept_name = 'Sales')
    AS SalesDept (dept_name, city_name, ...)
 WHERE city_name = 'New York';
```

and the query optimizer would then "flatten it out" into

```
SELECT *
 FROM Departments
 WHERE (dept_name = 'Sales')
  AND (city_name = 'New York');
```

Though this sounds like a nice approach, it had problems in early systems where the in-line expansion does not result in proper SQL. An earlier version of DB2 was one such system. To illustrate the problem, imagine that you are given a DB2 table that has a long identification number and some figures in each row. The long identification number is like those 40-digit monsters they give you on a utility bill—they are unique only in the first few characters, but the utility company prints the whole thing out anyway. Your task is to create a report that is grouped according to the first six characters of the long identification number. The immediate naive query uses the SUBSTRING() function:

```
SELECT SUBSTRING(long_id FROM 1 TO 6), SUM(amt1), SUM(amt2), ...
 FROM TableA
 GROUP BY id;
```

This does not work; it is incorrect SQL, since the SELECT and GROUP BY lists do not agree. Other common attempts include GROUP BY SUBSTRING(long_id FROM 1 TO 6), which will fail because you cannot use a function, and GROUP BY 1, which will fail because you can use a column position only in a UNION statement, (column position is now deprecated in Standard SQL) and in the ORDER BY in some products.

The GROUP BY has to have a list of simple column names drawn from the tables of the FROM clause. The next attempt is to build a VIEW:

```
CREATE VIEW BadTry (short_id, amt1, amt2, ...)
AS
SELECT SUBSTRING(long_id FROM 1 TO 6), amt1, amt2, ...
 FROM TableA;
```

and then do a grouped select on it. This is correct SQL, but it does not work in older versions DB2. The compiler apparently tried to insert the VIEW into the FROM clause, as we have seen, but when it expands it out, the results are the same as those of the incorrect first query attempt with a function call in the GROUP BY clause. The trick was to force DB2 to materialize the VIEW so that you can name the column constructed with the SUBSTRING() function. Anything that causes a sort will do this—the SELECT DISTINCT, UNION, GROUP BY, and HAVING clauses, for example.

Since we know that the short identification number is a key, we can use this VIEW:

```
CREATE VIEW Shorty (short_id, amt1, amt2, ...)
AS
SELECT DISTINCT SUBSTRING(long_id FROM 1 TO 6), amt1, amt2, ...
 FROM TableA;
```

Then the report query is

```
SELECT short_id, SUM(amt1), SUM(amt2), ...
 FROM Shorty
 GROUP BY short_id;
```

This works fine in DB2. I am indebted to Susan Vombrack of Loral Aerospace for this example. Incidentally, this can be written in Standard SQL as

```
SELECT *
 FROM (SELECT SUBSTRING(long_id FROM 1 TO 6) AS short_id,
        SUM(amt1), SUM(amt2), ...
      FROM TableA
      GROUP BY long_id)
 GROUP BY short_id;
```

The name on the substring result column in the subquery expression makes it recognizable to the parser.

6.4.4 Pointer Structures

Finally, the system can handle VIEWs with special data structures for the VIEW. This is usually an array of pointers into a base table constructed from the VIEW definition. This is a good way to handle updatable VIEWs in Standard SQL, since the target row in the base table is at the end of a pointer chain in the VIEW structure. Access will be as fast as possible.

The pointer structure approach cannot easily use existing indexes on the base tables. But the pointer structure can be implemented as an index with restrictions. Furthermore, multi-table VIEWs can be constructed as pointer structures that allow direct access to the related rows in the table involved in the JOIN. This is very product-dependent, so you cannot make any general assumptions.

6.4.5 Indexing and Views

Note that VIEWs cannot have their own indexes. However, VIEWs can inherit the indexing on their base tables in some implementations. Like tables, VIEWs have no inherent ordering, but a programmer who knows his particular SQL implementation will often write code that takes advantage of the quirks of that product. In particular, some implementations allow you to use an ORDER BY clause in a VIEW (they are allowed only on cursors in standard SQL). This will force a sort and could materialize the VIEW as a working table. When the SQL engine has to do a sequential read of the entire table, the sort might help or hinder a particular query. There is no way to predict the results.

6.5 WITH CHECK OPTION Clause

If WITH CHECK OPTION is specified, the viewed table has to be updatable. This is actually a fast way to check how your particular SQL implementation handles updatable VIEWs. Try to create a version of the VIEW in question using the WITH CHECK OPTION and see if your product will allow you to create it. The WITH CHECK OPTION was part of the SQL-89 standard, which was extended in Standard SQL by adding an optional <levels clause>. CASCADED is implicit if an explicit LEVEL clause is not given. Consider a VIEW defined as:

```
CREATE VIEW V1
AS SELECT *
   FROM Foobar
  WHERE col1 = 'A';
```

and now UPDATE it with

```
UPDATE V1 SET col1 = 'B';
```

The UPDATE will take place without any trouble, but the rows that were previously seen now disappear when we use V1 again. They no longer meet the WHERE clause condition! Likewise, an INSERT INTO statement with VALUES (col1 = 'B') would insert just fine, but its rows would never be seen again in this VIEW. VIEWs created this way will always have all the rows that meet the criteria and that can be handy. For example, you can set up a VIEW of rows with a status code of 'to be done,' work on them, and change a status code to 'finished,' and they will disappear from your view. The important

point is that the WHERE clause condition was checked only at the time when the VIEW was invoked.

The WITH CHECK OPTION makes the system check the WHERE clause condition upon insertion or UPDATE. If the new or changed row fails the test, the change is rejected and the VIEW remains the same. Thus, the previous UPDATE statement would get an error message and you could not change certain columns in certain ways. For example, consider a VIEW of salaries under $30,000 defined with a WITH CHECK OPTION to prevent anyone from giving a raise above that ceiling.

The WITH CHECK OPTION clause does not work like a CHECK constraint.

```
CREATE TABLE Foobar (col_a INTEGER);

CREATE VIEW TestView (col_a)
AS
SELECT col_a FROM Foobar WHERE col_a > 0
WITH CHECK OPTION;
INSERT INTO TestView VALUES (NULL); -- This fails!

CREATE TABLE Foobar_2 (col_a INTEGER CHECK (col_a > 0));
INSERT INTO Foobar_2(col_a)
VALUES (NULL); -- This succeeds!
```

The WITH CHECK OPTION must be TRUE while the CHECK constraint can be either TRUE or UNKNOWN. Once more, you need to watch out for NULLs.

Standard SQL has introduced an optional <levels clause>, which can be either CASCADED or LOCAL. If no <levels clause> is given, a <levels clause> of CASCADED is implicit. The idea of a CASCADED check is that the system checks all the underlying levels that built the VIEW, as well as the WHERE clause condition in the VIEW itself. If anything causes a row to disappear from the VIEW, the UPDATE is rejected. The idea of a WITH LOCAL check option is that only the local WHERE clause is checked. The underlying VIEWs or tables from which this VIEW is built might also be affected, but we do not test for those effects. Consider two VIEWs built on each other from the salary table:

```
CREATE VIEW Lowpay
AS SELECT *
  FROM Personnel
 WHERE salary <= 250;
```

```
CREATE VIEW Mediumpay
AS SELECT *
     FROM Lowpay
   WHERE salary >= 100;
```

If neither VIEW has a WITH CHECK OPTION, the effect of updating Mediumpay by increasing every salary by $1000 will be passed without any check to Lowpay. Lowpay will pass the changes to the underlying Personnel table. The next time Mediumpay is used, Lowpay will be rebuilt in its own right and Mediumpay rebuilt from it, and all the employees will disappear from Mediumpay.

If only Mediumpay has a WITH CASCADED CHECK OPTION on it, the UPDATE will fail. Mediumpay has no problem with such a large salary, but it would cause a row in Lowpay to disappear, so Mediumpay will reject it. However, if only Mediumpay has a WITH LOCAL CHECK OPTION on it, the UPDATE will succeed. Mediumpay has no problem with such a large salary, so it passes the change along to Lowpay. Lowpay, in turn, passes the change to the Personnel table and the UPDATE occurs. If both VIEWs have a WITH CASCADED CHECK OPTION, the effect is a set of conditions, all of which have to be met. The Personnel table can accept UPDATEs or INSERTs only where the salary is between $100 and $250.

This can become very complex. Consider an example from an ANSI X3H2 paper by Nelson Mattos of IBM (Celko 1993). Let us build a five-layer set of VIEWs, using xx and yy as place holders for CASCADED or LOCAL, on a base table T1 with columns c1, c2, c3, c4, and c5, all set to a value of 10, thus:

```
CREATE VIEW V1 AS SELECT * FROM T1 WHERE (c1 > 5);

CREATE VIEW V2 AS SELECT * FROM V1 WHERE (c2 > 5)
    WITH xx CHECK OPTION;

CREATE VIEW V3 AS SELECT * FROM V2 WHERE (c3 > 5);

CREATE VIEW V4 AS SELECT * FROM V3 WHERE (c4 > 5)
    WITH yy CHECK OPTION;

CREATE VIEW V5 AS SELECT * FROM V4 WHERE (c5 > 5);
```

When we set each one of the columns to zero, we get different results, which can be shown in this chart, where 'S' means success and 'F' means failure:

xx/yy	c1	c2	c3	c4	c5
CASCADE/CASCADE	F	F	F	F	S
LOCAL/CASCADE	F	F	F	F	S
LOCAL/LOCAL	S	F	S	F	S
CASCADE/LOCAL	F	F	S	F	S

To understand the chart, look at the last line. If xx = CASCADED and yy = LOCAL, updating column c1 to zero via V5 will fail, whereas updating c5 will succeed. Remember that a successful UPDATE means the row(s) disappear from V5.

Follow the action for UPDATE V5 SET c1 = 0; VIEW V5 has no with check options, so the changed rows are immediately sent to V4 without any testing. VIEW V4 does have a WITH LOCAL CHECK OPTION, but column c1 is not involved, so V4 passes the rows to V3. VIEW V3 has no with check options, so the changed rows are immediately sent to V2. VIEW V2 does have a WITH CASCADED CHECK OPTION, so V2 passes the rows to V1 and awaits results. VIEW V1 is built on the original base table and has the condition c1 > 5, which is violated by this UPDATE. VIEW V1 then rejects the UPDATE to the base table, so the rows remain in V5 when it is rebuilt. Now the action for

```
UPDATE V5 SET c3 = 0;
```

VIEW V5 has no with check options, so the changed rows are immediately sent to V4, as before. VIEW V4 does have a WITH LOCAL CHECK OPTION, but column c3 is not involved, so V4 passes the rows to V3 without awaiting the results. VIEW V3 is involved with column c3 and has no with check options, so the rows can be changed and passed down to V2 and V1, where they UPDATE the base table. The rows are not seen again when V5 is invoked, because they will fail to get past VIEW V3. The real problem comes with UPDATE statements that change more than one column at a time. For example,

```
UPDATE V5 SET c1 = 0, c2 = 0, c3 = 0, c4 = 0, c5 = 0;
```

will fail for all possible combinations of <levels clause> in the example schema.

Standard SQL defines the idea of a set of conditions that are inherited by the levels of nesting. In our sample schema, these implied tests would be added to each VIEW definition:

local/local

```
V1 = none
V2 = (c2 > 5)
V3 = (c2 > 5)
V4 = (c2 > 5) AND (c4 > 5)
V5 = (c2 > 5) AND (c4 > 5)
```

cascade/cascade

```
V1 = none
V2 = (c1 > 5) AND (c2 > 5)
V3 = (c1 > 5) AND (c2 > 5)
V4 = (c1 > 5) AND (c2 > 5) AND (c3 > 5) AND (c4 > 5)
V5 = (c1 > 5) AND (c2 > 5) AND (c3 > 5) AND (c4 > 5)
```

local/cascade

```
V1 = none
V2 = (c2 > 5)
V3 = (c2 > 5)
V4 = (c1 > 5) AND (c2 > 5) AND (c4 > 5)
V5 = (c1 > 5) AND (c2 > 5) AND (c4 > 5)
```

cascade/local

```
V1 = none
V2 = (c1 > 5) AND (c2 > 5)
V3 = (c1 > 5) AND (c2 > 5)
V4 = (c1 > 5) AND (c2 > 5) AND (c4 > 5)
V5 = (c1 > 5) AND (c2 > 5) AND (c4 > 5)
```

6.5.1 WITH CHECK OPTION as CHECK() clause

Lothar Flatz, an instructor for Oracle Software Switzerland made the observation that while Oracle cannot put subqueries into CHECK() constraints and triggers would not be possible because of the mutating table

problem, you can use a VIEW that has a WITH CHECK OPTION to enforce subquery constraints.

For example, consider a hotel registry that needs to have a rule that you cannot add a guest to a room that another is or will be occupying. Instead of writing the constraint directly, like this:

```
CREATE TABLE Hotel
(room_nbr INTEGER NOT NULL,
 arrival_date DATE NOT NULL,
 departure_date DATE NOT NULL,
 guest_name CHAR(30) NOT NULL,
 CONSTRAINT schedule_right
 CHECK (H1.arrival_date <= H1.departure_date),
 CONSTRAINT no_overlaps
 CHECK (NOT EXISTS
    (SELECT *
      FROM Hotel AS H1, Hotel AS H2
     WHERE H1.room_nbr = H2.room_nbr
      AND H2.arrival_date < H1.arrival_date
      AND H1.arrival_date < H2.departure_date)));
```

The schedule_right constraint is fine, since it has no subquery, but many products will choke on the no_overlaps constraint. Leaving the no_overlaps constraint off the table, we can construct a VIEW on all the rows and columns of the Hotel base table and add a WHERE clause which will be enforced by the WITH CHECK OPTION.

```
CREATE VIEW Hotel_V (room_nbr, arrival_date, departure_date, guest_name)
AS SELECT H1.room_nbr, H1.arrival_date, H1.departure_date, H1.guest_name
   FROM Hotel AS H1
  WHERE NOT EXISTS
     (SELECT *
       FROM Hotel AS H2
      WHERE H1.room_nbr = H2.room_nbr
       AND H2.arrival_date < H1.arrival_date
       AND H1.arrival_date < H2.departure_date)
   AND H1.arrival_date <= H1.departure_date
  WITH CHECK OPTION;
```

For example,

```
INSERT INTO Hotel_V
VALUES (1, '2006-01-01', '2006-01-03', 'Ron Coe');
COMMIT;
INSERT INTO Hotel_V
VALUES (1, '2006-01-03', '2006-01-05', 'John Doe');
```

will give a WITH CHECK OPTION clause violation on the second INSERT INTO statement, as we wanted.

6.6 Dropping VIEWs

VIEWs, like tables, can be dropped from the schema. The Standard SQL syntax for the statement is:

```
DROP VIEW <table name> <drop behavior>
<drop behavior> ::= [CASCADE | RESTRICT]
```

The <drop behavior> clause did not exist in SQL-86, so vendors had different behaviors in their implementation. The usual way of storing VIEWs was in a schema-level table with the VIEW name, the text of the VIEW, and other information. When you dropped a VIEW, the engine usually removed the appropriate row from the schema tables. You found out about dependencies when you tried to use VIEWs built on other VIEWs that no longer existed. Likewise, dropping a base table could cause the same problem when the VIEW was accessed.

The CASCADE option will find all other VIEWs that use the dropped VIEW and remove them also. If RESTRICT is specified, the VIEW cannot be dropped if there is anything that is dependent on it. This implies a structure for the schema tables that is different from just a simple single table.

The bad news is that some older products will let you drop the table(s) from which the view is built, but not drop the view itself.

```
CREATE TABLE Foobar (col_a INTEGER);
CREATE VIEW TestView
AS SELECT col_a
   FROM Foobar;
DROP TABLE Foobar; -- drop the base table
```

Unless you also cascaded the DROP TABLE statement, the text of the view definition was still in the system. Thus, when you re-use the table and column names, they are resolved at run-time with the view definition.

```
CREATE TABLE Foobar
(foo_key CHAR(5) NOT NULL PRIMARY KEY,
 col_a REAL NOT NULL);
INSERT INTO Foobar VALUES ('Celko', 3.14159);
```

This is a potential security flaw and a violation of the SQL Standard, but be aware that it exists. Notice that the data type of TestView.col_a changed from INTEGER to REAL along with the new version of the table.

6.7 Materialized Query Tables

DB2 has a feature know as "Materialized Query Table" (MQT) which is based upon the result of a query. MQTs can be used for summary tables and staging tables. You can think of an MQT as a kind of materialized view. Both views and MQTs are defined on the basis of a query. The query on which a view is based is run whenever the view is referenced; however, an MQT actually stores the query results as data, and you can work with the data that is in the MQT instead of the data that is in the underlying tables.

6.7.1 CREATE TABLE

MQTs are created by executing a special form of the CREATE TABLE statement:

```
CREATE TABLE <table name>
AS
(<select statement>)
DATA INITIALLY DEFERRED
REFRESH [DEFERRED | IMMEDIATE]
[ENABLE | DISABLE] QUERY OPTIMIZATION
MAINTAINED BY [SYSTEM | USER]
```

A system-maintained MQTs and user-maintained MQTs are the major options. INSERT, UPDATE, and DELETE operations cannot be performed against system-maintained MQTs. These operations are known as "database events" when they are detected by triggers.

REFRESH IMMEDIATE system-maintained MQT is updated automatically, as changes are made to all underlying tables upon which the MQT is based. The REFRESH keyword lets you control how the data in the MQT is to be maintained: REFRESH IMMEDIATE indicates that changes made to underlying tables are cascaded to the MQT as they happen, and REFRESH DEFERRED means that the data in the MQT will be refreshed only when the REFRESH TABLE statement is executed.

User-maintained MQTs allow INSERT, UPDATE, or DELETE operations to be executed against them and can be populated with import and load operations. However, they cannot be populated by executing the REFRESH TABLE statement, nor can they be created with the REFRESH IMMEDIATE option specified. Essentially, a user-defined MQT is a summary table that the DBA is responsible for populating, but one that the DB2 optimizer can utilize to improve query performance. If you do not want the optimizer to utilize an MQT, simply specify the DISABLE QUERY OPTIMIZATION option with the CREATE TABLE statement used to construct the MQT.

6.7.2 REFRESH TABLE Statement

The REFRESH TABLE statement refreshes the data in a materialized query table.

REFRESH TABLE <materialized table name list>
[[NOT] INCREMENTAL]
[ALLOW [NO | READ | WRITE] ACCESS]

The INCREMENTAL options allows the user to refresh the whole table or to use the delta in the data since the last refresh. If neither INCREMENTAL nor NOT INCREMENTAL is specified, the system will determine whether incremental processing is possible; if not, full refresh will be performed.

You can specify the accessibility of the table while it is being processed. This is a version of the usual session options in the transaction levels.

ALLOW NO ACCESS = Specifies that no other users can access the table while it is being refreshed.

ALLOW READ ACCESS = Specifies that other users have read-only access to the table while it is being refreshed.

ALLOW WRITE ACCESS = Specifies that other users have read and write access to the table while it is being refreshed.

There are more options that deal with optimization, but this give you the flavor of the statement.

Auxiliary Tables

Auxiliary tables are a declarative way of performing functions and look up tables that would be difficult if not impossible to do with the limited computational power of SQL. SQL is a declarative language for working with tables. If you are really old, like the author, you will remember text books with look-up table in the back. Trigonometry text had trig tables, finance texts had compound intersect and internal rate of return (IRR) functions, and statistics text had all kinds of functions! Auxiliary tables are not really a part of the data model and should not be part of an E-R diagram, but serve as adjuncts to do queries via joins rather than computations.

They are usually very static and constructed from an outside data source. These data are easy to find on the Internet. Thus, they do not require the same constraints for safety; however, since the optimizer can use the constraints for queries, you should include them. As a general statement, they need to have a primary key declared so that it will create a fast access method for searching and joining the auxiliary table to other tables in the schema, *not* to protect the data from redundancy.

The most important auxiliary table is a Calendar because the Common Era calendar is too irregular for computations and because time is a fundamental dimension in the real world. Holidays fall on lunar and solar cycles; there are hundreds of fiscal calendars and so forth. The discussion of Calendar tables will be given in Section 12.9 on temporal data. This section will look at various kinds of auxiliary tables.

7.1 Series Table

The Series table is a simple list of integers from 1 to (n) that is used in place of looping constructs in a procedural language. Rather than incrementing a counter value, we try to work in parallel with a complete set of values.

I previously used the name "Sequence" for this table. But now SEQUENCE is a reserved word for a construct in ANSI/ISO Standard SQL that builds a sequence of whole numbers and dispenses them one at a time. Other people use the name "Numbers" or "Tally" for the table, but it is more than some random collection of integers or a count. This table has the general declaration:

```
CREATETABLE Series
(seq INTEGER NOT NULL PRIMARY KEY
   CONSTRAINT non_negative_nbr
   CHECK (seq > 0)
 -- cardinal_name VARCHAR(25) NOT NULL,
 -- ordinal_name VARCHAR(25) NOT NULL,
 ...
 CONSTRAINT numbers_are_complete
 CHECK ((SELECT COUNT(*) FROM Series) =
     (SELECT MAX(seq) FROM Series));
```

with data like:

```
INSERT INTO Series
VALUES
(1, 'one','first'),
(2, 'two', 'second'),
(3, 'three', 'third'),
 ..
 (101, 'One hundred and one',' One hundred and first');
```

This table is a list of all the integers from 1 to some value (n). The ordinal and cardinal columns are simply examples of handy things that you might want to do with an integer, such as turn it into English words, which would be difficult in a procedural language or with the limitations of SQL.

I have found that is it a bad idea to start with zero, though that seems more natural to computer programmers. The reason for omitting zero is that this auxiliary table is often used to provide row numbering by being CROSS JOIN-ed to another table and the zero would throw off the one-to-one mapping.

7.1.1 Enumerating a List

Given a table in a data warehouse for a report that uses the monthly sales data shown as an attribute (the monthly amounts have to be NULL-able to hold missing values for the future), thus:

```
CREATE TABLE AnnualSales1
(salesman CHAR(15) NOT NULL PRIMARY KEY,
 jan DECIMAL(5,2),
 feb DECIMAL(5,2),
 mar DECIMAL(5,2),
 apr DECIMAL(5,2),
 may DECIMAL(5,2),
 jun DECIMAL(5,2),
 jul DECIMAL(5,2),
 aug DECIMAL(5,2),
 sep DECIMAL(5,2),
 oct DECIMAL(5,2),
 nov DECIMAL(5,2),
 "dec" DECIMAL(5,2)); -- DEC is short for DECIMAL
```

The goal is to "flatten" it out so that it looks like this:

```
CREATE TABLE AnnualSales2
(salesman_name CHAR(15) NOT NULL PRIMARY KEY,
 sales_month CHAR(3) NOT NULL
  CONSTRAINT valid_month_code
    CHECK (sales_month
        IN ('Jan', 'Feb', 'Mar', 'Apr',
          'May', 'Jun', 'Jul', 'Aug',
          'Sep', 'Oct', 'Nov', 'Dec'),
 sales_amt DECIMAL(5,2) NOT NULL,
 PRIMARY KEY(salesman, sales_month));
```

The trick is to build a VIEW of the original table with a number beside each month:

```
CREATE VIEW NumberedSales
AS SELECT salesman,
     1 AS M01, jan,
     2 AS M02, feb,
     3 AS M03, mar,
     4 AS M04, apr,
     5 AS M05, may,
     6 AS M06, jun,
     7 AS M07, jul,
     8 AS M08, aug,
     9 AS M09, sep,
     10 AS M10, oct,
     11 AS M11, nov,
     12 AS M12, "dec" -- reserved word
 FROM AnnualSales1;
```

Now you can use the Series table or a VALUES table constructor to build one. The flatten VIEW is

```
CREATE VIEW AnnualSales2 (salesman, sales_month, sales_amt)
AS SELECT S1.salesman_name,
    (CASE WHEN A.nbr = M01 THEN 'Jan'
       WHEN A.nbr = M02 THEN 'Feb'
       WHEN A.nbr = M03 THEN 'Mar'
       WHEN A.nbr = M04 THEN 'Apr'
       WHEN A.nbr = M05 THEN 'May'
       WHEN A.nbr = M06 THEN 'Jun'
       WHEN A.nbr = M07 THEN 'Jul'
       WHEN A.nbr = M08 THEN 'Aug'
       WHEN A.nbr = M09 THEN 'Sep'
       WHEN A.nbr = M10 THEN 'Oct'
       WHEN A.nbr = M11 THEN 'Nov'
       WHEN A.nbr = M12 THEN 'Dec'
       ELSE NULL END),
    (CASE WHEN A.nbr = M01 THEN jan
       WHEN A.nbr = M02 THEN feb
```

```
        WHEN A.nbr = M03 THEN mar
        WHEN A.nbr = M04 THEN apr
        WHEN A.nbr = M05 THEN may
        WHEN A.nbr = M06 THEN jun
        WHEN A.nbr = M07 THEN jul
        WHEN A.nbr = M08 THEN aug
        WHEN A.nbr = M09 THEN sep
        WHEN A.nbr = M10 THEN oct
        WHEN A.nbr = M11 THEN nov
        WHEN A.nbr = M12 THEN "dec" -- reserved word
        ELSE NULL END)
  FROM NumberedSales AS S1
   CROSS JOIN
   (SELECT seq FROM Series WHERE seq <= 12) AS A(month_nbr);
```

If your SQL product has derived tables, this can be written as a single VIEW query.

7.1.2 Mapping a Series into a Cycle

It is sometimes handy to map a sequence of numbers to a cycle. The general formula is

```
SELECT seq, MOD (((seq + (:n-1))/ :n), :n)
 FROM Series;
```

As an example, consider the following problem in which we want to display an output with what is called "snaking" in a report. Each id has several descriptions and we want to see them in cycles of four (n = 4); when a department has more than four job descriptions, we want to start a new row with an incremented position each subset of four or fewer job descriptions.

```
CREATE TABLE Companies
(dept_nbr INTEGER NOT NULL,
 job_nbr INTEGER NOT NULL, -- sequence within department
 company_descr CHAR(6) NOT NULL,
 PRIMARY KEY (dept_nbr, job_nbr));

INSERT INTO Companies
VALUES (1, 1, 'desc01'), (1, 2, 'desc02'), (1, 3, 'desc03'),
```

```
    (2, 1, 'desc04'), (2, 2, 'desc05'), (2, 3, 'desc06'),
    (2, 4, 'desc07'), (2, 5, 'desc08'), (2, 6, 'desc09'),
    (3, 1, 'desc10'), (3, 2, 'desc11'), (3, 3, 'desc12');
```

I am going to use a VIEW rather than a derived table to make the logic in the intermediate step easier to see.

```
CREATE VIEW Foo2 (dept_nbr, row_grp, d1, d2, d3, d4)
AS
SELECT dept_nbr, (MOD((job_nbr + 3)/4), 4),
    MAX(CASE WHEN MOD(job_nbr, 4) = 1
        THEN company_descr ELSE ' ' END) AS d1,
    MAX(CASE WHEN MOD(job_nbr, 4) = 2
        THEN company_descr ELSE ' ' END) AS d2,
    MAX(CASE WHEN MOD(job_nbr, 4) = 3
        THEN company_descr ELSE ' ' END) AS d3,
    MAX(CASE WHEN MOD(job_nbr, 4) = 0
        THEN company_descr ELSE ' ' END) AS d4
 FROM Companies AS F1
 GROUP BY dept_nbr, job_nbr;

SELECT dept_nbr, row_grp,
    MAX(d1) AS d1, MAX(d2) AS d2, MAX(d3) AS d3, MAX(d4) AS d4
 FROM Foo2
 GROUP BY dept_nbr, row_grp
 ORDER BY dept_nbr, row_grp;
```

dept_nbr	row_grp	d1	d2	d3	d4
1	1	desc1	desc2	desc3	
2	1	desc4	desc5	desc6	desc7
2	2	desc8	desc9		
3	1	desc10	desc11	desc12	

This is a bad coding practice. Display is a function of a presentation layer and should not be done in the database layer. And there is also the CYCLE option in the CREATE SEQUENCE statement.

7.1.3 Building Buckets of Fixed Size

A useful trick to create "buckets" of equal size, given a sub-series and size of the desired bucket. For example, to split the integers between 11 and 98 into 7 buckets would take the 88 numbers in the range and slice them into buckets of 1 to 13 units each. The cut points would be

12

25

37

50

62

75

A quick solution is shown below; notice that there is no valuation of the parameters:

```
CREATE PROCEDURE Buckets
(IN start_seq INTEGER,
 IN end_seq INTEGER,
 IN part_cnt INTEGER)
BEGIN
SELECT (seq - 1) * (start_seq - end_seq + 1) / part_cnt )
FROM Series
WHERE seq BETWEEN 1 AND part_cnt
 AND start_seq <= end_seq;
END;
```

7.1.4 Replacing an Iterative Loop

While it is not recommended as a technique, and it will vary from SQL dialect to dialect, it is a good exercise in learning to think in sets. You are given a quoted string that is made up of integers separated by commas and your goal is to break each of integers out as a row in a table.

The obvious approach is to write procedural code that will loop over the input string and cut off all characters from the start up to, but not including, the first comma, cast the substring as an integer and then iterate through the rest of the string.

```
CREATE PROCEDURE ParseList (IN inputstring VARCHAR(1000))
LANGUAGE SQL
BEGIN DECLARE i INTEGER;
```

```
SET i = 1; -- iteration control variable
-- add sentinel comma to end of input string
SET inputstring = TRIM (BOTH '' FROM inputstring || ', ');
WHILE i < CHAR_LENGTH(inputstring)
   DO WHILE SUBSTRING(inputstring, i, 1) <> ', '
         DO SET i = i + 1;
   END WHILE;
 SET outputstring = SUBSTRING(inputstring, 1, i-1);
 INSERT INTO Outputs VALUES (CAST (outputstring AS INTEGER));
 SET inputstring = SUBSTRING(inputstring, i+1);
 END WHILE;
END;
```

Another way to do this is with a Series table and this strange looking query.

```
CREATE PROCEDURE ParseList (IN inputstring VARCHAR(1000))
LANGUAGE SQL
INSERT INTO ParmList (parameter_position, param)
 SELECT S1.i,
    CAST (SUBSTRING ((', ' || inputstring ||', ')
          FROM (S1.i + 1)
          FOR (S2.i - S1.i - 1))
       AS INTEGER)
  FROM Series AS S1,
    Series AS S2
  WHERE SUBSTRING((', ' || inputstring ||', ') FROM S1.i FOR 1) = ', '
  AND SUBSTRING((', ' || inputstring ||', ') FROM S2.i FOR 1) = ', '
  AND S2.i
  = (SELECT MIN(S3.i)
       FROM Series AS S3
      WHERE S1.i < S3.i
       AND SUBSTRING((', ' || inputstring ||', ')
            FROM S3.i
            FOR 1) = ', ')
  AND S1.i < CHAR_LENGTH (inputstring+ 1);
```

The trick here is to concatenate commas on the left and right sides of the input string. To honest, you would probably want to trim blanks and perhaps do other tests on the string, such as seeing that LOWER(:instring) = UPPER(:instring) to avoid alphabetic characters, and so forth, and that edited result string would be kept in a local variable and used in the INSERT INTO statement.

The integer substrings are located between the i-th and ((i+1)-th comma pairs. In effect, the sequence table replaces the loop counter. The Series table has to have enough numbers to cover the entire string, but unless you really like to type in long parameter list, this should not be a problem. The last two predicates are to avoid a Cartesian product with the Series table.

7.2 Look-up Auxiliary Tables

In the old days, when engineers used slide rulers, other people went to the back of their math and financial book to use printed tables of functions. Here you could find trigonometry, compound interest, or statistical functions. Today, you would more likely calculate the function because computing power is so cheap. Pocket calculators that sold for hundreds of dollars in the 1960s and are now on spikes next to chewing gum in the check-out line at office supply stores.

In the days of keypunch data entry, there would be loose-leaf notebooks of the encoding schemes to use sitting next to the incoming paper forms. Today, you would more likely see a WIMP (Windows, Icons, Menus, and Pulldowns or Pop-ups) interface.

While the physical mechanisms have changed, the idea of building a table (in the nonrelational sense) is still valid. An auxiliary table holds a static or relatively static set of data. The users do not change the data. Updating one of these tables is a job for the Database Administrator or the Data Repository Administrator, if your shop is that sophisticated. One of the problems with even a simple look-up table change is that the existing data often have to be changed to the new encoding scheme, and this required Administrative privileges.

The primary key of an auxiliary table is never an identifier; an identifier is unique in the schema and refers to one entity anywhere it appears. These are *values, not entities*. Look-up tables work with values are not entities by definition. Monstrosities like "value_id," "<something>_code_id" are absurd on the face of them.

This is a short list of postfixes that can be used as the name of the key column in auxiliary tables. There is a more complete list of postfixes in my book *SQL Programming Style* (ISBN 978-0-12-088797-2, Morgan_Kaufmann, 2005).

"_nbr" or "_num" = tag number; this is a string of digits that names something. Do not use "_no" since it looks like the Boolean yes/no value. I prefer "nbr" to "num" since it is used as a common abbreviation in several European languages.

"_name" or "_nm" = this is an alphabetic name and it explains itself. It is also called a nominal scale.

"_code" or "_cd" = A code is a standard maintained by a trusted source, usually outside of the enterprise. For example, the ZIP code is maintained by the United States Postal Service. A code is well understood in its context, so you might not have to translate it for humans.

"_cat" or _ category = Category, an encoding that has an external source that has very distinct groups of entities. There should be strong formal criteria for establishing the category. The classification of Kingdom is in biology is an example.

"_class" = an internal encoding that does not have an external source that reflects a sub-classification of the entity. There should be strong formal criteria for the classification. The classification of plants in biology is an example.

"_type" = an encoding that has a common meaning both internally and externally. Types are usually less formal than a class and might overlap. For example, a driver's license might be motorcycle, automobile, taxi, truck, and so forth.

The differences among type, class, and category are an increasing strength of the algorithm for assigning the type, class, or category. A category is very distinct; you will not often have to guess if something "animal, vegetable, or mineral" to put it in one of those categories.

A class is a set of things that have some commonality; you have rules for classifying an animal as a mammal or a reptile. You may have some cases where it is harder to apply the rules, such as the egg laying mammal in Australia, but the exceptions tend to become their own classification—monotremes in this example.

A type is the weakest of the three, and it might call for a judgment. For example, in some states a three-wheeled motorcycle is licensed as a motorcycle. In other states, it is licensed as an automobile. And in some states, it is licensed as an automobile only if it has a reverse gear.

The three terms are often mixed in actual usage. Stick with the industry standard, even if violates the definitions given above.

"_status" = an internal encoding that reflects a state of being which can be the result of many factors. For example, "credit_status" might be computed from several sources.

"_addr" or "_loc" = an address or location for an entity. There can be a subtle difference between an address and location.

"_date" or "dt" = date, temporal dimension. It is the date of something—employment, birth, termination, and so forth; there is no such column name as just a date by itself.

7.2.1 Simple Translation Auxiliary Tables

The most common form of look-up has two columns, one for the value to be looked up and one for the translation of that value into something the user needs. A simple example would be the two-letter ISO-3166 country codes in a table like this:

```
CREATE TABLE CountryCodes
(country_code CHAR(2) NOT NULL PRIMARY KEY, -- iso-3166
 country_name VARCHAR(20) NOT NULL);
```

You can add a unique constraint on the descriptive column, but most programmers do not bother since these tables do not change much and when they do change, it is done with data provided by a trusted source. This makes OLTP database programmers a bit uneasy, but Data Warehouse database programmers understand it.

Another trick is to pack the data on the disk without allowing any fill factor. This means that more data are loaded per page and the system runs faster and smaller.

7.2.2 Multiple Translation Auxiliary Tables

While we want the encoding value to stay the same, we often need to have multiple translations. There can be a short description, a long description, or just a different one depending on who was looking at the data. For example, consider displaying error messages in various languages in a single table:

```
CREATE TABLE Error_Messages
(err_code CHAR(5) NOT NULL PRIMARY KEY,
```

```
english_err_msg CHAR(25) NOT NULL ...
french_err_msg NCHAR(25) NOT NULL ..
...
esperanto_err_msg NCHAR (25) NOT NULL);
```

Yes, this does require a structure change to add a new language. However, since the data are static the convenience of having all the related translations in one place is probably worth it. This inherently forces you to have all the languages for each error code, while a strict First Normal Form (1NF) table does not.

Your first thought is that an application using this table would be full of code like:

```
SELECT CASE :my_language
    WHEN 'English' THEN english_err
    WHEN 'French' THEN french_err
    ... END AS err_msg
 FROM ErrorMessages
 WHERE err_code = '42';
```

This is not usually the case. You have another table that finds the language preferences of the CURRENT_USER and presents a VIEW to him in the language he desires.

You don't invent or add languages very often. Tho I do know of one product that was adding Klingon to its error messages. Seriously, it was for a demo at a trade show to show off the internationalization features. ("Unknown error = Die in ignorance!!," sort of a user surly interface instead of user friendly).

7.2.3 Multiple Parameter Auxiliary Tables

This type of auxiliary table has two or more parameters that it uses to seek a value. The classic example from college freshman statistics courses is the Student's *t*-distribution for small samples. The value of (*r*) is the size of the sample minus one and the percentages are the confidence intervals. Loosely speaking, the Student's *t*-distribution is the best guess at the population distribution that we can make without knowing the standard deviation with a certain level of confidence.

This look-up table is easier to code in SQL than the calculus shown above, isn't it?

One sided	75%	80%	85%	90%	95%	97.5%	99%	99.5%	99.75%	99.9%	99.95%
Two sided	50%	60%	70%	80%	90%	95%	98%	99%	99.5%	99.8%	99.9%
1	1.000	1.376	1.963	3.078	6.314	12.71	31.82	63.66	127.3	318.3	636.6
2	0.816	1.061	1.386	1.886	2.920	4.303	6.965	9.925	14.09	22.33	31.60
3	0.765	0.978	1.250	1.638	2.353	3.182	4.541	5.841	7.453	10.21	12.92
4	0.741	0.941	1.190	1.533	2.132	2.776	3.747	4.604	5.598	7.173	8.610
5	0.727	0.920	1.156	1.476	2.015	2.571	3.365	4.032	4.773	5.893	6.869
6	0.718	0.906	1.134	1.440	1.943	2.447	3.143	3.707	4.317	5.208	5.959
7	0.711	0.896	1.119	1.415	1.895	2.365	2.998	3.499	4.029	4.785	5.408
8	0.706	0.889	1.108	1.397	1.860	2.306	2.896	3.355	3.833	4.501	5.041
9	0.703	0.883	1.100	1.383	1.833	2.262	2.821	3.250	3.690	4.297	4.781
10	0.700	0.879	1.093	1.372	1.812	2.228	2.764	3.169	3.581	4.144	4.587
11	0.697	0.876	1.088	1.363	1.796	2.201	2.718	3.106	3.497	4.025	4.437
12	0.695	0.873	1.083	1.356	1.782	2.179	2.681	3.055	3.428	3.930	4.318
13	0.694	0.870	1.079	1.350	1.771	2.160	2.650	3.012	3.372	3.852	4.221
14	0.692	0.868	1.076	1.345	1.761	2.145	2.624	2.977	3.326	3.787	4.140
15	0.691	0.866	1.074	1.341	1.753	2.131	2.602	2.947	3.286	3.733	4.073
16	0.690	0.865	1.071	1.337	1.746	2.120	2.583	2.921	3.252	3.686	4.015
17	0.689	0.863	1.069	1.333	1.740	2.110	2.567	2.898	3.222	3.646	3.965
18	0.688	0.862	1.067	1.330	1.734	2.101	2.552	2.878	3.197	3.610	3.922

Continued

19	0.688	0.861	1.066	1.328	1.729	2.093	2.539	2.861	3.174	3.579	3.883
20	0.687	0.860	1.064	1.325	1.725	2.086	2.528	2.845	3.153	3.552	3.850
21	0.686	0.859	1.063	1.323	1.721	2.080	2.518	2.831	3.135	3.527	3.819
22	0.686	0.858	1.061	1.321	1.717	2.074	2.508	2.819	3.119	3.505	3.792
23	0.685	0.858	1.060	1.319	1.714	2.069	2.500	2.807	3.104	3.485	3.767
24	0.685	0.857	1.059	1.318	1.711	2.064	2.492	2.797	3.091	3.467	3.745
25	0.684	0.856	1.058	1.316	1.708	2.060	2.485	2.787	3.078	3.450	3.725
26	0.684	0.856	1.058	1.315	1.706	2.056	2.479	2.779	3.067	3.435	3.707
27	0.684	0.855	1.057	1.314	1.703	2.052	2.473	2.771	3.057	3.421	3.690
28	0.683	0.855	1.056	1.313	1.701	2.048	2.467	2.763	3.047	3.408	3.674
29	0.683	0.854	1.055	1.311	1.699	2.045	2.462	2.756	3.038	3.396	3.659
30	0.683	0.854	1.055	1.310	1.697	2.042	2.457	2.750	3.030	3.385	3.646
40	0.681	0.851	1.050	1.303	1.684	2.021	2.423	2.704	2.971	3.307	3.551
50	0.679	0.849	1.047	1.299	1.676	2.009	2.403	2.678	2.937	3.261	3.496
60	0.679	0.848	1.045	1.296	1.671	2.000	2.390	2.660	2.915	3.232	3.460
80	0.678	0.846	1.043	1.292	1.664	1.990	2.374	2.639	2.887	3.195	3.416
100	0.677	0.845	1.042	1.290	1.660	1.984	2.364	2.626	2.871	3.174	3.390
120	0.677	0.845	1.041	1.289	1.658	1.980	2.358	2.617	2.860	3.160	3.373
∞	0.674	0.842	1.036	1.282	1.645	1.960	2.326	2.576	2.807	3.090	3.291

William Gosset created this statistic in 1907. His employer, Guinness Breweries, required him to publish under a pseudonym, so he chose "Student" and that name stuck.

7.2.4 Range Auxiliary Tables

In a range auxiliary table, there is one parameter, but it must fall inside a range of values. The most common example would be reporting periods or ranges. There is no rule that prevents these ranges from overlapping. For example, "Swimsuit Season" and "BBQ Grill Sale" might have a large number of days in common at a department store. However, it is usually a good idea not to have disjoint ranges.

```
CREATE TABLE Report_Periods
(period_name CHAR(15) NOT NULL,
 period_start_date DATE NOT NULL,
 period_end_date DATE NOT NULL,
 CHECK(period_start_date < period_end_date),
 PRIMARY KEY (period_start_date, period_end_date));
```

The searching is done with a BETWEEN predicate. A NULL can be useful as a marker for an open-ended range. Consider a table for grades in a school. The CHECK() constraint is not needed because of the static nature of the data, but it gives the optimizer extra information about the two columns and might help improve performance.

```
CREATE TABLE Letter_Grades
(letter_grade CHAR(1) NOT NULL PRIMARY KEY,
 low_score DECIMAL(6,3) NOT NULL,
 high_score DECIMAL(6,3));

INSERT INTO LetterGrades
VALUES ('F', '0.000, 60.000),
       ('D', 60.999, 70.000),
       ('C', 70.999, 80.000),
       ('B', 80.999, 90.000),
       ('A', 90.999, NULL);
```

If we had made the last range ('A,' 90.999, 100.000), then a student who did extra work and got a total score over 100.000 would not have gotten

a grade. The alternatives are to use a dummy value, such as ('A,' 90.999, 999.999) or to use a NULL and add the predicate.

```
SELECT ..
 FROM ..
 WHERE Exams.score
    BETWEEN LetterGrades.low_score
      AND COALESCE (LetterGrades.high_score, Exams.score);
```

The choice of using a dummy value or a NULL will depend on the nature of the data.

7.2.5 Set Auxiliary Tables

In the January 2005 issue of *The Data Administration Newsletter* (www.TDAN.com), I published an article on a look-up table solution to a more difficult problem. If you watch the Food channel on cable or if you just like Memphis-style BBQ, you know the name "Corky's." The chain started in 1984 in Memphis by Don Pelts and has grown by franchise at a steady rate ever since. They will never be a McDonald's because all the meats are slow cooked for up to 22 hours over hickory wood and charcoal, and then every pork shoulder is hand-pulled. No automation, no mass production.

They sell a small menu of items by mail order via a toll-free number or from their website (www.corkysbbq.com) and ship the merchandise in special boxes sometimes using dry ice. Most of the year, their staff can handle the orders. But at Christmas time, they have the problem of success.

Their packing operation consists of two lines. At the start of the line, someone pulls a box of the right size, and puts the pick list in it. As it goes down the line, packers put in the items, and when it gets to the end of the line, it is ready for shipment. This is a standard business operation in lots of industries. Their people know what boxes to use for the standard gift packs and can pretty accurately judge any odd sized orders.

At Christmas time, however, mail-order business is so good that they have to get outside temp help. The temporary help does not have the experience to judge the box sizes by looking at a pick list. If a box that is too small starts down the line, it will jam up things at some point. The supervisor has to get it off the line, and re-pack the order by hand. If a box that is too large goes down the line, it is a waste of money and creates extra shipping costs.

Mark Tutt (On The Mark Solutions, LLC) has been consulting with Corky's for years and set up a new order system for them on Sybase. One of the goals of the new system is print the pick list and shipping labels with all of the calculations done, including what box size the order requires.

Following the rule that you do not re-invent the wheel, Mr. Tutt went to the newsgroups to find out if anyone had a solution already. The suggestions tended to be along the lines of getting the weights and shapes of the items and using a Tetris program to figure out the packing.

Programmers seem to love to face every new problem as if nobody has ever done it before and nobody will ever do it again. The "Code first, research later!" mentality is hard to overcome.

The answer was not in complicated 3-D math, but in the past 4 or 5 years of orders in the database. Human beings with years of experience had been packing orders and leaving a record of their work to be mined. Obviously the standard gift packs are easy to spot. But most of the orders tend to be something that had occurred before, too. Here are the answers, if you will bother to dig them out.

First, Mr. Tutt found all of the unique configurations in the orders, how often they occurred and the boxes used to pack them. If the same configuration had two or more boxes, then you should go with the smaller size. As it turned out, there were ~5000 unique configurations in the custom orders which covered about 99.5% of the cases.

Next, this table of configurations was put into a stored procedure that did a slightly modified exact relational division to obtain the box size required. A fancy look-up table with the divisor set as its parameter!

7.2.6 Hierarchical Auxiliary Tables

In a hierarchical auxiliary table, there is one parameter, but it must fall inside one or more ranges of values and those ranges must be nested inside each other. We want to get an entire path of categories back as a result.

A common example would be the Dewey decimal classification system, which we might encode as:

```
CREATE TABLE Dewey_Decimal_Classification
(category_name CHAR(35) NOT NULL,
 low_ddc INTEGER NOT NULL
    CHECK (low_ddc BETWEEN 000 AND 999),
 high_ddc INTEGER NOT NULL
```

```
    CHECK (high_ddc BETWEEN 000 AND 999),
 CHECK (low_ddc <= high_ddc),
 PRIMARY KEY (low_ddc, high_ddc));

INSERT INTO Dewey_Decimal_Classification
VALUES ('Natural Sciences & Mathematics', 500, 599),
    ('Mathematics', 510, 519),
    ('General Topics', 511, 511),
    ('Algebra & Number Theory', 512, 512),
    ...

    ('Probabilities & Applied Mathematics', 519, 519);
```

Thus a search on 511 returns three rows in the look-up table. The leaf nodes of the hierarchy always have (low_ddc = high_ddc) and the relative nesting level can be determined by (high_ddc - low_ddc) or by the range values themselves.

Again, you can have a constraint on the table that prevents overlapping ranges, but this is not usually placed on the table since it is checked when the table is loaded. However, the CHECK (low_ddc <= high_ddc) can pass along information to the optimizer and the PRIMARY KEY (low_ddc, high_ddc) will create a useful index for the joins.

Notice I showed this example with INTEGER ranges. It would be fine to use CHAR(3) with constraints and string functions.

7.2.7 One True Look-up Table

I think that Paul Keister was the first person to coin the phrase "OTLT" (One True Look-up Table) for a common SQL programming technique that is popular with newbies. Later D. C. Peterson called it a "MUCK" (massively unified code-key) table. The technique crops up time and time again, but I'll give him credit as the first guy to give it a name. Simply put, the idea is to have *one table to do all of the code look-ups in the schema.* It usually looks like this:

```
CREATE TABLE Magical_Universal_Lookups
(code_type CHAR(10) NOT NULL,
 code_value VARCHAR(255) NOT NULL,
 code_description VARCHAR(255) NOT NULL,
 PRIMARY KEY (code_value, code_type));
```

So if we have Dewey decimal classification (library codes), ICD (international classification of diseases), and two-letter ISO-3166 country codes in the schema, we have them all in one, honking big table.

Let's start with the problems in the DDL and then look at the awful queries you have to write (or hide in VIEWs). So we need to go back to the original DDL and add a CHECK() constraint on the code_type column. (Otherwise, we might "invent" a new encoding system by typographical error.)

The Dewey decimal and ICD codes are numeric, and the ISO-3166 is alphabetic. Oops, need another CHECK constraint that will look at the code_type and make sure that the string is in the right format. Now the table looks something like this, if anyone attempted to do it right, which is not usually the case:

```
CREATE TABLE Magical_Universal_Lookups
(code_type CHAR(10) NOT NULL
    CHECK(code_type IN ('DDC', 'ICD', 'ISO3166', ..),
 code_value VARCHAR(255) NOT NULL,
    CHECK
    (CASE WHEN code_type = 'DDC'
          AND code_value
            SIMILAR TO '[0-9][0-9][0-9].[0-9][0-9][0-9]'
       THEN 1
       WHEN code_type = 'ICD'
          AND code_value
            SIMILAR TO '[0-9][0-9][0-9].[0-9][0-9][0-9]'
       THEN 1
       WHEN code_type = 'ISO3166'
          AND code_value
            SIMILAR TO '[A-Z][A-Z]'
       THEN 1 ELSE 0 END = 1),
 code_description VARCHAR(255) NOT NULL,
 PRIMARY KEY (code_value, code_type));
```

Since the typical application database can have dozens and dozens of codes in it, just keep extending this pattern for as long as required. Not very pretty is it? That is why most OTLT programmers do not bother with it and thus destroy data integrity.

The next thing you notice about this table is that the columns are pretty wide VARCHAR(n), or even worse, that they NVARCHAR(n). The size of the string is most often the largest one allowed in that particular SQL product.

Since you have no idea what is going to be shoved into the table, there is no way to predict and design with a safe, reasonable maximum size. The size constraint has to be put into the WHEN clause of that second CHECK() constraint between code_type and code_value.

These large sizes tend to invite bad data. You give someone a VARCHAR(n) column, and you eventually get a string with a lot of white space and a small odd character sitting at the end of it. You give someone an NVARCHAR(255) column and eventually it will get a Buddhist sutra in Chinese Unicode. I am sure of this because I load the Heart Sutra (247 Han characters) when I get called to evaluate a database.

If you make an error in the code_type or code_description among codes with the same structure, it might not be detected. You can turn 500.000 from "Natural Sciences and Mathematics" in Dewey decimal classification into "Coal Workers Pneumoconiosis" in ICD and vice versa. This can be really hard to find when one of the similarly structured schemes had unused codes in it.

Now let's consider the problems with actually using the OTLT in the DML. It is always necessary to add the code_type as well as the value that you are trying to look up.

```
SELECT P1.ssn, P1.last_name, ..., L1.code_description
 FROM Magical_Universal_Lookups AS L1, Personnel AS P1
 WHERE L1.code_type = 'ICD'
  AND L1.code_value = P1.icd
  AND ..;
```

In this sample query, I need to know the code_type of the Personnel table sickness column and of every other encoded column in the table. If you got a code_type wrong, you can still get a result.

I also need to allow for some overhead for type conversions. It would be much more natural to use DECIMAL (6,3) for Dewey decimal codes instead of VARCHAR(n), so that is probably how it appears in the Personnel table. But why not use CHAR(7) for the code? If I had a separate table for each encoding scheme, then I would have used a FOREIGN KEY and matched the data types in the referenced and referencing tables. There is no definitive guide for data type choices in the OTLT approach.

When I go to execute a query, I have to pull in the entire OTLT table, even if I only use one code. If one code is at the start of the physical storage, and another is at the end of physical storage, I can do a lot of paging. When I update the OTLT table, I have to lock out everyone until I am finished. It is like having to carry an encyclopedia set with you when all you needed was a magazine article.

I am going to venture a guess that this idea came from OO programmers who think of it as some kind of polymorphism done in SQL. They say to themselves that a table is a class, which it is not, and therefore it ought to have polymorphic behaviors, which it does not.

Maybe there are good reasons for the data modeling principle that a well-designed table is a set of things of the same kind, instead of a pile of unrelated items.

7.3 Advance Auxiliary Function Tables

SQL is not a computational language like FORTRAN and the specialized math packages. It typically does not have the numerical analysis routines to compensate for floating point rounding errors, or algebraic reductions in the optimizer. But it is good at joins.

Most auxiliary look-up tables are for simple decoding, but they can be used for more complex functions. Let's consider two financial calculations that you cannot do easily; the net present value (NPV) and its related IRR. Let me stop and ask how would you program the NPV and IRR in SQL? The answer posted on most Newsgroups replies was to write a procedure directly from the equation in the vendor-specific 4GL language and then call it.

As a quick review, let's start with the NPV calculation. Imagine that you just won the lottery. You can get the money in a lump sum or have it in monthly payouts over 20 years. What is the best deal? The lottery will pay you more total money over time than in a single payment. But if you can invest the single lump sum at a given interest rate yourself, you might do better. The NPV tells you what a series of payouts is worth as a lump sum at a given interest rate.

To make this more concrete, let's show a little code and data for your two investments options.

```
CREATE TABLE CashFlows
(project_name CHAR(15) NOT NULL,
 time_period INTEGER NOT NULL,
 CHECK (time_period >= 0),
 payment_amt DECIMAL(12,4) NOT NULL,
 PRIMARY KEY (project_id, time_period));

INSERT INTO CashFlows
VALUES ('Acme', 0, -1000.0000), ('Acme', 1, 500.0000),
    ('Acme', 2, 400.0000),('Acme', 3, 200.0000),
    ('Acme', 4, 200.0000),
    ('Beta', 0, -1000.0000), ('Beta', 1, 100.0000),
    ('Beta', 2, 200.0000), ('Beta', 3, 200.0000),
    ('Beta', 4, 700.0000);
```

At the start, I invest $1000 at the start of each project; the time period is zero and the amount is always negative. Every year I get a different amount back on my investment so that at the end of the fourth year, I've received a total of $13,000 on the Acme project less my initial $1000 for a profit of $12,000. Likewise the Beta project returns $15,000 at the end.

Beta looks like a better investment. Let's assume we can get 10% return on an investment and that we put our cash flows into that investment. The NPV function is

```
SELECT project_name,
    CAST(SUM(payment_amt/POWER ((1.00 + .10), time_period))
     AS DECIMAL(12,2)) AS npv
 FROM Cashflows
 GROUP BY project_name;
```

Acme has an NPV of $72.49 and Beta is worth –$113.97, which means the faster payback from Acme is worth more than waiting for Project Beta when we have high interest rates. This is a bit counter-intuitive.

7.3.1 Inverse Functions with Auxiliary Tables

The IRR depends on the NPV. It finds the interest rate at which your investment would break even if you invested back into the same project. Thus if you can get a better rate, this is a good investment.

Let's build another table.

```
CREATE TABLE Rates
(rate DECIMAL(6,4) NOT NULL PRIMARY KEY);
```

Now let's populate it with some values. One trick to fill the Rates table with values is to use a CROSS JOIN and keep values inside a reasonable range.

```
CREATE TABLE Digits(digit DECIMAL (6,4) PRIMARY KEY);
INSERT INTO Digits
VALUES (0.0000), (0.0001), (0.0002), (0.0003), (0.0004),
    (0.0005), (0.0006), (0.0007), (0.0008), (0.0009);

INSERT INTO Rates (rate)
SELECT DISTINCT (D1.digit *1000) + (D2.digit *100) + (D3.digit *10) +
D4.digit
 FROM Digits AS D1, Digits AS D2, Digits AS D3, Digits AS D4
 WHERE ((D1.digit *1000) + (D2.digit *100) + (D3.digit *10) + D4.digit)
  BETWEEN {{lower limit}} AND {{upper limit}}; -- pseudo-code
DROP TABLE Digits;
```

We now have two choices. We can build a VIEW or CTE that uses the cash flow table, thus:

```
CREATE VIEW NPV_by_Rate(project_id, rate, npv)
AS
SELECT CF.project_id, R1.rate,
  SUM(amount / POWER((1.00 + R1.rate), time_period))
FROM CashFlows AS CF, Rates AS R1
GROUP BY R1.rate, CF.project_id;
```

or we can set the amount in the formula to 1 and store the multiplier for the (rate, time_period) pair in another table:

```
INSERT INTO NPV_Mulipliers (time_period, rate, npv_multiplier)
SELECT S.seq, R1.rate,
  SUM(1.00/(POWER((1.00 + R1.rate), seq)))
 FROM Series AS S, Rates AS R1
 WHERE S.seq <= {{ upper limit }} --pseudo-code
 GROUP BY S.seq, R1.rate;
```

The Series table contains integers 1 to (n) and it is a standard auxiliary table used to avoid iteration.

Assuming we use the VIEW, the IRR is now the single query:

```
SELECT 'Acme', rate AS irr, npv
 FROM NPV_by_Rate
 WHERE ABS(npv)
 = (SELECT MIN(ABS(npv))
   FROM NPV_by_Rate)
 AND project_id = 'Acme';
```

In my sample data, I get an IRR of 13.99% at an NPV of −0.04965 for the Acme project. Assume you have hundreds of projects to consider; would you rather write one query or hundreds of procedure calls?

This website has a set of slides that deal with the use of interpolation to find the IRR: www.yorku.ca/adms3530/Interpolation.pdf. Using the method described on the website, we can write the interpolation for the Acme example as:

```
SELECT R1.rate + (R1.rate * (R1.npv/(R1.npv - R2.npv))) AS irr
 FROM NPV_by_Rate AS R1, NPV_by_Rate AS R2
 WHERE R1.project_id = 'Acme'
  AND R2.project_id = 'Acme'
  AND R1.rate = 0.1000
  AND R2.rate = 0.2100
  AND R1.npv > 0
  AND R2.npv < 0;
```

The important points are that the NPVs from R1 to R2 have to be on both sides of the zero point, so that you can do a linear interpolation between the two rates with which they are associated.

The trade-off is speed for accuracy. The IRR function is slightly concave and not linear; that means that if you graph it, the shape of the curve buckles toward the origin. Picking good (R1.rate, R2.rate) pairs is important, but if you want to round off to the nearest whole percentage, you probably have a larger range than you might think. The answer, 0.1399 from the original table look-up method, rounds to 14% as do all of the following interpolations.

RI	R2	IRR
0.1	0.21	0.14
0.1	0.2	0.143537
0.1	0.2	0.143457

RI	R2	IRR
0.1	0.2	0.143492
0.08	0.17	0.135658

The advantages of using an auxiliary function table are

(1) All host programs will be using the same calculations.

(2) The formula can be applied to hundreds or thousands of projects at one time instead doing one project, as you would with a spreadsheet or financial calculator.

Robert J. Hamilton (bobha@seanet.com) posted proprietary T-SQL functions for the NPV and IRR functions. The NPV function was straight forward, but he pointed out several problems with finding the IRR.

By definition IRR is the rate at which the NPV of the cash flows equals zero. When IRR is well behaved the graph of NPV as a function of rate is a curve that crosses the *x*-axis once and only once. When IRR is not well behaved, the graph crosses the *x*-axis many times which means the IRR is either multivalued or is undefined.

At this point, we need to ask what the appropriate domain is for IRR. As it turns out NPV is defined for all possible rates, both positive and negative, except where NPV approaches an asymptote at rate of −100% and the power function blows up. What does a negative rate mean when calculating NPV? What does it mean to have a negative IRR? Well it depends on how you look at it.

If you take a mathematical approach a negative IRR is just another solution to the equation. If you take an economic approach, a negative IRR means you are losing money on the project. Perhaps if you live in a deflationary economy, then a negative cash flow might be profitable in terms of real money, but that is a very unusual situation and we can dismiss negative IRRs as unreasonable.

This means that a table look-up approach to the IRR has to have a very fine granularity and enough of a scope to cover a lot of situation for the general case. It also means that it is probably not the way to go. Expressing rates to 5 or 6 decimal places is common in home mortgage finance (i.e., APR 5.6725%) and this degree of precision using the set-based approach does not scale well. Moreover, this is exacerbated by the requirements of using IRR in hyperinflationary economies where solutions of 200%, 300%, and higher are meaningful.

Here are Mr. Hamilton's functions written in SQL/PSM; one uses a straight-line algorithm as you find in Excel and other spreadsheets and a bounding box algorithm. The bounding box algorithm has better domain integrity but can inadvertently "skip over" a solution when widening its search.

```
CREATE TABLE CashFlows
(t INTEGER NOT NULL CHECK (t >= 0),
 amount DECIMAL(12,4) NOT NULL);

CREATE TABLE Rates
(rate DECIMAL(7,5) NOT NULL);

CREATE TABLE Digits
(digit DECIMAL(6,4));
INSERT INTO Digits
VALUES (0.0000), (0.0001), (0.0002), (0.0003), (0.0004),
    (0.0005), (0.0006), (0.0007), (0.0008), (0.0009);

INSERT INTO Rates
SELECT D1.digit * 1000 + D2.digit * 100 + D3.digit * 10 + D4.digit FROM
Digits AS D1, Digits AS D2, Digits AS D3, Digits AS D4;

INSERT INTO Rates
SELECT rate-1 FROM Rates WHERE rate >= 0;

INSERT INTO Rates
SELECT rate-2 FROM Rates WHERE rate >= 0;

DROP TABLE Digits;

CREATE FUNCTION NPV (IN my_rate FLOAT)
RETURNS FLOAT
DETERMINISTIC
CONTAINS SQL
RETURN (CASE WHEN -- prevent divide by zero at rate = -100%
       ABS (1.0 + my_rate) >= 1.0e-5
       THEN (SELECT SUM (amount * POWER ((1.0 + my_rate), -t))
           FROM CashFlows)
       ELSE NULL END);

CREATE FUNCTION irr_bb (IN guess FLOAT)
RETURNS FLOAT
```

```
DETERMINISTIC
CONTAINS SQL
BEGIN
 DECLARE maxtry INTEGER;
 DECLARE x1 FLOAT;
 DECLARE x2 FLOAT;
 DECLARE f1 FLOAT;
 DECLARE f2 FLOAT;
 DECLARE x FLOAT;
 DECLARE dx FLOAT;
 DECLARE x_mid FLOAT;
 DECLARE f_mid FLOAT;

 -- initial bounding box around guess
 SET x1 = guess - 0.005;
 SET f1 = NPV (x1);
 IF f1 IS NULL THEN RETURN (f1); END IF;

 SET x2 = guess + 0.005;
 SET f2 = NPV (x2);
 IF f2 IS NULL THEN RETURN (f2); END IF;

 -- expand bounding box to include a solution
 SET maxtry = 50;
 WHILE maxtry > 0 -- try until solution is bounded
    AND (SIGN(f1) * SIGN(f2)) <> -1
 DO IF ABS (f1) < ABS (f2)
   THEN -- move lower bound
     SET x1 = x1 + 1.6 * (x1 - x2);
     SET f1 = NPV (x1);
     IF f1 IS NULL -- no irr
     THEN RETURN (f1);
     END IF;
   ELSE -- move upper bound
     SET x2 = x2 + 1.6 * (x2 - x1);
     SET f2 = NPV (x2);
     IF f2 IS NULL -- no irr
     THEN RETURN (f2);
     END IF;
  END IF;
```

```
  SET maxtry = maxtry - 1;
  END WHILE;
 IF (SIGN(f1) * SIGN(f2)) <> -1
 THEN RETURN (CAST (NULL AS FLOAT));
 END IF;
END;

 -- now find solution with binary search
 SET x = CASE WHEN f1 < 0
        THEN x1
        ELSE x2 END;
 SET dx = CASE WHEN f1 < 0
        THEN (x2 - x1)
        ELSE (x1 - x2) END;
 SET maxtry = 50;
 WHILE maxtry > 0
 DO SET dx = dx / 2.0; -- reduce steps by half
   SET x_mid = x + dx;
   SET f_mid = NPV (x_mid);
   IF f_mid IS NULL -- no irr
   THEN RETURN (f_mid);
   ELSE IF ABS (f_mid) < 1.0e-5 -- epsilon for problem
     THEN RETURN (x_mid); -- irr found
     END IF;
   END IF;
   IF f_mid < 0
   THEN SET x = x_mid;
   END IF;
   SET maxtry = maxtry - 1;
 END WHILE;
 RETURN (CAST (NULL AS FLOAT));
END;
```

If you prefer to compute the IRR as a straight line, you can use this function.

```
CREATE FUNCTION irr_sl (IN guess FLOAT)
RETURNS FLOAT
DETERMINISTIC
CONTAINS SQL
```

```
BEGIN
 DECLARE maxtry INTEGER;
 DECLARE x1 FLOAT; DECLARE x2 FLOAT;
 DECLARE f1 FLOAT; DECLARE f2 FLOAT;

 SET maxtry = 50; -- iterations
 WHILE maxtry > 0
 DO SET x1 = guess;
   SET f1 = NPV (x1);
   IF f1 IS NULL -- no irr
   THEN RETURN (f1);
   ELSE IF ABS (f1) < 1.0e-5 -- irr within epsilon range
     THEN RETURN (x1);
     END IF;
   END IF;

   -- try again with new guess using two-point formula
   SET x2 = x1 + 1.0e-5;
   SET f2 = NPV (x2);
   IF f2 IS NULL -- no irr
   THEN RETURN (f2);
   END IF;
   IF ABS (f2 - f1) < 1.0e-5
   THEN RETURN (CAST (NULL AS FLOAT)); -- check for divide by zero
   END IF;
   SET guess = x1 - f1 * (x2 - x1)/ (f2 - f1);
   SET maxtry = maxtry - 1;
 END WHILE;
END;

-- Test table, holds results of straight line algorithm
CREATE TABLE Test_StraightLine
(rate DECIMAL(7,5) NOT NULL,
 npv FLOAT,
 irr DECIMAL(7,5));

CREATE TABLE Test_BoundedBox
(rate DECIMAL(7,5) NOT NULL,
 npv FLOAT,
 irr DECIMAL(7,5));
```

```
-- original scenario
-- try t = 0 cashflow of: - 391, irr undefined;
-- try t = 0 cashflow of: -350, irr multi-valued;
-- 0, irr single-valued (well-behaved)

DELETE FROM CashFlows
INSERT INTO CashFlows
VALUES (0, -350), (1, 100), (2, 100), (3, 100), (4, 100),
    (5, 100), (6, 100), (7, 100), (8, 100), (9, 100),
    (10, 100), (11, 100), (12, 100), (13, 100), (14, 100),
    (15, -1500);

-- scenario 1a: single valued irr
DELETE FROM CashFlows
INSERT INTO CashFlows
VALUES (0, -800), (1, 100), (2, 100), (3, 100), (4, 100),
    (5, 100), (6, 100), (7, 100), (8, 100), (9, 100),
    (10, 100);

-- scenario 1b: single valued irr, signs reversed
DELETE FROM CashFlows;
INSERT INTO CashFlows
VALUES (0, 800), (1, -100), (2, -100), (3, -100), (4, -100),
    (5, -100), (6, -100), (7, -100), (8, -100), (9, -100),
    (10, -100);

-- scenario 2: double valued irr
DELETE FROM CashFlows;
INSERT INTO CashFlows
VALUES (0, -300), (1, 100), (2, 100), (3, 100), (4, 100),
    (5, 100), (6, 100),(7, 100), (8, 100), (9, 100),
    (10, -690);

-- scenario 3: double valued irr with solutions very close together
DELETE FROM CashFlows;
INSERT INTO CashFlows
VALUES (0, -310), (1, 100), (2, 100), (3, 100), (4, 100),
    (5, 100), (6, 100), (7, 100), (8, 100), (9, 100),
    (10, -690);
```

```
-- scenario 4: undefined irr
DELETE FROM CashFlows;
INSERT INTO CashFlows
VALUES (0, -320), (1, 100), (2, 100), (3, 100), (4, 100),
    (5, 100), (6, 100), (7, 100), (8, 100), (9, 100),
    (10, -690);

-- run the test
DELETE FROM Test_StraightLine;
INSERT INTO Test_StraightLine (rate, npv, irr)
SELECT rate, NPV (rate), irr_sl(rate)
 FROM Rates;

DELETE FROM Test_BoundedBox;
INSERT INTO Test_BoundedBox (rate, npv, irr)
SELECT rate, NPV (rate), irr_bb(rate)
 FROM Rates;

-- View results of the test
SELECT SL.rate, SL.npv AS npv_sl, SL.irr AS irr_sl,
    BB.npv AS npv_bb,
    BB.irr AS irr_bb
 FROM Test_StraightLine AS SL, Test_BoundedBox
 WHERE BB.rate = SL.rate;
```

A computational version of the IRR due to Richard Romley returns approximations that become more and more accurate as you feed estimates back into the formula.

```
CREATE FUNCTION IRR(IN project_name CHAR(15), IN my_i DECIMAL(12,8))
RETURNS DECIMAL(12,8)
LANGUAGE SQL
DETERMINISTIC
RETURN (SELECT CASE WHEN ROUND(my_i, 4) = ROUND(T.i, 4)
          THEN 100 * (my_I - 1)
          ELSE IRR(project_id, T.i) END
     FROM (SELECT SUM((amount * (time_period + 1))
             /(POWER(my_i, time_period)))
             / SUM((amount * (time_period))
```

```
            /(POWER(my_i, time_period + 1)))
    FROM CashFlows
    WHERE project_id = my_project_id));
```

7.3.2 Interpolation with Auxiliary Function Tables

SQL is not a computational programming language, so you often have to depend on vendor extensions providing a good library or on being able to write the functions with the limited power in standard SQL.

However, SQL is good at handling tables and you can often set up auxiliary tables of the general form:

```
CREATE TABLE SomeFunction
(parameter <data type> NOT NULL PRIMARY KEY,
 result <data type> NOT NULL);
```

when the range of the function is relatively small. Thus, the pseudo-code expression:

```
SELECT SomeFunction(T1.x), ...
  FROM TableOne AS T1
 WHERE etc
```

is replaced by

```
SELECT F1.result,
  FROM TableOne AS T1, SomeFunction AS F1
 WHERE T1.x = F1.parameter
  AND etc
```

However, if the function has a large range, the SomeFunction table can become huge or completely impractical.

A technique that has fallen out of favor since the advent of cheap, fast computers is interpolation. It consists of using two known functional values, a and b, and their results in the function, $f(a)$ and $f(b)$, to find the result of a value, x, between them.

Linear interpolation is the easiest method and if the table has a high precision, it will work quite well for most applications. It is based on the idea that a straight line drawn between two function values $f(a)$ and $f(b)$ will approximate the function well enough that you can take a proportional increment of x relative to (a, b) and get a usable answer for $f(x)$.

The algebra looks like this:

$$f(x) = f(a) + (x - a) * ((f(b) - f(a)) / (b - a))$$

where ($a \leq x \leq b$) and x is not in the table. This can be translated into SQL like this, where x is :myparameter, F1 is related to the variable a, and F2 is related to the variable b (Figure 7.1).

```
SELECT :myparameter AS my_input,
   (F1.answer + (:myparameter - F1.param)
   * ((F2.answer - F1.answer)
     / (CASE WHEN F1.param = F2.param
         THEN 1.00
         ELSE F2.param - F1.param END)))
   AS answer
  FROM SomeFunction AS F1, SomeFunction AS F2
 WHERE F1.param -- establish a and f(a)
  = (SELECT MAX(param)
       FROM SomeFunction
      WHERE param <= :myparameter)
  AND F2.param -- establish b and f(b)
  = (SELECT MIN(param)
       FROM SomeFunction
      WHERE param >= :myparameter);
```

The CASE expression in the divisor is to avoid division by zero errors when $f(x)$ is in the table.

The rules for interpolation methods are always expressible in four-function arithmetic, which is good for standard SQL. In the old days, the function tables gave an extra value with each parameter and result pair, called delta squared, which was based on finite differences. Delta squared was like a second derivative and could be used in a formula to improve the accuracy of the approximation.

$$f(t) = \frac{\Gamma\left(\frac{(v+1)}{2}\right)}{\sqrt{v\pi}\,\Gamma\left(\frac{(v)}{2}\right)}\left(1 + \frac{t^2}{v}\right)^{-\left(\frac{(v+1)}{2}\right)}$$

Figure 7.1 Student's *t*-distribution formula.

This is not a book on numerical analysis, so you will have to go to a library to find details—or ask an old engineer.

7.4 Global Constants Tables

When you configure a system, you might want to have a way to set and keep constants in the schema. One method for doing this is to have a one-row table that can be set with default values at the start, and then updated only by someone with administrative privileges.

```
CREATE TABLE Constants
(lock CHAR(1) DEFAULT 'X'
   NOT NULL PRIMARY KEY
   CHECK (lock = 'X'),
 pi FLOAT DEFAULT 3.142592653 NOT NULL,
  e FLOAT DEFAULT 2.71828182 NOT NULL,
 phi FLOAT DEFAULT 1.6180339887 NOT NULL,
 ...);
```

To initialize the row, execute this statement.

INSERT INTO Constants VALUES DEFAULTS;

The lock column assures there is only one row and the default values load the initial values. These defaults can include the current user and current timestamp, as well as numeric and character values.

Another version of this idea that does not allow for any updates is a VIEW defined with a table constructor.

```
CREATE VIEW Constants (pi, e, phi, ..)
AS VALUES (3.142592653), (2.71828182), (1.6180339887), ..;
```

The next step is to put in a formula for the constants so that they will be computed on any platform to which this DDL is moved, using the local math library and hardware precision.

7.4.1 Prime Numbers

I was teaching SQL classes for YAPC-10 (“Yet Another PERL Conference” #10) at Carnegie Mellon University at the end of June 2009. For the record, I have never used PERL and had to Google up an overview before I went; it is a very different creature from SQL. One of my students asked if you could write an SQL statement to generate the prime numbers less than 1000 (or any other limit) that scales well. He was bothered by the lack of loops in SQL and a Prime Number sieve is a common PERL programming exercise. You can Google it and see an animation http://www.hbmeyer.de/eratosiv.htm and some PERL code at http://www.perlmonks.org/?node_id=276103.

There are two useful facts from Number Theory:

(1) The prime factors of a given number (n) cannot be greater than ceiling ($\sqrt{n}$). Think about it; by definition ($\sqrt{n} * \sqrt{n}$)) = n, and by definition, ceiling ($\sqrt{n}$)≥floor ($\sqrt{n}$) so integer rounding up will be safe. This says that if I look at ($a * b = c$) where ($a < b$), then I don't have to look at ($b * a = c$), so I can start searching for prime factors with small values.

(2) All primes are of the form ($6 * n \pm 1$), but not all number of that form are Primes. For example, ($n = 1$) gives us {5, 7} and they are both primes. But for ($n = 4$) gives us {23, 25}, where ($25 = 5 * 5$). What this does is remove the multiples of 2 and 3 from consideration.

Let's get all of that into SQL statements. Let's start with a table for the primes:

```
CREATE TABLE Primes
(p INTEGER NOT NULL PRIMARY KEY
 CHECK (p > 1));
```

Now, your puzzle is to fill the table up to some limit, say 1000 just to keep it simple.

Let's assume we already have a table named Series with integers from 1 to (n) that we can use.

Method #1

For the first attempt, let's load the Primes table with candidate numbers using math fact #2 from above.

```
INSERT INTO Primes (p)
(SELECT (6 * seq) + 1
 FROM Series
WHERE (6 * seq) + 1 <= 1000
UNION ALL
SELECT (6 * seq) - 1
```

```
 FROM Series
WHERE (6 * seq) + 1 <= 1000);
```

An improvement which gets rid of the UNION ALL uses a table constant:

```
INSERT INTO Primes (p)
SELECT (6 * seq) + S.switch
 FROM Series
    CROSS JOIN
    (SELECT switch
     FROM (VALUES (-1), (+1)))
    AS S(switch)
 WHERE (6 * seq) + 1 <= 1000;
```

Now we have too many rows in Primes and need to remove the nonprimes. Now math fact #1 can come into play; test the set of numbers less than the square root to see if there is a factor among them.

```
DELETE FROM Primes
WHERE EXISTS
 (SELECT *
   FROM Primes AS P1
  WHERE P1.p <= CEILING (SQRT (Primes.p))
   AND MOD (Primes.p, P1.p) = 0);
```

Method #2

Another way to load the candidates into Primes is to have the first few known primes hardwired into a query. This is a generalization of the math fact #2, which dealt with multiples of only 2 and 3.

```
INSERT INTO Primes (p)
SELECT seq
 FROM Series
 WHERE 0 NOT IN (MOD(seq, 2), MOD(seq, 3), MOD(seq, 5), MOD(seq, 7),
..);
```

The idea is that if we can limit the candidate set for Primes, performance will improve. At the extreme, if the list of "MOD (seq, <prime>)" expressions goes to a value equal or higher than the upper limit we are looking at, we get the answer immediately.

This is a good trick; many SQL programmers think that an IN() list can only be constants. You might also want to look at how many values it can hold—It is larger than you think.

Method #3

Another candidate pruning trick is based on the math fact that integers with final digits {2, 4, 6, 8, 0} are even numbers; those with final digits {5, 0} are multiples of 5. Let's not look at them when we build a candidate table.

```
INSERT INTO Primes (p)
SELECT *
 FROM (WITH Digits(i)
     AS (SELECT i
   FROM (VALUES (1), (2), (3), (4), (5), (6), (7), (8), (9), (0)) AS
X(i),
-- last digit CTE
Units(i)
AS (SELECT i
  FROM (VALUES (1), (3), (7), (9)) AS X(i)

SELECT (D3.i * 1000 + D2.i * 100 + D1.i * 10 + Units.i)
 FROM Units, Digits AS D1, Digits AS D2, Digits AS D3);
```

Method #4

Another approach is to generate all of the non-primes and remove them from the Series table.

```
INSERT INTO Primes (p)
SELECT *
 FROM ((SELECT seq FROM Series WHERE seq <= 1000)
    EXCEPT
    (SELECT (F1.seq * F2.seq) AS composite_nbr
      FROM Series AS F1, Series AS F2
      WHERE F1.seq BETWEEN 2 AND CEILING (SQRT (1000))
       AND F2.seq BETWEEN 2 AND CEILING (SQRT (1000))
       AND F1.seq <= F2.seq
       AND (F1.seq * F2.seq) <= 1000);
```

Obviously, the Series table in the left-hand clause could be anyone of the trimmed candidate tables we previously constructed.

There are faster but more complicated algorithms, like the Sieve of Atkin and the various Wheel Sieves.

7.4.2 Fibonacci Numbers

Fibonacci numbers are defined recursively (as are many other mathematical series) so there is a temptation to use a recursive CTE.

If you are not familiar with Fibonacci series, it is defined by the formula:

$F(0)=1$—by convention

$F(1)=1$

$F(2)=1$

$F(n)=F(n-1)+F(n-2)$

In English, you start with a pair of numbers, (0,1) as the first two Fibonacci numbers and after than any Fibonacci number (greater than 2) is the sum of the two previous numbers. That gives us 1, 1, 2, 3, 5, 8, 13, 21, 34, 55, 89, etc.

This series occurs so often in nature and mathematical functions that you will find whole books devoted to it.

We can solve this using a recursive CTE, thus:

```
WITH RECURSIVE Fibonacci(n, f, f1)
AS(
(VALUES CAST(1 AS BIGINT), CAST(0 AS BIGINT), CAST(1 AS BIGINT))
UNION ALL
SELECT (n + 1),(f + f1), f
 FROM Fibonacci
 WHERE n < 100) - or other limit for BIGINT

SELECT n, f AS f_nbr
 FROM Fibonacci;
```

It looks nice and clever. But many such series have a closed form that is easy and faster than a recursive query. The constant phi and the formula:

```
ROUND (((POWER (phi, :n)- POWER (1.0 - phi, :n))/
SQRT (5.0)), 0);
```

Where phi = FLOOR(POWER(1.61803398874989, n)/SQRT(5) + 0.5)

You can load the table in one update statement. You can use more decimal places for phi, if you want more numbers.

7.4.3 Random Order Values

In many applications, we do not want to issue the sequence numbers in sequence. This pattern can give information that we do not wish to expose. Instead we want to issue generated values in random order. Do not get mixed up; we want known values that are supplied in random order and not random numbers. Most random number generators can repeat values, which would defeat the purpose of this drill.

While I usually avoid mentioning physical implementations, one of the advantages of random-order keys is to improve the performance of tree indexes. Tree structured indexes, such as a B-Tree, that have sequential insertions become unbalanced and have to be re-organized frequently. However, if the same set of keys is presented in a random order, the tree tends to stay balanced and you get much better performance.

The generator shown here is an implementation of the additive congruential method of generating values in pseudo-random order and is due to Roy Hann of Rational Commerce Limited, a CA-Ingres consulting firm. It is based on a shift-register and an XOR-gate, and it has its origins in cryptography. While there are other ways to do this, this code is nice because:

(1) The algorithm can be written in C or another low-level language for speed. But math is fairly simple even in base 10.

(2) The algorithm tends to generate successive values that are (usually) "far apart," which is handy for improving the performance of tree indexes. You will tend to put data on separate physical data pages in storage.

(3) The algorithm does not cycle until it has generated every possible value, so we don't have to worry about duplicates. Just count how many calls have been made to the generator.

(4) The algorithm produces uniformly distributed values, which is a nice mathematical property to have. It also does not include zero.

Let's walk through all the iterations of the 4-bit Generator illustrated in the diagram below:

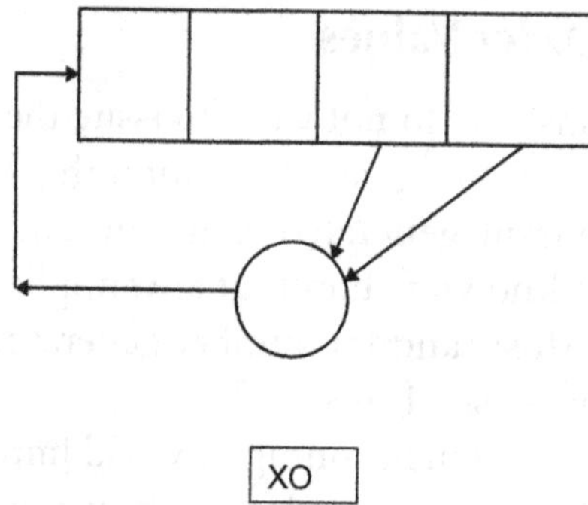

XO

Initially the shift register contains the value 0001. The two rightmost bits are XOR-ed together, giving 1, and the result is fed into the leftmost bit position and the previous register contents shift one bit right. The iterations of the register are shown in this table, with their base 10 values:

iteration 1: 0001 (1)

iteration 2: 1000 (8)

iteration 3: 0100 (4)

iteration 4: 0010 (2)

iteration 5: 1001 (9)

iteration 6: 1100 (12)

iteration 7: 0110 (6)

iteration 8: 1011 (11)

iteration 9: 0101 (5)

iteration 10: 1010 (10)

iteration 11: 1101 (13)

iteration 12: 1110 (14)

iteration 13: 1111 (15)

iteration 14: 0111 (7)

iteration 15: 0011 (3)

iteration 16: 0001 (1) wrap-around!

It might not be obvious that successive values are far apart when we are looking at a tiny 4-bit register. But it is clear that the values are generated in no obvious order, all possible values except 0 are eventually produced, and the termination condition is clear—the Generator cycles back to 1.

Generalizing the algorithm to arbitrary binary word sizes, and therefore longer number sequences, is not as easy as you might think. Finding the "tap" positions where bits are extracted for feedback varies according to the word-size in an extremely non-obvious way. Choosing incorrect tap positions results in an incomplete and usually very short cycle that is unusable. If you want the details and tap positions for words of 1-100 bits, see E. J. Watson, "Primitive polynomials (Mod 2)", *Mathematics of Computation*, vol. 16, 1962, pp. 368-369.

The table below shows the tap positions 8-, 16-, 31-, 32-, and 64-bit words. That should work with any computer hardware you have. The 31-bit word is the one that is probably the most useful since it gives billions of numbers, uses only two tap positions to make the math easier and matches most computer hardware. The 32-bit version is not easy to implement on a 32-bit machine because it will usually generate an overflow error.

Word Length

8 = {0, 2, 3, 4}

16 = {0, 2, 3, 5}

31 = {0, 3}

32 = {0, 1, 2, 3, 5, 7}

64 = {0 1, 3, 4}

Using the table above, we can see that we need to tap bits 0 and 3 to construct the 31-bit random-order generated value Generator (which is the one most people would want to use in practice):

```
UPDATE Generator31
  SET keyval =
    keyval/2 + MOD(MOD(keyval, 2) + MOD(keyval/8, 2), 2)*2^30;
```

Or if you prefer the algorithm in C:

```
int Generator31 ()
{static int n = 1;
 n = n >> 1 | ((n^n >> 3) & 1) << 30;
 return n;
}
```

7.5 A Note on Converting Procedural Code to Tables

Sometimes an idea is easier to see with an example. In 2010 February, a newsgroup poster asked for help with a user defied function they had written. What followed was a CASE expression with BETWEENs and ORs and CASE within CASE constructs. It took pairs of (x, y) and produced an answer from a set of three values, call them {'A', 'B', 'C'}. Again, the coding details are not my point. The body of the function could have been a complicated mathematical expression. The quick fix was in the CASE expression syntax for his immediate problem. His code looked like this skeleton:

```
CREATE FUNCTION FindFoobar (IN in_x INTEGER, IN in_y INTEGER)
RETURNS CHAR(1)
LANGUAGE SQL
DETERMINISTIC
BEGIN
<< horrible CASE expression with x and y >>;
END;
```

Now a second poster asked if the original posters if he had considered pre-calculating the CASE expression results and populating a table with them? This was a good piece of advice, since the number of (x, y) pairs involved came to a few thousand cases. Worrying about minimizing storage when the look-up table is this small is silly. Read-only tables this size tend to be in main storage or cache, so they can be shared among many sessions.

But the poster went on to say "You can use the table with your function or you could use it without the function," but he did not explain what the differences are. They are important. Putting the data in the read-only tables this size will tend to keep it in main storage or cache, If you are really that tight for primary and/or secondary storage that you cannot fit *a* ~5 K row table in your hardware, buy some chips and disks. It is cheap today. Now the data can be shared among many sessions. The table and its indexes can be used by the optimizer. In SQL Server you can include the single-column foobar in the index to get a covering index and performance improvement.

But when the data are locked inside the procedural code of a function, can it be shared or do computations get repeated with each invocation? What about indexes? Ouch! A function pretty much locks things inside. ANSI/ISO Standard SQL/PSM has a [NOT] DETERMINISTIC option in its procedure declarations. This tells the compiler if the procedure or function is going to always return the same answer for the same arguments (note about ANSI/ISO Standard SQL terms: a parameter is the formal place holder in the parameter list of a declaration and an argument is the value passed in the invocation of the procedure). A nondeterministic function has to be computed over and over; if you don't know about a procedure or function, this is what you have to assume.

Here is the skeleton of what was posted.

```
-- Create table
CREATE TABLE Foobar
(x INTEGER NOT NULL,
 y INTEGER NOT NULL,
 foobar CHAR(1) NOT NULL,
 PRIMARY KEY (x, y));

-- Populate table with data
INSERT INTO FooLookup (x, y, foobar)
SELECT X_CTE.x, Y_CTE.y, << horrible CASE expression >> AS foobar
 FROM (SELECT seq
     FROM Series
     WHERE seq BETWEEN 100 AND 300) AS X_Range (x)
    CROSS JOIN
    (SELECT seq
     FROM Series
     WHERE seq BETWEEN 1 AND 100) AS Y_Range (y);
```

Now let's go on with the rest of the skeleton code for the function:

```
CREATE FUNCTION Find_Foobar
(IN in_x INTEGER, IN in_y INTEGER)
RETURNS CHAR(1)
LANGUAGE SQL
DETERMINISTIC
BEGIN
RETURN
COALESCE
```

```
((SELECT foobar
  FROM FooLookup
  WHERE x = in_x
   AND y = in_y), 'A');
END;
```

The reason for COALESCE() is that 'A' is a default value in the outer CASE expression, but also a valid result in various THEN and ELSE clauses inside inner CASE expressions. The scalar query will return a NULL if it cannot find an (x, y, foobar) row in the table. If we know that the query covers the entire (x, y) universe, then we did not need the COALESCE() and could have avoided a function completely.

Now, let's think about declarative programming. In SQL that means constraints in the table declaration in the DDL. This skeleton has none except the PRIMARY KEY. Ouch! Here is a problem with magazine articles and newsgroup postings; you often skip over the constraints when you post a skeleton table. You did not need them when you declared a file, do you? What is forgotten is that the three SQL sub-languages (DDL, DML, and DCL) work together. In particular, the DDL constraints are used by the DML optimizer.

The ≪horrible CASE expression≫ implied expectations for x and y. We were given lower limits (100 and 1), but the upper limits were open after a small range of (x, y) pairs. I think we can assume that the original poster expected the vast majority of cases (or all of them) to fall in that small range and wanted to handle anything else as an error. In the real world, there is usually what Jerry Weinberg called "reasonableness checking" in data. The principle is also known as Zipf's Law or the "look for a horse and not a zebra" principle in medicine.

The simple first shot would be to assume we always know the limits and can simply use:

```
CREATE TABLE FooLookup
(x INTEGER NOT NULL
  CHECK (x BETWEEN 100 AND 300),
 y INTEGER NOT NULL
  CHECK (y BETWEEN 1 AND 100),
 foobar CHAR(1)
  DEFAULT 'A'
```

```
  NOT NULL
  CHECK (foobar) IN ('A', 'B', 'C'),
 PRIMARY KEY (x, y));
```

The DEFAULT 'A' subclause will take care of situation where we did not have an explicit value for foobar. This avoids the COALESCE(). But what if one of the parameters can be anything? That is easy; drop the CHECK() and add a comment. What if one of the parameters is half open or has a huge but sparse space? That is, we know a lower (upper) limit, but not the matching upper (lower) limit. Just use a simple comparison, such as CHECK (y≥1), instead of a BETWEEN.

A common situation, which was done with nested CASE expression in the original, is that you know a range for a parameter and what the results for the other parameter within that range are. That might be easier to see with code. Here is a CASE expression for some of the possible (x,y) pairs:

```
CASE
WHEN x BETWEEN 100 AND 200
THEN CASE
   WHEN y IN (2, 4, 6, 8) THEN 'B'
   WHEN y IN (1, 3, 5, 7, 9) THEN 'C'
   END
WHEN x BETWEEN 201 AND 300
THEN CASE
   WHEN y IN (2, 4, 6, 8, 99) THEN 'C'
   WHEN y IN (3, 5, 7, 9, 100) THEN 'B'
   END
ELSE 'A'
END;
```

This is the DML version of a constraint. It lives only in the INSERT. UPDATE, INSERT, or SELECT statement where it appears. What we really want is constraints in the DDL so that all statements, present and future, use it. The trick is to create the table with low and high values for each parameter range; a single value is shown with the low and high values equal to each other.

```
CREATE TABLE FooLookup
(low_x INTEGER NOT NULL,
```

```
high_x INTEGER NOT NULL,
 CHECK (low_x <= high_x),
low_y INTEGER NOT NULL,
high_y INTEGER NOT NULL,
CHECK (low_y <= high_y),
foobar CHAR(1) NOT NULL
 CHECK (foobar) IN ('A', 'B', 'C'),
PRIMARY KEY (x, y));
```

CASE expression now becomes this table:

low_x	high_x	low_y	high_y	foobar
100	200	2	2	'B'
100	200	6	6	'B'
100	200	8	8	'B'
100	200	1	1	'C'
100	200	3	3	'C'
100	200	5	5	'C'
100	200	7	7	'C'
100	200	9	9	'C'
201	300	2	2	'C'
201	300	4	4	'C'
201	300	6	6	'C'
201	300	8	8	'C'
201	300	99	99	'C'
201	300	3	3	'B'
201	300	5	5	'B'
201	300	7	7	'B'
201	300	9	9	'B'
201	300	100	100	'B'
301	9999	101	9999	'A'
-9999	99	-9999	0	'A'

As a safety device, put the default 'A' in ranges outside the rest of the table. I used –9999 and 9999 for the least and greatest limits, but you get the idea.

The query has to use BETWEENs on the high and low limits:

```
SELECT F.foobar, ..
 FROM FooLookup AS F, ..
 WHERE my_x BETWEEN F.low_x AND F.high_x
  AND my_y BETWEEN F.low_y AND F.high_y
  AND ..;
```

Is this always going to be the best way to do something? Who knows? Test it.

Other Schema Objects

THERE IS A CREATE SCHEMA statement defined in the standards which bring an entire schema into existence all at once. In practice, each product has very different utility programs to allocate physical storage and define a schema.

A schema is the "skeleton" of an SQL database; it defines the structures of the schema objects and the rules under which they operate. But not the data in that skeleton.

The only data structure in SQL is the table. Tables can be persistent (base tables), used for working storage (temporary tables) or virtual (VIEWs). The differences among these types are in implementation, not performance. One advantage of having only one data structure is that the results of all operations are also tables—you never have to convert structures, write special operators, or deal with any irregularity in the language.

The <grant statement> has to do with limiting access by users to only certain schema elements. The <assertion definition> is not widely implemented yet, but it is like constraint that applies to the schema as a whole. Finally, the <character set definition>, <collation definition>, and <translation definition> deal with the display of data. We are not really concerned with any of these schema objects; they are usually set in place by the DBA (Database Administrator) for the users and we mere programmers do not get to change them.

Conceptually, a table is a set of zero or more rows, and a row is a set of one or more columns. Each column has a specific data type and constraints that make up an implementation of an abstract domain. *The way a table is physically implemented does not matter, because you access it only with SQL.* The database engine handles all the details for you and you never worry about the internals as you would with a physical file. In fact, almost no two SQL products use the same internal structures.

There are two common conceptual errors made by programmers who are accustomed to file systems or PCs. The first is thinking that a table is a file; the second is thinking that a table is a spreadsheet. Tables do not behave like either one of these, and you will get surprises if you do not understand the basic concepts.

It is easy to imagine that a table is a file, a row is a record, and a column is a field. This is familiar and when data moves from SQL to the host language, it has to be converted into host language data types and data structures to be displayed and used.

The big differences between working with a file system and working with SQL are in the way SQL fits into a host program. Using a file system, your programs must open and close files individually. In SQL, the *whole schema* is connected to or disconnected from the program in one step. The host program might not be authorized to see or manipulate only some or all of the tables and other schema objects, but that is established as part of the connection.

The program defines fields within a file, FORTRAN uses the FORMAT statements to define what it is in a file. Likewise, a COBOL program uses a DATA DIVISION for the same purpose, and so on for every 3GL's programming. Their syntax and options vary, but the data is defined in each program. This means that in a file system, you can reference the same data by a different name in each program. If a file's layout changes, you must rewrite all the programs that use that file. When a file is empty, it looks exactly like all other empty files. When you try to read an empty file, the EOF (end of file) flag pops up and the program takes some action.

A schema is independent of the host programs. Column names and data types in a table are defined within the database schema. Within reasonable limits, the tables can be changed without the knowledge of the host program. The host program only worries about transferring the values to its own variables from the database. Remember the empty set from your high school math class? It is still a valid set. When a table is empty, *it still has columns, but has zero rows*. There is no EOF flag to signal an exception because there is no final record in a sequence.

Another major difference is that tables and columns can have constraints attached to them. A constraint is a rule that defines what must be true about the database after each transaction. In this sense, a database is more like a collection of active objects than a traditional passive file system.

A table is not a spreadsheet, even though they look very much alike when you view them on a screen or in a printout. In a spreadsheet, you can access a row, a column, a cell, or a collection of cells by navigating with a location co-ordinate (row, column, sheet). A table has no concept of navigation or location. Furthermore, cells in a spreadsheet can store instructions and not just data. There is no real difference between a row and column in a spreadsheet; you could flip them around completely and still get valid results.

Let's look at the details.

8.1 CREATE SCHEMA Statement

There is a CREATE SCHEMA statement defined in the standards which bring an entire schema into existence all at once. In practice, each product has very different utility programs to allocate physical storage and define a schema.

A schema is the skeleton of an SQL database; it defines the structures of the schema objects and the rules under which they operate.

```
<schema definition> ::=
 CREATE SCHEMA <schema name clause>
   [<schema character set specification>]
   [<schema element>...]

<schema name clause > ::=
   <schema name>
  | AUTHORIZATION <schema authorization identifier>
  | <schema name> AUTHORIZATION <schema authorization identifier>

<schema authorization identifier> ::= <authorization identifier>

<schema character set specification> ::=
 DEFAULT CHARACTER SET <character set specification>

<schema element> ::=
   <domain definition>
  | <table definition>
```

```
| <view definition>
| <grant statement>
| <assertion definition>
```

The schema can be created with an optional password or <schema authorization identifier>, set by the system administrator. The DEFAULT CHARACTER SET clause is self-explanatory; it was added to satisfy ISO requirements for international use.

The logical model for schema creation is that the whole schema comes into existence all at once. This is important because it means you can have circular references that would be impossible to add to the schema after creation. There is the classic joke that you cannot get a job without experience, and you cannot get experience without a job. The solution is deferrable constraints that can be "turned off" during a session while otherwise illegal work is done (i.e., we give the new man a job), then turned back on at the end of the session.

The only data structure in SQL is the table. Tables can be persistent (base tables), used for working storage (temporary tables) or virtual (VIEWs). The differences among these types are in implementation, not performance. One advantage of having only one data structure is that the results of all operations are also tables—you never have to convert structures, write special operators, or deal with any irregularity in the language.

The <grant statement> has to do with limiting access by users to only certain schema elements. The <assertion definition> is not widely implemented yet, but it is like constraint that applies to the schema as a whole. Finally, the <character set definition>, collation definition> and <translation definition> deal with the display of data. We are not really concerned with any of these schema objects; they are usually set in place by the DBA (Database Administrator) for the users and we mere programmers do not get to change them.

Conceptually, a table is a set of zero or more rows, and a row is a set of one or more columns. Each column has a specific data type and constraints that make up an implementation of an abstract domain. The way a table is physically implemented does not matter, because you access it only with SQL. The database engine handles all the details for you and you never worry about the internals as you would with a physical file. In fact, almost no two SQL products use the same internal structures.

There are two common conceptual errors made by programmers who are accustomed to file systems or PCs. The first is thinking that a table is a file; the second is thinking that a table is a spreadsheet. Tables do not behave like either one of these, and you will get surprises if you do not understand the basic concepts.

It is easy to imagine that a table is a file, a row is a record, and a column is a field. This is familiar and when data moves from SQL to the host language, it has to be converted into host language data types and data structures to be displayed and used.

The big differences between working with a file system and working with SQL are in the way SQL fits into a host program. Using a file system, your programs must open and close files individually. In SQL, the whole schema is connected to or disconnected from the program in one step. The host program might not be authorized to see or manipulate all of the tables and other schema objects, but that is established as part of the connection.

The program defines fields within a file, whereas SQL defines its columns in the schema. FORTRAN uses the FORMAT and READ statements to get data from a file. Likewise, a COBOL program uses a Data Division to define the fields and a READ to fetch it. And so on for every 3GL's programming, the concept is the same, though the syntax and options vary.

A file system lets you reference the same data by a different name in each program. If a file's layout changes, you must rewrite all the programs that use that file. When a file is empty, it looks exactly like all other empty files. When you try to read an empty file, the EOF (end of file) flag pops up and the program takes some action. Column names and data types in a table are defined within the database schema. Within reasonable limits, the tables can be changed without the knowledge of the host program.

The host program only worries about transferring the values to its own variables from the database. Remember the empty set from your high school math class? It is still a valid set. When a table is empty, it still has columns, but has zero rows. There is no EOF flag to signal an exception, because there is no final record.

Another major difference is that tables and columns can have constraints attached to them. A constraint is a rule that defines what must be true about the database after each transaction. In this sense, a database is more like a collection of objects than a traditional passive file system.

A table is not a spreadsheet, even though they look very much alike when you view them on a screen or in a printout. In a spreadsheet, you can access a row, a column, a cell, or a collection of cells by navigating with a cursor. A table has no concept of navigation. Cells in a spreadsheet can store instructions and not just data. There is no real difference between a row and column in a spreadsheet; you could flip them around completely and still get valid results. This is not true for an SQL table.

8.2 Schema Tables

The usual way an SQL engine keeps the information it needs about the schema is to put it in SQL tables. The standard also includes tables for timezone functions, collations, character sets, and so forth. No two vendors agree on how the schema tables should be named or structured. The standard defines a set of standard schema tables, and vendors must at least present them in VIEWs to assure they can pass information to other products.

Every SQL product will allow users to query the schema tables. Vendor and user groups will have libraries of queries for getting useful information out of the schema tables of your particular product; you should take the time to get copies of them.

8.3 Temporary Tables

Tables can be defined as persistent base tables, local temporary tables, or global temporary tables. The syntax is:

```
<table definition> ::=
  CREATE [{ GLOBAL | LOCAL } TEMPORARY] TABLE <table name>
    <table element list>
    [ON COMMIT { DELETE | PRESERVE } ROWS]
```

A local temporary table belongs to a single user. A global temporary table is shared by more than one user and exists at the schema level.

When a session using a temporary table is over and the work is COMMITed, the table can be either emptied or saved for the next transaction in the user's session. This is a way of giving the users working storage without giving them CREATE TABLE (and therefore DROP TABLE and ALTER TABLE) privileges.

8.4 CREATE ASSERTION Statement

This schema object creates a constraint that is at the schema level, not attached to any table. The syntax is:

```
<assertion definition> ::=
  CREATE ASSERTION <constraint name> CHECK (<search condition>)
  [<constraint attributes>]
```

As you would expect, there is a DROP ASSERTION statement, but no ALTER statement. The constraint name on any CHECK() clause is global to avoid conflicts with and among table level constraint names.

An assertion can do things that a CHECK() clause attached to a table cannot do because it is at the schema level and theretofore reference multiple tables. A CHECK() constraint is always TRUE if the table is empty, so there is no way to check for empty tables at that level, but an assertion can be FALSE.

```
CREATE ASSERTION Leftovers
CHECK (EXISTS (SELECT * FROM Refrigerator));
```

For a multiple table example, it is very hard to make a rule that the total number of employees in the company must be equal to the total number of employees in all the company health plan tables.

```
CREATE ASSERTION Total_health_Coverage
CHECK (SELECT COUNT(*) FROM Personnel) =
      + (SELECT COUNT(*) FROM HealthPlan_1)
      + (SELECT COUNT(*) FROM HealthPlan_2)
      + (SELECT COUNT(*) FROM HealthPlan_3);
```

As a generalization, the assertions will use a lot of EXISTS() and aggregations because they at a the schema level and do not care about the details of the data inside tables.

8.5 CREATE DOMAIN Statement

The DOMAIN is a new schema element in that allows you to declare an "in-line macro" that will allow you to put a commonly used column definition in one place in the schema. The syntax is:

```
<domain definition> ::=
 CREATE DOMAIN <domain name> [AS] <data type>
```

```
    [<default clause>]
    [<domain constraint>...]
    [<collate clause>]

<domain constraint> ::=
  [<constraint name definition>]
  <check constraint definition> [<constraint attributes>]

<alter domain statement> ::=
  ALTER DOMAIN <domain name> <alter domain action>

<alter domain action> ::=
    <set domain default clause>
  | <drop domain default clause>
  | <add domain constraint definition>
  | <drop domain constraint definition>
```

It is important to note that a DOMAIN has to be defined with a basic data type and not with other DOMAINs. Once declared, a DOMAIN can be used in place of a data type declaration on a column.

The CHECK() clause is where you can put the code for validating data items with check digits, ranges, lists, and other conditions. Since the DOMAIN is in one place, you can make a good argument for writing.

```
CREATE DOMAIN State_Code AS CHAR(2)
     DEFAULT '??'
     CONSTRAINT valid_state_code
     CHECK (VALUE IN ('AL', 'AK', 'AZ', ...));
```

instead of

```
CREATE DOMAIN State_Code AS CHAR(2)
     DEFAULT '??'
     CONSTRAINT valid_state_code
     CHECK (VALUE IN (SELECT state FROM State_Code_Table));
```

The second method would have been better if you did not have a DOMAIN and had to replicate the CHECK() clause in multiple tables in the database. This would collect the values and their changes in one place instead of many.

8.6 CREATE COLLATION Statement

A collation is the order in which strings are sorted. In the pre-SQL days, this meant EBCDIC if you were on IBM mainframe equipment and ASCII for the rest of the world. You used whatever your vendor gave you.

The bad news was that each alphabetic language had its own collations. Notice that was plural. In several languages, the rules have changed over time, and so older dictionaries may use a different order than modern ones. For example, German dictionaries and telephone directories use different collations. Spanish used to treat the digraphs *ch* and *ll* were treated as single letters until 1994 that sort after C and L, respectively. Esperanto (and many other languages) put accented letters after their unaccented versions, while the Nordic newspaper ordering puts all the accented letters after Z.

SQL added the ability to use an existing collation, modify it, and produce a new collation. Collations can be explicitly added to column declarations, but when they are not given, the schema has a default. The basic syntax is simple:

```
CREATE COLLATION <collation name> FOR <character set specification>
FROM <existing collation name> [<pad characteristic>]

<pad characteristic> ::= NO PAD | PAD SPACE
```

The <pad characteristic> tells us if the SQL engine will pad a string with blanks or not. The SQL Standard includes a standard character set specifies the name of a character set that is defined by a national or international standard. This character repertoire defines the order of the characters in the standard and has the PAD SPACE characteristic.

8.7 CREATE TRANSLATION Statement

A translation replaces the characters in the input or source string with corresponding characters in the target string. This can be a one to one, one to many, many to one, or many to many transformation.

```
CREATE TRANSLATION <transliteration name> FOR <source character set
specification>
TO <target character set specification> FROM <transliteration source>
```

This structure is part of the schema, and you can use with this built in function.

```
<character transliteration> ::=
TRANSLATE <left paren> <character value expression>
USING <transliteration name> <right paren>
```

There are other string functions, of course, but collation and translations work on the schema level.

8.8 CREATE PROCEDURE Statement

You need to see Chapter 38 for an overview of the SQL/PSM, the Persistent Stored Module language that works with the basic SQL language standard. It is a procedural programming language that is based on ADA and allows you to mix pure declarative SQL with more traditional programming constructs.

It was intended to replace various proprietary 4GL tools from vendors, such as T-SQL (Microsoft SQL Server), Informix/4GL (IBM Informix), PL/SQL(Oracle), and others.

8.9 TRIGGERs

There is a feature in many versions of SQL, called a TRIGGER that will execute a block of procedural code against the database when a *table event* occurs. The term table event refers to an INSERT, UPDATE or DELETE, but not to SELECT statement. An event touches a table and either changes the data or not. Since we are a set-oriented language, changing zero.

You can think of a TRIGGER as a generalization of the referential actions. This is actually where they started in the early days of SQL before declarative referential actions were part of the ANSI/ISO Standards. They are declared on one table but can effect more than one table.

The Standards assume that the procedural code body is written in SQL/PSM, but in the real world, it is usually written in a proprietary language and some products let you attach programs in other standard procedural languages. You should look at what your particular vendor has given you if you want to work with TRIGGERs.

The advantages of TRIGGERs over declarative referential integrity is that you can do everything that declarative referential integrity can and almost anything else, too. The disadvantages are that the optimizer cannot get any data from the procedural code, the TRIGGERs take longer to execute, and they are not portable from product to product.

8.10 The TRIGGER Model

The basic syntax is a header that names trigger, tells you which database events fires it, and how the SQL engine attempts to apply it to the table.

```
CREATE TRIGGER <trigger name> <trigger action time> <trigger event>
ON <table name> [REFERENCING <transition table or variable list>]
<triggered SQL statement>

<triggered SQL statement> ::=
<SQL procedure statement> | BEGIN ATOMIC { <SQL procedure statement> ;
}... END
```

The event clause tells us if the trigger is fired on an insertion, a deletion or an update. The update is the tricky one. You can give a list of specific columns in the table that will fire the trigger and ignore the rest.

```
<trigger event> ::=
INSERT | DELETE | UPDATE [OF <trigger column list>]
```

The next questions the time of the action relative to the event. The BEFORE option applies the trigger action and then performs (or attempts to perform) that triggered statement code. The AFTER does the event and then fires the triggered statement code. The INSTEAD OF trigger is a little weird.

```
<trigger action time> ::=
BEFORE | AFTER | INSTEAD OF
```

Not all VIEWs are updatable, and in fact, determining this is known to be an NP complete problem in general. The INSTEAD OF option does not perform the trigger event at all; it jumps to the trigger body immediately. We meant this feature to solve the VIEW updating problem and it cannot be used on base tables.

The next clause tell us how and where we "aim" the trigger. The trigger code can be applied once for the firing on the whole table, or we can apply to each row in the table with the option of a search condition to select a subset of rows to which we apply the code.

```
<triggered action> ::= [FOR EACH { ROW | STATEMENT }]
 [WHEN (<search condition>)]
```

The conceptual model of the table with a trigger is that we create images of the data before and after the event in local tables that we can reference in the triggered statement code. The key words for these virtual tables or rows are NEW and OLD, but you can give them correlation names. These tables are read only.

```
<transition table or variable>
 ::= OLD [ROW | TABLE] [AS] <old name>
 | NEW {ROW | TABLE] [AS] <new name>
```

There are a few rules that make sense if you stop and think about them.

1. You cannot declare a trigger on a local temporary table. Which copy would the trigger use?
2. If the trigger event is an INSERT, then neither OLD ROW nor OLD TABLE can be specified. There is no old image to reference.
3. If the trigger event is a DELETE, then neither NEW ROW nor NEW TABLE can be specified. There is no new image to reference.
4. If you do not use FOR EACH ROW, the default is FOR EACH STATEMENT. This is how most triggers are used.
5. If BEFORE is specified, then neither OLD TABLE nor NEW TABLE can be specified. There are no images yet.
6. The user has to have applicable privileges for the TRIGGER.
7. It is possible to create multiple triggers for the same event and time and if so the triggers will be executed in the order they are created. This is a bad programming practice.
8. As expected, we have a DROP TRIGGER <trigger name> statement.
9. If the SQL statement is a compound statement, it must be ATOMIC. The trigger action must not contain a COMMIT or ROLLBACK statement.

My advice would be to avoid TRIGGERs when you can use declarative referential integrity instead. If you do use them, check the code very carefully and keep it simple so that you will not hurt performance.

8.10.1 DECLARE CURSOR Statement

I will not spend much time with CURSORs in this book, but you should understand them at a high level since you will see them in actual code. A CURSOR is a way of converting a SQL result set into a sequential data structure that looks like a simple sequential file that can be handled by the procedural host language.

In fact, the whole cursor process looks like an old fashion magnetic tape system. This is the model we used in the ANSI X3H2 Committee, literally. The idea was that you would go to your 3GL host program (this was COBOL and FORTRAN in those days), replace the host language code one-for-one with SQL with SQL code.

You might have noticed that in SQL, the keyword CREATE builds persistent schema objects. The keyword DECLARE builds transient objects that disappear with the end of the session in which they are build. This is why you say DECLARE CURSOR and not CREATE CURSOR.

8.10.2 Allocate Storage in the Host Program

First, you allocate working storage in the host program with a BEGIN DECLARE … END DECLARE section. This sets up an area where SQL variables can be converted into host language data types and vice versa. NULLs are handled by declaring INDICATOR variables in the host language BEGIN DECLARE section, which are paired with the appropriate host variables. An INDICATOR is an exact numeric data type with a scale of zero—that is, some kind of integer in the host language. I am going to skip over this.

8.10.3 DECLARE CURSOR Statement

The DECLARE CURSOR statement must appear next. This gives the CURSOR a name and has the SELECT statement that makes up the body of the cursor. It also defines the cursor properties. here is an optional ORDER BY clause at the end which will sort the result set into the cursor.

The original tape drives and file systems were limited. The first Sybase cursors could only read forward, like the first tape drives. Later, the drives could scroll the tape forward and backward by counting records. Tape drives got buffers and other features, but the basic data model is that a tape is mounted on *one drive* and attached to *one program*. A table is shared by many

sessions, however, and we need more options. These are something like the transaction levels in declarative SQL. Here is the syntax, but not all vendors have all options.

```
DECLARE [<cursor sensitivity>] [<cursor scrollability>] CURSOR
[<cursor holdability>] [<cursor returnability>]

<cursor sensitivity> ::= SENSITIVE | INSENSITIVE | ASENSITIVE
<cursor scrollability> ::= SCROLL | NO SCROLL
<cursor holdability> ::= WITH HOLD | WITHOUT HOLD
<cursor returnability> ::= WITH RETURN | WITHOUT RETURN
```

CURSOR SENSITIVITY:

```
SENSITIVE | INSENSITIVE | ASENSITIVE
```

Scrollable cursors can potentially access the same row in the result set multiple times. That means insert, update, and delete operations from other transactions could change the result set. A cursor can be SENSITIVE, INSENSITIVE, or ASENSITIVE to such data modifications. A SENSITIVE cursor picks up data modifications impacting the result set of the cursor. All changes are visible through the cursor, including changes through the cursor and *from other transactions*. Higher isolation levels may hide some changes made in other transactions because of locking.

An INSENSITIVE cursors always return rows that match the query's selection criteria, in the order specified by any ORDER BY clause. The result set has to be fully materialized as a temporary table when the cursor is opened. You have to wait for this result set to take up space on disk before you can use it. INSENSITIVE cursors are not affected by ROLLBACK since there are in a temporary table.

An ASENSITIVE cursor has few restrictions on the result set. These cursors do not guarantee to return rows that match the query's selection and order. The row membership is fixed at cursor open time, but subsequent changes to the underlying values are reflected in the results. They always return rows that matched the customer's WHERE and ORDER BY clauses *at the time the cursor membership is established.* If column values change *after* the cursor is opened, rows may be returned that no longer match WHERE and ORDER BY clauses.
CURSOR SCROLLABILITY:

```
SCROLL | NO SCROLL
```

A scrolling cursor can move using the FETCH options. We will get to that shortly. Scrollable cursors can potentially access the same row in the result set multiple times. Thus, data modifications (insert, update, delete operations) from other transactions could have an impact on the result set.

CURSOR HOLDABILITY:

```
WITH HOLD | WITHOUT HOLD
```

Cursors are usually closed automatically when a COMMIT or ROLLBACK (or an implicit termination of the transaction) occurs. A holdable cursor is kept open over COMMIT and only closed upon ROLLBACK. Some DBMS deviate from this standard behavior and also keep holdable cursors open over ROLLBACK. When a COMMIT occurs, a holdable cursor is positioned *before* the next row. Thus, a positioned UPDATE or positioned DELETE statement will only succeed after a FETCH operation occurred first in the transaction.

CURSOR RETURNABILITY:

```
WITH RETURN | WITHOUT RETURN
```

This optional clause specifies that the cursor, if it is declared in a stored procedure, can return a result set to the caller.

8.10.4 OPEN Cursor Statement

The OPEN statement is like the open statement for a file. Well, almost. The ANSI/ISO Standards require that an aggregate function must send a warning about the elimination if NULLs before the computations. But when the warning is sent is implementation defined. It could be in the DECLARE CURSOR, in the OPEN statement or when that row is fetched.

8.10.5 FETCH FROM Cursor Statement

FETCH <cursor name> INTO <local variable list>

Once an application has processed all available rows or the fetch operation is to be positioned on a nonexisting row (compare scrollable cursors below), the DBMS returns a SQLSTATE '02000' (usually accompanied by an SQLCODE+100) to indicate the end of the result set.

The FETCH statement positions a cursor on a specific row in the result set and then transfers the data of the row into the host program. The simple

options mimic magnetic tapes; you move the imaginary read/write head to the next or prior row (record) or "rewind the tape" to the first or last row (record). The syntax is simple:

```
FETCH [ NEXT | PRIOR | FIRST | LAST ] FROM <cursor name>
```

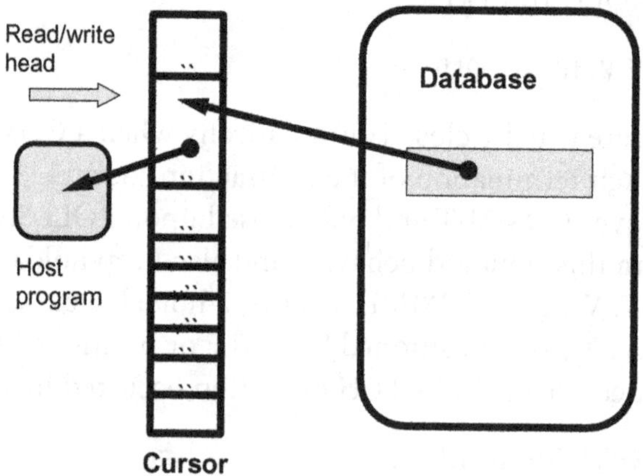

Simple Read-Only Cursor.

But there are other options. You can move the read/write head to a particular row with the absolute option. The result set is treated as if it has row numbering from first to last, so you can find each row by location in the sequence.

```
FETCH ABSOLUTE <non-negative integer> FROM <cursor name>
```

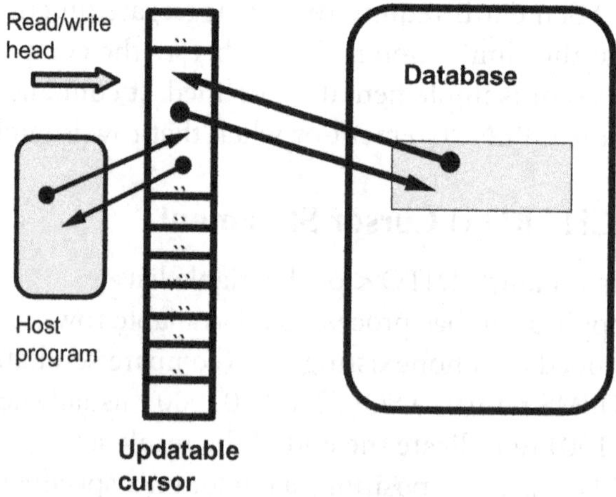

Simple Read/Write Cursor.

You can move the read/write head to a row from the current position with the relative option. It is a shorthand for either multiple NEXT or PRIOR fetches.

```
FETCH RELATIVE <integer> FROM <cursor name>
```

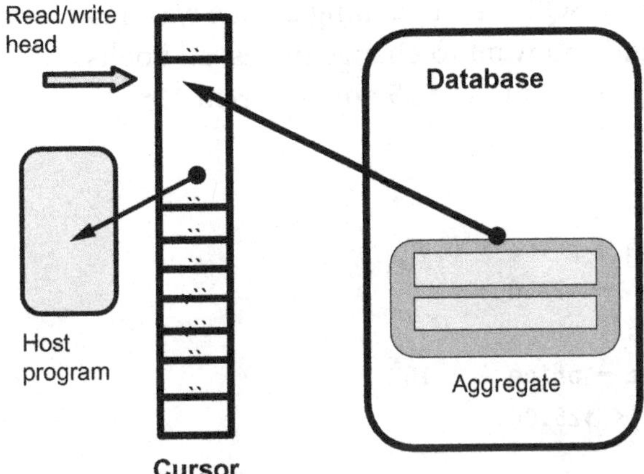

Cursor with Aggregates.

The FETCH statement takes one row from the cursor, converts each SQL data type into a host-language data type, and then puts result into the appropriate host variable. If the SQL value was a NULL, the INDICATOR is set to −1; if no indicator was specified, an exception condition is raised. As you can see, the host program must be sure to check the INDICATORs because otherwise the value of the parameter will be garbage. If the parameter is passed to the host language without any problems, the INDICATOR is set to zero. If the value being passed to the host program is a non-NULL character string and it has an indicator, the indicator is set to the length of the SQL string and can be used to detect string overflows or to set the length of the parameter.

8.10.6 CLOSE Cursor Statement

The CLOSE cursor statement closes the cursor. If it does not have a HOLD option, the cursor will disappear taking any working tables and structures like table locks with it.

8.10.7 The DEALLOCATE CURSOR Statement

The DEALLOCATE CURSOR statement frees up storage in the host program. Exactly what that means depends on how that language handles its storage.

8.10.8 Remarks About Cursors

Cursors are typically orders of magnitude slower than pure SQL code. I have written five cursors in my career; I know that if I had the CASE expression, I could have avoided three of them. The old argument for cursors in the original Sybase SQL Server training course was this example. You own a bookstore and you want to change prices; all books $25 and over are reduced 10%, and all books under $25 are increased 15%.

```
BEGIN ATOMIC
UPDATE Books
   SET price = price * 0.90
WHERE price >= $25.00;
UPDATE Books
   SET price = price * 1.15
WHERE price < $25.00;
END;
```

Opps! Look at a book which was $25.00 ((25.00 * .90) *1.10) = $24.75. So you were told to cursor through the table and change each row with a cursor.

Today you write:

```
UPDATE Books
   SET price
       = CASE WHEN price < $25.00;
              THEN price * 1.15
              WHEN price >= $25.00
              THEN price * 0.90
              ELSE price END;
```

But Steve Kass pointed out that even back then, it was possible to avoid a cursor:

```
BEGIN ATOMIC
UPDATE Books
   SET price = price * 1.80
WHERE price >= $25.00;
UPDATE Books
```

```
   SET price = price * 1.15
WHERE price < $25.00;
UPDATE Books
   SET price = price * 0.50
WHERE price >= $45.00;
END;
```

This means three passes through the Books table instead of just one.

DDL Flaws to Avoid

NOW WE HAVE the basic tools to build the DDL we need for a schema. But having tools is the same as knowing how to use them. Ask anyone who has tried to do his own plumbing.

9.1 Tibbling and Related Errors

Back in the days of punch cards and magnetic tapes, identifiers were short and had to carry metadata for the simple compilers and repeating systems. The classic example was FORTRAN I and FORTRAN II. They were languages based on algebra and used GOTO statements for process flow control. They had only two numeric data types, INTEGER and REAL. Variables were six or fewer characters long, had to begin with a letter, and be unique in the program. You declared them by using them in a statement, so the compiler had to deduce the data type by the name. Variables that begin with the letters I through N were integers; every other name was a REAL (floating point).

This mix of metadata in the prefixes of data element names also appeared in operating systems, where hardware (say, a tape or a disk drive) had hardwired names with short letters or numbers. Neither did we have modern compilers, nor had we separated the abstraction of a program from the implementation.

Yet, even today, you will see data type prefixes like "vch_" for VARCHAR(n), "int_" for INTEGER, and so forth. The term "tibble" comes

from "tbl_" for tables. We also have "vw_" to give us "Volkswagen Views" and worse.

9.1.1 ISO-11179 Standards

Today, we have the ISO-11179 Standards and the *INCITS*: L8 Meta Data Committees. These standards say to *name a thing for what it is by its nature.* That means:

1. No data types; that is, the how of physical storage.
2. No "pk_" or "fk_" affixes to tell you how the data element is used in a table (primary or foreign keys).
3. No table-column names to tell you about the location of one concurrence of the data element.
4. Tables are sets, so their names should be collective or plural nouns. That means "Employee" is wrong; "Employees" is better; "Personnel" is correct. Likewise, "Tree" is wrong; "Trees" is better; "Forest" is correct. Get the idea?
5. A data element name is made of an attribute name, underscore, and an attribute property. If the same data element appears in one table, its name is prefixed with a role name.

The ISO-11179 data element-naming conventions have the format [<role>_]<attribute>_<property>. The example used in the base document was an attribute of "tree" with properties like "tree_diameter," "tree_species," and so forth. Some properties do not apply to some attributes—"employee_diameter" is not something we need to model just yet and "employee_species" is a bit insulting. The attribute properties that deal with encodings for scales are the candidates for look-up tables. Here is a list and definitions for some of the basic ones I had introduced in my book *SQL Programming Style*.

- "**_id**" = Identifier, it is unique in the schema and refers to one *entity* anywhere it appears in the schema. A look-up table deals with attributes and their values, not entities, so by definition, this is not used in such tables. That is why things like "**_category_id**" or "**_type_id**" are garbage names. Never use "<table name>**_id**", that is a name based on location and tell you this is probably not a real key at all. Just plain "id" is too vague to be useful to anyone and will screw up your data dictionary when you have to find a zillion of them, all different, but with the same data element name and perhaps the same oversized data type.

- "**_date**" or "dt" = date, temporal dimension. It is the date of something—employment, birth, termination, and so forth; there is no such column name as just a date by itself.
- "**_nbr**" or "num" = tag number; this is a string of digits or even alphanumrics that names something. Do not use "**_no**," as it looks like the Boolean yes/no value. I prefer "nbr" to "num" since it is used as a common abbreviation in several European languages.
- "**_name**" or "nm" = this is an alphabetic name and it explains itself. It is also called a nominal scale.
- "**_code**" or "**_cd**" = a code is a standard maintained by a trusted source outside of the enterprise. For example, the ZIP code is maintained by the U.S. Postal Service. It has some legal authority to it.
- "**_size**" = an industry standard or company scale for a commodity, such as clothing, shoes, envelopes, or machine screws. There is usually a prototype that defines the sizes kept with a trusted source.
- "**_seq**" = sequence, ordinal numbering. This is not the same thing as a tag number, since it cannot have gaps. It also has a rule for successors in the sequence.
- "**_status**" = an internal encoding that reflects a state of being which can be the result of many factors. For example, "**credit_status**" might be computed from several sources. The word "status" comes from "state," and we expect that there are certain allowed state changes. For example, your marital status can change to "Divorced" only if it is "Married" currently.
- "**_cat**" = Category, an encoding that has an external source that has very distinct groups of entities. There should be strong formal criteria for establishing the category. The classification of Kingdom in biology is an example.
- "**_class**" = an internal encoding that does not have an external source that reflects a sub-classification of the entity. There should be strong

formal criteria for the classification. The classification of plants in biology is an example.

- "**_type**" = an encoding that has a common meaning both internally and externally. Types are usually less formal than a class and might overlap. For example, a driver's license might be for multiple kinds of vehicles: motorcycle, automobile, taxi, truck, and so forth. The differences among type, class, and category are an increasing strength of the algorithm for assigning the type, class, or category.

A category is very distinct; you will not often have to guess if something "animal, vegetable, or mineral" to put it in one of those categories.

A class is a set of things that have some commonality; you have rules for classifying an animal as a mammal or a reptile. You may have some cases where it is harder to apply the rules, such as the egg-laying mammal in Australia, but the exceptions tend to become their own classification—monotremes in this example.

A type is the weakest of the three, and it might call for a judgment. For example, in some states, a three-wheeled motorcycle is licensed as a motorcycle. In other states, it is licensed as an automobile. And in some states, it is licensed as an automobile only if it has a reverse gear.

The three terms are often mixed in actual usage. For example, a **blood_type** has a laboratory procedure to obtain a value of {A, B, AB, O} of what you want to know for sure. Stick with the industry standard even if violates the definitions given above.

9.1.2 Data Type and Constraint Errors

Think about the data type used. If the data element is used in computations, then it needs to be a numeric. Not a string or temporal type. Likewise, use temporal types for temporal data, not strings. Strings are for scales and tag numbers. Please read *SQL Programming Style* for the details (Morgan Kaufmann, 2005; ISBN: 978-0120887972).

The most common error with constraints is not having them. They are passed to the optimizer and improve the quality of the code; they protect the data integrity. They stay in place for every statement made against the DDL after their creation. And they are executed *the same way every time.*

9.2 Attribute Splitting

Attribute splitting takes many forms. It occurs when you have a single attribute but put its values in more than one place in the schema. You have to reassemble the original fact to use it. The most common form of attribute splitting is to create separate tables for each value. Another form of attribute splitting is to create separate rows in the same table for part of each value. These concepts are probably easier to show with examples.

9.2.1 Schema Level Attribute Splitting

This is putting one schema into many databases. Instead of having a single enterprise database, each enterprise unit is in a disjointed database of its own. The split parts have to be assembled to get a complete data model. This is not the same as a partitioned schema. The partitioned schema is still one logical unit.

9.2.2 Column Level Attribute Splitting

A column is supposed to be a *scalar* value. This is not the same as being an *atomic* value. Atomic is from the Greek word "a-toma," meaning without parts. Scalar is the property of being a measurement on a scale. Think about a geographical location. A (longitude, latitude) pair gives us a *single* location, but it has *two* columns. You can also use a single HTM (Hierarchical Triangular Mesh) number to locate a position on the globe.

If the value is not atomic, then you need constraints to assure that the components are valid when assembled.

9.2.3 Table Level Attribute Splitting

If I were to create a database with a table for male employees and a separate table for female employees, you would immediately see that there should be one table with a column for a sex code. I would have split a table on sex_code. This case is very obvious, but it can also be subtler.

9.3 Overloading Design Flaws

The attribute splitting flaws leave "bits and pieces" of a fact in the table. Overloading flaws are the opposite; they put too much in the schemas, tables, and columns.

9.3.1 Schema Level Overloading

I coined the phrase "Automobile, Squid, and Lady Gaga" to describe mixed and unrelated data put into one logical unit. As a schema, this is the attempt to put too many tasks in a single database. This can happen when two systems looked alike, so the programmer extended the existing data model.

9.3.2 Table Level Overloading

While you can overload a table in many ways, The One True Look-up Table (OTLT) is a nightmare that keeps showing up. The idea is that you put ALL the encodings into one huge table rather than have one table for each one. I think that Paul Keister was the first person to coin the phrase "OTLT," and Don Peterson (www.SQLServerCentral.com) gave the same technique the name "Massively Unified Code-Key" or MUCK tables in one of his articles.

The rationale is that you will only need one procedure to maintain *all* of the encodings, and one generic function to invoke them: the "Automobiles, Squids, and Lady GaGa" function. The technique crops up time and time again, but I will give him credit as the first writer to give it a name. Simply put, the idea is to have one table to do all of the code look-ups in the schema. It usually looks like this:

```
CREATE TABLE OTLT -- Generic_Look_Ups?
(generic_code_typeCHAR(10) NOT NULL, -- horrible names!
 generic_code_valueVARCHAR(255) NOT NULL, -- notice size!
 generic_descriptionVARCHAR(255) NOT NULL, -- notice size!
PRIMARY KEY (generic_code_value,generic_code_type));
```

The data elements are metadata now, so we wind up with horrible names for them. They are nothing in particular, but magical generics for anything in the universe of discourse. So if we have Dewey Decimal Classification (library codes), ICD (International Classification of Diseases), and two-letter ISO-3166 country codes in the schema, we have them all in one, honking big table.

Let's start with the problems in the DDL and then look at the awful queries you have to write (or hide in VIEWs). So we need to go back to the original DDL and add a CHECK() constraint on the generic_code_type column. Otherwise, we might "invent" a new encoding system by typographical error.

The basic Dewey Decimal and ICD codes are digits and have the same format—three digits, a decimal point, and more digits (usually three); the ISO-3166 is alphabetic. Oops, need another CHECK constraint that will look at the generic_code_type and make sure that the string is in the right format. Now, the table looks something like this, if anyone attempted to do it right, which is not usually the case:

```
CREATE TABLE OTLT
(generic_code_type CHAR(10) NOT NULL
   CHECK(generic_code_type IN ('DDC', 'ICD', 'ISO3166', ..),
 generic_code_value VARCHAR(255) NOT NULL,
   CONSTRAINT Valid_Generic_Code_Type
    CHECK (CASE WHEN generic_code_type  = 'DDC'
                   AND generic_code_value
                     LIKE '[0-9][0-9][0-9].[0-9][ 0-9][ 0-9]'
                THEN 'T'
                WHEN generic_code_type= 'ICD'
                   AND generic_code_value
                     LIKE '[0-9][0-9][0-9].[0-9][0-9][0-9]'
                THEN 'T'
                WHEN generic_code_type= 'ISO3166'
                   AND generic_code_value LIKE '[A-Z][A-Z]'
                THEN 'T' ELSE 'F' END = 'T'),
 generic_description VARCHAR(255) NOT NULL,
PRIMARY KEY (generic_code_value, generic_code_type));
```

Since the typical application database can have dozens and dozens of codes in it, just keep extending this pattern for as long as required. Not very pretty is it? Now let us consider adding new rows to the OTLT.

```
INSERT INTO OTLT
(generic_code_type, generic_code_value, generic_description)
  VALUES ('ICD', 259.0, 'Inadequate Genitalia after Puberty'),
         ('DDC', 259.0, 'Christian Pastoral Practices & Religious
  Orders');
```

If you make an error in the generic_code_type during insert, update, or delete, you have screwed up a totally unrelated value. If you make an error in thegeneric_code_type during a query, the results could be

interesting. This can be really hard to find when one of the similarly structured schemes had unused codes in it.

The next thing you notice about this table is that the columns are pretty wide VARCHAR(n), or even worse, that they are NVARCHAR(n) which can store characters from a strange language. The value of (n) is most often the largest one allowed.

Since you have no idea what is going to be shoved into the table, there is no way to predict and design with a safe, reasonable maximum size. The size constraint has to be put into the WHEN clause of that second CHECK() constraint between generic_code_type and generic_code_value. Or you can live with fixed length codes that are longer than what they should be.

These large sizes tend to invite bad data. You give someone a VARCHAR(n) column, and you eventually get a string with a lot of white space and a small odd character sitting at the end of it. You give someone an NVARCHAR(255) column, and eventually, it will get a Buddhist sutra in Chinese Unicode.

Now, let's consider the problems with actually using the OTLT in a query. It is always necessary to add the generic_code_type as well as the value which you are trying to look-up.

```
SELECT P1.ssn, P1.lastname, ..., L1.generic_description
   FROM OTLT AS L1, Personnel AS P1
  WHERE L1.generic_code_type  = 'ICD'
    AND L1.generic_code_value  = P1.disease_code
    AND ..;
```

In this sample query, you need to know the generic_code_type of the Personnel table disease_code column and of every other encoded column in the table. If you got a generic_code_type wrong, you can still get a result.

You also need to allow for some overhead for data type conversions. It might be more natural to use numeric values instead of VARCHAR(n) for some encodings to ensure a proper sorting order. Padding a string of digits with leading zeros adds overhead and can be risky if programmers do not agree on how many zeros to use.

When you execute a query, the SQL engine has to pull in the entire look-up table even if it only uses a few codes. If one code is at the start of the physical storage and another is at the end of the physical storage, I can do a lot of caching and paging. When I update the OTLT table, I have to lock out everyone until I am finished. It is like having to carry an encyclopedia set with you when all you needed was a magazine article.

Now consider the overhead with a two-part FOREIGN KEY in a table:

```
CREATE TABLE EmployeeAbsences
(..
 generic_code_typeCHAR(3) -- min length needed
       DEFAULT 'ICD' NOT NULL
       CHECK (generic_code_type  = 'ICD'),
generic_code_valueCHAR(7) NOT NULL, -- min length needed
  FOREIGN KEY (generic_code_type,generic_code_value)
   REFERENCES OTLT (generic_code_type,generic_code_value),
..);
```

Now, I have to convert the character types for more overhead. Even worse, ICD has a natural DEFAULT value (000.000 means "undiagnosed"), whereas Dewey Decimal does not. Older encoding schemes often used all 9s for "miscellaneous," so they would sort to the end of the reports in COBOL programs. Just as there is no Magical Universal "id," there is no Magical Universal DEFAULT value. I just lost one of the most important features of SQL.

I am going to venture a guess that this idea came from OO programmers who think of it as some kind of polymorphism done in SQL. They say to themselves that a table is a class, which it isn't, and therefore it ought to have polymorphic behaviors, which it doesn't.

9.3.3 Column Level Overloading

If the name of a column should have a conjunction in it, then it is wrong. Consider table to mimic a sign-in sheet on a clip board.

```
CREATE TABLE Clipboard
(emp_name CHAR(35) NOT NULL,
 signature_timestamp TIMESTAMP DEFAULT CURRENT_TIMESTAMP NOT NULL,
 signature_type CHAR(3) DEFAULT 'IN' NOT NULL
 CHECK (signature_type IN ('IN', 'OUT')),
 PRIMARY KEY (emp_name, signature_type));
```

The real name of signature_timestamp should have been "in_or_out_signature_timestamp" instead. To answer any basic query, you need to use

two rows in a self-outer join to get the sign-in and sign-out pairs for each employee.

The correct design would have been:

```
CREATE TABLE Clipboard
(emp_name CHAR(35) NOT NULL,
 sign_in_time TIMESTAMP DEFAULT CURRENT_TIMESTAMP NOT NULL,
 sign_out_time TIMESTAMP, -- null means current
 PRIMARY KEY (emp_name, sign_in_time));
```

The single attribute, duration, has to be modeled as *two columns* in Standard SQL, but it was split into rows identified by a metadata code to tell which end of the duration each one value represented. If this were longitude and latitude, you would immediately see the problem and put the two parts of the one attribute (geographical location) in the same row.

At the extreme, this error uses a metadata flag to mark the column as totally different and unrelated attributes.

9.4 Non-Normal Form Redundancy

Consider a table used to compute the linear distance between a list of cities on the globe.

```
CREATE TABLE City_Coords
(city_name VARCHAR(25) NOT NULL PRIMARY KEY,
 city_latitude FLOAT NOT NULL
 CHECK (city_latitude BETWEEN -1.57079633AND + 1.57079633)
 city_longitude FLOAT NOT NULL,
 CHECK (city_longitude BETWEEN -3.14159265 AND +3.14159265));
```

You then query with the spherical distance formula to get the distance. This table is very compact, but the math for each pair is a bit of overhead.

Now, consider a table for the same purpose which looks up the distance between any two cities in our universe of discourse:

```
CREATE TABLE City_Distances
(origin_city_name VARCHAR(25) NOT NULL,
 destination_city_name VARCHAR(25) NOT NULL,
  PRIMARY KEY (origin_city_name, destination_city_name),
 CHECK (origin_city_name < destination_city_name)
```

```
linear_distance DECIMAL (7,2) NOT NULL
 CHECK (linear_distance >= 0));
```

You then sort the two city names and look at the distance. For (n) cities, you will have ~($n^2/2$) rows in this table. You can make arguments about performance, etc., but the point is that they both do the same task in the schema. Both are normalized, *but one of them is redundant.* There is an old IT proverb that a programmer with two wrist watches is never sure what time it is. This is where I got my heuristic "one fact, one way, place, one time" to define normalization.

9.4.1 Conflicting Relationships

Here is a business rule that sounds fine until you think about it. A sales team is responsible for every customer that a member of that team (a salesperson) is assigned to and not responsible for any other customer. So we look for the assigned sales person, then if we cannot find them, we go to the team. This has two options for a redundant relationship.

Eliminate the redundancy by removing the is-responsible-for relationship from the sales team to their customer. The model is just as expressive as it was before the redundancy was eliminated.

```
-- this is the simplest table in the schema
CREATE TABLE SalesTeams
(sales_team_id INTEGER NOT NULL PRIMARY KEY,
 sales_team_name CHAR(10) NOT NULL);

CREATE TABLE Salespersons
(sales_person_id INTEGER NOT NULL PRIMARY KEY,
 sales_person_name CHAR(15) NOT NULL,
 sales_team_id INTEGER NOT NULL
  REFERENCES SalesTeams(sales_team_id)
  ON UPDATE CASCADE);
```

What if we have no responsible sales person? Then we need a NULL and have to go to the team level to help the customer:

```
CREATE TABLE Customer_Assignments
(customer_id INTEGER NOT NULL PRIMARY KEY,
 responsible_sales_team_id INTEGER NOT NULL
 REFERENCES SalesPerson(sales_team_id)
```

```
  ON UPDATE CASCADE,
 responsible_sales_person_id INTEGER
 REFERENCES Salespersons(sales_person_id)
  ON UPDATE CASCADE);
```

The second option is to control the redundancy by adding DRI actions. Because the two foreign keys that must be kept synchronized are in the same row, only one update is required. A team identifier may or may not have a sales person, but a sales person must have a team.

```
-- this is the same simple table
CREATE TABLE SalesTeams
(sales_team_id INTEGER NOT NULL PRIMARY KEY,
 sales_team_name CHAR(10) NOT NULL);

CREATE TABLE Salespersons
(sales_person_id INTEGER NOT NULL PRIMARY KEY,
 sales_person_name CHAR(15) NOT NULL,
 sales_team_id INTEGER NOT NULL
 REFERENCES SalesTeams(sales_team_id)
 ON UPDATE CASCADE,
 UNIQUE (sales_person_id, sales_team_id));

CREATE TABLE Customer_Assignments
(customer_id INTEGER NOT NULL PRIMARY KEY,
 sales_team_id INTEGER NOT NULL,
 sales_person_id INTEGER
 REFERENCES Salespersons(sales_person_id)
  ON UPDATE CASCADE
  ON DELETE SET NULL,
 FOREIGN KEY (sales_person_id, sales_team_id)
 REFERENCES Salespersons (sales_person_id, sales_team_id)
  ON UPDATE CASCADE);
```

Data Types

Numeric Data in SQL

SQL IS NOT a computational language; the arithmetic capability of the SQL is weaker than that of almost any other language you have ever used. But there are some tricks that you need to know working with numbers in SQL and when passing them to a host program. Much of the arithmetic and the functions are implementations defined, so you should experiment with your particular product and make notes on the default precision, and tools in the math library of your database.

This section deals with the arithmetic that you would use across a row instead of down a column; they are not quite the same.

The SQL Standard has a very wide range of numeric types. The idea is that *any host language* can find an SQL numeric type that matches one of its own. Remember that SQL is meant to be used with a host language and not by itself.

Numbers in SQL are classified as either exact or approximate. An exact numeric value has a precision, p, and a scale, s. The precision is a positive integer that determines the number of significant digits in a particular radix. The standard says the radix can be either binary or decimal, so you need to know what your implementation does. The scale is a nonnegative integer that tells you how many radix places the number has.

Today, there are not many base-ten platforms, so you almost certainly have a binary machine. However, a number can have one of many binary

representations — twos-complement, ones-complement, high end or low end and various word sizes. *The proper mental model of numbers in SQL is not to worry about the "bits and bytes" level of the physical representation, but to think in abstract terms.*

10.1 Exact Numeric Data Types

The data types INTEGER, BIGINT, SMALLINT, NUMERIC(p,s), and DECIMAL(p,s) are exact numeric types. An integer has a scale of zero but the syntax simply uses the word INTEGER or the abbreviation INT but if you use it you will look like a C family programmer. SMALLINT has a scale of zero, but the range of values it can hold is less than or equal to the range that INTEGER can hold in the implementation. Likewise, BIGINT has a scale of zero, but the range of values it can hold is greater than or equal to the range that INTEGER can hold in the implementation.

DECIMAL(p,s) can also be written DEC(p,s) . For example, DECIMAL(8,2) could be used to hold the number 123456.78, which has eight significant digits and two decimal places.

The difference between NUMERIC(p,s) and DECIMAL(p,s) is subtle. NUMERIC(p,s) specifies the *exact precision and scale* to be used. DECIMAL(p,s) specifies the exact *scale*, but *the precision is implementation-defined* to be equal to or greater than the specified value. That means DECIMAL(p,s) can have some room for rounding and NUMERIC(p,s) does not. Mainframe COBOL programmers can think of NUMERIC(p,s) as a PICTURE numeric type, whereas DECIMAL(p,s) is like a BCD. The use of BCD is not common today, but was popular on older mainframe business computers. I recommend using DECIMAL(p,s) because it might enjoy some extra precision.

10.1.1 Bit, Byte, and Boolean Data Types

The ANSI/ISO Standards provide for BOOLEAN, BINARY and BINARY VARYING data types and operations. Machine level things like a bit or byte data type have no place in SQL and are almost never used. SQL has a three-valued logic and it does not naturally accommodate Boolean algebra. The value TRUE is greater than the value FALSE, and any comparison involving NULL or an UNKNOWN truth value will return an UNKNOWN result. But what does

```
SELECT
CASE WHEN((x=1) >= (y=42))
THEN'TRUE'ELSE'FALSE'END
FROM Foobar;
```

mean conceptually? And are not there better ways to express the intent?

SQL is a high-level language; it is abstract and defined without regard to *physical* implementation. This basic principle of data modeling is called data abstraction. Bits and bytes are the lowest units of hardware-specific, physical implementation you can get. Are you on a high-end or low-end machine? Does the machine have 8, 16, 32, 64, or 128 bit words? Twos complement or ones complement math? Hey, the SQL Standards allow decimal machines, so bits do not have to exist at all!

What about NULLs in this data type? To be an SQL data type, you should have NULLs, so what is a NULL bit? By definition a bit, is in one of two states, on or off and has no NULL. If your vendor adds NULLs to bit, how are the bit-wise operations defined? Oh what a tangled web we weave when first we mix logical and physical models.

What do the host languages do? Did you know that +1, +0, −0 and −1 are all used for BOOLEANs, but not consistently? In C#, Boolean values are 0/1 for FALSE/TRUE, while VB.NET has Boolean values of 0/−1 for FALSE/TRUE and they are *proprietary languages from the same vendor*. That means all the host languages—present, future and not-yet-defined—can be different.

For standard programming languages C and COBOL, BOOLEAN values are mapped to integer variables in the host language. For standard programming languages Ada, FORTRAN, Pascal, and PL/I, BOOLEAN variables are directly supported. All data types in SQL have to be NULL-able, so the SQL Standard requires that a NULL Boolean is UNKNOWN; unfortunately, this makes the behavior of the data type inconsistent. The rule for NULLs has always been that they propagate. Consider the expressions:

```
(1=1)OR NULL yields NULL which is UNKNOWN
 (1=1)OR UNKNOWN yields TRUE
 (1=1)AND UNKNOWN yields UNKNOWN
 (1=1)AND NULL yields NULL which is UNKNOWN
```

Using assembly language style bit flags has its own problems.

There are usually two situations for using bits in practice. Either the bits are individual attributes or they are used as a vector to represent a single

attribute. In the case of a single attribute, the encoding is limited to two values, which do not port to host languages or other SQL products, cannot be easily understood by an end user, and which cannot be expanded.

In the second case what some Newbies, who are still thinking in terms of second and third generation programming languages or even punch cards, do is build a vector for a series of "yes/no" status codes, failing to see the status vector as a single attribute. Did you ever play the children's game "20 Questions" when you were young?

Imagine you have six components for a medical patient, so you allocate bits in your second-generation model of the world.

1. Patient is male
2. Patient is pregnant
3. Patient is under-weight
4. Patient is over-weight
5. Patient has a fever
6. Patient has high blood pressure

You have 64 possible bit patterns, but only some of the 64 bit patterns are valid (i.e., you cannot be pregnant and be a man; you cannot be both under-weight and over-weight). For your data integrity, you can:

(1) Ignore the problem. This is actually what most newbies do. I have spent three decades cleaning up bad SQL and I see it all the time.

(2) Write elaborate CHECK() constraints with user defined functions or proprietary bit level library functions that cannot port and that run like cold glue.

Now we add a seventh condition to the bit vector—which end does it go on? Why? How did you get it in the right place on all the possible hardware that it will ever use? Did all the code that references a bit in a word by its position do it right after the change?

You need to sit down and think about how to design an encoding of the data that is high level, general enough to expand, abstract and portable. For example, is that loan approval a hierarchical code? or a concatenation code? or a vector code? Did you provide codes for unknown, missing and N/A values? It is not easy to design such things!

BINARY and BINARY VARYING data types were meant provide a standard term for storing data in various formats that are not part of the SQL data types, such as images, video, audio and so forth.

Once upon a time, long, long time ago, programming languages were tied to the hardware. Obviously, assembly and machine languages were designed for one particular family of computers. But even the higher level languages still clung to the hardware. FORTRAN and COBOL standards were defined on the assumption that files were sequential, main storage was contiguous and all machine were binary.

The hardware affected the design of the languages. The hardware used a lot of bit flags and bit masks for control inside the machine. Flags were also used in the file system to mark deleted records and other things. Storage was expensive and very slow by today's standards. Bit flags were small and relatively fast to write. Since this was the style of coding we saw, we tended to mimic that programming style in higher level code. The bad news is that even as our programming languages became more abstract, the programmer's mind set did not.

When we got to SQL, we were in a very different game. The BIT data type in T-SQL and other SQL products was originally a bit in the way that computer people think of it; one or zero indicating an open or closed circuit. Code was written on the assumption that if a BIT column was not zero, it was one and if it was not one, it was zero.

Then BIT became a numeric data type. All data types in SQL are NULL-able. This change caught a lot of old programmers off-guard. Unexpected NULLs showed up. In spite of being a numeric data type, you cannot do any math on it.

This is even worse with bit masks. They are defined by hardware-specific, physical implementations. Are you on a high-end or low-end machine? Does the machine have 8, 16, 32, 64, or 128 bit words? Twos complement or ones complement math? Can a single bit in the mask be NULL-able? Hey, the SQL Standards say nothing about hardware, so bits do not have to exist at all! The most obvious problems with using an INTEGER (or other exact numeric data type) as a bit mask are:

1. The data is unreadable. Can you easily figure out what each bit means by looking at without a guide? Looking at `"WHERE auction_status & 42 <> 0"` is not very clear to a maintenance programmer whose languages do not use & for bit-wise conjunction. This is why

we design encoding schemes like Dewey Decimal codes for libraries; they are easy to read and to use.

2. Constraints are a bitch to write. The two choices are to use a lot of proprietary bit-wise and/or operators that are hard to optimize, or to a set of INTEGER values with a [NOT] IN() predicate.
3. You are limited to two values per column. That is very restrictive; even the ISO sex code cannot fit into such a column. What is fun is using two or more fields for more values. You start off with {00, 01, 10, 11} in contiguous positions. But when need more values, the next bit is not contiguous and the predicates are really horrible.
4. Think about a "is_completed_flg" bit flag on an auction. Did it complete because a bid was accepted? Because the bid was withdrawn? Because the reserve price was not met? Because the item was withdrawn? Because it expired?
5. There is no temporal element to the bit mask (or to single bit flags). For example, a flag "is_legal_adult_flg" does not tell you if the person is 18 or 80. Nor does it tell you exactly *what kind* of legal adult is involved. In Texas, you can be a stripper or porn star at 18 years of age, but cannot buy or serve a drink until you are 21. A DATE for the birth date (just 3 bytes) would hold complete fact and let us compute what we need to know; it would always be correct, too. How do you know a bit flag is still current?
6. You will find out that using the flags will tend to split the status of an entity over multiple tables. Let me give an actual example in one of my consulting jobs. The client conducts on-line auctions. A request for bids is posted, then it moves thru a series of steps over time until it expires, is withdrawn or finds a winning bid. The auction can be in about a dozen states, but the state changes have an ordering. A bid cannot be rejected until it is made, and so forth.
7. In the old system, it was necessary to go to the Invoices table, and see if a payment had been made on a bid. The date of the payment of the invoice sets one of many bit flags that were supposed to tell us the status of auctions. Now go over to shipments and see that the matching shipment left *after* the invoice was paid. You get the idea; tracking an auction involved between eight to ten tables. The bad

news was that people who worked with one of the process steps did not know or much care about the big picture. Data integrity suffered. Trying to track an auction history was hard enough, but when a flag had not be set correctly, it became a nightmare.

8. Bit flags invite redundancy. In the system I just mentioned, we had "is_active_flg" and "is_completed_flg" in the same table. A completed auction is not active and vice verse. It is the same fact in two flags. Human psychology (and the English language) prefers to hear an affirmative wording (remember the old song "Yes, we have no bananas today!"?). All of these bit flags, and sequence validation are being replaced by two sets of state transition tables, one for bids and one for shipments. For details on state transition constraints. The history of each auction is now in one place and has to follow business rules.

9. By the time you disassemble a bit mask column, and throw out the fields you did not need performance is not going to be improved over simpler data types. Remember we have 64 bit machinery today and it does comparisons quite fast.

10. Grouping and ordering on the individual fields is a real pain. Try it.

11. You have to index the whole column, so unless you luck up and have them in the right order, you are stuck with table scans.

12. Since a bit mask is not in First Normal Form (1NF), you have all the anomalies we wanted to avoid in RDBMS.

SQL is a "predicate language" and not a "flag language" like assembler. We use predicates and declarative code to discover the current state of the database in queries and to maintain data integrity in DDL. Try finding personnel that are legal adults. With a flag, I look use something like `"Personnel.legal_adult_flg = CAST(1 AS BIT)"` as my test. If the legal age changes to 21 for our purposes, as it did when the US raised the drinking age, then the search condition code change is easy; I have two slightly different predicates for two kinds of legal age. Some insurance benefits can apply to children up to age 25, which gives us three kinds of legal age. The assembly language programer is busy trying to add more flags to his Personnel table. Then he has to update them with my predicates before every execution of his query. This is not saving you anything.

10.2 Approximate Numeric Data Types

An approximate numeric value consists of a mantissa and an exponent. The mantissa is a signed numeric value; the exponent is a signed integer that specifies the magnitude of the mantissa. An approximate numeric value has a precision. The precision is a positive integer that specifies the number of significant binary digits in the mantissa. The value of an approximate numeric value is the mantissa multiplied by 10 to the exponent. FLOAT(p), REAL, and DOUBLE PRECISION are the approximate numeric types. There is a subtle difference between FLOAT(p), which has a binary precision equal to or greater than the value given, and REAL, which has an implementation-defined precision.

10.2.1 Float Versus Real Versus Double Precision

In the real world REAL and DOUBLE PRECISION are the IEEE Standard 754 for floating point numbers; FLOAT(p) is almost never used. IEEE math functions are built into processor chips so they will run faster than a software implementation. IEEE Standard 754 is binary and uses 32 bits for single precision and 64 bits for double precision, which is just right for personal computers and most Unix and Linux platforms.

The range for single precision numbers is approximately $\pm 10^{-44.85}$ to $10^{38.53}$ and for double precision, approximately $\pm 10^{-323.3}$ to $10^{308.3}$, respectively. However, there are some special values in the IEEE standard.

Zero cannot be directly represented in this format, so it is modeled as a special value denoted with an exponent field of zero and a fraction field of zero. The sign field can make this either −0 or +0, which are distinct values that compare as equal.

If the exponent is all zeroes, but the fraction is non-zero (else it would be interpreted as zero), then the value is a denormalized number. This denormalization has nothing to do with RDBMS and the normalization of tables. Because of the distribution of binary representations near zero, is not uniform, a "bias" has to be subtracted from these numbers to avoid gaps. The basic rules are:

1. The sign bit is 0 for positive, 1 for negative.
2. The exponent's base is two.
3. The exponent field contains 127 plus the true exponent for single-precision, or 1023 plus the true exponent for double precision.

4. The first bit of the mantissa is typically assumed to be 1.*f*, where *f* is the field of fraction bits.

Most SQL programmers will not see problems in computation because the IEEE standards make the adjustments in software or hardware.

10.2.2 IEEE Floating Point Extensions

The two values "+infinity" and "–infinity" are denoted with an exponent of all ones and a fraction of all zeroes. The sign bit distinguishes between negative infinity and positive infinity. Being able to denote infinity as a specific value is useful because it allows operations to continue past overflow situations. Operations with infinite values are well defined in IEEE floating point.

The value NaN ("Not a Number") is used to represent a bit configuration that does not represent number. NaN's are represented by a bit pattern with an exponent of all ones and a nonzero fraction. There are two categories of NaN: QNaN (Quiet NaN) and SNaN (Signaling NaN).

A QNaN is a NaN with the most significant fraction bit set. QNaN's propagate freely through most arithmetic operations. These values pop out of an operation when the result is not mathematically defined, like division by zero.

An SNaN is a NaN with the most significant fraction bit clear. It is used to signal an exception when used in operations. SNaN's can be handy to assign to uninitialized variables to trap premature usage. Semantically, QNaN's denote indeterminate operations, while SNaN's denote invalid operations.

SQL has not accepted the IEEE model for mathematics for several reasons. Much of the SQL Standard allows implementation defined rounding, truncation and precision so as to avoid limiting the language to particular hardware platforms. If the IEEE rules for math were allowed in SQL, then we need type conversion rules for infinite and a way to represent an infinite exact numeric value after the conversion. People have enough trouble with NULLs, so let's not go there.

10.3 Numeric Type Conversions

There are a few surprises in converting from one numeric type to another. The SQL Standard left it up to the implementation to answer a lot of basic questions, so the programmer has to know his SQL package.

10.3.1 Rounding and Truncating

When an exact or approximate numeric value is assigned to an exact numeric column, it may not fit. SQL says that the database engine will use an approximation that preserves leading significant digits of the original number after rounding or truncating. The choice of whether to truncate or round is implementation-defined, however. This can lead to some surprises when you have to shift data among SQL implementations, or storage values from a host language program into an SQL table. It is probably a good idea to create the columns with more decimal places than you think you need.

Truncation is defined as truncation toward zero; this means that 1.5 would truncate to 1, and −1.5 would truncate to −1. This is not true for all programming languages; everyone agrees on truncation toward zero for the positive numbers, but you will find that negative numbers may truncate away from zero (i.e., −1.5 would truncate to −2).

SQL is also indecisive about rounding, leaving the implementation free to determine its method. There are two major types of rounding in programming.

The scientific method looks at the digit to be removed. If this digit is 0, 1, 2, 3, or 4, you drop it and leave the higher-order digit to its left unchanged. If the digit is 5, 6, 7, 8, or 9, you drop it and increment the digit to its left. This method works with a small set of numbers and was popular with FORTRAN programmers because it is what engineers use.

The commercial methods look at the digit to be removed. If this digit is 0, 1, 2, 3, or 4, you drop it and leave the digit to its left unchanged. If the digit is 6, 7, 8, or 9, you drop it and increment the digit to its left. However, when the digit is 5, you want to have a rule that will round up about half the time.

One rule is to look at the digit to the left: If it is odd, then leave it unchanged; if it is even, increment it. The "Round half to even" is called "banker's rounding" (http://en.wikipedia.org/wiki/Rounding#Round_half_to_even). There are other versions of the decision rule, but they all try to make the rounding error as small as possible. This method works with a large set of numbers and is popular with bankers because it reduces the total rounding error in the system. This rule keeps commercial rounding symmetric. The usual ROUND() functions uses the scientific method, but you can use the MOD() function to implement the commercial method. Assume a simple list of two decimal place numbers we wish to round to one decimal place:

```
CREATE TABLE Accounts(amount DECIMAL(5,2)NOT NULL);

SELECT amount,
       ROUND(amount,1)AS scientific,
       CASE WHEN MOD((100 * amount),10) <>5
       THEN ROUND(amount,1)
       ELSE CASE WHEN MOD(FLOOR(MOD((10 * amount),10)),2) =0
            THEN TRUNC(amount,1) --even,down
            ELSE ROUND(amount,1) --odd,up
            END
       END AS commercial
FROM Accounts;
```

In commercial transactions, you carry money amounts to four or more decimal places, but round them to two decimal places for display. This is a GAAP (Generally Accepted Accounting Practice) in the United States for US Dollars and laws in the European Union for working with Euros. Check with an accountant to be sure.

Statistical and scientific software has special routines to correct floating point rounding problems, but most SQL databases do not. Floating math is rare in commercial applications and most commercial computers do not have floating point processors.

10.3.2 CAST() Function

Standard SQL defined the general CAST(<cast operand> AS <data type>) function for all data type conversions. The <cast operand> to be either a <column name>, a <value expression>, or a NULL.

For numeric-to-numeric conversion, you can do anything you wish, but you have to watch for the rounding errors. The comparison predicates can hide automatic type conversions, so be careful. Some castings are not legal in particular cases (i.e. not all strings cast to numbers or temporal values).

10.4 Four Function Arithmetic

SQL was originally weaker than a pocket calculator. Today, the Standards include most of the basic math functions. The dyadic arithmetic operators +, −, *, and / stand for addition, subtraction, multiplication, and division, respectively. The multiplication and division operators are of equal precedence and are performed before the dyadic plus and minus operators.

In algebra and in some programming languages, the precedence of arithmetic operators is more strict, so those programmers have to use parentheses to force an order of exception. They use the "My Dear Aunt Sally" rule; that is, multiplication is done before division, which is done before addition, which is done before subtraction. This can lead to subtle errors.

For example, consider (largenum+largenum–largenum), where largenum is the maximum value that can be represented in its numeric data type. If you group the expression from left to right, you get ((largenum+largenum)–largenum)=overflow error! However, if you group the expression from right to left, you get (largenum+(largenum–largenum))=largenum.

Because of these differences, an expression that worked one way in the host language may get different results in SQL and vice versa. SQL could reorder the expressions to optimize them. The best way to be safe is always to make extensive use of parentheses in complicated expressions, whether they are in the host language or in your SQL.

The monadic plus and minus signs are allowed and you can string as many of them in front of a numeric value of variables as you like. The bad news about this decision is that SQL also uses Ada-style comments, which put the text of a comment line between a double dash and a new line-character. This means that the parser has to figure out whether "--" is two minus signs or the start of a comment. Standard SQL also support C-style comment brackets (i.e., /* comment text */). Such brackets can be used in international data transmission standards which do not recognize a new line in a transmission so the double-dash convention will not work.

If both operands are exact numeric, the data type of the result is exact numeric, as you would expect. Likewise, an approximate numeric in a calculation will cast the results to approximate numeric. The kicker is in how the results are assigned in precision and scale.

Let S1 and S2 be the scale of the first and second operands, respectively. The precision of the result of addition and subtraction is implementation-defined, and the scale is the maximum of S1 and S2. The precision of the result of multiplication is implementation-defined, and the scale is (S1+S2). The precision and scale of the result of division are implementation-defined, and so are some decisions about rounding or truncating results.

The INCITS/H2 Database Standards Committee debated about requiring precision and scales in the standard in the early days of SQL and finally gave up. This means I can start losing high-order digits, especially with a division operation, where it is perfectly legal to make all results single-digit integers.

Nobody does anything that stupid in practice. In the real world, some vendors allow you to adjust the number of decimal places as a system parameter, some default to a known number of decimal places, and some display as many decimal places as they can so that you can round off to what you want. You will simply have to learn what your implementation does by experimenting with it.

10.4.1 Arithmetic and NULLs

NULLs are probably one of the most formidable database concepts for the beginner. This book has a detailed study of how NULLs work in SQL, but this section is concerned with how they act in arithmetic expressions.

The NULL in SQL is only one way of handling missing values. The usual description of NULLs is that they represent currently unknown values that might be replaced later with real values when we know something. Missing values actually cover a lot of territory. The Interim Report 75-02-08 to the ANSI X3 (SPARC Study Group 1975) showed 14 different kinds of incomplete data that could appear as the results of operations or as attribute values. They included such things as arithmetic underflow and overflow, division by zero, string truncation, raising zero to the zero-th power, and other computational errors, as well as missing or unknown values.

The NULL is a global creature, not belonging to any particular data type, but able to replace any of their values. This makes arithmetic a bit easier to define. You have to specifically forbid NULLs in a column by declaring the column with a NOT NULL constraint. But in Standard SQL you can use the CAST function to declare a specific data type for a NULL, such as CAST (NULL AS INTEGER). One reason for this convention is completeness; another is to let you pass practicable implementation information about how to create a column to the database engine.

The basic rule for math with NULLs is that they propagate. An arithmetic operation with a NULL will return a NULL. That makes sense; if a NULL is a missing value, then you cannot determine the results of a calculation with it. However, the expression (NULL / 0) looks strange to people. The first thought is that a division by zero should return an error; if NULL is a *missing value to be determined later*, there is no value to which it can resolve and make that expression valid. However, SQL propagates the NULL,

while a non-NULL divided by zero will cause a runtime error. NULL has no expectation of ever resolving to a value; it is "nonvalue", not just a place marker.

10.5 Converting Values to and from NULL

Since host languages do not support NULLs, the programmer can elect either to replace them with another value that is expressible in the host language or to use INDICATOR variables to signal the host program to take special actions for them.

An indicator parameter is an integer host parameter that is specified immediately following another host parameter. When the first host parameter gets a NULL, the indicator is set as a negative value. Indicators also show positive numbers to show string data truncation occurred during a transfer between a host program and SQL. A zero means there were no problems with the conversion.

10.5.1 NULLIF() Function

Standard SQL specifies two functions, NULLIF() and the related COALESCE(), that can be used to replace expressions with NULL and vice versa. They are part of the CASE expression family. The NULLIF(V1, V2) function has two parameters. It is equivalent to the following CASE expression:

```
NULLIF(V1,V2) :=CASE
         WHEN(V1=V2)
         THEN NULL
         ELSE V1 END;
```

That is, when the first parameter is equal to the second, the function returns a NULL; otherwise, it returns the first parameter's value. The properties of this function allow you to use it for many purposes. The important properties are these:

(1) NULLIF(x, x) will return NULL for all values of x. This includes NULL, since (NULL=NULL) is UNKNOWN, not TRUE.

(2) NULLIF(0, (x−x)) will convert all non-NULLs of a numeric x into NULL. But it will convert a NULL into zero, since (NULL−NULL) is NULL and the equality test will fail.

(3) NULLIF(1, (x−x+1)) will convert all non-NULLs of x into NULL. But it will convert a NULL into a 1. This can be generalized for all numeric data types and values.

10.5.2 COALESCE() Function

The COALESCE(<value expression>, ..., <value expression>) function scans the list of < value expression> s from left to right, determines the highest data type in the list and returns the first non-NULL in the list, casting it to the highest data type. If all the <value expression> s are NULL, the result is NULL.

The most common use of this function in math expressions is in a SELECT list where there are columns that have to be added, but one can be a NULL. For example, to create a report of the total pay for each employee, you might write this query:

```
SELECT emp_nbr, emp_name, (salary_amt + commission_amt)AS pay_tot
 FROM Personnel;
```

But salesmen may work on commission_amt only or on a mix of salary_amt and commission_amt. The office staff is on salary_amt only. This means an employee could have NULLs in his salary_amt or commission_amt column, which would propagate in the addition and produce a NULL result. A better solution would be

```
SELECT emp_nbr, emp_name
      COALESCE(salary_amt, 0.00) + COALESCE(commission_amt, 0.00))
       AS paycheck_amt
 FROM Personnel;
```

As an example of the use of COALESCE(), create a table of payments made for each month of a single year. (Yes, this could be done with a column for the months, but bear with me.)

```
CREATE TABLE Payments
(cust_nbr INTEGER NOT NULL,
 jan DECIMAL(8,2),
 feb DECIMAL(8,2),
 mar DECIMAL(8,2),
 apr DECIMAL(8,2),
 may DECIMAL(8,2),
 jun DECIMAL(8,2),
 jul DECIMAL(8,2),
 aug DECIMAL(8,2),
 sep DECIMAL(8,2),
 oct DECIMAL(8,2),
```

```
nov DECIMAL(8,2),
"dec" DECIMAL(8,2), --DEC is a reserved word
PRIMARY KEY cust_nbr);
```

The problem is to write a query that returns the customer and the amount of the last payment he made. Unpaid months are shown with a NULL in them. We could use a COALESCE function like this:

```
SELECT cust_nbr,
    COALESCE("dec", nov, oct, sep,
        aug, jul, jun, may, apr, mar, feb, jan)
  FROM Payments;
```

Of course this query is a bit incomplete, since it does not tell you in what month this last payment was made. This can be done with the rather ugly-looking expression that will turn a month's non-NULL payment into a character string with the name of the month. The general case for a column called "mon", which holds the number of a month within the year, is NULLIF (COALESCE (NULLIF (0, mon-mon), 'Month'), 0) where 'Month' is replaced by the string for the actual name of the particular month. A list of these statements in month order in a COALESCE will give us the name of the last month with a payment. The way this expression works is worth working out in detail.

Case 1: mon is a numeric value

```
NULLIF(COALESCE(NULLIF(0, mon - mon), 'Month'), 0)
NULLIF(COALESCE(NULLIF(0, 0), 'Month'), 0)
NULLIF(COALESCE(NULL, 'Month'), 0)
NULLIF('Month', 0)
('Month')
```

Case 2: mon is NULL

```
NULLIF(COALESCE(NULLIF(0, mon-mon), 'Month'), 0)
NULLIF(COALESCE(NULLIF(0, NULL-NULL), 'Month'), 0)
NULLIF(COALESCE(NULLIF(0, NULL), 'Month'), 0)
NULLIF(COALESCE(0, 'Month'), 0)
NULLIF(0, 0)
(NULL)
```

You can do a lot of work by nesting SQL functions. LISP programmers are used to thinking this way, but most procedural programmers are not. It just takes a little practice and time.

10.6 Mathematical Functions

The SQL:2003 Standard extended the original four-function math to include a small library of functions. Most of them have been in actual products for decades. SQL is not a computational language, so it should not have a math function library like, say, FORTRAN. Nor a string function library like ICON.

10.6.1 Number Theory Operators

ABS(n) = Absolute value function. Returns the absolute value of n. If (n) is NULL, then the result is NULL.

SIGN(n) = Signum function. Returns −1 if n is negative, 0 if n is zero and +1 if n is positive. If (n) is NULL, then the result is NULL. This function is the "signum" in mathematical terminology.

MOD(n, m) = modulo or remainder function. If either n or m is NULL, then the result is NULL. If m is zero, then we get a division by zero exception. Otherwise, the result is the unique non-negative exact numeric value r with scale zero such that.

(1) r has the same sign as n.

(2) the absolute value of r is less than the absolute value of m.

(3) n = m * k + r for some exact numeric value k with scale zero.

This is tricky when the values of n and m are not cardinals (i.e., positive, nonzero integers). Experiment and find out how your package handles negative numbers and decimal places. In particular, many other procedural languages have slightly different definitions. If you are foolish enough to use "features" that allow other programming languages to be embedded in the DDL, then you cannot have consistent data. This was a major issue for the Pascal at one time, among others.

In 1996 September, Len Gallagher of NIST proposed an amendment for the MOD function in the SQL3 working papers. Originally, the working draft defined MOD(n, m) only for positive values of both m and n, and leaves the result to be implementation-dependent when either of m or n is negative.

Negative values of n have no required mathematical meaning and that many implementations of MOD either do not define it at all, or give some result that is the easiest to calculate on a given hardware platform.

However, negative values for (m) do have a very nice mathematical interpretation that we wanted to see preserved in the SQL definition of MOD(). Len propose the following:

(1) If n is positive, then the result is the unique non_negative exact numeric quantity r with scale zero such that r is less than m and n = (m * k) + r for some exact numeric quantity k with scale zero.

(2) Otherwise, the result is an implementation-defined exact numeric quantity r with scale zero which satisfies the requirements that r is strictly between m and (−m), and that n = (m * k) + r for some exact numeric quantity k with scale zero, and a completion condition is raised: warning—implementation-defined result.

This definition guarantees that the MOD() function, for a given positive value of n, will be a homomorphism under addition from the mathematical group of all integers, under integer addition, to the modular group of integers {0, 1..., m − 1} under modular addition. This mapping then preserves the following group properties:

(1) The additive identity is preserved: MOD(0, m) = 0

(2) Additive inverse is preserved in the modular group defined by MOD(−MOD(n, m), m) = m − MOD(n, m): MOD(−n, m) = − MOD(n, m)

(3) The addition property is preserved where "{{ circled plus sign }}" is modular addition defined by MOD((MOD(m, m) + MOD(n, m)), m). MOD((m + n), m) = MOD(m, m) {{ circled plus sign }} MOD(n, m)

(4) Subtraction is preserve under modular subtraction, which is defined as MOD((MOD(m, m) {{ circled minus sign }} MOD(n, m)), m)

MOD(m − n, m) = MOD(m, m) {{ circled minus sign }} MOD(n, m)
From this definition, we would get the following:
MOD(12, 5) = 2
MOD(−12, 5) = 3

There are some applications where the "best" result to MOD(−12, 5) might "−2" or "−3" rather than "3"; and that is probably why various implementations of the MOD function differ. But the advantages of being able to rely on the above mathematical properties outweigh any other considerations. If a user knows what the SQL result will be, then it is easy to modify the expressions of a particular application to get the desired application result. Here is a chart of the differences in some SQL implementations.

Test	m	n	Type A	Type B	Type C	Proposal
a	12	5	2	2	2	2
b	–12	5	–2	–2	–2	3
c	–12	–5	–2	–2	(–2, 3)	(2, –3)
d	–12	–5	2	2	2	–2
e	NULL	5	NULL	NULL	NULL	NULL
f	NULL	NULL	NULL	NULL	NULL	NULL
g	12	NULL	NULL	NULL	NULL	NULL
h	12	0	12	NULL	error	12
i	–12	0	–12	NULL	error	–12
j	0	5	0	0	0	0
k	0	–5	0	0	0	0

Type A:

Oracle 7.0 and Oracle 8.0

Type B:

DataFlex—ODBC:

SQL Server 6.5, SP2

SQLBase Version 6.1 PTF level 4

Xbase

Type C:

DB2/400, V3r2:

DB2/6000 V2.01.1

Sybase SQL Anywhere 5.5

Sybase System 11

10.6.2 Exponential Functions

The exponential functions use powers and roots, so they are concerned with floating point numbers

POWER(x, n) = Raise the number x to the n-th power. If either parameter is NULL, then the result is NULL. If x is zero and n is negative, then an exception condition is raised: data exception — invalid. A non-negative number to the zero power is always one. and VE is positive, then the result is zero.

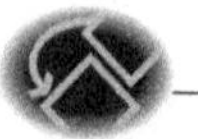

SQRT(x) = Return the square root of x. It is defined as a shorthand for POWER (x, 0.5).

LN(x) = Natural logarithm of x. If x is zero or negative, then an exception condition is raised: data exception—invalid argument for natural logarithm.

EXP(x) = Returns the constant e (~2.71828182845904523536.) to the x power; the inverse of a natural logarithm. If x is NULL then the result is NULL. If the result is not representable in the declared type of the result, then an exception is raised.

10.6.3 Scaling Functions

FLOOR(x) = The largest integer less than or equal to x. If x is NULL then the result is NULL.

CEILING(x) = The smallest integer greater than or equal to x. If x is NULL then the result is NULL.

While not part of the Standards, these are very common in actual products. They can be written with multiplication and division, which would be subject the local truncation and rounding rules of their product.

ROUND(x, p) = Round the number x to p decimal places. If either parameter is NULL, the result is NULL.

TRUNCATE(x, p) = Truncate the number x to p decimal places. If either parameter is NULL, the result is NULL.

10.6.4 Other Mathematical Functions

Vendors often include trigonometry and other math functions. These were easy to add from existing compilers for other languages, but are not part of the standard and do not port very well. Two proprietary functions that use an expression list are:

LEAST (<expression list>) = The expressions have to be of the same data type. This function returns the lowest value, whether numeric, temporal or character.

GREATEST(<expression list>) = As above, but it returns the highest value.

These functions are in MySQL, Oracle, Mimer and other SQL products, but are often mimicked with CASE expressions in actual code.

10.6.5 Converting Numbers to Words

A common function in report writers converts numbers into words so that they can be used to print checks, legal documents and other reports. This is not a common function in SQL products, nor is it part of the standards.

A method for converting numbers into words using only standard SQL by Stu Bloom follows. This was posted on 2002 Jan 02 on the SQL Server Programming newsgroup. First, create a table

```
CREATE TABLE Nbr_Words
number INTEGER PRIMARY KEY,
 word VARCHAR(30) NOT NULL);
```

Then populate it with the literal strings of Nbr_Words from 0 to 999. Assuming that your range is 1-999, 999, 999 use the following query; it should be obvious how to extend it for larger numbers and fractional parts.

```
CASE WHEN:num < 1000
  THEN(SELECT word FROM Nbr_Words
      WHERE number = :num)
  WHEN:num < 1000000
  THEN(SELECT word FROM Nbr_Words
      WHERE number = :num/1000)
     || 'thousand'
     || (SELECT word FROM Nbr_Words
       WHERE MOD(number = :num,1000))
  WHEN:num < 1000000000
  THEN(SELECT word FROM Nbr_Words
       WHERE number = :num/1000000)
     || 'million'
     || (SELECT word FROM Nbr_Words
       WHERE number = OD((:num/1000),1000))
     || CASE WHEN MOD((:num/1000),1000) > 0
          THEN'thousand'
          ELSE''END
     || (SELECT word FROM Nbr_Words
       WHERE number = MOD(:num,1000))
END;
```

Whether 2500 is “Twenty-Five Hundred” or “Two Thousand Five Hundred” is a matter of taste and not science. This can be done with a shorter list of words and a different query, but this is probably the best compromise between code and the size of the table.

10.7 IP Addresses

While they are not a numeric data type, IP addresses are common enough to deserve a section and this is the best place to put it in this book.

Internet Protocol version 6 (IPv6) replaces Internet Protocol version (IPv4), which was made up of four integers each in the range 0 to 255, separated by dots. The problem was that we are running out of IP space. Version 6 requires eight sets of four hexadecimal digits separated by colons.

While technically a numeric data type, IP addresses are stored as binary and displayed with digital strings. IPv6 was defined in December 1998 by the Internet Engineering Task Force (IETF) with the publication of an Internet standard specification, RFC 2460. There was no version five; it was an experimental flow-oriented streaming protocol (Internet Stream Protocol) intended to support video and audio.

The new standard uses of a 128-bit address, whereas IPv4 uses only 32 bits. There are a lot of details and new things in the standards, but I do not care about them for this discussion; this is only about data representation.

Most of the world is still on IPv4 and it will be awhile before we are converted to the new standard.

10.7.1 CHAR(39) Storage

You could keep the IP address as a CHAR (39) that is (8 * 4 digits+7 colons) and an easy regular expression in the DDL. The main advantage is that this is human readable and binary is not. But it is legal to drop leading zeroes in each group for readability. While that is a good goal, it makes comparisons a bit harder.

10.7.2 Binary Storage

Most current hardware supports 64 bit integers, but not 128 bits. Thankfully, the IPv6 standard uses a host identifier portion of 64 bits to facilitate an automatic mechanism for forming the host identifier from Link Layer media addressing information (MAC address). It is possible to use two BIGINTs for the data.

10.7.3 Separate SMALLINTs

The IP address is displayed as groups which each have meaning in the system, so we can model an IP address in separate columns. Notice that the IP address is still an atomic data element, but it is being modeled as scalar values. Check that you have such a data type in your product; if not, you can define it as

```
CREATE DOMAIN SmallInt
AS INTEGER DEFAULT 0 CHECK(VALUE BETWEEN 0 AND 65535);
```

Then use that data type to declare a nonscalar atomic data element, thus:

```
ip1 SMALLINT NOT NULL,
ip2 SMALLINT NOT NULL,
 ..
ip8 SMALLINT NOT NULL
```

The trick here is to index the octets in reverse order, since the final grouping is the most selective.

Character Data Types in SQL

SQL-89 DEFINED A CHARACTER(n) or CHAR(n) data type, which represents a fixed-length string of (n) printable characters, where (n) is always greater than zero. Some implementations allow the string to contain control characters, but this is not the usual case. The allowable characters are usually drawn from ASCII or EBCDIC character sets and most often use those collation sequences for sorting.

SQL-92 added the VARYING CHARACTER(n) or VARCHAR(n), which was already present in many implementations. A VARCHAR(n) represents a string that varies in length from 1 to (n) printable characters. This is important; SQL does not allow a string column of zero length, but you may find vendors who do so that you can store an empty string.

SQL-92 also added NATIONAL CHARACTER(n) and NATIONAL VARYING CHARACTER(n) data types (or NCHAR(n) and NVARCHAR(n), respectively), which are made up of printable characters drawn from ISO-defined UNICODE character sets. The literal values use the syntax N'<string>' in these data types.

SQL-92 also allows the database administrator to define collation sequences and do other things with the character sets. A Consortium (http://www.unicode.org/) maintains the Unicode standards and makes them available in book form (UNICODE STANDARD, VERSION 5.0; ISBN-13: 978-0321480910) or on the Website.

When the Standards got to SQL:2006, we had added a lot of things to handle Unicode and XML data but kept the basic string manipulations pretty simple compared to what vendors have. I am not going to deal with the Unicode and XML data in any detail because most working SQL programmers are using ASCII or a national character set exclusively in their databases.

11.1 Problems with SQL Strings

Different programming languages handle strings differently. You simply have to do some unlearning with you to get SQL. Here are the major problem areas for programmers.

In SQL, character strings are printable characters enclosed in single quotation marks. Many older SQL implementations and several programming languages use double quotation marks or make it an option so that the single quotation mark can be used as an apostrophe. SQL uses two apostrophes together to represent a single apostrophe in a string literal. SQL Server uses the square brackets for double quotes.

Double quotation marks are reserved for column names that have embedded spaces or that are also SQL reserved words.

Character sets fall into three categories: those defined by national or international standards, those provided by implementations, and those defined by applications. All character sets, however defined, always contain the <space> character. Character sets defined by applications can be defined to "reside" in any schema chosen by the application. Character sets defined by standards or by implementations reside in the Information Schema (named INFORMATION_SCHEMA) in each catalog, as do collations defined by standards and collations and form-of-use conversions defined by implementations. There is a default collating sequence for each character repertoire, but additional collating sequences can be defined for any character repertoire. This can be important in languages that have more than one collating sequence in use. For example, in German dictionaries, "öf" would come before "of," but in German telephone, it is the opposite ordering. It is a good idea to look at http://userguide.icu-project.org/collation for a guide to the current Unicode rules.

11.1.1 Problems of String Equality

No two languages agree on how to compare character strings as equal unless they are identical in length and match position for position, *exactly* character for character.

The first problem is whether uppercase and lowercase versions of a letter compare as equal to each other. Only Latin, Greek, Cyrillic, and Arabic have cases; the first three have upper and lower cases, whereas Arabic is a connected script that has initial, middle, terminal, and stand-alone forms of its letters. Most programming languages, including SQL, ignore case in the program text, but not always in the data. Some SQL implementations allow the DBA to set uppercase and lowercase matching as a system configuration parameter.

The Standard SQL has two folding functions (yes, that is the name) that change the case of a string:

LOWER(<string expression>) shifts all letters in the parameter string to corresponding lowercase letters;

UPPER(<string expression>) shifts all letters in the string to uppercase. Most implementations have had these functions (perhaps with different names) as vendor library functions.

Equality between strings of unequal length is calculated by first padding out the shorter string with blanks on the right-hand side until the strings are of the same length. Then they are matched, position for position, for identical values. If one position fails to match, then the equality fails.

In contrast, the Xbase languages (FoxPro, dBase, and so on) truncate the longer string to the length of the shorter string and then match them position for position. Other programming languages ignore upper- and lowercase differences.

11.1.2 Problems of String Ordering

SQL-89 was silent on the collating sequence to be used. In practice, almost all SQL implementations used either ASCII or EBCDIC, which are both Latin I character sets in ISO terminology. A few implementations have a Dictionary or Library order option (uppercase and lowercase letters mixed together in alphabetic order: {A, a, B, b, C, c, etc.}, and many vendors offer a national-language option that is based on the appropriate ISO Standard.

National language options can be very complicated. The Nordic languages all share a common ISO character set, but they do not sort the same letters in the same position. German was sorted differently in Germany and Austria. Spain decided to quit sorting 'ch' and 'll' as if they were single characters. You really need to look at the ISO Unicode implementation for your particular product.

The Standard SQL allows the DBA to define a collating sequence that is used for comparisons. The feature is becoming more common as we come more globalized, but you have to see what the vendor of your SQL product actually supports.

11.1.3 Problems of String Grouping

Because the SQL equality test has to pad out the shorter of the two strings with spaces, you may find doing a GROUP BY on a VARCHAR(n) that has unpredictable results:

```
CREATE TABLE Foobar (x VARCHAR(5) NOT NULL);
INSERT INTO Foobar VALUES ('a'), ('a '), ('a '), ('a ');
```

Now, execute the query:

```
SELECT x, CHAR_LENGTH(x)
  FROM Foobar
 GROUP BY x;
```

The value for CHAR_LENGTH(x) will vary for different products. The most common answers are 1 and 4, 5 in this example. A length of 1 is returned because it is the length of the shortest string or because it is the length of the first string physically in the table. A length of 4 because it is the length of the longest string in the table. A length of 5 because it is the greatest possible length of a string in the table.

SQL has two equivalence class operators; if you do not know what that means, go back to your Set Theory course. They partition an entire set into disjoint subsets. The first one is simple, vanilla scalar equality (=). The second is grouping, as in GROUP BY. This second operator treats all NULLs as part of the same class and follows the padding rule for strings. Yo will see this later in SQL.

You might want to add a constraint that makes sure to trim the trailing blanks to avoid problems.

11.2 Standard String Functions

SQL-92 defines a set of string functions that appear in most products, but with vendor-specific syntax. You will probably find that products will continue to support their own syntax but will also add the Standard SQL syntax in new releases. Let's look at the basic operations.

String concatenation is shown with the || operator, taken from PL/I. However, you can also find the plus sign being overloaded in the Sybase/SQL Server family and some products using a function call like CONCAT(s1, s2) instead.

The SUBSTRING(<string> FROM <start> FOR <length>) function uses three arguments: the source string, the starting position of the substring, and the length of the substring to be extracted. Truncation occurs when the implied starting and ending positions are not both within the given string.

DB2 and other products have a LEFT and a RIGHT function. The LEFT function returns a string consisting of the specified number of left-most characters of the string expression, and RIGHT, well, that is kind of obvious.

The fold functions are a pair of functions for converting all the lowercase characters in a given string to uppercase, UPPER(<string>), or all the uppercase ones to lowercase LOWER(<string>). We already mentioned them.

The TRIM([[<trim specification>] [<trim character>] FROM] <trim source>) produces a result string that is the source string with an unwanted character removed. The <trim source> is the original character value expression. The <trim specification> is LEADING, TRAILING, or BOTH and the <trim character> is the single character that is to be removed. If you don't give a <trim character>, then space is assumed. Most products still do not have the <trim character> option and work with only space.

The TRIM() function removes the leading and/or trailing occurrences of a character from a string. The default character if one is not given is a space. The SQL-92 version is a very general function, but you will find that most SQL implementations have a version that works only with spaces. Many early SQLs had two functions: LTRIM for left-most (leading) blanks and RTRIM for right-most (trailing) blanks.

A character translation is a function for changing each character of a given string according to some many-to-one or one-to-one mapping between two not necessarily distinct character sets.

The syntax TRANSLATE(<string expression> USING <translation>) assumes that a special schema object, called a translation, has already been created to hold the rules for doing all of this.

CHAR_LENGTH(<string>), also written CHARACTER_LENGTH(<string>), determines the length of a given character string, as an integer, in characters. In most current products, this function is usually expressed as LENGTH() and the next two functions do not exist at all; they assume that the database will only hold ASCII or EBCDIC characters.

BIT_LENGTH(<string>) determines the length of a given character string, as an integer, in bits.

OCTET_LENGTH(<string>) determines the length of a given character string, as an integer, in octets. Octets are units of 8 bits that are used by the one and two (Unicode) octet characters sets. This is the same as TRUNCATE (BIT_LENGTH (<string>)/8).

The POSITION(<search string> IN <source string>) determines the first position, if any, at which the <search string> occurs within the <source string>. If the <search string> is of length zero, then it occurs at position 1 for any value of the <source string>. If the <search string> does not occur in the <source string>, zero is returned. You will also see LOCATE() in DB2 and CHAR_INDEX() in SQL Server.

11.3 Common Vendor Extensions

The original SQL-89 standard did not define any functions for CHAR(n) data types. The Standard SQL added the basic functions that have been common to implementations for years. However, there are other common or useful functions, and it is worth knowing how to implement them outside of SQL.

Many vendors also have functions that will format dates for display by converting the internal format to a text string. A vendor whose SQL is tied to a 4GL is much more likely to have these extensions simply because the 4GL can use them.

These functions generally use either a COBOL-style picture parameter or a globally set default format. Some of this conversion work is done with the CAST() function in Standard SQL, but since SQL does not have any output statements, such things will be vendor extensions for some time to come.

Vendor extensions are varied, but there are some that are worth mentioning. The names will be different in different products, but the functionality will be the same.

SPACE(n) produces a string of (n) spaces for (n>0).

REPLICATE (<string expression>, n) produces a string of (n) repetitions of the <string expression>. DB2 calls this one REPEAT() and you will see other local names for it.

REPLACE (<target string>, <old string>, <new string>) replaces the occurrences of the <old string> with the <new string> in the <target string>.

As an aside, a nice trick to reduce several contiguous spaces in a string to a single space to format text:

```
UPDATE Foobar
 SET sentence
   = REPLACE(
     REPLACE(
      REPLACE(sentence, SPACE(1), ‘<>’)
     ‘><’, SPACE(0))
     ‘<>’, SPACE(1));
```

REVERSE(<string expression>) reverses the order of the characters in a string to make it easier to search.

11.3.1 Phonetic Matching

People’s names are a problem for designers of databases. Names are variable-length, can have strange spellings, and are not unique. American names have a diversity of ethnic origins, which give us names pronounced the same way but spelled differently and vice versa.

Ignoring this diversity of names, errors in reading or hearing a name lead to mutations. Anyone who gets junk mail is aware of this; I get mail addressed to “Selco,” “Selko,” “Celco,” as well as “Celko,” which are phonetic errors, and also some that result from typing errors, such as “Cellro,” “Chelco,” and “Chelko” in my mail stack. Such errors result in the mailing of multiple copies of the same item to the same address. To solve this problem, we need phonetic algorithms that can find similar sounding names.

11.3.1.1 Soundex Functions

The Soundex family of algorithms is named after the original algorithm. A Soundex algorithm takes a person’s name as input and produces a character string that identifies a set of names that are (roughly) phonetically alike.

SQL products often have a Soundex algorithm in their library functions. It is also possible to compute a Soundex in SQL, using string functions and the CASE expression in the Standard SQL. Names that sound alike do not always have the same Soundex code. For example, “Lee” and “Leigh” are pronounced alike but have different Soundex codes because the silent ‘g’ in “Leigh” is given a code.

Names that sound alike but start with a different first letter will always have a different Soundex, such as “Carr” and “Karr” will be separate codes.

Finally, Soundex is based on English pronunciation, so European and Asian names may not encode correctly. Just looking at French surnames like "Beaux" with a silent 'x' and "Beau" without it, we will create two different Soundex codes.

Sometimes names that don't sound alike have the same Soundex code. Consider the relatively common names "Powers," "Pierce," "Price," "Perez," and "Park" which all have the same Soundex code. Yet "Power," a common way to spell Powers 100 years ago, has a different Soundex code.

11.3.1.2 The Original Soundex

Margaret O'Dell and Robert C. Russell patented the original Soundex algorithm in 1918. The method is based on the phonetic classification of sounds by how they are made.

In case you wanted to know, the six groups are bilabial, labiodental, dental, alveolar, velar, and glottal. The algorithm is fairly straightforward to code and requires no backtracking or multiple passes over the input word. This should not be too surprising, since it was in use before computers and had to be done by hand by clerks. Here is the algorithm:

1.0 Capitalize all letters in the word. Pad the word with right-most blanks as needed during each procedure step.

2.0 Retain the first letter of the word.

3.0 Drop all occurrences of the following letters after the first position: A, E, H, I, O, U, W, Y.

4.0 Change letters from the following sets into the corresponding digits given:
1 = B, F, P, V
2 = C, G, J, K, Q, S, X, Z
3 = D, T
4 = L
5 = M, N
6 = R

5.0 Retain only one occurrence of consecutive duplicate digits from the string that resulted after step 4.0.

6.0 Pad the string that resulted from step 5.0 with trailing zeros and return only the first four positions, which will be of the form<uppercase letter><digit><digit><digit>.

An alternative version of the algorithm, due to Russell, changes the letters in step 3.0 (A, E, H, I, O, U, W, Y) to '9's, retaining them without dropping them. Then step 5.0 is replaced by two steps:

5.1: Remove redundant duplicates '22992345' → 29245

5.2: Remove all '9's and close the spaces. 29245 → 2245

This allows pairs of duplicate digits to appear in the result string. This version has more granularity and will work better for a larger sample of names.

This allows pairs of duplicate digits to appear in the result string. This version has more granularity and will work better for a larger sample of names.

The problem with the Soundex is that it was a manual operation used by the Census Bureau long before computers. The algorithm used was not always applied uniformly from place to place. Surname prefixes, such as "La," "De," "von," or "van," are generally dropped from the last name for Soundex, but not always.

If you are searching for surnames such as "DiCaprio" or "LaBianca," you should try the Soundex for both with and without the prefix. Likewise leading syllables like "Mc," "Mac," and "O'" were also dropped.

Then there was a question about dropping 'H' and 'W' along with the vowels. The U.S. Census Soundex did it both ways, so a name like "Ashcraft" could be converted to "Ascrft" in the first pass, and finally Soundexed to "A261," as it is in the 1920 New York Census. The Soundex code for the 1880, 1900, and 1910 censuses followed both rules. In this case, Ashcraft would be "A226" in some places. The reliability of Soundex is 95.99% with selectivity factor of 0.213% for a name inquiry.

This version is easy to translate into various dialects. The WHILE loop would be better done with a REPEAT loop, but not all products have that construct. The TRANSLATEs could be one statement, but this is easier to read. Likewise, the REPLACE functions could be nested.

```
CREATE FUNCTION Soundex(IN in_name VARCHAR(50))
RETURNS CHAR(4)
DETERMINISTIC
LANGUAGE SQL
BEGIN ATOMIC
DECLARE header_char CHAR(1);
DECLARE prior_name_size INTEGER;
```

```
-- split the name into a head and a tail
SET header_char = UPPER (SUBSTRING (in_name FROM 1 FOR 1));
SET in_name = UPPER (SUBSTRING (in_name FROM 2 FOR
CHAR_LENGTH(in_name)));
-- clean out vowels
SET in_name = TRANSLATE (in_name, ' ', 'AEHIOUWY');
-- clean out spaces and add zeros
SET in_name = REPLACE (in_name, ' ', '') || '0000';
-- consonant changes
SET in_name = TRANSLATE(in_name, '1111', 'BFPV');
SET in_name = TRANSLATE(in_name, '22222222', 'CGJKQSXZ');
SET in_name = TRANSLATE(in_name, '33', 'DT');
SET in_name = TRANSLATE(in_name, '4', 'L');
SET in_name = TRANSLATE(in_name, '55', 'MN');
SET in_name = TRANSLATE(in_name, '6', 'R');
-- loop to clean out duplicate digits
WHILE 1 = 1
DO
  SET prior_name_size = CHAR_LENGTH (in_name);
  SET in_name = REPLACE(in_name, '11', '1');
  SET in_name = REPLACE(in_name, '22', '2');
  SET in_name = REPLACE(in_name, '33', '3');
  SET in_name = REPLACE(in_name, '44', '4');
  SET in_name = REPLACE(in_name, '55', '5');
  SET in_name = REPLACE(in_name, '66', '6');
-- no size change means no more duplicate digits, time to
output the answer
  IF prior_name_size = CHAR_LENGTH (in_name)
  THEN RETURN header_char || SUBSTRING (in_name FROM 1 FOR 3);
  END IF;
END WHILE;
END;
```

11.3.1.3 Metaphone

Metaphone is another improved Soundex that first appeared in Computer Language magazine (Philips 1990). A Pascal version written by Terry Smithwick (Smithwick 1991), based on the original C version by Lawrence Philips, is reproduced with permission here:

```
FUNCTION Metaphone (p : STRING) : STRING;
CONST
VowelSet = ['A', 'E', 'I', 'O', 'U'];
FrontVSet = ['E', 'I', 'Y'];
VarSonSet = ['C', 'S', 'T', 'G'];
  { variable sound - modified by following 'h' }
FUNCTION SubStr (A : STRING;
 Start, Len : INTEGER) : STRING;
BEGIN
SubStr := Copy (A, Start, Len);
END;
FUNCTION Metaphone (p : STRING) : STRING;
VAR
  i, l, n: BYTE;
  silent, new: BOOLEAN;
  last, this, next, nnext : CHAR;
  m, d: STRING;
BEGIN { Metaphone }
IF (p = '')
THEN BEGIN
  Metaphone := '';
  EXIT;
  END;
{ Remove leading spaces }
FOR i := 1 TO Length (p)
DO p[i] := UpCase (p[i]);
{ Assume all alphas }
{ initial preparation of string }
d := SubStr (p, 1, 2);
IF d IN ('KN', 'GN', 'PN', 'AE', 'WR')
THEN p := SubStr (p, 2, Length (p) - 1);
IF (p[1] = 'X')
THEN p := 'S' + SubStr (p, 2, Length (p) - 1);
IF (d = 'WH')
THEN p := 'W' + SubStr (p, 2, Length (p) - 1);
{ Set up for Case statement }
l := Length (p);
m := '';
```

```
    { Initialize the main variable }
new := TRUE;
    { this variable only used next 10 lines!!! }
n := 1;
    { Position counter }
WHILE ((Length (m) < 6) AND (n <> 1))
DO BEGIN { Set up the 'pointers' for this loop-around }
  IF (n > 1)
  THEN last := p[n-1]
  ELSE last := #0;
  { use a nul terminated string }
  this := p[n];
  IF (n < 1)
  THEN next := p[n+1]
  ELSE next := #0;
  IF ((n+1) < 1)
  THEN nnext := p[n+2]
  ELSE nnext := #0;
  new := (this = 'C') AND (n > 1) AND (last = 'C');
  { 'CC' inside word }
  IF (new)
  THEN BEGIN
    IF ((this IN VowelSet) AND (n = 1))
    THEN m := this;
  CASE this OF
  'B' : IF NOT ((n = 1) AND (last = 'M'))
    THEN m := m + 'B';
  { -mb is silent }
'C' : BEGIN { -sce, i, y = silent }
  IF NOT ((last = 'S') AND (next IN FrontVSet))
  THEN BEGIN
    IF (next = 'i') AND (nnext = 'A')
    THEN m := m + 'X'{ -cia- }
    ELSE IF (next IN FrontVSet)
      THEN m := m + 'S' { -ce, i, y = 'S' }
      ELSE IF (next = 'H') AND (last = 'S')
        THEN m := m + 'K' { -sch- = 'K' }
        ELSE IF (next = 'H')
```

```
        THEN IF (n = 1) AND ((n+2) < = 1)
          AND NOT (nnext IN VowelSet)
          THEN m := m + 'K'
          ELSE m := m + 'X';
    END { Else silent }
  END;
 { Case C }
'D' : IF (next = 'G') AND (nnext IN FrontVSet)
    THEN m := m + 'J'
    ELSE m := m + 'T';
'G' : BEGIN
  silent := (next = 'H') AND (nnext IN VowelSet);

  IF (n > 1) AND (((n+1) = 1) OR ((next = 'n') AND
    (nnext = 'E') AND (p[n+3] = 'D') AND ((n+3) = 1))
{ Terminal -gned }
  AND (last = 'i') AND (next = 'n'))
  THEN silent := TRUE;
{ if not start and near -end or -gned.) }
  IF (n > 1) AND (last = 'D'gnuw) AND (next IN FrontVSet)
  THEN { -dge, i, y }
  silent := TRUE;
  IF NOT silent
  THEN IF (next IN FrontVSet)
    THEN m := m + 'J'
    ELSE m := m + 'K';
  END;
'H' : IF NOT ((n = 1) OR (last IN VarSonSet)) AND (next IN
VowelSet)
    THEN m := m + 'H';
   { else silent (vowel follows) }
'F', 'J', 'L', 'M', 'N', 'R' : m := m + this;
'K' : IF (last <> 'C')
    THEN m := m + 'K';
'P' : IF (next = 'H')
    THEN BEGIN
      m := m + 'F';
      INC (n);
```

```
        END { Skip the 'H' }
      ELSE m := m + 'P';
'Q' : m := m + 'K';
'S' : IF (next = 'H')
      OR ((n > 1) AND (next = 'i') AND (nnext IN ['O', 'A']))
    THEN m := m + 'X'
    ELSE m := m + 'S';
'T' : IF (n = 1) AND (next = 'H') AND (nnext = 'O')
      THEN m := m + 'T' { Initial Tho- }
      ELSE IF (n > 1) AND (next = 'i') AND (nnext IN ['O', 'A'])
      THEN m := m + 'X'
      ELSE IF (next = 'H')
        THEN m := m + '0'
        ELSE IF NOT ((next = 'C') AND (nnext = 'H'))
          THEN m := m + 'T';
{ -tch = silent }
'V' : m := m + 'F';
'W', 'Y' : IF (next IN VowelSet)
      THEN m := m + this;
  { else silent }
'X' : m := m + 'KS';
'Z' : m := m + 'S';
END;
 { Case }
INC (n);
END; { While }
END; { Metaphone }
Metaphone := m
END;
```

11.3.1.4 NYSIIS Algorithm

The New York State Identification and Intelligence System, or NYSIIS algorithm is more reliable and selective than Soundex, especially for grouped phonetic sounds. It does not perform well with 'Y' groups because 'Y' is not translated. NYSIIS yields an alphabetic string key that is filled or rounded to 10 characters.

(1) Translate first characters of name:
    MAC =>MCC
    KN =>NN

K => C

PH => FF

PF => FF

SCH => SSS

(2) Translate last characters of name:

EE => Y

IE => Y

DT,RT,RD,NT,ND => D

(3) The first character of key = first character of name.

(4) Translate remaining characters by following rules, scanning one character at a time

a. EV => AF else A,E,I,O,U => A
b. Q => G Z => S M => N
c. KN => N else K => C
d. SCH => SSS PH => FF
e. H => If previous or next character is a consonant use the previous character.
f. W => If previous character is a vowel, use the previous character.

Add the current character to result if the current character is to equal to the last key character.

(5) If last character is S, remove it

(6) If last characters are AY, replace them with Y

(7) If last character is A, remove it

The stated reliability of NYSIIS is 98.72% with a selectivity factor of .164% for a name inquiry. This was taken from Robert L. Taft, "Name Search Techniques", New York State Identification and Intelligence System.

11.4 Cutter Tables

Another encoding scheme for names has been used for libraries for over 100 years. The catalog number of a book often needs to reduce an author's name to a simple fixed-length code. While the results of a Cutter table look much like those of a Soundex, their goal is different. They attempt to preserve the original alphabetical order of the names in the encodings.

But the librarian cannot just attach the author's name to the classification code. Names are not the same length, nor are they unique within their first letters. For example, "Smith, John A." and "Smith, John B." are not unique until the last letter.

What librarians have done about this problem is to use Cutter tables. These tables map authors' full names into letter-and-digit codes. There are several versions of the Cutter tables. The older tables tended to use a mix of letters (both upper- and lowercase) followed by digits. The three-figure single letter followed by three digits. For example, using that table.

"Adams, J" becomes "A214"

"Adams, M" becomes "A215"

"Arnold" becomes "A752"

"Dana" becomes "D168"

"Sherman" becomes "S553"

"Scanlon" becomes "S283"

The distribution of these numbers is based on the actual distribution of names of authors in English-speaking countries. You simply scan down the table until you find the place where your name would fall and use that code.

Cutter tables have two important properties. They preserve the alphabetical ordering of the original name list, which means that you can do a rough sort on them. The second property is that each grouping tends to be of approximately the same size as the set of names gets larger. These properties can be handy for building indexes in a database.

If you would like copies of the Cutter tables, you can find some of them on the Internet. Princeton University Library has posted their rules for names, locations, regions, and other things (http://infoshare1.princeton.edu/katmandu/class/cutter.html).

You can also get hardcopies from this publisher.

Hargrave House
7312 Firethorn
Littleton, CO 80125
Website = http://www.cuttertables.com

Temporal Data Types in SQL

CLIFFORD SIMAK WROTE a science fiction novel entitled *Time is the Simplest Thing* in 1977. He was wrong. And the problems did not start with the Y2K problems we had in 2000, either. The calendar is irregular and the only standard unit of time is the second, years, months, weeks, hours, minutes, and so forth are not part of the metric (SI units) system but are mentioned in the ISO standards as conventions.

SQL is the first programming language to have temporal data types in it. If COBOL had done this, we would never have had the "Y2K Crisis" in IT. SQL-92 added temporal data to the language, acknowledging what was already in most SQL product by that time. The problem is that each vendor made a trade-off internally. We will get into SQL code later, but since this is an area where people do not have a good understanding, it is better to start with foundations.

12.1 Notes on Calendar Standards

The current calendar is known as the Common Era Calendar, and not the Western, Christian, or Gregorian Calendar. We want to use a universal, nonethnic, nonreligious name for it. The abbreviations for postfixes on dates are CE and BCE for "Common Era" and "Before Common Era," respectively. The abbreviations A.D. (Anno Domini—Latin for "in the year of Our Lord") and B.C. ("Before Christ") were dropped to avoid religious references.

Unfortunately, the solar year is not an even number of days; there are 365.2422 days in a year and the fraction adds up over time. This is why we have leap year in the Common Era Calendar. Leap years did not exist in the Roman or Egyptian solar calendars prior to the year 708 AUC ("ab urbe condita," Latin for "from the founding of the City [Rome]"). As a result, they were useless for agriculture, so the Egyptians relied on the stars to predict the flooding of the Nile. To realign the calendar with the seasons, Julius Caesar decreed that the year 708 (that is, the year 46 BCE to us) would have 445 days. Caesar, on the advice of Sosigenes, also introduced leap years (known as bissextile years) at this time. Many Romans simply referred to 708 AUC as the "year of confusion" and thus began the Julian calendar that was the standard for the world from that point forward.

The Julian calendar had a leap year day every 4 years and was reasonably accurate in the short or medium range, but it drifted by approximately 3 days every 400 years. This is a result of the 0.0022 fraction of a day adding up.

It had gotten 10 days out of step with the seasons by 1582 (a calendar without a leap year would have drifted completely around slightly more than once between 708 AUC and 2335 AUC—that is, 1582 CE to us). The Summer Solstice, so important to planting crops, had no relationship to 21 June. Scientists finally convinced Pope Gregory to realign the calendar by dropping almost 2 weeks from the month of October in 1582 CE. The years 800 CE and 1200 CE were leap years anywhere in the Christian world. But whether 1600 CE was a leap year depended on where you lived. European countries did not move to the new calendar at the same time or follow the same pattern of adoption.

The calendar corrections had economic and social ramifications. In Great Britain and its colonies, September 02, 1752 was followed by September 14, 1752. The calendar reform bill of 1751 was entitled "An Act for Regulating the Commencement of the Year and for Correcting the Calendar Now in Use." The bill included provisions to adjust the amount of money owed or collected from rents, leases, mortgages, and similar legal arrangements so that rents and so forth were prorated by the number of actual elapsed days in the time period affected by the calendar change. Nobody had to pay the full monthly rate for the short month of September in 1752 and nobody had to pay the full yearly rate for the short year.

The serious, widespread, and persistent rioting was not due to the commercial problems that resulted, but to the common belief that each person's days were "numbered" and that everyone was preordained to be born and die at a divinely ordained time that no human agency could alter in any way.

Thus the removal of 11 days from the month of September shortened the lives of everyone on Earth by 11 days. And there was also the matter of the missing 83 days due to the change of the New Year's Day from March 25 to January 01, which was believed to have a similar effect.

If you think this behavior is insane, consider the number of people today who get upset about the yearly 1-hour clock adjustments for Daylight Saving Time.

To complicate matters, the beginning of the year also varied from country to country. Great Britain preferred to begin the year on March 25, whereas other countries began at Easter, December 25, or perhaps March 01 and January 01—all important details for historians to keep in mind.

In Great Britain and its colonies, the calendar year 1750 began on March 25 and ended on March 25—that is, the day after March 24, 1750 and March 25, 1751. The leap year day was added to the end of the last full month in the year, which was then February. The extra leap year day comes at the end of February, as this part of the calendar structure was not changed.

In Latin, "septem" means seventh, from which we derived September. Likewise, "octem" means eighth, "novem" means ninth, and "decem" means tenth. Thus, September should be the seventh month, October should be the eighth, November should be the ninth, and December should be the tenth.

So, how come September is the ninth month? September was the seventh month until 1752 when the New Year was changed from March 25 to January 01.

Until fairly recently, nobody agreed on the proper display format for dates. Every nation seems to have its own commercial conventions. Most of us know that Americans put the month before the day and the British do the reverse, but do you know any other national conventions? National date formats may be confusing when used in an international environment. When it was '12/16/95' in Boston, it was '16/12/95' in London, '16.12.95' in Berlin and '95-12-16' in Stockholm. Then there are conventions within industries within each country that complicate matters further.

At one time, NATO tried to use Roman numerals for the month to avoid language problems among treaty members. The United States Army did a study and found that the four-digit year, three-letter month, and two-digit day format was the least likely to be missorted, misread, or miswritten by English speakers. That is also the reason for "24 hour" or "military" time.

Today, we have a standard for this: ISO-8601 "Data Elements and Interchange Formats—Information Interchange—Representation of Dates and Times" that is part of Standard SQL and other ISO standards.

The full ISO-8601 timestamp can be either a local time or a UTC time. UTC is the code for "Universal Coordinated Time," which replaced the older GMT, which was the code for "Greenwich Mean Time," which is still improperly used in popular media.

In 1970, the Coordinated Universal Time system was devised by an international advisory group of technical experts within the International Telecommunication Union (ITU). The ITU felt it was best to designate a single abbreviation for use in all languages in order to minimize confusion. The two alternative original abbreviation proposals for the "Universal Coordinated Time" were CUT (English: Coordinated Universal Time) and TUC (French: Temps Universel Coordinne). UTC was selected both as a compromise between the French and English proposals because the C at the end looks more like an index in UT0, UT1, UT2 and a mathematical-style notation is always the most international approach.

Universal Coordinated Time is not quite the same thing as astronomical time. The Earth wobbles a bit and the UTC had to be adjusted to the solar year with a leap second added or removed once a year to keep them in synch. As of this writing, Universal Coordinated Time will be based on an atomic clock without a leap second adjustment.

This extra second has screwed up software. In 1998, the leap second caused a mobile-phone blackout across the southern United States because different regions were suddenly operating with time differences outside the error tolerances. Then in 2012, an airline's booking system went belly-up for hours after a leap second insertion. Most nations want to move to an atomic clock, but not all. Britain wants to keep the leap second. Most countries are happy to let the clocks drift away from "solar time." The reason for Britain's reticence is largely a Luddite reaction to change. In 2014, the UK government launched a public opinion poll on the issue. As of this writing, the outcome is not known, so you will have to Google it.

Another problem is the use of local time zones (four of them in the United States) and "lawful time" to worry about. This is the technical term for time required by law for commerce. Usually, this means whether or not you use Daylight Saving Time (DST) and how it is defined locally. A date without a time zone is ambiguous in a distributed system. A transaction created with

DATE '1995-12-17' in London may be younger than a transaction created with DATE '1995-12-16' in Boston.

12.2 The Nature of Temporal Data Models

There is a joke about a father showing his young son, who has only seen digital clocks and watches, an old pocket watch with a sweeping second hand.

"What is it, Daddy?"

"It's a watch! This is how we used to tell time."

"HOW!? It is always changing!"

Time is not a simple thing. Most data processing done with data that is discrete by its nature. An account number is or is not equal to a value. A measurement has a value to so many decimal places. But time is a continuum, which means that given any two values on the time line, you can find an infinite number of points between them. Then we have the problem of which kind of infinite. Most nonmath majors do not even know that some transfinite numbers are bigger than others.

Do not panic. For purposes of a database, the rule we need to remember is that "Nothing happens instantaneously" in the real world. Einstein declared that duration in time is the fourth dimension that everything must have to exist. But before Einstein, the Greek philosopher Zeno of Elea (circa 490 to 430 BCE) wrote several paradoxes, but the one that will illustrate the point about a continuum versus a discrete set of points is the Arrow Paradox.

Informally, imagine you shoot an arrow into the air. It moves continuously from your bow to the target in some finite amount of time. Look at any *instant* in that period of time. The arrow cannot be moving during that instant because an instant has no duration as your arrow cannot be in two different places at the same time. Therefore, at every instant in time, the arrow is motionless. If this is true for all instants of time, then the arrow is motionless during the entire interval. The fallacy is that there is no such thing as an instant in time. But the Greeks only had geometry and the ideas of the continuum had to wait for Calculus. If you want more details on the topic, get a copy of A TOUR OF THE CALCULUS by David Berlinski (ISBN10: 0-679-74788-5) that traces the historical development of calculus from Zeno (about 450 BC) to Cauchy in the 19th Century.

The ISO model for temporal values is based on half-open intervals. This means there is a starting point, but the interval never gets to the ending

point. For example, the day begins at '2016-01-01 00:00:00' exactly, but it does not end at '2016-01-02 00:00:00'; instead, it *approaches the start of the next day as limit*. Depending on how much decimal precision we have, '2016-01-01 23:59:59.999..' is the end point approximation. I just need to have at least one more fractional part than my data (Figure 12.1).

Half-open intervals can be abutted to each other to produce another half-open interval. Two overlapping half-open intervals produce a half-open interval. Likewise, if you remove a half-open interval from another half-open interval, you get one or two half-open intervals. This is called closure and it is a nice mathematical property to have.

12.3 SQL Temporal Data Types

Standard SQL has a very complete description of its temporal data types. There are rules for converting from numeric and character strings into these data types, and there is a schema table for global time-zone information that is used to make sure that temporal data types are synchronized. It is so complete and elaborate that smaller SQLs have not implemented it yet. As an international standard, SQL has to handle time for the whole world and most of us work with only local time. If you have ever tried to figure out the time in a foreign city to place a telephone call, you have some idea of what is involved.

The common terms and conventions related to time are also confusing. We talk about "an hour" and use the term to mean a particular point within the cycle of a day (The train arrives at 13:00 Hrs) or to mean an interval of time not connected to another unit of measurement (The train takes three hours to get there), the number of days in a month is not uniform, the number of days in a year is not uniform, weeks are not easily related to months, and so on.

Standard SQL has a set of date, time (DATE, TIME, and TIMESTAMP), and INTERVALs (DAY, HOUR, MINUTE, and SECOND with decimal fraction) data types. They are made up of fields which are ordered within the

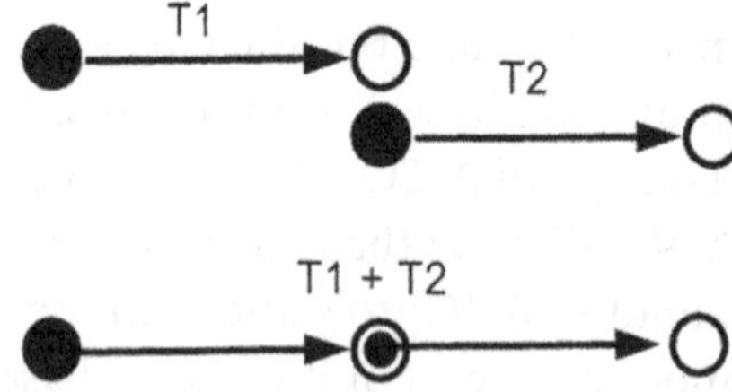

Figure 12.1 Abutted Half-Open Time Intervals.

value; they are YEAR, MONTH, DAY, HOUR, MINUTE, and SECOND. This is the only place in SQL that we use the term "field"; new SQL programmers too often confuse the term field as used in file systems with the column concept in RDBMS. They are very different.

Both of these are temporal data types, but datetimes represent points in the time line, while the interval data types are *durations* of time, not anchored at a point on the timeline. Standard SQL also has a full set of operators for these data types. But you will still find vendor syntax in most SQL implementations today.

12.3.1 Tips for Handling Dates, Timestamps, and Times

The syntax and power of date, timestamp, and time features vary so much from product to product that it is impossible to give anything but general advice. This chapter will assume that you have simple date arithmetic in your SQL, but you might find that some library functions would let you do a better job than what you see here. Please continue to check your manuals until the Standard SQL operators are implemented.

As a general statement, there are two ways of representing temporal data internally. The "UNIX representation" is based on keeping a single binary string of 64 or more bits that counts the computer clock ticks from a base starting date and time. The other representation is I will call the "COBOL method," as it uses separate fields for the year, month, day, hours, minutes, and seconds. These fields can be characters, BCD, or other another internal format.

The UNIX method is very good for calculations, but the engine must convert from the external ISO-8601 format to the internal format and vice versa. The COBOL format is the opposite, good for display purposes, but weaker on calculations.

12.3.2 Date Format Standards

There are three basic display formats in the ISO standards. They are all digits separated by punctuation of some kind.

Calendar date: It is a string of digits that is made up of the four-digit year, a dash, two-digit month, dash, and a two-digit day within the month. Example: '2015-06-25' for June 25, 2015. *This is the only date display format allowed in ANSI/ISO Standard SQL*. However, The ISO-8601 standards allow you to drop the dashes and write the data as a string of all digits.

Ordinal date: It is a string of digits that is made up of the four-digit year, a dash, and the three-digit ordinal number of the day within the year expressed as '001' through '365' or '366' as appropriate. Example: '2015-176' for June 25, 2015.

Week date: It is a string of digits that is made up of the four-digit year, a 'W,' the two-digit ordinal number of the week within the year expressed as '01' through '52' or '53' as appropriate, a dash, and a single digit from 1 to 7 for day within the week (1 = Monday, 7 = Sunday). Very often the week day is not used. Example: '2015W26' is the week from '2015-06-22' to '2015-06-28,' which includes '2015W26-05' for June 25, 2015.

Weeks do not align to calendar dates, so a week can cross over year boundaries. The first week of the year is the week that contains that year's first Thursday (first four-day week of the year). The highest week number in a year is either 52 or 53.

Time Periods: Longer periods can be modeled by truncating the finer fields in these display formats. Thus a whole year can be shown with four digits, the year-month period with "yyyy-mm," and we are also ready to show a whole week. None of this is part of SQL but the concept is useful, and you may have to invent your own names for such things in look-up tables.

I like the MySQL convention of using double zeroes for months and years, That is, 'yyyy-mm-00' for a month within a year and 'yyyy-00-00' for the whole year. The advantages are that it will sort with the ISO-8601 data format required by Standard SQL and it is language independent. The regular expression patterns for validation are '[12][0-9][0-9][0-9]-00-00' and '[12][0-9][0-9][0-9]-[01][0-9]-00,' respectively. You will need to create a look-up table with the time period name and the start and end timestamps for it.

12.3.3 Time Format Standards

TIME(n) is made up of a two-digit hour between '00' and '23,' colon, a two-digit minute between '00' and '59,' colon, and a two-digit second between '00' and '59' or '60,' if the leap second is still in use. Seconds can also have decimal places shown by (n) from zero to an implementation-defined accuracy. The FIPS-127 standard requires at least five decimal places after the second and modern products typically go to seven decimal places.

We do not use the old AM and PM postfixes any ISO Standards. There is no such time as 24:00:00; this *00:00:00 of the next day*. However, some SQLs will accept 24:00:00 as input and put it in the proper format. These values make little sense outside of a timestamp.

TIMESTAMP(n) values is made up of a date, a space, and a time. The ISO standards allow the space to be replaced by the letter 'T' to put the timestamp into a single string and for the punctuation to be removed. *The SQL standard does not.*

Remember that a TIMESTAMP will read the system clock once and use that same time on all the items involved in a transaction. It does not matter if the actual time it took to complete the transaction was days; a transaction in SQL is done as a whole unit or is not done at all. This is not usually a problem for small transactions, but it can be in large batched ones where very complex updates have to be done.

TIMESTAMP as a source of unique identifiers is fine in many single-user systems, as all transactions are serialized and of short enough duration that the clock will change between transactions-peripherals are slower than CPUs. But in a client/server system, two transactions can occur at the same time on different local workstations. Using the local client machine clock can create duplicates and adds the problem of coordinating all the clients. The coordination problem has two parts:

1. How do you get the clocks to start at the same time? I do not mean just the technical problem of synchronizing multiple machines to the microsecond but also the one or two clients who forgot about Daylight Saving Time.
2. How do you make sure the clocks stay the same? Using the server clock to send a timestamp back to the client increases network traffic yet does not always solve the problem.

The modern solution is to use the NIST time signal to set and synchronize all clocks, not just those in computers. Official U.S. Government time, as provided by NIST and USNO (U.S. Naval Observatory), is available on the Internet at http://www.time.gov. NIST also offers an Internet Time Service (ITS) and an Automated Computer Time Service (ACTS) that allow setting of computer and other clocks through the Internet or over standard commercial telephone lines. Free software for using these services on several types of popular computers can be downloaded there. The NIST Website has information on time and frequency standards and research.

Many operating systems represent the system time as a long binary string based on a count of machine cycles since a starting date. One trick is to pull off the least significant digits of this number and use them as a

key. But this will not work as transaction volume increases. Adding more decimal places to the timestamp is not a solution either. The real problem lies in statistics.

Open a telephone book (white pages) at random. Mark the last two digits of any 13 consecutive numbers, which will give you a sample of numbers between 00 and 99. What are the odds that you will have a pair of identical numbers? It is not 1 in 100, as you might first think. Start with one number and add a second number to the set; the odds that the second number does not match the first are 99/100. Add a third number to the set; the odds that it matches neither the first nor the second number are 98/100. Continue this line of reasoning and compute (0.99 * 0.98 * ··· * 0.88) = 0.4427 as the odds of not finding a pair. Therefore, the odds that you will find a pair are 0.5572, a bit better than even. By the time you get to 20 numbers, the odds of a match are about 87%; at 30 numbers, the odds exceed a 99% probability of one match. You might want to carry out this model for finding a pair in three-digit numbers and see when you pass the 50% mark.

A good key generator needs to eliminate (or at least minimize) identical keys and give a statistical distribution that is fairly uniform to avoid excessive index reorganization problems. Most key-generator algorithms that use the system clock depend on one or more "near key" values, such as employee name, to create a unique identifier.

The mathematics of such algorithms is much like that of a hashing algorithm. Hashing algorithms also try to obtain a uniform distribution of unique values. The difference is that a hashing algorithm must ensure that a hash result is both unique (after collision resolution) and repeatable so that it can find the stored data. A key generator needs only to ensure that the resulting key is unique in the database, which is why it can use the system clock and a hashing algorithm cannot.

You can often use a random-number generator in the host language to create pseudo-random numbers to insert into the database for these purposes. Most pseudo-random number generators will start with an initial value, called a seed, and then use it to create a sequence of numbers. Each call will return the next value in the sequence to the calling program. The sequence will have some of the statistical properties of a real random sequence, but the same seed will produce the same sequence each time, which is why the numbers are called pseudo-random numbers. This also means that if the sequence ever repeats a number it will begin to cycle. (This is not usually a problem, as the size of the cycle can be hundreds of thousands or even millions of numbers.)

12.3.4 Basic Time

You should use a "24-hour" time format, which is less prone to errors than 12-hour (AM/PM) time, as it is less likely to be misread or miswritten. This format can be manually sorted more easily and is less prone to computational errors. Americans use a colon as a field separator between hours, minutes, and seconds; some Europeans use a period. This is not a problem for them, as they also use a comma for a decimal point.

One of the major problems with time is that there are three kinds: fixed events (He arrives at 13:00 Hrs), intervals (The trip takes three hours), and durations (The train leaves at 10:00 Hrs and arrives at 13:00 Hrs)—which are all interrelated. An INTERVAL is a *unit of duration* of time rather than a *fixed point* in time. This comes from the fact that time is an interval scale.

12.3.5 Time Zones

Older, smaller databases live and work in one time zone. The system clock is set to local time and the DBA ignores the complications like leap seconds, DST, and time zones. Standard SQL uses only UTC and converts it to local time with TIMEZONE_HOUR and TIMEZONE_MINUTE fields at the end. These fields give the time-zone displacement for local times in that column or temporal variable.

There are also three-letter and four-letter codes for the time zones of the world, such as EST, for Eastern Standard Time, in the United States. But these codes are not universal. For example, all of these time zones are UTC—3 hours

Time-Zone Code	Time-Zone Name	Where Used
ADT	Atlantic Daylight Time	Atlantic
BRT	Brasília Time	South America
CLST	Chile Summer Time	South America
GFT	French Guiana Time	South America
WGT	West Greenland Time	North America

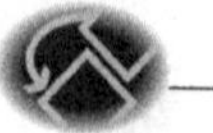

The closest thing to a universal naming convention for time zones is the Military alphabet code.

Time-Zone Code	Time-Zone Name	Displacement from UTC
A	Alpha Time Zone	+1 hour
B	Bravo Time Zone	+2 hours
C	Charlie Time Zone	+3 hours
D	Delta Time Zone	+4 hours
E	Echo Time Zone	+5 hours
F	Foxtrot Time Zone	+6 hours
G	Golf Time Zone	+7 hours
H	Hotel Time Zone	+8 hours
I	India Time Zone	+9 hours
K	Kilo Time Zone	+10 hours
L	Lima Time Zone	+11 hours
M	Mike Time Zone	+12 hours
N	November Time Zone	−1 hour
O	Oscar Time Zone	−2 hours
P	Papa Time Zone	−3 hours
Q	Quebec Time Zone	−4 hours
R	Romeo Time Zone	−5 hours
S	Sierra Time Zone	−6 hours
T	Tango Time Zone	−7 hours
U	Uniform Time Zone	−8 hours
V	Victor Time Zone	−9 hours
W	Whiskey Time Zone	−10 hours
X	X-ray Time Zone	−11 hours
Y	Yankee Time Zone	−12 hours
Z	Zulu Time Zone	UTC

This is why UTC is sometimes called "Zulu time" and the letter Z is used as punctuation between the timestamp and the displacement in ISO-8601.

The offset is usually a positive or negative number of hours, but there are still a few odd zones that differ by 15 or 30 minutes from the expected pattern.

The TIMESTAMP data type is a DATE and a TIME put together in one values (e.g., '2017-05-03 05:30:06.123'). There are some variations from DBMS to DBMS though. For example, the time component of DB2 TIMESTAMP data is configurable and can be more precise than DB2 TIME data. This is what CURRENT_TIMESTAMP returns from the system clock in a program, query, or statement. However, SQL dialects will still use NOW, getdate(), and other proprietary reserved words.

TIMESTAMP WITH TIME ZONE or TIMESTAMPTZ data types are a TIMESTAMP but include the time zone's displacement from UTC. The standards allow for TZD (time-zone designator), 'Z' or a positive or negative hour to minute interval (+hh:mm or –hh:mm). Standard SQL uses the last option.

CURRENT_TIMESTAMP is a representation of the current date and time with time zone. LOCALTIMESTAMP is a representation of the current date and time but without a time zone.

Now you have to factor in Daylight Saving Time on top of that to get what is called "lawful time" which is the basis for legal agreements. The U.S. government uses DST on federal lands inside of states that do not use DST. You can get a mix of gaps and duplicate times in the local lawful time display over a year. This is why Standard SQL uses UTC internally.

Vendors often have a system configuration parameter to set the local time zone and other options. You need to know your SQL and not get caught in this.

12.4 INTERVAL Data Types

INTERVAL data types are used to represent temporal duration. They come in two basic types, intervals that deal with the calendar and those that deal with the clock. The year-month intervals have an express or implied precision that includes no fields other than YEAR and MONTH, though it is not necessary to use both. The other class, called day-time intervals, has an express or implied interval precision that can include any fields other than YEAR or MONTH—that is, DAY, HOUR, MINUTE, and SECOND (with decimal places).

The units of time in an SQL temporal value are called fields; do not confuse this with the term "fields" are use with non_RDBMS file systems. The fields in the interval have to be in high to low order without missing fields.

Field	Inclusive Value Limit
YEAR	'0001' to '9999'; follows the ISO-8601 Standard
MONTH	'01' to '12'; the value 12 might be rounded to 1 year
DAY	'01' to '31'; must be valid for month and year
HOUR	'00' to '23'; value 24 might be rounded to the day
MINUTE	'00' to '59'; watch for leap seconds!
SECOND	'00' to '59.999..'; precision is implementation defined

SECOND are integers and have precision 2 when not the first field. SECOND, however, can be defined to have an <interval fractional seconds precision> that indicates the number of decimal digits maintained following the decimal point in the seconds value. When not the first field, SECOND has a precision of two places before the decimal point.

The datetime literals are not surprising in that they follow the syntax used by ISO-8601 Standards with the dashes between the fields in dates and colons between the field times. The strings are always quoted. The interval qualifier follows the keyword `INTERVAL` when specifying an `INTERVAL` data type.

The following table lists the valid interval qualifiers for `YEAR-MONTH` intervals:

Interval Qualifier	Description
YEAR	An interval class describing a number of years
MONTH	An interval class describing a number of months
YEAR TO MONTH	An interval class describing a number of years and months

The following table lists the valid interval qualifiers for DAY-TIME intervals:

Interval Qualifier	Description
DAY	Plus or minus a number of days
HOUR	Plus or minus a number of hours
MINUTE	Plus or minus a number of minutes
SECOND(s)	Plus or minus a number of seconds (decimals are allowed)
DAY TO HOUR	Plus or minus a number of days and hours
DAY TO MINUTE	Plus or minus a number of days, hours, and minutes
DAY TO SECOND(s)	Plus or minus a number of days, hours, minutes, and seconds
HOUR TO MINUTE	Plus or minus a number of hours and minutes
HOUR TO SECOND(s)	Plus or minus a number of hours, minutes, and seconds
MINUTE TO SECOND(s)	Plus or minus a number of minutes and seconds

Here is a sample query that shows all of the INTERVAL types in use:

```
SELECT CURRENT_TIMESTAMP + INTERVAL '+7' YEAR,
       CURRENT_TIMESTAMP + INTERVAL '-3' MONTH,
       CURRENT_TIMESTAMP + INTERVAL '0007 03' YEAR TO MONTH,
       CURRENT_TIMESTAMP + INTERVAL '+5' DAY,
       CURRENT_TIMESTAMP + INTERVAL '-5' HOUR,
       CURRENT_TIMESTAMP + INTERVAL '12' MINUTE,
       CURRENT_TIMESTAMP + INTERVAL '3' SECOND,
       CURRENT_TIMESTAMP + INTERVAL '1 12' DAY TO HOUR,
       CURRENT_TIMESTAMP + INTERVAL '1 12:35' DAY TO MINUTE,
       CURRENT_TIMESTAMP + INTERVAL '1 12:35:45' DAY TO SECOND,
       CURRENT_TIMESTAMP + INTERVAL '01:12' HOUR TO MINUTE,
       CURRENT_TIMESTAMP + INTERVAL '01:12:35' HOUR TO SECOND,
       CURRENT_TIMESTAMP + INTERVAL '01:12' MINUTE TO SECOND
  FROM Dummy;
```

Notice that the quoted strings in the HOUR TO MINUTE and MINUTE TO SECOND example are the same but have different meanings. A timestamp literal can also include a time-zone interval to change it from a UTC time to a local time.

12.5 Queries with Date Arithmetic

Almost every SQL implementation has a DATE data type, but the proprietary functions available for them vary quite a bit. The most common ones are a constructor that builds a date from integers or strings; extractors to pull out the month, day, or year; and some display options to format output.

You can assume that your SQL implementation has simple date arithmetic functions, although with different syntax from product to product, such as

1. A date plus or minus a number of days yields a new date.
2. A date minus a second date yields an integer number of days between the dates.

Here is a table of the valid combinations of <datetime> and <interval> data types in the Standard SQL standard:

<datetime> − <datetime> = <interval>

<datetime>+<interval>=<datetime>

<interval> (* or/) <numeric>=<interval>

<interval>+<datetime>=<datetime>

<interval>+<interval>=<interval>

<numeric> * <interval>=<interval>

There are other rules, which deal with time zones and the relative precision of the two operands that are intuitively obvious.

The Standard CURRENT_DATE function that returns the current date from the system clock. However, you will still find vendor dialects with odd names for the same function, such as TODAY, SYSDATE, Now(), and getdate(). There may also be a function to return the day of the week from a date, which is sometimes called DOW() or WEEKDAY(). Standard SQL provides for CURRENT_DATE, CURRENT_TIME [(<time precision>)], CURRENT_TIMESTAMP [(<timestamp precision>)], and LOCALTIMESTAMP functions, which are self-explanatory.

12.6 Use of NULL for "Eternity"

The temporal model in SQL does not have a symbol for "eternity in the future" or "eternity in the past," so you have to work around it for some applications. The IEEE floating point standard does have both a "–inf" and "+inf" symbol to handle this problem in the continuum model for real numbers. In fact, SQL can "only" represent timestamps in the range of years from 0001 CE up to 9999 CE. Usually, this range is good enough for most applications outside of archeology.

For example, when someone checks into a hotel, we know their arrival data, but we not know their departure date (an expected departure date is not the same thing as an actual one). All we know for certain is that it has to be after their arrival date. A NULL will act as a "place holder" until we get the actual departure date. The skeleton DDL for such a table would look like this:

```
CREATE TABLE Hotel_Register
(patron_id INTEGER NOT NULL
  REFERENCES Patrons (patron_id),
 arrival_date TIMESTAMP(0) DEFAULT CURRENT_TIMESTAMP NOT NULL,
```

```
departure_date TIMESTAMP(0), -- null means guest still here
CONSTRAINT arrive_before_depart
  CHECK (arrival_date <= departure_date),
..);
```

When getting reports, you will need to use the current timestamp in place of the NULL to accurately report the current billing.

```
SELECT patron_id, arrival_date,
       COALESCE (CURRENT_TIMESTAMP, departure_date)
       AS departure_date
  FROM HotelRegister
WHERE ..;
```

12.7 The OVERLAPS() Predicate

The OVERLAPS() predicate is a feature still not available in most SQL implementations because it requires more of the Standard SQL temporal data features than most implementations have. You can "fake it" in many products with the BETWEEN predicate and careful use of constraints.

The result of the <OVERLAPS predicate> is formally defined as the result of the following expression:

```
(S1 > S2 AND NOT (S1 >= T2 AND T1 >= T2))
OR (S2 > S1 AND NOT (S2 >= T1 AND T2 >= T1))
OR (S1 = S2 AND (T1 <> T2 OR T1 = T2))
```

where S1 and S2 are the starting times of the two time periods and T1 and T2 are their termination times. The rules for the OVERLAPS() predicate sound like they should be intuitive, but they are not. The principles that we wanted in the Standard were:

1. A time period includes its starting point but does not include its end point. We have already discussed this model and its closure properties.

2. If the time periods are not "instantaneous," they overlap when they share a common time period.

3. If the first term of the predicate is an INTERVAL and the second term is an instantaneous event (a <datetime> data type), they overlap when the second term is in the time period (but is not the end point of the time period). That follows the half-open model.

4. If the first and second terms are both instantaneous events, they overlap only when they are equal.
5. If the starting time is NULL and the finishing time is a <datetime> value, the finishing time becomes the starting time and we have an event. If the starting time is NULL and the finishing time is an INTERVAL value, then both the finishing and starting times are NULL.

Please consider how your intuition reacts to these results, when the granularity is at the YEAR-MONTH-DAY level. Remember that a day begins at 00:00:00 Hrs.

(today, today) OVERLAPS (today, today) = TRUE
(today, tomorrow) OVERLAPS (today, today) = TRUE
(today, tomorrow) OVERLAPS (tomorrow, tomorrow) = FALSE
(yesterday, today) OVERLAPS (today, tomorrow) = FALSE

Alexander Kuznetsov wrote this idiom for History Tables in T-SQL, but it generalizes to any SQL. It builds a temporal chain from the current row to the previous row. With a self-reference. This is easier to show with code:

```
CREATE TABLE Tasks
(task_id INTEGER NOT NULL,
 task_score CHAR(1) NOT NULL,
 previous_end_date DATE, -- null means first task
 current_start_date DATE DEFAULT CURRENT_TIMESTAMP NOT NULL,
 CONSTRAINT previous_end_date_and_current_start_in_sequence
   CHECK (prev_end_date <= current_start_date)
 DEFERRABLE INITIALLY IMMEDIATE,
 current_end_date DATE, -- null means unfinished current task
 CONSTRAINT current_start_and_end_dates_in_sequence
   CHECK (current_start_date <= current_end_date),
 CONSTRAINT end_dates_in_sequence
   CHECK (previous_end_date <> current_end_date),
 PRIMARY KEY (task_id, current_start_date),
 UNIQUE (task_id, previous_end_date), -- null first task
 UNIQUE (task_id, current_end_date), -- one null current task
```

```
FOREIGN KEY (task_id, previous_end_date) -- self-reference
  REFERENCES Tasks (task_id, current_end_date));
```

Well, that looks complicated. Let's look at it column by column. **Task_id** explains itself. The **previous_end_date** will not have a value for the first task in the chain, so it is NULL-able. The **current_start_date** and **current_end_date** are the same data elements, temporal sequence and PRIMARY KEY constraints we had in the simple history table schema.

The two UNIQUE constraints will allow one NULL in their pairs of columns and prevent duplicates. Remember that UNIQUE is NULL-able, not like PRIMARY KEY, which implies UNIQUE NOT NULL.

Finally, the FOREIGN KEY is the real trick. Obviously, the previous task has to end when the current task started for them to abut, so there is another constraint. This constraint is a self-reference that makes sure this is true. Modifying data in this type of table is easy but requires some thought.

Just one little problem with that FOREIGN KEY constraint. It will not let you put the first task into the table. There is nothing for the constraint to reference. In Standard SQL, we can declare constraints to be DEFERABLE with some other options. The idea is that you can turn a constraint ON or OFF during a session, so the database can be in state that would otherwise be illegal. But at the end of the session, all constraints have to be TRUE or UNKNOWN.

When a disabled constraint is re-enabled, the database does not check to ensure any of the existing data meets the constraints. You will want to hide this in a procedure body to get things started.

12.8 State-Transition Constraints

Transition constraints force status changes to occur in a particular order over time. A state-transition diagram is the best to show the rules. There is at least one initial state, flow lines that show what are the next legal states, and one or more termination states. Here is a simple state change diagram of possible marital states (Figure 12.2).

This state-transition diagram was deliberately simplified, but it is good enough to explain principles. To keep the discussion as simple as possible, my table is for only one person's marital status over his life. Here is a skeleton DDL with the needed FOREIGN KEY reference to valid state changes and the date that the current state started.

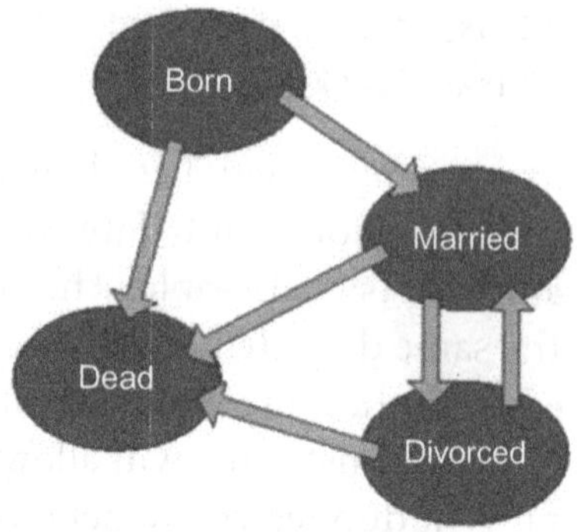

Figure 12.2 Simple Marital State Change Diagram.

```
CREATE TABLE MyLife
(previous_state VARCHAR(10) NOT NULL,
 current_state VARCHAR(10) NOT NULL,
 CONSTRAINT Improper_State_Change
   FOREIGN KEY (previous_state, current_state)
   REFERENCES StateChanges (previous_state, current_state),
  start_date DATE NOT NULL PRIMARY KEY,
  --etc.
);
```

What is not shown on it are which nodes are initial states (in this case "Born") and which are terminal or final states (in this case "Dead," a very terminal state of being). A terminal node can be the current state of a middle node, but not a prior state. Likewise, an initial node can be the prior state of a middle node, but not the current state. I did not write any CHECK() constraints for those conditions. It is easy enough to write a quick query with an EXISTS() predicate to do this, and I will leave that as an exercise for the reader. Let's load the diagram into an auxiliary table with some more constraints.

```
CREATE TABLE StateChanges
(previous_state VARCHAR(10) NOT NULL,
 current_state VARCHAR(10) NOT NULL,
 PRIMARY KEY (previous_state, current_state),
 state_type CHAR(1) DEFAULT 'M' NOT NULL
 CHECK (state_type IN ('I', 'T', 'M')), -- initial, terminal, middle
```

```
CONSTRAINT Node_Type_Violations
CHECK (CASE WHEN state_type IN ('I', 'T')
            AND previous_state = current_state
            THEN 'T'
            WHEN state_type = 'M'
            AND previous_state <> current_state
            THEN 'T' ELSE 'F' END = 'T'));

INSERT INTO StateChanges
 VALUES ('Born', 'Born', 'I'), -- initial state
        ('Born', 'Married', 'M'),
        ('Born', 'Dead', 'M'),
        ('Married', 'Divorced', 'M'),
        ('Married', 'Dead', 'M'),
        ('Divorced', 'Married', 'M'),
        ('Divorced', 'Dead', 'M'),
        ('Dead', 'Dead', 'T'); -- terminal state
```

We want to see a temporal path from an initial state to a terminal state. State changes do not happen all at once but are spread over time. Some of the changes are controlled by time, some by an agent. I cannot get married immediately after being born but have to wait to be of legal age. Then I have to consent.

For a real production system, you would need a more state pairs, but it is easy to expand the table.

```
CREATE PROCEDURE Change_State
(in_change_date DATE,
 in_change_state VARCHAR(10))
LANGUAGE SQL
DETERMINISTIC
BEGIN
DECLARE most_recent_state VARCHAR(10);
SET most_recent_state
    = (SELECT current_state
         FROM MyLife
        WHERE start_date
              = (SELECT MAX(start_date) FROM MyLife));
```

```
-- insert initial state if empty
IF NOT EXISTS (SELECT * FROM MyLife)
   AND in_change_state
       IN (SELECT previous_state
            FROM StateChanges
           WHERE state_type = 'I')
THEN
INSERT INTO MyLife (previous_state, current_state, start_date)
VALUES (in_change_state, in_change_state, in_change_date);
END IF;

-- must be a real state change
IF in_change_state = most_recent_state
THEN SIGNAL SQLSTATE '75002'
         SET MESSAGE_TEXT = 'This does not change the state.';
END IF;

-- must move forward in time
IF in_change_date <= (SELECT MAX(start_date) FROM MyLife)
THEN SIGNAL SQLSTATE '75003'
         SET MESSAGE_TEXT = 'Violates time sequence.';
END IF;

INSERT INTO MyLife (previous_state, current_state, start_date)
VALUES (most_recent_state, in_change_state, in_change_date);
END;
```

The first block of code locates the most recent state of my life based on the date. The second block of code will insert an initial state if the table is empty. This is a safety feature but there probably ought to be a separate procedure to create the set of initial states. The new state has to be an actual change, so there is a block of code to be sure. The changes have to move forward in time. Finally, we build a row using the most recent state as the new previous state, the input change state and the date. If the state change is illegal, the FOREIGN KEY is violated and we get an error.

If you had other business rules, you could also add them to the code in the same way. You should have noticed that if someone makes changes directly to the MyLife Table, they are pretty much free to screw up the data. It is a good idea to have a procedure that checks to see that MyLife is in order. Let's load the table with bad data:

```
INSERT INTO MyLife (previous_state, current_state, start_date)
VALUES ('Born', 'Married', '1990-09-05'),
       ('Married', 'Divorced', '1999-09-05'),
       ('Married', 'Dead', '2010-09-05'),
       ('Dead', 'Dead', '2011-05-10'),
       ('Dead', 'Dead', '2012-05-10');
```

This poor guy popped into existence without being properly born, committed bigamy and died twice. And you think your life is tough. You will need a simple validation procedure to catch those errors.

What is still missing is the temporal aspect of state changes. In this example, the ('Born,' 'Married') change would have to deal with the minimum age of consent. The ('Married,' 'Divorced') change often has a legal waiting period. While technically a business rule, you know that no human being has lived over 150 years, so a gap that size is a data error. The terminal and initial states are instantaneous, however. Let's add more flesh to the skeleton table:

```
CREATE TABLE StateChanges
(previous_state VARCHAR(10) NOT NULL,
 current_state VARCHAR(10) NOT NULL,
 PRIMARY KEY (previous_state, current_state),
 state_type CHAR(1) DEFAULT 'M' NOT NULL
 CHECK (state_type IN ('I', 'T', 'M')), -- initial, terminal, middle
 state_duration INTEGER NOT NULL -- unit of measure is months
   CHECK (state_duration >= 0),
 CONSTRAINT Node_type_violations
 CHECK (CASE WHEN state_type IN ('I', 'T')
             AND previous_state = current_state
             THEN 'T'
             WHEN state_type = 'M'
             AND previous_state <> current_state
             THEN 'T' ELSE 'F' END = 'T')
);
```

To make up some data, let's assume that the age of consent is 18 (12 months * 18 years = 216), that you have to wait 3 months into your marriage before getting a divorce, and that you have to be divorced 2 months before you can remarry. Of course, you can die instantly.

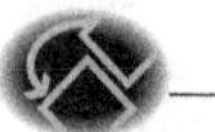

```
INSERT INTO StateChanges
 VALUES ('Born', 'Born', 'I', 0), -- initial state
        ('Born', 'Married', 'M', 216),
        ('Born', 'Dead', 'M', 0),
        ('Married', 'Divorced', 'M', 3),
        ('Married', 'Dead', 'M', 0),
        ('Divorced', 'Married', 'M', 2),
        ('Divorced', 'Dead', 'M', 0),
        ('Dead', 'Dead', 'T', 0); -- terminal state
```

The first question is where to check for temporal violations; during insertion or with validation procedures? My answer is both. Whenever possible, do not knowingly put bad data into a schema, so this should be done in the ChangeState() procedure. But someone or something will subvert the schema, and you have to be able to find and repair the damage.

A lot of commercial situations have a fixed lifespan. Warranties, commercial offers, and bids expire in a known number of days. This means adding another column to the StateChanges table that tells the insertion program if the expiration date is optional (shown with a NULL) or mandatory (computed from the duration).

Here is some skeleton DDL for a bid application to explain this better.

```
CREATE TABLE MyBids
(bid_nbr INTEGER NOT NULL,
 previous_state VARCHAR(10) NOT NULL,
 current_state VARCHAR(10) NOT NULL,
 CONSTRAINT Improper_State_Change
   FOREIGN KEY (previous_state, current_state)
   REFERENCES StateChanges (previous_state, current_state),
  start_date DATE NOT NULL PRIMARY KEY,
  expiry_date DATE, -- null means still open.
    CHECK (start_date <= expiry_date),
 PRIMARY KEY (bid_nbr, start_date),
 etc.
);
```

The DDL has a bid number as the primary key and a new column for the expiration date. Obviously, the bid has to exist for a while, so add a constraint to keep the date order right.

```
CREATE TABLE StateChanges
(previous_state VARCHAR(10) NOT NULL,
 current_state VARCHAR(10) NOT NULL,
 PRIMARY KEY (previous_state, current_state),
 state_duration INTEGER NOT NULL,
 duration_type CHAR(1) DEFAULT 'O' NOT NULL
    CHECK ('O', 'M')), -- optional, mandatory
 etc.
);
```

The DDL for the state changes gets a new column to tell us if the duration is optional or mandatory. The insertion procedure is a bit trickier. The VALUES clause has more power than most programmers use. The list can be more than just constants or simple scalar variables. But using CASE expressions lets you avoid if-then-else procedural logic in the procedure body.

All it needs is the bid number and what state you want to use. If you don't give me a previous state, I assume that this is an initial row and repeat the current state you just gave me. If you don't give me a start date, I assume you want the current date. If you don't give me an expiration date, I construct one from the State Changes table with a scalar subquery. Here is the skeleton DDL for an insertion procedure.

12.9 Calendar Tables

Because the calendar and temporal math are so irregular, build axillary tables for various single day calendars and for period calendars, one column for the calendar date and other columns to show whatever your business needs in the way of temporal information. Do not try to calculate holidays in SQL—Easter alone requires too much math. Oh, which Easter? Catholic or Orthodox?

1. Derek Dongray came up with a classification of the public holidays and weekends he needed to work within multiple countries. Here is his list with more added.
2. Fixed date every year.
3. Days relative to Easter.
4. Fixed date but will slide to next Monday if on a weekend.
5. Fixed date but slides to Monday if Saturday or Tuesday if Sunday (UK Boxing Day is the only one).

6. Specific day of week after a given date (usually first/last Monday in a month but can be other days, e.g., First Thursday after November 22 = Thanksgiving).
7. Days relative to Greek Orthodox Easter (not always the same as Western Easter) Fixed date in Hijri (Muslim) Calendar—this turns out to only be approximate due to the way the calendar works. An Imam has to see a full moon to begin the cycle and declare it.
8. Days relative to previous Winter Solstice (Chinese holiday of Qing Ming Ji). Civil holidays set by decree, such as a National Day of Mourning due to an unscheduled event.
9. Fixed date except Saturday slides to Friday, and Sunday slides to Monday.
10. Fixed date, but Tuesday slides to Monday, and Thursday to Friday. The day Columbus discovered America is a national holiday in Argentina. Except when it's a Tuesday, they back it one day to Monday.

As you can see, some of these are getting a bit esoteric and a bit fuzzy. A calendar table for U.S. Secular holidays can be built from the data at http://www.smart.net/~mmontes/ushols.html.

You will probably want a fiscal calendar in this table. Which fiscal calendar? The GAAP (General Accepted Accounting Practices) lists over a hundred of them.

I would add the ordinal date and week date, which we discussed earlier. They make temporal math much easier.

The Julian business day is a good trick. Number the days from whenever your calendar starts and repeat a number for a weekend or company holiday. This counts business days.

```
CREATE TABLE Calendar
CREATE TABLE Calendar
(cal_date DATE NOT NULL PRIMARY KEY,
 julian_business_nbr INTEGER NOT NULL,
 ...);
INSERT INTO Calendar VALUES ('2007-04-05', 42),
 ('2007-04-06', 43), -- good Friday
 ('2007-04-07', 43),
 ('2007-04-08', 43), -- Easter Sunday
 ('2007-04-09', 44),
```

```
('2007-04-10', 45); --Tuesday
```

To compute the business days from Thursday of this week to next Tuesdays:

```
SELECT (C2.julian_business_nbr - C1.julian_business_nbr)
  FROM Calendar AS C1, Calendar AS C2
 WHERE C1.cal_date = '2007-04-05',
   AND C2.cal_date = '2007-04-10';
```

12.9.1 Report Period Tables

Since SQL is a database language, we prefer to do look ups and not calculations. They can be optimized while temporal math messes up optimization. A useful idiom is a report period calendar that everyone uses, so there is no way to get disagreements in the DML.

The report period table gives a name to a range of dates that is common to the entire enterprise.

```
CREATE TABLE Something_Report_Periods
(something_report_name CHAR(10) NOT NULL PRIMARY KEY
   CHECK (something_report_name LIKE <pattern>),
 something_report_start_date DATE NOT NULL,
 something_report_end_date DATE NOT NULL,
  CONSTRAINT date_ordering
    CHECK (something_report_start_date <= something_report_end_date),
etc);
```

These report periods can overlap or have gaps. Avoid period names that are language dependent; they will have trouble porting. If possible the periods name should sort in temporal order. Again, I like the MySQL convention of using double zeroes for months and years, That is, 'yyyy-mm-00' for a month within a year and 'yyyy-00-00' for the whole year. The advantages are that it will sort with the ISO-8601 date format and will go to the top of each year and month within the year.

Overlapping periods are useful for reporting things like sales promotions. You can quickly see if the overlap between your "Bikini Madness Week" and "Three Day Suntan Lotion Promotion" helped increase total sales.

Multiple Column Data Elements

THE CONCEPT OF a data element being atomic or scalar is usually taken to mean that it is represented with a single column in a table. This is not always true. A data element is *atomic* when it cannot be decomposed into independent, meaningful parts. Doing so would result in attribute splitting, a very serious design flaw we discussed in other parts of this book. But *scalar* means it is measured on a scale and has only a magnitude.

Multiple column data elements come in two broad classes. They can be vectors or coordinate systems, in which each column is in some sense equal to the others. Or they can be hierarchical schemes in which the columns have some ordering relationship among themselves.

13.1 Vector and Coordinate Data Elements

A vector is made up of parts that are different in some way, and coordinates are made up of parts that are similar in some way. Consider an (x, y, z) coordinate system. A single x or y or z value identifies a continuum of points, while the pair has to be taken together to give you a plane, still an infinite number of points. It would be inconvenient to put all three coordinates into one column, so we model them in three columns. The math is easier. *This is notation and representation versus the abstract data element.* It is the difference between a number and a numeral system.

An example of a vector encoding might be product codes which require several attributes to make sense. One example is the ISO code for tires; it is made of the diameter of the wheel, the width of the tire, and the material from which it is made, plus other physical characteristics.

Vectors are often written in one column, the parsed out in computed columns or views. Here are some examples of common data elements.

13.1.1 Longitude and Latitude

The (longitude, latitude) pairs we use for geographical locations is the most common example. But if you use the HTM (Hierarchical Triangular Mesh) numbers for a location, you have a single 16-digit number prefixed with a quadrant code instead.

Since geographical data are important, you might find it handy to locate places by their longitude and latitude and then calculate the distances between two points on the globe. This is not a standard function in most SQL products, but it is handy to know.

Assume that we have points (Latitude1, Longitude1) and (Latitude2, Longitude2) which locate the two points, and that they are in radians, and we have trig functions.

To convert decimal degrees to radians, multiply the number of degrees by $\pi/180 = 0.017453293$ radians/degree, where π is approximately 3.14159265358979. If you can get more decimals, do it.

```
CREATE FUNCTION Distance
(IN latitude1 FLOAT, IN longitude1 FLOAT,
 IN latitude2 FLOAT, IN longitude2 FLOAT)
RETURNS FLOAT
LANGUAGE SQL
DETERMINISTIC
BEGIN
  DECLARE r FLOAT;
  DECLARE lat FLOAT;
  DECLARE lon FLOAT;
  DECLARE a FLOAT;
  DECLARE c FLOAT;
  SET r = 6367.00 * 0.6214;
```

```
-- calculate the Deltas...
  SET lon = longitude2 - longitude1;
  SET lat = latitude2 - latitude1;

--Intermediate values...
SET a = SIN(lat / 2) + COS(latitude1)
          * COS(latitude2) * SIN(lon / 2);

--Intermediate result c is the great circle distance in radians...
  SET c = 2 * ARCSIN(CASE WHEN 1.00 < SQRT(a)
                      THEN 1.00 ELSE SQRT(a)END );

--Multiply the radians by the radius to get the distance
  RETURN (r * c);
END;
```

The CASE expression protects against possible round off errors that could sabotage computation of the ARCSIN() if the two points are very nearly antipodal. Scott Coleman pointed out that the calculation of distance between two points using standard spherical geometry can be inaccurate for short distances (10 miles or less) because the sine function of very small angles approaches zero. The haversine approach (http://en.wikipedia.org/wiki/Haversine_formula) turns this around, so it is very accurate at small distances but has larger errors (about 10 miles) for points on opposite sides of the earth.

```
CREATE FUNCTION Haversine_Distance
      (rlat1 FLOAT, rlon1 FLOAT, rlat2 FLOAT, rlon2 FLOAT)
RETURNS FLOAT
LANGUAGE SQL
DETERMINISTIC
BEGIN
--parameters are in radians

DECLARE c FLOAT;
SET c = POWER(SIN((rlat2 - rlat1) / 2.0)), 2)
     + COS(rlat1) * COS(rlat2) * POWER (SIN((rlon2 - rlon1) / 2.0), 2);

RETURN (3956.088331329 * (2.0 * ATN2(SQRT(c), SQRT(1.0 - c))));
END;
```

Notice there is an assumption of trig functions in your SQL. If you need to convert from degrees, use:

```
SET DegToRad = CAST (180.0 / PI AS DOUBLE PRECISION)
```

And use it as a divisor. The atan2(x, y) function is used to convert from Cartesian(x, y) to polar (theta, radius) coordinates.

13.1.2 Storing an IPv4 Address in SQL

While not exactly a data type, IP addresses are being used as unique identifiers for people or companies. If you need to verify them, you can send an email or ping them. There are three popular ways to store an IP address: a string, an integer, and a set of four octets.

In a test conducted in SQL Server, all three methods required about the same amount of time, work, and I/O to return data as a string. The latter two have some additional computations, but the overhead was not enough to affect performance very much.

The conclusion was that the octet model with four TINYINT columns had three advantages: simpler programming indexes on individual octets, and human readability. But you should look at what happens in your own environment. TINYINT is a one-bit integer data type found in SQL Server and other products; SMALLINT is the closest to it in Standard SQL.

13.1.3 A Single VARCHAR(15) Column

The most obvious way to store IP addresses in a VARCHAR(15) column, like this '63.246.173.210,' with a CHECK() constraint that uses a SIMILAR TO predicate to be sure that it has the "dots and digits" in the right positions. You have to decide the meaning of leading zeros in an octet and trim them to do string comparisons.

The good points are that programming is reasonably simple and it is immediately human readable. The bad points are that this has a higher storage costs and it needs pattern matching string functions in searches. It is also harder to pass to some host programs that expect to see the octets to make their IP connections.

To convert the string into octets, you need to use a string procedure. You can write one based on the code given for parsing a comma-separated string into individual integers in Section 22.1 on using the Sequence auxiliary table.

13.1.4 One INTEGER Column

This has the lowest storage requirements of all the methods, and it keeps the address in one column. Searching and indexing are also minimal.

The bad side is more that programming is much more complex and you need to write user functions to break it apart into octets. It is also not very human readable. Given an INTEGER value like 2130706433, can you tell me it represents '127.0.0.1' on sight?

```
CREATE FUNCTION IP_Integer_To_String (IN ip INTEGER)
RETURNS VARCHAR(15)
LANGUAGE SQL
DETERMINISTIC
BEGIN
DECLARE o1 INTEGER;
DECLARE o2 INTEGER;
DECLARE o3 INTEGER;
DECLARE o4 INTEGER;

IF ABS(ip) > 2147483647
THEN RETURN '255.255.255.255';
END IF;

SET o1 = ip / 16777216;
IF o1 = 0
THEN SET o1 = 255;
     SET ip = ip + 16777216;
ELSE IF o1 < 0
     THEN IF MOD(ip, 16777216) = 0
  THEN SET o1 = o1 + 256;
  ELSE SET o1 = o1 + 255;
       IF o1 = 128
       THEN SET ip = ip + 2147483648;
       ELSE SET ip = ip + (16777216 * (256 - o1));
       END IF;
  END IF;
    ELSE SET ip = ip - (16777216 * o1);
    END IF;
END IF;
```

```
SET ip = MOD(ip, 16777216);
SET o2 = ip / 65536;
SET ip = MOD(ip, 65536);
SET o3 = ip / 256;
SET ip = MOD(ip, 256);
SET o4 = ip;

-- return the string
RETURN
CAST(o1 AS VARCHAR(3)) || '.' ||
CAST(o2 AS VARCHAR(3)) || '.' ||
CAST(o3 AS VARCHAR(3)) || '.' ||
CAST(o4 AS VARCHAR(3));
END;
```

13.1.5 Four SMALLINT Columns

The good points are that this has a lower storage cost than VARCHAR(15), searching is easy and relatively fast, and you can index on each octet of the address. If you have an SQL with a TINYINT (usually one byte) data type, then you can save even more space.

The bad point is that programming is slightly more complex.

```
CREATE TABLE FourColumnIP
(octet1 SMALLINT NOT NULL
        CHECK (octet1 BETWEEN 0 AND 255),
 octet2 SMALLINT NOT NULL
        CHECK (octet2 BETWEEN 0 AND 255),
 octet3 SMALLINT NOT NULL
        CHECK (octet3 BETWEEN 0 AND 255),
 octet4 SMALLINT NOT NULL
        CHECK (octet4 BETWEEN 0 AND 255),
..);
```

You will need a view for display, but that is straightforward.

```
CREATE VIEW DisplayIP (IP_address_display)
AS
SELECT (CAST(octet1 AS VARCHAR(3))||'.'||
```

```
        CAST(octet2 AS VARCHAR(3))||'.'||
        CAST(octet3 AS VARCHAR(3))||'.'||
        CAST(octet4 AS VARCHAR(3))
FROM FourColumnIP;
```

13.1.6 Storing an IPv6 Address in SQL

The original designers of TCP/IP defined an IP address as a 32-bit number. The Internet Assigned Numbers Authority (IANA) manages the IP address space allocations globally. IANA works in cooperation with five Regional Internet Registries (RIRs) to allocate IP address blocks to Local Internet Registries (Internet service providers) and other entities.

The IP version 6 addresses are huge compared to IPv4 and are not likely to run out anytime soon. The problem is that it is a redesign of the Internet Protocol and not a simple extension. The address size was increased from 32 to 128 bits (16 bytes). The new design is so large that subnet routing prefixes are easy to construct without any kludges. Large blocks can be assigned for efficient routing. Windows Vista, Apple Computer's Mac OS X, Linux distributions, and most other operating systems include native support for the IPv6 protocol.

13.1.7 A Single CHAR(32) Column

The most obvious way to store IPv6 addresses in a CHAR(32) column without the colons or a CHAR(40) column with colons. The hexadecimal display format is a simple fixed format. The letters for 10 (a) through 15 (d) are usually done in lowercase to avoid confusion with digits. Use a CHECK() constraint that uses a SIMILAR TO predicate to be sure that it has the "colons and digits" in the right positions.

```
ipv6 CHAR(40) NOT NULL
 CHECK (ipv6 SIMILAR TO '([0-9a-d]:){7}[0-9a-d]')
```

Since the string is fixed length, it is easy to slice it up into substrings. The trick with searching for the substrings is to use underscores in a LIKE predicate instead of an ampersand wildcard or a regular expression. The simple LIKE predicate will match character for character rather than create a finite automaton under the covers.

13.1.8 Quantity and Unit Vectors

There are data elements made up of a measurement and a unit of measure. Currency is the most common example, as it has to be expressed in both a decimal amount and a unit of currency. The ISO 4217 currency code gives you a standard way of identifying the unit. Two countries in the world use nondecimal currencies. These are Mauritania (1 ouguiya=5 khoums) and Madagascar (1 ariary=5 iraimbilanja). The official currency of the Sovereign Military Order of Malta, which retains its claims of sovereignty under international law, is the scud (1 scudo=12 tari; 1 taro=20 grani; 1 grano=6 piccioli).

You will need to talk to the accounting department about the number of decimal places to use in computations. The rules for Euros are established by the European Union and those for dollars are part of the GAAP (Generally Accepted Accounting Practices).

```
CREATE TABLE International_Money
( ..
currency_code CHAR(3) NOT NULL,
currency_amt DECIMAL (12,4) NOT NULL,
..);
```

This mixed table is not easy to work with, so it is best to create VIEWs with a single currency for each group of users. This will entail maintaining an exchange rate table to use in the VIEWs.

```
CREATE VIEW Euro_Money (.. euro_amt, ..)
AS
SELECT .. (M1.currency_amt * E1.conversion_factor),
  FROM International_Money AS M1,
       Exchange_Rate AS E1
 WHERE E1.to_currency_code = 'EUR'
   AND E1.from_currency_code = M1.curency_code;
```

But there is a gimmick. There are specific rules about precision and rounding which are mandatory in currency conversion to, from, and through the Euro. Conversion between two national currencies must be "triangulated"; this means that you first convert currency #1 to Euros, then convert the Euros to currency #2. Six-figure conversion rates are mandatory, but you should check the status of "Article 235 Regulation" to be sure that nothing has changed since this writing.

13.2 Hierarchical Data Elements

There is usually an organizing principle in the hierarchy. For example, the pair (city_name, county_code, state_code) is ordered by geography. Cites are contained within states. Before you ask, the *most common* named *city* in the *United States* is Greenville. It occurs 50 times in many *U.S.* places. The (city_name, state_code) pair is not good enough because we can have duplicate city names in the same state.

13.2.1 Social Security Numbers

The closest thing the United States has to a Universal identification number is the Social Security Number (SSN). You are supposed to validate the SSN when you hire a new employee, but a lot of programmers have no idea how to do it. I am not going to go into the privacy issues, recent laws, or anything to do with legal aspects. This is a book for working programmers, and all we care about is how to use these numbers in our code.

The Social Security Number (Social Security Number) is composed of three parts, all digits and separated by dashes in the format "XXX-XX-XXXX." These parts are called the Area, Group, and Serial. For the most part (there are a few exceptions) the Area was determined by where the individual applied for the Social Security Number (before 1972) or resided at time of application (after 1972). The chart below shows the Area numbers used in the United States and its possessions.

SSN Area Number	Issuance Location
000-000	Always invalid
001-003	New Hampshire
004-007	Maine
008-009	Vermont
010-034	Massachusetts
035-039	Rhode Island
040-049	Connecticut
050-134	New York
135-158	New Jersey
159-211	Pennsylvania
212-220	Maryland
221-222	Delaware
223-231	Virginia

SSN Area Number	Issuance Location
232-232	North Carolina
232-236	West Virginia
237-246	Not issued
247-251	South Carolina
252-260	Georgia
261-267	Florida
268-302	Ohio
303-317	Indiana
318-361	Illinois
362-386	Michigan
387-399	Wisconsin
400-407	Kentucky
408-415	Tennessee
416-424	Alabama
425-428	Mississippi
429-432	Arkansas
433-439	Louisiana
440-448	Oklahoma
449-467	Texas
468-477	Minnesota
478-485	Iowa
486-500	Missouri
501-502	North Dakota
503-504	South Dakota
505-508	Nebraska
509-515	Kansas
516-517	Montana
518-519	Idaho
520-520	Wyoming
521-524	Colorado
525585	New Mexico
526-527	Arizona
528-529	Utah
530-680	Nevada
531-539	Washington
540-544	Oregon

SSN Area Number	Issuance Location
545-573	California
574-574	Alaska
575-576	Hawaii
577-579	District of Columbia
580-580	Virgin Islands
580-584	Puerto Rico
586-586	Guam
586-586	American Samoa
586-586	Philippine Islands
587-665	Not issued
667-679	Not issued
681-690	Not issued
691-699	Not issued
700-728	Railroad board ended in 1963
729-733	Enumeration at entry
900-999	Always invalid

If an Area number is shown more than once, it means that certain numbers had been transferred from one State to another, or that an Area has been divided for use among certain geographic locations. The actual assignment is done based on the ZIP code given on the application.

While 900-999 are not valid Area numbers, they were used for program purposes when state aid to the aged, blind, and disabled was converted to a federal program administered by Social Security Administration. You might also see this range of Area numbers used to construct student id numbers for foreign students in the days when schools used SSN as the student id number.

The Group portion of the Social Security Number has no meaning other than to determine whether or not a number has been assigned. There was an Urban Myth that the ethnicity of the card holder was coded in the Group number, and I have no idea how that one got started. The Social Security Administration publishes a list of the highest group assigned for each Area once a month. You can download these data at: http://www.ssa.gov/employer/highgroup.txt.

The only validation check on SSN was the way the Group numbers are issued. The first numbers issued are the odd numbers from 01 through 09, followed by the even numbers from 10 through 98, within each Area number. After all numbers in Group 98 of a particular area have been issued, then issue even Groups 02 through 08, followed by odd Groups 11 through 99.

For example, if the highest group assigned for area XXX is 72, then we knew that the number XXX-04-XXXX is an invalid Group number because even Groups under 9 have not yet been assigned.

Fifty or 60 years ago, wallets came with fake Social Security cards already in them to make them look good when they were on display—much like the photos of a family in a dime store picture frame that looks better than your real family. Many people simply used these fake cards. The numbers look valid, but the IRS and other government agencies have a list of them.

The Serial portion of the Social Security Number has no meaning. The Serial number ranges from 0001 to 9999, but it is not assigned in strictly numerical order. The Serial number 0000 is never assigned.

There are commercial firms and nonprofit Websites that will verify Social Security Numbers for living and deceased persons. They usually tell you if the person holding that number is alive or dead, along with the year and place of issue. Some of these sites are set up by government agencies or universities to help employers, hospitals, or other concerned parties validate SSNs. The commercial sites can do bulk validations from files that you submit to them, at a cost of about one cent per SSN.

Here is a small sample to get you started. I am not recommending one source over another in this listing.

http://www.veris-ssn.com
http://www.searchbug.com/peoplefinder/ssn.aspx
http://privacy.cs.cmu.edu/dataprivacy/projects/ssnwatch/
http://info.dhhs.state.nc.us/olm/manuals/dma/eis/man/Eis1103.htm
http://www.comserv-inc.com/products/ssndtect.htm

Having said all of this, it does not apply any more. As of June 25, 2011, numbers are assigned with a randomization process for security and to extend the life of the nine-digit pattern. SSN randomization will keep group number 00 or serial number 0000 invalid, but the Area numbers are no longer allocated to states for assignment.

13.2.2 Rational Numbers

A rational number is defined as a fraction (*a/b*), where *a* and *b* are both integers and (*b*<>0). Likewise, an irrational number cannot be defined that way. The classic examples of an irrational number are $\sqrt{2}$ and π. Technically, a binary computer can only represent a subset of the rational numbers. But for some purposes, it is handy to actually model them as (numerator, denominator) pairs. The whole number part is superior to fractional part of the number in the hierarchy.

For example, Vadim Tropashko uses rational numbers in the nested interval model for hierarchies in SQL (see my book *Trees and Hierarchies in SQL for Smarties*, Morgan-Kaufmann, 2004; ISBN 1-55860-920-2). This means that you need a set of user-defined functions to do basic four-function math and to reduce the fractions.

Elementary school students, when questioned what the sum of 1/2 and 1/4 is, will add the denominators and numerators like this: 1/2 + 1/4 = (1 + 1)/(2 + 4) = 2/6 = 1/3. This operation called the mediant and it returns the simplest number between the two fractions, if we use smallness of denominator as a measure of simplicity. Indeed, the average of 1/4 and 1/2 has denominator 8 while the mediant has 3.

13.2.3 Nondecimal and Mixed Units

The Metric system (more correctly, SI or "International System of Units") allows us to DECIMAL data types for any attribute we can measure with SI units to the required precision. However, the U.S. customary system developed from English units which were in use in the British Empire *before* American independence. The British system was overhauled in 1824, changing the definitions of some units used there, so several differences existed between the two systems. The U.K. is metric today, but many of the old Imperial units do not match U.S. units.

If you have some time, get a good book on the history of measurements. It will be informative.

For the database guy in the United States, we often have to deal with nondecimal, mixed units. That is we say "5 feet 8 inches" and record this single fact as a feet column and an inches column. But what if we have "5 feet 13 inches" in the row?

We have to normalize this two-column measure to "6 feet 1 inches" for display. Today in SQL, we have computed columns, so we could keep the measurement in inches and have this for display:

```
CREATE TABLE Personnel_Height
(employee_hgt INTEGER NOT NULL
   CHECK (employee_hgt >= 0), -- kept in inches
 employee_hgt_feet GENERATED ALWAYS
     AS (employee_hgt/12),
```

```
 employee_hgt_inches GENERATED ALWAYS
       AS (employee_hgt - employee_hgt/12.0
),
 ..
);
```

13.2.4 Interrelated Columns

While not exactly a single data element, it is often the case that two or more attributes are interrelated by a business rule. Clothing is an example that is easy to understand. Certain sizes are not available in all the colors, materials, and styles.

This can be enforced with a multicolumn CHECK() constraint that allows valid combinations or rejects invalid combinations. Here is a skeleton for this.

```
CREATE TABLE Catalog
(..
 dress_size INTEGER NOT NULL
  CHECK (dress_size BETWEEN 0 AND 25),
 color_code CHAR(3) NOT NULL
  CHECK (color_code) IN ('blk', 'wht', 'red'),
 CONSTRAINT color_size_combination
 CHECK(CASE WHEN (dress_size BETWEEN 0 AND 10
                AND color_code = 'red')
           THEN 'f'
           WHEN (dress_size BETWEEN 5 AND 10
                AND color_code IN ('blk', 'wht')
           THEN 't'
            ..
           ELSE 'f' END = 't'),
 ..);
```

Obviously, the predicates can be elaborate.

Shoe sizes are made up of width and length. ISO 9407:1991, "Shoe sizes—Mondopoint system of sizing and marking" is a shoe-size system known as Mondopoint. It is based on the mean foot length and width of the foot for which the shoe is suitable, measured in millimeters. The length appears first, so 280/110 is a large, but possible, human foot, but 110/280 is absurd.

NULLs—Missing Data in SQL

A DISCUSSION OF HOW to handle missing data enters a sensitive area in relational database circles. Dr. E. F. Codd, creator of the relational model, favored *two* types of missing-value tokens in his book on the second version of the relational model, one for "unknown" (the eye color of a man wearing sunglasses) and one for "not applicable" (the eye color of an automobile). Chris Date, leading author on relational databases, advocates not using any general-purpose tokens for missing values at all. Standard SQL uses one token, based on Dr. Codd's original relational model.

Perhaps Dr. Codd was right—again. In Standard SQL, adding ROLLUP and CUBE created a need for a function to test NULLs to see if they were in fact "real NULLs" (i.e., present in the data and therefore assumed to model a missing value) or "created NULLs" (i.e., created as place holders for summary rows in the result set).

In their book *A Guide to Sybase And SQL Server*, David McGoveran and C. J. Date (ISBN 978-0201557107, 1992) said: "It is this writer's opinion that NULLs, at least as currently defined and implemented in SQL, are far more trouble than they are worth and should be avoided; they display very strange and inconsistent behavior and can be a rich source of error and confusion. (Please note that these comments and criticisms apply to any system that supports SQL-style NULLs, not just to SQL Server specifically.)"

SQL takes the middle ground and has a single general-purpose NULL for missing values. Rules for NULLs in particular statements appear in the appropriate sections of this book. This section will discuss NULLs and missing values *in general*.

People have trouble with things that "are not there" in some sense. There is no concept of zero in Egyptian, Mayan, Chinese, Roman numerals, and virtually all other traditional numeral systems. It was centuries before Hindu-Arabic numerals and a true zero became popular in Europe. In fact, many early Renaissance accounting firms advertised that they did *not* use the fancy, newfangled notation and kept records in well-understood Roman numerals instead.

Many of the conceptual problems with zero arose from not knowing the difference between ordinal and cardinal numbers. Ordinal numbers measure position (an ordering); cardinal numbers measure quantity or magnitude. The argument against the zero was this: If there is no quantity or magnitude there, how can you count or measure it? What does it mean to multiply or divide a number by zero? There was considerable linguistic confusion over words that deal with the lack of something.

There is a Greek paradox that goes like this:

1. No cat has 12 tails.
2. A cat has one more tail than no cat.
3. Therefore, a cat has 13 tails.

See how "no" is used two different ways? This was part of the Greek language. A blank as a character had to wait for typesetting to replace manuscripts. Likewise, it was a long time before the idea of an empty set found its way into mathematics. The argument was that if there are no elements, how could you have a set of them? Is the empty set a subset of itself? Is the empty set a subset of all other sets? Is there only one universal empty set or one empty set for each type of set?

Computer science now has its own problem with missing data. The Interim Report 75-02-08 to the ANSI X3 (SPARC Study Group 1975) had 14 different kinds of incomplete data that could appear as the result of queries or as attribute values. These types included overflows, underflows, errors, and other problems in trying to represent the real world within the limits of a computer.

Instead of discussing the theory for the different models and approaches to missing data, I would rather explain why and how to use NULLs in SQL. In the rest of this book, I will be urging you not to use them, which may seem contradictory, but it is not. Think of a NULL as a drug; use it properly and it works for you, but abuse it and it can ruin everything. Your best policy is to avoid them when you can use them properly when you have to.

14.1 Empty and Missing Tables

An empty table or view is a different concept from a missing table. An empty table is one that is defined with columns and constraints, but that has zero rows in it. This can happen when a table or view is created for the first time, or when all the rows are deleted from the table. It is a perfectly good table. By definition, all of its constraints are TRUE.

A missing table has been removed from the database schema with a DROP TABLE statement, or it never existed at all (you probably typed the name wrong). A missing view is a bit different. It can be absent because of a DROP VIEW statement or a typing error, too. But it can also be absent because a table or view from which it was built has been removed. This means that the view cannot be constructed at run time and the database reports a failure. If you used CASCADE behavior when you dropped a table, the view would also be gone, but more on that later.

The behavior of an empty TABLE or VIEW will vary with the way it is used. The reader should look at sections of this book that deal with predicates that use a subquery. In general, an empty table can be treated either as a NULL or as an empty set, depending on context.

14.2 Missing Values in Columns

The usual description of NULLs is that they represent currently unknown values that may be replaced later with real values when we know something. Actually, the NULL covers a lot more territory, as it is the only way of showing any missing values. Going back to basics for a minute, we can define a row in a database as an entity, which has one or more attributes (columns), each of which is drawn from some domain. Let us use the notation E(A) = V to represent the idea that an entity, E, has an attribute, A, which has a value, V. For example, I could write "John(hair) = black" to say that John has black hair.

SQL's general-purpose NULLs do not quite fit this model. If you have defined a domain for hair color and one for car color, then a hair color should not be comparable to a car color, because they are drawn from two different domains. You would need to make their domains comparable with an implicit or explicit casting function. This is done in Standard SQL, which has a CREATE DOMAIN statement. Trying to find out which employees drive cars that match their hair is a bit weird outside of Los Angeles, but in the case of NULLs, do we have a hit when a bald-headed man walks to work? Are no hair and no car somehow equal in color? In SQL-89 and higher, we would get an UNKNOWN result, rather than an error, if we compared these two NULLs directly. The domain-specific NULLs are conceptually different from the general NULL because we know what kind of thing is UNKNOWN. This could be shown in our notation as E(A) = NULL to mean that we know the entity, we know the attribute, but we do not know the value.

Another flavor of NULL is "Not Applicable," shown as N/A on forms and spreadsheets and called "I-marks" by Dr. E. F. Codd in his second version of the Relational Model. To pick an example near to my heart, a bald man's hair-color attribute is a missing-value NULL drawn from the hair-color domain, but his feather-color attribute is a "Not Applicable" NULL. The attribute itself is missing, not just the value. This missing-attribute NULL could be written as E(NULL) = NULL in the formula notation.

How could an attribute not belonging to an entity show up in a table? Consolidate medical records and put everyone together for statistical purposes. You should not find any male pregnancies in the result table. The programmer has a choice as to how to handle pregnancies. He can have a column in the consolidated table for "number of pregnancies" and put a zero or a NULL in the rows where sex_code = 1 ('male' in the ISO Standards) and then add some CHECK() clauses to make sure that this integrity rule is enforced.

The other way is to have a column for "medical condition" and one for "number of occurrences" beside it. Another CHECK() clause would make sure male pregnancies do not appear. But what happens when the sex is known to be person rather than a lawful entity like a corporation and all we have is a name like 'Alex Morgan,' who could be either sex? Can we use the presence of one or more pregnancies to determine that Alex is a woman? What if Alex is a woman who never had children? The case where we have NULL(A) = V is a bit strange. It means that we do not know the entity, but we are looking for a known attribute, A, which has a value of V. This is like asking "What things are colored red?," which is a perfectly good, though insanely vague, question that is very hard to ask in an SQL database. It is possible to ask in some columnar databases, however.

If you want to try writing such a query in SQL, you have to get to the system tables to get the table and column names, then JOIN them to the rows in the tables and come back with the PRIMARY KEY of that row.

For completeness, we could play with all eight possible combinations of known and unknown values in the basic E(A) = V formula. But such combinations are of little use or meaning. The "total ignorance" NULL, shown as NULL(NULL) = NULL, means that we have no information about the entity, even about its existence, its attributes, or their values. But NULL(NULL) = V would mean that we know a value, but not the entity or the attribute. This is like the running joke from Douglas Adam's HITCHHIKER'S GUIDE TO THE GALAXY, in which the answer to the question, "What is the meaning of life, the universe, and everything?" is 42. I found that interesting since I also teach a domino game named Forty-two that is only played in Texas.

14.3 Context and Missing Values

Create a domain called Tricolor that is limited to the values 'Red,' 'White,' and 'Blue' and a column in a table drawn from that domain with a UNIQUE constraint on it. If my table has a 'Red' and two NULL values in that column, I have some information about the two NULLs. I know they will be either ('White,' 'Blue') or ('Blue,' 'White') when their rows are resolved. This is what Chris Date calls a "distinguished NULL," which means we have some information in it.

If my table has a 'Red,' a 'White,' and a NULL value in that column, can I change the last NULL to 'Blue' because it can only be 'Blue' under the rule? Or do I have to wait until I see an actual value for that row? There is no clear way to handle this situation. Multiple values cannot be put in a column, nor can the database automatically change values as part of the column declaration.

This idea can be carried farther with marked NULL values. For example, we are given a table of hotel rooms that has columns for check-in date and check-out date. We know the check-in date for each visitor, but we do not know his or her check-out dates. Instead, we know relationships among the NULLs. We can put them into groups—Mr. and Mrs. X will check out on

the same day, members of tour group Y will check out on the same day, and so forth. We can also add conditions on them: Nobody checks out before his check-in date, tour group Y will leave after 2025-01-07, and so forth. Such rules can be put into SQL database schemas, but it is very hard to do. The usual method is to use procedural code in a host language to handle such things.

Another context is statistical and probabilistic. Using my previous example of "Alex Morgan" as an ambiguous sex_code, I can take the birth date and make a guess. In the 1940-1950 time period, Alex was almost exclusively a male first name; in the 1990-2000 time period, Alex was more than half female. This gets into fuzzy logic and probabilistic data; I do not want to deal with it in this book.

David McGoveran has proposed that each column that can have missing data should be paired with a column that encodes the reason for the absence of a value (McGoveran, 1993, 1994a,b,c). The cost is a bit of extra logic, but the extra column makes it easy to write queries that include or exclude values based on the semantics of the situation.

You might want to look at solutions statisticians have used for missing data. In many kinds of computations, the missing values are replaced by an average, median, or other value constructed from the data set.

14.4 Comparing NULLs

A NULL cannot be compared to another NULL (equal, not equal, less than, greater than, and so forth). This is where we get SQL's three-valued logic instead of two-valued logic. Most programmers do not easily think in three values. But think about it for a minute. Imagine that you are looking at brown paper bags and are asked to compare them without seeing inside of either of them. What can you say about the predicate "Bag A has more tuna fish than Bag B"—TRUE or FALSE? You cannot say one way or the other, so you use a third logical value, UNKNOWN.

If I execute "SELECT * FROM SomeTable WHERE SomeColumn = 2"; and then execute "SELECT * FROM SomeTable WHERE SomeColumn <> 2"; I expect to see all the rows of SomeTable between these two queries in a world of two-valued logic. However, I also need to execute "SELECT * FROM SomeTable WHERE SomeColumn IS NULL"; to do that. The IS [NOT] NULL predicate will return only TRUE or FALSE.

A special predicate was introduced in the SQL:2003 Standard with the syntax:

```
<expression 1> IS DISTINCT FROM <expression 2>
```

Which is logically equivalent to:

```
((<expression 1> = <expression 2> OR (<expression 1>IS NULL AND
<expression 2> IS NULL))
```

Likewise the infixed comparison operator

```
<expression 1> IS NOT DISTINCT FROM <expression 2>

NOT (<expression 1> IS DISTINCT FROM <expression 2>)
```

or equivalent to:

```
((<expression 1> <> <expression 2>
  OR (<expression 1> IS NULL AND <expression 2> IS NOT NULL)
  OR (<expression 1> IS NOT NULL AND <expression 2> IS NULL))
```

Besides being simpler and lending itself to better optimization, the IS [NOT] DISTINCT FROM operator gives you traditional two-valued logic. It is based on another concept in SQL—the difference between equality and grouping. Grouping, the equivalence relation used in the GROUP BY clause and other places in the language, treats all NULLs as one equivalence class.

14.5 NULLs and Logic

George Boole developed two-valued logic and attached his name to Boolean algebra forever (*An Investigation of the Laws of Thought* by George Boole, 1854; there several reprints in paper and e-formats). This is not the only possible logical system. Do a Google search on "Multi-valued logics" and you will come up with lots of material. SQL's search conditions look a lot like a proposal from Jan Łukasiewicz, the inventor of Polish Notation, for a three-valued logic.

Two-valued logic is the one that works best with a binary (two-state) computer and with a lot of mathematics. But SQL has three-valued logic: TRUE, FALSE, and UNKNOWN. The UNKNOWN value results from using NULLs in comparisons and other predicates, but UNKNOWN is a logical value and not the same as a NULL, which is a data value marker. That is why you have to say (x IS [NOT] NULL) in SQL and not use (x=NULL) instead.

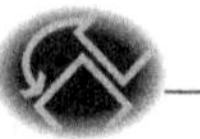

Here are the tables for the three logical operators that come with SQL.

	NOT
TRUE	FALSE
UNKNOWN	UNKNOWN
FALSE	TRUE

AND	TRUE	UNKNOWN	FALSE
TRUE	TRUE	UNKNOWN	FALSE
UNKNOWN	UNKNOWN	UNKNOWN	FALSE
FALSE	FALSE	FALSE	FALSE

OR	TRUE	UNKNOWN	FALSE
TRUE	TRUE	TRUE	TRUE
UNKNOWN	TRUE	UNKNOWN	UNKNOWN
FALSE	TRUE	UNKNOWN	FALSE

A comparison between known values gives you a result of TRUE or FALSE. This is Boolean logic, embedded in the SQL operators.

This is where we invented the logical value UNKNOWN. Well, rediscovered it. There were already a lot of multivalued logics in the mathematical literature. Some of them are based on discrete values and some on continuous values (i.e., fuzzy logic). SQL first looks like the system developed by Polish logician Jan Łukasiewicz (the L-bar is a "W" sound in English). Programmers know him as the guy who invented Polish Notation which inspired Reverse Polish Notation for HP calculators and stack architecture (aka zero address machines) computers like the old Burroughs computers.

In the Łukasiewicz multivalued logic systems, the AND, OR, and NOT are *almost* the same as in SQL's three-valued logic. The general case is based on the following Polish notation formulas in which 1 is TRUE, 0 is FALSE, and fractions are the other values.

- $Cab = 1$ for $a <= b$
- $Cab = 1 - a + b$ for $(a > b)$
- $Na = 1 - a$

N is the negation operator, and C is the implication operator. What is important about this system is that implication cannot be built from the AND, OR, and NOT operators. From the N and C pair, we define all other operators:

Operator	Symbol	Definition
OR	Oab	CCabb
AND	Aab	NONaNb
Equivalence	Eab	ACabCba
Maybe	Ma	CNaa

Maybe is defined as "not false" in this system. Then Tarski and Łukasiewicz had rules of inference to prove theorems. David McGoveran pointed out that SQL is not really a logic system because it lacks inference rules for deductions and proofs. The idea is that the UNKNOWN might be resolved to {TRUE, FALSE}, so we can sometimes determine the result regardless of how one value resolves. If we cannot determine a result, then return UNKNOWN.

Let me sum up. SQL is *not* a formal logical system. We have no inference rules and what we informally call "predicates" are actually "search conditions" in the ANSI/ISO Standards. What we have is a collection of look-up tables to compute a value of {TRUE, FALSE, UNKNOWN} to control ON and WHERE clauses in SQL statements.

The symbol for material implication in Boolean logic is a two-tailed right arrow defined by this table. It is often read as "a true premise cannot imply a false conclusion" in English.

⇒	TRUE	FALSE
TRUE	TRUE	FALSE
FALSE	TRUE	TRUE

This is properly called "material implication" and it can be read as "a true premise cannot imply a false conclusion" in English. But implication can also be written as $(a \Rightarrow b) = \Rightarrow(a \Rightarrow \Rightarrow b)$. There is also the "Smisteru rule"

that rewrites material implication as (a ⇒ b) = (⇒a ⇒ b), which is the same in two valued logic. If we use then old Algol operator IMP for three valued implication, things do not work well. Let's write some look-up tables.

Traditional implication

IMP	TRUE	UNKNOWN	FALSE
TRUE	TRUE	UNKNOWN	FALSE
UNKNOWN	TRUE	UNKNOWN	UNKNOWN
FALSE	TRUE	TRUE	TRUE

Compare this with Łukasiewicz implication

L-IMP	TRUE	UNKNOWN	FALSE
TRUE	TRUE	UNKNOWN	FALSE
UNKNOWN	TRUE	TRUE	UNKNOWN
FALSE	TRUE	TRUE	TRUE

The tables are not the same. In the first version, we have (UNKNOWN IMP FALSE) expanding out to:

⇒ (UNKNOWN ⇒ ⇒ UNKNOWN)
⇒ (UNKNOWN ⇒ UNKNOWN)
⇒ (UNKNOWN)
UNKNOWN

But the second version, Łukasiewicz, gives us:

L-IMP (½, ½) = CASE WHEN ½ <= ½ THEN 1 ELSE (1- ½ + ½) END
= 1 = TRUE

This is why we call the search logic in the SQL Standards is called a "search condition" and not a predicate. It will not actually hurt too much to make this error in practice.

14.5.1 NULLS in Subquery Predicates

People forget that a subquery often hides a comparison with a NULL. Consider these two tables:

```
CREATE TABLE Table1 (col1 INTEGER);
INSERT INTO Table1 (col1) VALUES (1), (2);

CREATE TABLE Table2 (col1 INTEGER);
INSERT INTO Table2 (col1) VALUES (1), (2), (3), (4), (5);
```

Notice that the columns are NULL-able. Execute this query:

```
SELECT col1
  FROM Table2
 WHERE col1 NOT IN (SELECT col1 FROM Table1);
```

Result

col1
3
4
5

Now insert a NULL and reexecute the same query:

```
INSERT INTO Table1 (col1) VALUES (NULL);
SELECT col1
  FROM Table2
 WHERE col1 NOT IN (SELECT col1 FROM Table1);
```

The result will be empty. This is counter-intuitive, but correct. The NOT IN predicate is defined as:

```
SELECT col1
 FROM Table2
 WHERE NOT (col1 IN (SELECT col1 FROM Table1));
```

The IN predicate is defined as:

```
SELECT col1
  FROM Table2
 WHERE NOT (col1 = ANY (SELECT col1 FROM Table1));
```

which becomes:

```
SELECT col1
  FROM Table2
```

```
WHERE NOT ((col1 = 1)
   OR (col1 = 2)
   OR (col1 = 3)
   OR (col1 = 4)
   OR (col1 = 5)
   OR (col1 = NULL));
```

The last expression is always UNKNOWN, so by applying DeMorgan's laws, the query is really:

```
SELECT col1
 FROM Table2
 WHERE ((col1 <> 1)
   AND (col1 <> 2)
   AND (col1 <> 3)
   AND (col1 <> 4)
   AND (col1 <> 5)
   AND UNKNOWN);
```

Look at the truth tables and you will see this always reduces to UNKNOWN and an UNKNOWN is always rejected in a search condition in a WHERE clause.

14.5.2 Logical Value Predicate

Standard SQL solved some of the 3VL (Three-Valued Logic) problems by adding this predicate:

```
<search condition> IS [NOT] TRUE | FALSE | UNKNOWN
```

which will let you map any combination of three-valued logic to two values. For example, ((credit_score<750) OR (eye_color='Blue')) IS NOT FALSE will return TRUE if (credit_score IS NULL) or (eye_color IS NULL) and the remaining condition does not matter.

14.6 Math and NULLs

NULLs propagate when they appear in arithmetic expressions (+, −, *, /) and return NULL results. See the chapter on numeric data types for more details. The principle of NULL propagation appears throughout SQL.

Aggregate functions (SUM, AVG, MIN, MAX, COUNT, COUNT(*)) drop the NULLs before doing their computation. This means that an all-NULL table will be empty. Now special rules apply to the results, and the aggregate of an empty set is NULL and COUNT(*) and COUNT are zero. Chris Date and other people do not like this convention. They are willing to agree to MIN, MAX, AVG, and COUNT sold be NULL, but they freak out on SUM.

The reason is that there is a convention in mathematics that when you do the summation of a series with the Σ_i notation, if the summation has one summand, then it returns that value, just like SQL. Technically, this makes addition (a binary operator) and summation different. If the summation has no summands, then it returns zero because zero is the identity element for addition. This is known as the empty sum. This convention makes formal manipulations easier.

Likewise, for the same reasons of formal convenience, when you do products of a series with the Π_i notation, if the product has one factor, then it returns that value. If the product has no factors, then it returns one, because one is the identity element for multiplication. This is known as the empty product.

14.7 Functions for NULLs

All standard computational functions propagate NULLs; that means a NULL argument gives NULL result of the appropriate data type. Most vendors propagate NULLs in the functions they offer as extensions of the standard ones required in SQL. For example, the cosine of a NULL will be NULL. There are two functions that convert NULLs into values.

1. NULLIF (V1, V2) returns a NULL when the first parameter equals the second parameter. The function is equivalent to the following case specification:

```
CASE WHEN (V1 = V2)
  THEN NULL
  ELSE V1 END
```

2. COALESCE (V1, V2, V3, ..., Vn) processes the list from left to right and returns the first parameter that is not NULL. If all the values are NULL, it returns a NULL.

14.8 NULLs and Host Languages

This book does not discuss using SQL statements embedded in any particular host language. You will need to pick up a book for your particular

language. However, you should know how NULLs are handled when they have to be passed to a host program. No standard host language for which an embedding is defined supports NULLs, which is another good reason to avoid using NULLs in your database schema.

Roughly speaking, the programmer mixes SQL statements bracketed by EXEC SQL and a language-specific terminator (the semicolon in Pascal and C, END-EXEC in COBOL, and so on) into the host program. This mixed-language program is run through an SQL preprocessor that converts the SQL into procedure calls the host language can compile; then the host program is compiled in the usual way.

There is an EXEC SQL BEGIN DECLARE SECTION, EXEC SQL END DECLARE SECTION pair that brackets declarations for the host parameter variables that will get values from the database via CURSORs. This is the "neutral territory" where the host and the database pass information. SQL knows that it is dealing with a host variable because these have a colon prefix added to them when they appear in an SQL statement. A CURSOR is an SQL query statement that executes and creates a structure that looks like a sequential file. The records in the CURSOR are returned, one at a time, to the host program in the BEGIN DECLARE section with the FETCH statement. This avoids the impedance mismatch between record processing in the host language and SQL's set orientation.

NULLs are handled by declaring INDICATOR variables in the host language BEGIN DECLARE section, which are paired with the host variables. An INDICATOR is an exact numeric data type with a scale of zero—that is, some kind of integer in the host language.

The FETCH statement takes one row from the cursor, and then converts each SQL data type into a host-language data type and puts that result into the appropriate host variable. If the SQL value was a NULL, the INDICATOR is set to minus one; if no indicator was specified, an exception condition is raised. As you can see, the host program must be sure to check the INDICATORs, because otherwise the value of the parameter will be garbage. If the parameter is passed to the host language without any problems, the INDICATOR is set to zero. If the value being passed to the host program is a non-NULL character string and it has an indicator, the indicator is set to the length of the SQL string and can be used to detect string overflows or to set the length of the parameter.

Other SQL interfaces such as ODBC, JDBC, etc., have similar mechanisms for telling the host program about NULLs even though they might not use cursors.

14.9 Design Advice for NULLs

"If you're that concerned with NULLs, then use the ISNULL function, that's what it's there for."

-- Jay, 2009-12-20 in a posting on the Microsoft SQL Server Programming Newsgroup

I wish this quotation was a fake. First of all, Jay did not know that MS SQL Server has had COALESCE() for years, so he was writing SQL in a Hillbilly dialect with the proprietary ISNULL() syntax. And then the content of the sentence is just wrong. Yet, I fear that he is not alone. A competent SQL programmer has a simple process for handling NULLs in his DDL.

First, declare all your base tables with NOT NULL constraints on all columns and then justify using NULLs in them. NULLs still confuse people who do not know SQL and NULLs are expensive. NULLs are usually implemented with an extra bit somewhere in the row where the column appears, rather than in the column itself. They adversely affect storage requirements, indexing, and searching.

NULLs are not permitted in PRIMARY KEY columns. Think about what a PRIMARY KEY that was NULL (or even partially NULL) would mean. A NULL in a key means that the data model does not know what makes the entities in that table unique from each other. That in turn says that the RDBMS cannot decide whether the PRIMARY KEY does or does not duplicate a key that is already in the table.

NULLs should be avoided in FOREIGN KEYs. SQL allows this "benefit of the doubt" relationship, but it can cause a loss of information in queries that involve joins. For example, given a part number code in Inventory that is referenced as a FOREIGN KEY by an Orders table, you will have problems getting a listing of the parts that have a NULL. This is a mandatory relationship; you cannot order a part that does not exist.

An example of an optional foreign key is a relationship between a Personnel table, a Jobs table and a Job_Assignments table. The new hire has all of his personnel information and we have a bunch of open jobs, but we have not assigned him a job yet. We might want to show his job as a NULL in Job_Assignments.

NULLs should not be allowed in encoding schemes that are known to be complete. For example, employees are people and people are either male or female. On the other hand, if you are recording lawful persons (corporations and other legal entities), you need the ISO sex codes, which use 0 = unknown, 1 = male, 2 = female, and 9 = legal persons, such as corporations.

The use of all zeros and all nines for "Unknown" and "N/A" is quite common in numeric encoding schemes. This convention is a leftover from the old punch card days, when a missing value was left as a field of blanks that could punched into the card later. Early versions of FORTRAN read blanks in numeric fields as zeroes.

Likewise, a field of all nines would sort to the end of the file, and it was easy to hold the "nine" key down when the keypunch machine was in numeric shift. This was a COBOL programmer convention.

However, you have to use NULLs in date columns when a DEFAULT date does not make sense. For example, if you do not know someone's birth date, a default date does not make sense; if a warranty has no expiration date, then a NULL can act as an "eternity" symbol. Unfortunately, you often know relative times, but it is difficult to express them in a database. For example, you cannot get a pay raise before you are hired, you cannot die before you are born, etc. A convict serving on death row should expect a release date resolved by an event: his execution or death by natural causes. This leads to extra columns to hold the status and to control the transition constraints.

There is a proprietary extension to date values in MySQL. If you know the year but not the month, you may enter '2017-00-00.' If you know the year and month but not the day, you may enter '2017-09-00.' You cannot reliably use date arithmetic on these values, but they do help in some instances, such as sorting people's birth dates or calculating their (approximate) age.

For people's names, you are probably better off using a special dummy string for unknown values rather than the general NULL. In particular, you can build a list of 'John Doe #1,' 'John Doe #2,' and so forth to differentiate them; and you cannot do that with a NULL. Quantities have to use a NULL in some cases. There is a difference between an unknown quantity and a zero quantity; it is the difference between an empty gas tank and not having a car at all. Using negative numbers to represent missing quantities does not work because it makes accurate calculations too complex.

When the host programming languages had no DATE data type, this could have been handled with a character string of '9999-99-99' for 'eternity' or 'the end of time'; it is actually the last date in the ISO-8601 Standard. When 4GL products with a DATE data type came onto the market, programmers usually inserted the maximum possible date for 'eternity.' But again, this will show up in calculations and in summary statistics. The best trick was to use two columns, one for the date and one for a flag. But this made for fairly complex code in the 4GL. For example, if there are a lot of flags that signal "this birthdate is approximated±3 years," then you have to do special statistics to computer the average age of a population.

14.9.1 Avoiding NULLs from the Host Programs

You can avoid putting NULLs into the database from the Host Programs with some programming discipline.

1. Initialization in the host program: initialize all the data elements and displays on the input screen of a client program before inserting data into the database. Exactly how you can make sure that all the programs use the same default values is another problem.

2. Automatic Defaults: The database is the final authority on the default values.

3. Deducing Values: infer the missing data from the given values. For example, patients reporting a pregnancy are female; patients reporting prostate cancer are male. This technique can also be used to limit choices to valid values for the user.

4. Tracking missing data: data is tagged as missing, unknown, in error, out of date, or whatever other condition makes it missing. This will involve a companion column with special codes. Most commercial applications do not need this, but a data quality audit could use this kind of detail.

5. Determine impact of missing data on programming and reporting. Numeric columns with NULLs are a problem because queries using aggregate functions can provide misleading results. Aggregate functions drop out the NULLs before doing the math and the programmer has to trap the SQLSTATE 01003 for this to make corrections. It is a Warning and will not create a ROLLBACK.

6. Prevent missing data: use batch process to scan and validate data elements before it goes into the database. In the early 2000's, there was a sudden concern for data quality when CEOs started going to jail for failing audits. This has lead to a niche in the software trade for data quality tools.

7. The data types and their NULL-ability constraints have to be consistent across databases (e.g., the chart of account should be defined the same way in both the desktop spreadsheets and enterprise level databases).

14.10 A Note on Multiple NULL Values

In a discussion on CompuServe in 1996 July, Carl C. Federl came up with an interesting idea for multiple missing value tokens in a database.

If you program in embedded SQL, you are used to having to work with an INDICATOR column. This is used to pass information to the host program, mostly about the NULL or NOT NULL status of the SQL column in the database. What the host program does with the information is up to the programmer. So why not extend this concept a bit and provide an indicator column? Let's work out a simply example:

```
CREATE TABLE Bob
(keycol INTEGER NOT NULL PRIMARY KEY,
 val_col INTEGER NOT NULL,
 multi_indicator INTEGER NOT NULL
 CHECK (multi_indicator IN (0, -- Known value
           1, -- Not applicable value
           2, -- Missing value
           3 -- Approximate value));
```

Let's set up the rules: When all values are known, we do a regular total. If a value is "not applicable," then the whole total is "not applicable." If we have no "not applicable" values, then "missing value" dominates the total; if we have no "not applicable" and no "Missing" values, then we give a warning about approximate values. The general form of the queries will be:

```
SELECT SUM (val_col),
   (CASE WHEN NOT EXISTS (SELECT multi_indicator
               FROM Bob
              WHERE multi_indicator > 0)
      THEN 0
      WHEN EXISTS (SELECT *
              FROM Bob
```

```
              WHERE multi_indicator = 1)
       THEN 1
       WHEN EXISTS (SELECT *
              FROM Bob
              WHERE multi_indicator = 2)
       THEN 2
       WHEN EXISTS (SELECT *
              FROM Bob
              WHERE multi_indicator = 3)
       THEN 3
       ELSE NULL END) AS totals_multi_indicator
   FROM Bob;
```

Why would I muck with the val_col total at all? The status is over in the multi_indicator column, just like it was in the original table. Here is an exercise for the reader:

1. Make up a set of rules for multiple missing values and write a query for the SUM(), AVG(), MAX(), MIN() and COUNT() functions.
2. Set degrees of approximation (plus or minus five, plus or minus ten, etc.) in the multi_indicator. Assume the val_col is always in the middle. Make the multi_indicator handle the fuzziness of the situation.

```
CREATE TABLE MultiNull
(groupcol INTEGER NOT NULL,
 keycol INTEGER NOT NULL,
 val_col INTEGER NOT NULL CHECK (val_col >= 0),
 val_col_null INTEGER NOT NULL DEFAULT 0,
 CHECK(val_col_null IN
 (0, -- Known Value
 1, -- Not applicable
 2, -- Missing but applicable
 3, -- Approximate within 1%
 4, -- Approximate within 5%
 5, -- Approximate within 25%
 6 -- Approximate over 25% range)),
 PRIMARY KEY (groupcol, keycol),
 CHECK (val_col = 0 OR val_col_null NOT IN (1,2));
```

```
CREATE VIEW Group_MultiNull
(groupcol, val_col_sum, val_col_avg, val_col_max, val_col_min,
row_cnt, notnull_cnt, na_cnt, missing_cnt, approximate_cnt,
appr_1_cnt, approx_5_cnt, approx_25_cnt, approx_big_cnt)
AS
SELECT groupcol, SUM(val_col), AVG(val_col), MAX(val_col),
   MIN(val_col), COUNT(*),
    SUM (CASE WHEN val_col_null = 0 THEN 1 ELSE 0 END)
     AS notnull_cnt,
    SUM (CASE WHEN val_col_null = 1 THEN 1 ELSE 0 END)
     AS na_cnt,
    SUM (CASE WHEN val_col_null = 2 THEN 1 ELSE 0 END)
     AS missing_cnt,
    SUM (CASE WHEN val_col_null IN (3,4,5,6) THEN 1 ELSE 0 END)
     AS approximate_cnt,
    SUM (CASE WHEN val_col_null = 3 THEN 1 ELSE 0 END)
     AS appr_1_cnt,
    SUM (CASE WHEN val_col_null = 4 THEN 1 ELSE 0 END)
     AS approx_5_cnt,
    SUM (CASE WHEN val_col_null = 5 THEN 1 ELSE 0 END)
     AS approx_25_cnt,
    SUM (CASE WHEN val_col_null = 6 THEN 1 ELSE 0 END)
     AS approx_big_cnt
  FROM MultiNull
  GROUP BY groupcol;
SELECT groupcol, val_col_sum, val_col_avg, val_col_max, val_col_min,
    (CASE WHEN row_cnt = notnull_cnt
       THEN 'All are known'
       ELSE 'Not all are known' END) AS warning_message,
   row_cnt, notnull_cnt, na_cnt, missing_cnt, approximate_cnt,
   appr_1_cnt, approx_5_cnt, approx_25_cnt, approx_big_cnt
 FROM Group_MultiNull;
```

While this is a bit complex for the typical application, it is not a bad idea for a "staging area" database that attempts to scrub the data before it goes to a data warehouse.

Table Operations

THERE ARE ONLY four things you can do with a set of rows in an SQL table: insert them into a table, delete them from a table, update the values in their rows, or query them. The unit of work is a set of whole rows inside a base table.

When you worked with file systems, access was one record at a time, then one field within a record. As you had repeated groups and other forms of variant records, you could change the structure of each record in the file.

The mental mode in SQL is that you grab a subset, as a unit, all at once in a base table and insert, update or delete, as a unit, all at once. Imagine that you have enough computer power that you can allocate one processor to every row in a table. When you blow your whistle, all the processors do their work in parallel.

15.1 DELETE FROM Statement

The DELETE FROM statement in SQL removes a set of zero or more rows of one table. Interactive SQL tools will tell the user how many rows were affected by an update operation and Standard SQL requires the database engine to raise a completion condition of "no data" if there were zero rows. There are two forms of DELETE FROM in SQL: positioned and searched. The positioned deletion is done with cursors; the searched deletion uses a WHERE clause like the search condition in a SELECT statement.

15.1.1 The DELETE FROM Clause

The syntax for a searched deletion statement is

```
<delete statement: searched> ::=
  DELETE FROM <table name> [[AS] <table name>]
  [WHERE <search condition>]
```

The DELETE FROM clause simply gives the name of the table or updatable view to be changed. Before SQL:2003, no correlation name was allowed in the DELETE FROM clause.

The SQL model for a correlation or alias table name is that the engine effectively creates a new table with that new name and populates it with rows identical to the base table or updatable view from which it was built. If you had a correlation name, you would be deleting from this system-created temporary table and it would vanish at the end of the statement. The base table would never have been touched.

After the SQL:2003 Standard, the correlation name is effectively an updatable VIEW build on its base table. I strongly recommend avoiding this newer feature.

For this discussion, we will assume the user doing the deletion has applicable DELETE privileges for the table. The positioned deletion removes the row in the base table that is the source of the current cursor row. The syntax is:

```
<delete statement: positioned> ::=
 DELETE FROM <table name> [[AS] <table name>]
  WHERE CURRENT OF <cursor name>
```

Cursors in SQL are generally much more expensive than declarative code and, in spite of the existence of standards, they vary widely in implementations. If you have a properly designed table with a key, you should be able to avoid them in a DELETE FROM statement.

15.1.2 The WHERE Clause

The most important thing to remember about the WHERE clause is that it is optional. If there is no WHERE clause, *all rows* in the table are deleted. The table structure still exists, but there are no rows.

Most, but not all, interactive SQL tools will give the user a warning when he is about to do this and ask for confirmation. Unless you wanted to clear out the table, immediately do a ROLLBACK to restore the table; if you COMMIT or have set the tool to automatically commit the work, then the data is pretty much gone. The DBA will have to do something to save you. And do not feel bad about doing it at least once while you are learning SQL.

Because we wish to remove a subset of rows all at once, we cannot simply scan the table one row at a time and remove each qualifying row as it is encountered; we need to have the whole subset all at once. The way most SQL implementations do a deletion is with two passes on the table. The first pass marks all of the candidate rows that meet the WHERE clause condition. This is also when most products check to see if the deletion will violate any constraints. The most common violations involve trying to remove a value that is referenced by a foreign key (Hey, we still have orders for those Pink Lawn Flamingos; you cannot drop them from inventory yet!). But other constraints can also cause a ROLLBACK.

After the subset is validated, the second pass removes it, either immediately or by marking them so that a housekeeping routine can later reclaim the storage space. Then any further housekeeping, such as updating indexes, is done last.

The important point is that while the rows are being marked, the entire table is still available for the WHERE condition to use. In many, if not most, cases this two-pass method does not make any difference in the results. The WHERE clause is usually a fairly simple predicate that references constants or relationships among the columns of a row. For example, we could clear out some Personnel with this deletion:

```
DELETE FROM Personnel
 WHERE iq <= 100;      -- constant in simple predicate
```

or

```
DELETE FROM Personnel
 WHERE hat_size = iq; -- uses columns in the same row
```

A good optimizer could recognize that these predicates do not depend on the table as a whole and would use a single scan for them. The two passes make a difference when the table references itself. Let's fire employees whose IQs are below average for their departments.

```
DELETE FROM Personnel
WHERE iq < (SELECT AVG(P1.iq)
              FROM Personnel AS P1 -- correlation name
             WHERE Personnel.dept_nbr = P1.dept_nbr);
```

We have the following data:

Personnel

emp_nbr	dept_nbr	iq
'Able'	'Acct'	101
'Baker'	'Acct'	105
'Charles'	'Acct'	106
'Henry'	'Mkt'	101
'Celko'	'Mkt'	170
'Popkin'	'HR'	120

If this were done one row at a time, we would first go to Accounting and find the average IQ, (101+105+106)/3.0=104, and fire Able. Then we would move sequentially down the table and again find the average accountant's IQ, (105+106)/2.0=105.5 and fire Baker. Only Charles would escape the downsizing, but being the last man standing.

Now sort the table a little differently so that the rows are visited in reverse alphabetic order. We first read Charles's IQ and compute the average for Accounting (101+105+106)/3.0=104, and retain Charles. Then we would move sequentially down the table, with the average IQ unchanged, so we also retain Baker. Able, however, is downsized when that row comes up.

15.1.3 Deleting Based on Data in a Second Table

The WHERE clause can be as complex as you wish. This means you can have subqueries that use other tables. For example, to remove customers who have paid their bills from the Deadbeats table, you can use a correlated EXISTS predicate, thus:

```
DELETE FROM Deadbeats
 WHERE EXISTS (SELECT *
```

```
        FROM Payments AS P1
       WHERE Deadbeats.cust_nbr = P1.cust_nbr
         AND P1.paid_amt > = Deadbeats.due_amt);
```

The scope rules from SELECT statements also apply to the WHERE clause of a DELETE FROM statement, but it is a good idea to qualify all of the column names.

15.1.4 Deleting Within the Same Table

SQL allows a DELETE FROM statement to use columns, constants, and aggregate functions drawn from the table itself. For example, it is perfectly all right to remove everyone who is below average in a class with this statement:

```
DELETE FROM Students
 WHERE grade < (SELECT AVG(grade) FROM Students);
```

The DELETE FROM clause now allows for correlation names on the table in the DELETE FROM clause, but this hides the original name of the table or view.

```
DELETE FROM Personnel AS B1 -- error!
 WHERE Personnel.boss_emp_nbr = B1.emp_nbr
   AND Personnel.salary_amt > B1.salary_amt;
```

There are ways to work around this. One trick is to build a VIEW of the table and use the VIEW instead of a correlation name. Consider the problem of finding all employees who are now earning more than their boss and deleting them. The employee table being used has a column for the employee's identification number, emp_nbr, and another column for the boss's employee identification number, boss_emp_nbr.

```
CREATE VIEW Bosses
AS SELECT emp_nbr, salary_amt FROM Personnel;
 DELETE FROM Personnel
  WHERE EXISTS
      (SELECT *
         FROM Bosses AS B1
        WHERE Personnel.boss_emp_nbr = B1.emp_nbr
          AND Personnel.salary_amt > B1.salary_amt);
```

Simply using the Personnel table in the subquery will not work. We need an outer reference in the WHERE clause to the Personnel table in the subquery, and we cannot get that if the Personnel table were in the subquery. Such views should be as small as possible so that the SQL engine can materialize them in main storage. Some products will allow a CTE to be used in place of a VIEW.

15.1.5 Redundant Duplicates in a Table

Redundant duplicates are unneeded copies of a row in a table. You most often get them because you did not put a UNIQUE constraint on the table, and then you inserted the same data twice. Removing the extra copies from a table in SQL is much harder than you would think. If fact, if the rows are exact duplicates, you cannot do it with a simple DELETE FROM statement. Removing redundant duplicates involves saving one of them while deleting the other(s). But if SQL has no way to tell them apart, it will delete all rows that were qualified by the WHERE clause. Another problem is that the deletion of a row from a base table can trigger referential actions, which can have unwanted side effects.

For example, if there is a referential integrity constraint that says a deletion in Table1 will cascade and delete matching rows in Table2, removing redundant duplicates from T1 can leave me with no matching rows in T2. Yet I still have a referential integrity rule that says there must be at least one match in T2 for the single row I preserved in T1. SQL allows constraints to be deferrable or nondeferrable, so you might be able to suspend the referential actions that the transaction below would cause.

The brute force method is to use "SELECT DISTINCT * FROM Personnel," clean out the redundancy, write it to a temp table and finally reload the data in the base table. This is awful programming.

The better tricks are based on "unique-ifying" the rows in the table so that one can be saved. Oracle has a nonrelational, proprietary ROWID which is a table property, not a column at all. It is the physical "track and sector" location on the disk of the record that holds the row.

Let's assume that we have a nontable, with redundant employee rows.

```
CREATE TABLE Personnel
(emp_id INTEGER NOT NULL, -- dups
 emp_name CHAR(30) NOT NULL, --dups
 ...);
```

The classic Oracle solution is the statement:

```
DELETE FROM Personnel
 WHERE ROWID < (SELECT MAX(P1.ROWID)
                  FROM Personnel AS P1
                 WHERE P1.emp_id = Personnel.emp_id
                   AND P1.emp_name = Personnel.emp_name);
```

ROWID can change after a user session but not during the session. It is the fastest possible physical access method into an Oracle table because it goes directly to the physical address of the data. It is also a complete violation of Dr. Codd's rules that require that the physical representation of the data be hidden from the users.

Another approach is to notice that set of all rows in the table minus set of rows we want to keep defines the set of rows to delete. This gives us the following statement:

```
DELETE FROM Personnel
 WHERE ROWID
       IN (SELECT P2.ROWID FROM Personnel AS P2
           EXCEPT
           SELECT MAX(P3.ROWID)
             FROM Personnel AS P3
            GROUP BY P3.emp_id, P3.emp_name);
```

This is faster than the short classic version because it avoids a correlated subquery expression in the WHERE clause. You can mimic the ROWID with the ROW_NUMBER() function.

```
CREATE VIEW Clustered_Personnel
AS
SELECT emp_id, emp_name,
       ROW_NUMBER() OVER (PARTITION BY emp_id)
       AS unique_row_nbr
  FROM Personnel;

DELETE FROM Clustered_Personnel
 WHERE unique_row_nbr > 1;
```

We are sure that the VIEW is updatable, so this will work. You have to a VIEW and not a CTE.

15.2 INSERT INTO Statement

The INSERT INTO statement is the only way to get new data into a base table in Standard SQL. In practice, there are *always* other tools for loading large amounts of data into a table, but they are very vendor dependent.

15.2.1 INSERT INTO Clause

The syntax for INSERT INTO is

```
<insert statement> ::=
  INSERT INTO <table name>
    <insert columns and source>

<insert columns and source> ::=
    [(<insert column list>)]
   <query expression>
  | VALUES <table value constructor list>
  | DEFAULT VALUES

<table value constructor list> ::=
   <row value constructor> [{<comma> <row value constructor>}...]

<row value constructor> ::=
     <row value constructor element>
   | ( <row value constructor list> )
   | <row subquery>

<row value constructor list> ::=
   <row value constructor element>
       [{<comma> <row value constructor element>}...]

<row value constructor element> ::=
     <value expression> | NULL |DEFAULT
```

The two basic forms of an INSERT INTO are a table constant insertion and a query insertion. The table constant insertion is done with a VALUES() clause. The list of insert values usually consists of constants or explicit NULLs, but in theory they could be almost any scalar expression, including scalar subqueries. The handiest trick is the use of CREATE SEQUENCE and the use of NEXT VALUE FOR <sequence_name> OVER (<over_order_by_clause>) in the insertion list.

The DEFAULT VALUES clause is a shorthand for VALUES (DEFAULT, DEFAULT, …, DEFAULT), so it is just shorthand for a particular single row insertion. Almost nobody knows it exists.

The tabular constant insertion is a simple tool, mostly used in interactive sessions to put in small amounts of data. A query insertion executes the query and produces a working table, which is inserted into the target table all at once. In both cases, the optional list of columns in the target table has to be union-compatible with the columns in the query or with the values in the VALUES clause. Any column not in the list will be assigned NULL or its explicit DEFAULT value.

15.2.2 The Nature of Inserts

In theory, an insert using a query will place the rows from the query in the target table all at once. The set-oriented nature of an insertion means that a statement with CURRENT_TIMESTAMP, CURRENT_DATE, and other dynamic system values will have *one value* for transaction_time in all the rows of the result, no matter how long it takes to physically load them into the target table. Keeping things straight requires a lot of checking behind the scenes. The insertion can fail if *just one row* violates a constraint on the target table. The usual physical implementation is to put the rows into the target table, but to mark the work as uncommitted until the whole transaction has been validated. Once the system knows that the insertion is to be committed, it must rebuild all the indexes. Rebuilding indexes will lock out other users and might require sorting the table if the table had a sorted index. If you have had experience with a file system, your first thought might be to drop the indexes, insert the new data, sort the table, and reindex it. The utility programs for index creation can actually benefit from having a known ordering. Unfortunately, this trick does not always work in SQL. The indexes maintain the uniqueness and referential integrity constraints and cannot be easily dropped and restored. Files stand independently of each other; tables are part of a whole database.

15.2.3 Bulk Load and Unload Utilities

All versions of SQL have a language extension or utility program that will let you read data from an external file directly into a table. There is no standard for this tool, so they are all different. Most of these utilities require the name of the file and the format it is written in. The simpler versions of the utility

just read the file and put it into a single target table. At the other extreme, Oracle uses a miniature language that can do simple editing as each record is read. If you use a simpler tool, it is a good idea to build a working table in which you stage the data for cleanup before loading it into the actual target table. You can apply edit routines, look for duplicates, and put the bad data into another working table for inspection.

The corresponding output utility, which converts a table into a file, usually offers a choice of format options; any computations and selection can be done in SQL. Some of these programs will accept a SELECT statement or a VIEW; some will only convert a base table. Most tools now have an option to output INSERT INTO statements along with the appropriate CREATE TABLE and CREATE INDEX statements.

15.3 The UPDATE Statement

The function of the UPDATE statement in SQL is to change the values in zero or more columns of zero or more of rows of one table. SQL implementations will tell you how many rows were affected by an update operation or as a minimum return the SQLSTATE value for zero rows effected.

The theory is that an UPDATE is a deletion and an insertion done together, via two fictional system_created tables. This lets triggers see the deleted rows (the OLD pseudo-table) and the inserted rows (the NEW pseudo-table).

There are two forms of UPDATE statements: positioned and searched. The positioned UPDATE is done with cursors; the searched UPDATE uses a WHERE that resembles the search condition in a SELECT statement.

Cursors allow the updating of the "CURRENT OF <cursor name>" row and that is covered in the chapter on CURSORs.

15.3.1 The UPDATE Clause

The syntax for a searched update statement is

```
<update statement> ::=
  UPDATE <table name> [[AS] <correlation name>]
     SET <set clause list>
  [WHERE <search condition>]
```

```
<set clause list> ::=
  <set clause> [{, <set clause>}...]

<set clause> ::= <object column> = <update source>

<update source> ::= <value expression> | NULL | DEFAULT

<object column> ::= <column name>
```

The UPDATE clause simply gives the name of the base table or updatable view to be changed.

15.3.2 The SET Clause

The SET clause is a list of columns to be changed or made; the WHERE clause tells the statement which rows to use. For this discussion, we will assume the user doing the update has applicable UPDATE privileges for each <object column>.

Standard SQL allows a row constructor in the SET clause. The syntax looks like this.

```
UPDATE Foobar
   SET (a, b, c) = (1, 2, 3)
 WHERE x < 12;
```

This is shorthand for the usual syntax, where the row constructor values are matched position for position with the SET clause column list.

Each assignment in the <set clause list> is executed in parallel and each SET clause changes all the qualified rows at once. Or at least that is the theoretical model. In practice, implementations will first mark all of the qualified rows in the table in one pass, using the WHERE clause. If there were no problems, then the SQL engine makes a copy of each marked row in working storage. Each SET clause is executed based on the old row image and the results are put in the new row image. Finally, the old rows are deleted and the new rows are inserted. If an error occurs during all of this, then system does a ROLLBACK, the table is left unchanged, and the errors are reported. This parallelism is not like what you find in a traditional third-generation programming language, so it may be hard to learn. This feature lets you write a statement that will swap the values in two columns, thus:

```
UPDATE MyTable
SET a = b, b = a;
```

This is not the same thing as

```
BEGIN ATOMIC
UPDATE MyTable
SET a = b;
UPDATE MyTable
SET b = a;
END;
```

In the first UPDATE, columns a and b will swap values in each row. In the second pair of UPDATEs, column a will get all of the values of column b in each row. In the second UPDATE of the pair, a, which now has the same value as the original value of b, will be written back into column b—no change at all. There are some limits as to what the value expression can be. The same column cannot appear more than once in a <set clause list>—which makes sense, given the parallel nature of the statement. Since both go into effect at the same time, you would not know which SET clause to use.

The CASE expression allows a programmer to put a lot of computing power into an UPDATE. I am going to assume that everyone has used Netflix or a similar service where they set up a queue and have to maintain it by rearranging the elements in the queue.

```
CREATE TABLE Movie_Queue
(movie_queue_seq INTEGER NOT NULL PRIMARY KEY
 CHECK (movie_queue_seq > 0),
 movie_title CHAR(25) NOT NULL);
```

Let's write a procedure to rearrange the display order based on the movie_queue_seq column. The inputs will be the current or old sequence number in the queue and the desired or new sequence.

```
CREATE PROCEDURE Swap_Movies
(IN old_movie_queue_seq INTEGER,
 IN new_movie_queue_seq INTEGER)
LANGUAGE SQL
DETERMINISTIC
```

```
UPDATE Movie_Queue
   SET movie_queue_seq
       = CASE movie_queue_seq
         WHEN old_movie_queue_seq
         THEN new_movie_queue_seq
         ELSE movie_queue_seq + SIGN(old_movie_queue_seq
- new_movie_queue_seq)
         END

 WHERE movie_queue_seq
       BETWEEN SYMMETRIC old_movie_queue_seq AND
new_movie_queue_seq;
```

When you want to drop a few rows, remember to close the gaps with this:

```
CREATE PROCEDURE Close_Movie_Queue_Gaps()
LANGUAGE SQL
DETERMINISTIC
UPDATE Movie_Queue
   SET movie_queue_seq
       = (SELECT M1.new_movie_queue_seq
            FROM (SELECT movie_queue_seq,
                         ROW_NUMBER()
                         OVER (ORDER BY movie_queue_seq)
                         AS new_movie_queue_seq
                    FROM Movie_Queue) AS M1
          WHERE M1.movie_queue_seq = Movie_Queue.movie_queue_seq);
```

SQL Server and perhaps other SQL products at the time you are reading this will allow you to use a CTE in the UPDATE statement in place of the derived table.

15.3.3 The WHERE Clause

As mentioned, the most important thing to remember about the WHERE clause is that it is optional. If there is no WHERE clause, all rows in the table are changed. This is a common error; if you make it, immediately execute a ROLLBACK statement or call the Database Administrator for help.

All rows that test TRUE for the <search condition> are marked as a subset and not as individual rows. It is also possible that this subset will be empty. This subset is used to construct a new set of rows that will be inserted into the table when the subset is deleted from the table. Note that the empty subset is a valid update that will fire declarative referential actions and triggers.

15.3.4 Updating with a Second Table Before MERGE

Most updating is done with simple expressions of the form SET <column name>=<constant value>, because UPDATEs are done via data entry programs. It is also possible to have the <column name> on both sides of the equal sign. This will not change any values in the table, but can be used as a way to trigger referential actions that have an ON UPDATE condition. However, the <set clause list> does not have to contain only simple expressions. It is possible to use one table to post summary data to another. The scope of the <table name> is the entire <update statement>, so it can be referenced in the WHERE clause. This is easier to explain with an example. Assume we have the following tables:

```
CREATE TABLE Customers
(cust_nbr CHAR(10) NOT NULL PRIMARY KEY,
 acct_amt DECIMAL(8,2) NOT NULL);

CREATE TABLE Payments
(trans_nbr CHAR(10) NOT NULL PRIMARY KEY,
 cust_nbr CHAR(10) NOT NULL,
 trans_amt DECIMAL(8,2) NOT NULL);
```

The problem is to post all of the payment amounts to the balance in the Customers table, overwriting the old balance. Such a posting is usually a batch operation, so a searched UPDATE statement seems the logical approach. After SQL-92, you can use the updated table's names in a subquery, thus:

```
UPDATE Customers
   SET acct_amt
       = acct_amt
         - (SELECT COALESCE (SUM(amt), 0.00)
              FROM Payments AS P1
             WHERE Customers.cust_nbr = P1.cust_nbr)
```

```
WHERE EXISTS
      (SELECT *
         FROM Payments AS P2
        WHERE Customers.cust_nbr = P2.cust_nbr);
```

When there is no payment, the scalar query will return an empty set. The SUM() of an empty set is always NULL, so coalesce it to zero. One of the most common programming errors made when using this trick is to write a query that may return more than one row. If you did not think about it, you might have written the last example as

```
UPDATE Customers
   SET acct_amt
       = acct_amt
         - (SELECT payment_amt
              FROM Payments AS P1
             WHERE Customers.cust_nbr = P1.cust_nbr)
 WHERE EXISTS
       (SELECT *
          FROM Payments AS P2
         WHERE Customers.cust_nbr = P2.cust_nbr);
```

But consider the case where a customer has made more than one payment and we have both of them in the Payments table; the whole transaction will fail. The UPDATE statement should return an error message about cardinality violations and ROLLBACK the entire UPDATE statement. In the first example, however, we know that we will get a scalar result because there is only one SUM(amt).

The second common programming error that is made with this kind of UPDATE is to use an aggregate function that does not return zero when it is applied to an empty table, such as the AVG(). Suppose we wanted to post the average payment amount made by the Customers, we could not just replace SUM() with AVG() and acct_amt with average balance in the above UPDATE. Instead, we would have to add a WHERE clause to the UPDATE that gives us only those customers who made a payment, thus:

```
UPDATE Customers
   SET payment = (SELECT AVG(P1.amt)
                    FROM Payments AS P1
```

```
                WHERE Customers.cust_nbr = P1.cust_nbr)
 WHERE EXISTS (SELECT *
               FROM Payments AS P1
              WHERE Customers.cust_nbr = P1.cust_nbr);
```

You can use the WHERE clause to avoid NULLs in cases where a NULL would propagate in a calculation.

Another solution was to use a COALESCE() function to take care of the empty subquery result problem. The general form of this statement is

```
UPDATE T1
   SET c1
       = COALESCE ((SELECT c1
                     FROM T2
                    WHERE T1.keycol = T2.keycol),
                  T1.c1),
       c2 = COALESCE ((SELECT c2
                        FROM T2
                       WHERE T1.keycol = T2.keycol),
                     T1.c2),

       ...
 WHERE ... ;
```

This will also leave the unmatched rows alone, but it will do a table scan on T1. Jeremy Rickard improved this by putting the COALESCE() inside the subquery SELECT list. This assumes that you have row constructors in your SQL product. For example:

```
UPDATE T2
   SET (c1, c2, ...)
     = (SELECT COALESCE (T1.c1, T2.c1),
               COALESCE (T1.c2, T2.c2),
               ...
          FROM T1
         WHERE T1.keycol = T2.keycol)
 WHERE ... ;
```

Again, these examples are presented only so that you can replace it with a MERGE statement

15.3.5 Using the CASE Expression in UPDATEs

The CASE expression is very handy for updating a table. The first trick is to realize that you can write "SET a=a" to do nothing. The statement given above can be rewritten as:

```
UPDATE Customers
   SET payment
     = CASE WHEN EXISTS
            (SELECT *
               FROM Payments AS P1
             WHERE Customers.cust_nbr = P1.cust_nbr)
            THEN (SELECT AVG(P1.amt)
                    FROM Payments AS P1
                  WHERE Customers.cust_nbr = P1.cust_nbr)
            ELSE payment END;
```

This statement will scan the entire table, as there is no WHERE clause. That might be a bad thing in this example—I would guess that only a small number of customers make a payment on any given day. But very often you were going to do table scans anyway and this version can be faster.

But the real advantage of the CASE expression is the ability to combine several UPDATE statements into one statement. The execution time will be greatly improved and will save you a lot of procedural code or really ugly SQL. Consider this example. We have an inventory of books and we want to (1) reduce the books priced $25.00 and over by 10% and (2) increase the item_price of the books under $25.00 by 15% to make up the difference. The immediate thought is to write:

```
BEGIN ATOMIC -- wrong!
UPDATE Books
   SET item_price = item_price * 0.90
 WHERE item_price > = 25.00;
UPDATE Books
   SET item_price = item_price * 1.15
 WHERE item_price < 25.00;
END;
```

But this does not work. Consider a book priced at $25.00; it goes through the first UPDATE and it is repriced at $22.50; it then goes through the second

UPDATE and is repriced $25.88, which is not what we wanted. Flipping the two statements will produce the desired results for this book, but given a book priced at $24.95, we will get $28.69 and then $25.82 as a final item_price.

```
UPDATE Books
   SET item_price = CASE WHEN item_price < 25.00
                    THEN item_price = item_price * 1.15
                    ELSE item_price = item_price * 0.90 END;
```

This is not only faster, but it is correct. However, you have to be careful and be sure that you did not really want a series of functions applied to the same columns in a particular order. If that is the case, then you need to try to make each assignment expression within the SET clause stand by itself as a complete function instead of one step in a process. Consider this example:

```
BEGIN ATOMIC
UPDATE Foobar
   SET a = x
 WHERE r = 1;
UPDATE Foobar
   SET b = y
 WHERE s = 2;
UPDATE Foobar
   SET c = z
 WHERE t = 3;
UPDATE Foobar
   SET c = z + 1
 WHERE t = 4;
END;
```

This can be replaced by:

```
UPDATE Foobar
   SET a = CASE WHEN r = 1 THEN x ELSE a END,
       b = CASE WHEN s = 2 THEN y ELSE b END,
       c = CASE WHEN t = 3 THEN z
                WHEN t = 4 THEN z + 1
                ELSE c END
```

```
WHERE r = 1
   OR s = 2
   OR t IN (3, 4);
```

The WHERE clause is optional but might improve performance if the index is right and the candidate set is small. Notice that this approach is driven by the destination of the UPDATE—the columns appear only once in the SET clause. The traditional approach is driven by the source of the changes—you first make updates from one data source, then the next, and so forth. Think about how you would do this with a set of magnetic tapes applied against a master file.

15.4 A Note on Flaws in a Common Vendor Extension

While I do not like to spend much time discussing nonstandard SQL-like languages, the T-SQL language from Sybase and Microsoft had a horrible flaw in it that users need to be warned about. They have a proprietary syntax that allows a FROM clause in the UPDATE statement.

Neither works correctly. The original Sybase statement would do multiple updates of the target table when the source table was in a many-to-one relationship with the base table being updated.

```
UPDATE T1
   SET T1.x = 2 * T1.x
  FROM T2
 WHERE T1.x = T2.x;
```

The column T1.x will be doulbed and redoubled for each x in T2.

The Microsoft version solved the cardinality problem by simply grabbing *one of the values based on the current physical arrangement of the rows in the table.* This is a simple example from Adam Mechanic:

```
CREATE TABLE Foo
(col_a CHAR(1) NOT NULL,
 col_b INTEGER NOT NULL);

INSERT INTO Foo VALUES ('A', 0), ('B', 0), ('C', 0);

CREATE TABLE Bar
(col_a CHAR(1) NOT NULL,
 col_b INTEGER NOT NULL);
```

```
INSERT INTO Bar
VALUES ('A', 1), ('A', 2), ('B', 1), ('C', 1);
```

You run this proprietary UPDATE with a FROM clause:

```
UPDATE Foo
   SET Foo.col_b = Bar.col_b
  FROM Foo INNER JOIN Bar
       ON Foo.col_a = Bar.col_a;
```

The result of the UPDATE cannot be determined. The value of the column will depend upon either order of insertion (if there are no clustered indexes present), or on order of clustering (but only if the cluster is not fragmented).

15.5 MERGE Statement

SQL-99 added a single statement to mimic a common magnetic tape file system "merge and insert" procedure. The simplest business logic, in a pseudo-code is like this.

```
FOR EACH row IN the Transactions table
DO IF working row NOT IN Master table
   THEN INSERT working row INTO the Master table;
   ELSE UPDATE Master table
           SET Master table columns to the Transactions table values
         WHERE they meet a matching criteria;
   END IF;
END FOR;
```

In the 1950s, we would sort the transaction tape(s) and Master tapes on the same key, read each one looking for a match, and then perform whatever logic is needed. In its simplest form, the MERGE statement looks like this (Figure 15.1):

```
MERGE INTO <table name> [AS [<correlation name>]]
USING <table reference> ON <search condition>
{WHEN [NOT] MATCHED [AND <search condition>]
 THEN <modification operation>} ...
[ELSE IGNORE];
```

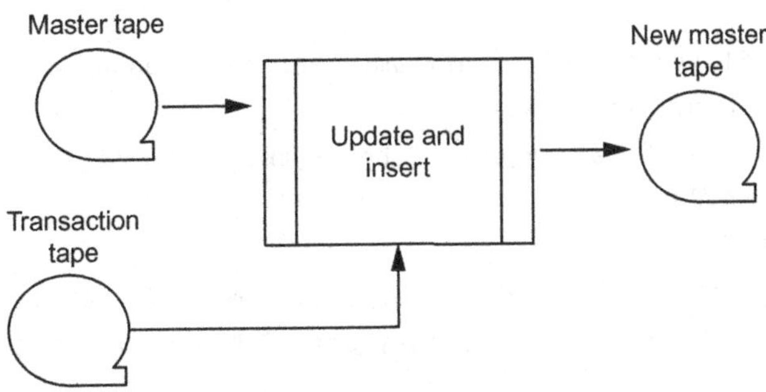

Figure 15.1 Tape merging.

You will notice that use of a correlation name in the MERGE INTO clause is in complete violation of the principle that a correlation name effectively creates a temporary table. There are several other places where SQL:2003 destroyed the original SQL language model, but you do not have to write irregular syntax in all cases.

After a row is MATCHED (or not) to the target table, you can add more <search condition>s in the WHEN clauses in the Standards. Some of the lesser SQLs do not allow extra <search condition>s, so be careful. You can often work around this limitation with logic in the ON, WHERE clauses and CASE expressions.

The <modification operation> clause can include insertion, update, or delete operations that follow the same rules as those single statements. This can hide complex programming logic in a single statement. But the NOT MATCHED indicates the operation to be performed on the rows where the ON search condition is FALSE or UNKNOWN. Only INSERT or signal-statement to raise an exception can be specified after THEN.

Let's assume that that we have a table of Personnel salary_amt changes at the branch office in a staging table called Personnel_Changes. Here is a MERGE statement, which will take the contents of the Personnel_Changes table and merge them with the Personnel table. Both of them use the emp_nbr as the key. Here is a typical, but very simple use of MERGE INTO.

```
MERGE INTO Personnel
USING (SELECT emp_nbr, salary_amt, bonus_amt, commission_amt
         FROM Personnel_Changes) AS C
  ON Personnel.emp_nbr = C.emp_nbr
WHEN MATCHED
```

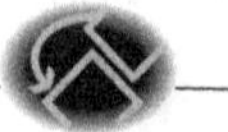

```
THEN UPDATE
        SET (Personnel.salary_amt, Personnel.bonus_amt,
Personnel.commission_amt)
            = (C.salary_amt, C.bonus_amt, C.commission_amt)
WHEN NOT MATCHED
THEN INSERT
     (emp_nbr, salary_amt, bonus_amt, commission_amt)
     VALUES (C.emp_nbr, C.salary_amt, C.bonus_amt, C.commission_amt);
```

If you think about it for a minute, if there is a match, then all you can do is UPDATE the row. If there is no match, then all you can do is INSERT the new row.

Consider a fancier version of the second clause, and an employee type that determines the compensation pattern.

```
WHEN MATCHED AND c.emp_type = 'sales'
THEN UPDATE
        SET (Personnel.salary_amt, Personnel.bonus_amt,
Personnel.commission_amt)
            = (C.salary_amt, C.bonus_amt, C.commission_amt)
WHEN MATCHED AND c.emp_type = 'executive'
THEN UPDATE
        SET (Personnel.salary_amt, Personnel.bonus_amt,
Personnel.commission_amt)
            = (C.salary_amt, C.bonus_amt, 0.00)
WHEN MATCHED AND c.emp_type = 'office'
THEN UPDATE
        SET (Personnel.salary_amt, Personnel.bonus_amt,
Personnel.commission_amt)
            = (C.salary_amt, 0.00, 0.00)
```

There are proprietary versions of this statement in particular, look for the term "upsert" in the literature. These statements are most often used for adding data to a data warehouse in their product.

Your first thought might be that MERGE is a shorthand for this code skeleton:

```
BEGIN ATOMIC
UPDATE T1
```

```
   SET (a, b, c, ..
       = (SELECT a, b, c, ..
            FROM T2
           WHERE T1.somekey = T2.somekey),
 WHERE EXISTS
       (SELECT *
          FROM T2
         WHERE T1.somekey = T2.somekey);
INSERT INTO T1
SELECT *
  FROM T2
 WHERE NOT EXISTS
       (SELECT *
          FROM T2
         WHERE T1.somekey = T2.somekey);
END;
```

But there are some subtle differences. The MERGE is a single statement, so it can be optimized as a whole. The two separate UPDATE and INSERT clauses can be optimized as a single statement. The first pass splits the working set into two buckets, and then each MATCHED/NOT MATCHED bucket is handled by itself. The WHEN [NOT] MATCHED clauses with additional search conditions can be executed in parallel or rearranged on the fly, but they have to effectively perform them in left-to-right order.

Set Operations

BY SET OPERATIONS, I mean union, intersection, and set differences where the sets in SQL are tables. These are the basic operators used in elementary set theory, which has been taught in the United States public school systems for decades. Since the relational model is based on sets, you would expect that SQL would have had a good variety of set operators. But there is a problem in SQL that you did not have in high school set theory. SQL tables are multisets (also called bags), which means that, unlike sets, they allow duplicate elements (rows or tuples). SQL handles these duplicate rows with an ALL or DISTINCT modifier in different places in the language; ALL preserves duplicates and DISTINCT removes them.

So that we can discuss the result of each operator formally, let R be a row that is a duplicate of some row in TableA, or of some row in TableB, or of both. Let m be the number of duplicates of R in TableA and let n be the number of duplicates of R in TableB, where (m>=0) and (n>=0). Informally, the engines will pair off the two tables on a row-per-row basis in set operations. We will see how this works for each operator.

For the rest of this discussion, let us create two skeleton tables with the same structure, which we can use for examples.

```
CREATETABLE S1 (a1 CHAR(1));
INSERT INTO S1
VALUES ('a'), ('a'), ('b'), ('b'), ('c');
```

```
CREATE TABLE S2 (a2 CHAR(1));
INSERT INTO S2
VALUES ('a'), ('b'), ('b'), ('b'), ('c'), ('d');
```

16.1 UNION and UNION ALL

UNIONs have been supported since SQL-86, with this infixed syntax:

<table expression> UNION [ALL] <table expression>

The two versions of the UNION statement take two tables and build a result table from them. The two tables must be union compatible, which means that they have exactly the same number of columns, and that each column in the first table has the *same data type* (or automatically cast to it) as the column in *the same position* in the second table. That is, their rows have the same structure, so they can be put in the same final result table. Most implementations will do some data type conversions to create the result table, but this can be implementation-dependent and you should check it out for yourself.

There are two forms of the UNION statement: the UNION and the UNION ALL. The simple UNION is the same operator you had in high school set theory; it returns the rows that appear in either or both tables and removes redundant duplicates from the result table.

The phrase "redundant duplicates" sounds funny; but it means that you leave one copy of the row in the table. The problem is that string equality in SQL works by padding the shorter string with trailing blanks, then comparing them position by position. Which string is retained is implementation defined.

The sample tables will yield:

```
(SELECT a1 FROM S1
 UNION
 SELECT a2 FROM S2)
```

a
b
c
d

In many early SQL implementations, merge-sorting the two tables discarding duplicates during the sorting did this removal. This had the side effect that the result table is sorted, but you cannot depend on that. Later implementations use hashing, indexing and parallel processing to find the duplicates.

The UNION ALL preserves the duplicates from both tables in the result table. Most early implementations simply appended one table to the other in physical storage. They used file systems based on physically contiguous storage, so this was easy and used the file system code. But, again, you cannot depend on any ordering in the results of either version of the UNION statement. Again, the sample tables will yield:

```
(SELECT a1 FROM S1
 UNION ALL
 SELECT a2 FROM S2)
```

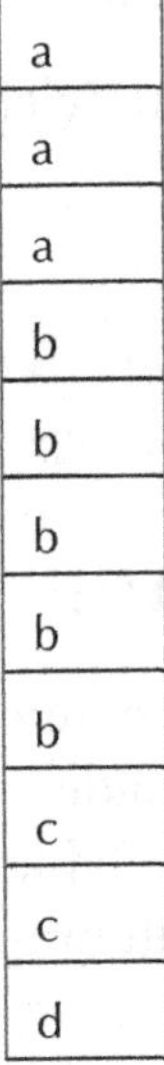

a
a
a
b
b
b
b
b
c
c
d

You can assign names to the columns by using the AS operator to make the result set into a derived table, thus:

```
SELECT rent, utilities, phone
  FROM (SELECT a, b, c
          FROM Old_Locations
         WHERE city_name = 'Boston'
```

```
UNION
SELECT x, y, z
  FROM New_Locations
 WHERE city_name = 'New York')
AS Cities (rent, utilities, phone);
```

A few SQL products will attempt to optimize UNIONs if they are made on the same table. Those UNIONs can often be replaced with OR-ed predicates. For example:

```
SELECT city_name 'Western'
  FROM Cities
 WHERE market_code = 't'
UNION ALL
SELECT city_name 'Eastern'
  FROM Cities
 WHERE market_code = 'v';
```

could be rewritten (probably more efficiently) as follows:

```
SELECT city_name
       CASE market_code
       WHEN 't' THEN 'Western'
       WHEN 'v' THEN 'Eastern' END
FROM Cities
WHERE market_code IN ('v', 't');
```

It takes system architecture based on domains rather than tables to optimize UNIONs if they are made on different tables.

Doing a UNION to the same table is the same as a SELECT DISTINCT, but the SELECT DISTINCT will probably run faster and preserve the column names too.

16.1.1 Order of Execution

UNION and UNION ALL operators are executed from left to right unless parentheses change the order of execution. Since the UNION operator is associative and commutative, the order of a chain of UNIONs will not affect the results. However, order and grouping can affect performance. Consider two tables that have many duplicates between them. If the optimizer does not consider table sizes, this query

```
(SELECT * FROM Small_Table1)
 UNION
(SELECT * FROM Big_Table)
 UNION
(SELECT * FROM Small_Table2);
```

will merge Small_Table1 into Big_Table, and then merge Small_Table2 into that first result. If the rows of Small_Table1 are spread out in the first result table, locating duplicates from Small_Table2 will take longer than if we had written the query thus:

```
(SELECT * FROM Small_Table1)
 UNION
(SELECT * FROM Small_Table2)
   UNION
(SELECT * FROM Big_Table);
```

Again, optimization of UNIONs is highly product-dependent, so you should experiment with it.

16.1.2 Mixed UNION and UNION ALL Operators

If you know that there are no duplicates, or that duplicates are not a problem in your situation, use UNION ALL instead of UNION for speed. For example, if we are sure that Big_Table has no duplicates in common with Small_Table1 and Small_Table2, this query will produce the same results as before but should run much faster:

```
((SELECT * FROM Small_Table1)
UNION
(SELECT * FROM Small_Table2)) -- intermediate set
UNION ALL
(SELECT * FROM Big_Table);
```

But be careful when mixing UNION and UNION ALL operators. The left-to-right order of execution will cause the last operator in the chain to have an effect on the results.

16.1.3 UNION of Columns from the Same Table

A useful trick for building the union of columns from the same table is to use a CROSS JOIN and a CASE expression, thus

```
SELECT CASE WHEN S1.seq = 1 THEN F1.col1
            WHEN S1.seq = 2 THEN F1.col2
            ELSE NULL END
  FROM Foobar AS F1
       CROSS JOIN
       Series AS S1(seq)
 WHERE S1.seq IN (1, 2)
```

This acts like the UNION ALL statement, but change the SELECT to SELECT DISTINCT and you have a UNION. The advantage of this statement over the more obvious UNION is that it makes one pass through the table. Given a large table, that can be important for good performance.

16.2 INTERSECT and EXCEPT

The INTERSECT and EXCEPT set operators take two tables and build a new table from them. The two tables must be union compatible, just like with the UNION [ALL] operator. Like the UNION [ALL], the result of an INTERSECT [ALL] or EXCEPT [ALL] should use an AS operator if you want to have names for the result table and its columns.

Oracle was the first major vendor to have the EXCEPT operator with the keyword MINUS. The set difference is the rows in the first table, except for those that also appear in the second table. It answers questions like "Give me all the employees except the salesmen" in a natural manner.

Let's take our two multisets and use them to explain the basic model, by making a mapping between them:

```
S1 = {a, a, b, b,    c   }
      ↕    ↕  ↕      ↕
S2 = {a,   b, b, b,   c, d}
```

The INTERSECT and EXCEPT operators remove all duplicates from both sets, so we would have:

```
S1 = {a, b, c }
      ↕  ↕  ↕
S2 = {a, b, c, d}
```

and therefore,

```
S1 INTERSECT S2 = {a, b, c}
```

and

```
S2 EXCEPT S1 = {d}
S1 EXCEPT S2 = {}
```

When you add the ALL option, things are trickier. The mapped pairs become the unit of work. The INTERSECT ALL keeps each pairing, so that

```
S1 INTERSECT ALL S2 = {a, b, b, c}
```

and the EXCEPT ALL throws them away, retain what is left in the first set, thus.

```
S2 EXCEPT ALL S1 = {b, d}
```

Trying to write the INTERSECT and EXCEPT with other operators is trickier than it looks. It has to be general enough to handle situations where there is no key available and the number of columns is not known.

Standard SQL defines the actions for duplicates in terms of the count of duplicates of matching rows. Let (m) be the number of rows of one kind in S1 and (n) be the number in S2. The UNION ALL will have (m+n) copies of the row. The INTERSECT ALL will have LEAST(m, n) copies. EXCEPT ALL will have the greater of either the first table's count minus the second table's count or zero copies.

The immediate impulse of a programmer is to write the code with EXISTS() predicates. The bad news is that it does not work because of NULLs. This is easier to show with code. Let's redo our two sample tables.

```
CREATE TABLE S1 (a1 CHAR(1));
INSERT INTO S1
VALUES ('a'), ('a'), ('b'), ('b'), ('c'), (NULL), (NULL);

CREATE TABLE S2 (a2 CHAR(1));
INSERT INTO S2
VALUES ('a'), ('b'), ('b'), ('b'), ('c'), ('d'), (NULL);
```

Now build a view to hold the duplication_cnt of each value in each table.

```
CREATE VIEW DupCounts (a, s1_dup, s2_dup)
AS
SELECT S.a, SUM(s1_dup), SUM(s2_dup)
  FROM (SELECT S1.a1, 1, 0
           FROM S1
         UNION ALL
        SELECT S2.a2, 0, 1
          FROM S2) AS S(a, s1_dup, s2_dup)
 GROUP BY S.a, s1_dup, s2_dup;
```

The GROUP BY will put the NULLs into a separate group giving them the right tallies. Now code is a straightforward implementation of the definitions in Standard SQL.

```
-- S1 EXCEPT ALL S2
 SELECT DISTINCT D1.a, (s1_dup - s2_dup) AS dups
   FROM DupCounts AS D1,
        Series AS S1
 WHERE S1.seq <= (s1_dup - s2_dup);

-- S1 INTERSECT ALL S2
 SELECT DISTINCT D1.a,
                CASE WHEN s1_dup <= s2_dup
                     THEN s1_dup ELSE s2_dup END
                AS duplication_cnt
   FROM DupCounts AS D1,
        Series AS S1
  WHERE S1.seq <= CASE WHEN s1_dup <= s2_dup
                     THEN s1_dup ELSE s2_dup END;
```

Notice that we had to use SELECT DISTINCT. Without it, the sample data will produce this table.

a	duplication_cnt
NULL	1
a	1
b	2
b	2 ◄ redundant row
c	1

The nonduplicated versions are easy to write from the definitions in the Standards. In effect their duplication tallies are set to one.

```
-- S1 INTERSECT S2
 SELECT D1.a
   FROM DupCounts AS D1
  WHERE s1_dup > 0
    AND s2_dup > 0;

-- S1 EXCEPT S2
 SELECT D1.a
   FROM DupCounts AS D1
  WHERE s1_dup > 0
    AND s2_dup = 0;

-- S2 EXCEPT S1
 SELECT D1.a
   FROM DupCounts AS D1
  WHERE s2_dup > 0
    AND s1_dup = 0;
```

16.2.1 INTERSECT and EXCEPT Without NULLs and Duplicates

INTERSECT and EXCEPT are much easier if each of the two tables does not have NULLs and duplicate values in them. Intersection is simply

```
SELECT *
  FROM S1
 WHERE EXISTS
       (SELECT *
          FROM S2
         WHERE S1.a1 = S2.a2);
```

or

```
SELECT *
  FROM S2
 WHERE EXISTS
       (SELECT *
          FROM S1
         WHERE S1.a1 = S2.a2);
```

You can also use

```
SELECT DISTINCT S2.*
  FROM (S2 INNER JOIN S1 ON S1.a1 = S2.a2);
```

This is given as a motivation for the next piece of code, but you may find that some SQL engines do joins faster than EXISTS() predicates and vice versa, so it is a good idea to have more than one trick in your bag.

The set difference can be written with an OUTER JOIN operator. This code is due to Jim Panttaja.

```
SELECT DISTINCT S2.*
  FROM (S2 LEFT OUTER JOIN S1
        ON S1.a1 = S2.a2)
 WHERE S1.a1 IS NULL;
```

This was all we had in the early days, and you should not use it today. But you will see it in old code.

16.2.2 INTERSECT and EXCEPT with NULLs and Duplicates

These versions of INTERSECT and EXCEPT are due to Itzak Ben-Gan. They make very good use of the UNION and DISTINCT operators to implement set theory definitions.

```
-- S1 INTERSECT S2
SELECT D.a
FROM (SELECT DISTINCT a1 FROM S1
      UNION ALL
      SELECT DISTINCT a2 FROM S2) AS D(a)
GROUP BY D.a
HAVING COUNT(*) > 1;

-- S1 INTERSECT ALL S2
SELECT D2.a
FROM (SELECT D1.a, MIN(cnt) AS mincnt
      FROM (SELECT a1, COUNT(*)
              FROM S1
             GROUP BY a1
            UNION ALL
```

```
                SELECT a2, COUNT(*)
                  FROM S2
                 GROUP BY a2) AS D1(a, cnt)
         GROUP BY D1.a
         HAVING COUNT(*) > 1) AS D2
     INNER JOIN
     Series
   ON seq <= min_cnt;

-- S1 EXCEPT ALL S2
SELECT D2.a
  FROM (SELECT D1.a, SUM(cnt)
          FROM (SELECT a1, COUNT(*)
                 FROM S1
                 GROUP BY a1
                UNION ALL
                SELECT a2, -COUNT(*)
                  FROM S2
                 GROUP BY a2)
               AS D1(a, cnt)
         GROUP BY D1.a
         HAVING SUM(cnt) > 0)
       AS D2(a, dups)
       INNER JOIN
       Series ON seq <= D2.dups;
```

The Series table is discussed in other places in this book. It is a table of integers from 1 to (n) that is used to replace iteration and counting in SQL. Obviously, (n) has to be large enough for these statements to work.

16.3 A Note on ALL and SELECT DISTINCT

Here is a series of observations about the relationship between the ALL option in set operations and the SELECT DISTINCT options in a query from Beught Gunne. The multiset model does not behave like the traditional set theory we know from school.

Given two tables with duplicate values:

```
CREATE TABLE A (i INTEGER NOT NULL);
INSERT INTO A VALUES (1), (1), (2), (2), (4), (4);
```

```
CREATE TABLE B (i INTEGER NOT NULL);
INSERT INTO B VALUES (2), (2), (3), (3);
```

The UNION and INTERSECT operations have regular behavior in that

```
(A UNION B) = SELECT DISTINCT (A UNION ALL B) = ((1), (2), (3))
```

and

```
(A INTERSECT B) = SELECT DISTINCT (A INTERSECT ALL B) = (2)
```

However,

```
(A EXCEPT B) <> SELECT DISTINCT (A EXCEPT ALL B)
```

Or more literally, (1) <> ((1), (2)) for the tables given in the example. And likewise, we have

```
(B EXCEPT A) = SELECT DISTINCT (B EXCEPT ALL A) = (3)
```

by a coincidence of the particular values used in these tables.

16.4 Equality and Proper Subsets

At one point, when SQL was still in the laboratory at IBM, there was a CONTAINS operator that would tell you if one table was a subset of another. It disappeared in later versions of the language and no vendor picked it up. Set equality was never part of SQL as an operator, so you would have to have used the two expressions ((A CONTAINS B) AND (B CONTAINS A)) to find out.

Today, you can use the methods shown in the section on Relational Division to determine containment or equality. Or you can use set theory expressions, such as NOT EXISTS ((A EXCEPT B) UNION (B EXCEPT A)). Which method is fastest is going to depend on the SQL product and the access method used.

However, Itzak Ben-Gan came up with a novel approach for finding containment and equality that is worth a mention.

```
SELECT SUM(DISTINCT match_col)
  FROM (SELECT CASE
               WHEN S1.col
                    IN (SELECT S2.col FROM S2)
```

```
                THEN 1 ELSE -1 END
        FROM S1) AS X(match_col)
HAVING SUM(DISTINCT match_col) = :n;
```

You can set (:n) to 1, 0, or −1 for each particular test.

When I find a matching row in S1, I get a one; when I find a mismatched row in S1, get a −1 and they sum together to give me a zero. Therefore, S1 is a proper subset of S2. If they sum to one, then they are equal. If they sum to −1, they are disjoint.

Another trick for equality is based on the principle that if two sets are equal, then they have the same cardinality. This is necessary but not sufficient. They have the same elements. We can use a windowed count(*) to get the cardinality

```
EXISTS (SELECT a, COUNT(a) OVER() AS alpha_cardinality
          FROM Alphas
        EXCEPT
        SELECT b, COUNT(b) OVER() AS beta_cardinality
          FROM Betas)
```

Row and Column Level Features

Comparison or Theta Operators

DR. CODD INTRODUCED the term "theta operators" in his early papers for what a programmer would have called a comparison predicate or operator. The large number of data types in SQL makes doing comparisons a little harder than in other programming languages; we have to do more casting. Values of one data type have to be promoted to values of the other data type before the comparison can be done. The available data types are implementation- and hardware-dependent so read the manuals for your product.

The comparison operators are overloaded and will work for numeric, character, and temporal data types. The symbols and meanings for comparison operators are shown in the table below.

OPERATOR	NUMERIC	CHARACTER	DATETIME
<	less than	collates before	earlier than
=	equal to	collates equal to	same time as
>	greater than	collates after	later than
<=	at most	collates before or equal	no earlier than
<>	not equal	not the same as	not the same time as
>=	at least	collates after or equal	no later than

You will also see! = or ¬=for "not equal to" in some older SQL implementations. These symbols are borrowed from the C and PL/I programming languages, respectively, and have never been part of standard SQL. It is a bad habit to use them since it destroys portability of your code and makes it harder to read.

The comparison operators will return a logical value of TRUE, FALSE, or UNKNOWN. The values TRUE and FALSE follow the usual rules and UNKNOWN is always returned when one or both of the operands is a NULL. Please pay attention to Section 17.3 on the new IS [NOT] DISTINCT FROM Operator and look at functions that work with NULLs.

17.1 Converting Data Types

Numeric data types are all mutually comparable and mutually assignable. If an assignment would result in a loss of the most significant digits, an exception condition is raised. If least significant digits are lost, the implementation defines what rounding or truncating occurs and does not report an exception condition. Most often, one value is converted to the same data type as the other and then the comparison is done in the usual way. The chosen data type is the "higher" of the two, using the following ordering: SMALLINT, INTEGER, BIGINT, DECIMAL, NUMERIC, REAL, FLOAT, DOUBLE PRECISION.

Floating-point hardware will often affect comparisons for REAL, FLOAT, and DOUBLE PRECISION numbers. There is no good way to avoid this, since it is not always reasonable to use DECIMAL or NUMERIC in their place. A host language will probably use the same floating-point hardware, so at least errors will be constant across the application.

CHARACTER (or CHAR) and CHARACTER VARYING (or VARCHAR) data types are comparable if and only if they are taken from the same character repertoire. This means that ASCII characters cannot be compared with graphics characters, English cannot be compared to Arabic, and so on. In most implementations this is not a problem, because the database usually has only one repertoire.

The comparison takes the shorter of the two strings and pads it with spaces. The strings are compared position by position from left to right, using the collating sequence for the repertoire—ASCII or EBCDIC in most cases.

Temporal (or <datetime>, as they are called in the standard) data types are mutually assignable only if the source and target of the assignment have the same <datetime> fields. That is, you cannot compare a date and a time. The CAST() operator can do explicit type conversions before you do a comparison.

Here is a table of the valid combinations of source (rows in the table) and target (columns) data types in Standard SQL. Y ("yes") means that the combination is syntactically valid without restriction; M ("maybe") indicates that the combination is valid subject to other syntax rules; and N ("no") indicates that the combination is not valid.

	EN	AN	VC	FC	VB	FB	D	T	TS	YM	DT
EN	Y	Y	Y	Y	N	N	N	N	N	N	M
AN	Y	Y	Y	Y	N	N	N	N	N	N	N
C	Y	Y	M	M	Y	Y	Y	Y	Y	Y	Y
B	N	N	Y	Y	Y	Y	N	N	N	N	N
D	N	N	Y	Y	N	N	Y	N	Y	N	N
T	N	N	Y	Y	N	N	N	Y	Y	N	N
TS	N	N	Y	Y	N	N	Y	Y	Y	N	N
YM	M	N	Y	Y	N	N	N	N	N	Y	N
DT	M	N	Y	Y	N	N	N	N	N	N	Y

Where:

EN = Exact Numeric

AN = Approximate Numeric

C = Character (Fixed- or Variable-length)

FC = Fixed-length Character

VC = Variable-length Character

B = Bit String (Fixed- or Variable-length)

FB = Fixed-length Bit String

VB = Variable-length Bit String

D = Date

T = Time

TS = Timestamp

YM = Year-Month Interval

DT = Day-Time Interval

17.1.1 Date Display Formats

SQL is silent about formatting data for display, as it should be. Dates have many different national formats and you will find many vendor extensions that allow the user to format temporal data into strings and to input dates in various display formats. The only subset of the ISO-8601 formats used in Standard SQL is "yyyy-mm-dd hh:mm:ss.sssss". The year field is between "0001" and "9999", months and days follow the Common Era Calendar. Hours are between "00" and "23"; minutes are between "00" and "59"; seconds are between "00" and" 59.999.." with the decimal precision being defined by implementation. The FIPS (Federal Information Processing Standards) requires at least 5 decimal places and most modern hard will provide nanosecond accuracy.

17.1.2 Other Display Formats

Character and exact numeric data types are usually displayed as you would expect. Today this means Unicode rules. Approximate numeric data might be shown in decimal or exponential formats. This is implementation defined. However, the Standard defines an approximate numeric literal as:

<approximate numeric literal> ::= <mantissa> E <exponent>

<mantissa> ::= <exact numeric literal>

<exponent> ::= <signed integer>

But some host languages do not require a <mantissa> and some allow a lowercase 'e' for the separator. SQL requires a leading zero where other languages might not.

17.2 Row Comparisons in SQL

Standard SQL generalized the theta operators so they would work on row expressions and not just on scalars. This is not a popular feature yet, but it is very handy for situations where a key is made from more than one column, and so forth. This makes SQL more orthogonal and it has an intuitive feel to it. Take three row constants:

A=(10, 20, 30, 40);

B=(10, NULL, 30, 40);

C=(10, NULL, 30, 100);

It seems reasonable to define a row comparison as valid only when the data types of each corresponding column in the rows are union-compatible. If not, the operation is an error and should report a warning. It also seems reasonable to define the results of the comparison to the AND-ed results of each corresponding column using the same operator. That is, (A = B) becomes:

((10, 20, 30, 40) = (10, NULL, 30, 40));

becomes:

((10 = 10) AND (20 = NULL) AND (30 = 30) AND (40 = 40))

becomes:

(TRUE AND UNKNOWN AND TRUE AND TRUE);

becomes:

(UNKNOWN);

This seems to be reasonable and conforms to the idea that a NULL is a missing value that we expect to resolve at a future date, so we cannot draw a conclusion about this comparison just yet. Now consider the comparison (A = C), which becomes:

((10, 20, 30, 40) = (10, NULL, 30, 100));

becomes:

((10 = 10) AND (20 = NULL) AND (30 = 30) AND (40 = 100));

becomes:

(TRUE AND UNKNOWN AND TRUE AND FALSE);

becomes:

(FALSE);

There is no way to pick a value from column 2 of row C such that the UNKNOWN result will change to TRUE because the fourth column is always FALSE. This leaves you with a situation that is not very intuitive. The first case can resolve to TRUE or FALSE, but the second case can only go to FALSE.

Standard SQL decided that the theta operators would work as shown in the table below. The expression RX <comp op> RY is shorthand for a row RX compared to a row RY; likewise, RXi means the i-th column in the row RX. The results are still TRUE, FALSE, or UNKNOWN, if there is no error in type matching. The rules favor solid tests for TRUE or FALSE, using UNKNOWN as a last resort.

The idea of these rules is that as you read the rows from left to right, the values in one row are always greater than or less than) those in the other row after some column. This is how it would work if you were alphabetizing words. The rules are:

1. RX = RY is TRUE if and only if RXi = RYi for all i.
2. RX <> RY is TRUE if and only if RXi <> RYi for some i.
3. RX < RY is TRUE if and only if RXi = RYi for all i < n and RXn < RYn for some n.
4. RX > RY is TRUE if and only if RXi = RYi for all i < n and RXn > RYn for some n.
5. RX <= RY is TRUE if and only if Rx = Ry or Rx < Ry.
6. RX >= RY is TRUE if and only if Rx = Ry or Rx > Ry.
7. RX = RY is FALSE if and only if RX <> RY is TRUE.
8. RX <> RY is FALSE if and only if RX = RY is TRUE.
9. RX < RY is FALSE if and only if RX >= RY is TRUE.
10. RX > RY is FALSE if and only if RX <= RY is TRUE.
11. RX <= RY is FALSE if and only if RX > RY is TRUE.
12. 17. RX >= RY is FALSE if and only if RX < RY is TRUE.
13. RX <comp op> RY is UNKNOWN if and only if RX <comp op> RY is neither TRUE nor FALSE.

The negations are defined so that the NOT operator will still have its usual properties. Notice that a NULL in a row will give an UNKNOWN result in a comparison. Consider this expression:

(a, b, c) < (x, y, z)

which becomes

((a < x)

OR ((a = x) AND (b < y))

OR ((a = x) AND (b = y) AND (c < z)))

The standard allows a single-row expression of any sort, including a single-row subquery, on either side of a comparison. Likewise, the BETWEEN predicate can use row expressions in any position in Standard SQL.

17.3 IS [NOT] DISTINCT FROM Operator

The SQL 2003 Standards added a verbose but useful theta operator. SQL has two kinds of comparisons, or equivalence classes; equality and grouping.

Equality treats NULLs as incomparable and gets us into the three valued logic that returns {TRUE, FALSE, UNKNOWN}.

Grouping treats NULLs as equal values and gets us into the usual two valued logic that returns {TRUE, FALSE}. This is why a GROUP BY puts all the NULLs in one group and you get that behavior in other places.

The theta operators we have discussed so far are based on the equality model, so if you wanted a comparison that grouped NULLs, you had to write elaborate CASE expressions. Now you can do it in one infix operator for either rows or scalars.

```
<expression 1> IS NOT DISTINCT FROM <expression 2>
```

is logically equivalent to

```
(<expression 1> IS NOT NULL
AND <expression 2> IS NOT NULL
AND <expression 1>=<expression 2>)
OR (<expression 1> IS NULL AND <expression 2> IS NULL)
```

Thus following the usual pattern for adding NOT into SQL constructs

```
<expression 1> IS DISTINCT FROM <expression 2>
```

is a shorthand for

```
NOT (<expression 1> IS NOT DISTINCT FROM <expression 2>)
```

This double negative was because the IS NOT DISTINCT FROM was defined first. I have no idea why.

You will see an attempt to get this functionality with search conditions like:
COALESCE (<expression 1>, <absurd non-null value>) = COALESCE (<expression 2>, <absurd non-null value>)

This avoids the problem that if the second parameter, an absurd value, was NULL, then COALESCE will be "NULL=NULL" which will result in UNKNOWN.

17.4 Monadic Operators

A monadic operator returns a logical value. But the problem in SQL is that we have scalar values, row values and table values. These operators are defined for one or more levels.

17.4.1 IS NULL

<null predicate> ::=<row value constructor> IS [NOT] NULL

It is the only way to test to see if an expression is NULL or not, and it has been in SQL-86 and all later versions of the standard. The SQL-92 standard extended it to accept <row value constructor> instead of a single column or a scalar expression.

This extended version will start showing up in implementations when other row expressions are allowed. If all the values in the row R are the NULL value, then R IS NULL is TRUE; otherwise, it is FALSE. If none of the values in R are NULL value, R IS NOT NULL is TRUE; otherwise, it is FALSE. The case where the row is a mix of NULL and non-NULL values is defined by the table below, where Degree means the number of columns in the row expression.

Degree of R	R IS NULL	R IS NOT NULL	NOT (R IS NULL)	NOT (R IS NOT NULL)
Degree = 1				
NULL	TRUE	FALSE	FALSE	TRUE
Not NULL	FALSE	TRUE	TRUE	FALSE
Degree > 1				
All NULLs	TRUE	FALSE	FALSE	TRUE
Some NULLs	FALSE	FALSE	TRUE	TRUE
No NULLs	FALSE	TRUE	TRUE	FALSE

Note that R IS NOT NULL has the same result as NOT R IS NULL if and only if R is of degree one. This is a break in the usual pattern of predicates with a NOT option in them. Here are some examples:

(1, 2, 3) IS NULL = FALSE

(1, NULL, 3) IS NULL = FALSE

(1, NULL, 3) IS NOT NULL = FALSE

(NULL, NULL, NULL) IS NULL = TRUE

(NULL, NULL, NULL) IS NOT NULL = FALSE

NOT (1, 2, 3) IS NULL = TRUE

NOT (1, NULL, 3) IS NULL = TRUE

NOT (1, NULL, 3) IS NOT NULL = TRUE

NOT (NULL, NULL, NULL) IS NULL = FALSE

NOT (NULL, NULL, NULL) IS NOT NULL = TRUE

It is important to remember where NULLs can occur. They are more than just a possible value in a column. Aggregate functions on empty sets, OUTER JOINs, arithmetic expressions with NULLs, and so forth all return NULLs. These constructs often show up as columns in VIEWs.

17.4.2 IS [NOT] {TRUE | FALSE | UNKNOWN}

This predicate tests a condition that has the truth-value TRUE, FALSE, or UNKNOWN, and returns TRUE or FALSE. The syntax is:

<Boolean test> ::=

<Boolean primary> [IS [NOT] <truth value>]

<truth value> ::= TRUE | FALSE | UNKNOWN

<Boolean primary> ::=

<predicate> | <left paren> <search condition> <right paren>

As you would expect, the expression IS NOT <logical value> is the same as NOT (x IS < logical value>), so the predicate can be defined by the table below.

IS < logical value>	TRUE	FALSE	UNKNOWN
TRUE	TRUE	FALSE	FALSE
FALSE	FALSE	TRUE	FALSE
UNKNOWN	FALSE	FALSE	TRUE

If you are familiar with some of Date's writings, his MAYBE(x) predicate is not the same as the ANSI (x) IS NOT FALSE predicate, but it is equivalent to the (x) IS UNKNOWN predicate. Date's predicate excludes the case where all conditions in the predicate are TRUE.

Date points out that it is difficult to ask a conditional question in English. To borrow one of Chris Date's examples (Date 1990), consider the problem of finding employees who might be programmers born before 1975 January 18 with a salary less than $50,000. The statement of the problem is a bit unclear as to what the "might be" covers—just being a programmer, or all three conditions. Let's assume that we want some doubt on any of the three conditions. With this predicate, the answer is fairly easy to write:

```
SELECT*
  FROM Personnel
 WHERE (job_title = 'Programmer'
        AND birth_date < CAST ('1975-01-18' AS DATE)
        AND (salary_amt < 50000.00) IS UNKNOWN;
```

could be expanded in the old SQLs as:

```
SELECT *
  FROM Personnel
 WHERE (job_title IS NULL
        AND birth_date < CAST ('1975-01-18' AS DATE)
        AND salary_amt < 50000.00.00)
    OR (job_title = 'Programmer'
        AND birth_date IS NULL
        AND salary_amt < 50000.00.00)
    OR (job_title = 'Programmer'
        AND birth_date < CAST ('1975-01-18' AS DATE)
        AND salary_amt IS NULL)
    OR (job_title IS NULL
        AND birth_date IS NULL
        AND salary_amt < 50000.00.00)
    OR (job_title IS NULL
        AND birth_date < CAST ('1975-01-18' AS DATE)
        AND salary_amt IS NULL)
```

```
OR (job_title = 'Programmer'
    AND birth_date IS NULL
    AND salary_amt IS NULL)
OR (job_title IS NULL
    AND birth_date IS NULL
    AND salary_amt IS NULL);
```

The problem is that every possible combination of NULLs and non-NULLs has to be tested. Since there are three predicates involved, this gives us (3^2)−1=7 combinations to check out (when none of the columns are NULL, we can get a TRUE or FALSE result). The IS NOT UNKNOWN predicate does not have to bother with the combinations, only the final logical value.

17.4.3 IS [NOT] NORMALIZED

<string> IS [NOT] NORMALIZED determines if a Unicode string is one of the four normal forms (D, C, KD and KC). The use of the words "normal form" here are not the same as in a relational context. In the Unicode model, a single character can be built from several other characters. Accent marks can be put on basic Latin letters. Certain combinations of letters can be displayed as ligatures ('ae' becomes 'æ'). Some languages, such as Hangul (Korean) and Vietnamese, build glyphs from concatenating symbols in two dimensions. Some languages have special forms of one letter that are determined by context, such as the terminal lowercase sigma in Greek or accented 'u' in Czech. In short, writing is more complex than putting one letter after another.

The Unicode standard defines the order of such constructions in their normal forms. You can still produce the same results with different orderings and sometimes with different combinations of symbols. But it is very handy when you are searching such text to know that it is normalized rather than trying to parse each glyph on the fly. You can find details about normalization and links to free software at www.unicode.org.

Subquery Predicates

MOST PROGRAMMING LANGUAGES use simple scalar predicates with theta operators. They apply to a single scalar value. SQL also has them, but it also has set-oriented predicates. Since SQL is a set-oriented language this is should not be a surprise. These predicates apply to subsets that are built with subqueries.

18.1 The UNIQUE Predicate

The UNIQUE *predicate* is a test for the absence of redundant duplicate rows in a subquery. The UNIQUE keyword is also used as a table or column *constraint*. This predicate is used to define the constraint. The syntax for this predicate is:

```
<unique predicate> ::= UNIQUE <table subquery>
```

If any two rows in the subquery are equal to each other, the predicate is FALSE. However, the definition in the standard is worded in the negative, so that NULLs get the benefit of the doubt. The query can be written as an EXISTS predicate that counts rows, thus:

```
EXISTS (SELECT <column list>
          FROM <subquery>
        WHERE (<column list>) IS NOT NULL
         GROUP BY <column list>
        HAVING COUNT(*) > 1);
```

An empty subquery is always TRUE, since you cannot find two rows, and therefore duplicates do not exist. This makes sense on the face of it.

NULLs are easier to explain with an example, say a table with only two rows, ('a', 'b') and ('a', NULL). The first columns of each row are non-NULL and are equal to each other, so we have a match so far. The second column in the second row is NULL and cannot compare to anything, so we skip the second column pair, and go with what we have, and the test is TRUE. This is giving the NULLs the benefit of the doubt, since the NULL in the second row could become 'b' some day and give us a duplicate row.

Now consider the case where the subquery has two rows, ('a', NULL) and ('a', NULL). The predicate is still TRUE, because the NULLs do not test equal or unequal to each other—not because we are making NULLs equal to each other.

As you can see, it is a good idea to avoid NULLs in UNIQUE constraints.

The UNIQUE column constraint is implemented in most SQL products with a "CREATE UNIQUE INDEX <index name> ON <table> (<column list>)" statement hidden under the covers. Standard SQL does not have indexes or any physical data access methods defined, but a vendor consortium agreed on this basic syntax.

Another way to do check uniqueness is to use hashing. When you get a hash clash (also known as a hash collision), then you look to see if the values are identical or not. A lot of research work is being done with Perfect and Minimal Perfect Hashing for databases. This technique is much faster than indexing for large databases since it requires only one hash probe instead of several index tree traversals.

The row version of IS [NOT] DISTINCT FROM theta operator is part of this family. It is a test of whether two row values are distinct from each other.

```
<distinct predicate> ::=
<row value predicand 1>
IS [NOT] DISTINCT FROM  <row value predicand 2>
```

Following the usual pattern

```
<row value predicand 1> IS NOT DISTINCT FROM <row value predicand 2>
```

means

```
NOT (<row value predicand 1> IS DISTINCT FROM  <row value predicand 2>)
```

This operator treats NULLs as equal, in the same way that GROUP BY does. You can expand it as a shorthand for:

```
((value1 IS NOT NULL AND value2 IS NOT NULL
 AND value1 = value 2)
 OR
 (value1 IS NULL AND value2 IS NULL))
```

18.2 The [NOT] IN() Predicate

The IN() predicate is one of the "abbreviations" that are allowed in SQL. It can be expanded into the usual AND, OR and NOT logical operators, but it is easier to see the intent of the programmer with this syntax. New SQL programmers stick to the more familiar "non-abbreviated" logic for two reasons: (1) it looks like their procedural language (2) they think the optimizer will do better with "non-abbreviated" logic; this is not true at all.

The IN () syntax is very natural and was borrowed and generalized from the Pascal language. It takes a value on the left side and sees if it is in a list of comparable values on the right side.

Most of the time, this predicate is done with a scalar value and a set of scalar values But Standard SQL allows row value expressions in the list or for you to use a query to construct the list. The syntax is:

```
<in predicate> ::=  <row value predicand = [NOT] IN  <in predicate
value>

<in predicate value> ::=  <table subquery> | <left paren> <in value
list> <right paren>

<in value list> ::=  <row value expression> [{<comma> <row value
expression> } ...]
```

The expression

```
<row value constructor> NOT IN <in predicate value>
```

means

```
NOT (<row value constructor> IN <in predicate value>)
```

This pattern for the use of the keyword NOT is found in most of the other SQL predicates.

The SQL:2006 Standards say that if the <in value list> consists of a single <row value expression> , then that <row value expression> shall not be a <scalar subquery>. This syntax rule resolves an ambiguity in which <in predicate value> might be interpreted either as a <table subquery> or as a <scalar subquery>. This means that:

```
(<in predicate value>)
```

is equivalent to the <table value constructor> :

```
(VALUES <in predicate value>)
```

It is safer and better documentation to use the second syntax. With DB2 version 9.7 as an example, the following will not work:

```
SELECT *
  FROM Foobar
 WHERE (x, y) IN (('x1', y1));
```

It returns an error—SQL0104N An unexpected token "," was found following ", y) in (('x1'". Expected tokens may include: "+". SQLSTATE=42601. However, this *does* work:

```
SELECT *
  FROM Foobar
 WHERE (x, y) IN (VALUES ('x1', 1));
```

The <row value constructor> IN <in predicate value> has the same effect as <row value constructor>=ANY <in predicate value> by definition. Most optimizers will recognize this and execute the same code for both. This means that if the <in predicate value> is empty, such as one you would get from a subquery that returns no rows, the results will be equivalent to (<row value constructor>= (NULL, …, NULL)), which is always evaluated to UNKNOWN. Likewise, if the <in predicate value> is an explicit list of NULLs, the results will be UNKNOWN. However, please remember that there is a difference between an empty table and a table with rows of all NULLs.

IN() predicates with a subquery can *sometimes* be converted into EXISTS predicates, but there are some problems and differences in the predicates. The conversion to an EXISTS predicate might be a good way to improve performance, but it will not be as easy to read as the original IN() predicate. An EXISTS predicate can use indexes to find (or fail to find) a single value that confirms (or denies) the predicate, whereas the IN()

predicate often has to build the results of the subquery in a working table. Know your SQL product.

18.2.1 Optimizing the IN() Predicate

Many database engines have no statistics about the relative frequency of the values in a list of constants, so they will scan that list in the order in which they appear. People like to order lists alphabetically or in numeric order, but it would be better to order the list from most frequently occurring values to least frequent. It is also pointless to have duplicate values in the constant list, since the predicate will return TRUE if it matches the first duplicate it finds and never get to the second occurrence. Likewise, if the predicate is FALSE for that value, it wastes computer time to traverse a needlessly long list.

The IN() predicate with a subquery can be optimized by using an implicit SELECT DISTINCT when building the result set of the subquery as a temporary working table. For example, in a query to find employees in a city with a major sport team (we want them to get tickets for us), we could write:

```
SELECT *
  FROM Personnel AS P
 WHERE P.city_name
       IN (SELECT S.city_name
             FROM SportTeams AS S);
```

Let us further assume that our personnel are located in (n) cities and the sports teams are in (m) cities. If (m) is much greater than (n), then we would want a different optimization than if (n) is much greater than (m). Today, all major versions of SQL remove duplicates in the result table of the subquery, so you do not have to use an explicit SELECT DISTINCT in the subquery. You might see this in legacy code. A scan, a binary search or a hash might be the best way. Trust the optimizer.

Standard SQL allows row expression comparisons, so if you have a Standard SQL implementation with separate columns for the city and state, you could write:

```
SELECT *
  FROM Personnel
 WHERE (city_name, state_code)
       IN (SELECT city_name, state_code
             FROM SportTeams);
```

The major SQL products also kick in optimizations where the list gets to a certain size. This can lead to weird behavior from a human viewpoint; a list with (n < k) items takes longer to search a list with (n >=k) items.

Some of the optimizer tricks are

(1) construct a working table with an index

(2) construct a working table with a hidden column of the frequency of each value and sort on it. The initial frequency values can come from the statistics on the left side table.

(3) Organize the list as a heap in an array. A heap is an array such that for each element in position (n) in the list, the (n+1) element is lower and the (2n+1) element is greater. It is a quick way to do a binary search.

Another trick is to replace the IN() predicate with a JOIN operation. For example, you have a table of restaurant telephone numbers and a guidebook and you want to pick out the three-star places, so you write this query:

```
SELECT R.restaurant_name, R.phone_nbr
  FROM Restaurants AS R
 WHERE E.restaurant_name
       IN (SELECT Q.restaurant_name
             FROM QualityGuide AS Q
            WHERE Q.michelin_stars = 3);
```

If there is an index on QualityGuide.michelin_stars, the SQL engine will probably build a temporary table of the three-star places and pass it on to the outer query. The outer query will then handle it as if it were a list of constants. In the case of a list of three-star restaurants, it will be short.

However, this is not the sort of column that you would normally index. Without an index on Michelin stars, the engine will simply do a sequential search of the QualityGuide table. This query can be replaced with a JOIN query, thus:

```
SELECT R.restaurant_name, R.phone_nbr
  FROM Restaurants AS R, QualityGuide AS Q
 WHERE michelin_stars = 4
   AND R.restaurant_name = Q.restaurant_name;
```

This query should run faster, since restaurant_name is a key for both tables and will be indexed to ensure uniqueness. However, this can return duplicate rows in the result table that you can handle with a

SELECT DISTINCT. Consider a more budget-minded query, where we want places with a meal under $10 and the menu guidebook lists all the meals. The query looks about the same:

```
SELECT R.restaurant_name, R.phone_nbr
  FROM Restaurants AS R
 WHERE R.restaurant_name
       IN (SELECT M.restaurant_name
             FROM Menu_Guide AS M
            WHERE M.meal_price <= 10.00);
```

And you would expect to be able to replace it with

```
SELECT R.restaurant_name, R.phone_nbr
  FROM Restaurants AS R, MenuGuide AS M
 WHERE M.meal_price <= 10.00
   AND R.restaurant_name = M.restaurant_name;
```

Every item in Murphy's Two-Dollar Hash House will get a line in the results of the JOIN-ed version, however. This can be fixed by changing SELECT restaurant_name, phone_nbr to SELECT DISTINCT restaurant_name, phone_nbr, but it will cost more time to remove the duplicates. There is no good general advice, except to experiment with your particular query and product.

The NOT IN() predicate is often better replaced with a NOT EXISTS predicate. Using the restaurant example again, our friend John has a list of eateries and we want to see those that are not in the guidebook. The natural formation of the query is

```
SELECT J.*
  FROM Johns_Book AS J
 WHERE J.restaurant_name
       NOT IN (SELECT Q.restaurant_name
                 FROM QualityGuide AS Q);
```

But you can write the same query with a NOT EXISTS predicate and it will probably run faster:

```
SELECT J.*
  FROM Johns_Book AS J
 WHERE NOT EXISTS
```

```
       (SELECT *
          FROM QualityGuide AS Q
         WHERE Q.restaurant_name = J.restaurant_name);
```

The reason the second version will probably run faster is that it can test for existence using the indexes on both tables. The NOT IN() version has to test all the values in the subquery table for inequality. Many SQL implementations will construct a temporary table from the IN() predicate subquery if it has a WHERE clause, but the temporary table will not have any indexes. The temporary table can also have duplicates and a random ordering of its rows, so that the SQL engine has to do a full-table scan.

18.2.2 Replacing ORs with the IN() Predicate

A simple trick that beginning SQL programmers often miss is that an IN() predicate can often replace a set of OR-ed predicates. For example:

```
SELECT *
  FROM Quality_Control_Report
 WHERE test_1 = 'passed'
    OR test_2 = 'passed'
    OR test_3 = 'passed'
    OR test_4 = 'passed';
```

can be rewritten as:

```
SELECT *
  FROM Quality_Control_Report
 WHERE 'passed' IN (test_1, test_2, test_3, test_4);
```

The reason this is hard to see is that programmers get used to thinking of a constant on the right side of theta operators, not the left.

18.2.3 NULLs and the IN() Predicate

NULLs make some special problems in a NOT IN() predicate with a subquery. Consider these two tables:

```
CREATE TABLE Table1 (x INTEGER);
INSERT INTO Table1 VALUES (1), (2), (3), (4);

CREATE TABLE Table2 (x INTEGER);
INSERT INTO Table2 VALUES (1), (NULL), (2);
```

Now execute the query:

```
SELECT *
 FROM Table1
 WHERE x NOT IN (SELECT x FROM Table2)
```

Let's work it out step by painful step:

(1) do the subquery

```
 SELECT *
   FROM Table1
  WHERE x NOT IN (1, NULL, 2);
```

(2) convert the NOT IN() to its definition

```
 SELECT *
   FROM Table1
  WHERE NOT (x IN (1, NULL, 2));
```

(3) expand IN() predicate

```
 SELECT *
   FROM Table1
  WHERE NOT ((x = 1) OR (x = NULL) OR (x = 2));
```

(4) apply DeMorgan's law:

```
 SELECT *
   FROM Table1
  WHERE ((x <> 1) AND (x <> NULL) AND (x <> 2);
```

(5) constant logical expression

```
 SELECT *
   FROM Table1
  WHERE ((x <> 1) AND UNKNOWN AND (x <> 2));
```

(6) Reduction of OR to constant

```
SELECT *
 FROM Table1
 WHERE UNKNOWN;
```

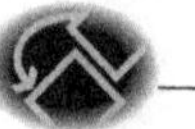

(7) Results are always empty.

Now try this with another set of tables

```
CREATE TABLE Table3 (x INTEGER);
INSERT INTO Table3 VALUES (1), (2), (NULL), (4);

CREATE TABLE Table4 (x INTEGER);
INSERT INTO Table3 VALUES (1), (3), (2);
```

Let's work out the same query step by painful step again.

(1) do the subquery

```
SELECT *
  FROM Table3
 WHERE x NOT IN (1, 3, 2);
```

(2) convert the NOT IN() to Boolean expression

```
SELECT *
  FROM Table3
 WHERE NOT (x IN (1, 3, 2));
```

(3) expand IN() predicate

```
SELECT *
  FROM Table3
 WHERE NOT ((x = 1) OR (x = 3) OR (x = 2));
```

(4) DeMorgan's law:

```
SELECT *
  FROM Table3
 WHERE ((x <> 1) AND (x <> 3) AND (x <> 2));
```

(5) Computed result set; I will show it as a UNION with substitutions

```
 SELECT *
   FROM Table3
  WHERE ((1 <> 1) AND (1 <> 3) AND (1 <> 2)) -- FALSE
UNION ALL
 SELECT *
   FROM Table3
  WHERE ((2 <> 1) AND (2 <> 3) AND (2 <> 2)) -- FALSE
```

```
UNION ALL
 SELECT * FROM Table3
  WHERE ((CAST(NULL AS INTEGER) <> 1)
          AND (CAST(NULL AS INTEGER) <> 3)
          AND (CAST(NULL AS INTEGER) <> 2)) -- UNKNOWN
UNION ALL
 SELECT *
   FROM Table3
  WHERE ((4 <> 1) AND (4 <> 3) AND (4 <> 2)); -- TRUE
```

(6) Result is one row = (4).

18.2.4 IN() Predicate and Referential Constraints

One of the most popular uses for the IN() predicate is in a CHECK() clause on a table. The usual form is a list of values that are legal for a column, such as:

```
CREATE TABLE Addresses
(addressee_name CHAR(25) NOT NULL PRIMARY KEY,
 street_loc CHAR(25) NOT NULL,
 city_name CHAR(20) NOT NULL,
 state_code CHAR(2) NOT NULL
       CONSTRAINT valid_state_code
       CHECK (state_code IN ('AL', 'AK', ...)),
 ...);
```

This method works fine with a small list of values, but it has problems with a longer list. Please note that "short" and "long" are very relative as storage gets bigger, cheaper, and faster. While DML could have optimizations, the DDL might not! You also have to remember that DML and DDL treat NULLs differently. An UNKNOWN is treated as a TRUE in the DDL and a FALSE in the DML.

In full Standard SQL, a constraint can reference other tables, so you could write the same constraint as:

```
CREATE TABLE Addresses
(addressee_name CHAR(25) NOT NULL PRIMARY KEY,
 street_loc CHAR(25) NOT NULL,
 city_name CHAR(20) NOT NULL,
 state_code CHAR(2) NOT NULL,
 CONSTRAINT valid_state_code
```

```
CHECK (state_code
       IN (SELECT state_code
             FROM Zip_Codes AS Z
            WHERE Z.state_code = Addresses.state_code)),
 ...);
```

This is not a common feature at this time!

The advantage of this feature is that you can change the Zip_Codes table and thereby change the effect of the constraint on the Addresses table. This is fine for adding more data in the outer reference (i.e., Quebec joins the Union and gets the code 'QB'), but it has a bad effect when you try to delete data in the outer reference (i.e., California secedes from the Union and every row with 'CA' for a state code is now invalid).

As a rule of thumb, use the IN() predicate in a CHECK() constraint when the list is short, static, and unique to one table. When the list is short, static but not unique to one table, then use a CREATE DOMAIN statement and put the IN() predicate in a CHECK() constraint on the domain.

Use a REFERENCES clause to a look-up table when the list is long and dynamic, or when several other schema objects (VIEWs, stored procedures, etc.) reference the values. A separate table can have an index and that makes a big difference in searching and doing joins.

18.2.5 IN() Predicate and Scalar Queries

As mentioned before, the list of an IN() predicate can be any scalar expression. This includes scalar subqueries, but most people do not seem to know that this is possible. For example, given tables that model warehouses, trucking centers, and so forth, we can find if we have a product, identified by its UPC code, somewhere in the enterprise.

```
SELECT P.upc
  FROM Picklist AS P
 WHERE P.upc
       IN ((SELECT upc
              FROM Warehouse AS W
             WHERE W.upc = P.upc),
           (SELECT upc
              FROM Stores AS S
             WHERE S.upc = P.upc),
```

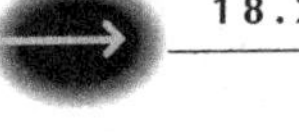


```
(SELECT upc
   FROM Garbage AS G
  WHERE G.upc = P.upc));
```

The empty result sets will become NULLs in the list. The alternative to this is usually a chain of OUTER JOINs or an OR-ed list of EXISTS() predicates.

This is a strange construction at the time I am writing this chapter and might not work very well. But check it out when you are reading this book. The trend in SQL is toward parallel query processing so each of the scalar expressions could be done at the same time.

A more useful version is in stored procedures with a long parameter list of related values. The simplest version is to use a list of constants like this:

```
SELECT *
  FROM Parameter_List
 WHERE Parameter_List.i
       IN (SELECT X.i
             FROM (VALUES (1), (2), (3)) AS X(i));
```

this can be generalized to row constructors;

```
SELECT Parameter_List.*
  FROM Parameter_List
 WHERE (Parameter_List.i, Parameter_List.j)
        IN (SELECT X.i, X.j
              FROM (VALUES (1, 'a'), (2, 'b'), (3, 'c'))
           AS X(i, j));
```

But the real power comes from taking an input list of parameters and converting it into a table with the VALUES() construct. For example, given a variable list of GTIN (Global Trade Item Number) item identifiers, you can construct a procedure to return a result based on that list. If not all parameters are given in the CALL, then NULLs will passed instead.

```
CREATE PROCEDURE Foobar
(IN in_gtin_1 CHAR(15), .. IN in_gtin_n CHAR(15))
LANGUAGE SQL
SQL DATA
..
BEGIN
 ..
```

```
SELECT << something here > >
  FROM Products AS P
 WHERE gtin
       IN (SELECT Picklist.item
             FROM (VALUES (in_gtin_1),
                          ..., (in_gtin_n)) AS Picklist(item)
            WHERE Picklist.item IS NOT NULL);
 ..
END;
```

Alternatively, the VALUES() list elements can be expressions such as COALESCE (in_gtin_n, '123456789012345') or anything that returns an appropriate scalar value.

18.3 [NOT] EXISTS() Predicate

The EXISTS predicate is very natural. It is a test for a nonempty set (read: table). If there are any rows in its subquery, it is TRUE; otherwise, it is FALSE; this predicate does not give an UNKNOWN result. The syntax is

```
<exists predicate> ::= EXISTS <table subquery>
```

It is worth mentioning that a <table subquery> is always inside parentheses to avoid problems in the grammar during parsing.

In SQL-89, the rules stated that the subquery had to have a SELECT clause with one column or an asterisk (*). If the SELECT * option was used, the database engine would (in theory) pick one column and use it. This fiction was needed because SQL-89 defined subqueries as having only one column. Things are much better today.

Some early SQL implementations would work better with "EXISTS(SELECT <column> ..)", " EXISTS(SELECT <constant> ..)" or "EXISTS(SELECT * ..)" versions of the predicate. Today, there is no difference in the three forms in the major products, so the "EXISTS(SELECT * ..)" is now the preferred form since it shows that we are working at the table and row level, without regard to columns.

Indexes are very useful for EXISTS() predicates because they can be searched while the base table is left *completely alone*. For example, we want to find all the employees who were born on the same day as *any* famous person. The query could be

```
SELECT P.emp_name AS famous_person_birth_date_guy
  FROM Personnel AS P
 WHERE EXISTS
       (SELECT *
          FROM Celebrities AS C
         WHERE P.birth_date = C.birth_date);
```

If the table Celebrities has an index on its birth_date column, the optimizer will get the current employee's birth_date P.birth_date and look up that value in the index. If the value is in the index, the predicate is TRUE and we do not need to look at the Celebrities table at all.

If it is not in the index, the predicate is FALSE and there is still no need to look at the Celebrities table. This should be fast, since indexes are smaller than their tables and are structured for very fast searching.

However, if Celebrities has no index on its birth_date column, the query may have to look at every row to see if there is a birth_date that matches the current employee's birth_date. There are some tricks that a good optimizer can use to speed things up in this situation. Some SQLs, such as Microsoft SQL Server, can put values from columns not used by the index to build the tree with an INCLUDE option. This says put this column value in the leaf nodes of the index tree to save an access to the base table.

18.3.1 EXISTS and NULLs

A NULL might not be a value, but it does exist in SQL. This is often a problem for a new SQL programmer who is having trouble with NULLs and how they behave.

Think of them as being like a brown paper bag—you know that something is inside because you lifted it up and felt a weight, but you do not know exactly what that something is. If you felt an empty bag, you know to stop looking. For example, we want to find all the Personnel who were not born on the same day as a famous person. This can be answered with the negation of the original query, like this:

```
SELECT P.emp_name AS famous_birth_date_person
  FROM Personnel AS P
 WHERE NOT EXISTS
       (SELECT *
          FROM Celebrities AS C
         WHERE P.birth_date = C.birth_date);
```

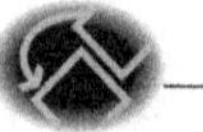

But assume that among the Celebrities, we have a movie star who will not admit her age, shown in the row ('Gloria Glamour', NULL). A new SQL programmer might expect that Ms. Glamour would not match to anyone, since we do not know her birth_date yet. Actually, she will match to everyone, since there is a chance that they may match when some tabloid newspaper finally gets a copy of her birth certificate. But work out the subquery in the usual way to convince yourself:

```
...
WHERE NOT EXISTS
      (SELECT *
         FROM Celebrities
        WHERE P.birth_date = NULL);
```

becomes

```
...
WHERE NOT EXISTS
        (SELECT *
           FROM Celebrities
          WHERE UNKNOWN);
```

becomes

```
...
WHERE TRUE;
```

and you will see that the predicate tests to UNKNOWN because of the NULL comparison and therefore fails whenever we look at Ms. Glamour.

Another problem with NULLs is found when you attempt to convert IN predicates to EXISTS predicates. Using our example of matching our Personnel to famous people, the query can be rewritten as:

```
SELECT P.emp_name AS famous_birth_date_person
  FROM Personnel AS P
 WHERE P.birth_date
       NOT IN
       (SELECT C.birth_date
          FROM Celebrities AS C);
```

However, consider a more complex version of the same query, where the celebrity has to have been born in New York City. The IN predicate would be

```
SELECT P.emp_name, ' was born on a day without a famous New Yorker!'
  FROM Personnel AS P
 WHERE P.birth_date
       NOT IN
      (SELECT C.birth_date
         FROM Celebrities AS C
        WHERE C.birth_city_name = 'New York');
```

and you would think that the EXISTS version would be:

```
SELECT P.emp_name, ' was born on a day without a famous New Yorker!'
  FROM Personnel AS P
 WHERE NOT EXISTS
       (SELECT *
          FROM Celebrities AS C
         WHERE C.birth_city_name = 'New York'
           AND C.birth_date = P.birth_date);
```

Assume that Gloria Glamour is our only New Yorker and we still do not know her birth_date. The subquery will be empty for every employee in the NOT EXISTS predicate version, because her NULL birth_date will not test equal to the known employee birthdays.

That means that the NOT EXISTS predicate will return TRUE and we will get every employee to match to Ms. Glamour. But now look at the IN predicate version, which will have a single NULL in the subquery result. This predicate will be equivalent to (Personnel.birth_date = NULL), which is always UNKNOWN, and we will get no Personnel back.

Likewise, you cannot, in general, transform the quantified comparison predicates into EXISTS predicates because of the possibility of NULL values. Remember that "x <> ALL <subquery> " is shorthand for "x NOT IN <subquery> " and "x = ANY <subquery> " is shorthand for "x IN <subquery> " and it will not surprise you.

In general, the EXISTS predicates will run faster than the IN predicates. The problem is in deciding whether to build the query or the subquery first; the optimal approach depends on the size and distribution of values in each and that cannot usually be known until run-time.

18.3.2 EXISTS and INNER JOINs

The [NOT] EXISTS predicate is almost always used with a correlated subquery. Very often the subquery can be "flattened" into a JOIN, which will often run faster than the original query. Our sample query can be converted into:

```
SELECT P.emp_name AS famous_birth_date_person
  FROM Personnel AS P, Celebrities AS C
 WHERE P.birth_date = C.birth_date;
```

The advantage of the JOIN version is that it allows us to show columns from both tables. We should make the query more informative by rewriting the query:

```
SELECT P.emp_name, C.emp_name
  FROM Personnel AS P, Celebrities AS C
 WHERE P.birth_date = C.birth_date;
```

This new query could be written with an EXISTS() predicate but that is a waste of resources.

```
SELECT P.emp_name, ' has the same birth_date as ', C.emp_name
  FROM Personnel AS P, Celebrities AS C
 WHERE EXISTS
       (SELECT *
          FROM Celebrities AS C2
         WHERE P.birth_date = C2.birth_date
           AND C.emp_name = C2.emp_name);
```

18.3.3 NOT EXISTS and OUTER JOINs

The NOT EXISTS version of this predicate is almost always used with a correlated subquery. Very often the subquery can be "flattened" into an OUTER JOIN, which will often run faster than the original query. Our other sample query was

```
SELECT P.emp_name AS Non_famous_New_Yorker_birth_date
  FROM Personnel AS P
 WHERE NOT EXISTS
      (SELECT *
         FROM Celebrities AS C
```

```
      WHERE C.birth_city_name = 'New York'
        AND C.birth_date = P.birth_date);
```

Which we can replace with:

```
SELECT P.emp_name AS famous_New_Yorker_birth_date
  FROM Personnel AS P
       LEFT OUTER JOIN
       Celebrities AS C
       ON C.birth_city_name = 'New York'
          AND C.birth_date = E2.birth_date
 WHERE C.emp_name IS NULL;
```

This is assuming that we know each and every celebrity name in the Celebrities table. If the column in the WHERE clause could have NULLs in its base table, then we could not prune out the generated NULLs. The test for NULL should always be on (a column of) the primary key, which cannot be NULL. Relating this back to the example, how could a celebrity be a celebrity with an unknown name? Even The Unknown Comic had a name ("The Unknown Comic").

18.3.4 EXISTS() and Referential Constraints

Standard SQL was designed so that the declarative referential constraints could be expressed as EXISTS() predicates in a CHECK() clause. For example:

```
CREATE TABLE Addresses
(addressee_name CHAR(25) NOT NULL PRIMARY KEY,
 street_addr CHAR(25) NOT NULL,
 city_name CHAR(20) NOT NULL,
 state_code CHAR(2) NOT NULL
    REFERENCES ZipCodes(state_code),
...);
```

could be written as:

```
CREATE TABLE Addresses
(addressee_name CHAR(25) NOT NULL PRIMARY KEY,
 street_addr CHAR(25) NOT NULL,
 city_name CHAR(20) NOT NULL,
```

```
state_code CHAR(2) NOT NULL,
CONSTRAINT valid_state_code
 CHECK (EXISTS(SELECT *
                FROM ZipCodes AS Z1
               WHERE Z1.state_code = Addresses.state_code)),
...);
```

There is no advantage to this expression for the Database Administrator, since you cannot attach referential actions with the CHECK() constraint. However, an SQL database can use the same mechanisms in the SQL compiler for both constructions.

18.3.5 EXISTS() and Quantifiers

Formal logic makes use of quantifiers that can be applied to propositions. The two forms are "For all x, P(x)" and "For some x, P(x)". If you want to look up formulas in a textbook, the traditional symbol for the universal quantifier is ∀, an inverted letter 'A' and the symbol for the existential quantifier is ∃, a rotated letter E.

The big question over 100 years ago was that of existential import in formal logic. Everyone agreed that saying "All men are mortal" implies that "No men are not mortal," but does it also imply that "some men are mortal"—that we have to have at least one man who is mortal?

Existential import lost the battle and the modern convention is that "All men are mortal" has the same meaning as "There are no men who are immortal", but does not imply that any men exist at all. This is the convention followed in the design of SQL. Consider the statement "Some salesmen are liars" and the way we would write it with the EXISTS() predicate in SQL:

```
...
EXISTS(SELECT *
         FROM Personnel AS P, Liars AS L
        WHERE P.job = 'Salesman'
          AND P.emp_name = L.emp_name);
```

If we are more cynical about salesmen, we might want to formulate the predicate "All salesmen are liars" with the EXISTS predicate in SQL, using the transform rule just discussed:

```
...
NOT EXISTS(SELECT *
             FROM Personnel AS P
            WHERE P.job = 'Salesman'
              AND P.emp_name
                  NOT IN
                  (SELECT L.emp_name
                     FROM Liars AS L));
```

which, informally, says "There are no salesmen who are not liars" in English. In this case, the IN predicate can be changed into a JOIN, which should improve performance and be a bit easier to read.

18.3.6 EXISTS and Three Valued Logic

This example is due to an article by Lee Fesperman at FirstSQL. Using Chris Date's "SupplierParts" table with three rows

```
CREATE TABLE SupplierPart
(sup_nbr CHAR(2) NOT NULL PRIMARY KEY,
 part_nbr CHAR(2) NOT NULL,
 onhand_qty INTEGER CHECK (onhand_qty > 0));
```

sup_nbr	part_nbr	onhand_qty
'S1'	'P'	NULL
'S2'	'P'	200
'S3'	'P'	1000

The row ('S1', 'P', NULL) means that supplier 'S1' supplies part 'P' but we do not know what quantity he has.

The query we wish to answer is "Find suppliers of part 'P', but not in a quantity of 1000 on hand"; the correct answer is 'S2'. All suppliers in the table supply 'P', but we do know if 'S3' supplies the part in quantity 1000 and we do not know in what quantity 'S1' supplies the part. The only supplier we eliminate for certain is 'S2'.

An SQL query to retrieve this result would be:

```
SELECT SPX.sup_nbr
  FROM SupplierParts AS SPX
 WHERE px.part_nbr = 'P'
   AND 1000
       NOT IN (SELECT SPY.onhand_qty
                 FROM SupplierParts AS SPY
                WHERE SPY.sup_nbr = SPX.sup_nbr
                  AND SPY.part_nbr = 'P');
```

According to Standard SQL, this query should return only 'S2', but when we transform the query into what *looks like* an equivalent version, using EXISTS instead, we obtain:

```
SELECT SPX.sup_nbr
  FROM SupplierParts AS SPX
 WHERE SPX.part_nbr = 'P'
   AND NOT EXISTS
       (SELECT *
          FROM SupplierParts AS SPY
         WHERE SPY.sup_nbr = SPX.sup_nbr
           AND SPY.part_nbr = 'P'
           AND SPY.onhand_qty = 1000);
```

Which will return ('S1', 'S2'). You can argue that this is the wrong answer because we do not definitely know whether or not 'S1' supplies 'P' in quantity 1000 or less or more. The EXISTS() predicate will return TRUE or FALSE, even in situations where a subquery's predicate returns an UNKNOWN (i.e., NULL = 1000).

The solution is to modify the predicate that deals with the quantity in the subquery to explicitly say that you do or not want to give the "benefit of the doubt" to the NULL. You have several alternatives:

```
(1) (SPY.onhand_qty = 1000) IS NOT FALSE
```

This uses the valued predicates in Standard SQL for testing logical values. Frankly, this is confusing to read and worse to maintain.

```
(2) (SPY.onhand_qty = 1000 OR SPY.onhand_qty IS NULL)
```

This uses another test predicate, but the optimizer can probably use any index on the "onhand_qty" column.

```
(3) (COALESCE(SPY.onhand_qty, 1000) = 1000)
```

This is portable an easy to maintain. The only disadvantage is that some SQL products might not be able to use an index on the "onhand_qty" column because it is in an expression.

The real problem is that the query was formed with a double negative in the form of a NOT EXISTS and an implicit IS NOT FALSE condition. The problem stems from the fact that the EXISTS() predicate is one of the few two-value predicates in SQL and that (NOT (NOT UNKNOWN)) = UNKNOWN.

For another approach based on Dr. Codd's second relational model, visit www.FirstSQL.com and read some of the white papers there by Lee Fesperman. He used the two NULLs proposed by Dr. Codd to develop a product.

18.4 <theta> [SOME | ANY] <subquery>

There are two shorthand notations that compare a single value to those of a subquery, and take the general form <value expression> <theta op> <quantifier> <subquery> . The first predicate "<value expression> <theta op> [ANY | SOME] <table expression> " is equivalent to taking each row, s, (assume that they are numbered from 1 to n) of <table expression> and testing "<value expression> <theta op> s" with ORs between the expanded expressions:

```
((<value expression> <theta op> s1)
OR (<value expression> <theta op> s2)
   ...
OR (<value expression> <theta op> sn))
```

When you get a single TRUE result, the whole predicate is TRUE. As long as <table expression> has cardinality greater than zero and one non-NULL value, you will get a result of TRUE or FALSE. The keyword SOME is the same as ANY, and the choice is just a matter of style and readability.

If you think about it, the IN() predicate is equivalent to a simple " = ANY" predicate. In fact, that is how it is defined in the ANSI/ISO Standard. But the <theta op> can be any of =, <, > , <> , <=, >=, and (in theory, but practice) any other theta operator.

18.5 <theta> ALL <subquery>

Likewise, "<value expression> <comp op> ALL <table expression> " takes each row, s, of <table expression> and tests <value expression> <comp op> s with ANDs between the expanded expressions:

```
((<value expression> <comp op> s1)
AND (<value expression> <comp op> s2)
   ...
AND (<value expression> <comp op> sn))
```

When you get a single FALSE result, the whole predicate is FALSE. As long as <table expression> has cardinality greater than zero and all non-NULL values, you will get a result of TRUE or FALSE.

That sounds reasonable so far. Now let Empty_Set be an empty table (no rows, cardinality zero) and NullTable be a table with only NULLs in its rows and a cardinality greater than zero. The rules for SQL say that "<value expression> <comp op> ALL NullTable" always returns UNKNOWN, and likewise "<value expression> <comp op> ANY NullTable" always returns UNKNOWN. This makes sense, because every row comparison test in the expansion would return UNKNOWN, so the series of OR and AND operators would behave in the usual way.

However, "<value expression> <comp op> ALL Empty_Set" always returns TRUE and "<value expression> <comp op> ANY Empty_Set" always returns FALSE. Most people have no trouble seeing why the ANY predicate works that way; you cannot find a match, so the result is FALSE. But most people have lots of trouble seeing why the ALL predicate is TRUE. This convention is called existential import, and it was a big debate at the start of modern logic. It boiled down to deciding if the statement "All x are y" implies that "some x exists" by definition. The modern convention is that it does not. Lewis Carroll went with existential import, John Venn and George Boole did not.

If I were to walk into a bar and announce that I can beat any pink elephant in the bar, that would be a true statement. The fact that there are no pink elephants in the bar merely shows that the problem is reduced to the minimum case. If this seems unnatural, then convert the ALL and ANY predicates into EXISTS predicates and look at the way that this rule preserves the formal mathematical properties that:

(1) $(\forall x)P(x) = \neg(\exists x) \neg P(x)$

(2) $(\exists x)P(x) = \neg(\forall x)\neg P(x)$

The "Table1.x <comp op> ALL (SELECT y FROM Table2 WHERE <search condition>)" predicate converts to:

```
... NOT EXISTS
     (SELECT *
        FROM Table1, Table2
       WHERE Table1.x <comp op> Table2.y
         AND NOT <search condition>). . .
```

The "Table1.x <comp op> ANY (SELECT y FROM Table2 WHERE <search condition>)" predicate converts to

```
... EXISTS
     (SELECT *
        FROM Table1, Table2
       WHERE Table1.x <comp op> Table2.y
         AND <search condition>) . . .
```

Of the two quantified predicates, the "<comp op> ALL" predicate is used more. The ANY predicate is more easily replaced and more naturally written with an EXISTS() predicate or an IN() predicate. In fact, the standard defines the IN() predicate as shorthand for "= ANY" and the NOT IN() predicate as shorthand for "<> ANY", which is how most people would construct them in English.

The <comp op> ALL predicate is probably the more useful of the two, since it cannot be written in terms of an IN() predicate. The trick with it is to make sure that its subquery defines the set of values in which you are interested. For example, to find the authors whose books *all* sell for $49.95 or more, you could write

```
SELECT *
  FROM Authors AS A1
 WHERE 49.95
       <= ALL (SELECT book_price
                 FROM Books AS B1
                WHERE A1.author_name = B1.author_name);
```

The best way to think of this is to reverse the usual English sentence "Show me all x that are y" in your mind so that it says "y is the value of all x" instead.

18.5.1 The ALL Predicate and Extrema Functions

It is counter-intuitive at first that these two predicates are *not* the same in SQL:

```
x >= (SELECT MAX(y) FROM Table1)
x >= ALL (SELECT y FROM Table1)
```

but you have to remember the rules for the extrema functions—they drop out all the NULLs before returning the greater or least values. The ALL predicate does not drop NULLs, so you can get them in the results.

However, if you know that there are no NULLs in a column or are willing to drop the NULLS yourself, then you can use the ALL predicate to construct single queries to do work that would otherwise be done by two queries. For example, given the table of products and store managers, to find which manager handles the largest number of products, you would first construct a grouped VIEW or CTE and group it again. Assume we have a table of the managers responsible for each product we stock:

```
CREATE TABLE Product_Managers
(manager_name VARCHAR(35) NOT NULL,
 product_nbr CHAR(15) NOT NULL,
 PRIMARY KEY (manager_name, product_nbr));
```

Now, the query:

```
WITH TotalProducts (manager_name, product_tally)
AS
(SELECT manager_name, COUNT(*)
   FROM Product_Managers
  GROUP BY manager_name)

SELECT manager_name
  FROM TotalProducts
 WHERE product_tally
       = (SELECT MAX(product_tally)
            FROM TotalProducts);
```

But Alex Dorfman found a single query solution instead:

```
SELECT manager_name, COUNT(*) AS product_tally
  FROM Product_Managers
 GROUP BY manager_name
```

```
HAVING COUNT(*) + 1
       > ALL (SELECT DISTINCT COUNT(*)
                FROM Product_Managers
               GROUP BY manager_name);
```

The use of the SELECT DISTINCT in the subquery is to guarantee that we do not get duplicate rows when two managers handle the same number of products. You can also add a ".. WHERE dept IS NOT NULL" clause to the subquery to get the effect of a true MAX() aggregate function.

BETWEEN and OVERLAPS Predicates

THE BETWEEN AND OVERLAPS predicates both offer a shorthand way of showing that one value lies within a range defined by two other values. BETWEEN works with scalar range limits of any type; the OVERLAPS predicate looks at two time periods (defined either by start and end points or by a starting time and an INTERVAL) to see if they overlap in time.

19.1 The BETWEEN Predicate

The BETWEEN predicate is a feature of SQL that is used enough to deserve special attention. It is also just tricky enough to fool beginning programmers.

```
<between predicate>
  ::= <row value predicand> <between predicate part 2>

<between predicate part 2> ::=
[NOT] BETWEEN [ASYMMETRIC | SYMMETRIC]
<row value predicand> AND <row value predicand>
```

If neither SYMMETRIC nor ASYMMETRIC is specified, then ASYMMETRIC is implicit. This is the original definition of the shorthand that only worked with single valued predicands. This is not likely what you will see in your product.

Let x, y, and z be the first, second, and third row value predicands, respectively, so we can start defining this predicate.

```
1. x NOT BETWEEN SYMMETRIC y AND z
```

means

```
NOT (x BETWEEN SYMMETRIC y AND z)
```

No surprises here, since that is how SQL has handled optional NOT in all constructs.

```
2. X BETWEEN SYMMETRIC y AND z
```

means

```
((x BETWEEN ASYMMETRIC y AND z)
OR (x BETWEEN ASYMMETRIC z AND y))
```

There is a historical note about the early days of ANSI X3H2. We voted to make this the definition of "x BETWEEN y AND z" at one meeting. This was revoked at the next committee meeting, but Microsoft had gone ahead and changed it in their ACCESS database product. They failed to read the follow up papers.

```
3. x NOT BETWEEN ASYMMETRIC y AND z
```

means

```
NOT (x BETWEEN ASYMMETRIC y AND z)
```

No surprises here, since that is how SQL has handled optional NOT in all constructs.

```
4. x BETWEEN ASYMMETRIC y AND z
```

means

```
x >= y AND x <= z
```

Please note that the end points are included in this definition. This predicate works with any data types that can be compared. Most programmers miss this fact and use it only for numeric values. It can be used for character strings and temporal data as well. The <row value predicand>s can be expressions or constants, but again programmers tend to use just constants or column names.

Many optimizers will take special steps for the BETWEEN because SQL implementations often use B+ and other tree indexes that have ranges in their nodes. It is also more human readable than its definition and shows a higher level of abstraction.

19.1.1 Results with NULL Values

The results of this predicate with NULL values for the <row value predicand>s follow directly from the definition. If either <row value predicand>s is NULL, the result is UNKNOWN for any value of <value expression>.

19.1.2 Results with Empty Sets

Notice that if first second <row value predicand> is less than the third <row value predicand>, the ASYMMETRIC expression will always be FALSE unless the value is NULL; then it is UNKNOWN. That is a bit confusing, since there is no value to which <value expression> could resolve itself that would produce a TRUE result. But this follows directly from expanding the definition.

```
x BETWEEN ASYMMETRIC 12 AND 15 -- depends on x
x BETWEEN ASYMMETRIC 15 AND 12 -- always FALSE
x BETWEEN ASYMMETRIC NULL AND 15 -- always UNKNOWN
NULL BETWEEN ASYMMETRIC 12 AND 15 -- always UNKNOWN
x BETWEEN ASYMMETRIC 12 AND NULL -- always UNKNOWN
x BETWEEN ASYMMETRIC x AND x -- always TRUE

x BETWEEN SYMMETRIC 12 AND 15 -- depends on x
x BETWEEN SYMMETRIC 15 AND 12 -- depends on x
x BETWEEN SYMMETRIC NULL AND 15 -- always UNKNOWN
NULL BETWEEN SYMMETRIC 12 AND 15 -- always UNKNOWN
x BETWEEN SYMMETRIC 12 AND NULL -- always UNKNOWN
x BETWEEN SYMMETRIC x AND x -- always TRUE
```

19.1.3 Programming Tips

The BETWEEN range includes the end points, so you have to be careful. For example, changing a percent range on a test into a letter grade

Grades

low_score	high_score	grade
90	100	'A'
80	90	'B'
70	80	'C'
60	70	'D'
0	60	'F'

will not work when a student gets a grade on the borderlines (90, 80, 70, or 60). One way to solve the problem is to change the table by adding 1 to the low scores. Of course, the student who got 90.1 will argue that he should have gotten an 'A' and not a 'B'. If you add 0.01 to the low scores, the student who got 90.001 will argue that he should have gotten an 'A' and not a 'B' and so forth. This is a problem with a continuous variable. A better solution might be to change the predicate to (score BETWEEN low_score AND high_score) AND (score > low_score) or simply to ((low_score < score) AND (score <= high_score)). Neither approach will be much different in this example, since few values will fall on the borders between grades and this table is very, very small.

However, some indexing schemes might make the BETWEEN predicate the better choice for larger tables of this sort. They will keep index values in trees whose nodes hold a range of values (look up a description of the B tree family in a computer science book). An optimizer can compare the range of values in the BETWEEN predicate to the range of values in the index nodes as a single action. If the BETWEEN predicate were presented as two comparisons, it might execute them as separate actions against the database, which would be slower.

19.2 OVERLAPS Predicate

The OVERLAPS predicate requires the Standard SQL temporal data features that might not be in your implementation yet.

19.2.1 Time Periods and OVERLAPS Predicate

Temporal data types and functions are the most irregular features in SQL products. By the time the ANSI/ISO Standards were written, each dialect had its own set of functions and features. But let's start with the concept of an INTERVAL, which is a measure of temporal duration, expressed in units such as days, hours, minutes, and so forth. This is how you add or subtract days to or from a date, hours and minutes to or from a time, and so forth. A time period is defined by a fixed starting point and fixed stopping point in time.

The OVERLAPS predicate compares two time periods. These time periods are defined as row values with two columns. The first column (the starting time) of the pair is always a <datetime> data type, and the second column (the termination time) is a <datetime> data type that can be used to compute a <datetime> value. If the starting and termination time are the same, this is an instantaneous event.

The BNF for this predicate is

```
<overlaps predicate>
   ::= <overlaps predicate part 1> <overlaps predicate part 2>
<overlaps predicate part 1> ::= <row value predicand 1>
<overlaps predicate part 2> ::= OVERLAPS <row value predicand 2>
<row value predicand 1> ::= <row value predicand>
<row value predicand 2> ::= <row value predicand>
```

The result of the <overlaps predicate> is formally defined as the result of the following expression:

```
(S1 > S2 AND NOT (S1 >= T2 AND T1 >= T2))
OR (S2 > S1 AND NOT (S2 >= T1 AND T2 >= T1))
OR (S1 = S2 AND (T1 <> T2 OR T1 = T2))
```

where S1 and S2 are the starting time of the two time periods and T1 and T2 are their respective termination time.

The rules for the OVERLAPS predicate should be intuitive, but they are not. The principles that we wanted in the Standard were

1. A time period includes its starting point but does not include its end point. The reason for this model is that it follows the ISO convention that there is no TIME '24:00:00' h today; it is TIME '00:00:00' h tomorrow. Half-open durations have closure properties that are useful. The overlap, intersection, and concatenation of two half-open durations is an half-open duration.

2. If the time periods are not instantaneous, they overlap when they share a common time period.

3. If the first term of the predicate is an INTERVAL and the second term is an instantaneous event (a <datetime> data type), they overlap when the second term is in the time period (but is not the end point of the time period).

4. If the first and second terms are both instantaneous events, they overlap only when they are equal.
5. If the starting time is NULL and the finishing time is a known <datetime> value, the finishing time becomes the starting time and we have an event. If the starting time is NULL and the finishing time is an INTERVAL value, then both the finishing and starting time are NULL.

Please consider how your intuition reacts to these results, when the granularity is at the YEAR-MONTH-DAY level. Remember that a day begins at 00:00:00 h.

```
(today, today) OVERLAPS (today, today) is TRUE
(today, tomorrow) OVERLAPS (today, today) is TRUE
(today, tomorrow) OVERLAPS (tomorrow, tomorrow) is FALSE
(yesterday, today) OVERLAPS (today, tomorrow) is FALSE
```

This is still not very intuitive, so let's draw pictures. Consider a table of hotel guests with the days of their stays and a table of special events being held at the hotel. The tables might look like this:

```
CREATE TABLE Guests
(guest_name CHARACTER(30) NOT NULL PRIMARY KEY,
 arrival_date DATE NOT NULL,
 departure_date DATE NOT NULL,
 . . .);
```

Guests

guest_name	arrival_date	departure_date
'Doroth yGale'	'2016-02-01'	'2016-11-01'
'Indiana Jones'	'2016-02-01'	'2016-02-01'
'Don Quixote'	'2016-01-01'	'2016-10-01'
'JamesT.Kirk'	'2016-02-01'	'2016-02-28'
'Santa Claus'	'2016-12-01'	'2016-12-25'

```
CREATE TABLE Celebrations
 (celeb_name CHARACTER(30) PRIMARY KEY,
  celeb_start_date DATE NOT NULL,
  celeb_end_date DATE NOT NULL,
  . . .);
```

Celebrations

celeb_name	celeb_start_date	celeb_end_date
'Apple Month'	'2016-02-01'	'2016-02-28'
'Christmas Season'	'2016-12-01'	'2016-12-25'
'Garlic Festival'	'2016-01-15'	'2016-02-15'
'National Pear Week'	'2016-01-01'	'2016-01-07'
'New Year's Day'	'2016-01-01'	'2016-01-01'
'St. Fred's Day'	'2016-02-24'	'2016-02-24'
'Year of the Prune'	'2016-01-01'	'2016-12-31'

The BETWEEN operator will work just fine with single dates that fall between the starting and finishing dates of these celebrations, but please remember that the BETWEEN predicate will include the end point of an interval and that the OVERLAPS predicate will not. To find out if a particular date occurs during an event, you can simply write queries like

```
SELECT guest_name, celeb_name
  FROM Guests, Celebrations
 WHERE arrival_date BETWEEN celeb_start_date AND celeb_end_date
   AND arrival_date <> celeb_end_date;
```

which will find the guests who arrived at the hotel during each event. The final predicate can be kept, if you want to conform to the ANSI convention, or dropped if that makes more sense in your situation. From now on, we will keep both end points to make the queries easier to read.

```
SELECT guest_name, celeb_name
  FROM Guests, Celebrations
 WHERE arrival_date BETWEEN celeb_start_date AND celeb_end_date;
```

Results

guest_name	celeb_name
'Dorothy Gale'	'Apple Month'
'Dorothy Gale'	'Garlic Festival'
'Dorothy Gale'	'Year of the Prune'
'Indiana Jones'	'Apple Month'
'Indiana Jones'	'Garlic Festival'

guest_name	celeb_name
'Indiana Jones'	'Year of the Prune'
'Don Quixote'	'National Pear Week'
'Don Quixote'	'New Year's Day'
'Don Quixote'	'Year of the Prune'
'James T. Kirk'	'Apple Month'
'James T. Kirk'	'Garlic Festival'
'James T. Kirk'	'Year of the Prune'
'Santa Claus'	'Christmas Season'
'Santa Claus'	'Year of the Prune'

The obvious question is which guests were at the hotel during each event. A common programming error when trying to find out if two intervals overlap is to write the query with the BETWEEN predicate, thus:

```
SELECT guest_name, celeb_name
  FROM Guests, Celebrations
 WHERE arrival_date BETWEEN celeb_start_date AND celeb_end_date
    OR departure_date BETWEEN celeb_start_date AND celeb_end_date;
```

This is wrong, because it does not cover the case where the event began and finished during the guest's visit. Seeing his error, the programmer will sit down and draw a timeline diagram of all four possible overlapping cases, like this:

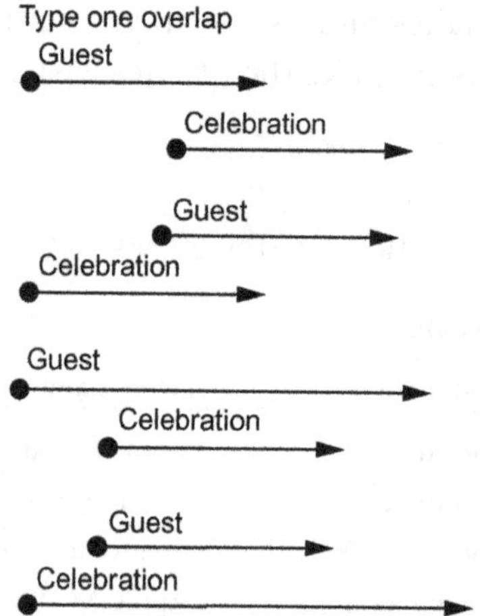

So the programmer adds more predicates, thus:

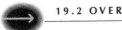

```
SELECT guest_name, celeb_name
  FROM Guests, Celebrations
WHERE arrival_date BETWEEN celeb_start_date AND celeb_end_date
   OR departure_date BETWEEN celeb_start_date AND celeb_end_date
   OR celeb_start_date BETWEEN arrival_date AND departure_date
   OR celeb_end_date BETWEEN arrival_date AND departure_date;
```

A thoughtful programmer will notice that the last predicate is not needed and might drop it, but either way, this is a correct query. But it is not the best answer. In the case of the overlapping intervals, there are two cases where a guest's stay at the hotel and an event do not both fall within the same time frame: Either the guest checked out before the event started or the event ended before the guest arrived. If you want to do the logic, that is what the first predicate will work out to be when you also add the conditions that arrival_date <= departure_date and celeb_start_date <= celeb_end_date. But it is easier to see in a timeline diagram, thus:

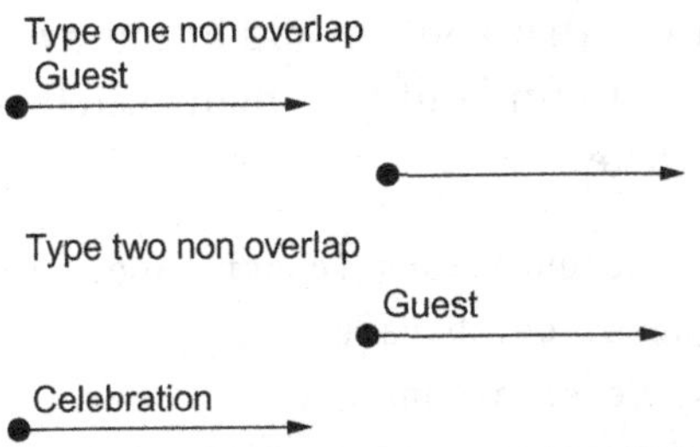

Both cases can be represented in one SQL statement as

```
SELECT guest_name, celeb_name
  FROM Guests, Celebrations
 WHERE NOT ((departure_date < celeb_start_date) OR
(arrival_date > celeb_end_date));
```

VIEW GuestsEvents

guest_name	celeb_name
'Dorothy Gale'	'Apple Month'
'Dorothy Gale'	'Garlic Festival'
'Dorothy Gale'	'St. Fred's Day'
'Dorothy Gale'	'Year of the Prune'
'Indiana Jones'	'Apple Month'
'Indiana Jones'	'Garlic Festival'

guest_name	celeb_name
'Indiana Jones'	'Year of the Prune'
'Don Quixote'	'Apple Month'
'Don Quixote'	'Garlic Festival'
'Don Quixote'	'National Pear Week'
'Don Quixote'	'New Year's Day'
'Don Quixote'	'St. Fred's Day'
'Don Quixote'	'Year of the Prune'
'James T. Kirk'	'Apple Month'
'James T. Kirk'	'Garlic Festival'
'James T. Kirk'	'St. Fred's Day'
'James T. Kirk'	'Year of the Prune'
'Santa Claus'	'Christmas Season'
'Santa Claus'	'Year of the Prune'

This VIEW is handy for other queries. The reason for using the NOT in the WHERE clause is that you can add or remove it to reverse the sense of the query. For example, to find out how many celebrations each guest could have seen, you would write

```
CREATE VIEW Guest_Celebrations (guest_name, celeb_name)
AS SELECT guest_name, celeb_name
     FROM Guests, Celebrations
    WHERE NOT ((departure_date < celeb_start_date) OR (arrival_date >
celeb_end_date));

SELECT guest_name, COUNT(*) AS celebcount
  FROM Guest_Celebrations
 GROUP BY guest_name;
```

Results

guest_name	celeb_cnt
'Dorothy Gale'	4
'Indiana Jones'	3
'Don Quixote'	6
'James T. Kirk'	4
'Santa Claus'	2

and then to find out how many guests were at the hotel during each celebration, you would write

```
SELECT celeb_name, COUNT(*) AS guest_cnt
  FROM Guest_Celebrations
 GROUP BY celeb_name;
```

Result

celeb_name	guest_cnt
'Apple Month'	4
'Christmas Season'	1
'Garlic Festival'	4
'National Pear Week'	1
'New Year's Day'	1
'St. Fred's Day'	3
'Year of the Prune'	5

This last query is only part of the story. What the hotel management really wants to know is how many room nights were sold for a celebration. A little algebra tells you that the length of an event is (celeb_end_date – celeb_start_date + INTERVAL '1' DAY) and that the length of a guest's stay is ((Guest.departure_date – Guest.arrival_date) + 1) because the difference is an integer count of the days. Let's do one of those timeline charts again:

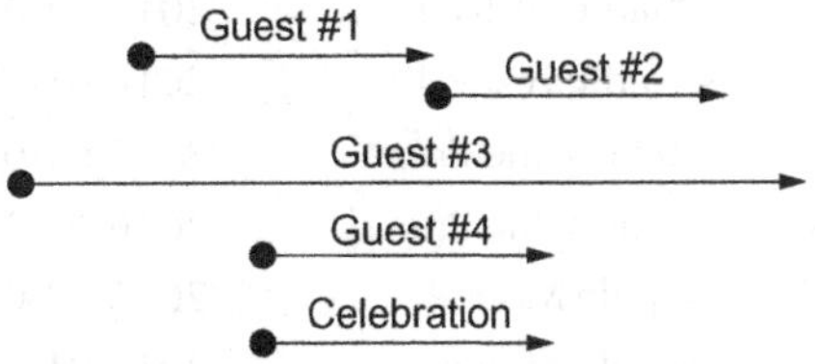

What we want is the part of the Guests interval that is inside the Celebrations interval.

Guests 1 and 2 spent only part of their time at the celebration; Guest 3 spent all of his time at the celebration; and Guest 4 stayed even longer than the celebration. That interval is defined by the two points (CASE WHEN arrival_date > celeb_start_date THEN arrival_date ELSE celeb_start_date END) and (CASE WHEN departure_date < celeb_end_date THEN departure_date ELSE celeb_end_date END).

Instead, you can use the aggregate functions in SQL to build a VIEW on a VIEW, like this:

```
CREATE VIEW Working (guest_name, celeb_name, entry_date, exit_date)
AS
SELECT GE.guest_name, GE.celeb_name, celeb_start_date, celeb_end_date
  FROM Guest_Celebrations AS GE, Celebrations AS E1
 WHERE E1.celeb_name = GE.celeb_name
UNION
SELECT GE.guest_name, GE.celeb_name, arrival_date, departure_date
  FROM Guest_Celebrations AS GE, Guests AS G1
 WHERE G1.guest_name = GE.guest_name;
```

VIEW Working

guest_name	celeb_name	entry_date	exit_date
'Dorothy Gale'	'Apple Month'	'2016-02-01'	'2016-02-28'
'Dorothy Gale'	'Apple Month'	'2016-02-01'	'2016-11-01'
'Dorothy Gale'	'Garlic Festival'	'2016-02-01'	'2016-11-01'
'Dorothy Gale'	'Garlic Festival'	'2016-01-15'	'2016-02-15'
'Dorothy Gale'	'St. Fred's Day'	'2016-02-01'	'2016-11-01'
'Dorothy Gale'	'St. Fred's Day'	'2016-02-24'	'2016-02-24'
'Dorothy Gale'	'Year of the Prune'	'2016-02-01'	'2016-11-01'
'Dorothy Gale'	'Year of the Prune'	'2016-01-01'	'2016-12-31'
'Indiana Jones'	'Apple Month'	'2016-02-01'	'2016-02-01'
'Indiana Jones'	'Apple Month'	'2016-02-01'	'2016-02-28'
'Indiana Jones'	'Garlic Festival'	'2016-02-01'	'2016-02-01'
'Indiana Jones'	'Garlic Festival'	'2016-01-15'	'2016-02-15'
'Indiana Jones'	'Year of the Prune'	'2016-02-01'	'2016-02-01'
'Indiana Jones'	'Year of the Prune'	'2016-01-01'	'2016-12-31'
'Don Quixote'	'Apple Month'	'2016-02-01'	'2016-02-28'
'Don Quixote'	'Apple Month'	'2016-01-01'	'2016-10-01'
'Don Quixote'	'Garlic Festival'	'2016-01-01'	'2016-10-01'
'Don Quixote'	'Garlic Festival'	'2016-01-15'	'2016-02-15'
'Don Quixote'	'National Pear Week'	'2016-01-01'	'2016-01-07'
'Don Quixote'	'National Pear Week'	'2016-01-01'	'2016-10-01'
'Don Quixote'	'New Year's Day'	'2016-01-01'	'2016-01-01'
'Don Quixote'	'New Year's Day'	'2016-01-01'	'2016-10-01'
'Don Quixote'	'St. Fred's Day'	'2016-02-24'	'2016-02-24'
'Don Quixote'	'St. Fred's Day'	'2016-01-01'	'2016-10-01'
'Don Quixote'	'Year of the Prune'	'2016-01-01'	'2016-12-31'
'Don Quixote'	'Year of the Prune'	'2016-01-01'	'2016-10-01'

guest_name	celeb_name	entry_date	exit_date
'James T. Kirk'	'Apple Month'	'2016-02-01'	'2016-02-28'
'James T. Kirk'	'Garlic Festival'	'2016-02-01'	'2016-02-28'
'James T. Kirk'	'Garlic Festival'	'2016-01-15'	'2016-02-15'
'James T. Kirk'	'St. Fred's Day'	'2016-02-01'	'2016-02-28'
'James T. Kirk'	'St. Fred's Day'	'2016-02-24'	'2016-02-24'
'James T. Kirk'	'Year of the Prune'	'2016-02-01'	'2016-02-28'
'James T. Kirk'	'Year of the Prune'	'2016-01-01'	'2016-12-31'
'Santa Claus'	'Christmas Season'	'2016-12-01'	'2016-12-25'
'Santa Claus'	'Year of the Prune'	'2016-12-01'	'2016-12-25'
'Santa Claus'	'Year of the Prune'	'2016-01-01'	'2016-12-31'

This will put the earliest and latest points in both intervals into one column. Now we can construct a VIEW like this:

```
CREATE VIEW Attendees (guest_name, celeb_name, entry_date, exit_date)
AS
SELECT guest_name, celeb_name,
       MAX(entry_date), MIN(exit_date)
  FROM Working
 GROUP BY guest_name, celeb_name;
```

VIEW Attendees

guest_name	celeb_name	entry_date	exit_date
'Dorothy Gale'	'Apple Month'	'2016-02-01'	'2016-02-28'
'Dorothy Gale'	'Garlic Festival'	'2016-02-01'	'2016-02-15'
'Dorothy Gale'	'St. Fred's Day'	'2016-02-24'	'2016-02-24'
'Dorothy Gale'	'Year of the Prune'	'2016-02-01'	'2016-11-01'
'Indiana Jones'	'Apple Month'	'2016-02-01'	'2016-02-01'
'Indiana Jones'	'Garlic Festival'	'2016-02-01'	'2016-02-01'
'Indiana Jones'	'Year of the Prune'	'2016-02-01'	'2016-02-01'
'Don Quixote'	'Apple Month'	'2016-02-01'	'2016-02-28'
'Don Quixote'	'Garlic Festival'	'2016-01-15'	'2016-02-15'
'Don Quixote'	'National Pear Week'	'2016-01-01'	'2016-01-07'
'Don Quixote'	'New Year's Day'	'2016-01-01'	'2016-01-01'
'Don Quixote'	'St. Fred's Day'	'2016-02-24'	'2016-02-24'
'Don Quixote'	'Year of the Prune'	'2016-01-01'	'2016-10-01'
'James T. Kirk'	'Apple Month'	'2016-02-01'	'2016-02-28'

guest_name	celeb_name	entry_date	exit_date
'James T. Kirk'	'Garlic Festival'	'2016-02-01'	'2016-02-15'
'James T. Kirk'	'St. Fred's Day'	'2016-02-24'	'2016-02-24'
'James T. Kirk'	'Year of the Prune'	'2016-02-01'	'2016-02-28'
'Santa Claus'	'Christmas Season'	'2016-12-01'	'2016-12-25'
'Santa Claus'	'Year of the Prune'	'2016-12-01'	'2016-12-25'

The Attendees VIEW can be used to compute the total number of room days for each celebration. Assume that the difference of two dates will return an integer that is the number of days between them:

```
SELECT celeb_name,
      SUM(exit_date - entry_date + INTERVAL '1' DAY)
     AS room_days
  FROM Attendees
  GROUP BY celeb_name;
```

Result

celeb_name	room_days
'Apple Month'	85
'Christmas Season'	25
'Garlic Festival'	63
'National Pear Week'	7
'New Year's Day'	1
'St. Fred's Day'	3
'Year of the Prune'	602

If you would like to get a count of the room days sold in the month of January, you could use this query, which avoids a BETWEEN or OVERLAPS predicate completely.

```
SELECT SUM(CASE WHEN depart > DATE '2016-01-31'
               THEN DATE '2016-01-31'
                ELSE depart END
          - CASE WHEN arrival_date < DATE '2016-01-01'
                 THEN DATE '2016-01-01'
```

```
                ELSE arrival_date END + INTERVAL '1' DAY)
       AS room_days
  FROM Guests
 WHERE depart > DATE '2016-01-01'
   AND arrival_date <= DATE '2016-01-31';
```

CASE Expression Family

SQL-92 ADDED NEW expressions and extended the rules for old ones to make the language more orthogonal. Basically, anything that looks reasonable is probably legal syntax. But SQL is declarative, so we do not have the concept of flow control in procedural languages. Instead, we use expressions that come from primitive recursive function theory to select a result from among possible values.

In English, it means we do not use IF-THEN-ELSE control flow logic and its various forms but have CASE expressions and those various forms.

20.1 CASE Expression

The CASE expression is probably the most useful addition to SQL-92. This is a quick overview of how to use the expression, but you will find other tricks spread throughout the book. It allows the programmer to pick a value based on a logical expression in his code. ANSI stole the idea and the syntax from the ADA programming language and the selection operators from recursive function theory. Here is the BNF for a <case specification>:

```
<case specification> ::= <simple case> | <searched case>

<simple case> ::=
   CASE <case operand>
```

```
      <simple when clause>. . .
      [<else clause>]
    END

<searched case> ::=
    CASE
      <searched when clause>. . .
      [<else clause>]
    END

<simple when clause> ::= WHEN <when operand> THEN <result>

<searched when clause> ::= WHEN <search condition> THEN <result>

<else clause> ::= ELSE <result>

<case operand> ::= <value expression>

<when operand> ::= <value expression>

<result> ::= <result expression> | NULL

<result expression> ::= <value expression>
```

The searched CASE expression is probably the most used version of the expression. The WHEN… THEN… clauses are executed in left to right order. The first WHEN clause that tests TRUE returns the value given in its THEN clause. And, yes, you can nest CASE expressions inside each other. If no explicit ELSE clause is given for the CASE expression, then the database will insert a default ELSE NULL clause. If you wish to return a NULL from a THEN, however, you must use a CAST (NULL AS <data type>) expression to establish the data type for the compiler.

```
--this works
 CASE WHEN 1 = 1
      THEN NULL
      ELSE CAST(NULL AS INTEGER) END

--this works
  CASE WHEN 1 = 1
       THEN CAST(NULL AS INTEGER)
       ELSE NULL END
```

```
--this does not work; no <result> to establish a data type
  CASE WHEN 1 = 1
       THEN NULL
       ELSE NULL END

--might or might not work in your SQL
 CAST (CASE WHEN 1 = 1
       THEN NULL
       ELSE NULL END AS INTEGER)
```

I recommend always writing an explicit ELSE clause, so that you can change it later when you find a value to return. I would also recommend that you explicitly cast a NULL in the CASE expression THEN clauses to the desired data type.

If the THEN clauses have results of different data types, the compiler will find the most general one and CAST() the others to it. But again, actual implementations might have slightly different ideas about how this casting should be done.

The <simple case expression> is defined as a searched CASE expression in which all the WHEN clauses are made into equality comparisons against the <case operand>. For example

```
CASE sex_code
WHEN 0 THEN 'Unknown'
WHEN 1 THEN 'Male'
WHEN 2 THEN 'Female'
WHEN 9 THEN 'N/A'
ELSE NULL END
```

could also be written as:

```
CASE
WHEN sex_code = 0 THEN 'Unknown'
WHEN sex_code = 1 THEN 'Male'
WHEN sex_code = 2 THEN 'Female'
WHEN sex_code = 9 THEN 'N/A'
ELSE NULL END
```

There is a gimmick in this definition, however. The expression

```
CASE foo
WHEN 1 THEN 'bar'
WHEN NULL THEN 'no bar'
END
```

becomes

```
CASE WHEN foo = 1 THEN 'bar'
     WHEN foo = NULL THEN 'no_bar' -- error!
     ELSE NULL END
```

The second WHEN clause is always UNKNOWN. This definition can get really weird with a random number generator in the expression. Let's assume that RANDOM() uses a seed value and returns a uniformly distributed random floating point number between 0.0000 and 0.99999999…99 when it is called.

This expression will spend most of its time in the ELSE clause instead of returning a number word between one and five.

```
SET pick_one = CASE CAST((5.0 * RANDOM()) + 1 AS INTEGER)
               WHEN 1 THEN 'one'
               WHEN 2 THEN 'two'
               WHEN 3 THEN 'three'
               WHEN 4 THEN 'four'
               WHEN 5 THEN 'five'
               ELSE 'This should not happen' END;
```

The expansion will reproduce the CAST() expression for each WHEN clause and the RANDOM() function will be reevaluated each time. You need to be sure that it is evaluated only once.

```
BEGIN
  DECLARE tmp INTEGER;
  SET tmp = CAST((5.0 * RANDOM()) + 1 AS INTEGER);
  SET pick_one = CASE tmp
                 WHEN 1 THEN 'one'
                 WHEN 2 THEN 'two'
                 WHEN 3 THEN 'three'
                 WHEN 4 THEN 'four'
                 WHEN 5 THEN 'five'
                 ELSE 'This should not happen' END;
END;
```

The variable tmp is also expanded into the WHEN clause, but because it is not a function call, it is not evaluated over and over.

20.1.1 The COALESCE() and NULLIF() Functions

The SQL Standard defines other functions in terms of the CASE expression, which makes the language a bit more compact and easier to implement. For example, the COALESCE() function can be defined for one or two expressions by

```
1) COALESCE (<value exp #1>) is equivalent to (<value exp #1>)

2) COALESCE (<value exp #1>, <value exp #2>) is equivalent to


   CASE WHEN <value exp #1> IS NOT NULL
        THEN <value exp #1>
        ELSE <value exp #2> END
```

then we can recursively define it for (n) expressions, where (n >=3), in the list by COALESCE (<value exp #1>, <value exp #2>,..., n), as equivalent to:

```
   CASE WHEN <value exp #1> IS NOT NULL
        THEN <value exp #1>
        ELSE COALESCE (<value exp #2>,. . ., n)
   END
```

Likewise, NULLIF (<value exp #1>, <value exp #2>) is equivalent to:

```
   CASE WHEN <value exp #1> = <value exp #2>
        THEN NULL
        ELSE <value exp #1> END
```

20.1.2 CASE Expressions with GROUP BY

A CASE expression is very useful with a GROUP BY query. For example, to determine how many employees of each gender by department you have in your personnel table, you can write:

```
SELECT dept_nbr,
        SUM(CASE WHEN gender = 'M' THEN 1 ELSE 0) AS males,
        SUM(CASE WHEN gender = 'F' THEN 1 ELSE 0) AS females
  FROM Personnel
 GROUP BY dept_nbr;
```

or

```
SELECT dept_nbr,
       COUNT(CASE WHEN gender = 'M' THEN 1 ELSE NULL) AS males,
       COUNT(CASE WHEN gender = 'F' THEN 1 ELSE NULL) AS females
  FROM Personnel
 GROUP BY dept_nbr;
```

I am not sure if there is any general rule as to which form will run faster.

The previous example shows the CASE expression inside the aggregate function; it is possible to put aggregate functions inside a CASE expression. For example, assume you are given a table of employee's skills:

```
CREATE TABLE Personnel_Skills
(emp_id CHAR(11) NOT NULL,
 skill_id CHAR(11) NOT NULL,
 primary_skill_ind CHAR(1) NOT NULL
                   CONSTRAINT primary_skill_given
                   CHECK (primary_skill_ind IN ('Y', 'N'),
 PRIMARY KEY (emp_id, skill_id));
```

Each employee has a row in the table for each of his skills. If the employee has multiple skills they will have multiple rows in the table and the primary skill indicator will be a 'Y' for their main skill. If they only have one skill (which means one row in the table), the value of primary_skill_ind is indeterminate. The problem is to list each employee once along with:

(a) his only skill if he has only one row in the table or

(b) his primary skill if he has multiple rows in the table.

```
SELECT emp_id,
      CASE WHEN COUNT(*) = 1
           THEN MAX(skill_id)
           ELSE MAX(CASE WHEN primary_skill_ind = 'Y'
                         THEN skill_id END)
                         ELSE NULL END)
      END AS main_skill
  FROM Personnel_Skills
 GROUP BY emp_id;
```

This solution looks at first like a violation of the rule in SQL that prohibits nested aggregate functions, but if you look closely, it is not. The aggregate functions are inside the CASE expression and the CASE expression is also inside an aggregate function. The reason this works is that every branch of the CASE expression resolves to an aggregate function, MAX() or a NULL.

20.1.3 CASE, CHECK() Clauses and Logical Implication

Complicated logical predicates can be put into a CASE expression which returns either 'T' (TRUE) or 'F' (FALSE)

```
CONSTRAINT implication_example
CHECK (CASE WHEN dept_nbr = 'D1'
            THEN CASE WHEN salary < 44000.00
                      THEN 'T' ELSE 'F' END
            ELSE 'T' END = 'T')
```

This is a logical implication operator. It is usually written as an arrow with two stems ⇒ and its definition is usually stated as "a true premise cannot imply a false conclusion" of as "If a then b" in English.

In English, this condition says "if an employee is in department 'D1', then his salary is less than $44,000.00," which is not the same as saying "(dept_nbr = 'D1' AND salary < 44000.00)" in the constraint. In standard Boolean logic, there is a simple transformation called the "Smisteru rule" after the engineer who discovered it which says that $(A \Rightarrow B)$ is equivalent to $(\neg A \wedge B)$.

But in SQL, the rule is that a CHECK() constraint succeeds when the answer is TRUE or UNKNOWN while an ON or WHERE clause fails when the answer is FALSE or UNKNOWN. This leads to all kinds of problems with implication in 3-valued logic with two sets of rules. One for DDL and one for DML!

Let's try the Smisteru transform first:

```
CREATE TABLE Foobar_DDL_1
(a CHAR(1) CHECK (a IN ('T', 'F')),
 b CHAR(1) CHECK (b IN ('T', 'F')),
CONSTRAINT implication_example
CHECK (NOT (A ='T') OR (B = 'T')));

INSERT INTO Foobar_DDL_1VALUES ('T', 'T');
INSERT INTO Foobar_DDL_1 VALUES ('T', 'F'); -- fails
INSERT INTO Foobar_DDL_1 VALUES ('T', NULL);
INSERT INTO Foobar_DDL_1 VALUES ('F', 'T');
```

```
INSERT INTO Foobar_DDL_1 VALUES ('F', 'F');
INSERT INTO Foobar_DDL_1 VALUES ('F', NULL);
INSERT INTO Foobar_DDL_1 VALUES (NULL, 'T');
INSERT INTO Foobar_DDL_1 VALUES (NULL, 'F');
INSERT INTO Foobar_DDL_1 VALUES (NULL, NULL);

SELECT * FROM Foobar_DDL_1;
```

a	b
T	T
T	NULL
F	T
F	F
F	NULL
NULL	T
NULL	F
NULL	NULL

Now my original version is

```
CREATE TABLE Foobar_DDL
(a CHAR(1) CHECK (a IN ('T', 'F')),
 b CHAR(1) CHECK (b IN ('T', 'F')),
CONSTRAINT implication_example_2
CHECK(CASE WHEN A = 'T'
           THEN CASE WHEN B = 'T'
                THEN 1 ELSE 0 END
           ELSE 1 END = 1));

INSERT INTO Foobar_DDL VALUES ('T', 'T');
INSERT INTO Foobar_DDL VALUES ('T', 'F'); -- fails
INSERT INTO Foobar_DDL VALUES ('T', NULL);
INSERT INTO Foobar_DDL VALUES ('F', 'T');
INSERT INTO Foobar_DDL VALUES ('F', 'F');
INSERT INTO Foobar_DDL VALUES ('F', NULL);
INSERT INTO Foobar_DDL VALUES (NULL, 'T');
INSERT INTO Foobar_DDL VALUES (NULL, 'F');
INSERT INTO Foobar_DDL VALUES (NULL, NULL);
```

```
SELECT * FROM Foobar_DDL;
```

a	b
T	T
F	T
F	F
F	NULL
NULL	T
NULL	F
NULL	NULL

Both agree that a TRUE premise cannot lead to a FALSE conclusion, but Smisteru allows ('T', NULL). Not quite the same implication operators!

Let's now look at the query side of the house:

```
CREATE TABLE Foobar
(a CHAR(1) CHECK (a IN ('T', 'F')),
 b CHAR(1) CHECK (b IN ('T', 'F')));

INSERT INTO Foobar
VALUES ('T', 'T'),
       ('T', 'F'),
       ('T', NULL),
       ('F', 'T'),
       ('F', 'F'),
       ('F', NULL),
       (NULL, 'T'),
       (NULL, 'F'),
       (NULL, NULL);
```

Using the Smisteru rule as the search condition:
SELECT * FROM Foobar WHERE (NOT (a = 'T') OR (b = 'T'));

a	b
T	T
F	T
F	F
F	NULL
NULL	T

Using the original predicate:

```
SELECT * FROM Foobar
WHERE CASE WHEN A = 'T'
           THEN CASE WHEN B = 'T'
                THEN 1 ELSE 0 END
           ELSE 1 END = 1;
```

a	b
T	T
F	T
F	F
F	NULL
NULL	T
NULL	F
NULL	NULL

This is why I used the CASE expression; it works the same way in both the DDL and DML.

20.2 Subquery Expressions and Constants

Subquery expressions are SELECT statements inside of parentheses. Well, there is more to it than that.

The four flavors of subquery expressions are tabular, columnar, row, and scalar subquery expressions. As you might guess from the names, the tabular or table subquery returns a table as a result, so it has to appear any place that a table is used in SQL, which usually means it is in the FROM clause.

The columnar subquery returns a table with a single column in it. This was the important one in the original SQL-89 standards because the IN, <comp op> ALL and <comp op> ANY predicates were based on the ability of the language to convert the column into a list of comparisons connected by ANDs or ORs. Later versions of SQL allow for row comparison.

The row subquery returns a single row. It can be used anywhere a row can be used. This sort of query is the basis for the singleton SELECT statement used in the embedded SQL. It is not used too much right now, but with the extension of theta operators to handle row comparisons, it might become more popular.

The scalar subquery returns a single scalar value. It can be used anywhere a scalar value can be used, which usually means it is in the SELECT or WHERE clauses.

A scalar subquery is better thought of as the SQL version of a subroutine or in-line function. That is, it is a body of code in the native language, available to the program. The use of the scalar subquery will be discussed as needed in the following sections when we get to programming tricks and techniques. I will make the very general statement now that the performance of scalar subqueries depends a lot on the architecture of the hardware upon which your SQL is implemented. A massively parallel machine can allocate a processor to each scalar subquery and get drastic performance improvement.

A table of any shape can be constructed using the VALUES() expression. The idea is that you can build a row as a comma separated list of scalar expressions and build a table as a comma separated list of row constructors.

LIKE and SIMILAR TO Predicates

THE LIKE PREDICATE is a string pattern-matching test with the syntax

```
<like predicate> ::=
    <match value> [NOT] LIKE <pattern>
        [ESCAPE <escape character>]

<match value> ::= <character value expression>
<pattern> ::= <character value expression>
<escape character> ::= <character value expression>
```

The expression "m NOT LIKE p" is equivalent to "NOT (m LIKE p)", which follows the usual syntax pattern in SQL. There are two wild cards allowed in the <pattern> string. They are the '%' and '_' characters. The '_' character represents a single arbitrary character; the '%' character represents an arbitrary substring, possibly of length zero. Notice that there is no way to represent zero or one arbitrary character. This is not the case in many text-search languages and can lead to problems or very complex predicates.

Any other character in the <pattern> represents that character itself. This means that SQL patterns are case-sensitive, but many vendors allow you to set case sensitivity on or off at the database system level.

The <escape character> is used in the <pattern> to specify that the character that follows it is to be interpreted as a literal rather than a wild

card. This means that the escape character is followed by the escape character itself, an '_' or a '%'. Old C programmers are used to this convention, where the language defines the escape character as '\', so this is a good choice for SQL programmers too.

21.1 Tricks with Patterns

The '_' character tests much faster than the '%' character. The reason is obvious: the parser that compares a string to the pattern needs only one operation to match an underscore before it can move to the next character but has to do some look-ahead parsing to resolve a percentage sign. The wild cards can be inserted in the middle or beginning of a pattern. Thus, 'B%K' will match 'BOOK', 'BLOCK', and 'BK', but it will not match 'BLOCKS'.

The parser would scan each letter and classify it as a wild card match or an exact match. In the case of 'BLOCKS', the initial 'B' would be an exact match and the parser would continue; 'L', 'O', and 'C' have to be wild card matches, since they don't appear in the pattern string; 'K' cannot be classified until we read the last letter. The last letter is 'S', so the match fails.

For example, given a column declared to be seven characters long, and a LIKE predicate looking for names that start with 'Mac', you would usually write

```
SELECT *
  FROM People
 WHERE last_name LIKE 'Mac%';
```

but this might actually run faster:

```
SELECT *
  FROM People
 WHERE last_name LIKE 'Mac_   '
    OR last_name LIKE 'Mac__  '
    OR last_name LIKE 'Mac___ '
    OR last_name LIKE 'Mac____';
```

The trailing blanks are also characters that can be matched exactly.

Putting a '%' at the front of a pattern is very time-consuming. For example, you might try to find all names that end in 'son' with the query

```
SELECT *
  FROM People
  WHERE last_name LIKE '%son';
```

The use of underscores instead will make a real difference in most SQL implementations for this query, because most of them always parse from left to right.

```
SELECT *
  FROM People
 WHERE last_name LIKE '_son '
    OR last_name LIKE '__son '
    OR last_name LIKE '___son '
    OR last_name LIKE '____son';
```

Remember that the '_' character requires a matching character and the '%' character does not. Thus, the query

```
SELECT *
  FROM People
 WHERE last_name LIKE 'John_%';
```

and the query

```
SELECT *
  FROM People
 WHERE last_name LIKE 'John%';
```

are subtly different. Both will match to 'Johnson' and 'Johns', but the first will not accept 'John' as a match. This is how you get a "one-or-more-characters" pattern match in SQL.

Remember that the <pattern> as well as the <match value> can be constructed with concatenation operators, SUBSTRING(), and other string functions. For example, let's find people whose first names are part of their last names with the query

```
SELECT *
  FROM People
 WHERE last_name LIKE '%' || first_name || '%';
```

which will show us people like 'John Johnson', 'Anders Andersen', and 'Bob McBoblin'. This query will also run very slowly. However, this is

case-sensitive and would not work for names such as 'Jon Anjon', so you might want to modify the statement to:

```
SELECT *
  FROM People
 WHERE UPPER (last_name) LIKE '%' || UPPER(first_name) || '%';
```

21.2 Results with NULL Values and Empty Strings

As you would expect, a NULL in the predicate returns an UNKNOWN result. The NULL can be the escape character, pattern, or match value.

If both M and P are character strings of length zero, M LIKE P defaults to TRUE. If one or both are longer than zero characters, you use the regular rules to test the predicate.

21.3 LIKE is Not Equality

A very important point that is often missed is that two strings can be equal but not LIKE in SQL. The test of equality first pads the shorter of the two strings with rightmost blanks, then matches the characters in each, one for one. Thus 'Smith' and 'Smith' (with three trailing blanks) are equal. However, the LIKE predicate does no padding, so 'Smith' LIKE 'Smith' tests FALSE because there is nothing to match to the blanks.

A good trick to get around these problems is to use the TRIM() function to remove unwanted blanks from the strings within either or both of the two arguments.

21.4 Extending the LIKE Predicate with a Join

Beginners often want to write something similar to "<string> IN LIKE (<pattern list>)" rather than a string of OR-ed LIKE predicates. That syntax is illegal, but you can get the same results with a table of patterns and a join.

CREATE TABLE Patterns

```
(template VARCHAR(10) NOT NULL PRIMARY KEY);

INSERT INTO Patterns
VALUES ('Celko%'),
       ('Chelko%'),
       ('Cilko%'),
       ('Selko%),
```

```
       ('Silko%');
SELECT A1.last_name
  FROM Patterns AS P1, Authors AS A1
 WHERE A1.last_name LIKE P1.template;
```

21.5 CASE Expressions and LIKE Predicates

The CASE expression in Standard SQL lets the programmer use the LIKE predicate in some interesting ways. The simplest example is counting the number of times a particular string appears inside another string. Assume that text_col is CHAR(25) and we want the count of a particular string, 'term', within it.

```
SELECT text_col,
      CASE
       WHEN text_col LIKE '%term%term%term%term%term%term%'
       THEN 6
       WHEN text_col LIKE '%term%term%term%term%term%'
       THEN 5
       WHEN text_col LIKE '%term%term%term%term%'
       THEN 4
       WHEN text_col LIKE '%term%term%term%'
       THEN 3
       WHEN text_col LIKE '%term%term%'
       THEN 2
       WHEN text_col LIKE '%term%'
       THEN 1
       ELSE 0 END AS term_tally
  FROM Foobar
 WHERE text_col LIKE '%term%';
```

This depends on the fact that a CASE expression executes the WHEN clauses in order of their appearance. We know that a substring can repeat no more than six times because of the length of text_col.

Another use of the CASE is to adjust the pattern within the LIKE predicate.

```
name LIKE CASE
          WHEN language = 'English'
```

```
THEN 'Red%'
WHEN language = 'French'
THEN 'Rouge%'
ELSE 'R%' END
```

21.6 SIMILAR TO Predicates

As you can see, the LIKE predicate is pretty weak, especially if you have used a version of grep(), a utility program from the UNIX operating system. The name is short for "general regular expression parser" and before you ask, a regular expression is a class of formal languages. If you are a computer science major, you have seen them; otherwise, don't worry about it. The bad news is that there are several versions of grep() in the UNIX community, such as egrep(), fgrep(), xgrep(), and a dozen or so others.

The SQL-99 standard added a regular expression predicate of the form "<string expression> SIMILAR TO <pattern>", which is based on the POSIX version of grep() found in ISO/IEC 9945.

The special symbols in a pattern are

| means alternation (either of two alternatives)

* means repetition of the previous item zero or more times

+ means repetition of the previous item one or more times

Parentheses () may be used to group items into a single unit.

A bracket expression [...] specifies a match to any of the characters inside the brackets.

There are abbreviations for lists of commonly used character subsets, taken from POSIX.

[:ALPHA:] match any alphabetic character, regardless of case.

[:UPPER:] match any upper case alphabetic character.

[:LOWER:] match any lower case alphabetic character.

[:DIGIT:] match any numeric digit.

[:ALNUM:] match any numeric digit or alphabetic character.

Examples:

(1) The letters 'foo' or 'bar' followed by any string

```
Foobar SIMILAR TO '(foo|bar)%'
```

(2) The 'SER #' followed by one or more digits

```
serial_nbr SIMILAR TO ' SER #[0-9]+'
serial_nbr SIMILAR TO ' SER [:DIGIT:]+'
```

You should still read your product manual for details, but most grep() functions accept other special symbols for more general searching than the SIMILAR TO predicate.

. any character (same as the SQL underscore)

^ start of line (not used in an SQL string)

$ end of line (not used in an SQL string)

\ The next character is a literal and not a special symbol; this is called an ESCAPE in SQL

[^] match anything but the characters inside the brackets, after the caret

Regular expressions have a lot of nice properties.

21.7 Tricks with Strings

This is a list of miscellaneous tricks that you might not think about when using strings. They are not always a good idea, but you might see them and need to know what they are trying to do.

21.7.1 String Character Content

A weird way of providing an edit mask for a varying character column to see if it has only digits in it was proposed by Ken Sheridan on the ACCESS forum of Compuserve in 1999 October. If the first character is not a zero, then you can check that the VARCHAR(n) string is all digits with:

```
CAST (LOG10 (CAST (test_column AS INTEGER) AS INTEGER) = n
```

If the first (*n*) characters are not all digits then it will not return (*n*). If they are all digits, but the (*n*+1) character is also a digit it will return (*n*+1) and so forth. If there are non-digit characters in the string, then the innermost CAST() function will fail to convert the test_column into a number. If you do have to worry about leading zeros or blanks then concatenate '1' to the front of the string.

Another trick is to think in terms of whole strings and not in a "character at a time" mind set. So how can I tell if a string is all alphabetic, partly alphabetic, or complete nonalphabetic without scanning each character? The answer from the folks at Ocelot software is surprisingly easy:

```
CREATE TABLE Foobar
(no_alpha VARCHAR(6) NOT NULL
            CHECK (UPPER(no_alpha) = LOWER(no_alpha)),
 some_alpha VARCHAR(6) NOT NULL
            CHECK (UPPER(some_alpha) <> LOWER(some_alpha)),
 all_alpha VARCHAR(6) NOT NULL
           CHECK (UPPER(all_alpha) <> LOWER(all_alpha)
                 AND LOWER (all_alpha)
                     BETWEEN 'aaaaaa' AND 'zzzzzz'),
  . . .);
```

Letters have different upper and lowercase values, but other characters do not. This lets us edit a column for no alphabetic characters, some alphabetic characters, and all alphabetic characters.

21.7.2 Searching Versus Declaring a String

You need to be very accurate when you declare a string column in your DDL, but thanks to doing that, you can slack off a bit when you search on those columns in your DML. For example, most credit card numbers are made up of four groups of four digits, and each group has some validation rule, thus.

```
CREATE TABLE CreditCards
(card_nbr CHAR(17) NOT NULL PRIMARY KEY
 CONSTRAINT valid_card_nbr_format
   CHECK (card_nbr SIMILAR TO
          '[0-9][0-9][0-9][0-9]-[0-9][0-9][0-9][0-9]-[0-9][0-9][0-9]
[0-9]-[0-9][0-9][0-9][0-9]'),
 CONSTRAINT valid_bank_nbr
   CHECK (SUBSTRING (card_nbr FROM 1 FOR 4)
          IN ('2349', '2345', ..),
 . .);
```

Since we are sure that the credit card number is stored correctly, we can search for it with a simple LIKE predicate. For example to find all the cards that 1234 in the third group, you can use this.

```
SELECT card_nbr
  FROM CreditCards
 WHERE card_nbr LIKE '____-____-1234-____';
```

Or even

```
SELECT card_nbr
  FROM CreditCards
 WHERE card_nbr LIKE '________1234____';
```

The SIMILAR TO predicate will build an internal finite state machine to parse the pattern, while the underscores in the LIKE can be optimized so that it can run in parallel down the whole column.

21.7.3 Creating an Index on a String

Many string encoding techniques have the same prefix because we read from left to right and tend to put the codes for the largest category to the left. For example, the first group of digits in the credit card numbers is the issuing bank. The syntax might look like this:

```
CREATE INDEX Acct_Searching
    ON CreditCards
  WITH REVERSE(card_nbr);
```

If your SQL has the ability to define a function in an index, you can reverse or rearrange the string to give faster access. This is very vendor dependent, but often the query must explicitly use the same function as the index.

An alternative is to store the rearranged value in the base table and show the actual value in a view. When the view is invoked, the rearranged value will be used for the query without the users knowing it.

Basic SELECT Statement

HERE IS HOW a SELECT works in SQL ... at least in theory. Real products will optimize things, but the code has to produce the same results.

The high level skeleton for a SELECT is

```
[WITH <cte list>]
SELECT <column list>
 FROM <table constructor>
[WHERE <row search condition>]
[GROUP BY <grouping list>]
[HAVING <group search condition>];
```

Please note that *the only required* clauses are SELECT and FROM. The WHERE clause is the most common additional clause. The clauses are not effectively executed in the order written. Let's take a high level look at each clause.

22.1 CTEs

CTE stands for "Common Table Expression" and it refers to factoring out a table expression much like we do in algebra. As an analogy, look at "$ax + bx = x(a + b)$"; we factor out x as a common expression in the terms.

SELECT statements can be nested so deeply that the code is unreadable. Before we had block structured languages, we had to use some form of a GOTO statement. The result was "spaghetti code"; the control flow was such a mess that it looked like spaghetti when you drew lines of control. When we moved to goto-less programming in block structured languages, we got a new problem. I invented the term "lasagna code" for programs in block structured languages nested so deeply that they were hard to understand.

SQL is a block structured language and we can get "lasagne code" in our queries. The syntax skeleton for each CTE is like that for a VIEW:

```
[<with clause>] <query expression body>

<with clause> ::= WITH [RECURSIVE] <with list>

<with list> ::= <with list element> [{,<with list element> }. . .]

<with list element> ::=
        <query name> [ (<with column list>)]
        AS (<query expression>) [<search or cycle clause>]

<with column list> ::= <column name list>
```

We effectively materialize the CTEs in the optional WITH clause wherever they are invoked. CTE's *come into existence in the order they are declared* so only backward references are allowed. A CTE can be recursive, but this is a sign of bad SQL, complicated and needs to be discussed separately.

Think of them as VIEWs that exist only in the scope of the query. In practice, if they are used once then they are implemented as an in-line macro. If they are used more than once in the query, then the optimizer might decide to actually materialize the CTE.

The use of RECURSIVE is complicated and should not be used much if at all. The <search or cycle clause> specify the generation of ordering and cycle detection information in the result of recursive query expressions.

If a column list is not given, then the column names from the original tables are exposed in the containing blocks. If a column list is given, then these column names are exposed in the containing blocks.

This might be easier to see with a skeleton example:

```
Foo
AS
(SELECT X.a, X.b, Y.b, Y.c
   FROM X, Y);
```

This CTE has to keep the table qualifiers on the column names when they are referenced. If the column is unique in its scope

```
Foo (r, s, t, u)
AS
(SELECT X.a, X.b, Y.b, Y.c
   FROM X, Y);
```

22.2 FROM Clause

The FROM clause is done first, since it builds a working table from all of the joins, unions, intersections, and whatever other table constructors are there. Without this virtual table, the SELECT, WHERE and other clauses would have nothing to use!

The column names in this working table are inherited from the base tables and views in the table expression.

The <table expression> AS <correlation name> option allows you give a name to this working table which you then have to use for the rest of the containing query. There are UNION, INTERSECT and EXCEPT set constructors, LATERAL tables, table-valued function, INNER JOINs, OUTER JOINs, and all kinds of things happening in here.

We will deal with them in detail later.

The important thing is that the clause effectively constructs a working for the query and that it exists within the scope of its SELECT.. FROM.

22.3 WHERE Clause

The WHERE clause removes rows that do not pass the search condition; that is, that do not test to TRUE (i.e., reject UNKNOWN and FALSE). The WHERE clause is applied to the working set in the FROM clause.

This is where the real work gets done. Rows are retained if they pass the search condition, which is a logical test. SQL has three-valued logic versions of classic AND, OR, and NOT logical operators found in all programming

languages. However, the language has special operators for handling NULLs and shorthand like IN (), BETWEEN, OVERLAPS, etc. for common programming situations.

The data types have the usual theta operators or comparison operators with an appropriate definition for that data type. But they are extended to handle NULLs. The rule for NULLs is that they do not compare to anything. Again, we will go into detail on this later.

The optimizer will combine the CHECK () constraints from the DDL and expand the shorthand operators then parse the search conditions to build an execution plan. Outside of the DDL and DML, SQL engines also keep statistics on the distribution of data in the tables, indexes, and other access methods available to use. You will see more details on this later.

22.4 GROUP BY Clause

The GROUP BY clause will partition the original table into groups and reduce each grouping to a *single* row, replacing the original working table with the new grouped table. The rows of a grouped table *must be only group characteristics*: (1) a grouping column, (2) a statistic about the group (i.e., aggregate functions), (3) a function or constant, (4) an expression made up of only those three items.

The partitions or groupings are what we call equivalence classes in set theory. Grouping has an extra rule; all NULLs are put in the same class or grouping when they appear in the grouping columns. The concepts of grouping versus equality appear in other places in the language.

The aggregate functions perform some computation on the grouping, but first they drop out the NULLs. If a column in an aggregate function is all NULLs, then we have an empty set. We will discuss aggregate functions in detail in Chapter 23.

22.5 HAVING Clause

The optional HAVING clause is like a WHERE clause applied against the grouped working table. If there was no GROUP BY clause, we treat the entire table as one group. Obviously, the search conditions refer to the columns of the grouped working table, and the aggregate functions cannot be given aliases in the GROUP BY clause.

22.6 SELECT Clause

The SELECT clause is done last of all. It constructs the expressions in the SELECT list. This means that the scalar subqueries, function calls, and expressions in the SELECT are done *after all the other clauses are done*. The AS operator can also give names to expressions in the SELECT list. These new column names come into existence all at once but after the WHERE clause, GROUP BY clause, and HAVING clause have been executed; you cannot use them in the SELECT list or the WHERE clause for that reason.

If there is a SELECT DISTINCT, then redundant duplicate rows are removed. For purposes of defining a duplicate row, NULLs are treated as matching (just like in the GROUP BY).

22.7 ORDER BY Clause

The ORDER BY clause is part of a cursor, *not a query*. However, most SQLs allow you to write it at the end of a query. The SQL engine creates a local cursor and the result set is passed to the cursor, which can only see the names in the SELECT clause list, and the sorting is done there. The ORDER BY clause cannot have expression in it or references to other columns because the result set has been converted into a sequential file structure and that is what is being sorted. The options on the sort columns are ascending order, descending order, and whether to place NULLs before or after values.

22.8 Nested Query Expressions and Orthogonality

SQL is an orthogonal language. That means if an expression returns a scalar value, you can use it wherever the language allows a scalar value; if it returns a table, you can use the query wherever the language allows a table. Nested query expressions follow the usual scoping rules you would expect from a block structured language like C, Pascal, Algol, etc. Namely, the innermost queries can reference to columns and tables in the queries in which they are contained.

Declarative languages like SQL use their scoping rules to replace the control flow that you learned in procedural languages.

As you can see, things happen "all at once" in SQL, not "from left to right" as they would in a sequential file/procedural language model.

In procedural languages, these two file read statements produce different results:

```
READ (a, b, c) FROM File_X;
READ (c, a, b) FROM File_X;
```

The File_X would open and an imaginary read-write head would scan the scan in left to right order, assigning values from the file to variables in the program while these two SELECT statements return the same data:

```
SELECT a, b, c FROM Table_X;
SELECT c, a, b FROM Table_X;
```

In the SQL model, the query connects to *a whole schema*, not a single file or even a group of files. Sets of data are manipulated as complete units of work, not row-by-row processing.

Think about what a confused mess this statement is in the SQL model.

```
SELECT f(c2) AS c1, f(c1) AS c2 FROM Foobar;
```

The f() function is invoked and creates columns c1 and c2 at the same time. And all the rows of the result set are created at the same time. That is why such nonsense is illegal syntax.

Basic Aggregate Functions

AN AGGREGATE FUNCTION reduces a set of values to a single value. Some of the basic ones are built into SQL, and they are usually fast because optimizers and index structures often store this data for their own use. The original functions are SUM(), AVG(), MAX(), MIN(), COUNT(), and COUNT(*).

Simple aggregate functions first construct a set of values as defined by the parameter. The parameter is usually a single column name, but it can be an expression with scalar functions and calculations. Pretty much the only things that cannot be used as parameters are other aggregate functions (e.g., SUM(AVG(x)) is illegal) and a subquery (e.g., AVG(SELECT col1 FROM SomeTable WHERE ...) is illegal). A subquery could return more than one value, so it would not fit into a column and an aggregate function would have to try to build a column within a column.

Once the working set is constructed, all the NULLs are removed and the function performs its operation. As you learn the definitions I am about to give, stress the words *known* values to remind yourself that the NULLs have been dropped.

There are two parameter options, ALL and DISTINCT, that are shown as keywords inside the parameter list. The keyword ALL is optional and is never really used in practice. It says that all the rows in the working column are retained for the final calculation. The keyword DISTINCT is not optional in these functions. It removes all *redundant* duplicate values from the working

column before the final calculation. Let's look at the particulars of each built-in aggregate function.

They fall into three categories:

1. The mathematical operations: The average (or arithmetic mean) AVG() and the sum (or arithmetic total) SUM(). These work for all numeric data types.
2. The extrema functions: minimum MIN() and maximum MAX() for all data types.
3. The counting functions: This is just the simple tally of the rows in the working table. The table cardinality is really a different animal that happens to look like the count function.

Let's go into details.

23.1 COUNT() Functions

There are two forms of the COUNT() function, cardinality and expression counting.

COUNT(*) returns the number of rows in a table (called the cardinality of a set); it is the only standard aggregate function that uses an asterisk as a parameter. This function is very useful and usually will run quite fast, since it can use system information about the table size. Remember that NULL values are also counted, because this function deals with *entire rows* and not column values. There is no such thing as "NULL row"—a row exists or it does not without regard to contents.

An empty table has a COUNT(*) of zero, which makes sense. However, all of the other aggregate functions we will discuss in this section will return an empty set as the result when they are given an empty set as input—"ab nilo, ex nilo" (from nothing, comes nothing). While it is too late to change SQL, we would have been better off with syntax that uses a table expression in a parameter for cardinality, much like the EXISTS() predicate. Frankly, this notation has problems; the parameter is a table, so we should have had something like "CARDINALITY(<table expression>)" instead of overloading the keyword COUNT.

You would think that using the COUNT(*) would be easy, but there are a lot of subtle tricks to it. Think of a database of the presidencies of the United States, with columns for the first name, middle initial(s), and last name of each US President who held that office, along with his political party and his term(s) in office. It might look like this:

```
CREATE TABLE Parties
(party_code CHAR(2) NOT NULL PRIMARY KEY,
 party_name CHAR(25) NOT NULL);

INSERT INTO Parties
VALUES ('D', 'Democratic'),
    ('DR', 'Democratic Republican'),
    ('R', 'Republican'),
    ('F', 'Federalist'),
    ('W', 'Whig'),
    ('L', 'Libertarian');

CREATE TABLE Presidencies
(first_name CHAR(11) NOT NULL,
 initial VARCHAR(4) DEFAULT ' ' NOT NULL, -- one space
 last_name CHAR(11) NOT NULL,
 party_code CHAR(2) NOT NULL
  REFERENCES Parties(party_code)
 start_term_year INTEGER NOT NULL UNIQUE
   CHECK (start_term_year > 1789),
 end_term_year INTEGER); -- null means current
```

Presidencies

first_name	initial	last_name	party	start_term_year	end_term_year
'George'	' '	'Washington'	'F'	1789	1797
'John'	' '	'Adams'	'F'	1797	1801
'Thomas'	' '	'Jefferson'	'DR'	1801	1809
'James'	' '	'Madison'	'DR'	1809	1817
'James'	' '	'Monroe'	'DR'	1817	1825
'John'	' '	'Adams'	'DR'	1825	1829
'Andrew'	' '	'Jackson'	'D'	1829	1837
'Martin'	' '	'Van Buren'	'D'	1837	1841
'William'	'H.'	'Harrison'	'W'	1841	1841
'John'	' '	'Tyler'	'W'	1841	1845

Continued

first_name	initial	last_name	party	start_term_year	end_term_year
'James'	'K.'	'Polk'	'D'	1845	1849
'Zachary'	' '	'Taylor'	'W'	1849	1850
'Millard'	' '	'Fillmore'	'W'	1850	1853
'Franklin'	' '	'Pierce'	'D'	1853	1857
'James'	' '	'Buchanan'	'D'	1857	1861
'Abraham'	' '	'Lincoln'	'R'	1861	1865
'Andrew'	' '	'Johnson'	'R'	1865	1869
'Ulysses'	'S.'	'Grant'	'R'	1869	1877
'Rutherford'	'B.'	'Hayes'	'R'	1877	1881
'James'	'A.'	'Garfield'	'R'	1881	1881
'Chester'	'A.'	'Arthur'	'R'	1881	1885
'Grover'	' '	'Cleveland'	'D'	1885	1889
'Benjamin'	' '	'Harrison'	'R'	1889	1893
'Grover'	' '	'Cleveland'	'D'	1893	1897
'William'	' '	'McKinley'	'R'	1897	1901
'Theodore'	' '	'Roosevelt'	'R'	1901	1909
'William'	'H.'	'Taft'	'R'	1909	1913
'Woodrow'	' '	'Wilson'	'D'	1913	1921
'Warren'	'G.'	'Harding'	'R'	1921	1923
'Calvin'	' '	'Coolidge'	'R'	1923	1929
'Herbert'	'C.'	'Hoover'	'R'	1929	1933
'Franklin'	'D.'	'Roosevelt'	'D'	1933	1945
'Harry'	'S.'	'Truman'	'D'	1945	1953
'Dwight'	'D.'	'Eisenhower'	'R'	1953	1961
'John'	'F.'	'Kennedy'	'D'	1961	1963
'Lyndon'	'B.'	'Johnson'	'D'	1963	1969
'Richard'	'M.'	'Nixon'	'R'	1969	1974
'Gerald'	'R.'	'Ford'	'R'	1974	1977
'James'	'E.'	'Carter'	'D'	1977	1981
'Ronald'	'W.'	'Reagan'	'R'	1981	1989
'George'	'H.W.'	'Bush'	'R'	1989	1993
'William'	'J.'	'Clinton'	'D'	1993	2001
'George'	'W.'	'Bush'	'R'	2001	2009
'Obama'	'H.'	'Barack'	'D'	2009	NULL

Your civics teacher has just asked you to tell her how many people have been President of the United States. So you write the query as SELECT COUNT(*) FROM Presidencies; and get the wrong answer. For those of you who have been out of high school too long, more than one Adams, more than one John, more than one Bush, and more than one Roosevelt have served as president. Many people have had more than one term in office, but Grover Cleveland served two *discontinuous* terms; this is important for counting. In short, this database is not a simple one-row, one-person system. What you really wanted was not COUNT(*), but something that is able to look at unique combinations of multiple columns. You cannot do this in one column, so you need to construct an expression that is unique. The point is that you need to be very sure that the expression you are using as a parameter is really what you wanted to count.

The COUNT([ALL] <value expression>) returns the number of members in the <value expression> set. The NULLs have been thrown away before the counting took place and an empty set returns zero. The best way to read this is as "Count the number of known values in this expression" with stress on the word known. In this example you might use COUNT(first_name || ' ' || initial || ' ' || last_name); if this was for display, you might also want to clean out the extra spaces.

The COUNT(DISTINCT <value expression>) returns the number of unique members in the <value expression> set. The NULLs have been thrown away before the counting took place and then all redundant duplicates are removed (i.e., we keep one copy). Again, an empty set returns a zero, just as with the other counting functions. Applying this function to a key or a unique column is the same as using the COUNT(*) function and the optimizer should be smart enough to spot it.

Notice that the use of the keywords ALL and DISTINCT follows the same pattern here as they did in the [ALL | DISTINCT] options in the SELECT clause of the query expressions. This is a common pattern in SQL.

23.1.1 Optimizing Aggregates with DISTINCT

This trick is due to Itzik Ben-Gan and it may or may not help you depending on your optimizer. Assume you have to optimize queries that use both regular aggregates and ones with DISTINCT.

```
SELECT cust_id, COUNT(*) AS order_cnt,
       COUNT(DISTINCT order_date) AS order_day_cnt,
       SUM(order_amt) AS order_amt_tot
 FROM Sales
GROUP BY cust_id;
```

The query groups the data by cust_id and returns for each customer the total count of orders, distinct count of order dates (number of days with order activity), and total amount due from the customer. Some optimizers will do separate scans for the nondistinct aggregates and the distinct aggregates.

You can achieve the same task with a query that requires only one scan of the data. We use a CTE that groups the data by both customer id and order date, and then use it at a higher level of aggregation. Here's the complete solution:

```
WITH Customer_Daily_Sales (cust_id, order_date, daily_order_cnt, order_
amt_tot)
AS
(SELECT cust_id, order_date, COUNT(*), SUM(order_amt)
   FROM Sales
  GROUP BY cust_id, order_date)
SELECT cust_id,
       SUM(daily_order_cnt) AS daily_order_cnt,
       COUNT(order_date) AS order_day_distinct_cnt,
       SUM(order_amt) AS order_amt_tot
  FROM Customer_Daily_Sales
 GROUP BY cust_id;
```

This time, the optimizer scans the base table once, groups the data first to calculate aggregates based on (cust_id, order_date), and then aggregates on just the cust_id.

23.2 SUM() Function

This function works only with numeric values. You should also consult your particular product's manuals to find out the precision of the results for exact and approximate numeric data types. This is implementation defined in the SQL Standards.

SUM([ALL] <value expression>) returns the numeric total of all known values. The NULLs are removed before the summation took place. An empty set returns an empty result set and not a zero. If there are other columns in the SELECT list, then that empty set will be converted into a NULL.

SUM(DISTINCT <value expression>) returns the numeric total of all known, unique values. The NULLs and all redundant duplicates have been removed before the summation took place. An empty set returns an empty result set and not a zero.

That last rule is hard for people to see. If there are other columns in the SELECT list, then that empty result set will be converted into a NULL. This is true for the rest of the Standard aggregate functions.

```
-- no rows
SELECT SUM(x)
  FROM Empty_Table;

--one row with (0, NULL) in it
SELECT COUNT(*), SUM(x)
  FROM Empty_Table;
```

The summation of a set of numbers looks as if it should be easy, but it is not. Make two tables with the same set of positive and negative approximate numeric values, but put one in random order and have the other sorted by absolute value. The sorted table will give more accurate results. The reason is simple; positive and negative values of the same magnitude will be added together and will get a chance to cancel each other out. There is also less chance of an overflow or underflow error during calculations. Most PC SQL implementations and a lot of mainframe implementations do not bother with this trick, because it would require a sort for every SUM() statement and would take a long time.

Whenever an exact or approximate numeric value is assigned to exact numeric, it may not fit into the storage allowed for it. SQL says that the database engine will use an approximation that preserves leading significant digits of the original number after rounding or truncating. The choice of whether to truncate or round is implementation defined, however. This can lead to some surprises when you have to shift data among SQL implementations, or storage values from a host language program into an SQL table. It is probably a good idea to create the columns with one more decimal place than you think you need.

Truncation is defined as truncation toward zero; this means that 1.5 would truncate to 1, and −1.5 would truncate to −1. This is not true for all programming languages; everyone agrees on truncation toward zero for the positive numbers, but you will find that negative numbers may truncate away from zero (e.g., −1.5 would truncate to −2). SQL is also wishy-washy on rounding, leaving the implementation free to determine its method. There are two major types of rounding, the scientific method and the commercial method, which are discussed in other places in this book.

23.3 AVG() Function

AVG([ALL] <value expression>) returns the average of the values in the value expression set. An empty set returns an empty result set. A set of all NULLs will become an empty set. Remember that in general AVG(x) is not the same as (SUM(x)/COUNT(*)); the SUM(x) function has thrown away the NULLs, but the COUNT(*) has not.

Likewise, AVG(DISTINCT <value expression>) returns the average of the distinct known values in the <value expression>set. Applying this function to a key or a unique column is the same as using AVG(<value expression>) function.

Remember that in general AVG(DISTINCT x) is not the same as AVG(x) or (SUM(DISTINCT x)/COUNT(*)). The SUM(DISTINCT x) function has thrown away the duplicate values and NULLs, but the COUNT(*) has not. An empty set returns an empty result set.

The SQL engine is probably using the same code for the totaling in the AVG() that it used in the SUM() function. This leads to the same problems with rounding and truncation, so you should experiment a little with your particular product to find out what happens.

But even more troublesome than those problems is the problem with the average itself, because it does not really measure central tendency and can be very misleading. Consider the chart below, from Darrell Huff's superlative little book, *How to Lie with Statistics* (Huff, 1954). Please note that this little book has been in print this long and that is why the salaries look funny. The Sample Company has 25 employees, earning the following salaries:

employee_cnt	salary_amt	Statistic
12	$2000.00	Mode, minimum
1	$3000.00	Median
4	$3700.00	
3	$5000.00	
1	$5700.00	Average
2	$10,000.00	
1	$15,000.00	
1	$45,000.00	Maximum

The average salary_amt (or, more properly, the arithmetic mean) is $5700. When the boss is trying to look good to the unions, he uses this figure. When the unions are trying to look impoverished, they use the mode, which is the most frequently occurring value, to show that the exploited workers are making $2000 (which is also the minimum salary_amt in this case).

A better measure in this case is the median, which will be discussed later; that is, the employee with just as many cases above him as below him. That gives us $3000. The rule for calculating the median is that if there is no actual entity with that value, you fake it in some way.

Most people take an average of the two values on either side of where the median would be; others jump to the higher or lower value. The mode also has a problem because not every distribution of values has one mode. Imagine a country in which there are as many very poor people as there are very rich people and nobody in between. This would be a bimodal distribution. If there were sharp classes of incomes, that would be a multimodal distribution.

Some SQL products have median and mode aggregate functions as extensions, but they are not part of the SQL Standard. We will discuss how to write them in pure SQL in detail.

23.3.1 Averages with Empty Groups

Sometimes you need to count an empty set as part of the population when computing an average. This is easier to explain with an example that was posted on CompuServe. A fish and game warden is sampling different bodies of water for fish populations. Each sample falls into one or more groups

(muddy bottoms, clear water, still water, and so on) and she is trying to find the average of something that is not there. This is neither quite as strange as it first sounds, nor quite as simple, either. She is collecting sample data on fish in a table like this:

```
CREATE TABLE Samples
(sample_id INTEGER NOT NULL,
 fish_name CHAR(20) NOT NULL,
 found_cnt INTEGER NOT NULL,
 PRIMARY KEY (sample_id, fish_name));
```

The samples are then aggregated into sample groups. A single sample might fall into more than one group.

```
CREATE TABLE Sample_Groups
(group_id INTEGER NOT NULL,
 sample_id INTEGER NOT NULL,
 PRIMARY KEY (group_id, sample_id);
```

Assume some of the data look like this:

Samples

sample_id	fish_name	found_cnt
1	'Seabass'	14
1	'Minnow'	18
2	'Seabass'	19

Sample_Groups

group_id	sample_id
1	1
1	2
2	2

She needs to get the average number of each species of fish in the sample groups. For example, using sample group 1 as shown, which has samples 1 and 2, we could use the parameters :my_fish_name = 'Minnow' and :my_group = 1 to find the average number of minnows in sample group 1, thus:

```
SELECT fish_name, AVG(found_cnt) AS found_cnt_avg
 FROM Samples
```

```
WHERE sample_id
   IN (SELECT sample_id
         FROM Sample_Groups
        WHERE group_id = :my_group)
  AND fish_name = :my_fish_name
GROUP BY fish_name;
```

But this query will give us an average of 18 minnows, which is wrong. There were no minnows for sample_id = 2, so the average is ((18 + 0)/2) = 9. The other way is to do several steps to get the correct answer—first use a SELECT statement to get the number of samples involved, then another SELECT to get the sum, and then manually calculate the average.

The obvious answer is to enter a count of zero for each animal under each sample_id, instead of letting it be missing, so you can use the original query. You can create the missing rows with:

```
INSERT INTO Samples
SELECT M1.sample_id, M2.fish_name, 0
  FROM Samples AS M1, Samples AS M2
 WHERE NOT EXISTS
        (SELECT *
           FROM Samples AS M3
          WHERE M1.sample_id = M3.sample_id
            AND M2.fish_name = M3.fish_name);
```

Unfortunately, it turns out that we have over 10,000 different species of fish and thousands of samples. This trick will fill up more disk space than we have on the machine. The best trick is to use this statement:

```
SELECT fish_name, SUM(found_cnt)/
         (SELECT COUNT(sample_id)
            FROM SampleGroups
           WHERE group_id = :my_group)
  FROM Samples
 WHERE fish_name = :my_fish_name
 GROUP BY fish_name;
```

This query is using the rule that the average is the sum of values divided by the count of the set. Another way to do this would be to use an OUTER JOIN and preserve all the group ids, but that would create NULLs for the fish

that are not in some of the sample groups and you would have to handle the NULLs as zero.

23.3.2 Averages Across Columns

The sum of several columns can be done with COALESCE() function to effectively remove the NULLs by replacing them with zeroes like this:

```
SELECT (COALESCE(c1, 0.0)
    + COALESCE(c2, 0.0)
    + COALESCE(c3, 0.0)) AS c_total
 FROM Foobar;
```

There are several vendor-specific functions that are *nearly* the same as COALESCE, For example, there is the ISNULL() function in SQL Server and another function of the same name in MySQL, which works differently from both.

Likewise, the minimum and maximum values of several columns can be done with a CASE expression, or the GREATEST() and LEAST() functions if you have that vendor extension.

Taking an average across several columns is easy if none of the columns are NULL. You simply add the values and divide by the number of columns. However, Getting rid of NULLs is a bit harder. The first trick is to count the NULLs.

```
SELECT (COALESCE(c1-c1, 1)
    + COALESCE(c2-c2, 1)
    + COALESCE(c3-c3, 1)) AS null_cnt
 FROM Foobar;
```

The trick is to watch out for a row with all NULLs in it. This could lead to a division by zero error.

```
SELECT CASE WHEN COALESCE(c1, c2, c3) IS NULL
       THEN NULL
       ELSE (COALESCE(c1, 0.0)
            + COALESCE(c2, 0.0)
            + COALESCE(c3, 0.0))
            / (3 - (COALESCE(c1-c1, 1)
               + COALESCE(c2-c2, 1)
```

```
                + COALESCE(c3-c3, 1))
        END AS horizontal_avg
  FROM Foobar;
```

23.4 Extrema Functions

The MIN() and MAX() functions are known as extrema functions in mathematics. They assume that the elements of the set have an ordering, so that it makes sense to select a first or last element based on its value. SQL provides two simple extrema functions, and you can write queries to generalize these to (n) elements.

23.4.1 Simple Extrema Functions

MAX([ALL | DISTINCT] <value expression>) returns the greatest known value in the <value expression> set. This function will also work on character, and temporal values, as well as numeric values. An empty set returns an empty result set. Technically, you can write MAX(DISTINCT <value expression>), but it is the same as MAX(ALL <value expression>) or MAX(<value expression>); this form exists only for completeness and nobody ever uses it.

MIN([ALL | DISTINCT] <value expression>) returns the smallest known value in the <value expression> set. This function will also work on character and temporal values, as well as numeric values. An empty set returns a NULL. Likewise, MIN(DISTINCT <value expression>) and MIN (ALL <value expression>) exist, but it is defined only for completeness and nobody ever uses it.

The MAX() for a set of numeric values is the largest. The MAX() for a set temporal data types is the one closest to '9999-12-31,' which is the final data in the ISO-8601 Temporal Standard. The MAX() for a set of character strings is the last one in the ascending sort order in the collation used. Likewise, the MIN() for a set of numeric values is the smallest. The MIN() for a set of temporal data types is furthest from '9999-12-31.' The MIN() for a set of character strings is the first one in the ascending sort order of the collation used.

People have a hard time understanding the MAX() and MIN() aggregate functions when they are applied to temporal data types. They seem to expect the MAX() to return the date closest to the current date. Likewise, if the set has no dates before the current date, they seem to expect the MIN() function to return the date closest to the current date. Human psychology wants to use the current time as an origin point for temporal reasoning.

Consider the predicate "billing_date<(CURRENT_DATE - INTERVAL '90' DAY)" as an example. Most people have to stop and figure out that this is looking for billings that are over 90 days past due. This same thing happens with MIN() and MAX() functions.

SQL also has funny rules about comparing VARCHAR strings, which can cause problems. When two strings are compared for equality, the shortest one is right-padded with blanks; then they are compared position for position. Thus, the strings 'John ' and 'John' are equal. You will have to check your implementation of SQL to see which string is returned as the MAX() and which as the MIN(), or whether there is any pattern to it at all. Likewise, if you do a GROUP BY which member of the group is picked as the representative of the group is implementation defined.

Another consideration is the collation used on columns. A column is sorted in an order defined by its collation; the same data element in different tables can have different local collations and therefore different extremas. Mixed collations like this are a sign of bad schema design.

There are some tricks with extrema functions in subqueries that differ from product to product. For example, to find the current employee status in a table of Salary Histories, the obvious query is

```
SELECT emp_status, ..
  FROM Salary_History AS S0
 WHERE S0.change_date
    = (SELECT MAX(S1.change_date)
         FROM Salary_History AS S1
        WHERE S0.emp_id = S1.emp_id);
```

But you can also write the query as:

```
SELECT emp_status, ..
  FROM Salary_History AS S0
 WHERE NOT EXISTS
    (SELECT *
       FROM Salary_History AS S1
      WHERE S0.emp_id = S1.emp_id
        AND S0.change_date < S1.change_date);
```

The correlated subquery with a MAX() will be implemented by going to the subquery and building a working table which is grouped by emp_id. Then for each group, you will keep track of the maximum and save it for the final result.

However, the NOT EXISTS version will find the first row that meets the criteria and when found, it returns TRUE. Therefore, the NOT EXISTS () predicate might run faster.

23.4.2 Generalized Extrema Functions

This is known as the Top (or Bottom) (n) value problem and it originally appeared in *Explain* magazine in 1991; it was submitted by Jim Wankowski of Hawthorne, CA. You are given a table of Personnel and their salaries. Write a single SQL query that will display the three highest salaries from that table. It is easy to find the maximum salary_amt with the simple query "SELECT MAX(salary_amt) FROM Personnel"; but SQL does not have a maximum function that will return a group of high values from a column. The trouble with this query is that the specification is bad for several reasons.

(1) How do we define "best salary_amt" in terms of an ordering? Is it base pay or does it include commissions? For the rest of this section, assume that we are using a simple table with a column that has the salary_amt for each employee.

(2) What if we have three or fewer Personnel in the company? Do we report all the Personnel we do have? Or do we return a NULL, empty result set or error message? This is the equivalent of calling the contest for lack of entries.

(3) How do we handle two employees who tied? Include them all and allow the result set to be bigger than three? Pick an arbitrary subset and exclude someone? Or do we return a NULL, empty result set or error message?

To make these problems more explicit, consider this table:
Personnel

emp_name	salary_amt
'Able'	1000
'Bill'	900
'Charles'	900
'Delta'	800
'Eddy'	700
'Fred'	700
'George'	700

Able, Bill, and Charles are the three highest paid Personnel, but \$1000.00, \$900.00, and \$800.00 are the three highest salaries. The highest salaries belong to Able, Bill, Charles, and Delta—a set with four elements.

The way that most new SQL programmers do this is produce a cursor with an ORDER BY clause, then read the first so many rows from that cursor result. In Standard SQL, cursors have an ORDER BY clause but no way to return a fixed number of rows. However, most SQL products have propriety syntax to clip the result set at exactly some number of rows. Oh, yes, did I mention that the whole table has to be sorted and that this can take some time if the table is large?

The best algorithm for this problem is the Partition algorithm by C. A. R. Hoare. This is the procedure in QuickSort that splits a set of values into three partitions—those greater than a pivot value, those less than the pivot, and those values equal to the pivot. The expected run time is only (2^n) operations.

In practice, it is a good idea to start with a pivot value at or near the k-th position you seek, because real data tend to have some ordering already in it. If the file is already in sorted order, this trick will return an answer in one pass. Here is the algorithm in Pascal.

```
CONST
  list_length = { some large number };
  ...
TYPE
  LIST = ARRAY [1..list_length] OF REAL;
  ...
PROCEDURE Find_Top_K (k-th INTEGER, records : LIST);
VAR pivot, left, right, start, finish: INTEGER;
BEGIN
start := 1;
finish := list_length;
WHILE start < finish
DO BEGIN
  pivot := records[k-th];
  left := start;
  right := finish;
  REPEAT
    WHILE (records[left] > pivot) DO left := left + 1;
    WHILE (records[right] < pivot) DO right := right - 1;
```

```
    IF (left >= right)
    THEN BEGIN { swap right and left elements }
       Swap (records[left], records[right]);
       left := left + 1;
       right := right - 1;
       END;
  UNTIL (left < right);
  IF (right < k-th) THEN start := left;
  IF (left > k-th) THEN finish := right;
  END;

{ the first k numbers are in positions 1 through k-th, in no particular
order except that the k-th highest number is in k-th position }
END.
```

The original articles in *Explain* magazine gave several solutions (Murchison; Wankowski). They are needlessly complicated and expensive today. One involved UNION operations on nested subqueries.

I am getting ahead of myself, but these days we have windowed queries that might perform better than any of these answers. But they might not; as usual, test alternate queries for yourself.

```
SELECT DISTINCT X.salary_amt
  FROM (SELECT salary_amt,
              DENSE_RANK()
               OVER (ORDER BY salary_amt DESC)
         FROM Personnel) AS X(salary_amt, sal_rank)
 WHERE X.sal_rank <= 3;
```

or if you prefer a CTE:

```
WITH X(salary_amt, sal_rank)
AS
(SELECT salary_amt,
        DENSE_RANK()
        OVER (ORDER BY salary_amt DESC)
   FROM Personnel)
SELECT DISTINCT X.salary_amt
  FROM X
 WHERE X.sal_rank <= 3;
```

23.4.3 Multiple Criteria Extrema Functions

There is an old Marie Severin cartoon of a British Sargent-Major in India telling his troops to line up alphabetically by height. While this was good for a laugh, we can generalize extrema functions by deciding ties are based on multiple columns in a table.

```
WITH X(emp_name, severin_rank)
AS
(SELECT emp_name,
        DENSE_RANK()
        OVER (ORDER BY emp_name ASC,
                       emp_height DESC,
                       emp_weight DESC)
   FROM Personnel)
SELECT X.emp_name
  FROM X
 WHERE X.severin_rank <= 3;
```

Unlike the old self-join solutions, this windowed solution generalizes and vendors are able to optimize it.

23.4.4 GREATEST() and LEAST() Functions

Oracle has a proprietary pair of functions which return greatest and least values, respectively—a sort of "horizontal" MAX() and MIN(). The syntax is GREATEST (<list of values>) and LEAST (<list of values>). Awkwardly enough, DB2 allows MIN and MAX as synonyms for LEAST and GREATEST.

If you have NULLs, then you have to decide if they sort high or low, exclude them or propagate the NULL, so that you can define this function several ways.

If you don't have NULLs in the data:

```
CASE WHEN col1 > col2
 THEN col1 ELSE col2 END
```

If you want the highest non-NULL value:

```
CASE WHEN col1 > col2
 THEN col1 ELSE COALESCE(col2, col1) END
```

If you want to return NULL where one of the cols is NULL:

```
CASE WHEN col1 > col2 OR col1 IS NULL
  THEN col1 ELSE col2 END
```

But for the rest of this section, let's assume (a<b) and NULL is high:

```
GREATEST (a, b) = b
GREATEST (a, NULL) = NULL
GREATEST (NULL, b) = NULL
GREATEST (NULL, NULL) = NULL
```

which we can write as:

```
GREATEST(x, y) ::= CASE WHEN (COALESCE (x, y) > COALESCE (y, x))
            THEN x
            ELSE y END
```

The rules for LEAST() are

```
LEAST (a, b) = a
LEAST (a, NULL) = a
LEAST (NULL, b) = b
LEAST (NULL, NULL) = NULL
```

which is written:

```
LEAST(x, y)
::= CASE WHEN (COALESCE (x, y) <= COALESCE (y, x))
        THEN COALESCE (x, y)
        ELSE COALESCE (y, x) END
```

This can be done in Standard SQL, but takes a little bit of work. Let's assume that we have a table that holds he scores for each player in a series of five games and we want to get his best score from all five games.

```
CREATE TABLE Games
(player CHAR(10) NOT NULL PRIMARY KEY,
 score_1 INTEGER NOT NULL DEFAULT 0,
 score_2 INTEGER NOT NULL DEFAULT 0,
 score_3 INTEGER NOT NULL DEFAULT 0,
 score_4 INTEGER NOT NULL DEFAULT 0,
 score_5 INTEGER NOT NULL DEFAULT 0);
```

and we want to find the GREATEST (score_1, score_2, score_3, score_4, score_5).

```
SELECT player, MAX(CASE X.seq_nbr
          WHEN 1 THEN score_1
          WHEN 2 THEN score_2
          WHEN 3 THEN score_3
          WHEN 4 THEN score_4
          WHEN 5 THEN score_5
          ELSE NULL END) AS best_score
 FROM Games
    CROSS JOIN
    (VALUES (1), (2), (3), (4), (5)) AS X(seq_nbr)
 GROUP BY player;
```

Another approach is to use a pure CASE expression:

```
CASE
WHEN score_1 <= score_2 AND score_1 <= score_3
  AND score_1 <= score_4 AND score_1 <= score_5
THEN score_1
WHEN score_2 <= score_3 AND score_2 <= score_4
  AND score_2 <= score_5
THEN score_2
WHEN score_3 <= score_4 AND score_3 <= score_5
THEN score_3
WHEN score_4 <= score_5
THEN score_4
ELSE score_5
END
```

A final trick is to use a bit of algebra for numeric values. You can define

```
GREATEST(a, b) ::= (a + b + ABS(a - b)) / 2
LEAST(a, b) ::= (a + b - ABS(a - b)) / 2
```

Then iterate on it as a recurrence relation on numeric values. For example, for three items, you can use GREATEST (a, GREATEST(b, c)) which expands out to:

```
((a + b) + ABS(a - b)
  + 2 * c + ABS((a + b) + ABS(a - b)
  - 2 * c))/4
```

You need to watch for possible overflow errors if the numbers are large and NULLs propagate in the math functions. Here is the answer for five scores.

```
(score_1 + score_2 + 2*score_3 + 4*score_4 + 8*score_5
 + ABS(score_1 - score_2) + ABS((score_1 + score_2)+
ABS(score_1 - score_2) - 2*score_3)
 + ABS(score_1 + score_2 + 2*score_3 - 4*score_4 +
ABS(score_1 - score_2) + ABS((score_1 + score_2 -
2*score_3) + ABS(score_1 - score_2)))
 + ABS(score_1 + score_2 + 2*score_3 + 4*score_4 -
8*score_5
 + ABS(score_1 - score_2) + ABS((score_1 + score_2) +
ABS(score_1 - score_2) - 2*score_3)
 + ABS(score_1 + score_2 + 2*score_3 - 4*score_4 +
ABS(score_1 - score_2) + ABS((score_1 + score_2 -
2*score_3) + ABS(score_1 - score_2))) )) / 16
```

23.5 The LIST() Aggregate Function

The LIST() aggregate function is not part of the ANSI/ISO Standards, but it is a common vendor extension (see Sybase, MySQL, Postgres, etc.) in some form. It takes a column of strings, removes the NULLs, and merges them into a single result string having commas between each of the original strings. The DISTINCT option removes duplicates as well as NULLs before concatenating the strings together. This function is a generalized, grouped version of concatenation, just as SUM() is a generalized, grouped version of addition. The Sybase syntax is

```
LIST([ALL | DISTINCT] <string expression>
[, <constant delimiter string>]
[ORDER BY order-by-expression [ASC | DESC], ...] )
```

The string expression is usually a column name. When ALL is specified (the default), for each row in the group, the value of <string expression> is concatenated to the result string, with values separated by the <constant delimiter string>. When DISTINCT is specified, only unique <string expression> values are concatenated.

The default setting is a comma. There is no delimiter if a value of NULL or an empty string is supplied. The ORDER BY orders the items returned by the

function. There is no comma preceding this argument, which makes it easy to use in the case where no delimiter string is supplied.

23.5.1 LIST Aggregate with Recursive CTE

The first thing you will need to do is to add a column to give a sequence number to order each item to be put in the list. This can be done with a ROW_NUMBER() function, but let's assume the table already has such a column:

```
CREATE TABLE Make_String
(list_seq INTEGER NOT NULL PRIMARY KEY,
 cat_string VARCHAR(10) NOT NULL);

INSERT INTO Make_String
VALUES (1, 'abc'), (2, 'bcd'), (3, 'cde'), (4, 'def'),
    (5, 'efg'), (6, 'fgh'), (7, 'ghi');
```

The desired result is

```
'abc, bcd, cde, def, efg, fgh, ghi'
```

This can be done with a recursive CTE:

```
WITH RECURSIVE
String_Tail(list_seq, cat_string)
AS
(SELECT list_seq, cat_string
  FROM Make_String
 WHERE list_seq > 1),

String_Head(list, max_list_seq)
AS
(SELECT cat_string, 1
  FROM String_Head
UNION ALL
SELECT String_Head.cat_string || ', ' ||
String_Tail.cat_string,
    String_Head.max_list_seq + 1
```

```
 FROM String_Tail, String_Head
 WHERE String_Tail.list_seq = String_Head.max_list_seq + 1)

SELECT cat_list
 FROM String_Head
 WHERE max_list_seq
    = (SELECT MAX(list_seq)
       FROM Make_String);
```

The interesting side effect is that you get all of the left to right concatenations.

23.5.2 The LIST() Function by Crosstabs

Carl Federl used this to get a similar result:

```
CREATE TABLE People
(person_id INTEGER NOT NULL PRIMARY KEY,
person_name VARCHAR(10) NOT NULL);

INSERT INTO People
VALUES ('1, 'John'), (2, 'Mary'), ('3, 'Fred'), (4, 'Jane');

CREATE TABLE Clothes
(id INTEGER NOT NULL,
 seq INTEGER NOT NULL,
 PRIMARY KEY (id, seq),
 clothing_item VARCHAR(10) NOT NULL,
 worn_flg CHAR(1) NOT NULL
CHECK (worn_flg IN ('Y', 'N'))
);

INSERT INTO Clothes
VALUES
(1, 1, 'Hat', 'Y'), (1, 2, 'Coat', 'N'), (1, 3, 'Glove', 'Y'),
(2, 1, 'Hat', 'Y'), (2, 2, 'Coat', 'Y'),
(3, 1, Shoes', 'N'),
(4, 1, 'Pants', 'N'), (4, 2, 'Sock', 'Y');
```

```
CREATE TABLE Crosstabs
(seq_nbr INTEGER NOT NULL PRIMARY KEY,
 seq_nbr_1 INTEGER NOT NULL,
 seq_nbr_2 INTEGER NOT NULL,
 seq_nbr_3 INTEGER NOT NULL,
 seq_nbr_4 INTEGER NOT NULL,
 seq_nbr_5 INTEGER NOT NULL);

INSERT INTO Crosstabs
VALUES (1, 1, 0, 0, 0, 0),
    (2, 0, 1, 0, 0, 0),
    (3, 0, 0, 1, 0, 0),
    (4, 0, 0, 0, 1, 0),
    (5, 0, 0, 0, 0, 1);

SELECT Clothes.id,
  TRIM (MAX(SUBSTRING(item_name FROM 1 FOR seq_nbr_1 * 10))
 || ' ' || MAX(SUBSTRING(item_name FROM 1 FOR seq_nbr_2 * 10))
 || ' ' || MAX(SUBSTRING(item_name FROM 1 FOR seq_nbr_3 * 10))
 || ' ' || MAX(SUBSTRING(item_name FROM 1 FOR seq_nbr_4 * 10))
 || ' ' || MAX(SUBSTRING(item_name FROM 1 FOR seq_nbr_5 * 10)))
 FROM Clothes, Crosstabs
 WHERE Clothes.seq_nbr = Crosstabs.seq_nbr
  AND Clothes.worn_flag = 'Y'
 GROUP BY Clothes.id;
```

person_id	person_name	list
1	'John'	'Hat, Glove'
2	'Mary'	'Hat, Coat'
3	'Fred'	''
4	'Jane'	'Socks'

23.6 The Mode Aggregate Function

The mode is the most frequently occurring value in a set. If there are two such values in a set, statisticians call it a bimodal distribution; three such values make it trimodal, and so forth. Most SQL implementations do not have a mode function, since it is easy to calculate. This version is from Shepard Towindo and it will handle multiple modes.

```
SELECT salary_amt, COUNT(*) AS frequency
  FROM Personnel
 GROUP BY salary_amt
HAVING COUNT(*) >= ALL (SELECT COUNT(*)
                          FROM Personnel
                         GROUP BY salary_amt);
```

The mode is a weak descriptive statistic, because it can be changed by small amounts of additional data. For example, if we have 101 cases where the value of the color variable is 'red' and 100 cases where the value is 'green,' the mode is 'red.' But when two more greens are added to the set, the mode switches to 'green.' A better idea is to allow for some variation, k, in the values. In general the best way to compute k is probably as a percentage of the total number of occurrences. Of course, knowledge of the actual situation could change this.

23.7 The Median Aggregate Function

The median is defined as the value for which there are just as many cases with a value below it as above it. If such a value exists in the data set, this value is called the statistical median by some authors. If no such value exists in the data set, the usual method is to divide the data set into two halves of equal size such that all values in one half are lower than any value in the other half. The median is then the average of the highest value in the lower half (called the lower median) and the lowest value in the upper half (called the upper median), and this average is called the financial median.

Let us use Date's famous Parts table, from several of his textbooks which has a column for weight in it, like this:

```
CREATE TABLE Parts
(part_nbr CHAR(2) NOT NULL PRIMARY KEY,
 part_name VARCHAR (15) NOT NULL,
 color_code CHAR(5) NOT NULL,
 part_wgt INTEGER NOT NULL
  CHECK (part_wgt > 0),
city_name VARCHAR(15) NOT NULL);
```

Parts

part_nbr	part_name	color_code	part_wgt	city_name
'p1'	'Nut'	'Red'	12	'London'
'p2'	'Bolt'	'Green'	17	'Paris'
'p3'	'Cam'	'Blue'	12	'Paris'
'p4'	'Screw'	'Red'	14	'London'
'p5'	'Cam'	'Blue'	12	'Paris'
'p6'	'Cog'	'Red'	19	'London'

First sort the table by weights and find the three rows in the lower half of the table. The greatest value in the lower half is 12; the smallest value in the upper half is 14; their average, and therefore the median, is 13. If the table had an odd number of rows, we would have looked at only one row after the sorting.

The median is a better measure of central tendency than the average and the mode, but it is also harder to calculate without sorting. At one time in the SQL world, the "programing problem du jour" was finding the median. This was because there were two newsstand data base magazines, *DBMS* and *Database Programming & Design*, in the 1990s with editorial columns by myself and Chris, respectively. The magazines had the same publisher, so to boost sales of both, Chris and I would do "dueling SQL" columns. You had to buy both to get the whole story. We each did several versions of the median with the SQL available at the time starting in 1992 and these articles ran for months. Date and I posted several versions and Rory Murchison and Philip Vaughan of San Jose, CA, and the team of Anatoly Abramovich, Yelena Alexandrova, and Eugene Birger presented a series of articles in *SQL Forum* magazine on computing the median (SQL Forum, 1993, 1994). The late Ken Henderson also added a stream-lined version of this code to the discussion.

23.7.1 The Weighted Median

The weighted median is an even better measure of central tendency than the plain median. It is also more "set-oriented" than the plain median. It factors in the number of times the two values in the middle subset of a table with an even number of rows appear. The table with

(1, 2, 2, 3, 3, 3) has a median of 3, the middle value. It returns the subset (2, 2, 3, 3, 3) in the middle, which gives us (13/5) = 2.6 for the weighted median. The weighted median is a more accurate description of the skew of the data.

23.7.2 Modern Median

We now have ROW_NUMBER() and can that function to do the sorting without the complicated self-joins, unions, and views of the older methods. Here is an elegant solution from Peso:

```
SELECT AVG(X.part_wgt) AS part_wgt_median
 FROM (SELECT part_wgt,
       (2 * ROW_NUMBER() OVER (ORDER BY part_wgt)
       - COUNT(*) OVER ()) AS middle_subset
    FROM Parts) AS X
 WHERE X.middle_subset BETWEEN 0 AND 2;
```

This can be modified to give us the weighted median.

```
SELECT (1.0 * SUM(X.y)/SUM(X.t)) AS part_wgtmedian
 FROM (SELECT SUM(part_wgt) OVER (PARTITION BY part_wgt) AS y,
       (2 * ROW_NUMBER() OVER (ORDER BY part_wgt)
       - COUNT(*) OVER ()) AS middle_subset,
       COUNT(*) OVER (PARTITION BY part_wgt) AS t
    FROM Parts) AS X
 WHERE X.middle_subset BETWEEN 0 AND 2;
```

The 1.0 factor is an old trick to switch from integer math to decimal, but you could use a CAST().

23.8 The PRD() Aggregate Function

Bob McGowan had a client, a financial institution, that tracks investment performance with a table something like this:

```
CREATE TABLE Performance
(portfolio_id CHAR(7) NOT NULL,
 execute_date DATE NOT NULL,
 rate_of_return DECIMAL(13,7) NOT NULL);
```

In order to calculate a rate of return over a date range, you use the formula:

```
 (1.0 + rate_of_return [day_1])
* (1.0 + rate_of_return [day_2])
* (1.0 + rate_of_return [day_3])
* (1.0 + rate_of_return [day_4])
 ...
* (1.0 + rate_of_return [day_N])
```

How would you construct a query that would return one row for each portfolio's return over the date range? What Mr. McGowan really wants is an aggregate function in the SELECT clause to return a columnar product, like the SUM() returns a columnar total.

If you were a math major, you would write these functions as capital Sigma (Σ) for summation and capital Pi for product (Π). If such an aggregate function existed in SQL, the syntax for it would probably look something like:

PRD ([DISTINCT] <expression>)

While I am not sure that there is any use for the DISTINCT option, the new aggregate function would let us write his problem simply as:

```
SELECT portfolio_id, PRD(1.00 + rate_of_return)
  FROM Performance
 WHERE execute_date BETWEEN start_date AND end_date
 GROUP BY portfolio_id;
```

23.8.1 PRD() Function by Expressions

There is a trick for doing this, but you need a second table that looks like this for a period of 5 days:

```
CREATE TABLE BigPi
(execute_date DATE NOT NULL,
 day_1 INTEGER NOT NULL,
 day_2 INTEGER NOT NULL,
 day_3 INTEGER NOT NULL,
 day_4 INTEGER NOT NULL,
 day_5 INTEGER NOT NULL);
```

Let's assume we wanted to look at January 6-10, so we need to update the execute_date column to that range, thus:

```
INSERT INTO BigPi
VALUES ('2017-01-06', 1, 0, 0, 0, 0),
    ('2017-01-07', 0, 1, 0, 0, 0),
    ('2017-01-08', 0, 0, 1, 0, 0),
    ('2017-01-09', 0, 0, 0, 1, 0),
    ('2017-01-10', 0, 0, 0, 0, 1);
```

The idea is that there is a one in the column when BigPi.execute_date is equal to the n-th date in the range and zero otherwise. The query for this problem is

```
SELECT portfolio_id,
   (SUM((1.00 + P1.rate_of_return) * M1.day_1) *
    SUM((1.00 + P1.rate_of_return) * M1.day_2) *
    SUM((1.00 + P1.rate_of_return) * M1.day_3) *
    SUM((1.00 + P1.rate_of_return) * M1.day_4) *
    SUM((1.00 + P1.rate_of_return) * M1.day_5))
     AS product
  FROM Performance AS P1, BigPi AS M1
 WHERE M1.execute_date = P1.execute_date
   AND P1.execute_date
       BETWEEN '2017-01-06' AND '2017-01-10'
 GROUP BY portfolio_id;
```

If anyone is missing a rate_of_return entry on a date in that range, their product will be zero. That might be fine, but if you needed to get a NULL when you have missing data, then replace each SUM() expression with a CASE expression like this:

```
CASE WHEN SUM((1.00 + P1.rate_of_return) * M1.day_N) = 0.00
   THEN CAST (NULL AS DECIMAL(6, 4))
   ELSE SUM((1.00 + P1.rate_of_return) * M1.day_N)
END
```

or if your SQL has the full SQL set of expressions, with this version:

```
COALESCE (SUM((1.00 + P1.rate_of_return) * M1.day_N), 0.00)
```

23.8.2 The PRD() Aggregate Function by Logarithms

Roy Harvey, another SQL guru, found a different solution, which only someone old enough to remember slide rules and that we can multiply by adding logs. The nice part of this solution is that you can also use the DISTINCT option in the SUM() function.

But there are a lot of warnings about this approach. The Standard allow only natural logarithms shown as LN(), but you will see LOG10() for the logarithm base 10 and perhaps LOG(<parameter>, <base>) for a general logarithm function. Since the logarithm of zero or less is undefined, the Standard requires an exception to be raised. But some older SQL might return a zero or a NULL. Likewise, the Standard also defines the exponential function as EXP() as its inverse.

The expression for the product of a column from logarithm and exponential functions is

```
SELECT ((EXP (SUM (LN (CASE WHEN nbr = 0.00
                       THEN CAST (NULL AS FLOAT)
                       ELSE ABS(nbr) END))))
       * (CASE WHEN MIN (ABS (nbr)) = 0.00
               THEN 0.00 ELSE 1.00 END)
       * (CASE WHEN MOD (SUM (CASE WHEN SIGN(nbr) = -1
               THEN 1 ELSE 0 END), 2) = 1
      THEN -1.00 ELSE 1.00 END) AS big_pi
 FROM Number_Table;
```

The nice part of this is that you can also use the SUM (DISTINCT <expression>) option to get the equivalent of PRD (DISTINCT <expression>).

You should watch the data type of the column involved and use either integer 0 and 1 or decimal 0.00 and 1.00 as is appropriate in the CASE statements. It is worth studying the three CASE expressions that make up the terms of the Prod() calculation.

The first CASE expression is to insure that all zeros and negative numbers are converted to a non-negative or NULL for the SUM() function, just in the case your SQL raises an exception.

The second CASE expression will return zero as the answer if there was a zero in the nbr column of any selected row. The MIN(ABS(nbr)) is a handy trick for detecting the existence of a zero in a list of both positive and negative numbers with an aggregate function.

The third CASE expression will return minus one if there was an odd number of negative numbers in the nbr column. The innermost CASE expression uses a SIGN() function which returns +1 for a positive number, −1 for a negative number, and 0 for a zero. The SUM() counts the −1 results then the MOD() functions determines if the count was odd or even.

I present this version of the query first, because this is how I developed the answer. We can do a much better job with a little algebra and logic:

```
SELECT CASE MIN (SIGN (nbr))
       -- all positive numbers
       WHEN 1 THEN EXP (SUM (LN (nbr)))
        -- some zeros
       WHEN 0 THEN 0.00
       -- some negative numbers
       WHEN -1
       THEN (EXP (SUM (LN (ABS(nbr))))
             * (CASE WHEN
                  MOD (SUM (ABS (SIGN(nbr)-1/ 2)), 2) = 1
                THEN -1.00 ELSE 1.00 END))
       ELSE CAST (NULL AS FLOAT) END AS big_pi
  FROM Number_Table;
```

The idea is that there are three special cases—all positive numbers, one or more zeros, and some negative numbers in the set. You can find out what your situation is with a quick test on the SIGN() of the minimum value in the set.

Within the case where you have negative numbers, there are two subcases: (1) an even number of negatives or (2) an odd number of negatives. You then need to apply some High School algebra to determine the sign of the final result.

Itzak Ben-Gan had problems in implementing this in an older version of SQL Server which are worth passing along in case your SQL product also has them. The query as written returns a domain error in SQL Server, even though it should not had the result expressions in the CASE expression been evaluated *after* the conditional flow had performed a short circuit evaluation. Examining the execution plan of the above query, it looks like the optimizer evaluates all of the possible result expressions in a step prior to handling the flow of the CASE expression.

This means that in the expression after WHEN 1 … the LN() function is also invoked in an intermediate phase for zeros and negative numbers, and in the expression after WHEN –1 … the LN(ABS()) is also invoked in an intermediate phase for zeroes. This explains the domain error.

To handle this, I had to use the ABS() and NULLIF() functions in the positive numbers when CLAUSE, and the NULLIF() function in the negative numbers when CLAUSE:

```
  ...
  WHEN 1 THEN EXP(SUM(LN(ABS(NULLIF(result, 0.00)))))
and
  ...
  WHEN -1
  THEN EXP(SUM(LN(ABS(NULLIF(result, 0.00)))))
     * CASE ...
```

If you are sure that you will have only positive values in the column being computed, then you can use:

```
PRD(<exp>) = EXP(SUM(LN (<exp>)))
```

As an aside, the book *Bypasses: A Simple Approach to Complexity* by Z. A. Melzak (Wiley-Interscience, 1983, ISBN 0-471-86854-X), is a short mathematical book on the general principle of conjugacy. This is the method of using a transform and its inverse to reduce the complexity of a calculation.

Advance Descriptive Statistics

DESCRIPTIVE STATISTICS ARE better done in the presentation layers of the system than the database. Those tools will do floating point math in ways that prevent errors. However, the SQL:2006 Standard defines many common descriptive statistics in terms of the basic aggregate functions with a DISTINCT and OVER() clauses.

24.1 Binary Table Functions

They are elaborate and you need to know at least freshman statistics to use them, which I will not explain here. They use tables that have two columns, the <dependent variable expression> and the <independent variable expression>. The functions are

VAR_POP = population variance, defined as the sum of squares of the difference of <value expression> from the mean of <value expression>, divided by the number of rows.

VAR_SAMP = the sample variance of <value expression>, defined as the sum of squares of the difference of <value expression> from the mean of <value expression>, divided by the number of rows remaining minus 1.

STDDEV_POP = the population standard deviation of <value expression>, defined as the square root of the population variance.

STDDEV_SAMP = the sample standard deviation of <value expression>, defined as the square root of the sample variance.

Neither DISTINCT nor ALL are allowed to be specified for VAR_POP, VAR_SAMP, STDDEV_POP, or STDDEV_SAMP; redundant duplicates are not removed when computing these functions.

REGR_COUNT = the number of rows remaining in the group.

COVAR_POP = the population covariance.

COVAR_SAMP = the sample covariance, defined as the sum of products of the difference of <independent variable expression> from its mean times the difference of <dependent variable expression> from its mean, divided by the number of rows remaining minus 1 (one).

CORR = the correlation coefficient, defined as the ratio of the population covariance divided by the product of the population standard deviation of <independent variable expression> and the population standard deviation of <dependent variable expression>.

REGR_R2 = the square of the correlation coefficient.

REGR_SLOPE = the slope of the least-squares-fit linear equation determined by the (<independent variable expression>, <dependent variable expression>) pairs.

REGR_INTERCEPT = the y-intercept of the least-squares-fit linear equation determined by the (<independent variable expression>, <dependent variable expression>) pairs.

REGR_SXX = the sum of squares of <independent variable expression>.

REGR_SYY = the sum of squares of <dependent variable expression>.

REGR_SXY = the sum of products of <independent variable expression> times <dependent variable expression>.

REGR_AVGX = the average of <independent variable expression>.

REGR_AVGY = the average of <dependent variable expression>.

There are two inverse distribution functions, PERCENTILE_CONT and PERCENTILE_DISC. Both inverse distribution functions specify an argument and an ordering of a value expression. The value of the argument should be between 0 (zero) and 1 (one) inclusive. The value expression is evaluated for each row of the group, NULLs are discarded, and the remaining rows are ordered. The computation concludes:

PERCENTILE_CONT = by considering the pair of consecutive rows that are indicated by the argument, treated as a fraction of the total number of rows in the group, and interpolating the value of the value expression evaluated for these rows.

PERCENTILE_DISC = by treating the group as a window partition of the CUME_DIST window function, using the specified ordering of the value expression as the window ordering, and returning the first value expression whose cumulative distribution value is greater than or equal to the argument.

If you need other statistics, consult your vendor's documentation for what functions they have implemented.

24.2 Correlation

A correlation is a measure of how much alike two sets of data are. There are many types of correlation in statistics, but the most common one is Pearson's r. It is worth be able to do without using the CORR() function if your SQL odes not have it.

This version of Pearson's r is due to van Heusden consulting in the Netherlands (http://www.vanheusden.com/misc/pearson.php). The data are the movie ratings of a set of films by all the pairs of reviewers. The population is (n) movies.

```
CREATE TABLE Movie_Reviews
(reviewer VARCHAR(15) NOT NULL,
 movie_title VARCHAR(15) NOT NULL,
 PRIMARY KEY (user, movie_title)
 rating DECIMAL(2,1) NOT NULL
  CHECK (rating BETWEEN 1.0 AND 5.0);
```

The computation is

```
SELECT reviewer_1, reviewer_2,
       ((psum - (sum1 * sum2 / n))
        / SQRT((sum1sq - POWER(sum1, 2.0) / n)
        * (sum2sq - POWER(sum2, 2.0) / n))) AS pearson_r, n
  FROM (SELECT N1.reviewer AS reviewer_1, N2.reviewer AS reviewer_2,
               SUM(N1.rating) AS sum1, SUM(N2.rating) AS sum2,
               SUM(N1.rating * N1.rating) AS sum1sq,
               SUM(N2.rating * N2.rating) AS sum2sq,
               SUM(N1.rating * N2.rating) AS psum,
               COUNT(*) AS N
```

```
    FROM Movie_Reviews AS N1
         LEFT OUTER JOIN
         Movie_Reviews AS N2
         ON N1.movie_title = N2.movie_title
   WHERE N1.reviewer > N2.reviewer
   GROUP BY N1.reviewer, N2.reviewer)
  AS step1;
```

OLAP Aggregation in SQL

MOST SQL PROGRAMMERS work with OLTP (online transaction processing) databases and write simple, one-level aggregations. This chapter reviews how the usual GROUP BY clause works. The result set is partitioned by the grouping columns, then *each group is reduced to a single row.* For example, if I group personnel by their departments, I can get the total salaries in each department, but I cannot see the salary of each employee. The employee is at a lower level of aggregation.

25.1 Querying Versus Reporting

Proper queries return tables. A table is a set and all the rows are of the same kind of thing. Reports, also known as OLAP queries, mix unlike things into the same row or the same table. To use the prior example, a row might have the salary of an individual employee in one column, the average salary in his department in a second column, and the total amount of all salaries in the company in a third column in the same row.

A reporting tool can format the data for display, each line on the printout can be different. But an SQL query is required to return something that looks like a table—columns of known data types and rows of a known number of columns. This means that I need to be able to determine the aggregation level of a row in an OLAP query, so I can display it. We need to use NULLs for columns that are "empty" because that level of aggregation does not include

a particular column; the row with the average departmental salary would not have an employee name.

Some of this is easier to explain with the actual extensions in SQL.

25.2 GROUPING Operators

OLAP functions add the ROLLUP and CUBE extensions to the GROUP BY clause. The ROLLUP and CUBE are often referred to as super-groups. They can be written in older Standard SQL using GROUP BY and UNION operators.

As expected, NULLs form their own group just as before. However, we now have a GROUPING(<column reference>) function which checks for NULLs that are the results of aggregation over that <column reference> during the execution of a grouped query containing CUBE, ROLLUP, or GROUPING SET, and returns 1 if they were created by the query and a zero otherwise.

SQL:2003 added a multicolumn version that constructs a binary number from the ones and zeros of the columns in the list in an implementation defined exact numeric data type. Here is a recursive definition:

```
GROUPING(<column ref 1>, ..., <column ref n-1>, <column ref n>)
```

is equivalent to:

```
(2 *(<column ref 1>, ..., <column ref n-1>) + GROUPING (<column ref n>))
```

25.2.1 GROUP BY GROUPING SET

The GROUPING SET(<column list>) is shorthand for a series of UNION-ed queries that are common in reports. For example, to find the total:

```
SELECT dept_name, CAST(NULL AS CHAR(10)) AS job_title, COUNT(*)
  FROM Personnel
 GROUP BY dept_name
UNION ALL
SELECT CAST(NULL AS CHAR(8)) AS dept_name, job_title, COUNT(*)
  FROM Personnel
 GROUP BY job_title;
```

The above can be rewritten like this:

```
SELECT dept_name, job_title, COUNT(*)
  FROM Personnel
 GROUP BY GROUPING SET (dept_name, job_title);
```

There is a problem with all of the OLAP grouping functions. They will generate NULLs for each dimension at the subtotal levels. How do you tell the difference between a real NULL and a generated NULL? This is a job for the GROUPING() function which returns 0 for NULLs in the original data and 1 for generated NULLs that indicate a subtotal.

```
SELECT CASE GROUPING(dept_name)
       WHEN 1 THEN 'department total'
       ELSE dept_name END AS dept_name,
       CASE GROUPING(job_title)
       WHEN 1 THEN 'job total'
       ELSE job_title_name END AS job_title
 FROM Personnel
GROUP BY GROUPING SETS (dept_name, job_title);
```

The grouping set concept can be used to define other OLAP groupings.

25.2.2 ROLLUP

A ROLLUP group is an extension to the GROUP BY clause in SQL-99 that produces a result set that contains subtotal rows in addition to the aregular' grouped rows. Subtotal rows are super-aggregate rows that contain further aggregates whose values are derived by applying the same column functions that were used to obtain the grouped rows. A ROLLUP grouping is a series of grouping sets:

```
GROUP BY ROLLUP (a, b, c)
```

is equivalent to:

```
GROUP BY GROUPING SETS
(a, b, c)
(a, b)
(a)
()
```

Notice that the (n) elements of the ROLLUP translate to (n+1) grouping set. Another point to remember is that the order in which the grouping-expression is specified is significant for ROLLUP.

The ROLLUP is basically the classic totals and subtotals report presented as an SQL table.

25.2.3 CUBES

The CUBE super-group is the other SQL-99 extension to the GROUP BY clause that produces a result set that contains all the subtotal rows of a ROLLUP aggregation and, in addition, contains 'cross-tabulation' rows. Cross-tabulation rows are additional 'super-aggregate' rows. They are, as the name implies, summaries across columns if the data were represented as a spreadsheet. Like ROLLUP, a CUBE group can also be thought of as a series of grouping sets. In the case of a CUBE, all permutations of the cubed grouping-expression are computed along with the grand total. Therefore, the n elements of a CUBE translate to 2n grouping sets:

```
GROUP BY CUBE (a, b, c)
```

is equivalent to:

```
GROUP BY GROUPING SETS
(a, b, c) (a, b) (a, c) (b, c) (a) (b) (c) ()
```

Notice that the three elements of the CUBE translate to eight grouping sets. Unlike ROLLUP, the order of specification of elements doesn't matter for CUBE:

CUBE (julian_day, sales_person) is the same as CUBE (sales_person, julian_day).

CUBE is an extension of the ROLLUP function. The CUBE function not only provides the column summaries we saw in ROLLUP but also calculates the row summaries and grand totals for the various dimensions.

25.2.4 OLAP Examples of SQL

The following example illustrates advanced OLAP function used in combination with traditional SQL. In this example, we want to perform a ROLLUP function of sales by region and city:

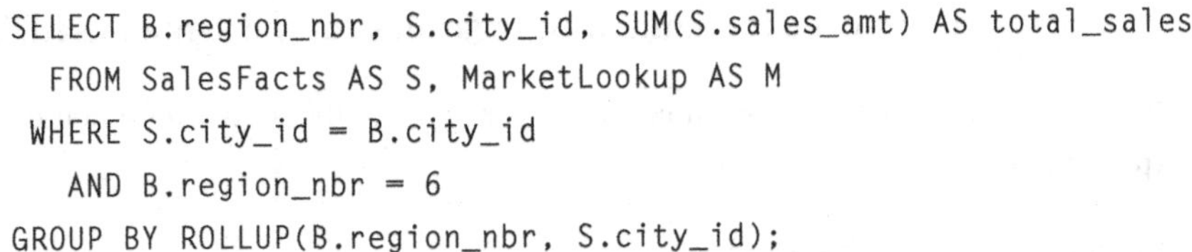

```
SELECT B.region_nbr, S.city_id, SUM(S.sales_amt) AS total_sales
  FROM SalesFacts AS S, MarketLookup AS M
 WHERE S.city_id = B.city_id
   AND B.region_nbr = 6
GROUP BY ROLLUP(B.region_nbr, S.city_id);
```

The resultant set is reduced by explicitly querying region 6. A sample result of the SQL is shown below. The result shows ROLLUP of two groupings (region, city) returning three totals, including region, city, and the grand total. Yearly sales by city and region:

region_nbr	city_id	total_sales	Aggregation levels
6	1	81,655	◄ city within region
6	2	131,512	
6	3	58,384	
...	...	...	
6	30	1733	
6	31	5058	
6	NULL	1,190,902	◄ region six total
NULL	NULL	1,190,902	◄ grand total

25.3 The Window Clause

The window clause is also called the OVER() clause informally. The idea is that the table is first broken into partitions with the PARTITION BY subclause. The partitions are then sorted by the ORDER BY clause. An imaginary cursor sits on the current row where the windowed function is invoked. A subset of the rows in the current partition is defined by the number of rows before and after the current row; if there is a <window frame exclusion> option then certain rows are removed from the subset. Finally, the subset is passed to an aggregate or ordinal function to return a scalar value. The window functions follow the rules of any function, but with a different syntax. The window part can be either a <window name> or a <window specification>. The <window specification> gives the details of the window in the OVER() clause and this is how most programmers use it. However, you can define a window and give it a name, then use the name in the OVER() clauses of several statements.

The window works the same way, regardless of the syntax used. The BNF is

```
<window function>::= <window function type> OVER <window name or
specification>

<window function type>::=
   <rank function type> | ROW_NUMBER ()| <aggregate function>

<rank function type>::= RANK() | DENSE_RANK() | PERCENT_RANK() | CUME_
DIST()

<window name or specification>::= <window name> | <in-line window
specification>

<in-line window specification>::= <window specification>
```

The window clause has three subclauses: partitioning, ordering, and aggregation grouping or window frame.

25.3.1 PARTITION BY Subclause

A set of column names specifies the partitioning, which is applied to the rows that the preceding FROM, WHERE, GROUP BY, and HAVING clauses produced. If no partitioning is specified, the entire set of rows composes a single partition and the aggregate function applies to the whole set each time. Though the partitioning looks a bit like a GROUP BY, it is not the same thing. A GROUP BY collapses the rows in a partition into a single row. The partitioning within a window, though, simply organizes the rows into groups without collapsing them.

25.3.2 ORDER BY Subclause

The ordering within the window clause is like the ORDER BY clause in a CURSOR. It includes a list of sort keys and indicates whether they should be sorted ascending or descending. The important thing to understand is that ordering is applied within each partition. The other subclauses are optional, but don't make any sense without an ORDER BY and/or PARTITION BY in the function:

```
<sort specification list>::= <sort specification> [{,<sort
specification>}...]
```

```
<sort specification>::= <sort key> [<ordering specification>] [<null ordering>]

<sort key>::= <value expression>

<ordering specification>::= ASC | DESC

<null ordering>::= NULLS FIRST | NULLS LAST
```

It is worth mentioning that the rules for an ORDER BY subclause have changed to be more general than they were in earlier SQL Standards:

1. A sort can now be a <value expression> and is not limited to a simple column in the select list. However, it is still a good idea to use only column names so that you can see the sorting order in the result set.

2. <sort specification> specifies the sort direction for the corresponding sort key. If DESC is not specified in the i-th <sort specification>, then the sort direction for Ki is ascending and the applicable <comp op> is the <less than operator>. Otherwise, the sort direction for Ki is descending and the applicable <comp op> is the <greater than operator>.

3. If <null ordering> is not specified, then an implementation defined <null ordering> is implicit. This was a big issue in earlier SQL Standards because vendors handled NULLs differently. NULLs are considered equal to each other, using the grouping model.

4. If one value is NULL and second value is not NULL, then
   4.1 If NULLS FIRST is specified or implied, then first value <comp op> second value is considered to be TRUE.
   4.2 If NULLS LAST is specified or implied, then first value <comp op> second value is considered to be FALSE.
   4.3 If first value and second value are not NULL and the result of "first value <comp op> second value" is UNKNOWN, then the relative ordering of first value and second value is implementation dependent.

5. Two rows that are not distinct with respect to the <sort specification> are said to be peers of each other. The relative ordering of peers is implementation dependent.

25.3.3 Window Frame Subclause

The tricky one is the window frame. Here is the BNF, but you really need to see code for it to make sense.

```
<window frame clause>::= <window frame units> <window frame extent>
[<window frame exclusion>]

<window frame units>::= ROWS | RANGE
```

RANGE works with a single-sort key of a numeric, datetime, or interval data type. It is for data that is a little fuzzy on the edges, if you will. If ROWS is specified, then sort list is made of exact numeric with scale zero.

```
<window frame extent>::= <window frame start> | <window frame between>

<window frame start>::=
UNBOUNDED PRECEDING | <window frame preceding> | CURRENT ROW

<window frame preceding>::= <unsigned value specification> PRECEDING
```

If the window starts at UNBOUNDED PRECEDING, then the lower bound is always the first row of the partition; likewise, CURRENT ROW explains itself. The <window frame preceding> is an actual count of preceding rows.

```
<window frame bound>::= <window frame start> | UNBOUNDED FOLLOWING |
<window frame following>

<window frame following>::= <unsigned value specification> FOLLOWING
```

If the window starts at UNBOUNDED FOLLOWING, then the lower bound is always the last row of the partition; likewise, CURRENT ROW explains itself. The <window frame following> is an actual count of following rows:

```
<window frame between>::= BETWEEN <window frame bound 1> AND <window
frame bound 2>

<window frame bound 1>::= <window frame bound>

<window frame bound 2>::= <window frame bound>
```

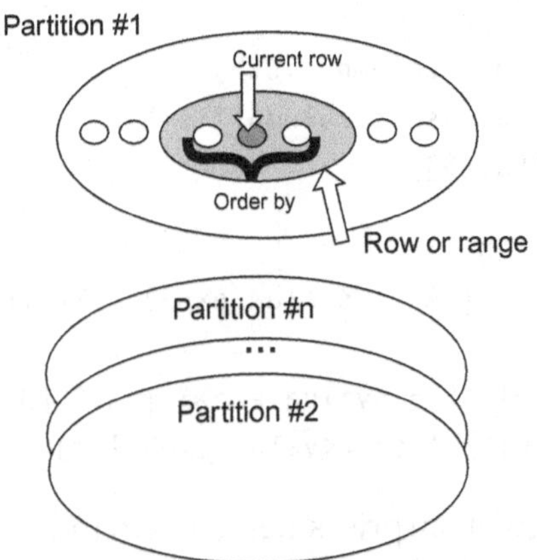

Figure 25.1 Window Function Partitioning and Ordering Model.

The current row and its window frame have to stay inside the partition, so the following and preceding limits can effectively change at either end of the frame:

```
<window frame exclusion>::= EXCLUDE CURRENT ROW | EXCLUDE GROUP
| EXCLUDE TIES | EXCLUDE NO OTHERS
```

The <window frame exclusion> is not used much or widely implemented. It is also hard to explain. The term "peer" refers to duplicate values.

(1) EXCLUDE CURRENT ROW removes the current row from the window.

(2) EXCLUDE GROUP removes the current row and any peers of the current row.

(3) EXCLUDE TIES removed any rows other than the current row that are peers of the current row.

(4) EXCLUDE NO OTHERS makes sure that no additional rows are removed (Figure 25.1).

25.4 Windowed Aggregate Functions

The regular aggregate functions can take a window clause:

```
<aggregate function>
OVER ([PARTITION BY <column list>]
          [ORDER BY <sort column list>]
      [<window frame>])

<aggregate function>::=
      MIN([DISTINCT | ALL] <value exp>) | MAX([DISTINCT | ALL]
<value exp>)
 | SUM([DISTINCT | ALL] <value exp>) | AVG([DISTINCT | ALL] <value exp>)
 | COUNT([DISTINCT | ALL] [<value exp> | *])
```

There are no great surprises here. The window that is constructed acts as if it was a group to which the aggregate function is applied.

25.5 Ordinal Functions

The ordinal functions use the window clause but must have an ORDER BY subclause to make sense. They return an ordering of the row within its partition or window frame relative to the rest of the rows in the partition. They have no parameters.

25.5.1 Row Numbering

ROW_NUMBER() uniquely identifies rows with a sequential number based on the position of the row within the window defined by an ordering clause (if one is specified), starting with 1 for the first row and continuing sequentially to the last row in the window. If an ordering clause, ORDER BY, isn't specified in the window, the row numbers are assigned to the rows in arbitrary order.

25.5.2 RANK() and DENSE_RANK()

RANK() assigns a sequential rank of a row within a window. The RANK() of a row is defined as one plus the number of rows that strictly precede the row. Rows that are not distinct within the ordering of the window are assigned equal ranks. If two or more rows are not distinct with respect to the ordering, then there will be one or more gaps in the sequential rank numbering. That is, the results of RANK() may have gaps in the numbers resulting from duplicate values.

DENSE_RANK() also assigns a sequential rank to a row in a window. However, a row's DENSE_RANK() is one plus the number of rows preceding it that are distinct with respect to the ordering. Therefore, there will be no gaps in the sequential rank numbering, with ties being assigned the same rank.

25.5.3 PERCENT_RANK() and CUME_DIST

These were added in the SQL:2003 Standard and are defined in terms of earlier constructs. Let <approximate numeric type> 1 be an approximate numeric type with implementation defined precision. PERCENT_RANK() OVER <window specification>is equivalent to:

```
CASE
WHEN COUNT(*)
      OVER (<window specification>
             RANGE BETWEEN UNBOUNDED PRECEDING
                      AND UNBOUNDED FOLLOWING) = 1
THEN CAST (0 AS <approximate numeric type>)
ELSE (CAST (RANK ()
             OVER (<window specification>) AS <approximate numeric
type>1) - 1)
      / (COUNT (*)
          OVER (<window specification>1
                RANGE BETWEEN UNBOUNDED PRECEDING
                          AND UNBOUNDED FOLLOWING) - 1)
END
```

Likewise, the cumulative distribution is defined with an <approximate numeric type>with implementation defined precision. CUME_DIST() OVER <window specification>is equivalent to:

```
 (CAST (COUNT (*)
         OVER (<window specification>
               RANGE UNBOUNDED PRECEDING) AS <approximate numeric type>)
      / COUNT(*)
         OVER (<window specification>1
                RANGE BETWEEN UNBOUNDED PRECEDING
                          AND UNBOUNDED FOLLOWING))
```

You can also go back and define the other windowed in terms of each other, but it is only a curiosity and has no practical value.

RANK() OVER <window specification> is equivalent to:

```
(COUNT (*) OVER (<window specification> RANGE UNBOUNDED PRECEDING)
 -COUNT (*) OVER (<window specification>RANGE CURRENT ROW) + 1)
```

DENSE_RANK() OVER (<window specification>) is equivalent to:

```
COUNT (DISTINCT ROW (<value exp 1>, ...,<value exp n>))
OVER (<window specification> RANGE UNBOUNDED PRECEDING)
```

Where <value exp i> is a sort key in the table.
ROW_NUMBER() OVER WNS is equivalent to:

```
COUNT (*)
OVER (<window specification> ROWS UNBOUNDED PRECEDING)
```

25.5.4 Some Examples

The <aggregation grouping> defines a set of rows upon which the aggregate function operates for each row in the partition. Thus, in our example, for each month, you specify the set including it and the two preceding rows:

```
SELECT SH.region_nbr, SH.sales_month, SH.sales_amt,
       AVG(SH.sales_amt)
       OVER (PARTITION BY SH.region_nbr
             ORDER BY SH.sales_month ASC
             ROWS 2 PRECEDING)
       AS moving_average,
       SUM(SH.sales_amt)
       OVER (PARTITION BY SH.region_nbr
             ORDER BY SH.sales_month ASC
             ROWS BETWEEN UNBOUNDED PRECEDING AND CURRENT ROW)
       AS moving_total
  FROM Sales_History AS SH;
```

Here, "AVG(SH.sales_amt) OVER (PARTITION BY…)" is the first OLAP function. The construct inside the OVER() clause defines the window of data to which the aggregate function, AVG() in this example, is applied.

The window clause defines a partitioned set of rows to which the aggregate function is applied. The window clause says to take Sales_History table and then apply the following operations to it.

1. Partition the sales history by region.
2. Order the data by month within each region.
3. Group each row with the two preceding rows in the same region.
4. Compute the windowed average on each grouping.

The database engine is not required to perform the steps in the order described here, but has to produce the same result set as if they had been carried out.

The second windowed function is a cumulative total to date for each region. It is a very column query pattern.

There are two main types of aggregation groups: physical and logical. In physical grouping, you count a specified number of rows that are before or after the current row. The Sales_History example used physical grouping. In logical grouping, you include all the data in a certain interval, defined in terms of a quantity that can be added to, or subtracted from, the current sort key. For instance, you create the same group whether you define it as the current month's row plus:

(1) The two preceding rows as defined by the ORDER BY clause.

(2) Any row containing a month no less than 2 months earlier.

Physical grouping works well for contiguous data and programmers who think in terms of sequential files. Physical grouping works for a larger variety of data types than logical grouping, because it does not require operations on values.

Logical grouping works better for data that has gaps or irregularities in the ordering and for programmers who think in SQL predicates. Logical grouping works only if you can do arithmetic on the values (such as numeric quantities and dates).

You will find another query pattern used with these functions. The function invocations need to get names to be referenced, so they are put into a derived table which is encased in a containing query.

```
SELECT X.*
  FROM (SELECT <window function 1> AS W1,
               <window function 2> AS W2,
                ..
```

```
                <window function n> AS Wn
          FROM ..
        [WHERE ..]
        ) AS X
 [WHERE..]
[GROUP BY ..];
```

Using the SELECT * in the containing query is a handy way to save repeating a select clause list over and over.

25.6 Vendor Extensions

You will find that vendors have added their own proprietary windowed functions to their products. While there is no good way to predict what they will do, there are two sets of common extensions. As a programming exercise, I suggest you try to write them in Standard SQL windowed functions so you can translate dialect SQL if you need to do so.

25.6.1 LEAD and LAG Functions

LEAD and LAG functions are nonstandard shorthands you will find in Oracle other SQL products. Rather than compute an aggregate value, they jump ahead or behind the current row and use that value in an expression. They take three arguments and an OVER() clause. The general syntax is shown below:

```
[LEAD | LAG] (<expr>, <offset>, <default>) OVER (<window specification>)
```

<expr>is the expression to compute from the leading or lagging row.

<offset>is the position of the leading or lagging row relative to the current row; it has to be a positive integer which defaults to 1.

<default>is the value to return if the <offset>points to a row outside the partition range. Here is a simple example:

```
SELECT dept_nbr, emp_id, sal_amt,
       LEAD(sal, 1, 0)
         OVER (PARTITION BY dept_nbr
                    ORDER BY sal DESC NULLS LAST)AS lead_sal_amt,
       LAG (sal, 1, 0)
          OVER (PARTITION BY dept_nbr
                    ORDER BY sal DESC NULLS LAST) AS lag_sal_amt
FROM Personnel;
```

Results

dept_nbr	emp_id	sal_amt	lead_sal_amt	lag_sal_amt
10	7839	5000	2450	0
10	7782	2450	1300	5000
10	7934	1300	0	2450
20	7788	3000	3000	0
20	7902	3000	2975	3000
20	7566	2975	1100	3000
20	7876	1100	800	2975
20	7369	800	0	1100

Look at employee 7782, whose current salary is $2450.00. Looking at the salaries, we see that the first salary greater than his is $5000.00 and the first salary less his is $1300.00. Look at employee 7934 whose current salary of $1300.00 puts him at the bottom of the company pay scale; his lead_salary_amt is defaulted to zero.

25.6.1.1 Example with Gaps

Given a sequence of data values, we often miss something. The classic example is reading a meter and getting a gap in the sequence. A common way to handle such missing is to assume that the missing value is the same as the prior known value. For example, every reading we score a foobar on the scale {'Alpha,' 'Beta,' Gamma'} or post a NULL if we could not get a reading.

```
CREATE TABLE Foobars
(reading_seq INTEGER NOT NULL PRIMARY KEY,
 foo_score CHAR(6)
   CHECK (foo_score IN ('Alpha', 'Beta', Gamma'))
);

INSERT INTO Foobars
VALUES
(1, 'Alpha'),
(2, 'Alpha'),
(3, NULL),
(4, NULL),
(5, NULL),
(6, 'Beta'),
```

```
(7, NULL),
(8, 'Beta'),
(9, 'Gamma');
```

What we want to do when we have a NULL is assume that we can use the last known value. But a simple LAG() or LEAD() will not work. We have no idea when we had a value. The trick is to use CTEs to get rid of NULLs, then look for ranges in the sequence:

```
WITH Known_Foo_Scores (reading_seq, foo_score)
AS
(SELECT reading_seq, foo_score
   FROM Foobars
  WHERE foo_score IS NOT NULL),

Known_Reading_Pairs (reading_seq, foo_score, prior_reading_seq, prior_
foo_score)
AS
(SELECT reading_seq, foo_score,
        LAG(reading_seq) OVER (ORDER BY reading_seq),
        LAG(foo_score) OVER (ORDER BY reading_seq)
   FROM Known_Foo_Scores)

SELECT DISTINCT F.foo_id,
        COALESCE (F.foo_score, X2.prior_foo_score)
  FROM Known_Reading_Pairs AS X2, Foobars AS F
 WHERE F.foo_id BETWEEN X2.prior_foo_id AND X2.foo_id;
```

1	Alpha
2	Alpha
3	Alpha
4	Alpha
5	Alpha
6	Beta
7	Beta
8	Beta
9	Gamma

25.6.2 FIRST and LAST Functions

FIRST and LAST functions are nonstandard shorthands you will find in SQL products in various forms. Rather than compute an aggregate value, they sort a partition on one set of columns, then return an expression from the first or last row of that sort. The expression usually has nothing to do with the sorting columns. This is a bit like the joke about the British Sargent-Major ordering the troops to line up alphabetically by height. The general syntax is

```
[FIRST | LAST](<expr>) OVER (<window specification>)
```

Using the imaginary Personnel table again:

```
SELECT emp_id, dept_nbr, hire_date,
       FIRST(hire_date)
        OVER (PARTITION BY dept_nbr
                  ORDER BY emp_id)
       AS first_hire_by_dept
  FROM Personnel;
```

The results get the hire date for the employee who has the lowest employee id in each department.

emp_id	dept_nbr	hire_date	first_hire_by_dept	
7369	20	'2017-01-01'	'2017-01-01'	◄ first emp_id in dept20
7566	20	'2017-01-02'	'2017-01-01'	
7902	20	'2017-01-02'	'2017-01-01'	
7788	20	'2017-01-04'	'2017-01-01'	
7876	20	'2017-01-07'	'2017-01-01'	◄ last emp_id in dept20
7499	30	'2017-01-27'	'2017-01-27'	◄ first emp_id in dept30
7521	30	'2017-01-09'	'2017-01-27'	
7844	30	'2017-01-17'	'2017-01-27'	
7654	30	'2017-01-18'	'2017-01-27'	
7900	30	'2017-01-20'	'2017-01-27'	◄ las temp_id in dept 30

If we had used LAST() instead, the two chosen rows would have been
(7876, 20, '2017-01-07,' '2017-01-01')
(7900, 30, '2017-01-20,' '2017-01-27')

The Oracle extensions FIRST_VALUE and LAST_VALUE are even stranger. They allow other ordinal and aggregate functions to be applied to

the retrieved values. If you want to use them, I suggest that you look product specific references and examples.

You can do these with Standard SQL and a little work. The skeleton:

```
WITH First_Last_Query
AS
(SELECT emp_id, dept_nbr,
        ROW_NUMBER()
          OVER (PARTITION BY dept_nbr
                      ORDER BY emp_id ASC) AS asc_order,
        ROW_NUMBER()
          OVER (PARTITION BY dept_nbr
                      ORDER BY emp_id DESC) AS desc_order
   FROM Personnel)
SELECT A.emp_id, A.dept_nbr,
       OA.hire_date AS first_value,
       OD.hire_date AS last_value
  FROM First_Last_Query AS A,
       First_Last_Query AS OA,
       First_Last_Query AS OD
 WHERE OD.desc_order = 1
   AND OA.asc_order = 1;
```

25.7 A Bit of History

IBM and Oracle jointly proposed these extensions in early 1999 and thanks to ANSI's uncommonly rapid (and praiseworthy) actions, they are part of the SQL-99 Standard. IBM implemented portions of the specifications in DB2 UDB 6.2, which was commercially available in some forms as early as mid-1999. Oracle 8i version 2 and DB2 UDB 7.1, both released in late 1999, contain beefed-up implementations.

Other vendors contributed, including database tool vendors Brio, MicroStrategy, and Cognos and database vendor Informix, among others. A team lead by Dr. Hamid Pirahesh of IBM's Almaden Research Laboratory played a particularly important role. After his team had researched the subject for about a year and come up with an approach to extending SQL in this area, he called Oracle. The companies then learned that each had independently done some significant work. With Andy Witkowski playing a pivotal role at Oracle, the two companies hammered out a joint standards proposal in about 2 months. Red Brick was actually the first product to implement this functionality before the standard, but in a less complete form. You can find details in the ANSI document *Introduction to OLAP Functions* by Fred Zemke, Krishna Kulkarni, Andy Witkowski, and Bob Lyle.

Advanced SELECT Statements

IN CHAPTER 22, WE took a look at the basic SELECT statement. Now we need to look at other ways to nest subqueries and build the working table in the FROM clause with JOINs and other syntax. This is a collection of solutions to problems for which you might not think about using SQL. I also give a bit history.

26.1 Correlated Subqueries

One of the classics of Software Engineering is a short paper by the late Edsger Dijkstra entitled *Go To Statement Considered Harmful* (communications of the ACM, Vol. 11, No. 3, March 1968, pp. 147–148). In this paper, he argued for dropping the GOTO statement from programming languages in favor of what we now called Structured Programming.

One of his observations was that programs that used only BEGIN-END blocks, WHILE loops and IF-THEN-ELSE statements were easier to read and maintain. Programs that jumped around via GOTO statements were harder to follow because the execution path could have arrived at a statement label from anywhere in the code. Algol, the first of the blocked structured programming languages, had all of those control structures but still kept the GOTO—it was considered a fundamental part of programming. Before Dijkstra, nobody had really understood the power of limiting the scope of variables and control structures in procedural code. The basic idea of a scope is that a block of code can only reference variables that are declared

in the block. Failing to find a local variable, the containing blocks are then inspected from the inside out.

We have the same concept in SQL queries. A correlated subquery is a subquery that references columns in the tables of its containing query. The general structure might look like:

```
SELECT T1.x, T1.y, T1.z
  FROM TableOne AS T1
 WHERE T1.x
       = (SELECT T2.x, T2.y, T2.z
            FROM TableTwo AS T2
           WHERE T2.y
                 = (SELECT foobar
                      FROM TableThree AS T3
                     WHERE T3.x = T1.x
                       AND T3.y = T2.y
                       AND T3.z = 42));
```

Look at the innermost query. The predicate (T3.z=42) is local to this query. The predicate (T3.y=T2.y) works because this query is in the scope of the query with T2 in the FROM clause. Likewise, The predicate (T3.x=T1.x) works because this query is in the scope of the query with T1 in the FROM clause. If I had not qualified the table names in the innermost WHERE clause, the predicate (T3.x=x) would refer to the most local x, which gives us (T3.x=T3.x), which is always TRUE or UNKNOWN. That is absurd.

But a predicate like (T3.z=floob) might reference table T1, T2, or T3, depending on which ones has the nearest column floob. Which table would be determined by working outward. This is why it is important to qualify column names.

The tables can reference the same table under a different correlation name. Consider a query to find all the students who are younger than the oldest student of their gender:

```
SELECT S1.stud_nbr, S1.stud_name, S1.sex_code, S1.stud_age
  FROM Students AS S1
 WHERE stud_age
       < (SELECT MAX(stud_age)
            FROM Students AS S2
           WHERE S1.sex_code = S2.sex_code);
```

1. Let's work it out in detail. The fiction in SQL is that we create local tables S1 and S2 which happen to have the same data and structure as the Students table. A copy of the Students table is made for each correlation name, S1 and S2. Obviously, this is not how it is implemented in a real SQL compiler. Following the same steps we used in simple SELECT Statements, expand the outer query.

stud_nbr	stud_name	sex_code	stud_age
1	Smith	1	16
2	Smyth	2	17
3	Smoot	2	16
4	Adams	2	17
5	Jones	1	16
6	Celko	1	17
7	Vennor	2	16
8	Murray	1	18

2. When you get to the WHERE clause, and find the innermost query, you will see that you need to get data from the containing query. The model of execution says that each outer row has the subquery executed on it in parallel with the other rows. Assume we are working on student (1, 'Smith'), who is male. The query in effect becomes:

```
SELECT 1, 'Smith', 1, 16
  FROM Students AS S1
 WHERE 16 < (SELECT MAX(stud_age)
               FROM Students AS S2
              WHERE 1 = S2.sex_code);
```

As an aside, the search conditions (1 = S2.sex_code) and (S2.sex_code = 1) are equivalent. The choice is largely a matter of the programmer's culture—do you read from left to right or right to left?

3. The subquery can now be calculated for male students; the maximum stud_age is 18. When we expand this out for all the other rows, this will give us the effect of this set of parallel queries.

```
SELECT 1, 'Smith', 1, 16 FROM Students AS S1 WHERE 16 < 18;
SELECT 2, 'Smyth', 2, 17 FROM Students AS S1 WHERE 17 < 17;
SELECT 3, 'Smoot', 2, 16 FROM Students AS S1 WHERE 16 < 17;
```

```
SELECT 4, 'Adams', 2, 17 FROM Students AS S1 WHERE 17 < 17;
SELECT 5, 'Jones', 1, 16 FROM Students AS S1 WHERE 16 < 18;
SELECT 6, 'Celko', 1, 17 FROM Students AS S1 WHERE 17 < 18;
SELECT 7, 'Vennor', 2, 16 FROM Students AS S1 WHERE 16 < 17;
SELECT 8, 'Murray', 1, 18 FROM Students AS S1 WHERE 18 < 18;
```

4. These same steps have been done for each row in the containing query. The model is that all of the subqueries are resolved at once. With cheaper and cheaper parallel hardware, this might be true some day, but no implementation really does it that way currently. The usual approach in real SQL compilers is to build procedural loops in the database engine that scan through both tables. What table is in what loop is decided by the optimizer. The final results are

stud_nbr	stud_name	sex_code	stud_age
1	Smith	1	16
3	Smoot	2	16
5	Jones	1	16
6	Celko	1	17
7	Vennor	2	16

Again, no real product works this way, but it has to produce the same results as this process.

There is no limit to the depth of nesting of correlated subqueries in theory. In practice, it is probably a good heuristic to keep the nesting under five levels.

These examples used scalar subqueries, but you can also use correlated subqueries that return a collection of tables. For example, to find all of Professor Celko's students, we might use this query.

```
SELECT S1.stud_nbr, S1.stud_name, S1.sex_code, S1.stud_age
  FROM Students AS S1
 WHERE S1.stud_nbr
       IN (SELECT T.stud_nbr
             FROM Teachers AS T1
            WHERE S1.stud_nbr = T1.stud_nbr
              AND T1.teacher_name = 'Celko');
```

Another problem is that many SQL programmers do not fully understand the rules for scope of derived table names. If an infixed join is given a derived table name, then all of the table names inside it are hidden from containing expressions. For example, this will fail

```
SELECT a, b, c -- wrong!
 FROM (Foo
       INNER JOIN
       Bar
       ON Foo.y >= Bar.x) AS Foobar (x, y)
         INNER JOIN
         Flub
         ON Foo.y <= Flub.z;
```

Because the table name Foo is not available to the second INNER JOIN. However, this will work:

```
SELECT a, b, c
 FROM (Foo
       INNER JOIN
       Bar
       ON Foo.y >= Bar.x) AS Foobar (x, y)
         INNER JOIN
         Flub
         ON Foobar.y <= Flub.z;
```

If you start nesting lots of derived table expressions, you can force an order of execution in the query. It is not a generally a good idea to try to outguess the optimizer.

So far, I have shown fully qualified column names. It is a good programming practice, but it is not required. Assume that Foo and Bar both have a column named w. These statements will produce an ambiguous name error:

```
SELECT a, b, c
  FROM Foo
       INNER JOIN
       Bar ON y >= x
       INNER JOIN
       Flub ON y <= w;
```

```
SELECT a, b, c
  FROM Foo, Bar, Flub
 WHERE y BETWEEN x AND w
```

But this statement will work from inside the parentheses first and then does the outermost INNER JOIN last.

```
SELECT a, b, c
 FROM Foo
      INNER JOIN
      (Bar
       INNER JOIN
       Flub ON y <= w)
      ON y >= x;
```

If Bar did not have a column named w, then the parser would go to the next containing expression, find Foo.w, and use it.

26.2 Infixed INNER JOINs

SQL-92 added new syntax for various JOINs using infixed operators in the FROM clause. The JOIN operators are quite general and flexible, allowing you to do things in a single statement that you could not do in the older notation. The basic syntax is

```
<joined table> ::=
   <cross join> | <qualified join> | (<joined table>)

<cross join> ::= <table reference> CROSS JOIN <table reference>

<qualified join> ::=
   <table reference> [NATURAL] [<join type>] JOIN
       <table reference> [<join specification>]

<join specification> ::= <join condition> | <named columns join>

<join condition> ::= ON <search condition>

<named columns join> ::= USING (<join column list>)

<join type> ::= INNER | <outer join type> [OUTER] | UNION

<outer join type> ::= LEFT | RIGHT | FULL
```

```
<join column list> ::= <column name list>

<table reference> ::=
   <table name> [[AS] <correlation name>[(<derived column list>)]]
       | <derived table>
          [AS] <correlation name> [(<derived column list>)]
       | <joined table>

<derived table> ::= <table subquery>

<column name list> ::=
   <column name> [{ <comma> <column name> }...]
```

An INNER JOIN is done by forming the CROSS JOIN and then removing the rows that do not meet the JOIN search conditions given in the ON clause, just like we did with the original FROM.. WHERE syntax. The ON clause can be as elaborate as you want to make it, as long as it refers to tables and columns within its scope. If a <qualified join> is used without a <join type>, INNER is implicit. But it is good documentation to spell out all of the JOIN operators.

However, in the real world, most INNER JOINs are done using equality tests on columns with the same names in different tables, rather than on elaborate search conditions. Equi-JOINs are so common that Standard SQL has two shorthand ways of specifying them. The USING (c1, c2, ..., cn) clause takes the column names in the list and replaces them with the clause ON ((T1.c1, T1.c2, ..., T1.cn) = (T2.c1, T2.c2, ..., T2.cn)). Likewise, the NATURAL option is shorthand for a USING() clause that is a list of all the column names that are common to both tables. If NATURAL is specified, a JOIN specification cannot be given; it is already there.

A strong warning: do *not* use NATURAL JOIN in production code. Any change to the column names or addition new columns will change the join at run time. This is also why you do not use "SELECT *" in production code. But the NATURAL JOIN is more dangerous. As Daniel Morgan pointed out a NATURAL JOIN between two tables with a vague generic column name like "comments" for unrelated data elements can give you a meaningless join containing megabytes of text.

The same sort of warning applies to the USING clause. Neither of these options is widely implemented or used. If you find out that "product_id," "product_nbr," and "upc" were all used for the same data element in your

schema, you should do a global change to make sure that one data element has one and only one name.

There was a myth among ACCESS programmers that the ON clause can contain only JOIN conditions and the WHERE can contain only search conditions. This is not true, and the difference in the position of the search conditions is not important. The product generated code in that format because this was the execution plan used by the simple compiler.

Having said this, separating the conditions this way can have some advantages for documentation. It becomes easy to remove the WHERE clause and have a candidate for a VIEW. But there are trade-offs.

26.3 OUTER JOINs

OUTER JOINs used to be done with proprietary vendor syntax. Today, the use of the Standard OUTER JOIN is universal. An OUTER JOIN is a JOIN that preserves all the rows in one or both tables, even when they do not have matching rows in the second table. The unmatched columns in the unpreserved table (this is the correct term) are filled with NULLs to complete the join and return rows with the right structure.

Let's take a real-world situation. I have a table of orders and a table of suppliers that I wish to JOIN for a report to tell us how much business we did with each supplier. With a traditional inner join, the query would be this:

```
SELECT S.sup_id, S.sup_name, O.order_nbr, O.order_amt
  FROM Suppliers AS S, Orders AS O
 WHERE S.sup_id = O.sup_id;
```

or with the infixed syntax

```
SELECT S.sup_id, S.sup_name, O.order_nbr, O.order_amt
  FROM Suppliers AS S -- preserved table
       INNER JOIN
       Orders AS O
       ON S.sup_id = O.sup_id;
```

Some supplier totals include credits for returned merchandise, and our total business with them works out to zero dollars. Other suppliers never got an order from us at all, so we did zero dollars worth of business with them, too. But the first case will show up in the query result and be passed on to the report, whereas the second case will disappear in the INNER JOIN.

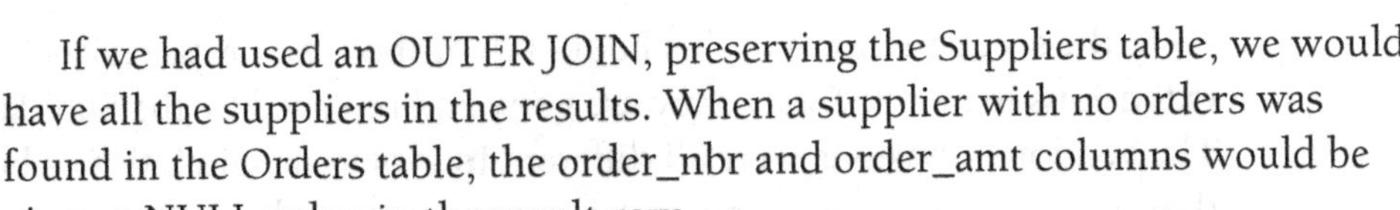
If we had used an OUTER JOIN, preserving the Suppliers table, we would have all the suppliers in the results. When a supplier with no orders was found in the Orders table, the order_nbr and order_amt columns would be given a NULL value in the result row.

```
SELECT S.sup_id, S.sup_name, O.order_nbr, O.order_amt
  FROM Suppliers AS S
       OUTER LEFT JOIN
       Orders AS O
       ON S.sup_id = O.sup_id;
```

26.3.1 A Bit of History

Before the SQL-99 Standard, there was no Standard OUTER JOIN syntax, so you had to construct it by hand with a messy UNION in products like very early versions of DB2 from IBM like this:

```
SELECT sup_id, sup_name, order_amt -- regular INNER JOIN
  FROM Suppliers, Orders
 WHERE Suppliers.sup_id = Orders.sup_id
UNION ALL
SELECT sup_id, sup_name, CAST(NULL AS INTEGER) -- preserved rows
  FROM Suppliers
 WHERE NOT EXISTS
      (SELECT *
         FROM Orders
        WHERE Suppliers.sup_id = Orders.sup_id);
```

You have to use a NULL with the correct data type to make the UNION work, hence the CAST() functions. Some products are smart enough that just NULL by itself will be given the correct data type, but this is portable and safer.

The other alternative is to insert a constant of some sort to give a more meaningful result. This is easy in the case of a CHARACTER column, where a message like '{{NONE}}' can be quickly understood. It is much harder in the case of a numeric column, where we could have a balance with a supplier that is positive, zero, or negative because of returns and credits. There really is a difference between a vendor that we did not use and a vendor whose returns and credits canceled out its orders.

In the second edition of this book, I described the proprietary OUTER JOIN extensions in detail. Today, they are gone and replaced by the Standard syntax. The vendor extensions were all different in syntax or semantics or both. Since they are mercifully gone, I am not going to tell you about them in this edition.

The name LEFT OUTER JOIN comes from the fact that the preserved table is on the left side of the operator. Likewise, a RIGHT OUTER JOIN would have the preserved table on the right-hand side and the FULL OUTER JOIN preserves both tables.

Here is how OUTER JOINs work in Standard SQL. Assume you are given:

Table1

a	b
1	w
2	x
3	y
4	z

Table2

a	c
1	r
2	s
3	t

and the OUTER JOIN expression

```
Table1
LEFT OUTER JOIN
Table2
ON Table1.a = Table2.a -- JOIN condition
   AND Table2.c = 't'; -- single table filter condition
```

We call Table1 the "preserved table" and Table2 the "unpreserved table" in the query. What I am going to give you is a little different, but equivalent to the ANSI/ISO standards.

(1) We build the CROSS JOIN of the two tables. Scan each row in the result set.

(2) If all search conditions in the ON clause test TRUE for that row, then you keep it.

(3) If the predicate tests FALSE or UNKNOWN for that row, then keep the columns from the preserved table, convert all the columns from the unpreserved table to NULLs and remove the duplicates. So let us execute this by hand:

Let ◄ = passed the join search condition
Let ● = passed the filter search condition
Step One and two:

Table1 CROSS JOIN Table2

a	b	a	c	Notes
1	w	1	r	◄
1	w	2	s	
1	w	3	t	●
2	x	1	r	
2	x	2	s	◄
2	x	3	t	●
3	y	1	r	
3	y	2	s	
3	y	3	t	◄ ●
4	z	1	r	
4	z	2	s	
4	z	3	t	●

Step three:

Table1 LEFT OUTER JOIN Table2

a	b	a	c	Notes
3	y	3	t	◄ row(s)from step two
1	w	NULL	NULL	Sets of duplicates
1	w	NULL	NULL	
1	w	NULL	NULL	
2	x	NULL	NULL	
2	x	NULL	NULL	
2	x	NULL	NULL	
3	y	NULL	NULL	◄ removed in step two
3	y	NULL	NULL	◄ removed in step two
4	z	NULL	NULL	
4	z	NULL	NULL	
4	z	NULL	NULL	

the final results:

Table1 LEFT OUTER JOIN Table2

a	b	a	c
1	w	NULL	NULL
2	x	NULL	NULL
3	y	3	t
4	z	NULL	NULL

The basic rule is that every row in the preserved table is represented in the results in at least one result row.

Consider the two famous Chris Date tables from his "Suppliers and Parts" database used in his textbooks.

SupParts

sup_id	part_nbr	part_qty
S1	P1	100
S1	P2	250
S2	P1	100
S2	P2	250

Suppliers

sup_id
S1
S2
S3

If you write the OUTER JOIN with only the join predicate in the ON clause, like this:

```
SELECT Suppliers.sup_id, SupParts.part_nbr, SupParts.part_qty
  FROM Suppliers
       LEFT OUTER JOIN
       SupParts
       ON Supplier.sup_id = SupParts.sup_id
 WHERE part_qty < 200;
```

You get:

sup_id	part_nbr	part_qty
S1	P1	100
S2	P1	100

but if we put the search predicate in the ON clause, we get this result.

```
SELECT Suppliers.sup_id, SupParts.part_nbr, SupParts.part_qty
  FROM Suppliers
       LEFT OUTER JOIN
       SupParts
       ON Supplier.sup_id = SupParts.sup_id
          AND part_qty < 200;
```

You get:

sup_id	part_nbr	part_qty
S1	P1	100
S2	P1	100
S3	NULL	NULL

Another problem was that you could not show the same table as preserved and unpreserved in the proprietary syntax options, but it is easy in Standard SQL. For example, to find the students who have taken Math 101 and might have taken Math 102:

```
SELECT C1.stud_nbr, C1.math_course, C2.math_course
  FROM (SELECT * FROM Courses WHERE math_course = 'Math 101') AS C1
       LEFT OUTER JOIN
       (SELECT * FROM Courses WHERE math_course = 'Math 102') AS C2
       ON C1.stud_nbr = C2.stud_nbr;
```

A third problem is that the order of execution matters with a chain of OUTER JOINs. That is to say, ((T1 OUTER JOIN T2) OUTER JOIN T3) does not produce the same results as (T1 OUTER JOIN (T2 OUTER JOIN T3)).

26.3.2 NULLs and OUTER JOINs

The NULLs that are generated by the OUTER JOIN can occur in columns derived from source table columns that have been declared to be NOT NULL. Even if you tried to avoid all the problems with NULLs by making every column in every table of your schema NOT NULL, they could still occur in OUTER JOIN and OLAP function results. However, a table can have NULLs and still be used in an OUTER JOIN. Consider different JOINs on the following two tables, which have NULLs in the common column:

T1

a	x
1	r
2	v
3	NULL

T2

b	x
7	r
8	s
9	NULL

A natural INNER JOIN on column x can only match those values that are equal to each other. But NULLs do not match to anything, even to other NULLs. Thus, there is one row in the result, on the value r in column x in both tables.

Now, do a LEFT OUTER JOIN on the tables, which will preserve table T1, and you get

T1 LEFT OUTER JOIN T2 ON T1.x = T2.x

a	T1.x	b	T2.x
1	r	7	r
2	v	NULL	NULL
3	NULL	NULL	NULL

Again, there are no surprises. The original INNER JOIN row is still in the results. The other two rows of T1 that were not in the equi-JOIN do show up in the results, and the columns derived from table T2 are filled with NULLs. The RIGHT OUTER JOIN would also behave the same way. The problems start with the FULL OUTER JOIN, which looks like this:

T1 FULL OUTER JOIN T2 ON (T1.x=T2.x)

a	T1.x	b	T2.x
1	r	7	r
2	v	NULL	NULL
3	NULL	NULL	NULL
NULL	NULL	8	s
NULL	NULL	9	NULL

The way this result is constructed is worth explaining in detail.

First do an INNER JOIN on T1 and T2, using the ON clause condition, and put those rows (if any) in the results. Then all rows in T1 that could not be joined are padded out with NULLs in the columns derived from T2 and inserted into the results. Finally, take the rows in T2 that could not be joined, pad them out with NULLs, and insert them into the results. The bad news is that the original tables cannot be reconstructed from an OUTER JOIN. Look at the results of the FULL OUTER JOIN, which we will call R1, and SELECT the first columns from it:

```
SELECT T1.a, T1.x FROM R1
```

a	x
1	r
2	v
3	NULL
NULL	NULL
NULL	NULL

The created NULLs remain and could not be differentiated from the original NULLs. But you cannot throw out those duplicate rows because they may be in the original table T1. There is now a function, GROUPING (<column name>), used with the CUBE, ROLLUP, and GROUPING SET() options which returns a 1 for original NULLs or data and 0 for created NULLs. Your vendor may allow this function to be used with the OUTER JOINs.

26.3.3 NATURAL Versus Searched OUTER JOINs

It is worth mentioning in passing that Standard SQL has a NATURAL LEFT OUTER JOIN, but it is not implemented in most versions of SQL.

A NATURAL JOIN has only one copy of the common column pairs in its result. The searched OUTER JOIN has both of the original columns, with their table-qualified names. The NATURAL JOIN has to have a correlation name for the result table to identify the shared columns. We can build a NATURAL LEFT OUTER JOIN by using the COALESCE() function to combine the common column pairs into a single column and put the results into a VIEW where the columns can be properly named, thus:

```
CREATE VIEW NLOJ12 (x, a, b)
AS SELECT COALESCE(T1.x, T2.x), T1.a, T2.b
     FROM T1 LEFT OUTER JOIN T2 ON T1.x = T2.x;
```

NLOJ12

x	a	b
r	1	7
v	2	NULL
NULL	3	NULL

Unlike the NATURAL JOINs, the searched OUTER JOIN does not have to use a simple one-column equality as the JOIN search condition. The search condition can have several search conditions, use other comparisons, and so forth. For example,

T1 LEFT OUTER JOIN T2 ON (T1.x < T2.x)

a	T1.x	b	T2.x
1	r	8	s
2	v	NULL	NULL
3	NULL	NULL	NULL

as compared to

T1 LEFT OUTER JOIN T2 ON (T1.x > T2.x)

a	T1.x	b	T2.x
1	r	NULL	NULL
2	v	7	r
2	v	8	s
3	NULL	NULL	NULL

26.3.4 Self OUTER JOINs

There is no rule that forbids an OUTER JOIN on the same table. In fact, this kind of self-join is a good trick for "flattening" a normalized table into a horizontal report. To illustrate the method, start with a skeleton table defined as

```
CREATE TABLE Credits
(student_nbr INTEGER NOT NULL,
 course_name CHAR(8) NOT NULL,
 PRIMARY KEY (student_nbr, course_name));
```

This table represents student ids and a course name for each class they have taken. However, our rules say that students cannot get credit for 'CS-102' until they have taken the prerequisite 'CS-101' course; they cannot get credit for 'CS-103' until they have taken the prerequisite 'CS-102' course, and so forth. Let's first load the table with some sample values.

Notice that student #10 has both courses, student #20 has only the first of the series, and student #3 jumped ahead of sequence and therefore cannot get credit for his 'CS-102' course until he goes back and takes 'CS-101' as a prerequisite.

Credits

student_nbr	course_name
1	CS-101
1	CS-102
2	CS-101
3	CS-102

What we want is basically a histogram (bar chart) for each student, showing how far he or she has gone in his or her degree programs. Assume that we are only looking at two courses; the result of the desired query might look like this (NULL is used to represent a missing value):

```
(1, 'CS-101', 'CS-102')
(2, 'CS-101', NULL)
```

Clearly, this will need a self-JOIN, since the last two columns come from the same table, Credits. You have to give correlation names to both uses of the Credits table in the OUTER JOIN operator when you construct a self OUTER JOIN, just as you would with any other SELF-JOIN, thus:

```
SELECT student_nbr, C1.course_name, C2.course_name
  FROM Credits AS C1
       LEFT OUTER JOIN
       Credits AS C2
       ON C1.stud_nbr_nbr = C2.stud_nbr_nbr
          AND C1.course_name = 'CS-101'
          AND C2.course_name = 'CS-102';
```

26.3.5 Two or More OUTER JOINs

Some relational purists feel that every operator should have an inverse, and therefore they do not like the OUTER JOIN. Others feel that the created NULLs are fundamentally different from the explicit NULLs in a base table and should have a special token. SQL uses its general-purpose NULLs and leaves things at that. Getting away from theory, you will also find that vendors have often done strange things with the ways their products work.

A major problem is that OUTER JOIN operators do not have the same properties as INNER JOIN operators. The order in which FULL OUTER JOINs are executed will change the results (a mathematician would say that they are not associative). To show some of the problems that can come up when you have more than two tables, let us use three very simple two column tables. Notice that some of the column values match and some do not match, but the three tables have all possible pairs of column names in them.

```
CREATE TABLE T1 (a INTEGER NOT NULL, b INTEGER NOT NULL);
INSERT INTO T1 VALUES (1, 2);

CREATE TABLE T2 (a INTEGER NOT NULL, c INTEGER NOT NULL);
INSERT INTO T2 VALUES (1, 3);

CREATE TABLE T3 (b INTEGER NOT NULL, c INTEGER NOT NULL);
INSERT INTO T3 VALUES (2, 100);
```

Now let's try some of the possible orderings of the three tables in a chain of LEFT OUTER JOINS. The problem is that a table can be preserved or unpreserved in the immediate JOIN and in the opposite state in the containing JOIN.

```
SELECT T1.a, T1.b, T3.c
  FROM ((T1 NATURAL LEFT OUTER JOIN T2)
       NATURAL LEFT OUTER JOIN T3);
```

Result

a	b	c
1	2	NULL

```
SELECT T1.a, T1.b, T3.c
  FROM ((T1 NATURAL LEFT OUTER JOIN T3)
       NATURAL LEFT OUTER JOIN T2);
```

Result

a	b	c
1	2	100

```
SELECT T1.a, T1.b, T3.c
  FROM ((T1 NATURAL LEFT OUTER JOIN T3)
       NATURAL LEFT OUTER JOIN T2);
```

Result

a	b	c
NULL	NULL	NULL

Even worse, the choice of column, in the SELECT list can change the output. Instead of displaying T3.c, use T2.c and you will get:

```
SELECT T1.a, T1.b, T2.c
  FROM ((T2 NATURAL LEFT OUTER JOIN T3)
       NATURAL LEFT OUTER JOIN T1);
```

Result

a	b	c
NULL	NULL	3

The compiler should give you error messages about ambiguous column names.

26.3.6 OUTER JOINs and Aggregate Functions

At the start of this chapter, we had a table of orders and a table of suppliers, which were to be used to build a report to tell us how much business we did with each supplier. The query that will do this is

```
SELECT Suppliers.sup_id, sup_name, SUM(order_amt)
  FROM Suppliers
       LEFT OUTER JOIN
       Orders
       ON Suppliers.sup_id = Orders.sup_id
 GROUP BY sup_id, sup_name;
```

Some suppliers' totals include credits for returned merchandise, such that our total business with them worked out to zero dollars. Each supplier with which we did no business will have a NULL in its order_amt column in the OUTER JOIN. The usual rules for aggregate functions with NULL values apply, so these suppliers will also show a zero total amount. It is also possible to use a function inside an aggregate function, so you could write SUM(COALESCE(T1.x, T2.x)) for the common column pairs.

If you need to tell the difference between a true sum of zero and the result of a NULL in an OUTER JOIN, use the MIN() or MAX() function on the questionable column. These functions both return a NULL result for a NULL input, so an expression inside the MAX() function could be used to print the message MAX(COALESCE(order_amt, 'No Orders')), for example.

Likewise, these functions could be used in a HAVING clause, but that would defeat the purpose of an OUTER JOIN.

26.3.7 FULL OUTER JOIN

The FULL OUTER JOIN is a mix of the LEFT and RIGHT OUTER JOINs, with preserved rows constructed from both tables. The statement takes two tables and puts them in one result table. Again, this is easier to explain with an example than with a formal definition.

T1

a	x
1	r
2	v
3	NULL

T2

b	x
7	r
8	s
9	NULL

T1 FULL OUTER JOIN T2 ON (T1.x = T2.x)

a	T1.x	b	T2.x	notes
1	r	7	r	-- T1 INNER JOIN T2
2	v	NULL	NULL	-- preserved from T1
3	NULL	NULL	NULL	-- preserved from T1
NULL	NULL	8	s	-- preserved from T2
NULL	NULL	9	NULL	-- preserved from T2

26.4 UNION JOIN Operators

There is also a UNION JOIN in Standard SQL which returns the results of a FULL OUTER JOIN without the rows that were in the INNER JOIN of the two tables. The only SQL product which has implemented it as of 2014 is MariaDB (www.mariadb.com) and it is part of the SAS statistical system (www.sas.com) in the PROC SQL options.

T1 UNION JOIN T2 ON(T1.x = T2.x)

a	T1.x	b	T2.x	Notes
2	v	NULL	NULL	-- preserved from T1
3	NULL	NULL	NULL	-- preserved from T1
NULL	NULL	8	s	-- preserved from T2
NULL	NULL	9	NULL	-- preserved from T2

As an example of this, you might want to combine the medical records of male and female patients into one table with this query.

```
SELECT *
  FROM (SELECT 'male', prostate_flg FROM Males)
        OUTER UNION
       (SELECT 'female', pregnancy_flg FROM Females);
```

to get a result table like this

Result

male	prostate_flg	female	pregnancy_flg
'male'	'no'	NULL	NULL
'male'	'no'	NULL	NULL
'male'	'yes'	NULL	NULL
'male'	'yes'	NULL	NULL
NULL	NULL	'female'	'no'
NULL	NULL	'female'	'no'
NULL	NULL	'female'	'yes'
NULL	NULL	'female'	'yes'

Frédéric Brouard came up with a nice trick for writing a similar join. That is, a join on one table, say a basic table of student data, with either a table of data particular to domestic students or another table of data particular to foreign students, based on the value of a parameter. This is one way to handle sub-types and supper-types in SQL. This differs from a true UNION JOIN in that it has to have a "root" table to use for the outer JOINs.

```
CREATE TABLE Students
(student_nbr INTEGER NOT NULL PRIMARY KEY,
 student_type CHAR(1) NOT NULL DEFAULT 'D'
     CHECK (student_type IN ('D', 2, ..))
...);

CREATE TABLE Domestic_Students
(student_nbr INTEGER NOT NULL PRIMARY KEY,
     REFERENCES Students(student_nbr),
...);

CREATE TABLE Foreign_Students
(student_nbr INTEGER NOT NULL PRIMARY KEY,
     REFERENCES Students(student_nbr),
...);

SELECT Students.*, Domestic_Students.*, Foreign_Students.*
  FROM Students
       LEFT OUTER JOIN
       Domestic_Students
```

```
ON CASE Students.stud_type
   WHEN 'D' THEN 1 ELSE NULL END
   = 1
   LEFT OUTER JOIN
   Foreign_Students
   ON CASE Student.stud_type WHEN 2 THEN 1 ELSE NULL END
     = 1;
```

26.5 Scalar SELECT Expressions

A SELECT expression that returns a single row with a single value can be used where a scalar expression can be used. If the result of the scalar query is empty, it is converted to a NULL. This will sometimes, but not always, let you write an OUTER JOIN as a query within the SELECT clause; thus, this query will work only if each supplier has one or zero orders:

```
SELECT sup_id, sup_name, order_nbr,
       (SELECT order_amt
          FROM Orders
         WHERE Suppliers.sup_id = Orders.sup_id)
       AS order_amt
  FROM Suppliers;
```

However, I could write

```
SELECT sup_id, sup_name,
       (SELECT COUNT(*)
          FROM Orders
         WHERE Suppliers.sup_id = Orders.sup_id)
  FROM Suppliers;
```

instead of writing

```
SELECT sup_id, sup_name, COUNT(*)
  FROM Suppliers
       LEFT OUTER JOIN
       Orders
       ON Suppliers.sup_id = Orders.sup_id
 GROUP BY sup_id, sup_name;
```

26.6 Old Versus New JOIN Syntax

The infixed OUTER JOIN syntax was meant to replace *several different* vendor options which all had different syntax and semantics. It was absolutely needed. The INNER JOIN and OUTER JOIN operators are universal now. They are binary operators and programmers are used to binary operators—add, subtract, multiply, and divide are all binary operators. E-R diagrams use lines between tables to show a relational schema.

But this leads to a linear approach to problem solving that might not be such a good thing in SQL. Consider this statement which would have been written in the traditional syntax as:

```
SELECT a, b, c
 FROM Foo, Bar, Flub
 WHERE Foo.y BETWEEN Bar.x AND Flub.z;
```

With the infixed syntax, I can write this same statement in any of several ways. For example:

```
SELECT a, b, c
  FROM (Foo
       INNER JOIN
       Bar
       ON Foo.y >= Bar.x)
        INNER JOIN
        Flub
        ON Foo.y <= Flub.z;
```

or

```
SELECT a, b, c
  FROM Foo
       INNER JOIN
       (Bar
        INNER JOIN
        Flub
        ON Foo.y <= Flub.z)
        ON Foo.y >= Bar.x;
```

I leave it to the reader to find all the permutations, with or without the parentheses.

Humans tend to see things that are close together as a unit or as having a relationship. It is a law of visual psychology and typesetting called the Law of Proximity. The extra reserved words in the infixed notation tend to work against proximity; you have to look in many places to find the parts of a.

The infixed notation invites a programmer to add one table at a time to the chain of JOINs. First I built and tested the Foo-Bar join and when I was happy with the results, I added Flub. Step-wise program refinement was one of the mantras of structured programming.

But look at the code; can you see that there is a BETWEEN relationship among the three tables? It is not easy, is it? In effect, you see only *pairs of tables* and not the *whole* problem. SQL is an "all-at-once" set-oriented language, not a "step-wise" language. This is much like the conceptual difference between addition with a simple binary+operator and the generalized n-ary summation operator with a Σ.

I am against infixed JOINs? No, but it is a bit more complicated than it first appears and if there are some OUTER JOINs in the mix, things can be very complicated. Just be careful with the new toys, kids.

26.7 Constrained Joins

We can relate two tables together based on quantities in each of them. These problems take the form of pairing items in one set with items in another. The extra restriction is that the set of pairs has constraints at the level of the result which a row-by-row join does not. Here the values are identifiers and cannot be repeated in the results.

Let us assume we have two tables, X and Y. Some possible situations are:

1. A row in X matches one and only one row in Y. There can be one matching function that applies to one set, or each set can have its own matching function.

An example of one matching function is an optimization with constraints. For example, you are filling an egg carton with a set of colored eggs given rules about how the colors can be arranged. A lot of logic puzzles use this model.

The classic example of two matching functions is the Stable Marriages problem where the men rank the women they want to marry and where the women rank the men they want to marry.

2. A row in X matches one or more rows in Y: knapsack or bin packing problems where one bin holds one or more items and we try to optimize the arrangement.

In all cases, there can be a unique answer or several answers or no valid answer at all. Let's give some examples and code for them.

26.7.1 Inventory and Orders

The simplest example is filling customer orders from the inventories that we have at various stores. To make life easier, assume that we have only one product, process orders in increasing customer_id order (this could be temporal order as well), and draw from store inventory by increasing store_id (this could be nearest store).

```
CREATE TABLE Inventory
(store_id INTEGER NOT NULL PRIMARY KEY,
 item_qty INTEGER NOT NULL CHECK (item_qty >=0));

INSERT INTO Inventory (store_id, item_qty)
VALUES (10, 2), (20, 3), (30, 2);

CREATE TABLE Orders
(customer_id CHAR(5) NOT NULL PRIMARY KEY,
 item_qty INTEGER NOT NULL CHECK (item_qty > 0));

INSERT INTO Orders (customer_id, item_qty)
VALUES ('Bill', 4), ('Fred', 2);
```

What we want to do is fill Bill's order for 4 units by taking 2 units from store #10, and 2 units from store #20. Next, we process Fred's order with the 1 unit left in store #10 and 1 unit from store #3.

```
SELECT I.store_id, O.customer_id,
       (CASE WHEN O.end_running_qty <= I.end_running_qty
             THEN O.end_running_qty
             ELSE I.end_running_qty END
       - CASE WHEN O.start_running_qty >=I.start_running_qty
             THEN O.start_running_qty
             ELSE I.start_running_qty END)
       AS items_consumed_tally
 FROM (SELECT I1.store_id,
             SUM(I2.item_qty) - I1.item_qty,
             SUM(I2.item_qty)
        FROM Inventory AS I1, Inventory AS I2
       WHERE I2.store_id <= I1.store_id
```

```
 GROUP BY I1.store_id, I1.item_qty)
AS I (store_id, start_running_qty, end_running_qty)
INNER JOIN
(SELECT O1.customer_id,
      SUM(O2.item_qty) - O1.item_qty,
      SUM(O2.item_qty) AS end_running_qty
   FROM Orders AS O1, Orders AS O2
  WHERE O2.customer_id <= O1.customer_id
 GROUP BY O1.customer_id, O1.item_qty)
AS O(customer_id, start_running_qty, end_running_qty)
ON O.start_running_qty < I.end_running_qty
   AND O.end_running_qty > I.start_running_qty;
```

store_id	customer_id	items_consumed_tally
10	Bill	2
20	Bill	2
20	Fred	1
30	Fred	1

This can also be done with ordinal functions.

26.7.2 Stable Marriages

This is a classic programming problem from procedural language classes. The set up is fairly simple; you have a set of potential husbands and an equal sized set of potential wives. We want to pair them up into stable marriages.

What is a stable marriage? In 25 words or less, a marriage in which neither partner can do better. You have a set of *n* men and a set of *n* women. All the men have a preference scale for all the women that ranks them from 1 to *n* without gaps or ties. The women have the same ranking system for the men. The goal is to pair off the men and women into *n* marriages such that there is no pair in your final arrangement where Mr. X and Ms. Y are matched to each other when they both would rather be matched to someone else.

For example, let's assume the husbands are ('Joe Celko,' 'Brad Pitt') and the wives are ('Jackie Celko,' 'Angelina Jolie'). If Jackie got matched to Mr. Pitt, she would be quite happy. And I would enjoy Ms. Jolie's company. However, Mr. Pitt and Ms. Jolie can both do better than us. Once they are paired up, they will stay that way, leaving Jackie and me still wed.

The classic Stable Marriage algorithms usually are based on backtracking. These algorithms try a combination of couples and then attempt to fix any unhappy matches. When the algorithm hits on a situation where nobody can improve their situation, they stop and give an answer.

Two important things to know about this problem: (1) there is always a solution and (2) there is often more than one solution. Remember that a stable marriage is not always a happy marriage. In fact, in this problem, while there is always at least one arrangement of stable marriages in any set, you most often find many different pairings that produce a set of stable marriages. Each set of marriages will tend to maximize either the happiness of the men or the women.

```
CREATE TABLE Husbands
(man CHAR(2) NOT NULL,
 woman CHAR(2) NOT NULL,
 PRIMARY KEY (man, woman),
 ranking INTEGER NOT NULL);

CREATE TABLE Wives
(woman CHAR(2) NOT NULL,
 man CHAR(2) NOT NULL,
 PRIMARY KEY (woman, man),
 ranking INTEGER NOT NULL);

CREATE TABLE Wife_Perms
(perm INTEGER NOT NULL PRIMARY KEY,
 wife_name CHAR(2) NOT NULL);

-- The men's preferences
INSERT INTO Husbands -- husband #10
VALUES ('h1', 'w1', 5), ('h1', 'w2', 2),
('h1', 'w3', 6), ('h1', 'w4', 8),
('h1', 'w5', 4), ('h1', 'w6', 3),
('h1', 'w7', 1), ('h1', 'w8', 7);

INSERT INTO Husbands -- husband #20
VALUES ('h2', 'w1', 6), ('h2', 'w2', 3),
('h2', 'w3', 2), ('h2', 'w4', 1),
('h2', 'w5', 8), ('h2', 'w6', 4),
('h2', 'w7', 7), ('h2', 'w8', 5);
```

```
INSERT INTO Husbands -- husband #3
VALUES ('h3', 'w1', 4), ('h3', 'w2', 2),
('h3', 'w3', 1), ('h3', 'w4', 3),
('h3', 'w5', 6), ('h3', 'w6', 8),
('h3', 'w7', 7), ('h3', 'w8', 5);

INSERT INTO Husbands -- husband #4
VALUES ('h4', 'w1', 8), ('h4', 'w2', 4),
('h4', 'w3', 1), ('h4', 'w4', 3),
('h4', 'w5', 5), ('h4', 'w6', 6),
('h4', 'w7', 7), ('h4', 'w8', 2);

INSERT INTO Husbands -- husband #5
VALUES ('h5', 'w1', 6), ('h5', 'w2', 8),
('h5', 'w3', 2), ('h5', 'w4', 3),
('h5', 'w5', 4), ('h5', 'w6', 5),
('h5', 'w7', 7), ('h5', 'w8', 1);

INSERT INTO Husbands -- husband #6
VALUES ('h6', 'w1', 7), ('h6', 'w2', 4),
('h6', 'w3', 6), ('h6', 'w4', 5),
('h6', 'w5', 3), ('h6', 'w6', 8),
('h6', 'w7', 2), ('h6', 'w8', 1);

INSERT INTO Husbands -- husband #7
VALUES ('h7', 'w1', 5), ('h7', 'w2', 1),
('h7', 'w3', 4), ('h7', 'w4', 2),
('h7', 'w5', 7), ('h7', 'w6', 3),
('h7', 'w7', 6), ('h7', 'w8', 8);

INSERT INTO Husbands -- husband #8
VALUES ('h8', 'w1', 2), ('h8', 'w2', 4),
('h8', 'w3', 7), ('h8', 'w4', 3),
('h8', 'w5', 6), ('h8', 'w6', 1),
('h8', 'w7', 5), ('h8', 'w8', 8);

-- The women's preferences
INSERT INTO Wives -- wife #1
VALUES ('w1', 'h1', 6), ('w1', 'h2', 3),
 ('w1', 'h3', 7), ('w1', 'h4', 1),
```

```
('w1', 'h5', 4), ('w1', 'h6', 2),
 ('w1', 'h7', 8), ('w1', 'h8', 5);

INSERT INTO Wives -- wife #2
VALUES ('w2', 'h1', 4), ('w2', 'h2', 8),
 ('w2', 'h3', 3), ('w2', 'h4', 7),
 ('w2', 'h5', 2), ('w2', 'h6', 5),
 ('w2', 'h7', 6), ('w2', 'h8', 1);

INSERT INTO Wives -- wife #3
VALUES ('w3', 'h1', 3), ('w3', 'h2', 4),
 ('w3', 'h3', 5), ('w3', 'h4', 6),
 ('w3', 'h5', 8), ('w3', 'h6', 1),
 ('w3', 'h7', 7), ('w3', 'h8', 2);

INSERT INTO Wives -- wife #4
VALUES ('w4', 'h1', 8), ('w4', 'h2', 2),
 ('w4', 'h3', 1), ('w4', 'h4', 3),
 ('w4', 'h5', 7), ('w4', 'h6', 5),
 ('w4', 'h7', 4), ('w4', 'h8', 6);

INSERT INTO Wives -- wife #5
VALUES ('w5', 'h1', 3), ('w5', 'h2', 7),
 ('w5', 'h3', 2), ('w5', 'h4', 4),
 ('w5', 'h5', 5), ('w5', 'h6', 1),
 ('w5', 'h7', 6), ('w5', 'h8', 8);

INSERT INTO Wives -- wife #6
VALUES ('w6', 'h1', 2), ('w6', 'h2', 1),
 ('w6', 'h3', 3), ('w6', 'h4', 6),
 ('w6', 'h5', 8), ('w6', 'h6', 7),
 ('w6', 'h7', 5), ('w6', 'h8', 4);

INSERT INTO Wives -- wife #7
VALUES ('w7', 'h1', 6), ('w7', 'h2', 4),
 ('w7', 'h3', 1), ('w7', 'h4', 5),
 ('w7', 'h5', 2), ('w7', 'h6', 8),
 ('w7', 'h7', 3), ('w7', 'h8', 7);

INSERT INTO Wives -- wife #8
VALUES ('w8', 'h1', 8), ('w8', 'h2', 2),
 ('w8', 'h3', 7), ('w8', 'h4', 4),
```

```
 ('w8', 'h5', 5), ('w8', 'h6', 6),
 ('w8', 'h7', 1), ('w8', 'h8', 3);

-- This auxiliary table helps us create all permutations of the wives.
INSERT INTO Wife_Perms
VALUES (1, 'w1'), (2, 'w2'), (4, 'w3'), (8, 'w4'),
       (16, 'w5'), (32, 'w6'), (64, 'w7'), (128, 'w8');
```

The query builds all permutation of wives and then filters them for blocking pairs in an elaborate NOT EXISTS() predicate.

```
SELECT A.wife_name AS h1, B.wife_name AS h2,
       C.wife_name AS h3, D.wife_name AS h4,
       E.wife_name AS h5, F.wife_name AS h6,
       G.wife_name AS h7, H.wife_name AS h8
  FROM Wife_Perms AS A, Wife_Perms AS B,
       Wife_Perms AS C, Wife_Perms AS D,
       Wife_Perms AS E, Wife_Perms AS F,
       Wife_Perms AS G, Wife_Perms AS H
 WHERE A.perm + B.perm + C.perm + D.perm
        + E.perm + F.perm + G.perm + H.perm = 255
   AND NOT EXISTS
     (SELECT *
        FROM Husbands AS W, Husbands AS X, Wives AS Y, Wives AS Z
       WHERE W.man = X.man
         AND W.ranking > X.ranking
         AND X.woman = Y.woman
         AND Y.woman = Z.woman
         AND Y.ranking > Z.ranking
         AND Z.man = W.man
         AND W.man||W.woman
            IN ('h1'||A.wife_name, 'h2'||B.wife_name,
                'h3'||C.wife_name, 'h4'||D.wife_name,
                'h5'||E.wife_name, 'h6'||F.wife_name,
                 h7'||G.wife_name, 'h8'||H.wife_name)
       AND Y.man||Y.woman
           IN ('h1'||A.wife_name, 'h2'||B.wife_name,
               'h3'||C.wife_name, 'h4'||D.wife_name,
               'h5'||E.wife_name, 'h6'||F.wife_name,
               'h7'||G.wife_name, 'h8'|| H.wife_name))
```

The results look like this:

h1	h2	h3	h4	h5	h6	h7	h8
w3	w6	w4	w8	w1	w5	w7	w2
w3	w6	w4	w1	w7	w5	w8	w2
w6	w4	w3	w8	w1	w5	w7	w2
w6	w3	w4	w8	w1	w5	w7	w2
w6	w4	w3	w1	w7	w5	w8	w2
w6	w3	w4	w1	w7	w5	w8	w2
w2	w4	w3	w8	w1	w5	w7	w6
w2	w4	w3	w1	w7	w5	w8	w6
w7	w4	w3	w8	w1	w5	w2	w6

REFERENCES:

Gusfierld, Dan and Irving, Robert W. The Stable Marriage Problem: Structure & Algorithms. ISBN 0-262-07118-5.

Knuth, Donald E. CRM Proceedings & Lecture Notes, Vol #10, "Stable Marriage and Its Relation to Other Combinatorial Problems" ISBN 0-8218-0603-3.

This booklet, which reproduces seven expository lectures given by the author in November 1975, is a gentle introduction to the analysis of algorithms using the beautiful theory of stable marriages as a vehicle to explain the basic paradigms of that subject.

Wirth, Nicklaus; Algorithms+Data Structures=Programs. Section 3.6. ISBN 0-13-022418-9

This section gives an answer in Pascal and a short analysis of the algorithm. In particular, I used his data for my example. He gives several answers which give a varying "degrees of happiness" for husbands and wives.

26.7.3 Ball and Box Packing

This example was taken from the BeyondRelational Website SQL Challenge #22 in 2010 January. We have got some boxes and balls. Our job is to put balls into those boxes. But, wait a second. The balls should be filled into the boxes based on some rules and preferences configured by the user. Here are the rules.

1. A box can have only one ball
2. A ball can be placed only in one box

3. Number of balls and number of boxes will always be the same.

4. All boxes should be filled and all balls should be used

5. There will be a configuration table where the preferences of the user will be stored. The preference setting should be followed when putting a ball into a box.

```
CREATE TABLE Boxes
(box_nbr INTEGER NOT NULL PRIMARY KEY,
 box_name VARCHAR(20) NOT NULL);

INSERT INTO Boxes (box_nbr, box_name)
VALUES (1, 'Box 1'), (2, 'Box 2'), (3, 'Box 3'),
       (4, 'Box 4'), (5, 'Box 5'), (6, 'Box 6');

CREATE TABLE Balls
(ball_nbr INTEGER NOT NULL PRIMARY KEY,
 ball_name VARCHAR(20) NOT NULL);

INSERT INTO Balls (ball_name)
VALUES (1, 'Ball 1'), (2, 'Ball 2'), (3, 'Ball 3'),
       (4, 'Ball 4'), (5, 'Ball 5'), (6, 'Ball 6');

CREATE TABLE Preferences
(box_nbr INTEGER NOT NULL
    REFERENCES Boxes (box_nbr),
 ball_nbr INTEGER NOT NULL
    REFERENCES Balls (ball_nbr),
 PRIMARY KEY (box_nbr, ball_nbr));

INSERT INTO Preferences (box_nbr, ball_nbr)
VALUES (1, 1),
       (2, 1), (2, 3),
       (3, 2), (3, 3),
       (4, 1), (4, 2), (4, 3), (4, 4), (4, 5), (4, 6),
       (5, 4), (5, 5),
       (6, 5);

Results
```

box_name	ball_name
1	1
2	3
3	2
4	6
5	4
6	5

This answer is done in parts to expose the logic via CTEs. The Balls_In_Boxes CTE gives us *all* the possible arrangements of six balls in six boxes. This is passed to the Preferred_Balls_In_Boxes CTE to apply the preference rules but allow duplicate balls if two or more boxes want them. Finally, the main query makes sure that we keep only the rows with unique balls.

The use of the IN() predicates to assure that the row has no duplicate columns is easy to extend to any number of items, but a bit bulky to read. But it is remarkably fast in the SQL engines where we tested it.

```
WITH
Balls_In_Boxes (bx1, bx2, bx3, bx4, bx5, bx6)
AS
(SELECT B1.ball_nbr, B2.ball_nbr, B3.ball_nbr,
        B4.ball_nbr, B5.ball_nbr, B6.ball_nbr
   FROM Balls AS B1, Balls AS B2, Balls AS B3,
        Balls AS B4, Balls AS B5, Balls AS B6
  WHERE B1.ball_nbr NOT IN (B2.ball_nbr, B3.ball_nbr, B4.ball_nbr, B5.
ball_nbr, B6.ball_nbr)
    AND B2.ball_nbr NOT IN (B3.ball_nbr, B4.ball_nbr, B5.ball_nbr, B6.
ball_nbr)
    AND B3.ball_nbr NOT IN (B4.ball_nbr, B5.ball_nbr, B6.ball_nbr)
    AND B4.ball_nbr NOT IN (B5.ball_nbr, B6.ball_nbr)
    AND B5.ball_nbr NOT IN (B6.ball_nbr)),

Preferred_Balls_In_Boxes (bx1, bx2, bx3, bx4, bx5, bx6)
AS
(SELECT bx1, bx2, bx3, bx4, bx5, bx6
   FROM Balls_In_Boxes AS BB
  WHERE BB.bx1
        IN (SELECT ball_nbr
```

```
                FROM Preferences AS P
               WHERE box_nbr = 1)
     AND BB.bx2
         IN (SELECT ball_nbr
                FROM Preferences AS P
               WHERE box_nbr = 2)
     AND BB.bx3
         IN (SELECT ball_nbr
                FROM Preferences AS P
               WHERE box_nbr = 3)
     AND BB.bx4
         IN (SELECT ball_nbr
                FROM Preferences AS P
               WHERE box_nbr = 4)
     AND BB.bx5
         IN (SELECT ball_nbr
                FROM Preferences AS P
               WHERE box_nbr = 5)
     AND BB.bx6
         IN (SELECT ball_nbr
                FROM Preferences AS P
               WHERE box_nbr = 6))

SELECT bx1, bx2, bx3, bx4, bx5, bx6
  FROM Preferred_Balls_In_Boxes AS PBB1
 WHERE PBB1.bx NOT IN (PBB2.bx, PBB3.bx, PBB4.bx, PBB5.bx, PBB6.bx)
   AND PBB2.bx NOT IN (PBB3.bx, PBB4.bx, PBB5.bx, PBB6.bx)
   AND PBB3.bx NOT IN (PBB4.bx, PBB5.bx, PBB6.bx)
   AND PBB4.bx NOT IN (PBB5.bx, PBB6.bx)
   AND PBB5.bx NOT IN (PBB6.bx);
```

26.8 Dr. Codd's T-Join

In the Second Version of the relationnal model in 1990, Dr. E. F. Codd introduced a set of new theta operators, called T-operators, which were based on the idea of a best-fit or approximate equality (Codd, 1990). The algorithm for the operators is easier to understand with an example modified from Dr. Codd.

The problem is to assign the classes to the available classrooms. We want (class_size<room_size) to be true after the assignments are made.

This will allow us a few empty seats in each room for late students. We can do this in one of two ways. The first way is to sort the tables in ascending order by classroom size and the number of students in a class. We start with the following tables and load them with the data that follows the DDL.

```
CREATE TABLE Rooms
(room_nbr CHAR(3) NOT NULL PRIMARY KEY,
 room_size INTEGER NOT NULL);
```

Classes

class_nbr	class_size
'c1'	80
'c2'	70
'c3'	65
'c4'	55
'c5'	50
'c6'	40

```
CREATE TABLE Classes
(class_nbr CHAR(3) NOT NULL PRIMARY KEY,
 class_size INTEGER NOT NULL);
```

Rooms

room_nbr	room_size
r1	70
r2	40
r3	50
r4	85
r5	30
r6	65
r7	55

The goal of the T-JOIN problem is to assign a class which is smaller than the classroom given it (class_size<room_size). Dr. Codd gives two approaches to the problem.

(1) Ascending Order Algorithm

Sort both tables into ascending order. Reading from the top of the Rooms table, match each class with the first room that will fit.

Classes

class_nbr	class_size
c6	40
c5	50
c4	55
c3	65
c2	70
c1	80

Rooms

room_nbr	room_size
r5	30
r2	40
r3	50
r7	55
r6	65
r1	70
r4	85

This gives us

Results

Classes		Rooms	
class_nbr	class_size	room_nbr	room_size
c2	70	r4	85
c3	65	r1	70
c4	55	r6	65
c5	50	r7	55
c6	40	r3	50

(2) Descending Order Algorithm

Sort both tables into descending order. Reading from the top of the Classes table, match each class with the first room that will fit.

Classes		Rooms	
class_nbr	class_size	room_nbr	room_size
c1	80	r4	85
c2	70	r1	70
c3	65	r6	65
c4	55	r7	55
c5	50	r3	50
c6	40	r2	40
NULL	NULL	r5	30

Results

class_nbr	class_size	room_nbr	room_size
c1	80	r4	85
c3	65	r1	70
c4	55	r6	65
c5	50	r7	55
c6	40	r3'	50

Notice that the answers are different. Dr. Codd has never given a definition in relational algebra of the T-Join, so I proposed that we need one. Informally, for each class, we want the smallest room that will hold it, while maintaining the T-JOIN condition. Or for each room, we want the largest class that will fill it, while maintaining the T-JOIN condition. These can be two different things, so you must decide which table is the driver. But either way, I am advocating a "best fit" over Codd's "first fit" approach.

Other theta conditions can be used in place of the "less than" shown here. If "less than or equal" is used, all the classes are assigned to a room in this case, but not in all cases. This is left to the reader as an exercise.

The first attempts in Standard SQL are versions of grouped by queries. They can, however, produce some rows that would be left out of the answers Dr. Codd was expecting. The first JOIN can be written as

```
SELECT class_nbr, class_size, MIN(room_size)
  FROM Rooms, Classes
 WHERE Classes.class_size < Rooms.room_size
 GROUP BY class_nbr, class_size;
```

This will give a result table with the desired room sizes, but not the room numbers. You cannot put the other columns in the SELECT list, since it would conflict with the GROUP BY clause. But also note that the classroom with 85 seats ('r4') is used twice, once by class 'c1' and then by class 'c2':

class_size	class_size	MIN(room_size)	Notes
c1	80	85	◄ room r4
c2	70	85	◄ room r4
c3	65	70	
c4	55	65	
c5	50	55	
c6	40	50	

If you do a little arithmetic on the data, you find that we have 360 students and 395 seats, 6 classes and 7 rooms. Do you want to use the smallest number of rooms?

As it works out, the best fit of rooms to classes will leave the smallest room empty and pack the other rooms to capacity, thus:

```
SELECT class_nbr, class_size, MIN(room_size)
  FROM Rooms, Classes
 WHERE Classes.class_size <= Rooms.room_size
 GROUP BY class_nbr, class_size;
```

26.8.1 A Procedural Approach

The place to start is with all the possible legal room assignments for a class. We have already seen this query:

```
SELECT R.room_nbr, C.class_nbr
  FROM Rooms AS R, Classes AS C
 WHERE C.class_size <= R.room_size
 ORDER BY R.room_nbr, C.class_nbr;
```

At the extreme, if all the rooms and classes are the same size, then your have (n!) solutions. If all the rooms are different sizes, we can save ourselves combinatorial explosions, so let us agree that we will juggle the data to get that condition. This query will give us the pairs that are an exact fit, but we know that there will not be any ties for room size.

```
SELECT R.room_nbr, C.class_nbr
  FROM Rooms AS R, Classes AS C
```

```
 WHERE C.class_size <= R.room_size
 GROUP BY R.room_nbr, C.class_nbr
HAVING MIN(R.room_size - C.class_size) = 0;
```

r1	c2
r6	c3
r7	c4
r3	c5
r2	c6

This leaves us with class {c1} and rooms {r4, r5} yet to be used. We can then repeat a limited version of the basic Pairs query.

```
SELECT R.room_nbr, C.class_nbr
  FROM Rooms AS R, Classes AS C
 WHERE C.class_size <= R.room_size
   AND R.room_nbr IN ('r4', 'r5')
   AND C.class_nbr IN ('c1');
```

r4	c1

We can now union these result sets and have an answer. I took some extra time to show the details to demonstrate how we can implement a best-fit, greedy algorithm. Let us get a bigger data set and work with it.

```
INSERT INTO Classes (class_nbr, class_size)
VALUES
('c01', 106), ('c02', 105), ('c03', 104), ('c04', 100), ('c05', 99),
('c06', 90), ('c07', 89), ('c08', 88), ('c09', 83), ('c10', 82),
('c11', 81), ('c12', 65), ('c13', 50), ('c14', 49), ('c15', 30),
('c16', 29), ('c17', 28), ('c18', 20), ('c19', 19);

INSERT INTO Rooms (room_nbr, room_size)
VALUES
('r01', 102), ('r02', 101), ('r03', 95), ('r04', 94), ('r05', 85),
('r06', 70), ('r07', 55), ('r08', 54), ('r09', 35), ('r10', 34),
('r11', 25), ('r12', 18);
```

To see how this will work, let's add another column to the table of legal (class_nbr, room_nbr) pairs to see how well they fit.

```
WITH Pairs (room_nbr, class_nbr, fit)
AS
(SELECT R.room_nbr, C.class_nbr,
       (R.room_size - C.class_size)
  FROM Rooms AS R, Classes AS C
 WHERE C.class_size <= R.room_size)

 SELECT P1.room_nbr, P1.class_nbr, fit
   FROM Pairs AS P1
  WHERE P1.fit
        = (SELECT MIN(P2.fit)
             FROM Pairs AS P2
            WHERE P1.room_nbr = P2.room_nbr);
```

r01	c04	2
r02	c04	1
r03	c06	5
r04	c06	4
r05	c09	2
r06	c12	5
r07	c13	5
r08	c13	4
r09	c15	5
r10	c15	4
r11	c18	5

This time we did not have an exact fit, so let's look for (fit = 1) into a working table and remove 'r02' and 'c04' from their tables. The second step is

r02	c04	1

We can now remove the best fit rooms and classes and look the next set of remaining best fits.

```
WITH Pairs (room_nbr, class_nbr, fit)
AS
(SELECT R.room_nbr, C.class_nbr,
       (R.room_size - C.class_size)
  FROM Rooms AS R, Classes AS C
 WHERE C.class_size <= R.room_size)

(SELECT P1.room_nbr, P1.class_nbr, fit
   FROM Pairs AS P1
  WHERE P1.fit = 2);
```

r05	c09	2

Here is the step for a fit of 3, 4, 5, and 6

r01	c05	3
r04	c06	4
r08	c13	4
r10	c15	4
r06	c12	5
r11	c18	5
r03	c07	6
r07	c14	6
r09	c16	6

At this point, the original tables of rooms and classes cannot be paired. Notice that as we removed rooms and classes, the fit numbers changed. This is a characteristic of greedy algorithms; taking the "big bites" can leave sub-optimal leftovers on the plate.

26.9 Missing Values in Data

In 2014, Dwain Camps published an article on filling gaps in a sequence with the nearest prior value and then doing a linear distribution of the delta (changes). His choice of a name for the problem was the 'Data Smear,' and he found several solutions with window functions. Let's begin with a table of fictional meter reading that is full of gaps.

```
CREATE TABLE Foo_Meters
(reading_nbr INTEGER NOT NULL PRIMARY KEY,
 foo_reading INTEGER NOT NULL);

INSERT INTO Foo_Meters
VALUES
(1, 121), (2, NULL), (3, NULL),
(4, 312), (5, NULL), (6, NULL), (7, NULL),
(8, 123), (9, NULL), (10, NULL),
(11, 415), (12, NULL), (13, NULL), (14, NULL), (15, NULL),
(16, 200);
```

26.9.1 Last Known Value

The number of NULL (unknown) values between known values is not consistently the same. I arranged them on the same line to make it easy to see which values would be carried over which rows.

```
SELECT reading_nbr, foo_reading,
        MAX(foo_reading)
        OVER (PARTITION BY reading_cnt) AS prior_foo_reading
  FROM (SELECT reading_nbr, foo_reading,
               COUNT(foo_reading)
                OVER (ORDER BY reading_nbr) AS reading_cnt
          FROM Foo_Meters)

       AS prior_foo_reading;
```

reading_nbr	foo_reading	prior_foo_reading
1	121	121
2	NULL	121
3	NULL	121
4	312	312
5	NULL	312
6	NULL	312
7	NULL	312

reading_nbr	foo_reading	prior_foo_reading
8	123	123
9	NULL	123
10	NULL	123
11	415	415
12	NULL	415
13	NULL	415
14	NULL	415
15	NULL	415
16	200	200

26.9.2 Sequence Missing Readings

Suppose we want something slightly different filling in the NULL values, for example, a sequence of the same PARTITION we constructed can be used in this case, and so can the ROW_NUMBER in the preceding example.

```
SELECT reading_nbr, foo_reading,
       COALESCE(foo_reading,
                ROW_NUMBER()
                OVER (PARTITION BY c
                          ORDER BY reading_nbr) -1) AS s
  FROM (SELECT reading_nbr, foo_reading,
               COUNT(foo_reading) OVER (ORDER BY reading_nbr) AS c
        FROM Foo_Meters) AS A;
```

Results:

reading_nbr	foo_reading	s
1	121	121
2	NULL	1
3	NULL	2
4	312	312
5	NULL	1
6	NULL	2
7	NULL	3
8	123	123
9	NULL	1

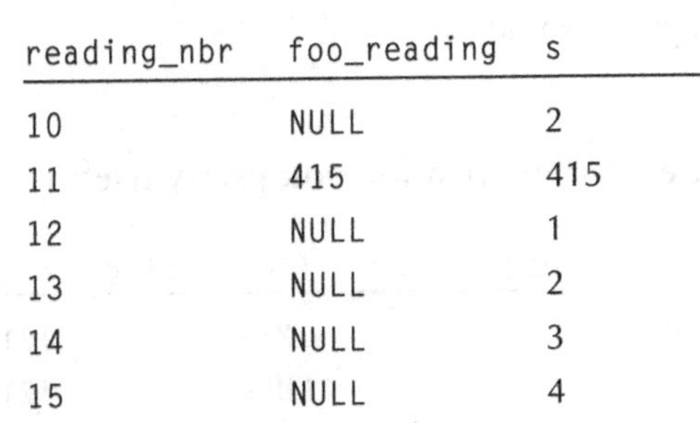

reading_nbr	foo_reading	s
10	NULL	2
11	415	415
12	NULL	1
13	NULL	2
14	NULL	3
15	NULL	4
16	200	200

26.9.3 Smoothed Result

Suppose we want a bit smoother transition from our trailing value to our following value. This could be particularly appealing if we have many NULL rows between sparse data points. Let's illustrate this by looking at the first four rows of the above results set.

reading_nbr	foo_reading	linear_reading
1	121	121
2	NULL	216.500000121+(1/3)*(312-121)=184.6667
3	NULL	216.500000121+(2/3)*(312-121)=248.3333
4	312	312

First let's look at some intermediate results using ROW_NUMBER() and the COUNT window aggregate.

```
SELECT reading_nbr, foo_reading, s, m, x
  FROM (SELECT reading_nbr, foo_reading,
              MAX(foo_reading)
                OVER (PARTITION BY c) AS s,
              ROW_NUMBER()
                OVER (PARTITION BY c ORDER BY reading_nbr DESC) AS n,
              ROW_NUMBER()
                OVER (PARTITION BY c ORDER BY reading_nbr) - 1 AS m,
              1 + COUNT(CASE WHEN foo_reading IS NULL THEN 1 END)
                    OVER (PARTITION BY c) AS x
 FROM (SELECT reading_nbr, foo_reading,
              COUNT(foo_reading) OVER (ORDER BY reading_nbr) AS c
```

```
 FROM Foo_Meters) AS A
) AS A;
```

Our intermediate results look pretty useful:

reading_nbr	foo_reading	s	m	x
1	121	121	0	3
2	NULL	121	1	3
3	NULL	121	2	3
4	312	312	0	4
5	NULL	312	1	4
6	NULL	312	2	4
7	NULL	312	3	4
8	123	123	0	3
9	NULL	123	1	3
10	NULL	123	2	3
11	415	415	0	5
12	NULL	415	1	5
13	NULL	415	2	5
14	NULL	415	3	5
15	NULL	415	4	5
16	200	200	0	1

You can see that all three of our calculated columns are what we need to produce the smoothing calculation shown prior. The first, s, is of course our original smear. The columns m and x, when m is divided by x, produce the multiplier we need. We have omitted the LEAD result, but in the end, we'll use that also (so n is likewise still required).

Putting that all together, we get this.

```
SELECT reading_nbr, foo_reading,
        CASE
        WHEN foo_reading IS NOT NULL
        THEN foo_reading
        ELSE s + (1.0 * m / x)
              * (LEAD(foo_reading, n, s)
               OVER (ORDER BY reading_nbr) - s)
       END AS computed_foo_reading
FROM (SELECT reading_nbr, foo_reading, (MAX(foo_reading) OVER (PARTITION
BY c)) AS s,
```

```
          (ROW_NUMBER() OVER (PARTITION BY c ORDER BY reading_nbr
DESC)) AS n,
          (ROW_NUMBER() OVER (PARTITION BY c ORDER BY reading_nbr) -
1) AS m,
          1 + COUNT(CASE WHEN foo_reading IS NULL
                    THEN 1 ELSE NULL END)
               OVER (PARTITION BY c) AS x
     FROM (SELECT reading_nbr, foo_reading,
                  (COUNT(foo_reading) OVER (ORDER BY reading_nbr)) AS c
              FROM Foo_Meters) AS F1
   ) AS F2;
```

We have just done a simple linear interpolation in T-SQL!

reading_nbr	foo_reading	computed_foo_reading
1	121	121.00
2	NULL	184.67
3	NULL	248.33
4	312	312.00
5	NULL	337.75
6	NULL	363.50
7	NULL	389.25
11	415	415.00
12	NULL	372.00
13	NULL	329.00
14	NULL	286.00
15	NULL	243.00
16	200	200.00

26.10 Missing and Mixed Data in Rows

Collecting data is not always easy. When you sample or stage data, you can wind up with rows that have missing data (usually shown with NULLs) or overlapping data. This data will be shown on one row. We will need business rules that will depend on the particulars of each problem. The rules we want in this example are:

1. If we have multiple starting dates, then use the earliest known date. If there is a NULL in the data, then use it since we are uncertain.

2. If we have multiple ending dates, then use the latest known date. If there is a NULL in the data, then use it since we are uncertain.

As an example, assume we are taking samples of some kind within a date range, but the data is messy and we have multiple rows for multiple samples we have to reduce to a single row. Here is the DDL and some sample data.

```
CREATE TABLE Samples
(sample_id INTEGER NOT NULL,
 first_date DATE,
 second_date DATE,
UNIQUE (sample_id, first_date, second_date),
 CHECK (first_date < second_date)
);
```

Note the use of UNIQUE versus PRIMARY KEY because of the NULL-able column. Many new SQL programmers do not know that UNIQUE does not imply NOT NULL, like PRIMARY KEY.

```
INSERT INTO Samples
VALUES
(1, '2012-02-24', '2012-02-27'),
(1, '2012-02-24', '2012-03-06'),
(2, '2012-02-24', '2012-03-06'),
(2, '2012-01-05', '2012-01-06'),
(3, NULL, '2012-03-07'),
(3, '2012-02-01', '2012-03-07'),
(4, '2012-02-01', NULL),
(4, '2012-01-01', '2012-02-10'),
(5, NULL, NULL);
```

Samples one and two have known values on their date ranges, so they are easy. But the other samples have missing dates. Normally, doing an aggregate will drop the NULLs instead of making them dominate. I am calling it "first_date" and "second_date" since we have not decided which start and end dates we will finally use. The names "candidate_start_date" and "candidate_end_date" are a bit stuffy. The decision is to use the latest ending date.

```
SELECT sample_id,
    CASE WHEN COUNT(*) <> COUNT(first_date)
    THEN NULL ELSE MIN(first_date) END AS first_date,
```

```
    CASE WHEN COUNT(*) <> COUNT(second_date)
    THEN NULL ELSE MAX(second_date) END
    AS second_date
 FROM Samples
GROUP BY sample_id, second_date;
```

The use of CASE has to be at the same level of aggregation as the grouping for the query allows for this construct.

Data Structures in SQL

Graphs in SQL

THE TERMINOLOGY IN graph theory pretty much explains itself; if it does not, you can read some of the books suggested in the appendix for graph theory. Graphs are important because they are a general way to represent many different types of data and their relationships. Here is a quick review of terms.

A graph is a data structure made up of nodes connected by edges. Edges can be directed (permit travel in only one direction) or undirected (permit travel in both directions). The number of edges entering a node is its indegree; likewise, the number of edges leaving a node is its outdegree. A set of edges that allow you to travel from one node to another is called a path. A cycle is a path that comes back to the node from which it started without crossing itself (this means that a big 'O' is fine but a figure '8' is not).

A tree is a type of directed graph that is enough important to have its own terminology. Its special properties and frequent use have made it enough important to be covered in a separate chapter. The following section will stress other useful kinds of generalized directed graphs. Generalized directed graphs are classified into nonreconvergent and reconvergent graphs. In a reconvergent graph, there are multiple paths between at least one pair of nodes. Reconvergent graphs are either cyclic or acyclic.

The most common way to model a graph in SQL is with an adjacency list model. Each edge of the graph is shown as a pair of nodes in which the ordering matters and then any values associated with that edge is shown in another column.

27.1 Basic Graph Characteristics

The following code is from John Gilson. It uses an adjacency list model of the graph, with nodes in a separate table. This is the most common method for modeling graphs in SQL.

```
CREATE TABLE Nodes
(node_id INTEGER NOT NULL PRIMARY KEY);

CREATE TABLE Adjacency_List_Graph
(begin_node_id INTEGER NOT NULL REFERENCES Nodes (node_id),
 end_node_id INTEGER NOT NULL REFERENCES Nodes (node_id),
 PRIMARY KEY (begin_node_id, end_node_id),
 CHECK (begin_node_id <> end_node_id));
```

It is also possible to load an acyclic-directed graph into a nested set model by splitting the nodes.

```
CREATE TABLE Nested_Sets_Graph
(node_id INTEGER NOT NULL REFERENCES Nodes (node_id),
 lft INTEGER NOT NULL CHECK (lft >= 1) PRIMARY KEY,
 rgt INTEGER NOT NULL UNIQUE,
 CHECK (rgt > lft),
 UNIQUE (node_id, lft));
```

You split nodes by starting at the sink nodes and move up the tree. When you come to a node of (indegree>1), replace it with that many copies of the node under each of its superiors. Continue to do this until you get to the root. The acyclic graph will become a tree, but with duplicated node values. There are advantages to this model. We will discuss them in Section 27.3.

27.1.1 All Nodes in the Graph

```
CREATE VIEW Graph_Nodes (node_id)
AS
SELECT DISTINCT node_id FROM Nested_Sets_Graph;
```

27.1.2 Path Endpoints

A path through a graph is a traversal of consecutive nodes along a sequence of edges. Clearly, the node at the end of one edge in the sequence must also be the node at the beginning of the next edge in the sequence. The length of the path is the number of edges that are traversed along the path.

Path endpoints are the first and last nodes of each path in the graph. For a path of length zero, the path endpoints are the same node. If there is more than one path between two nodes, then each path will be distinguished by its own distinct set of number pairs for the nested-set representation.

If there is only one path p between two nodes but this path is a sub-path of more than one distinct path, then the endpoints of p will have number pairs for each of these greater paths. As a canonical form, the least numbered pairs are returned for these endpoints.

```
CREATE VIEW Path_End_Points
(begin_node_id, end_node_id,
 begin_lft, begin_rgt,
 end_lft, end_rgt)
AS
SELECT G1.node_id, G2.node_id,
       G1.lft, G1.rgt, G2.lft, G2.rgt
  FROM (SELECT node_id, MIN(lft), MIN(rgt)
          FROM Nested_Sets_Graph
         GROUP BY node_id) AS G1 (node_id, lft, rgt)
        INNER JOIN
        Nested_Sets_Graph AS G2
        ON G2.lft >= G1.lft
           AND G2.lft < G1.rgt;
```

27.1.3 Reachable Nodes

If a node is reachable from another node, then a path exists from one node to the other. It is assumed that every node is reachable from itself.

```
CREATE VIEW Reachable_Nodes (begin_node_id, end_node_id)
AS
SELECT DISTINCT begin_node_id, end_node_id
  FROM Path_End_Points;
```

27.1.4 Edges

Edges are pairs of adjacent connected nodes in the graph. If edge E is represented by the pair of nodes (n0, n1), then (n1) is reachable from (n0) in a single traversal.

```
CREATE VIEW Edges (begin_node_id, end_node_id)
AS
SELECT begin_node_id, end_node_id
  FROM Path_Endpoints AS PE
 WHERE begin_node_id <> end_node_id
   AND NOT EXISTS
       (SELECT *
          FROM Nested_Sets_Graph AS G
         WHERE G.lft > PE.begin_lft
           AND G.lft < PE.end_lft
           AND G.rgt > PE.end_rgt);
```

27.1.5 Indegree and Outdegree

The indegree of a node n is the number of distinct edges ending at n. Nodes that have 0 indegree are not returned. Indegree of all nodes in the graph:

```
CREATE VIEW Indegree (node_id, node_indegree)
AS
SELECT N.node_id, COUNT(E.begin_node_id)
  FROM Graph_Nodes AS N
       LEFT OUTER JOIN
       Edges AS E
       ON N.node_id = E.end_node_id
 GROUP BY N.node_id;
```

Outdegree of a node (n) is the number of distinct edges beginning at (n). Nodes that have zero outdegree are not returned. Outdegree of all nodes in the graph:

```
CREATE VIEW Outdegree (node_id, node_outdegree)
AS
SELECT N.node_id, COUNT(E.end_node_id)
  FROM Graph_Nodes AS N
       LEFT OUTER JOIN
       Edges AS E
       ON N.node_id = E.begin_node_id
 GROUP BY N.node_id;
```

27.1.6 Source, Sink, Isolated, and Internal Nodes

A source node of a graph has a positive outdegree but 0 indegree, that is, it has edges leading from, but not to, the node. This assumes there are no isolated nodes (nodes belonging to no edges).

```
CREATE VIEW Source_Nodes (node_id, lft, rgt)
AS
SELECT node_id, lft, rgt
  FROM Nested_Sets_Graph AS G1
 WHERE NOT EXISTS
      (SELECT *
         FROM Nested_Sets_Graph AS G
        WHERE G1.lft > G2.lft
          AND G1.lft < G2.rgt);
```

Likewise, a sink node of a graph has positive indegree but 0 outdegree. It has edges leading to, but not from, the node. This assumes there are no isolated nodes.

```
CREATE VIEW Sink_Nodes (node_id)
AS
SELECT node_id
  FROM Nested_Sets_Graph AS G1
 WHERE lft = rgt - 1
   AND NOT EXISTS
       (SELECT *
          FROM Nested_Sets_Graph AS G2
         WHERE G1.node_id = G2.node_id
           AND G2.lft < G1.lft);
```

An isolated node belongs to no edges, i.e., it has zero indegree and zero outdegree.

```
CREATE VIEW Isolated_Nodes (node_id, lft, rgt)
AS
SELECT node_id, lft, rgt
  FROM Nested_Sets_Graph AS G1
 WHERE lft = rgt - 1
   AND NOT EXISTS
```

```
(SELECT *
   FROM Nested_Sets_Graph AS G2
  WHERE G1.lft > G2.lft
    AND G1.lft < G2.rgt);
```

An internal node of a graph has an (indegree>0) and an (outdegree>fPa0), that is, it acts as both a source and a sink.

```
CREATE VIEW Internal_Nodes (node_id)
AS
SELECT node_id
  FROM (SELECT node_id, MIN(lft) AS lft, MIN(rgt) AS rgt
          FROM Nested_Sets_Graph
         WHERE lft < rgt - 1
        GROUP BY node_id) AS G1
 WHERE EXISTS
      (SELECT *
         FROM Nested_Sets_Graph AS G2
        WHERE G1.lft > G2.lft
          AND G1.lft < G2.rgt)
```

27.2 Paths in a Graph

Finding a path in a graph is the most important operation done with graphs in commercial use. They mode transportation networks, electrical and cable systems, process control flow, and thousands of other things.

A path P of length L from a node (n0) to a node (nk) in the graph is defined as a traversal of (L+1) contiguous node along a sequence of edges where the first node is node number 0 and the last is node number (k).

```
CREATE VIEW Paths
(begin_node_id, end_node_id, this_node_id,
 seq_nbr,
 begin_lft, begin_rgt, end_lft, end_rgt,
 this_lft, this_rgt)
AS
SELECT PE.begin_node_id, PE.end_node_id, G1.node_id,
       (SELECT COUNT(*)
          FROM Nested_Sets_Graph AS G2
         WHERE G2.lft > PE.begin_lft
```

```
            AND G2.lft <= G1.lft
            AND G2.rgt >= G1.rgt),
        PE.begin_lft, PE.begin_rgt,
        PE.end_lft, PE.end_rgt,
        G1.lft, G1.rgt
  FROM Path_End_Points AS PE
       INNER JOIN
       Nested_Sets_Graph AS G1
       ON G1.lft BETWEEN PE.begin_lft
                     AND PE.end_lft
          AND G1.rgt >= PE.end_rgt
```

27.2.1 Length of Paths

The length of a path is the number of edges that are traversed along the path. A path of N nodes has a length of (N − 1).

```
CREATE VIEW Path_Lengths
(begin_node_id, end_node_id,
 path_length,
 begin_lft, begin_rgt,
 end_lft, end_rgt)
AS
SELECT begin_node_id, end_node_id, MAX(seq_nbr),
       begin_lft, begin_rgt, end_lft, end_rgt
  FROM Paths
 GROUP BY begin_lft, end_lft, begin_rgt, end_rgt,
          begin_node_id, end_node_id;
```

27.2.2 Shortest Path

This gives the shortest path length between all nodes, but it does not tell you what the actual path is. There are other queries that use the new CTE feature and recursion which we will discuss in Section 27.3.

```
CREATE VIEW Shortest_Path_Lengths
(begin_node_id, end_node_id, path_length,
 begin_lft, begin_rgt, end_lft, end_rgt)
AS
SELECT PL.begin_node_id, PL.end_node_id,
```

```
       PL.path_length,
       PL.begin_lft, PL.begin_rgt,
       PL.end_lft, PL.end_rgt
  FROM (SELECT begin_node_id, end_node_id,
               MIN(path_length) AS path_length
          FROM PathLengths
         GROUP BY begin_node_id, end_node_id) AS MPL
       INNER JOIN
       PathLengths AS PL
       ON MPL.begin_node_id = PL.begin_node_id
          AND MPL.end_node_id = PL.end_node_id
          AND MPL.path_length = PL.path_length;
```

27.2.3 Paths by Iteration

First let's build a graph with a cost associated with each edge and put it into an adjacency list model.

```
INSERT INTO Edges (out_node, in_node, cost)
VALUES ('A', 'B', 50),
 ('A', 'C', 30),
 ('A', 'D', 100),
 ('A', 'E', 10),
 ('C', 'B', 5),
 ('D', 'B', 20),
 ('D', 'C', 50),
 ('E', 'D', 10);
```

To find the shortest paths from one node to those that it can reach, we can write this recursive VIEW.

```
CREATE VIEW Shortest_Paths (out_node, in_node, path_length)
AS
WITH RECURSIVE Paths (out_node, in_node, path_length)
AS
(SELECT out_node, in_node, 1
  FROM Edges
 UNION ALL
```

```
 SELECT E1.out_node, P1.in_node, P1.path_length + 1
   FROM Edges AS E1, Paths AS P1
  WHERE E1.in_node = P1.out_node)
SELECT out_node, in_node, MIN(path_length)
  FROM Paths
 GROUP BY out_node, in_node;
```

out_node	in_node	path_length
'A'	'B'	1
'A'	'C'	1
'A'	'D'	1
'A'	'E'	1
'C'	'B'	1
'D'	'B'	1
'D'	'C'	1
'E'	'B'	2
'E'	'D'	1

To find the shortest paths without recursion, stay in a loop and add one edge at a time to the set of paths defined so far.

```
CREATE PROCEDURE Iterate_Paths()
LANGUAGE SQL
MODIFIES SQL DATA
BEGIN
DECLARE old_path_tally INTEGER;
SET old_path_tally = 0;
DELETE FROM Paths; -- clean out working table
INSERT INTO Paths
SELECT out_node, in_node, 1
  FROM Edges; -- load the edges
-- add one edge to each path
WHILE old_path_tally < (SELECT COUNT(*) FROM Paths)
DO SET old_path_tally = (SELECT COUNT(*) FROM Paths);
   INSERT INTO Paths (out_node, in_node, lgth)
   SELECT E1.out_node, P1.in_node, (1 + P1.lgth)
     FROM Edges AS E1, Paths AS P1
```

```
    WHERE E1.in_node = P1.out_node
      AND NOT EXISTS -- path is not here already
          (SELECT *
             FROM Paths AS P2
            WHERE E1.out_node = P2.out_node
              AND P1.in_node = P2.in_node);
END WHILE;
END;
```

The Least Cost Path is basically the same algorithm, but instead of a constant of one for the path length, we use the actual costs of the edges.

```
CREATE PROCEDURE Iterate_Cheap_Paths ()
LANGUAGE SQL
MODIFIES SQL DATA
BEGIN
DECLARE old_path_cost INTEGER;
SET old_path_cost = 0;
DELETE FROM Paths; -- clean out working table
INSERT INTO Paths
SELECT out_node, in_node, cost
  FROM Edges; -- load the edges
-- add one edge to each path
WHILE old_path_cost < (SELECT COUNT(*) FROM Paths)
DO SET old_path_cost = (SELECT COUNT(*) FROM Paths);
   INSERT INTO Paths (out_node, in_node, cost)
   SELECT E1.out_node, P1.in_node, (E1.cost + P1.cost)
     FROM Edges AS E1
          INNER JOIN
          (SELECT out_node, in_node, MIN(cost)
             FROM Paths
           GROUP BY out_node, in_node)
          AS P1 (out_node, in_node, cost)
          ON E1.in_node = P1.out_node
             AND NOT EXISTS
                 (SELECT *
                    FROM Paths AS P2
                   WHERE E1.out_node = P2.out_node
```

```
                AND P1.in_node = P2.in_node
                AND P2.cost <= E1.cost + P1.cost);
END WHILE;
END;
```

27.2.4 Listing the Paths

I got data for this table from the book Introduction to Algorithms by Cormen, Leiserson, and Rivest (ISBN 0-262-03141-8), page 518. This book was very popular in college courses in the United States. I made one decision that will be important later; I added self-traversal edges (i.e., the node is both the out_node and the in_node of an edge) with weights of zero.

```
INSERT INTO Edges
VALUES ('s', 's', 0);
INSERT INTO Edges
VALUES ('s', 'u', 3),
 ('s', 'x', 5),
 ('u', 'u', 0),
 ('u', 'v', 6),
 ('u', 'x', 2),
 ('v', 'v', 0),
 ('v', 'y', 2),
 ('x', 'u', 1),
 ('x', 'v', 4),
 ('x', 'x', 0),
 ('x', 'y', 6),
 ('y', 's', 3),
 ('y', 'v', 7),
 ('y', 'y', 0);
```

I am not happy about this approach, because I have to decide the maximum number of edges in path before I start looking for an answer. But this will work and I know that a path will have no more than the total number of nodes in the graph. Let's create a table to hold the paths:

```
CREATE TABLE Paths
(step1 CHAR(2) NOT NULL,
 step2 CHAR(2) NOT NULL,
 step3 CHAR(2) NOT NULL,
```

```
step4 CHAR(2) NOT NULL,
step5 CHAR(2) NOT NULL,
total_cost INTEGER NOT NULL,
path_length INTEGER NOT NULL,
PRIMARY KEY (step1, step2, step3, step4, step5));
```

The "step1" node is where I begin the path. The other columns are the second step, third step, fourth step, and so forth. The last step column is the end of the journey. The "total_cost" column is the total cost, based on the sum of the weights of the edges, on this path. The path length column is harder to explain, but for now, let's just say that it is a count of the nodes visited in the path.

To keep things easier, let's look at all the paths from 's' to 'y' in the graph. The INSERT INTO statement for constructing that set looks likes this:

```
INSERT INTO Paths
SELECT G1.out_node, -- it is 's' in this example
       G2.out_node,
       G3.out_node, G4.out_node,
       G4.in_node, -- it is 'y' in this example
       (G1.cost + G2.cost + G3.cost + G4.cost),
       (CASE WHEN G1.out_node NOT IN (G2.out_node,
G3.out_node, G4.out_node)            THEN 1 ELSE 0 END
        + CASE WHEN G2.out_node NOT IN (G1.out_node,
G3.out_node, G4.out_node)            THEN 1 ELSE 0 END
        + CASE WHEN G3.out_node NOT IN (G1.out_node,
G2.out_node, G4.out_node)            THEN 1 ELSE 0 END
        + CASE WHEN G4.out_node NOT IN (G1.out_node,
G2.out_node, G3.out_node)            THEN 1 ELSE 0 END)
  FROM Edges AS G1,
       Edges AS G2,
       Edges AS G3,
       Edges AS G4
 WHERE G1.out_node = 's'
   AND G1.in_node = G2.out_node
   AND G2.in_node = G3.out_node
   AND G3.in_node = G4.out_node
   AND G4.in_node = 'y';
```

I put in 's' and 'y' as the out_node and in_node of the path and made sure that the in_node of each step in the path was the out_node of the next step in the path. This is a combinatorial explosion, but it is easy to read and understand.

The sum of the weights is the cost of the path, which is easy to understand. The path_length calculation is a bit harder. This sum of CASE expressions looks at each node in the path. If it is unique within the row, it is assigned a value of one, if it is not unique within the row, it is assigned a value of zero.

All paths will have five steps in them because the way to table is declared. But what if a path exists between the two nodes which is shorter than five steps? That is where the self-traversal rows are used. Consecutive pairs of steps in the same row can be repetitions of the same node.

Here is what the rows of the Paths table look like after this INSERT INTO statement, ordered by descending path_length, and then by ascending cost.

Paths

step_1	step_2	step_3	step_4	step_5	total_cost	path_length
s	s	x	x	y	11	0
s	s	s	x	y	11	1
s	x	x	x	y	11	1
s	x	u	x	y	14	2
s	s	u	v	y	11	2
s	s	u	x	y	11	2
s	s	x	v	y	11	2
s	s	x	y	y	11	2
s	u	u	v	y	11	2
s	u	u	x	y	11	2
s	u	v	v	y	11	2
s	u	x	x	y	11	2
s	x	v	v	y	11	2
s	x	x	v	y	11	2
s	x	x	y	y	11	2

step_1	step_2	step_3	step_4	step_5	total_cost	path_length
s	x	y	y	y	11	2
s	x	y	v	y	20	4
s	x	u	v	y	14	4
s	u	v	y	y	11	4
s	u	x	v	y	11	4
s	u	x	y	y	11	4
s	x	v	y	y	11	4

Clearly, all pairs of nodes could be picked from the original Edges table and the same INSERT INTO run on them with a minor change in the WHERE clause. However, this example is big enough for a short magazine article. And it is too big for most applications. It is safe to assume that people really want the cheapest path. In this example, the total_cost column defines the cost of a path, so we can eliminate some of the paths from the Paths table with this statement.

```
DELETE FROM Paths
 WHERE total_cost
     > (SELECT MIN(total_cost)
          FROM Paths);
```

Again, if you had all the paths for all possible pairs of nodes, the subquery expression would have a WHERE clause to correlate it to the subset of paths for each possible pair.

In this example, it got rid of 3 out of 22 possible paths. It is helpful and in some situations we might like having all the options. But these are not distinct options.

As one of many examples, the paths

(s, x, v, v, y, 11, 2)

and

(s, x, x, v, y, 11, 2)

are both really the same path, (s, x, v, y). Before we decide to write a statement to handle these equivalent rows, let's consider another cost factor. People do not like to change airplanes or trains. If they can go from Amsterdam to New York City on one plane without changing planes for the same cost, they are happy. This is where that path_length column comes in. It is a quick way to remove the paths that have more edges than they need to get the job done.

```
DELETE FROM Paths
 WHERE path_length
       > (SELECT MIN(path_length)
            FROM Paths);
```

In this case, that last DELETE FROM statement will reduce the table to one row: (s, s, x, x, y, 11, 0) which reduces to (s, x, y). This single remaining row is very convenient for my article, but if you look at the table, you will see that there was also a subset of equivalent rows that had higher path_length numbers.

(s, s, s, x, y, 11, 1)
(s, x, x, x, y, 11, 1)
(s, x, x, y, y, 11, 2)
(s, x, y, y, y, 11, 2)

Your task is to write code to handle equivalent rows. *Hint*: the duplicate nodes will always be contiguous across the row.

27.3 Acyclic Graphs as Nested Sets

Let's start with a simple graph in an adjacency list model.

```
INSERT INTO Nodes (node_id)
VALUES ('a'), ('b'), ('c'), ('d'),
       ('e'), ('f'), ('g'), ('h');

INSERT INTO Adjacency_List_Graph (begin_node_id, end_node_id)
VALUES ('a', 'b'), ('a', 'c'), ('b', 'd'), ('c', 'd'),
       ('c', 'g'), ('d', 'e'), ('d', 'f'), ('e', 'h'),
       ('g', 'h');
```

We can convert this adjacency list model to the nested sets model with a simple stack algorithm.

```
-- Stack to keep track of nodes being traversed in depth-first fashion
CREATE TABLE NodeStack
(node_id INTEGER NOT NULL PRIMARY KEY
    REFERENCES Nodes (node_id),
 distance INTEGER NOT NULL CHECK (distance >= 0),
```

```
 lft INTEGER CHECK (lft >= 1),
 rgt INTEGER,
 CHECK (rgt > lft));

CREATE PROCEDURE Adjacency_Lists_To_Nested_Sets_Graph ()
LANGUAGE SQL
READS SQL DATA
BEGIN
DECLARE path_length INTEGER;
DECLARE current_number INTEGER;
SET path_length = 0;
SET current_number = 0;
-- Clear the table that will hold the result
DELETE FROM Nested_Sets_Graph;
-- Initialize stack by inserting all source nodes of graph
INSERT INTO NodeStack (node_id, distance)
SELECT DISTINCT G1.begin_node_id, path_length
  FROM Adjacency_List_Graph AS G1
 WHERE NOT EXISTS
       (SELECT *
          FROM Adjacency_List_Graph AS G2
         WHERE G2.end_node_id = G1.begin_node_id);

WHILE EXISTS (SELECT * FROM NodeStack)
DO
  SET current_number = current_number + 1;
  IF EXISTS (SELECT * FROM NodeStack WHERE distance = path_length)
  THEN UPDATE NodeStack
          SET lft = current_number
        WHERE distance = path_length
          AND NOT EXISTS
              (SELECT *
                 FROM NodeStack AS S2
                WHERE distance = path_length
                  AND S2.node_id < NodeStack.node_id);
       INSERT INTO NodeStack (node_id, distance)
       SELECT G.end_node_id, (S.distance + 1)
         FROM NodeStack AS S,
              Adjacency_List_Graph AS G
```

```
      WHERE S.distance = path_length
        AND S.lft IS NOT NULL
        AND G.begin_node_id = S.node_id;

     SET path_length = (path_length + 1);
  ELSE SET path_length = (path_length - 1);
     UPDATE NodeStack
        SET rgt = current_number
      WHERE lft IS NOT NULL
        AND distance = path_length;

     INSERT INTO Nested_Sets_Graph (node_id, lft, rgt)
     SELECT node_id, lft, rgt
       FROM NodeStack
      WHERE lft IS NOT NULL
        AND distance = path_length;
   DELETE FROM NodeStack
    WHERE lft IS NOT NULL
      AND distance = path_length;
 END IF;
END WHILE;
END;
```

You can now use modified versions of the nested set queries you already know on this kind of graph. However, be sure to use DISTINCT options to remove duplicate node references.

27.4 Adjacency Matrix Model

An adjacency matrix is a square array whose rows are out-node and columns are in-nodes of a graph. A one in a cell means that there is edge between the two nodes. Using the graph in figure 30.1, we would have an array like this:

	A	B	C	D	E	F	G	H
A	1	1	1	0	0	0	0	0
B	0	1	0	1	0	0	0	0
C	0	0	1	1	0	0	1	0

Continued

	A	B	C	D	E	F	G	H
D	0	0	0	1	1	1	0	0
E	0	0	0	0	1	0	0	1
F	0	0	0	0	0	1	0	0
G	0	0	0	0	0	0	1	1
H	0	0	0	0	0	0	0	1

Many graph algorithms are based on the adjacency matrix model and can be translated into SQL. Go back to the chapter on modeling matrices in SQL and in particular matrix multiplication in SQL. For example, Dijkstra's algorithm for the shortest distances between each pair of nodes in a graph looks like this in pseudo-code.

```
FOR k = 1 TO n
  DO FOR i = 1 TO n
     DO FOR j = 1 TO n
        IF a[i,k] + a[k,j] < a[i,j]
        THEN a[i,j] = a[i,k] + a[k,j]
        END IF;
     END FOR;
  END FOR;
END FOR;
```

You need to be warned that for a graph of (n) nodes, the table will be of size (n^2). The algorithms often run in (n^3) time. The advantage it has is that once you have completed a table it can be used for look ups rather than recomputing distances over and over.

27.5 Points Inside Polygons

While not actually part of graph theory, this seemed to be the reasonable place to put this section since it is also related to spatial queries. A polygon can be described as a set of corner point in an (x, y) coordinate system. The usual query is to tell if a given point is inside or outside of the polygon.

This algorithm is due to Darel R. Finley. The main advantage it has is that it can be done in Standard SQL without trigonometry functions. The disadvantage is that it does not work for concave polygons. The workaround is to dissect the convex polygons into concave polygons and then add column for the name of the original area.

-- set up polygon, with any ordering of the corners

```
CREATE TABLE Polygon
(x FLOAT NOT NULL,
 y FLOAT NOT NULL,
 PRIMARY KEY (x, y));

INSERT INTO Polygon
VALUES (2.00, 2.00), (1.00, 4.00),
       (3.00, 6.00), (6.00, 4.00), (5.00, 2.00);

--set up some sample points
CREATE TABLE Points
(xx FLOAT NOT NULL,
 yy FLOAT NOT NULL,
 location VARCHAR(10) NOT NULL, -- answer the question in advance!
 PRIMARY KEY (xx, yy));
INSERT INTO Points
VALUES (2.00, 2.00, 'corner'),
       (1.00, 5.00, 'outside'),
       (3.00, 3.00, 'inside'),
       (3.00, 4.00, 'inside'),
       (5.00, 1.00, 'outside'),
       (3.00, 2.00, 'side');

-- do the query
SELECT P1.xx, P1.yy, p1.location, SIGN(
SUM
 (CASE WHEN (polyY.y < P1.yy AND polyY.x >= P1.yy
          OR polyY.x < P1.yy AND polyY.y >= P1.yy)
       THEN CASE WHEN polyX.y + (P1.yy - polyY.y)
                     /(polyY.x - polyY.y) * (polyX.x - polyX.y) < P1.xx
                 THEN 1 ELSE 0 END
       ELSE 0 END))AS flag
  FROM Polygon AS polyY, Polygon AS polyX, Points AS P1
GROUP BY P1.xx, P1.yy, p1.location;
```

When flag = 1, the point is inside; when flag = 0, it is outside.

xx	yy	Location	Flag
1	5	Outside	0
2	2	Corner	0
3	3	Inside	1
3	4	Inside	1
5	1	Outside	0
3	2	Side	1

Sides are counted as inside, but if you want to count the corner points as inside, you should start the CASE expression with:

```
CASE WHEN EXISTS
        (SELECT * FROM Polygon
          WHERE x = P1.xx AND y = P1.yy)
    THEN 1 ..".
```

27.6 Taxicab Geometry

Taxicab geometry is a form of geometry in which the usual plane is replaced with a grid of points in a Cartesian coordinate system, connected by horizontal and vertical paths. Think of a city map, with streets and intersections. The usual distance function or metric of Euclidean geometry is replaced by a new metric, the taxi distance. This is a count of the number of blocks you have to travel (by taxi) to get from one point to another.

Imagine that you are in a taxi and want to get from point (x1, y1) to (x2, y2), how would you compute the distance? You would use high school math and the Euclidean distance: $d = \sqrt{((x1 - x2)^2 + (y1 - y2)^2)}$. To make this concrete, let's take a taxi from the center of town (0,0) and want to get to the Chez Vermin Hotel at (3,4), how far do you have to travel? (Figure 27.1)

Your Euclidean formula gives us five blocks, but look at the map. You go three block east and then four blocks north for a total of seven blocks in the taxi. He cannot fly, so he has to drive through the streets. The shortest distance is seven blocks in Taxicab geometry. But that means there are many ways to walk between two points. I could walk three blocks east and then four blocks north; four blocks north and then three blocks east; there are all kinds of zig-zags, but as long as the total number of blocks north is three and the total number of blocks east is four (Figure 27.2).

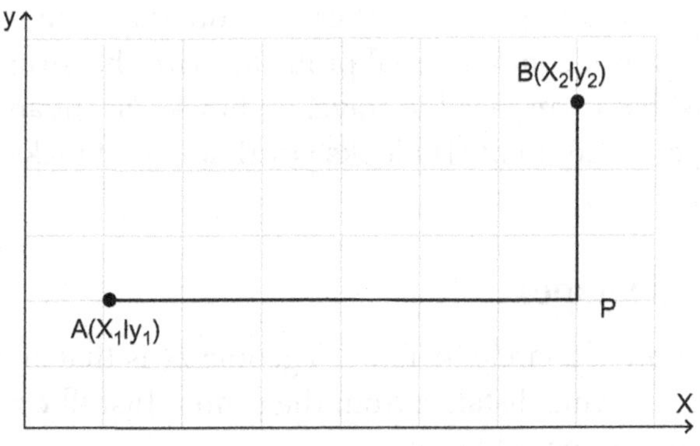

Figure 27.1 Taxicab Distance.

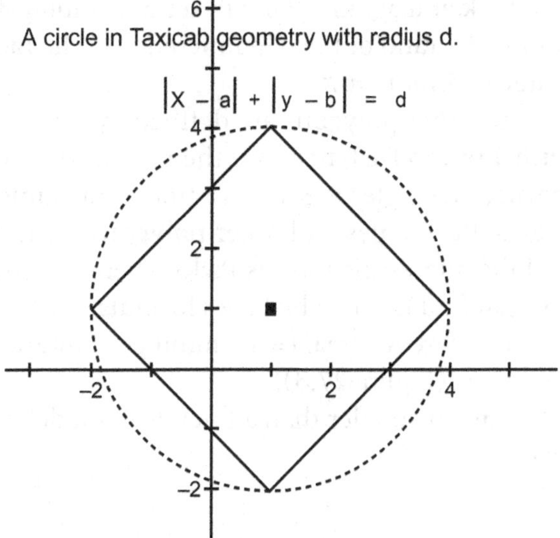

Figure 27.2 Taxicab Circle.

27.6.1 Taxi Versus Euclidean Distance

Let's invent some notations that we can turn into programs. Use uppercase letters for point (hotel) names:

A = (x1, y1), B = (x2, y2)

De (A, B) = Euclidean Distance = d = $\sqrt{((x1-x2)^2+(y1-y2)^2)}$

Dt (A, B) = Taxicab Distance = (|x1 − x2| + |y1 − y2|).

You might want to convince yourself that

Dt (A, A) = 0

Dt (A, B) = Dt (B, A)

Unlike Euclidean geometry, there is more than one shortest path between two points. It is a combinatorial problem, with the formula N = r!/(n!(r − n)!). The idea is that if you need to travel (i) blocks North and (j) blocks East, then any permutation of (i) blocks North and (j) blocks East will get you to your destination.

27.6.2 Taxi Shapes

The definition of a circle in Taxicab geometry is that all points (hotels) in the set are the same distance from the center. Just like a Euclidean circle, but with a finite number of points.

Circle = {X: Dt (X, P) = k}, k is the radius and P is the center

When you look at diagram, you will see a diamond shape. Remember the definition of π? The ratio of the circumference to the radius of a circle. This gives us a value of 4 for taxi-π.

Triangles and other polygons are defined by replacing Euclidean Distance with Taxicab Distance. But the results are not as pretty as the circle. Congruent triangles are hard to find; you cannot use the simple side and angle rules. Rectangles and other polygons are not visually obvious.

But one of the interesting tools is Pick's Theorem. Given a general polygon, you can find the area by Pick's formula,

$A = i + b/2 - 1$, where A = area, i = the number of interior points, b = number of boundary points (Figure 27.3).

The math is much simpler than a Euclidean model, which would involve trigonometry.

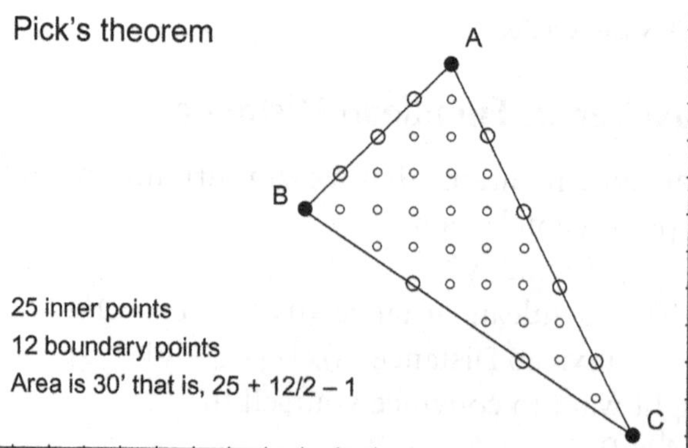

Figure 27.3 Pick's Theorem

27.7 Equivalence Classes and Cliques

We keep harping that SQL is based on sets, but how many of us ever go back and re-read any old text books on set theory? In particular, one concept gets forgotten is equivalence relations on sets, which create equivalence classes. These classes are disjoint, and we can put an element from a set into one of them with some kind of rule.

Let's use ~ as the notation for an equivalence relation. The definition is that it has three properties:

- The relation is reflexive: $A \sim A$. This means the relation applies to itself.
- The relation is symmetric: if $(A \sim B) \Leftrightarrow (B \sim A)$. This means when the relation applies to two different elements in the set, it applies both ways.
- The relation is transitive: $(A \sim B) \wedge (B \sim C) \Rightarrow (A \sim C)$. This means we can deduce all elements in a class by applying the relation to any known members of the class. This is pretty important for programming, as we will see.

So, if this is such a basic set operation, why isn't it in SQL? The problem is that it produces *classes*, not a set. A class is a set of sets, but a table is just a set. The notation for each class is a pair of square bracket that contains some representative of each set. Assume we have …

$a \in A$
$b \in B$

These expressions are all the same:

$A \sim B$
$[a] = [b]$
$[a] \cap [b] \neq \emptyset$

A common example is the set **Z** of integers and any MOD() operator will give you equivalence classes. The MOD(n, 2) operation gives you one class consisting of all even numbers, and the other consisting of all odd numbers. The nice part is that you can compute the MOD() function with arithmetic.

An equivalence classes can also be defined by a set of sets. This is an important concept in graph theory and graph database. If you have not seen it, Google "Six Degrees of Kevin Bacon" (http://en.wikipedia.org/wiki/Six_

Degrees_of_Kevin_Bacon). The idea is that any individual involved in the Hollywood film industry can be linked through his or her film roles to Kevin Bacon within six steps.

Let's steal a sample set from a SQL Forum posting of friends, where ~ now means "is a friend of" and that we can use "foaf"—"Friend of a friend"—to build cliches.

{Fred, Jessica, John, Mary}
{Albert, Nancy, Peter}
{Abby}
{Frank, Joe}

A complete graph means that each node is connected to every other node by one edge. If a subgraph is complete, it is actually called a Clique in graph theory.

The complete graph K_n of order n is a simple graph with n vertices in which every vertex is adjacent to every other. The complete graph on n vertices has n(n–1)/2 edges, which corresponding to all possible choices of pairs of vertices. But *this is not an equivalence relation* because it does not include the reference of each node to itself. Remember A~A? Think about Abby in this set, assuming that she likes herself, in spite of her lack of social skills.

Obviously, if you have a clique with (k) nodes in it, you can a complete subgraph of any size (j<k). A maximal clique is a clique that is not a subset of any other clique (some authors reserve the term clique for maximal clique.

SQL *seems* to have two equivalence relations that are major parts of the language. The first is plain old vanilla equal (=) for scalar values in the base data types. SQL is just like any other programming language, but we also have NULLs to consider. Opps! We all know that (NULL=NULL) is not true. So we have to exclude NULLs or work around them.

The other "almost" equivalence relation is GROUP BY in which the class is the grouping columns. A quick example would be "SELECT city_name, state_code FROM Customers GROUP BY state_code"; this is still not quite right because we have to do some kind of aggregation on the nongrouping columns in the query.

27.7.1 Graph for Equivalence Relations

As we have seen, the idiom for graphs in SQL is to use a table with the nodes involved and a second table with pairs of nodes (a, b) to model the edges, which model our ~ relation. The bad news is that when you use it for equivalence relations, it can get big. A class with one member is has one row to show the edge back to itself. A class with two members {a, b} has {(a, a), (b, b), (a, b), (b, a)} to show the ~ properties as edges. Three members give us six rows: {(a, a), (b, b), (c, c), (a, b), (a, c), (b, a), (b, c), (c, a), (c, b)}. The general formula is $(n*(n-1))+n$, which is pretty close to $(n!)$.

First, load the table a few facts we might already know:

```
CREATE TABLE Friends
(lft_member VARCHAR(20) NOT NULL,
 rgt_member VARCHAR(20) NOT NULL,
 PRIMARY KEY (lft_member, rgt_member))

INSERT INTO Friends (lft_member, rgt_member)
VALUES
('John', 'Mary'),
('Mary', 'Jessica'),
('Peter', 'Albert'),
('Peter', 'Nancy'),
('Abby', 'Abby'),
('Jessica', 'Fred'),
('Joe', 'Frank');
```

27.7.2 Reflexive Rows

The first thing we noticed is that only Abby has a reflexive property row. We need to add those rows and can do this with basic set operators. Bu it is not that easy, as you can see with this insertion statement:

```
INSERT INTO Friends
SELECT X.lft_member, X.rgt_member
 FROM
((SELECT lft_member, lft_member FROM Friends AS F1
UNION
SELECT rgt_member, rgt_member FROM Friends AS F2)
EXCEPT
SELECT lft_member, rgt_member FROM Friends AS F3)
AS X (lft_member, rgt_member);
```

The use of table aliases is tricky. You have to be sure that the SQL engine will construct a table in such a way that you do not get scoping problems.

The UNION and EXCEPT operators are used to assure that we do not have primary key violations.

Abby	Abby
Albert	Albert
Frank	Frank
Fred	Fred
Jessica	Jessica
Jessica	Fred
Joe	Joe
Joe	Frank
John	Mary
John	John
Mary	Mary
Mary	Jessica
Nancy	Nancy
Peter	Peter
Peter	Nancy
Peter	Albert

27.7.3 Symmetric Rows

Look at the update table and there are no {(a, b), (b, a)} pairs. We need to add this second property to the relation table. This follows the pattern of set operators we just used:

```
INSERT INTO Friends
SELECT X.lft_member, X.rgt_member
 FROM
(
(SELECT F1.rgt_member, F1.lft_member
  FROM Friends AS F1
 WHERE F1.lft_member <> F1.rgt_member)
```

```
EXCEPT
(SELECT F2.lft_member, F2.rgt_member FROM Friends AS F2)
) AS X (lft_member, rgt_member);
```

This will give us:

Abby	Abby
Albert	Peter
Albert	Albert
Frank	Joe
Frank	Frank
Fred	Jessica
Fred	Fred
Jessica	Mary
Jessica	Jessica
Jessica	Fred
Joe	Joe
Joe	Frank
John	Mary
John	John
Mary	Mary
Mary	John
Mary	Jessica
Nancy	Peter
Nancy	Nancy
Peter	Peter
Peter	Nancy
Peter	Albert

If you do quick GROUP BY query, you see that Abby is seriously antisocial with a count of 1, but Mary and Jessica look very social with a

count of 3. This is not quite true because the property could be the dreaded "Rock-paper-scissors-lizard-Spock" relationship. But this is what we are using.

27.7.4 Transitive Rows

Transitivity goes on forever. Well, until we have what mathematicians call a closure. This means we have gotten a set of elements that have all of the valid relationships. In some cases, these sets are infinite. But in database, we can only have insanely large tables. Let's pull a subset that is part of a clique of four friends.

Fred	Jessica
Fred	Fred
Jessica	Mary
Jessica	Jessica
Jessica	Fred
John	Mary
John	John
Mary	Mary
Mary	John
Mary	Jessica

Now apply the transitive relation to get some of the missing edges of a graph:

```
INSERT INTO Friends
SELECT X.lft_member, X.rgt_member
 FROM
((SELECT F1.lft_member, F2.rgt_member
  FROM Friends AS F1, Friends AS F2
 WHERE F1.rgt_member = F2.lft_member)
EXCEPT
(SELECT F3.lft_member, F3.rgt_member FROM Friends AS F3)
) AS X (lft_member, rgt_member);
```

This is a simple statement using the definition of transitivity, without a universal quantifier or loop on it. It will add these rows to this subset:

Fred	Mary
Jessica	John
John	Jessica
Mary	Fred

When you look at Mary and Jessica have all of their friends. However, Fred and John do not know that they are friends. So we invoke the statement again and get those two rows. If you try it for a third time, there are zero rows added.

The first thought is this sounds like a job for a recursive statement. But it is not that easy. If the original graph has a cycle in it, you can hang in an infinite loop if you try to use a recursive CTE. The assumption is that each clique has a spanning graph in the pairs in. Oops! New term: a spanning graph is a subgraph that includes the nodes and some or all of the edges of the graph. A complete graph is the spanning graph has all the possible edges, so each node is *directly* connected to any other node.

27.7.5 Cliques

Now change your mindset from graphs to sets. Let's look at the size of the cliques:

```
WITH X (member, clique_size)
AS
(SELECT lft_member, COUNT(*) FROM Friends GROUP BY lft_member)
SELECT * FROM X ORDER BY clique_size;
```

Abby	1
Frank	2
Joe	2
Nancy	3
Peter	3

Albert	3
Fred	4
Jessica	4
John	4
Mary	4

What we want to do it is assign a number to each clique. This sample data is biased by the fact that the cliques are all of different sizes. You cannot simply use the size to assign a clique_nbr.

Create this table and load it with the names.

```
CREATE TABLE Cliques
(clique_member VARCHAR(20) NOT NULL PRIMARY KEY,
 clique_nbr INTEGER);
```

We can start by assigning everyone their own clique, using whatever your favorite method is:

```
INSERT INTO Cliques
 VALUES
('Abby', 1),
('Frank', 2),
('Joe', 3),
('Nancy', 4),
('Peter', 5),
('Albert', 6),
('Fred', 7),
('Jessica', 8),
('John', 9),
('Mary', 10);
```

Everyone is equally a member of their clique in this model. That means we could start with anyone to get the rest of their clique. The update is very straight forward. Take any clique number, find the member to whom it belongs and use that name to build that clique. But which number to we use? We could use the MIN, MAX, or a random number in the clique; I will use the MAX for no particular reason.

I keep thinking that there is a recursive update statement that will do this in one statement. But I know it will not port (Standard SQL has no recursive update statement right now. We would do it with SQL/PSM or a host language) and I think it would be expensive. Recursion will happen for each member of the whole set, but if we consolidate a clique for one person, we have removed his friends from consideration.

The worst situation would be a bunch of hermits, so the number of clique would be the cardinality of set. That is not likely or useful in the real world. Let's put the update in the body of a loop.

```
BEGIN
DECLARE clique_loop INTEGER;
DECLARE node CHAR(10);
SET clique_loop = (SELECT MAX(clique_nbr) FROM Cliques);

WHILE clique_loop > 0
DO
SET node
    = (SELECT clique_member
         FROM Cliques
        WHERE clique_nbr = clique_loop);
UPDATE Cliques
   SET clique_nbr
       = (SELECT clique_nbr
            FROM Cliques
           WHERE clique_member = node)
 WHERE clique_member
        IN (SELECT rgt_member
              FROM Friends
             WHERE lft_member = mode);
SET clique_loop = clique_loop - 1;
END WHILE;
END;
```

As a programming assignment, replace the simple counting loop with one that does not do updates with clique_loop values that were removed in the prior iteration. This can save a lot of work in a larger social network than the sample data used here.

27.7.6 Adding Members

Now that we have a Cliques table, we can do a simple insertion if the new guy belongs to one clique. However, we can have someone who knows a people in different cliques. This will merge the two cliques into one.

```
CREATE PROCEDURE Clique_Merge
(IN clique_member_1 CHAR(10),
 IN clique_member_2 CHAR(10))
UPDATE Cliques
  SET clique_nbr
     =(SELECT MAX(clique_nbr)
         FROM Cliques
        WHERE clique_member
            IN (clique_member_1, clique_member_2))
 WHERE clique_nbr
       =(SELECT MIN (clique_nbr)
         FROM Cliques
        WHERE clique_member
            IN (clique_member_1, clique_member_2));
```

Deleting a member or moving him to another clique is trivial.

27.8 Conclusion

This chapter is full of handy tricks to use with SQL. But graphs are better handled with a graph database than with SQL. This is no surprise; that is what they were meant to do! The graph database can also handle relationships that do not have just the simple mathematical properties needed for a single relationship. Over Publications is a great source for books on math and they have a good offering in Graph Theory.

- "A First Course in Graph Theory" by Gary Chartrand, Ping Zhang (ISBN: 978-0486483689)
- "Graph Theory" by Ronald Gould (ISBN: 978-0486498065)
- "Introduction to Graph Theory" by Richard J. Trudeau (ISBN: 978-0486678702)
- "Introductory Graph Theory" by Gary Chartrand (ISBN: 978-0486247755)

Trees and Hierarchies in SQL

A TREE IS A special kind of directed graph. Graphs are data structures that are made up of nodes (usually shown as boxes) connected by edges (usually shown as lines with arrowheads). Each edge represents a one-way relationship between the two nodes it connects. In an organizational chart, the nodes are employees and each edge is the "reports to" relationship. In a parts explosion (also called a bill of materials), the nodes are assembly units (eventually resolving down to individual parts) and each edge is the "is made of" relationship.

The top of the tree is called the root. In an organizational chart, it is the highest authority; in a parts explosion, it is the final assembly. The number of edges coming out of the node is its outdegree, and the number of edges entering it is its indegree. A binary tree is one in which a parent can have at most two subordinates; more generally, an n-ary tree is one in which a node can have at most outdegree of (n).

The nodes of the tree that have no subtrees beneath them are called the leaf nodes. In a parts explosion, they are the individual parts, which cannot be broken down any further. The descendants, or subordinates, of a node (called the parent) are every node in the subtree that has the parent node as its root.

There are several ways to define a tree: It is a graph with no cycles; it is a graph where all nodes except the root have indegree 1 and the root has

indegree zero. Another defining property is that a path can be found from the root to any other node in the tree by following the edges in their natural direction.

All of Western thought has been based on hierarchies and top-down organizations. It should be no surprise that hierarchies were very easy to represent in hierarchical databases, where the structure of the data and the structure of the database were the same. IMS, IDMS, Total, and other early databases used pointer chains to build graph structures that could be traversed with procedural code.

The early arguments against SQL were largely based on the lack of such traversals in a declarative language. Dr. Codd himself introduced the adjacency list mode for trees in an early paper. This model dominated SQL programming for years, even though it is not set-oriented or declarative. It simply mimics the pointer chains from the pre-RDBMS network databases.

28.1 Adjacency List Model

Since the nodes contain the data, we can add columns to represent the edges of a tree. This is usually done in one of two ways in SQL: a single table or two tables. In the single-table representation, the edge connection appears in the same table as the node. In the two-table format, one table contains the nodes of the graph and the other table contains the edges, represented as pairs of end points. The two-table representation can handle generalized directed graphs, not just trees, so we defer a discussion of this representation here. There is very little difference in the actual way you would handle things, however. The usual reason for using a separate edge table is that the nodes are very complex objects or are duplicated and need to be kept separately for normalization.

In the single-table representation of hierarchies in SQL, there has to be one column for the identifier of the node and one column of the same data type for the parent of the node. In the organizational chart, the "linking column" is usually the employee identification number of the immediate boss_emp_id of each employee.

The single table works best for organizational charts because each employee can appear only once (assuming each employee has one and only one manager), whereas a parts explosion can have many occurrences of the same part within many different assemblies. Let us define a simple Personnel table.

```
CREATE TABLE Personnel
(emp_id CHAR(20) NOT NULL PRIMARY KEY
   CHECK (emp_id <> boss_emp_id), -- simple cycle check
 boss_emp_id CHAR(20), -- he has to be NULL-able!
 salary_amt DECIMAL(6,2) NOT NULL
   CHECK(salary_amt > 0.00));
```

This is a skeleton table and should not be used. There are no constraints to prevent cycles other than the simple case that nobody can be his own boss_emp_id. There is no constraint to assure one and only one root node in the tree. Yet this is what you will find in actual code (Figure 28.1).

Personnel

emp_id	boss_emp_id	salary_amt
'Albert'	NULL	$1,000.00
'Bert'	'Albert'	$900.00
'Chuck'	'Albert'	$900.00
'Donna'	'Chuck'	$800.00
'Eddie'	'Chuck'	$700.00
'Fred'	'Chuck'	$600.00

28.2 Finding the Root Node

The root of the tree has a boss_emp_id that is NULL—the root has no superior.

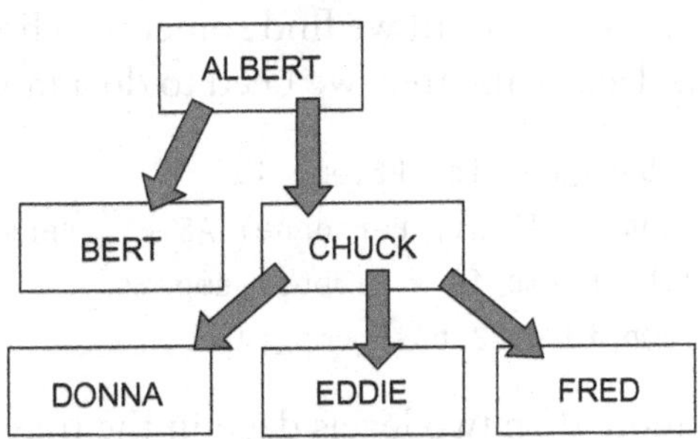

Figure 28.1 Simple Organizational Chart - Graph Model.

```
SELECT *
 FROM Personnel
 WHERE boss_emp_id IS NULL;
```

28.3 Finding Leaf Nodes

A leaf node is one that has no subordinates under it. In an adjacency list model, this set of nodes is fairly easy to find. They are going to be the employees who are not bosses to anyone else in the company, thus:

```
SELECT *
 FROM Personnel AS P1
WHERE NOT EXISTS (SELECT *
        FROM Personnel AS P2
         WHERE P1.emp_id = P2.boss_emp_id);
```

28.4 Finding Levels in a Tree

The length of a path from one node to another is measured by the number of levels of the hierarchy that you have to travel to get from the start to the finish. This is handy for queries such as "Does Mr. King have any authority over Mr. Jones?" or "Does a gizmo use a frammistat?" which are based on paths. To find the name of the boss_emp_id for each employee, the query is a self-JOIN, like this:

```
SELECT B1.boss_emp_id, P1.emp_id
 FROM Personnel AS B1, Personnel AS P1
 WHERE B1.boss_emp_id = P1.boss_emp_id;
```

But something is missing here. These are only the immediate bosses of the employees. Your boss_emp_id's boss_emp_id also has authority over you, and so forth up the tree until we find someone who has no subordinates. To go two levels deep in the tree, we need to do a more complex self-JOIN, thus:

```
SELECT B1.boss_emp_id, P2.emp_id
 FROM Personnel AS B1, Personnel AS P1, Personnel AS P2
 WHERE B1.boss_emp_id = P1.boss_emp_id
  AND P1.emp_id = P2.boss_emp_id;
```

To go more than two levels deep in the tree, just extend the pattern. Unfortunately, you have no idea just how deep the tree is, so you must keep

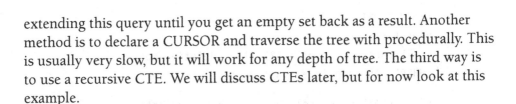

extending this query until you get an empty set back as a result. Another method is to declare a CURSOR and traverse the tree with procedurally. This is usually very slow, but it will work for any depth of tree. The third way is to use a recursive CTE. We will discuss CTEs later, but for now look at this example.

```
WITH RECURSIVE Subordinates (root_emp_id, emp_id, level)
AS
(SELECT P1.boss_emp_id, P1.emp_id, 0
  FROM Personnel AS P1
UNION ALL
SELECT S.root_emp_id, P2.emp_id, (S.level + 1)
  FROM Personnel AS P2, Subordinates AS S
 WHERE P2.boss_emp_id = S.emp_id)

SELECT * FROM Subordinates;
```

The anchor or fixpoint of the recursion is in the first SELECT. The second SELECT references the CTE, Subordinates, as a whole and joins to its rows. This UNION ALL is done over and over until it returns an empty set. The basic pattern we used to compute the organizational level can be used for hierarchical aggregations.

None of these queries are cheap to execute, but the recursive CTE is portable and go or any depth of hierarchy. It is usually a cursor and loop under the covers, it is a bitch to optimize even in theory.

28.5 Tree Operations

Tree operations are those that alter the size and shape of a tree, not the contents of the nodes of the tree. Some of these operations can be very complex, such as balancing a binary tree, but we will deal only with deletion and insertion of a whole subtree.

28.5.1 Subtree Deletion

Deleting a subtree is hard in the adjacency list model. You have to find all of the subordinates and then remove that subset from the table. One way of doing this is with a cursor, but you can also mark the subordinates and then delete them:

```
BEGIN ATOMIC
UPDATE Personnel
  SET boss_emp_id = '???????' -- deletion marker
 WHERE boss_emp_id = :subtree_root;

LOOP UPDATE Personnel     -- mark subordinates
    SET emp_id = CASE WHEN boss_emp_id = '???????'
            THEN '???????' ELSE emp_id END,
      boss_emp_id = CASE WHEN EXISTS
              (SELECT *
                FROM Personnel AS P1
               WHERE P1.emp_id = Personnel.boss_emp_id
                AND Personnel.boss_emp_id = '???????')
            THEN '???????' ELSE boss_emp_id END;
END LOOP;

DELETE FROM Personnel  -- delete marked nodes
 WHERE boss_emp_id = '???????';
END;
```

Obviously, you do not want to use a marker which has any real meaning in the table.

28.5.2 Subtree Insertion

Inserting a subtree under a given node is easy. Given a table with the subtree that is to be made subordinate to a given node, you simply write:

```
BEGIN
-- subordinate the subtree to his new boss_emp_id
INSERT INTO Personnel VALUES (:subtree_root, :new_boss_emp_id, …);
-- insert the subtree
INSERT INTO Personnel SELECT * FROM Subtree;
END;
```

Remember that a single row is just a subtree with one node, so you will that people will not try to build a subtree table. They mimic what they did with punch cards and sequential files; single row insertion statements.

28.6 Nested Sets Model

Since SQL is a set-oriented language, nested sets is a better model for trees and hierarchies. Let us redefine our simple Personnel table. The first three columns explain themselves and recopy from Section28.1. Ignore the lft and rgt columns for now, but note that their names are abbreviations for "left" and "right," which are reserved words in ANSI/ISO Standard SQL (Figure 28.2).

```
CREATE TABLE Personnel
(emp_id CHAR(10) NOT NULL PRIMARY KEY,
 boss_emp_id CHAR(10), -- this has to be NULL-able for the root node!!
 salary_amt DECIMAL(6,2) NOT NULL,
 lft INTEGER NOT NULL,
 rgt INTEGER NOT NULL);
```

Personnel

emp_id	boss_emp_id	salary_amt	lft	rgt
'Albert'	NULL	$1000.00	1	12
'Bert'	'Albert'	$900.00	2	3
'Chuck'	'Albert'	$900.00	4	11
'Donna'	'Chuck'	$800.00	5	6
'Eddie'	'Chuck'	$700.00	7	8
'Fred'	'Chuck'	$600.00	9	10

Which would look like this as a graph (Figure 28.2): To show a tree as nested sets, replace the boxes with ovals and then nest subordinate ovals inside their parents. Containment represents subordination. The root will be the largest oval and will contain every other node. The leaf nodes will be the

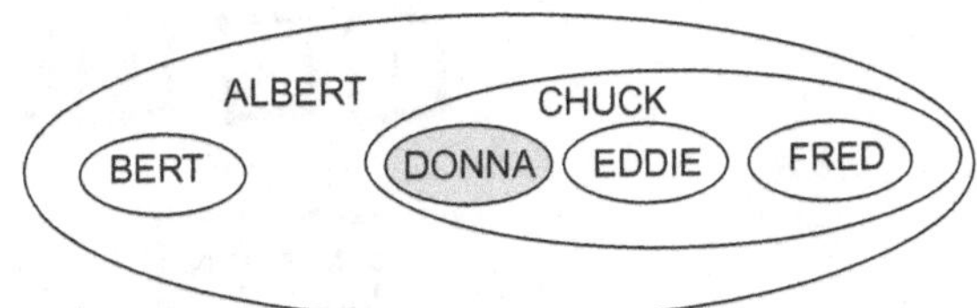

Figure 28.2 Simple Organizational Chart - Nested Sets.

innermost ovals, with nothing else inside them, and the nesting will show the hierarchical relationship. This is a natural way to model a parts explosion, as a final assembly is made of physically nested assemblies that finally break down into separate parts. This tree translates into this nesting of sets (Figures 28.2 and 28.3). Using this approach, we can model a tree with lft and rgt nested sets with number pairs. These number pairs will always contain the pairs of their subordinates so that a child node is within the bounds of its parent. This is a version of the nested sets, flattened onto a number line (Figure 28.4). If that mental model does not work for you, then visualize the nested sets model as a little worm with a Bates automatic numbering stamp crawling along the "boxes-and-arrows" version of the tree. The worm starts at the top, the root, and makes a complete trip around the tree. When he comes to a node, he puts a number in the cell on the side that he is visiting and his numbering stamp increments itself. Each node will get two numbers, one for the right (rgt) side and one for the left (lft) side. Computer science majors will recognize this as a modified preorder tree traversal algorithm. This numbering has some predictable results that we can use for building queries.

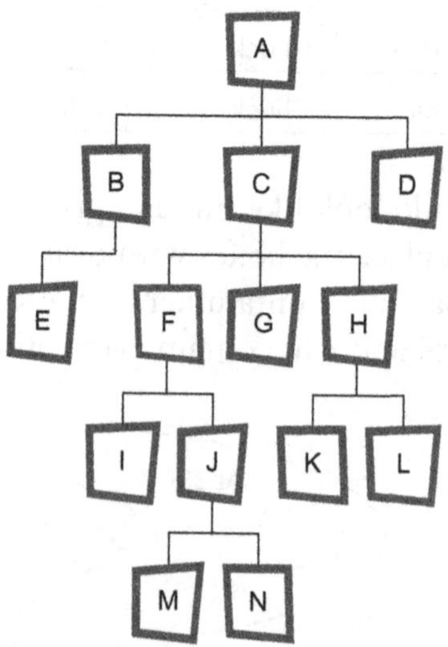

Figure 28.3 Bill of Materials - Graph Model.

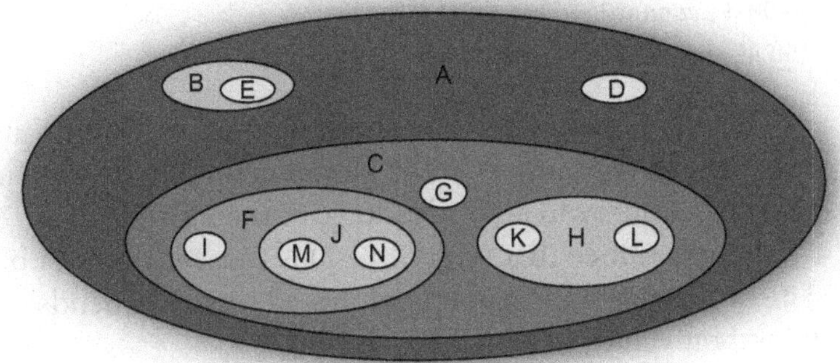

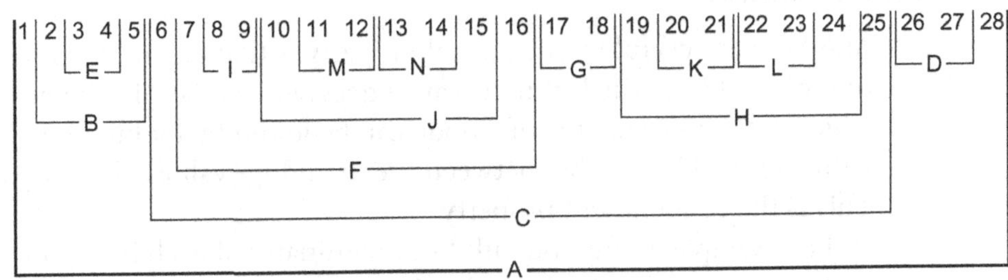

Figure 28.4 Bill of Materials - Nested Sets.

28.7 Finding Root and Leaf Nodes

The root will always have a 1 in its lft column and twice the number of nodes in its rgt column. This is easy to understand; the worm has to visit each node twice, once for the lft side and once for the rgt side, so the final count has to be twice the number of nodes in the whole tree. The root of the tree is found with the query.

```
SELECT *
 FROM Personnel
 WHERE lft = 1;
```

This query will take advantage of the index on the lft value. In the nested sets table, the difference between the lft and rgt values of leaf nodes is always 1. Think of the little worm turning the corner as he crawls along the tree. That means you can find all leaf nodes with the extremely simple query.

```
SELECT *
 FROM Personnel
 WHERE lft = (rgt- 1);
```

There is a further trick, to speed up queries. Build a unique index on either the lft column or on the pair of columns (lft, rgt) and then you can rewrite the query to take advantage of the index.

Did you notice that ((rgt−lft+1) is the size of the subtree at this node? This is the algebraic property of nested sets. It depends on incrementing the lft and rgt values to work.

28.8 Finding Subtrees

Another very useful mathematical property is that any node in the tree is the root of a subtree (the leaf nodes are a degenerate case). In the nested sets table, all the descendants of a node can be found by looking for the nodes with a rgt and lft number between the lft and rgt values of their parent node. This is the containment property.

For example, to find out all the subordinates of each boss_emp_id in the corporate hierarchy, you would write:

```
SELECT Mangers.emp_id AS boss, Workers.emp_id AS worker
 FROM Personnel AS Mgrs, Personnel AS Workers
 WHERE Workers.lft BETWEEN Mgrs.lft AND Mgrs.rgt
  AND Workers.rgt BETWEEN Mgrs.lft AND Mgrs.rgt;
```

Look at the way the numbering was done, and you can convince yourself that this search condition is too strict. We can drop the last predicate and simply use:

```
SELECT Mangers.emp_id AS boss, Workers.emp_id AS worker
 FROM Personnel AS Mgrs, Personnel AS Workers
 WHERE Workers.lft BETWEEN Mgrs.lft AND Mgrs.rgt;
```

This would tell you that everyone is also his own superior, so in some situations, you would also add the predicate.

.. AND Workers.lft <> Mgrs.lft

This simple self-JOIN query is the basis for almost everything that follows in the nested sets model.

28.9 Finding Levels and Paths in a Tree

The level of a node in a tree is the number of edges between the node and the root, where the larger the depth number, the farther away the node is from the root. A path is a set of edges which directly connect two nodes.

The nested sets model uses the fact that each containing set is "wider" (where width = (rgt − lft)) than the sets it contains.

Obviously, the root will always be the widest row in the table. The level function is the number of edges between two given nodes; it is fairly easy to calculate. For example, to find the level of each worker, you would use:

```
SELECT P2.emp_id, (COUNT(P1.emp_id) - 1) AS level
 FROM Personnel AS P1, Personnel AS P2
 WHERE P2.lft BETWEEN P1.lft AND P1.rgt
 GROUP BY P2.emp_id;
```

The reason for using the expression (COUNT(*) − 1) is to remove the duplicate count of the node itself because a tree starts at level zero. If you prefer to start at one, then drop the extra arithmetic.

28.9.1 Finding the Height of a Tree

The height of a tree is the length of the longest path in the tree. We know that this path runs from the root to a leaf node, so we can write a query to find like this:

```
SELECT MAX(level) AS height
 FROM (SELECT P2.emp_id, (COUNT(P1.emp_id) - 1)
     FROM Personnel AS P1, Personnel AS P2
     WHERE P2.lft BETWEEN P1.lft AND P1.rgt
     GROUP BY P2.emp_id) AS L(emp_id, level);
```

Other queries can be built from this tabular subquery expression of the nodes and their level numbers.

28.9.2 Finding Immediate Subordinates

The adjacency model allows you to find the immediate subordinates of a node immediately; you simply look in the column which gives the parent of every node in the tree.

This becomes complicated in the nested set model. You have to prune the subtree rooted at the node of boss_emp_id we are looking at to one level. Another way is to find his subordinates is to define them as personnel who have no other employee between themselves and the boss_emp_id in question.

```
CREATE VIEW Immediate_Subordinates (boss_emp_id, worker, lft, rgt)
AS SELECT Mgrs.emp_id, Workers.emp_id, Workers.lft, Workers.rgt
   FROM Personnel AS Mgrs, Personnel AS Workers
  WHERE Workers.lft BETWEEN Mgrs.lft AND Mgrs.rgt
   AND NOT EXISTS -- no middle manger between the boss_emp_id and us!
     (SELECT *
       FROM Personnel AS MidMgr
      WHERE MidMgr.lft BETWEEN Mgrs.lft AND Mgrs.rgt
       AND Workers.lft BETWEEN MidMgr.lft AND MidMgr.rgt
       AND MidMgr.emp_id NOT IN (Workers.emp_id, Mgrs.emp_id));
```

There is a reason for setting this up as a VIEW and including the lft and rgt numbers of the subordinates. The lft and rgt numbers for the parent can be reconstructed by

```
SELECT boss_emp_id, MIN(lft) - 1, MAX(rgt) + 1
  FROM Immediate_Subordinates AS S1
 GROUP BY boss_emp_id;
```

This illustrates a general principle of the nested sets model; it is easier to work with subtrees than to work with individual nodes or other subsets of the tree.

28.9.3 Finding Oldest and Youngest Subordinates

The third property of a nested sets model is sibling ordering. Do you remember the old Charlie Chan movies? Charlie Chan was the Chinese detective created by Earl Derr Biggers. There were 44 "Charlie Chan" movies made from 1931 to 1949. Detective Chan had varying number of children who were always helping him with his cases. The kids were referred to by their birth order, number one son, number two son, and so forth.

Organizations with a seniority system are much like the Chan family. Within each organizational level, the immediate subordinates have a left to right order implied by their lft value. The adjacency list model does not have a concept of such rankings, so the following queries are not possible without extra columns to hold the ordering in the adjacency list model. This lets you assign some significance to being the leftmost child of a parent. For example, the employee in this position might be the next in line for promotion in a corporate hierarchy.

Most senior subordinate is found by this query:

```
SELECT Workers.emp_id, ' is the oldest child of ', :my_employee
 FROM Personnel AS Mgrs, Personnel AS Workers
 WHERE Mgrs.emp_id = :my_employee
  AND Workers.lft + 1 = Mgrs.lft; -- leftmost child
```

Most junior subordinate:

```
SELECT Workers.emp_id, ' is the youngest child of ', :my_employee
 FROM Personnel AS Mgrs, Personnel AS Workers
 WHERE Mgrs.emp_id = :my_employee
  AND Workers.rgt = Mgrs.rgt - 1; -- rightmost child
```

The real trick is to find the nth sibling of a parent in a tree.

```
SELECT S1.worker, ' is the number ', :n, ' son of ', S1.boss_emp_id
 FROM Immediate_Subordinates AS S1
 WHERE S1.boss_emp_id = :my_employee
  AND 1 = (SELECT COUNT(S2.lft) - 1
        FROM Immediate_Subordinates AS S2
        WHERE S2.boss_emp_id = S1.boss_emp_id
         AND S2.boss_emp_id <> S1.worker
         AND S2.lft BETWEEN 1 AND S1.lft);
```

Notice that you have to subtract one to avoid counting the parent as his own child. Here is another way to do this and get a complete ordered listing of siblings.

```
SELECT P1.emp_id AS boss_emp_id, S1.worker,
        COUNT(S2.lft) AS sibling_order
  FROM Immediate_subordinates AS S1,
       Immediate_subordinates AS S2,
       Personnel AS P1
 WHERE S1.boss_emp_id = P1.emp_id
   AND S2.boss_emp_id = S1.boss_emp_id
   AND S2.lft <= S1.lft
 GROUP BY p1.emp_id, S1.worker;
```

28.9.4 Finding a Path

To find and number the nodes in the path from a :start_node to a :finish_node, you can repeat the nested sets "BETWEEN predicate trick" twice to form an upper and a lower boundary on the set.

```
SELECT T2.node,
   (SELECT COUNT(*)
     FROM Tree AS T4
    WHERE T4.lft BETWEEN T1.lft AND T1.rgt
     AND T2.lft BETWEEN T4.lft AND T4.rgt) AS path_nbr
 FROM Tree AS T1, Tree AS T2, Tree AS T3
 WHERE T1.node = :start_node
  AND T3.node = :finish_node
  AND T2.lft BETWEEN T1.lft AND T1.rgt
  AND T3.lft BETWEEN T2.lft AND T2.rgt;
```

Using the Parts explosion tree, this query would return the following table for the path from 'C' to 'N,' with 1 being the highest starting node and the other nodes numbered in the order they must be traversed.

node	path_nbr
C	1
F	2
J	3
N	4

However, if you just need a column to use in a sort for outputting the answer in a host language, then replace the subquery expression with "(T2.rgt−T2.lft) AS sort_col" and use an ORDER BY clause in a cursor.

28.10 Functions in the Nested Sets Model

JOINs and ORDER BY clauses will not interfere with the nested sets model as they will with the adjacency graph model. Nor are the results dependent on the order in which the rows are displayed as in vendor extensions. The LEVEL function for a given employee node is a matter of counting how many lft and rgt groupings (superiors) this employee node's lft or rgt is within. You can get this by modifying the sense of the BETWEEN predicate in the query for subtrees:

```
SELECT COUNT(Mgrs.emp_id) AS level
  FROM Personnel AS Mgrs, Personnel AS Workers
 WHERE Workers.lft BETWEEN Mgrs.lft AND Mgrs.rgt
   AND Workers.emp_id = :my_employee;
```

A simple total of the salaries of the subordinates of a supervising employee works out the same way. Notice that this total will include the boss_emp_id's salary_amt, too.

```
SELECT SUM (Workers.salary_amt) AS payroll
 FROM Personnel AS Mgrs, Personnel AS Workers
 WHERE Workers.lft BETWEEN Mgrs.lft AND Mgrs.rgt
  AND Mgrs.emp_id = :my_employee;
```

A slightly trickier function involves using quantity columns in the nodes to compute an accumulated total. This usually occurs in parts explosions, where one assembly may contain several occurrences of a subassembly.

```
SELECT SUM (Subassem.qty * Subassem.price) AS totalcost
  FROM Blueprint AS Assembly, Blueprint AS Subassem
 WHERE Subassem.lft
       BETWEEN Assembly.lft AND Assembly.rgt
   AND Assembly.part_nbr = :this_part;
```

28.11 Deleting Nodes and Subtrees

Deleting a single node in the middle of the tree is conceptually harder than removing whole subtrees. When you remove a node in the middle of the tree, you have to decide how to fill the hole. There are two ways. The first method is to promote one of the subordinates to the original node's position—Dad dies and the oldest son takes over the business. The second method is to connect the subordinates to the parent of the original node—Mom dies and the kids are adopted by Grandma.

28.11.1 Deleting Subtrees

This query will take the downsized employee as a parameter and remove the subtree rooted under him. The trick in this query is that we are using the key, but we need to get the lft and rgt values to do the work. The answer is scalar subqueries:

```
DELETE FROM Personnel
 WHERE lft BETWEEN
  (SELECT lft FROM Personnel WHERE emp_id = :downsized)
  AND
  (SELECT rgt FROM Personnel WHERE emp_id = :downsized);
```

The problem is that this will result gaps in the sequence of nested sets numbers. You can still do queries that depend on containment and sibling ordering, but the algebraic property gone. Closing the gaps is like garbage collection in other languages.

28.11.2 Deleting a Single Node

Deleting a single node in the middle of the tree is harder than removing whole subtrees. When you remove a node in the middle of the tree, you have to decide how to fill the hole. There are two ways. The first method is to connect the subordinates to the parent of the original node—Mom dies and the kids are adopted by Grandma.

Grandma gets the kids automatically in the nested sets model; you just delete the node and its subordinates are already contained in their ancestor nodes.

The second method is to promote one of the subordinates to the original node's position—Dad dies and a chid inherits the business, usually, the oldest son. There is a problem with this operation, however. If the older child has subordinates of his own, then you have to decide how to handle them and so on down the tree until you get to a leaf node.

Let's use a '??' as a marker for the downsized employee. This way we can promote the oldest subordinate to the vacant job and then decide if we want to fill his previous position with his oldest subordinate.

```
BEGIN
 UPDATE Personnel -- set removed emp_id to vacant position marker
  SET emp_id = '??'
 WHERE emp_id = :downsized;
```

```
 UPDATE Personnel -- promotion
  SET emp_id
    = CASE Personnel.emp_id
        WHEN '??' -- move oldest child into vacant position marker
        THEN (SELECT P1.emp_id
            FROM Personnel AS p1
           WHERE P1.lft = Personnel.lft + 1)
        WHEN (SELECT P2.emp_id -- move vacant position marker into
oldest child
            FROM Personnel AS P1, Personnel AS P2
           WHERE (P1.lft + 1) = P2.lft
            AND P1.emp_id = '??')
        THEN '??'
        ELSE emp_id END
 WHERE NOT (emp_id = '??' AND (lft + 1 = rgt)); -- vacancy is not at leaf
node
END;
```

28.11.3 Closing Gaps in the Tree

The important thing is to preserve the nested subsets based on lft and rgt numbers. As you remove nodes from a tree, you create gaps in the nested sets numbers. These gaps do not destroy the subset property or sibling ordering, but they can present other problems and should be closed. This is like garbage collection in other languages. The easiest way to understand the code is to break it up into a series of meaningful VIEWs and then use the VIEWs to UPDATE the tree table. This VIEW "flattens out" the whole tree into a list of nested sets numbers, regardless of whether they are lft or rgt numbers:

```
CREATE VIEW LftRgt(old_lftrgt, new_lftrgt)
AS
(WITH LftRgt (lftrgt)
 AS
 (SELECT lft from Personnel
   UNION ALL
  SELECT rgt from Personnel)

SELECT lftrgt, ROW_NUMBER() OVER (ORDER BY lftrgt)
  LftRgt;
```

```
UPDATE Personnel
  SET lft = CASE WHEN old_lftrgt = lft
                 THEN new_lftrgt
                 ELSE lft END,
      rgt = CASE WHEN old_lftrgt = rgt
                 THEN new_lftrgt
                 ELSE rgt END;
```

28.12 Summary Functions on Trees

There are tree queries that deal strictly with the nodes themselves and have nothing to do with the tree structure at all. For example, what is the name of the president of the company? How many people are in the company? Are there two people with the same name working here? These queries are handled with the usual SQL queries and there are no surprises.

Other types of queries do depend on the *tree structure*. For example, what is the total weight of a finished assembly (i.e., the total of all of its subassembly weights)? Do Harry and John report to the same boss_emp_id? And so forth. Let's consider a sample database that shows a parts explosion for a Frammis again, but this time in nested sets representation. The leaf nodes are the basic parts, the root node is the final assembly, and the nodes in between are subassemblies. Each part or assembly has a unique catalog number (in this case, a single letter), a weight, and the quantity of this unit that is required to make the next unit above it. The declaration looks like this:

```
CREATE TABLE Frammis
(part CHAR(2) PRIMARY KEY,
 qty INTEGER NOT NULL
   CONSTRAINT non_negative_qty
   CHECK (qty >= 0),
 wgt INTEGER NOT NULL
   CONSTRAINT non_negative_wgt
   CHECK (wgt >= 0),
 lft INTEGER NOT NULL UNIQUE
   CONSTRAINT valid_lft
   CHECK (lft > 0),
 rgt INTEGER NOT NULL UNIQUE
   CONSTRAINT valid_rgt
```

```
  CHECK (rgt > 1),
CONSTRAINT valid_range_pair
CHECK (lft < rgt));
```

We initially load it with this data:

Frammis

part	qty	wgt	lft	rgt
'A'	1	0	1	28
'B'	1	0	2	5
'C'	2	0	6	19
'D'	2	0	20	27
'E'	2	12	3	4
'F'	5	0	7	16
'G'	2	6	17	18
'H'	3	0	21	26
'I'	4	8	8	9
'J'	1	0	10	15
'K'	5	3	22	23
'L'	1	4	24	25
'M'	2	7	11	12
'N'	3	2	13	14

Notice that the weights of the subassemblies are initially set to zero and only parts (leaf nodes) have weights. You can easily insure this is true with this statement.

```
UPDATE Frammis
  SET wgt = 0
 WHERE lft < (rgt - 1);
```

The weight of an assembly will be calculated as the total weight of all its subassemblies. The tree initially looks like this (Figures 28.5–28.7).

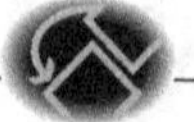

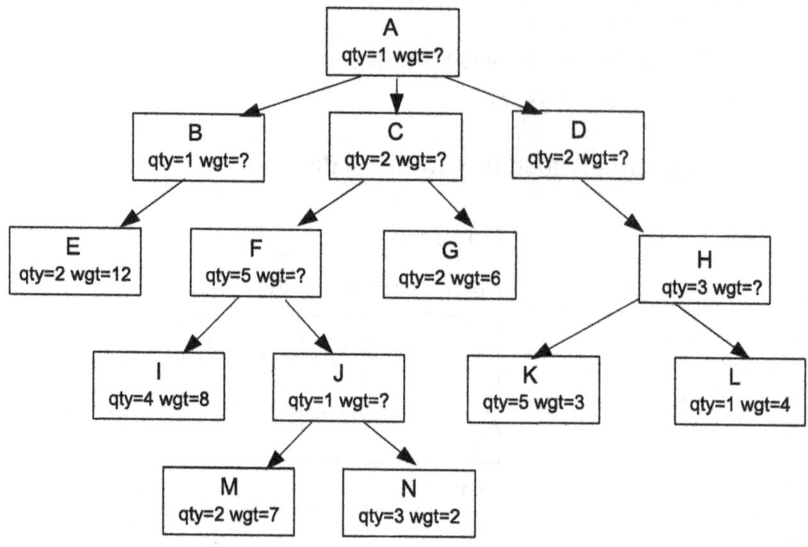

Figure 28.5 Bill of Materials - Initial State.

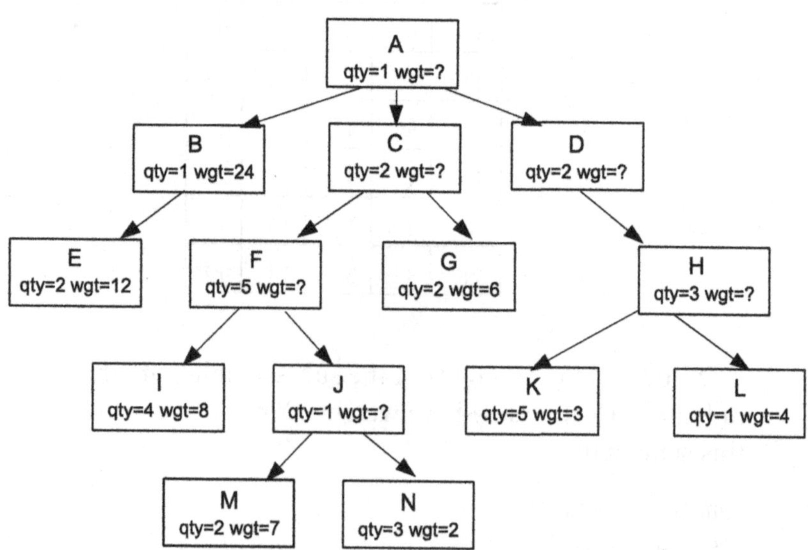

Figure 28.6 Bill of Materials - First Level Subassemblies.

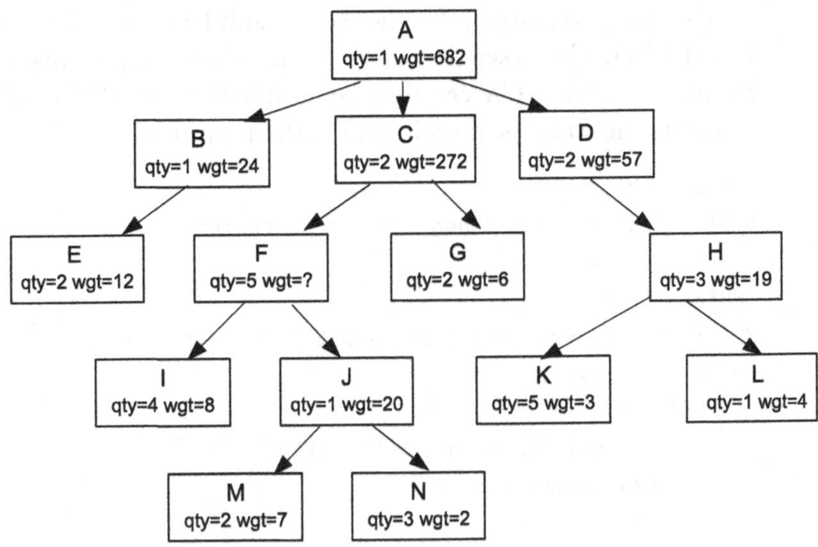

Figure 28.7 Bill of Materials - Final Assembly.

Look at the M and N leaf nodes. The table says that we need two M units weighing 7 kilograms each, plus three N units weighing 2 kilograms each, to make one J assembly. So that is $((2 * 7) + (3 * 2)) = 20$ kilograms per J assembly. That is, the weight of a nonleaf node is the sum of the products of the weights and quantities of its immediate subordinates.

The problem is that the nested sets model is good at finding subtrees, but not at finding a single level within the tree. The immediate subordinates of a node are found with this view:

```
CREATE VIEW Immediate_Kids (parent, child, wgt)
AS
SELECT F2.part, F1.part, F1.wgt
  FROM Frammis AS F1, Frammis AS F2
  WHERE F1.lft BETWEEN F2.lft AND F2.rgt
    AND F1.part <> F2.part
    AND NOT EXISTS
        (SELECT *
           FROM Frammis AS F3
         WHERE F3.lft BETWEEN F2.lft AND F2.rgt
           AND F1.lft BETWEEN F3.lft AND F3.rgt
         AND F3.part NOT IN (F1.part, F2.part));
```

The query says that F2 is the parent, and F1 is one of it's child. The EXISTS() checks to see that there are no other descendants strictly between F1 and F2. This VIEW can then be used with this UPDATE statement to calculate the weights of each level of the Frammis.

```
BEGIN ATOMIC
UPDATE Frammis -- set non-leaf nodes to zero
  SET wgt = 0
 WHERE lft < rgt - 1;
WHILE (SELECT wgt FROM Frammis WHERE lft = 1) = 0
DO UPDATE Frammis
    SET wgt
      = (SELECT SUM(F1.qty * F1.wgt)
         FROM Frammis AS F1
         WHERE EXISTS
            (SELECT *
             FROM Immediate_kids AS I1
             WHERE parent = Frammis.part
              AND I1.child = F1.part))
   WHERE wgt = 0 -- weight is missing
    AND NOT EXISTS -- subtree rooted here is completed
        (SELECT *
          FROM Immediate_kids AS I2
         WHERE I2.parent = Frammis.part
          AND I2.wgt = 0);
END WHILE;
END;
```

This is a bit tricky, but in English we are calculating the weights of the sub-assemblies by moving up the tree until we get to the root. A node is filled in with a weight when all of its subordinate assemblies have a weight assigned to them. The EXISTS() predicate in the WHERE clause says that this part in Frammis is a parent and the NOT EXISTS() predicate says that no sibling has a zero (i.e., unknown) weight. This query works from the leaf nodes up to the root and has been applied repeatedly.

If we change the weight of any part, we must correct the whole tree. Simply set the weight of all nonleaf nodes to zero first and redo this procedure. Once the proper weights and quantities are in place, it is fairly easy to find averages and other aggregate functions within a subtree.

Here is how the table changes after each execution:

First iteration (7 rows affected)

part	qty	wgt	lft	rgt
'A'	1	0	1	28
'B'	1	24	2	5
'C'	2	0	6	19
'D'	2	0	20	27
'E'	2	12	3	4
'F'	5	0	7	16
'G'	2	6	17	18
'H'	3	19	21	26
'I'	4	8	8	9
'J'	1	20	10	15
'K'	5	3	22	23
'L'	1	4	24	25
'M'	2	7	11	12
'N'	3	2	13	14

Second iteration (4 rows affected)

part	qty	wgt	lft	rgt
'A'	1	0	1	28
'B'	1	24	2	5
'C'	2	0	6	19
'D'	2	57	20	27
'E'	2	12	3	4
'F'	5	52	7	16
'G'	2	6	17	18
'H'	3	19	21	26
'I'	4	8	8	9
'J'	1	20	10	15
'K'	5	3	22	23
'L'	1	4	24	25
'M'	2	7	11	12
'N'	3	2	13	14

Third iteration (2 rows affected)

part	qty	wgt	lft	rgt
'A'	1	0	1	28
'B'	1	24	2	5
'C'	2	272	6	19
'D'	2	57	20	27
'E'	2	12	3	4
'F'	5	52	7	16
'G'	2	6	17	18
'H'	3	19	21	26
'I'	4	8	8	9
'J'	1	20	10	15
'K'	5	3	22	23
'L'	1	4	24	25
'M'	2	7	11	12
'N'	3	2	13	14

Fourth iteration (1 row, the root, is affected and looping halts)

part	qty	wgt	lft	rgt
'A'	1	682	1	28
'B'	1	24	2	5
'C'	2	272	6	19
'D'	2	57	20	27
'E'	2	12	3	4
'F'	5	52	7	16
'G'	2	6	17	18
'H'	3	19	21	26
'I'	4	8	8	9
'J'	1	20	10	15
'K'	5	3	22	23
'L'	1	4	24	25
'M'	2	7	11	12
'N'	3	2	13	14

28.13 Inserting and Updating Trees

Updates to the nodes are done by searching for the key of each node; there is nothing special about them. Inserting a subtree or a new node involves finding a place in the tree for the new node, spreading the other nodes apart by incrementing their (lft, rgt) numbers, and then renumbering the new subtree to fit. For example, let's insert a new node, G1, under part G. We can insert one node at a time like this:

```
BEGIN ATOMIC
DECLARE right_most_sibling INTEGER;

SET right_most_sibling
  = (SELECT rgt
     FROM Frammis
    WHERE part = 'G');
UPDATE Frammis
  SET lft = CASE WHEN lft > right_most_sibling
         THEN lft + 2
         ELSE lft END,
    rgt = CASE WHEN rgt >= right_most_sibling
         THEN rgt + 2
         ELSE rgt END
 WHERE rgt >= right_most_sibling;

 INSERT INTO Frammis (part, qty, wgt, lft, rgt)
 VALUES ('G1', 3, 4, parent, (parent + 1));
 COMMIT WORK;
END;
```

The idea is to spread the lft and rgt numbers after the youngest child of the parent, G in this case, over by two to make room for the new addition, G1. This procedure will add the new node to the rightmost child position, which helps to preserve the idea of an age order among the siblings.

28.13.1 Moving a Subtree Within a Tree

Yes, it is possible to move subtrees inside the nested sets model for hierarchies. But we need to get some preliminary things out of the way first. The nested sets model needs a few auxiliary tables to help it. The first is:

```
CREATE VIEW LftRgt (i)
AS SELECT lft FROM Tree
  UNION ALL
  SELECT rgt FROM Tree;
```

This is all lft and rgt values in a single column. Since we should have no duplicates, we use a UNION ALL to construct the VIEW. Yes, LftRgt can be written as a derived table inside queries, but there are advantages to use a VIEW. Self-joins are much easier to construct. Code is easier to read. If more than one user needs this table, it can be materialized only once by the SQL engine.

The next table is a working table to hold subtrees that we extract from the original tree. This could be declared as a local temporary table, but it would lose the benefit of a PRIMARY KEY declaration.

```
CREATE TABLE WorkingTree
(root CHAR(2) NOT NULL,
 node CHAR(2) NOT NULL,
 lft INTEGER NOT NULL,
 rgt INTEGER NOT NULL,
 PRIMARY KEY (root, node));
```

The root column is going to be the value of the root node of the extracted subtree. This gives us a fast way to find an entire subtree via part of the primary key. While this is not important for the stored procedure discussed here, it is useful for other operations that involve multiple extracted subtrees.

Let me move right to the commented code. The input parameters are the root node of the subtree being moved and the node which is to become its new parent. In this procedure, there is an assumption that new sibling are added on the right side of the immediate subordinates so that siblings are ordered by their age.

```
CREATE PROCEDURE MoveSubtree
         (IN my_root CHAR(2),
         IN new_parent CHAR(2))
AS
BEGIN
DECLARE right_most_sibling INTEGER,
    subtree_size INTEGER;

-- clean out and rebuild working tree
DELETE FROM WorkingTree;
```

```
INSERT INTO WorkingTree (root, node, lft, rgt)
SELECT my_root,
    T1.node,
    T1.lft - (SELECT MIN(lft)
          FROM Tree
         WHERE node = my_root),
    T1.rgt - (SELECT MIN(lft)
          FROM Tree
         WHERE node = my_root)
 FROM Tree AS T1, Tree AS T2
 WHERE T1.lft BETWEEN T2.lft AND T2.rgt
  AND T2.node = my_root;

-- Cannot move a subtree to itself, infinite recursion
IF (new_parent IN (SELECT node FROM WorkingTree))
THEN BEGIN
   PRINT 'Cannot move a subtree to itself, infinite recursion';
   DELETE FROM WorkingTree;
   END
ELSE BEGIN

   -- remove the subtree from original tree
   DELETE FROM Tree
   WHERE node IN (SELECT node FROM WorkingTree);

   -- get size and location for inserting working tree into new slot
   SET right_most_sibling
     = (SELECT rgt
       FROM Tree
       WHERE node = new_parent);

   SET subtree_size = (SELECT (MAX(rgt)+1) FROM WorkingTree);

   -- make a gap in the tree
   UPDATE Tree
    SET lft = CASE WHEN lft > right_most_sibling
               THEN lft + subtree_size
               ELSE lft END,
      rgt = CASE WHEN rgt >= right_most_sibling
               THEN rgt + subtree_size
```

```
         ELSE rgt END
 WHERE rgt >= right_most_sibling;

 -- insert the subtree and renumber its rows
 INSERT INTO Tree (node, lft, rgt)
 SELECT node,
    lft + right_most_sibling,
    rgt + right_most_sibling
  FROM WorkingTree;

 -- clean out working tree table
 DELETE FROM WorkingTree;

 -- close gaps in tree
 UPDATE Tree
  SET lft = (SELECT COUNT(*)
         FROM LftRgt
        WHERE LftRgt.i <= Tree.lft),
    rgt = (SELECT COUNT(*)
         FROM LftRgt
        WHERE LftRgt.i <= Tree.rgt);
END;
END; -- of MoveSubtree
```

As a minor note, the variables right_most_sibling and @subtree_size could have been replaced with their scalar subqueries in the UPDATE and INSERT INTO statements that follow their assignments. But that would make the code much harder to read at the cost of only a slight boost in performance.

28.14 Converting Adjacency List to Nested Sets Model

Most SQL databases have used the adjacency list model for two reasons. The first reason is that Dr. Codd came up with it in the early days of the relational model and nobody thought about it after that. The second reason is that the adjacency list is a way of "faking" pointer chains, the traditional programming method in procedural languages for handling trees.

It would be fairly easy to load an adjacency list model table into a host language program and then use a recursive preorder tree traversal program from a college freshman data structures textbook to build the nested sets model. This is not the fastest way to do a conversion, but since conversions are probably not going to be frequent tasks, it might be good enough when translated into your SQL product's procedural language.

28.15 Converting Nested Sets to Adjacency List Model

To convert a nested sets model into an adjacency list model, use this query:

```
SELECT P.node AS parent, P.node
 FROM Tree AS P
    LEFT OUTER JOIN
    Tree AS C
    ON P.lft = (SELECT MAX(lft)
           FROM Tree AS S
          WHERE P.lft > S.lft
           AND P.lft < S.rgt);
```

This single statement, originally written by Alejandro Izaguirre, replaces my own previous attempt that was based on a push-down stack algorithm. Once more, we see that best way to program SQL is to think in terms of sets and not procedures.

28.16 Comparing Nodes and Structure

There are *several kinds* of equality comparisons when you are dealing with a hierarchy:

(1) Same nodes in both tables

(2) Same structure in both tables

(3) Same nodes and structure in both tables—they are identical

Let me once more invoke my semi-quasi-famous Organization chart I used earlier to show the nested sets model and a second Personnel table to which we will compare it.

Case one: Same employees

Let's create a second table with the same nodes, but with a different structure

```
CREATE TABLE Personnel_2
(emp_id CHAR(10) NOT NULL PRIMARY KEY,
 lft INTEGER NOT NULL UNIQUE CHECK (lft > 0),
 rgt INTEGER NOT NULL UNIQUE CHECK (rgt > 1),
 CONSTRAINT order_okay CHECK (lft < rgt));
```

Insert sample data and flatten the organization to report directly to Albert.

Personnel_2

emp_id	lft	rgt
'Albert'	1	12
'Bert'	2	3
'Chuck'	4	5
'Donna'	6	7
'Eddie'	8	9
'Fred'	10	11

```
SELECT CASE WHEN COUNT(*) = 0
            THEN 'They have the same nodes'
            ELSE 'They are different node sets' END AS answer
  FROM (SELECT emp_id, COUNT(emp_id) OVER() AS emp_cnt FROM Personnel
AS P1
       EXCEPT
       SELECT emp_id, COUNT(emp_id) OVER() AS emp_cnt FROM
Personnel_2 AS P2)
       AS X;
```

The trick in this query is including the row count in a windowed function.

Case two: Same structure

I will not bother with an ASCII drawing, but let's present a table with sample data that has different people inside the same structure.

Personnel_3

emp_id	lft	rgt
'Alvin'	1	12
'Bobby'	2	3
'Charles'	4	11
'Donald'	5	6
'Edward'	7	8
'Frank'	9	10

If these things are really separate trees, then life is easy. You do the same join as before but with the (lft, rgt) pairs:

```
SELECT CASE WHEN COUNT(*) = 0
            THEN 'They have the same structure'
            ELSE 'They are different structure' END AS answer
  FROM (SELECT lft, rgt, COUNT(*) OVER() AS node_cnt FROM Personnel AS P1
        EXCEPT
        SELECT lft, rgt, COUNT(*) OVER() AS node_cnt FROM
Personnel_2 AS P2)
        AS X;
```

Case three: same nodes and same structure.

Just the last two queries:

```
SELECT CASE WHEN COUNT(*) = 0
            THEN 'They have the same structure and/or nodes'
            ELSE 'They are different structure and/or nodes' END AS
answer
  FROM (SELECT emp_id, lft, rgt, COUNT(*) OVER() AS node_cnt FROM
Personnel AS P1
        EXCEPT
        SELECT emp_id, lft, rgt, COUNT(*) OVER() AS node_cnt FROM
Personnel AS P3)
        AS X;
```

But more often than not, you will be comparing subtrees within the same tree. This is best handled by putting the two subtrees into a canonical form. First you need the root node (i.e., the emp_id in this sample data) and then you can renumber the (lft, rgt) pairs with a derived table of this form:

```
WITH P1 (emp_id, lft, rgt)
AS
(SELECT emp_id,
     lft - (SELECT MIN(lft FROM Personnel),
     rgt - (SELECT MIN(lft FROM Personnel)
  FROM Personnel
  WHERE ...),
```

For an exercise, try writing the same structure and node queries with the adjacency list model.

Several vendors have added extensions to SQL to handle trees. Since these are proprietary, you should look up the syntax and rules for your products. Most of them are based on the adjacency list model and involve a hidden cursor or repeated self-joins. They will not port.

This chapter is a quick overview. You really need to get a copy of *Joe Celko's Trees and Hierarchies in SQL for Smarties* (Second Edition; Morgan Kaufmann; 2012; ISBN: 978-012387733) which provides details and several other data models. I cannot include a 275+ age book in a chapter.

Queues

QUEUE IS A fancy name for a waiting line. The basic idea is that things enter one end of the queue (the tail), wait for awhile and get serviced at the other end of the queue (the head). This is what happens to people in a grocery store checkout line or to DVDs in your Netflix list.

Each element has a position in the queue, so we know that a table to model a queue will have the position in a column as well as the element. Basically, this is like a one dimensional array, but we want to manipulate the elements.

For my examples, I want to use something people know; a queue of DVD movies.

29.1 Basic DDL

The basic DDL is simple, and you can use new features to automate parts of the application. The obvious tool is the sequence, to give us the place numbers in the queue.

```
CREATE SEQUENCE Movie_Place
AS INTEGER
 START WITH 1
 INCREMENT BY 1
 MINVALUE 1
 MAXVALUE 1000000
 NO CYCLE;
```

On the assumption that I will never watch over one million movies in my life, I have set a safe upper limit. However, I could set the upper limit based on a company policy. The queue is a simple two-column table, which allows resubmitting a title later in the queue.

```
CREATE TABLE Movie_Queue
(movie_seq INTEGER DEFAULT NEXT VALUE FOR Movie_Place PRIMARY KEY,
 movie_title VARCHAR(35) NOT NULL);

INSERT INTO Movie_Queue(movie_title) VALUES ('The Best Exotic
Marigold Hotel');
INSERT INTO Movie_Queue(movie_title) VALUES ('Bad Girls from Mars');
INSERT INTO Movie_Queue(movie_title) VALUES ('Jiro Dreams of Sushi');
INSERT INTO Movie_Queue(movie_title) VALUES ('Hick');
```

This DDL assumes that the head of the queue is MIN(movie_seq). To make life easier, we would prefer that the head is one and the rest of the queue has no gaps in the sequence. The garbage collection is simple:

```
CREATE PROCEDURE Garbage_Collection()
LANGUAGE SQL
MERGE INTO Movie_Queue AS M1
USING (SELECT movie_seq AS old_movie_seq,
     ROW_NUMBER() OVER (ORDER BY movie_seq) AS new_movie_seq
     FROM Movie_Queue) AS M2
ON M1.movie_seq = M2.old_movie_seq
WHEN MATCHED
THEN UPDATE
 SET movie_seq = new_movie_seq;
```

It might be more useful to put the M2 subquery into a VIEW. This will be updatable and gives us sequential numbering for display.

29.2 Enqueue, Dequeue, and Empty Procedures

Putting a new movie in the list is easy as it is just a simple insertion. This is called enqueuing, if you like obscure words,

```
CREATE PROCEDURE Enqueue (IN movie_title VARCHAR(35))
LANGUAGE SQL
INSERT INTO Movie_Queue VALUES (movie_title);
```

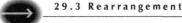

Dequeuing can be a trickier. It is not deterministic and has to return a value before it is deleted from the queue.

```
CREATE PROCEDURE Dequeue (OUT current_movie_title VARCHAR(35))
LANGUAGE SQL
BEGIN ATOMIC
SELECT movie_title
  INTO current_movie_title
  FROM Movie_Queue
 WHERE movie_seq = (SELECT MIN(movie_seq) FROM Movie_Queue);
DELETE FROM Movie_Queue
 WHERE movie_seq = (SELECT MIN(movie_seq) FROM Movie_Queue);
END;
```

The use of the singleton SELECT might surprise even experienced SQL programmers. But it has been part of the standards from the start. It is also handy to be able to empty the queue.

```
CREATE PROCEDURE Empty_Queue()
LANGUAGE SQL
BEGIN ATOMIC
DELETE FROM Movie_Queue;
ALTER SEQUENCE Movie_Place
RESTART WITH 1;
END;
```

29.3 Rearrangement

The Netflix queue management tool allows you to move a given movie to the head of the queue. This is actually a special case of rearrangement, but it is the most common one. People decided which video they wish to see next, so they move that video to the head of the queue.

```
CREATE PROCEDURE Move_to_Head (IN current_movie_title VARCHAR(35))
LANGUAGE SQL
UPDATE Movie_Queue
  SET movie_seq
      = CASE WHEN movie_title = current_movie_title
             THEN 1
             ELSE movie_seq + 1 END;
```

The more general rearrangement is move a queue element from position *i* to position *j*. If $(i=j)$ then we are done; this will not be done very often in the real world as it does nothing. But we can have $(i<j)$ or $(i>j)$ as two situations. It might be a good idea to run the garbage collection procedure first to give use easier math.

```
CREATE PROCEDURE Swap_Movies
       (IN first_movie_seq INTEGER,
        IN second_movie_seq INTEGER)

LANGUAGE SQL
UPDATE Movie_Queue
   SET movie_seq =
       CASE movie_seq
       WHEN first_movie_seq
       THEN second_movie_seq
       WHEN second_movie_seq
       THEN first_movie_seq
       ELSE movie_seq END --- do nothing
 WHERE movie_seq IN (first_movie_seq, second_movie_seq);
```

A more useful procedure takes the data element in the first position, moves it to the second position by sliding the intervening elements *up or down* in the queue.

```
CREATE PROCEDURE Slide_Movies
       (IN first_movie_seq INTEGER,
        IN second_movie_seq INTEGER)
LANGUAGE SQL
UPDATE Movie_Queue
   SET movie_seq =
       CASE
       WHEN movie_seq = first_movie_seq
       THEN second_movie_seq
       WHEN movie_seq BETWEEN first_movie_seq AND second_movie_seq
       THEN movie_seq - 1
       WHEN movie_seq BETWEEN second_movie_seq AND first_movie_seq
       THEN movie_seq + 1
       ELSE movie_seq END --- do nothing
```

```
WHERE movie_seq
      BETWEEN SYMMETRIC first_movie_seq AND second_movie_seq;
```

29.4 Queues and Math

The most important bit of math when working with queues is the average waiting time. The assumption is that new customers arrive at random, at a rate per unit of time, called λ. If the process can always handle jobs faster than they can arrive, the queue is never full. If the service is slightly slower, the queue will start to fill and empty into a shape called a Poisson distribution.

The shape waiting line will vary, but you will see what that little old lady for a full grocery cart in the express line can do when she increases λ (Figure 29.1).

Many years ago, banks and other retail stores had one check-out clerk per queue. This lead to a version of "Murphy's Law" that "the other line moves faster" in the folk lore. It also leads to banks and some retail stores instituted a single input queue with multiple serving clerks. The customer simply goes to the next available clerk when a signal light goes on at that cash register.

Too many clerks is a waste of salary, and too few the customer is not happy (and may abandon their shopping carts). Now the problem is to find the number of registers needed to keep the average wait down to an acceptable duration.

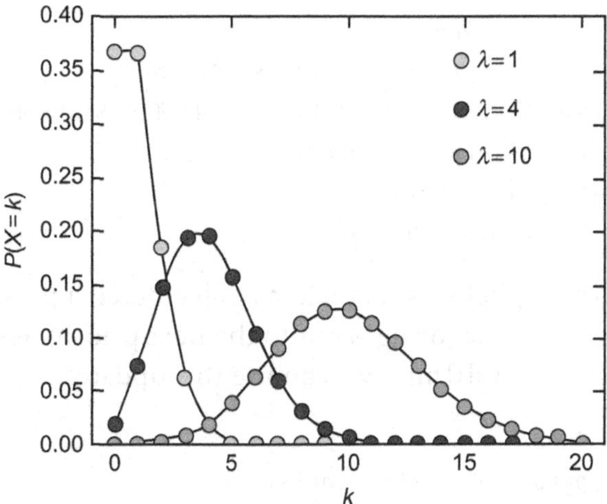

Figure 29.1 Poisson Distribution.

WalMart found that a policy of "If there are more than five customers in line, we will open a new register. We promise!" was optimal. Grocery stores have found that customers expect to wait longer for a larger purchase, but will abandon smaller purchases if the service time is too long. Express lines (10 or fewer items) create satisfaction by having a smaller value for λ.

If you want the mathematical theory of queueing, the classic book is Leonard Kleinrock; Queueing Systems. Volume 1: Theory; Wiley Interscience; 1975; ISBN 978-0471491101 and Queueing Systems. Volume 2: Computer Applications; 1976; ISBN 978-0471491118, you will need to be current on calculus and statistics.

29.5 Priority Queues

Mainframe computers still use batch processing. In these systems, jobs are put in a queue and processed one at a time as they come to the head of the queue. But not all jobs are of equal priority. The classic example is placing higher priority on doing the payroll or other regular corporate tasks than on software development. It is possible to get a "live lock" situation where software development is constantly bumped to the back of the queue.

One method is to insert new jobs into the queue at their appropriate priority level to start them. As time goes on, the priority level changes. The goal is to see that all jobs eventually clear the queue.

```
CREATE TABLE Job_Queue
(job_seq INTEGER DEFAULT NEXT VALUE FOR Job_Place,
 job_timestamp TIMESTAMP DEFAULT CURRENT_TIMESTAMP NOT NULL,
 job_priority INTEGER NOT NULL
   CHECK (job_priority >= 0),
 job_title VARCHAR(35) NOT NULL);
```

The timestamp tells us that when a job entered a priority level and we will reset it each time, the job ages out to the next priority level. If we want to advance a job every 10 min, we can use this update:

```
UPDATE Job_Queue
   SET job_priority = job_priority -1,
```

```
       job_timestamp = CURRENT_TIMESTAMP
 WHERE job_timestamp + INTERVAL '10:00' MINUTE TO SECOND
       <= CURRENT_TIMESTAMP;
```

The dequeue procedure needs to include the priority level, but it is the same logic as before, likewise the code to close up gaps in the job sequence and job priority numbering.

```
CREATE PROCEDURE Dequeue (OUT current_job_title VARCHAR(35))
LANGUAGE SQL
BEGIN ATOMIC
SELECT job_title
  INTO current_job_title
  FROM Job_Queue
 WHERE job_seq = (SELECT MIN(job_seq) FROM Job_Queue)
   AND job_priority = (SELECT MIN(job_priority) FROM Job_Queue);
DELETE FROM Job_Queue
 WHERE job_seq = (SELECT MIN(job_seq) FROM Job_Queue)
   AND job_priority = (SELECT MIN(job_priority) FROM Job_Queue);
END;
```

29.6 FIFO and LIFO Queues

The terms FIFO and LIFO stand for "first in, first out" and "last in, first out" respectively. They refer to how we value and allocate goods from an inventory. This will be easier to explain with an example for the readers who have not worked with an inventory system before. Imagine that we have a warehouse of one product to which we add stock once a day. Assume that today is 2016-01-05.

```
CREATE TABLE InventoryReceipts
(receipt_nbr INTEGER PRIMARY KEY,
 purchase_date DATETIME NOT NULL,
 qty_on_hand INTEGER NOT NULL
   CHECK (qty_on_hand >= 0),
 unit_price DECIMAL (12,4) NOT NULL);
```

with the following data.

InventoryReceipts

Receipt_nbr	Purchase_date	Qty_on_hand	Unit_price
1	2016-01-01	15	10
2	2016-01-02	25	12
3	2016-01-03	40	13
4	2016-01-04	35	12
5	2016-01-05	45	10

The business now sells 100 units on 2016-01-05. How do you calculate the value of the stock sold? There is not one right answer, but here are some options:

(1) Use the current replacement cost, which is $10.00 per unit as of 2016-01-05. That would mean the sale cost us $1000.00 because of a recent price break.

(2) Use the current average price per unit. We have a total of 160 units, for which we paid a total of $1840.00 and that gives us an average cost of $11.50 per unit, or $1150.00 in total inventory costs.

(3) Use LIFO. We start by looking at the most recent purchases and work *backwards* thru time until we have pulled 100 units from inventory.

Purchase Date	Extension	Total Units Picked so Far
2016-01-05	45×$10.00=$450.00	45
2016-01-04	35×$12.00=$420.00	80
2016-01-03	20×$13.00=$260.00	100

for a total of $1130.00 in inventory cost.

(4) Use FIFO. We start by looking at the earliest purchases and work *forward* thru time.

Purchase Date	Extension	Total Units Picked So Far
2016-01-01	15×$10.00=$150.00	15
2016-01-02	25×$12.00=$300.00	40
2016-01-03	40×$13.00=$520.00	80
2016-01-04	20×$12.00=$240.00	100

for a total of $1210.00 in inventory costs.

The first two scenarios are trivial to program. The LIFO and FIFO are more interesting because they involve looking at matching the order against blocks of inventory in a particular order. Consider this view:

```
CREATE VIEW LIFO (stock_date, unit_price, qty_on_hand_tot, tot_cost)
AS
SELECT R1.purchase_date, R1.unit_price, SUM(R2.qty_on_hand),
SUM(R2.qty_on_hand *
R2.unit_price)
 FROM InventoryReceipts AS R1,
      InventoryReceipts AS R2
 WHERE R2.purchase_date >= R1.purchase_date
 GROUP BY R1.purchase_date, R1.unit_price;
```

A row in this view tells us the total quantity on hand, the total cost of the goods in inventory, and what we were paying for items on each date. The quantity on hand is a running total. We can get the LIFO cost with this query.

```
SELECT (tot_cost - ((qty_on_hand_tot - :order_qty_on_hand) * unit_
price)) AS cost
  FROM LIFO AS L1
 WHERE stock_date
      = (SELECT MAX(stock_date)
           FROM LIFO AS L2
          WHERE qty_on_hand_tot >= :order_qty_on_hand);
```

This is straight algebra and a little logic. Find the most recent date that we had enough (or more) quantity on hand to meet the order. If by dumb blind luck, there is a day when the quantity on hand exactly matched the order, return the total cost as the answer. If the order was for more than we have in stock, then return nothing. If we go back to a day when we had more in stock than the order was for, then look at the unit price on that day, multiply by the overage, and subtract it.

Alternatively, you can use a derived table and a CASE expression. The CASE expression computes the cost of units which have a running total quantity less than the :order_qty_on_hand and then does algebra on the final block of inventory which would put the running total over the limit. The outer query does a sum on these blocks.

```
SELECT SUM(R3.v) AS inventory_cost
  FROM (SELECT R1.unit_price
               * CASE WHEN SUM(R2.qty_on_hand) <= :order_qty_on_hand
                      THEN R1.qty_on_hand
                      ELSE :order_qty_on_hand
                           - (SUM(R2.qty_on_hand) - R1.qty_on_hand)
  END
          FROM InventoryReceipts AS R1,
               InventoryReceipts AS R2
         WHERE R1.purchase_date <= R2.purchase_date
         GROUP BY R1.purchase_date, R1.qty_on_hand, R1.unit_price
        HAVING (SUM(R2.qty_on_hand) - R1.qty_on_hand)
               <= :order_qty_on_hand)
       AS R3(v);
```

FIFO can be done with a similar VIEW or derived table.

```
CREATE VIEW FIFO (stock_date, unit_price, qty_on_hand_tot, tot_cost)
AS
SELECT R1.purchase_date, R1.unit_price,
       SUM(R2.qty_on_hand), SUM(R2.qty_on_hand *
R2.unit_price)
 FROM InventoryReceipts AS R1,
       InventoryReceipts AS R2
 WHERE R2.purchase_date <= R1.purchase_date
 GROUP BY R1.purchase_date, R1.unit_price;
```

with the corresponding query

```
SELECT (tot_cost - ((qty_on_hand_tot - :order_qty_on_hand) *
unit_price)) AS inventory_cost
  FROM FIFO AS F1
 WHERE stock_date
       = (SELECT MIN (stock_date)
            FROM FIFO AS F2
           WHERE qty_on_hand_tot >= :order_qty_on_hand);
```

Matrices in SQL

ARRAYS ARE NOT the same thing as matrices. An array is a data structure whose elements are accessed by a numeric value called an index. A matrix is an array with mathematical operations defined on it. A matrix can be one, two, three, or more dimensional structures. The most common mathematical convention has been to use the letters i, j, and k for the indexes for the respective dimension.

SQL had neither arrays nor matrices because the only data structure is a table. Arrays violate the rules of First Normal Form (1NF) and the Information Principle required for a relational database, which say that all columns are scalars. Actually, DB2 supports arrays in SQL-stored procedures, as a vendor extension.

This was unfortunately changed in SQL:2003 with the addition of collection types. You can now declare a column to be an array of one of the SQL data types. The array is one-dimensional and has no mathematical operations on it. There is an array constructor and a comparison operation. The constructor can be a comma separated list or a query with an ORDER BY clause. *Fortunately, almost nobody uses any of this.*

There is no obvious way to display or transmit a multidimensional array column as a linear result set. Different languages and different compilers for the same language store arrays in column-major or row-major order, so there is no standard. There is no obvious way to write constraints on nonscalar values.

The goal of SQL is to be a database language that operates with a wide range of host languages. To meet that goal, the basic SQL scalar data types are designed to match the basic scalar data types in any host language. The transfer of data to the host language programs is to be as easy as possible. This is a huge advantage in a tiered architecture.

30.1 Arrays via Named Columns

An array in the other programming languages has a name and subscripts by which the array elements are referenced. The array elements are all of the same data type and the subscripts are all sequential integers. Some languages start numbering at zero, some start numbering at one, and some let the user set the upper and lower bounds. For example, a Pascal array declaration would look like this:

```
foobar : ARRAY [1..5] OF INTEGER;
```

Would have integer elements foobar[1], foobar[2], foobar[3], foobar[4], and foobar[5]. The same structure is most often mapped into an SQL declaration as

```
CREATE TABLE Foobar1
(element1 INTEGER NOT NULL,
 element2 INTEGER NOT NULL,
 element3 INTEGER NOT NULL,
 element4 INTEGER NOT NULL,
 element5 INTEGER NOT NULL);
```

The elements cannot be accessed by the use of a subscript in this table as they can in a true array. That is, to set the array elements equal to zero in Pascal takes one statement with a FOR loop in it:

```
FOR i := 1 TO 5 DO foobar[i] := 0;
```

The same action in SQL would be performed with the statement

```
UPDATE Foobar1
   SET element1 = 0,
       element2 = 0,
       element3 = 0,
       element4 = 0,
       element5 = 0;
```

because there is no subscript which can be iterated in a loop. Any access has to be based on column names and not on subscripts. These "pseudo-subscripts" lead to building column names on the fly in dynamic SQL, giving code that is both slow and dangerous. Even worse, some users will use the same approach in table names to destroy their logical data model.

Let's assume that we design a Personnel table with separate columns for the names of four children, and we start with an empty table and then try to use it.

1. What happens if we hire a man with fewer than four children?

   We can fire him immediately or make him have more children. We can restructure the table to allow for fewer children. The usual, and less drastic, solution is to put NULLs in the columns for the nonexistent children. We then have all of the problems associated with NULLs to handle.

2. What happens if we hire a man with five children?

   We can fire him immediately or order him to kill one of his children. We can restructure the table to allow five children. We can add a second row to hold the information on children 5 through 8; however, this destroys the uniqueness of the emp_id, so it cannot be used as a key. We can overcome that problem by adding a new column for record number, which will form a two-column key with the emp_id. This leads to needless duplication in the table.

3. What happens if the employee dies?

   We will delete all the data of his children along with his, even if the company owes benefits to the survivors. You could have a status of 'dead' for the employee and a lot of logic in any statement about his family; this will not be pretty.

4. What happens if the employee dies?

   We can fire him or order him to get another child immediately. We can restructure the table to allow only three children. We can overwrite the child's data with NULLs and get all of the problems associated with NULL values.

   This last one is the most common decision. But what if we had used the multiple-row trick and this employee had a fifth child—should that child be brought up into the vacant slot in the current row and the second row of the set deleted?

5. What happens if the employee replaces a current child with a new one?
   Should the new child's data overwrite the NULLs in the dead child's data? Should the new child's data be put in the next available slot and overwrite the NULLs in those columns?
   Some of these choices involve rebuilding the database. Others are simply absurd attempts to restructure reality to fit the database. The real point is that each insertion or deletion of a child involves a different procedure, depending on the size of the group to which he/she belongs. File systems had variant records that could change the size of their repeating groups.

Consider instead a table of employees and another table for the children:

```
CREATE TABLE Personnel
(emp_id INTEGER NOT NULL PRIMARY KEY,
 emp_name CHAR(30) NOT NULL,
 ...);

CREATE TABLE Dependents
(emp_id INTEGER NOT NULL
    REFERENCES Personnel(emp_id)
    ON UPDATE CASCADE,
 child_name CHAR(30) NOT NULL,
 PRIMARY KEY (emp_id, child_name),
 birth_date DATE NOT NULL,
 sex_code CHAR(1) NOT NULL);
```

To add a child, you insert a row into Children. To remove a child, you delete a row from Children. There is nothing special about the fourth or fifth child that requires the database system to use special procedures. There are no NULLs in either table.

The tradeoff is that the number of tables in the database schema increases, but the total amount of storage used will be smaller, because you will keep data only on children who exist rather than using NULLs to hold space. The goal is to have data in the simplest possible format so that any host program can use it.

The late Gabrielle Wiorkowski (1938-2012), in her excellent DB2 classes, used an example of a table for tracking the sales made by salespersons during the past year. That table could be defined as

```
CREATE TABLE AnnualSales1
(salesman CHAR(15) NOT NULL PRIMARY KEY,
 jan DECIMAL(5,2),
 feb DECIMAL(5,2),
 mar DECIMAL(5,2),
 apr DECIMAL(5,2),
 may DECIMAL(5,2),
 jun DECIMAL(5,2),
 jul DECIMAL(5,2),
 aug DECIMAL(5,2),
 sep DECIMAL(5,2),
 oct DECIMAL(5,2),
 nov DECIMAL(5,2),
 "dec" DECIMAL(5,2) -- DEC[IMAL] is a reserved word
);
```

We have to allow for NULLs in the monthly sales_amts in the first version of the table, but the table is actually quite a bit smaller than it would be if we were to declare it as:

```
CREATE TABLE AnnualSales2
(salesman CHAR(15) NOT NULL PRIMARY KEY,
 sale_month CHAR(3)
    CONSTRAINT valid_month_abbrev
    CHECK (sale_month IN ('Jan', 'Feb', 'Mar', 'Apr',
             'May', 'Jun', 'Jul', 'Aug',
             'Sep', 'Oct', 'Nov', 'Dec'),
 sales_amt DECIMAL(5,2) NOT NULL,
 PRIMARY KEY(salesman, sale_month));
```

In Wiorkowski's actual example in DB2, the break-even point for DASD storage was April; that is, the storage required for AnnualSales1 and AnnualSales2 is about the same in April of the given year.

Queries that deal with individual salespersons will run much faster against the AnnualSales1 table than queries based on the AnnualSales2 table, because all the data are in one row in the AnnualSales1 table. They may be a bit messy and may have to have function calls to handle possible NULL values, but they are not very complex.

The only reason for using AnnualSales1 is that you have a data warehouse and all you want to see is summary information, grouped into years. This design is not acceptable in an OLTP system.

30.2 Arrays via Subscript Columns

Another approach to faking a multidimensional array is to map arrays into a table with an integer column for each subscript, thus:

```
CREATE TABLE Foobar2
(i INTEGER NOT NULL PRIMARY KEY
  CONSTRAINT valid_array_index
  CHECK(i BETWEEN 1 AND 5),
 element REAL NOT NULL);
```

This looks more complex than the first approach, but it is closer to what the original Pascal declaration was doing behind the scenes. Subscripts resolve to unique physical addresses, so it is not possible to have two values for foobar[i]; hence, i is a key. The Pascal compiler will check to see that the subscripts are within the declared range; hence the CHECK() clause.

The first advantage of this approach is that multidimensional arrays are easily handled by adding another column for each subscript. The Pascal declaration

```
ThreeD : ARRAY [1..3, 1..4, 1..5] OF REAL;
```

is mapped over to

```
CREATE TABLE ThreeD
(i INTEGER NOT NULL
  CONSTRAINT valid_i
  CHECK(i BETWEEN 1 AND 3),
 j INTEGER NOT NULL
  CONSTRAINT valid_j
  CHECK(j BETWEEN 1 AND 4),
 k INTEGER NOT NULL
  CONSTRAINT valid_k
  CHECK(k BETWEEN 1 AND 5),
 element REAL NOT NULL,
 PRIMARY KEY (i, j, k));
```

Obviously, SELECT statements with GROUP BY clauses on the subscript columns will produce row and column totals, thus:

```
SELECT i, j, SUM(element) -- sum across the k columns
 FROM ThreeD
 GROUP BY i, j;

SELECT i, SUM(element) -- sum across the j and k columns
 FROM ThreeD
 GROUP BY i;

SELECT SUM(element) -- sum the entire array
 FROM ThreeD;
```

If the original one element/one column approach were used, the table declaration would have 120 columns, named "element_111" through "element_345". This would be too many names to handle in any reasonable way; you would not be able to use the GROUP BY clauses for array projection, either.

Another advantage of this approach is that the subscripts can be data types other than integers. DATE and TIME data types are often useful, but CHARACTER and approximate numerics can have their uses too.

30.3 Matrix Operations in SQL

A matrix is not quite the same thing as an array. Matrices are mathematical structures with particular properties that we cannot take the time to discuss here. You can find that information in a college freshman algebra book. Though it is possible to do many matrix operations in SQL, it is not a good idea, because such queries and operations will eat up resources and run much too long. SQL was never meant to be a language for calculations.

Let us assume that we have two-dimensional arrays that are declared as tables, using two columns for subscripts, and that all columns are declared with a NOT NULL constraint.

The presence of NULLs is not defined in linear algebra and I have no desire to invent a three-valued linear algebra of my own. Another problem is that a matrix has rows and columns that are not the same as the rows and columns of an SQL table; as you read the rest of this section, be careful not to confuse the two.

```
CREATE TABLE MyMatrix
(element INTEGER NOT NULL, -- could be any numeric data type
 i INTEGER NOT NULL CHECK (i > 0),
 j INTEGER NOT NULL CHECK (j > 0),
 CHECK ((SELECT MAX(i) FROM MyMatrix)
```

```
    = (SELECT COUNT(i) FROM MyMatrix)),
 CHECK ((SELECT MAX(j) FROM MyMatrix)
    = (SELECT COUNT(j) FROM MyMatrix)));
```

The constraints see that the subscripts of each element are within proper range. I am starting my subscripts at one, but a little change in the logic would allow any value.

30.3.1 Matrix Equality

This test for matrix equality is from the article "SQL Matrix Processing" by Mrdalj, Vujovic, and Jovanovic in 1996 July issue of *Database Programing & Design*. Two matrices are equal if their cardinality and the cardinality of their intersection are all equal.

```
SELECT COUNT(*) FROM MatrixA
UNION
SELECT COUNT(*) FROM MatrixB
UNION
SELECT COUNT(*)
  FROM MatrixA AS A, MatrixB AS B
 WHERE A.i = B.i
   AND A.j = B.j
   AND A.element = B.element;
```

You have to decide how to use this query in your context. If it returns one number, they are the same and otherwise they are different.

30.3.2 Matrix Addition

Matrix addition and subtraction are possible only between matrices of the same dimensions. The obvious way to do the addition is simply:

```
SELECT A.i, A.j, (A.element + B.element) AS total
  FROM MatrixA AS A, MatrixB AS B
 WHERE A.i = B.i
   AND A.j = B.j;
```

But properly, you ought to add some checking to be sure the matrices match. We can assume that both start numbering subscripts with either one or zero.

```
SELECT A.i, A.j, (A.element + B.element) AS total
  FROM MatrixA AS A, MatrixB AS B
```

```
WHERE A.i = B.i
  AND A.j = B.j
  AND (SELECT COUNT(*) FROM MatrixA)
       = (SELECT COUNT(*) FROM MatrixB)
  AND (SELECT MAX(i) FROM MatrixA)
      = (SELECT MAX(i) FROM MatrixB)
  AND (SELECT MAX(j) FROM MatrixA)
      = (SELECT MAX(j) FROM MatrixB));
```

Likewise, to make the addition permanent, you can use the same basic query in an UPDATE statement:

```
UPDATE MatrixA
   SET element = element
             + (SELECT element
                  FROM MatrixB
                 WHERE MatrixB.i = MatrixA.i
                   AND MatrixB.j = MatrixA.j)
 WHERE (SELECT COUNT(*) FROM MatrixA)
       = (SELECT COUNT(*) FROM MatrixB)
   AND (SELECT MAX(i) FROM MatrixA)
       = (SELECT MAX(i) FROM MatrixB)
   AND (SELECT MAX(j) FROM MatrixA)
       = (SELECT MAX(j) FROM MatrixB));
```

30.3.3 Matrix Multiplication

Multiplication by a scalar constant is direct and easy:

```
UPDATE MyMatrix
   SET element = element * :constant;
```

Matrix multiplication is not as big a mess as might be expected.

Remember that the first matrix must have the same number of rows as the second matrix has columns. That means A[i, k] * B[k, j] = C[i, j], which we can show with an example:

```
CREATE TABLE MatrixA
(i INTEGER NOT NULL
  CHECK (i BETWEEN 1 AND 10), -- pick your own bounds
 k INTEGER NOT NULL
  CHECK (k BETWEEN 1 AND 10), -- must match MatrixB.k range
```

```
 element INTEGER NOT NULL,
 PRIMARY KEY (i, k));
```

MatrixA

i	k	Element
1	1	2
1	2	–3
1	3	4
2	1	–1
2	2	0
2	3	2

```
CREATE TABLEMatrixB
(k INTEGER NOT NULL
  CHECK (k BETWEEN 1 AND 10), -- must match MatrixA.k range
 j INTEGER NOT NULL
  CHECK (j BETWEEN 1 AND 4), -- pick your own bounds
 element INTEGER NOT NULL,
 PRIMARY KEY (k, j));
```

MatrixB

k	j	Element
1	1	–1
1	2	2
1	3	3
2	1	0
2	2	1
2	3	7
3	1	1
3	2	1
3	3	–2

```
CREATE VIEW MatrixC(i, j, element)
AS
SELECT i, j, SUM(MatrixA.element * MatrixB.element)
```

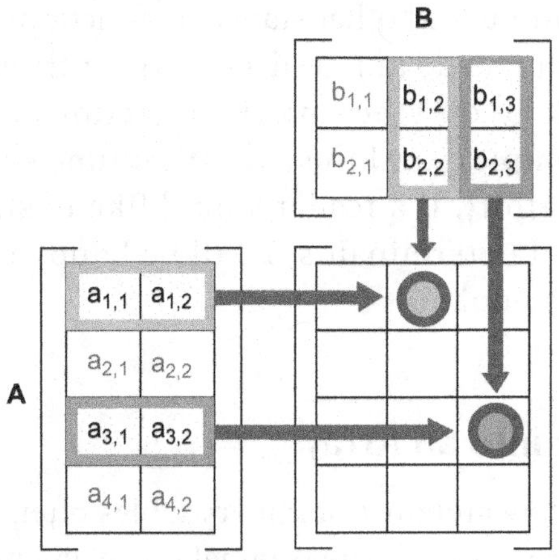

Figure 30.1 Matrix multiplication.

```
  FROM MatrixA, MatrixB
 WHERE MatrixA.k = MatrixB.k
 GROUP BY i, j;
```

This is taken directly from the definition of matrix multiplication (Figure 30.1).

30.3.4 Other Matrix Operations

The transpose of a matrix is easy to do:

```
CREATE VIEW TransA (i, j, element)
AS SELECT j, i, element FROM MatrixA;
```

Again, you can make the change permanent with an UPDATE statement:

```
UPDATE MatrixA
 SET i = j, j = i;
```

Multiplication by a column or row vector is just a special case of matrix multiplication, but a bit easier. Given the vector V and MatrixA:

```
SELECT i, SUM(A.element * V.element)
 FROM MatrixA AS A, VectorV AS V
 WHERE V.j = A.i
 GROUP BY A.i;
```

Cross tabulations and other statistical functions traditionally use an array to hold data. But you do not need a matrix for them in SQL.

It is possible to do other matrix operations in SQL, but the code becomes so complex, and the execution time so long, that it is simply not worth the effort. If a reader would like to submit queries for eigenvalues and determinants, I will be happy to put them in future editions of this book.

30.4 Flattening a Table into an Array

Reports and data warehouse summary tables often want to see an array laid horizontally across a line. The original one element/one column approach to mapping arrays was based on seeing such reports and duplicating that structure in a table. A subscript is often an enumeration, denoting a month or another time period, rather than an integer.

For example, a row in a "Salesmen" table might have a dozen columns, one for each month of the year, each of which holds the total commission earned in a particular month. The year is really an array, subscripted by the month. The subscripts-and-value approach requires more work to produce the same results. It is often easier to explain a technique with an example.

Let us imagine a company that collects time cards from its truck drivers, each with the driver's name, the week within the year (using the ISO-8601 format), and his total hours. We want to produce a report with one line for each driver and 6weeks of his time across the page. The Timecards table looks like this:

```
CREATE TABLE Timecards
(driver_name CHAR(25) NOT NULL,
 week_date CHAR(9) NOT NULL
   CONSTRAINT valid_week_date
   CHECK(week_date LIKE '[12][0-9][0-9][0-9]W[0-5][0-9]-[1-7]'),
 PRIMARY KEY (driver_name, week_date),
 work_hrs INTEGER
    CONSTRAINT zero_or_more_hours
    CHECK(work_hrs >= 0),
 PRIMARY KEY (driver_name, week_date));
```

We need to "flatten out" this table to get the desired rows for the report. First create a working storage table from which the report can be built.

```
CREATE TEMPORARY TABLE TimeReportWork -- working storage
(driver_name CHAR(25) NOT NULL,
 wk1 INTEGER, -- important that these columns are NULL-able
 wk2 INTEGER,
 wk3 INTEGER,
 wk4 INTEGER,
 wk5 INTEGER,
 wk6 INTEGER);
```

Notice two important points about this table. First, there is no primary key; second, the weekly data columns are NULL-able. This table is then filled with time card values, thus:

```
INSERT INTO TimeReportWork (driver_name, wk1, wk2, wk3, wk4, wk5, wk6)
SELECT driver_name,
    SUM(CASE SUBSTRING (week_date FROM 1 FOR 7) = :rpt_week_date_1)
        THEN work_hrs ELSE 0 END) AS wk1,
    SUM(CASE SUBSTRING (week_date FROM 1 FOR 7) = :rpt_week_date_2)
        THEN work_hrs ELSE 0 END) AS wk2,
    SUM(CASE SUBSTRING (week_date FROM 1 FOR 7) = :rpt_week_date_3)
        THEN work_hrs ELSE 0 END) AS wk3,
    SUM(CASE SUBSTRING (week_date FROM 1 FOR 7) = :rpt_week_date_4)
        THEN work_hrs ELSE 0 END) AS wk4,
    SUM(CASE SUBSTRING (week_date FROM 1 FOR 7) = :rpt_week_date_5)
        THEN work_hrs ELSE 0 END) AS wk5,
    SUM(CASE SUBSTRING (week_date FROM 1 FOR 7) = :rpt_week_date_6)
        THEN work_hrs ELSE 0 END) AS wk6
  FROM Timecards
 WHERE week_date BETWEEN :rpt_week_date_1 AND (:rpt_week_date_6);
```

The number of weeks in the WHERE clauses will vary with the period covered by the report. The parameter ":rpt_week_date_#" is week of the report. If a driver did not work in a particular week, the corresponding weekly column gets a zero hours total. However, if the driver has not worked at all in the last 6 weeks, we could lose him completely (no time

cards, no summary). Depending on the nature of the report, you might consider using an OUTER JOIN to a "Personnel" table to be sure you have all the driver's names.

The NULLs are coalesced to zero in this example, but if you drop the "..ELSE 0" clauses, the SUM() will have to deal with a week of all NULLs and return a NULL. This lets you tell the difference between a driver who was missing for the reporting period and a driver who worked zero hours and turned in a time card for that during the period. That difference could be important for computing the payroll.

30.5 Comparing Arrays in Table Format

It is often necessary to compare one array or set of values with another when the data is represented in a table. Remember that comparing a set with a set does not involve ordering the elements, whereas an array does. For this discussion, let us create two tables, one for employees and one for their dependents. The children are subscripted in the order of their births—that is, 1 is the oldest living child, and so forth.

```
CREATE TABLE Personnel
(emp_id INTEGER PRIMARY KEY,
 emp_name CHAR(15) NOT NULL,
 . . . );

CREATE TABLE Dependents
(emp_id INTEGER NOT NULL -- the parent
 dependent_name CHAR(15) NOT NULL, -- the array element
 birth_seq INTEGER NOT NULL, -- the array subscript
 PRIMARY KEY (emp_id, dependent_name));
```

The query "Find pairs of employees whose children have the same set of names" is very restrictive, but we can make it more so by requiring that the children be named in the same birth order. Both Mr. X and Mr. Y must have exactly the same number of dependents; both sets of names must match. We can assume that no parent has two children with the same name (George Foreman does not work here) or born at the same time (we will order twins). Let us begin by inserting test data into the Dependents table, thus:

Dependents

Emp_id	Dependent_name	Birth_seq
1	'Dick'	2
1	'Harry'	3
1	'Tom'	1
2	'Dick'	3
2	'Harry'	1
2	'Tom'	2
3	'Dick'	2
3	'Harry'	3
3	'Tom'	1
4	'Harry'	1
4	'Tom'	2
5	'Curly'	2
5	'Harry'	3
5	'Moe'	1

In this test data, employees 1, 2, and 3 all have dependents named 'Tom', 'Dick', and 'Harry'.

The birth order is the same for the children of employees 1 and 3, but not for employee 2.

For testing purposes, you might consider to adding an extra child to the family of employee 3, and so forth, to play with this data.

Though there are many ways to solve this query, this approach will give us some flexibility that others would not. Construct a VIEW that gives us the number of dependents for each employee:

```
CREATE VIEW FamilySize (emp_id, tally)
AS
SELECT emp_id, COUNT(*)
 FROM Dependents
 GROUP BY emp_id;
```

Create a second VIEW that holds pairs of employees who have families of the same size.

This VIEW is also useful for other statistical work, but that is another topic.

```
CREATE VIEW Samesize (emp_id1, emp_id2, tally)
AS SELECT F1.emp_id, F2.emp_id, F1.tally
    FROM Familysize AS F1, Familysize AS F2
  WHERE F1.tally = F2.tally
    AND F1.emp_id < F2.emp_id;
```

We will test for set equality by doing a self-JOIN on the dependents of employees with families of the same size. If one set can be mapped onto another with no children left over, and in the same birth order, then the two sets are equal.

```
SELECT D1.emp_id, ' named his ',
       S1.tally, ' kids just like ',
       D2.emp_id
  FROM Dependents AS D1, Dependents AS D2, Samesize AS S1
 WHERE S1.emp_id1 = D1.emp_id
   AND S1.emp_id2 = D2.emp_id
   AND D1.dependent_name = D2.dependent_name
   AND D1.birth_seq = D2.birth_seq
 GROUP BY D1.emp_id, D2.emp_id, S1.tally
HAVING COUNT(*) = S1.tally;
```

If birth order is not important, then drop the predicate D1.birth_seq = D2.birth_seq from the query.

This is a form of exact relational division with a second column equality test as part of the criteria.

30.6 Other Matrix Operations

It is possible to write Inverses and Determinants in SQL. It is insanely expensive even if you use proprietary tricks. Brian C. Brown, Manager of Solution Delivery, Data, and Analytics at Avanade, met this challenge in T-SQL and was able to perform simple regression (meaning, no ANOVA statistics) on a small data set consisting of four independent variables.

He was able to write Views named for the Determinants and Inverse, but without regression, he said "I wonder if your readers would see much point in understanding those operations."

Typical Queries

Partitioning and Aggregating Data in Queries

THIS CHAPTER IS concerned with how to break the data in SQL into meaningful subsets that can then be presented to the user or passed along for further reduction.

31.1 Coverings and Partitions

We need to define some basic set operations. A covering is a collection of subsets, drawn from a set, whose union is the original set. A partition is a covering whose subsets do not intersect each other. Cutting up a pizza is a partitioning; smothering it in two layers of pepperoni slices is a covering.

Partitions are the basis for most reports. The property that makes partitions useful for reports is aggregation: the whole is the sum of its parts. For example, a company budget is broken into divisions, divisions are broken into departments, and so forth. Each division budget is the sum of its department's budgets, and the sum of the division budgets is the total for the whole company again. We would not be sure what to do if a department belonged to two different divisions because that would be a covering and not a partition.

31.1.1 Partitioning by Ranges

A common problem in data processing is classifying things by the way they fall into a range on a numeric or alphabetic scale. The best approach to translating a code into a value when ranges are involved is to set up a table

with the high and the low values for each translated value in it. This was covered in the section on auxiliary tables in more detail, but here is a quick review.

Any missing values will easily be detected and the table can be validated for completeness. For example, we could create a table of ZIP code ranges and two-character state_code abbreviation codes like this:

```
CREATE TABLE State_Zip
(state_code CHAR(2) NOT NULL PRIMARY KEY,
 low_zip CHAR(5) NOT NULL UNIQUE,
 high_zip CHAR(5) NOT NULL UNIQUE,
 CONSTRAINT zip_order_okay CHECK(low_zip <= high_zip),
 . . . );
```

Here is a query that looks up the city_name customer_type and state_code code from the zip code in the Addressbook table to complete a mailing label with a simple JOIN that looks like this:

```
SELECT A1.customer_type, A1.street_address, SZ.city_name, SZ.state_code,
A1.zip
  FROM State_Zip AS SZ, Addressbook AS A1
 WHERE A1.zip BETWEEN SZ.low_zip AND SZ.high_zip;
```

You need to be careful with this predicate. If one of the three columns involved has a NULL in it, the BETWEEN predicate becomes UNKNOWN and will not be recognized by the WHERE clause. If you design the table of range values with the high value in one row equal to or greater than the low value in another row, both of those rows will be returned when the test value falls on the overlap.

If you know that you have a partitioning in the range value tables, you can write a query in SQL that will let you use a table with only the high value and the translation code. The grading system table would have (100%, 'A'), (89%, 'B'), (79%, 'C'), (69%, 'D'), and (59%, 'F') as its rows. Likewise, a table of the state_code code and the highest ZIP code in that state_code could do the same job as the BETWEEN predicate in the previous query.

```
CREATE TABLE State_Zip2
(high_zip CHAR(5) NOT NULL,
 state_code CHAR(2) NOT NULL,
 PRIMARY KEY (high_zip, state_code));
```

We want to write a query to give us the greatest lower bound or least upper bound on those values. The greatest lower bound (glb) operator finds the largest number in one column that is less than or equal to the target value in the other column. The least upper bound (lub) operator finds the smallest number greater than or equal to the target number. Unfortunately, this is not a good tradeoff, because the subquery is fairly complex and slow. The "high and low" columns are a better solution in most cases. Here is a second version of the Addressbook query, using only the high_zip column from the State_Zip2 table:

```
SELECT customer_type, street_address, city_name, state_code, zip
  FROM State_Zip2, Addressbook
 WHERE state_code =
       (SELECT state_code
          FROM State_Zip2
         WHERE high_zip =
               (SELECT MIN(high_zip)
                  FROM State_Zip2
                 WHERE Address.zip <= State_Zip2.high_zip));
```

If you want to allow for multiple-row matches by not requiring that the lookup table has unique values, the equality subquery predicate should be converted to an IN() predicate.

31.1.2 Partition by Functions

It is also possible to use a function that will partition the table into subsets that share a particular property. Consider the cases where you have to add a column with the function result to the table because the function is too complex to be reasonably written in SQL.

One common example of this technique is the Soundex function, which is often a vendor extension; the Soundex family assigns codes to names that are phonetically alike. The complex calculations in engineering and scientific databases that involve functions that SQL does not have are another example of this technique.

SQL was never meant to be a computational language. However, many vendors allow a query to access functions in the libraries of other programming languages. You must know what the cost in execution time for your product is before doing this. One version of SQL uses a threaded-code approach to carry parameters over to the other language's libraries and return

the results on each row—the execution time is horrible. Some versions of SQL can compile and link another language's library into the SQL.

Although this is a generalization, the safest technique is to unload the parameter values to a file in a standard format that can be read by the other language. Then use that file in a program to find the function results and create INSERT INTO statements that will load a table in the database with the parameters and the results. You can then use this working table to load the result column in the original table.

31.1.3 Partition by Sequential Order

We are looking for patterns over a history that has a sequential ordering to it. This ordering could be temporal or via a sequence numbering. For example, given a payment history we want to break it into groupings of behavior, say whether or not the payments were on time or late.

```
CREATE TABLE Payment_History
(payment_nbr INTEGER NOT NULL PRIMARY KEY,
 on_time_flg CHAR(1) DEFAULT 'Y' NOT NULL
     CHECK(on_time_flg IN ('Y', 'N')));

INSERT INTO Payment_History
VALUES (1006, 'Y'),
       (1005, 'Y'),
       (1004, 'N'),
       (1003, 'Y'),
       (1002, 'Y'),
       (1001, 'Y'),
       (1000, 'N');
```

The results that we want assign a grouping number to each run of on-time/late payments, thus.

Grp_nbr	Payment_nbr	On_time_flg
1	1006	'Y'
1	1005	'Y'
2	1004	'N'
3	1003	'Y'
3	1002	'Y'
3	1001	'Y'
4	1000	'N'

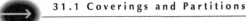

Here is a solution from Hugo Kornelis that depends on the payments always being numbered consecutively.

```
SELECT (SELECT COUNT(*)
          FROM Payment_History AS H2,
               Payment_History AS H3
         WHERE H3.payment_nbr = H2.payment_nbr + 1
           AND H3.on_time_flg <> H2.on_time_flg
           AND H2.payment_nbr >= H1.payment_nbr) + 1 AS grp,
      payment_nbr, on_time_flg
 FROM Payment_History AS H1;
```

This is very useful when looking for patterns in a history. A more complex version of the same problem would involve more than two categories. Consider a table with a sequential numbering and a list of products that have been received.

What we want is the average quality score value for a sequential grouping of the same Product. For example, I need an average of Entries 1, 2, and 3 because this is the first grouping of the same product type, but not want that average to include entry #8, which is also Product A, but in a different "group."

```
CREATE TABLE Product_Tests
(batch_nbr INTEGER NOT NULL PRIMARY KEY,
 prod_code CHAR(1) NOT NULL,
 prod_quality DECIMAL(8,4) NOT NULL);

INSERT INTO Product_Tests (batch_nbr, prod_code, prod_quality)
VALUES (1, 'A', 80),
       (2, 'A', 70),
       (3, 'A', 80),
       (4, 'B', 60),
       (5, 'B', 90),
       (6, 'C', 80),
       (7, 'D', 80),
       (8, 'A', 50),
       (9, 'C', 70);
```

The query then becomes:

```
SELECT X.prod_code, MIN(X.batch_nbr) AS start_batch_nbr, end_batch_nbr,
       AVG(B4.prod_quality) AS avg_prod_quality
```

```
FROM (SELECT B1.prod_code, B1.batch_nbr,
             MAX(B2.batch_nbr) AS end_batch_nbr
        FROM Product_Tests AS B1, Product_Tests AS B2
       WHERE B1.batch_nbr <= B2.batch_nbr
         AND B1.prod_code = B2.prod_code
         AND B1.prod_code
             = ALL (SELECT prod_code
                      FROM Product_Tests AS B3
                     WHERE B3.batch_nbr BETWEEN B1.batch_nbr
                       AND B2.batch_nbr)
      GROUP BY B1.prod_code, B1.batch_nbr) AS X
      INNER JOIN
      Product_Tests AS B4 -- join to get the quality measurements
      ON B4.batch_nbr BETWEEN X.batch_nbr AND X.end_batch_nbr
GROUP BY X.prod_code, X.end_batch_nbr ;
```

Results

Prod_code	Start_batch_nbr	End_batch_nbr	Avg_prod_quality
'A'	1	3	76.67
'B'	4	5	75
'C'	6	6	80
'D'	7	7	80
'A'	8	8	50
'C'	9	9	70

31.2 Advanced Grouping, Windowed Aggregation, and OLAP in SQL

Most SQL programmers work with OLTP (Online Transaction Processing) databases and have had no exposure to Online Analytic Processing (OLAP) and data warehousing. OLAP is concerned with summarizing and reporting data, so the schema designs and common operations are very different from the usual SQL queries.

As a gross generalization, everything you knew in OLTP is reversed in a data warehouse.

(1) OLTP changes data in short, frequent transactions. A data warehouse is bulk loaded with static data on a schedule. The data remains constant once it is in place.

(2) OLTP databases want to store only the data needed to do its current work. A data warehouse wants all the historical data it can hold. In 2008, Teradata Corporation announced that they had five customers running data warehouses larger than a petabyte. The "Petabyte Power Players" club included eBay, with 5 petabytes of data; Wal-Mart Stores, which has 2.5 petabytes; Bank of America, which is storing 1.5 petabytes; Dell, which has a 1 petabyte data warehouse; an unnamed bank. The definition of a petabyte is $2^{50} = 1{,}125{,}899{,}906{,}842{,}624$ bytes = 1024 terabytes or roughly 10^{15} bytes.

(3) OLTP queries tend to be for simple facts. Data warehouse queries tend to be aggregate relationships that are more complex. For example, an OLTP query might ask, "How much chocolate did Joe Celko buy?" while a data warehouse might ask, "What is the correlation between chocolate purchases, geographic location, and wearing tweed?"

(4) OLTP wants to run as fast as possible. A data warehouse is more concerned with the accuracy of computations and it is willing to wait to get an answer to a complex query.

(5) Properly designed OLTP databases are normalized. A data warehouse is usually a Star or Snowflake Schema, which is highly denormalized. The Star Schema is due to Ralph Kimball and you can get more details about it in his books and articles.

The Star Schema is a violation of basic normalization rules. There is a large central fact table. This table contains all the facts about an event that you wish to report on, such as sales, in one place. In an OLTP, the inventory would be in one table, the sale in another table, customers in a third table, and so forth. In the data warehouse, they are all in one huge table.

The dimensions of the values in the fact are in smaller tables that allow you to pick a scale or unit of measurement on that dimension in the fact table. For example, the time dimension for the Sales fact table might be grouped by year, month within year, week within month. Then a weight dimension could give you pounds, kilograms, or stock packaging sizes. A category dimension might classify the stocks by department. And so forth.

This lets me ask for my fact aggregated in any granularity of units I wish, and perhaps dropping some of the dimensions.

Until recent changes in SQL, OLAP queries had to be done with special OLAP-centric languages, such as Microsoft's Multidimensional Expressions (MDX). Be assured that the power of OLAP is not found in the wizards or GUIs presented in the vendor demos. The wizards and GUI are often the glitter that lures the uninformed.

Many aspects of OLAP are already integrated with the relational database engine, itself. This blending of technology blurs the distinction between an RDBMS and OLAP data management technology, effectively challenging the passive role often relegated to relational databases with regard to dimensional data. The more your RDBMS can address the needs of both traditional relational data and dimensional data, and then you can reduce the cost of OLAP-only technology and get more out of your investment in RDBMS technology, skills and resources. But do not confuse what SQL can do for you with a reporting tools or the power of a statistical package, either.

31.2.1 GROUPING Operators

OLAP functions add the ROLLUP and CUBE extensions to the GROUP BY clause. The ROLLUP and CUBE are often referred to as super-groups. They can be written in older Standard SQL using GROUP BY and UNION operators.

As expected, NULLs form their own group just as before. However, we now have a GROUPING (<column reference>) function which checks for NULLs that are the results of aggregation over that <column reference> during the execution of a grouped query containing CUBE, ROLLUP, or GROUPING SET, and returns one if they were created by the query and a zero otherwise.

SQL:2003 added a multicolumn version that constructs a binary number from the ones and zeros of the columns in the list in an implementation defined exact numeric data type. Here is a recursive definition:

GROUPING (<column ref 1>, …, <column ref n-1>, <column ref n>) is equivalent to

(2*(<column ref 1>, …, <column ref n-1>) + GROUPING (<column ref n>))

31.2.2 GROUP BY GROUPING SET

The GROUPING SET (<column list>) is short hand in SQL-99 for a series of UNION-ed queries that are common in reports. For example, to find the total

```
SELECT dept_name, CAST(NULL AS CHAR(10)) AS job_title, COUNT(*)
  FROM Personnel
 GROUP BY dept_name
UNION ALL
SELECT CAST(NULL AS CHAR(8)) AS dept_name, job_title, COUNT(*)
  FROM Personnel
 GROUP BY job_title;
```

The above can be rewritten like this.

```
SELECT dept_name, job_title, COUNT(*)
  FROM Personnel
 GROUP BY GROUPING SET (dept_name, job_title);
```

There is a problem with all of the OLAP grouping functions. They will generate NULLs for each dimension at the subtotal levels. How do you tell the difference between a real NULL and a generated NULL? This is a job for the GROUPING() function which returns 0 for NULLs in the original data and 1 for generated NULLs that indicate a subtotal.

```
SELECT CASE GROUPING(dept_name)
       WHEN 1 THEN 'department total'
       ELSE dept_name END AS dept_name,
       CASE GROUPING(job_title)
       WHEN 1 THEN 'job total'
       ELSE job_title_name END AS job_title
 FROM Personnel
GROUP BY GROUPING SETS (dept_name, job_title);
```

The grouping set concept can be used to define other OLAP groupings.

31.2.3 ROLLUP

A ROLLUP group is an extension to the GROUP BY clause in SQL-99 that produces a result set that contains subtotal rows in addition to the regular grouped rows. Subtotal rows are super-aggregate rows that contain further

aggregates whose values are derived by applying the same column functions that were used to obtain the grouped rows. A ROLLUP grouping is a series of grouping-sets.

```
GROUP BY ROLLUP (a, b, c)
```

is equivalent to

```
GROUP BY GROUPING SETS (a, b, c), (a, b), (a),()
```

Notice that the (n) elements of the ROLLUP translate to (n+1) grouping set. Another point to remember is that the order in which the grouping-expression is specified is significant for ROLLUP.

The ROLLUP is basically the classic totals and subtotals report presented as an SQL table.

31.2.4 CUBES

The CUBE super-group is the other SQL-99 extension to the GROUP BY clause that produces a result set that contains all the subtotal rows of a ROLLUP aggregation and, in addition, contains 'cross-tabulation' rows. Cross-tabulation rows are additional 'super-aggregate' rows. They are, as the name implies, summaries across columns if the data were represented as a spreadsheet. Like ROLLUP, a CUBE group can also be thought of as a series of grouping-sets. In the case of a CUBE, all permutations of the cubed grouping-expression are computed along with the grand total. Therefore, the n elements of a CUBE translate to 2n grouping-sets.

```
GROUP BY CUBE (a, b, c)
```

is equivalent to

```
GROUP BY GROUPING SETS
(a, b, c), (a, b), (a, c), (b, c), (a), (b), (c), ()
```

Notice that the three elements of the CUBE translate to eight grouping sets. Unlike ROLLUP, the order of specification of elements does not matter for CUBE:

CUBE (julian_day, sales_person) is the same as CUBE (sales_person, julian_day).

CUBE is an extension of the ROLLUP function. The CUBE function not only provides the column summaries that we saw in ROLLUP but also calculates the row summaries and grand totals for the various dimensions.

31.2.5 OLAP Examples of SQL

The following example illustrates the advanced OLAP function used in combination with traditional SQL. In this example, we want to perform a ROLLUP function of sales by region and city.

```
SELECT B.region_nbr, S.city_id, SUM(S.sales_amt) AS total_sales
  FROM SalesFacts AS S, MarketLookup AS M
 WHERE EXTRACT (YEAR FROM trans_date) = 2011
   AND S.city_id = B.city_id
   AND B.region_nbr = 6
GROUP BY ROLLUP(B.region_nbr, S.city_id);
```

The resultant set is reduced by explicitly querying region 6 and the year 1999. A sample result of the SQL is shown below. The result shows ROLLUP of two groupings (region, city) returning three totals, including region, city, and grand total.

Yearly Sales by city and region (only region 6 data)

Region_nbr	City_id	Total_sales
6	1	81,655 ◄ city within region total
6	2	131,512
6	3	58,384
..	..	..
6	NULL	1,190,902 ◄ region 6 total
NULL	NULL	1,190,902 ◄ grand total

31.2.6 The Window Clause

The window clause is also called the OVER() clause informally. The idea is that the table is first broken into partitions with the PARTITION BY subclause. The partitions are then sorted by the ORDER BY clause. An imaginary cursor sits on the current row where the windowed function is invoked. A subset of the rows in the current partition is defined by the

number of rows before and after the current row; if there is a <window frame exclusion> option then certain rows are removed from the subset. Finally, the subset is passed to an aggregate or ordinal function to return a scalar value. The window functions are functions that follow the rules of any function, but with a different syntax. The window part can be either a <window name> or a <window specification>. The <window specification> gives the details of the window in the OVER() clause and this is how most programmers use it. However, you can define a window and give it a name, then use the name in the OVER() clauses of several statements.

The window works the same way, regardless of the syntax used. The BNF is:

<window function>::= <window function type> OVER <window name or specification>

<window function type>::=

<rank function type> | ROW_NUMBER ()| <aggregate function>

<rank function type>::= RANK() | DENSE_RANK() | PERCENT_RANK() | CUME_DIST()

<window name or specification>::= <window name> | <in-line window specification>

<in-line window specification>::= <window specification>

The window clause has three subclauses: partitioning, ordering, and aggregation grouping or window frame.

31.2.6.1 Partition by Subclause

A set of column names specifies the partitioning, which is applied to the rows that the preceding FROM, WHERE, GROUP BY, and HAVING clauses produced. If no partitioning is specified, the entire set of rows composes a single partition and the aggregate function applies to the whole set each time. Though the partitioning looks a bit like a GROUP BY, it is not the same thing. A GROUP BY collapses the rows in a partition into a single row. The partitioning within a window, though, simply organizes the rows into groups without collapsing them.

31.2.6.2 ORDER BY Subclause

The ordering within the window clause is like the ORDER BY clause in a CURSOR. It includes a list of sort keys and indicates whether they should be sorted ascending or descending. The important thing to understand is that ordering is applied within each partition. The other subclauses are optional, but do not make any sense without an ORDER BY and/or PARTITION BY in the function.

<sort specification list>::= <sort specification> [{,<sort specification>}...]

<sort specification>::= <sort key> [<ordering specification>] [<null ordering>]

<sort key>::= <value expression>

<ordering specification>::= ASC | DESC

<null ordering>::= NULLS FIRST | NULLS LAST

It is worth mentioning that the rules for an ORDER BY subclause have changed to be more general than they were in earlier SQL Standards.

1. A sort can now be a <value expression> and is not limited to a simple column in the select list. However, it is still a good idea to use only column names so that you can see the sorting order in the result set

2. <sort specification> specifies the sort direction for the corresponding sort key. If DESC is not specified in the ith <sort specification>, then the sort direction for Ki is ascending and the applicable <comp op> is the <less than operator>. Otherwise, the sort direction for Ki is descending and the applicable <comp op> is the <greater than operator>.

3. If <null ordering> is not specified, then an implementation-defined <null ordering> is implicit. This was a big issue in earlier SQL Standards because vendors handled NULLs differently. NULLs are considered equal to each other.

4. If one value is NULL and second value is not NULL, then
   - 4.1 If NULLS FIRST is specified or implied, then first value <comp op> second value is considered to be TRUE.
   - 4.2 If NULLS LAST is specified or implied, then first value <comp op> second value is considered to be FALSE.
   - 4.3 If first value and second value are not NULL and the result of "first value <comp op> second value" is UNKNOWN, then the relative ordering of first value and second value is implementation dependent.

5. Two rows that are not distinct with respect to the <sort specification>s are said to be peers of each other. The relative ordering of peers is implementation dependent.

31.2.6.3 Window Frame Subclause

The tricky one is the window frame. Here is the BNF, but you really need to see code for it to make sense.

<window frame clause>::= <window frame units> <window frame extent>

[<window frame exclusion>]

<window frame units>::= ROWS | RANGE

RANGE works with a single sort key of numeric, datetime, or interval data type. It is for data that is a little fuzzy on the edges, if you will. If ROWS is specified, then sort list is made of exact numeric with scale zero.

<window frame extent>::= <window frame start> | <window frame between>

<window frame start>::=

UNBOUNDED PRECEDING | <window frame preceding> | CURRENT ROW

<window frame preceding>::= <unsigned value specification> PRECEDING

If the window starts at UNBOUNDED PRECEDING, then the lower bound is always the first row of the partition; likewise, CURRENT ROW explains itself. The <window frame preceding> is an actual count of preceding rows.

<window frame bound>::= <window frame start> | UNBOUNDED FOLLOWING | <window frame following>

<window frame following>::= <unsigned value specification> FOLLOWING

If the window starts at UNBOUNDED FOLLOWING, then the lower bound is always the last row of the partition; likewise, CURRENT ROW explains itself. The <window frame following> is an actual count of following rows.

<window frame between>::= BETWEEN <window frame bound 1> AND <window frame bound 2>

<window frame bound 1>::= <window frame bound>

<window frame bound 2>::= <window frame bound>

The current row and its window frame have to stay inside the partition, so the following and preceding limits can effectively change at either end of the frame.

<window frame exclusion>::= EXCLUDE CURRENT ROW | EXCLUDE GROUP

| EXCLUDE TIES | EXCLUDE NO OTHERS

The <window frame exclusion> is not used much or widely implemented. It is also hard to explain. The term "peer" refers to duplicate values (Figure 31.1).

(1) EXCLUDE CURRENT ROW removes the current row from the window.

(2) EXCLUDE GROUP removes the current row and any peers of the current row.

(3) EXCLUDE TIES removed any rows other than the current row that are peers of the current row.

(4) EXCLUDE NO OTHERS makes sure that no additional rows are removed.

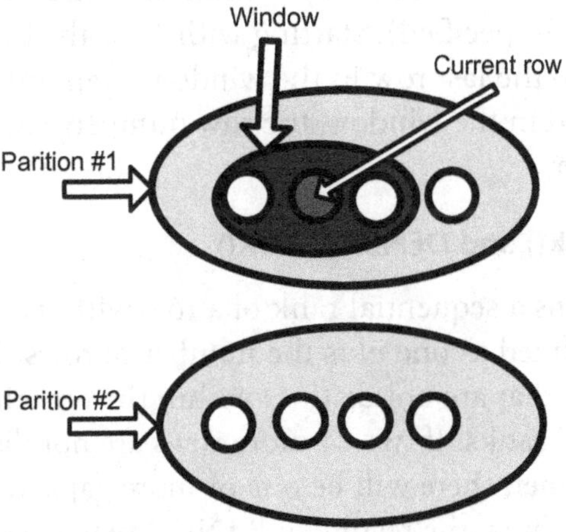

Figure 31.1 Window Clause Partition Model.

31.2.7 Windowed Aggregate Functions

The regular aggregate functions can take a window clause.

```
<aggregate function>
OVER ([PARTITION BY <column list>]
          [ORDER BY <sort column list>]
      [<window frame>])

<aggregate function>::=
     MIN([DISTINCT | ALL] <value exp>) | MAX([DISTINCT | ALL] <value exp>)
  | SUM([DISTINCT | ALL] <value exp>) | AVG([DISTINCT | ALL] <value exp>)
  | COUNT([DISTINCT | ALL] [<value exp> | *])
```

There are no great surprises here. The window that is constructed acts as if it were a group to which the aggregate function is applied.

31.2.8 Ordinal Functions

The ordinal functions use the window clause but must have an ORDER BY subclause to make sense. They have no parameters. They create an ordering of the row within each partition or window frame relative to the rest of the rows in that partition. The ordering is not for the whole table.

31.2.8.1 Row Numbering

ROW_NUMBER() uniquely identifies rows with a sequential number based on the position of the row within the window defined by an ordering clause (if one is specified), starting with 1 for the first row and continuing sequentially to the last row in the window. If an ordering clause, ORDER BY, is not specified in the window, the row numbers are assigned to the rows in arbitrary order.

31.2.8.2 RANK() and DENSE_RANK()

RANK() assigns a sequential rank of a row within a window. The RANK() of a row is defined as one plus the number of rows that strictly precede the row. Rows that are not distinct within the ordering of the window are assigned equal ranks. If two or more rows are not distinct with respect to the ordering, then there will be one or more gaps in the sequential rank numbering. That is, the results of RANK() may have gaps in the numbers resulting from duplicate values.

DENSE_RANK() also assigns a sequential rank to a row in a window. However, a row's DENSE_RANK() is one plus the number of rows preceding it that are distinct with respect to the ordering. Therefore, there will be no gaps in the sequential rank numbering, with ties being assigned the same rank.

31.2.8.3 PERCENT_RANK() and CUME_DIST

These were added in the SQL:2003 Standard and are defined in terms of earlier constructs. Let <approximate numeric type>1 be an approximate numeric type with implementation defined precision. PERCENT_RANK() OVER <window specification> is equivalent to:

```
CASE
WHEN COUNT(*)
      OVER (<window specification>
             RANGE BETWEEN UNBOUNDED PRECEDING
                       AND UNBOUNDED FOLLOWING) = 1
THEN CAST (0 AS <approximate numeric type>)
ELSE (CAST (RANK ()
             OVER (<window specification>) AS <approximate numeric
type>1) - 1)
      / (COUNT (*)
          OVER (<window specification>1
                RANGE BETWEEN UNBOUNDED PRECEDING
                          AND UNBOUNDED FOLLOWING) - 1)
END
```

Likewise, the cumulative distribution is defined with an <approximate numeric type> with implementation defined precision. CUME_DIST() OVER <window specification> is equivalent to:

```
 (CAST (COUNT (*)
         OVER (<window specification>
               RANGE UNBOUNDED PRECEDING) AS <approximate numeric type>)
       / COUNT(*)
          OVER (<window specification>1
                RANGE BETWEEN UNBOUNDED PRECEDING
                          AND UNBOUNDED FOLLOWING))
```

You can also go back and define the other windowed in terms of each other, but it is only a curiosity and has no practical value.

```
RANK() OVER <window specification> is equivalent to:

 (COUNT (*) OVER (<window specification> RANGE UNBOUNDED PRECEDING)
  -COUNT (*) OVER (<window specification>RANGE CURRENT ROW) + 1)

DENSE_RANK() OVER (<window specification>) is equivalent to:

COUNT (DISTINCT ROW (<value exp 1>, ...,<value exp n>))
OVER (<window specification> RANGE UNBOUNDED PRECEDING)
```

Where <value exp i> is a sort key in the table.

```
ROW_NUMBER() OVER WNS is equivalent to:

COUNT (*)
OVER (<window specification> ROWS UNBOUNDED PRECEDING)
```

31.2.8.4 Some Examples

The <aggregation grouping> defines a set of rows upon which the aggregate function operates for each row in the partition. Thus, in our example, for each month, you specify the set including it and the two preceding rows.

```
SELECT SH.region_nbr, SH.sales_month, SH.sales_amt,
       AVG(SH.sales_amt)
       OVER (PARTITION BY SH.region_nbr
             ORDER BY SH.sales_month ASC
             ROWS 2 PRECEDING)
       AS moving_average,
       SUM(SH.sales_amt)
       OVER (PARTITION BY SH.region_nbr
             ORDER BY SH.sales_month ASC
             ROWS BETWEEN UNBOUNDED PRECEDING AND CURRENT ROW)
       AS moving_total
  FROM Sales_History AS SH;
```

Here, "AVG(SH.sales_amt) OVER (PARTITION BY…)" is the first OLAP function. The construct inside the OVER() clause defines the window of data to which the aggregate function, AVG() in this example, is applied.

The window clause defines a partitioned set of rows to which the aggregate function is applied. The window clause says to take Sales_History table and then apply the following operations to it.

1. Partition Sales_History by region
2. Order the data by month within each region.
3. Group each row with the two preceding rows in the same region.
4. Compute the windowed average on each grouping.

The database engine is not required to perform the steps in the order described here but has to produce the same result set as if they had been carried out.

The second windowed function is a cumulative total to date for each region. It is a very common query pattern or SQL idiom.

There are two main types of aggregation groups: physical and logical. In physical grouping, you count a specified number of rows that are before or after the current row. The Sales_History example used physical grouping. In logical grouping, you include all the data in a certain interval, defined in terms of a quantity that can be added to, or subtracted from, the current sort key. For instance, you create the same group whether you define it as the current month's row plus:

(1) The two preceding rows as defined by the ORDER clause
(2) Any row containing a month no less than 2 months earlier.

Physical grouping works well for contiguous data and programmers who think in terms of sequential files. Physical grouping works for a larger variety of data types than logical grouping, because it does not require operations on values.

Logical grouping works better for data that has gaps or irregularities in the ordering and for programmers who think in SQL predicates. Logical grouping works only if you can do arithmetic on the values (such as numeric quantities and dates).

You will find another query pattern used with these functions. The function invocations need to get names to be referenced, so they are put into a derived table which is encased in a containing query

```
SELECT X.*
  FROM (SELECT <window function 1> AS W1,
               <window function 2> AS W2,
                ..
```

```
                <window function n> AS Wn
          FROM ..
        [WHERE ..]
       ) AS X
 [WHERE..]
[GROUP BY ..];
```

Using the SELECT * in the containing query is a handy way to save repeating a select clause list over and over.

One point will confuse older SQL programmers. These OLAP extensions are scalar functions, not aggregates. You cannot nest aggregates in Standard SQL because it would make no sense. Consider this example:

```
SELECT customer_id, SUM(SUM(purchase_amt)) --error
  FROM Sales
 GROUP BY dept_nbr, customer_id;
```

But you may or may not be able to nest a windowed function in a regular aggregate. This will vary from SQL to SQL. If you get an error message, then use a CTE to get the windowed result set or look to grouping sets.

31.2.9 Vendor Extensions

You will find that vendors have added their own proprietary windowed functions to their products. While there is no good way to predict what they will do, there are two sets of common extensions. As a programming exercise, I suggest you try to write them in Standard SQL windowed functions so you can translate dialect SQL if you need to do so.

31.2.9.1 LEAD and LAG Functions

LEAD and LAG functions are nonstandard shorthands that you will find in Oracle and other SQL products. Rather than compute an aggregate value, they jump ahead or behind the current row and use that value in an expression. They take three arguments and an OVER() clause. The general syntax is shown below:

```
[LEAD | LAG] (<expr>, <offset>, <default>) OVER (<window specification>)
```

<expr> is the expression to compute from the leading or lagging row.

<offset> is the position of the leading or lagging row relative to the current row; it has to be a positive integer which defaults to one.

<default> is the value to return if the <offset> points to a row outside the partition range. Here is a simple example:

```
SELECT dept_nbr, emp_id, sal_amt,
       LEAD(sal, 1, 0)
         OVER (PARTITION BY dept_nbr
                    ORDER BY sal DESC NULLS LAST)AS lead_sal_amt,
       LAG (sal, 1, 0)
          OVER (PARTITION BY dept_nbr
                    ORDER BY sal DESC NULLS LAST) AS lag_sal_amt
FROM Personnel;
```

Dept_nbr	Emp_id	Sal_amt	Lead_sal_amt	Lag_sal_amt
10	7839	$5000.00	$2450.00	$0.00
10	7934	$1300.00	$0.00	$2450.00
10	7782	$2450.00	$1300.00	$5000.00 ◄ example emp_id in dept10
20	7369	$800.00	$0.00	$1100.00
20	7876	$1100.00	$800.00	$2975.00
20	7566	$2975.00	$1100.00	$3000.00
20	7902	$3000.00	$2975.00	$3000.00
20	7788	$3000.00	$3000.00	$0.00

Look at employee 7782, whose current salary is $2450.00. Looking at the salaries, we see that the first salary greater than his is $5000.00 and the first salary less than his is $1300.00. Look at employee 7934 whose current salary of $1300.00 puts him at the bottom of the company pay scale; his lead_salary_amt is defaulted to zero.

31.2.9.2 FIRST and LAST Functions

FIRST and LAST functions are nonstandard shorthands that you will find in SQL products in various forms. Rather than compute an aggregate value, they sort a partition on one set of columns, then return an expression from the first or last row of that sort. The expression usually has nothing to do with the sorting columns. This is a bit like the joke about the British Sargent-Major ordering the troops to line up alphabetically by height. The general syntax is:

[FIRST | LAST](<expr>) OVER (<window specification>)

Using the imaginary Personnel table again:

```
SELECT emp_id, dept_nbr, hire_date,
       FIRST(hire_date)
        OVER (PARTITION BY dept_nbr
                   ORDER BY emp_id)
       AS first_hire_by_dept
  FROM Personnel;
```

The results get the hire date for the employee who has the lowest employee id in each department.

Emp_id	Dept_nbr	Hire_date	First_hire_by_dept
7369	20	'2011-01-01'	'2011-01-01' ◄ first emp_id in dept 20
7566	20	'2011-01-02'	'2011-01-01'
7902	20	'2011-01-02'	'2011-01-01'
7788	20	'2011-01-04'	'2011-01-01'
7876	20	'2011-01-07'	'2011-01-01' ◄ last emp_id in dept 20
7499	30	'2011-01-27'	'2011-01-27' ◄ first emp_id in dept 30
7521	30	'2011-01-09'	'2011-01-27'
7844	30	'2011-01-17'	'2011-01-27'
7654	30	'2011-01-18'	'2011-01-27'
7900	30	'2011-01-20'	'2011-01-27' ◄ last emp_id in dept 30

If we had used LAST() instead, the two chosen rows would have been:

(7876, 20, '2011-01-07', '2011-01-01')

(7900, 30, '2011-01-20', '2011-01-27')

The Oracle extensions FIRST_VALUE and LAST_VALUE are even stranger. They allow other ordinal and aggregate functions to be applied to the retrieved values. If you want to use them, I suggest that you look product-specific references and examples.

You can do these with Standard SQL and a little work. The skeleton

```
WITH FirstLastQuery
AS
(SELECT emp_id, dept_nbr,
        ROW_NUMBER()
```

```
            OVER (PARTITION BY dept_nbr
                      ORDER BY emp_id ASC) AS asc_order,
          ROW_NUMBER()
            OVER (PARTITION BY dept_nbr
                      ORDER BY emp_id DESC) AS desc_order
     FROM Personnel)

SELECT A.emp_id, A.dept_nbr,
       OA.hire_date AS first_value,
       OD.hire_date AS last_value
  FROM FirstLastQuery AS A,
       FirstLastQuery AS OA,
       FirstLastQuery AS OD
 WHERE OD.desc_order = 1
   AND OA.asc_order = 1;
```

31.2.9.3 NTILE Function

NTILE() splits a set into equal groups. It exists in SQL Server and Oracle, but it is not part of the SQL-99 Standards. Oracle adds the ability to sort NULLs either FIRST or LAST, but again this is a vendor extension.

NTILE(3) OVER (ORDER BY x)

x	NTILE
1	1
1	1
2	1
2	1
3	2
3	2
3	2
3	3
3	3
3	3

The SQL engine attempts to get the groups the same size, but this is not always possible. The goal is then to have them differ by just one row. NTILE(n) where (n) is greater than the number of rows in the query, it is effectively a ROW_NUMBER(), with groups of size one.

Obviously, if you use NTILE(100), you will get percentiles, but you need at least 100 rows in the result set.

Jeff Moss has been using it for quite some time to work out outliers for statistical analysis of data. An outlier is a value that is outside the range of the other data values. He uses NTILE (200) and drops the first and 200th bucket to rule out the 0.5% on either end of the normal distribution.

If you do not have an NTILE(n) function in your SQL, you can write it with other SQL functions. The SQL Server implementation NTILE(n) function uses a temporary worktable that can be expensive when the COUNT(*) is not a multiple of (n).

The NTILE(n) puts larger groups before smaller groups in the order specified by the OVER clause. In fact, Marco Russo tested a millions row table and the following code used 37 times less I/O than the built-in function in SQL Server 2005.

Most of the time, you really do not care about the order of the groups and their sizes; in the real world they will usually vary by one or two rows. You can take the row number, divide it by the bucket size and find the nearest number plus one.

```
CEILING (ROW_NUMBER()
        OVER (ORDER BY x)
       /((SELECT COUNT(*) + 1.0
            FROM Foobar)/:n))
   AS ntile_bucket_nbr
```

This expression is like this non-OLAP expression:

```
SELECT S1.seq,
       CEILING(((SELECT CAST(COUNT(*)+1 AS FLOAT)
                  FROM Sequence AS S2
                 WHERE S2.seq < S1.seq)/:n))
       AS ntile_bucket_nbr
  FROM Sequence AS S1;
```

Do not use this last piece code for a table of over a few hundred rows. It will run much too long on most products.

31.2.10 A Bit of History

IBM and Oracle jointly proposed these extensions in early 1999 and thanks to ANSI's uncommonly rapid (and praiseworthy) actions, they are part of the SQL-99 Standard. IBM implemented portions of the specifications in DB2 UDB 6.2, which was commercially available in some forms as early as mid-1999. Oracle 8i version 2 and DB2 UDB 7.1, both released in late 1999, contain beefed-up implementations.

Other vendors contributed, including database tool vendors Brio, MicroStrategy, and Cognos and database vendor Informix, among others. A team lead by Dr. Hamid Pirahesh of IBM's Almaden Research Laboratory played a particularly important role. After his team had researched the subject for about a year and come up with an approach to extending SQL in this area, he called Oracle. The companies then learned that each had independently done some significant work. With Andy Witkowski playing a pivotal role at Oracle, the two companies hammered out a joint standards proposal in about 2 months. Red Brick was actually the first product to implement this functionality before the standard, but in a less complete form. You can find details in the ANSI document "Introduction to OLAP Functions" by Fred Zemke, Krishna Kulkarni, Andy Witkowski, and Bob Lyle.

31.2.10 A Bit of History

Sub-sequences, Regions, Runs, Gaps, and Islands

WE HAVE ALREADY talked about the GROUP BY clause in queries. The groups in a GROUP BY do not depend on any orderings. But you will often want to make other groupings which depend on an ordering of some kind. Examples of this sort of data would be ticket numbers, time series data taken at fixed intervals, and the like which can have missing data or sub-sequences that are of interest. These things are easier to explain with examples. Consider a skeleton table with a sequential key and seven rows.

```
CREATE TABLE List
(list_seq INTEGER NOT NULL PRIMARY KEY,
 list_val INTEGER NOT NULL UNIQUE);

INSERT INTO List
VALUES (1, 99), (2, 10), (3, 11), (4, 12), (5, 13), (6, 14), (7, 0);
```

A sub-sequence in the list_val column can be increasing, decreasing, monotonic, or not. Let's look at rows where the values are increasing uniformly by steps of one. You can find sub-sequences of size three which follow the rule—(10, 11, 12), (11, 12, 13), and (12, 13, 14)—but the longest sub-sequence is (10, 11, 12, 13, 14) and it is of size five.

A run is like a sequence, but the numbers do not have to be consecutive, just increasing (or decreasing) and in sequence. For example, given the run {(1, 1), (2, 2), (3, 12), (4, 15), (5, 23)}, you can find sub-runs of size three: (1, 2, 12), (2, 12, 15), and (12, 15, 23).

A region is contiguous and all the values are the same. For example, {(1, 1), (2, 0), (3, 0), (4, 0), (5, 25)} has a region of zeros that is three items long.

In procedural languages, you would simply sort the data and scan it. In SQL, you used to have to define everything in terms of sets and fancy joins to get an ordering if it was not in the data. Today, we have ROW_NUMBER() to get us a sequence number for ordering the data.

32.1 Finding Subregions of Size (*n*)

This example is adapted from SQL and its applications (Lorie and Daudenarde, 1991).[1] You are given a table of theater seats, defined by

```
CREATE TABLE Theater
(seat_nbr INTEGER NOT NULL PRIMARY KEY, -- sequence
 occupancy_status CHAR(1) DEFAULT 'A' NOT NULL -- values
        CONSTRAINT valid_occupancy_status
        CHECK (occupancy_status IN ('A', 'S'));
```

where an occupancy_status code of 'A' means available and 'S' means sold. Your problem is to write a query that will return the subregions of (n) consecutive seats still available. Assume that consecutive seat numbers mean that the seats are also consecutive for a moment, ignoring rows of seating where seat_nbr(n) and seat_nbr((n)+1) might be on different physical theater rows. For (n)=3, we can write a self-JOIN query, thus:

```
SELECT T1.seat_nbr, T2.seat_nbr, T3.seat_nbr
  FROM Theater AT T1, Theater AT T2, Theater AT T3
 WHERE T1.occupancy_status = 'A'
   AND T2.occupancy_status = 'A'
   AND T3.occupancy_status = 'A'
   AND T2.seat_nbr = T1.seat_nbr + 1
   AND T3.seat_nbr = T2.seat_nbr + 1;
```

The trouble with this answer is that it works only for (n=3) and for nothing else. This pattern can be extended for any (n), but what we really want is a generalized query where we can use (n) as a parameter to the query.

[1] Lorie and Daudenarde (1991). Prentice Hall; ISBN: 978-0138379568.

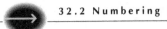

The solution given by Lorie and Daudenarde starts with a given seat_nbr and looks at all the available seats between it and $((n)-1)$ seats further up. The real trick is switching from the English-language statement "All seats between here and there are available" to the passive-voice version, "Available is the occupancy_status of all the seats between here and there", so that you can see the query.

```
SELECT seat_nbr, ' thru ', (seat_nbr + (:n - 1))
  FROM Theater AS T1
 WHERE occupancy_status = 'A'
   AND 'A' = ALL (SELECT occupancy_status
                    FROM Theater AS T2
                   WHERE T2.seat_nbr > T1.seat_nbr
                     AND T2.seat_nbr <= T1.seat_nbr + (:n - 1));
```

Please notice that this returns subregions. That is, if seats (1, 2, 3, 4, 5) are available, this query will return (1, 2, 3), (2, 3, 4), and (3, 4, 5) as its result set.

32.2 Numbering Regions

Instead of looking for a region, we want to number the regions in the order in which they appear. For example, given a view or table with a payment history we want to break it into grouping of behavior, say whether or not the payments were on time or late. This is a bad design; we should use a NULL-able payment date, but this is easier to read.

```
CREATE TABLE Payment_History
(payment_nbr INTEGER NOT NULL PRIMARY KEY,
 paid_on_time_flg CHAR(1) DEFAULT 'Y' NOT NULL
     CHECK(paid:on_time_flg IN ('Y', 'N')));

INSERT INTO Payment_History
VALUES (1006, 'Y'), (1005, 'Y'), (1004, 'N'),
(1003, 'Y'), (1002, 'Y'), (1001, 'Y'),
(1000, 'N');
```

The results we want assign a grouping number to each run of on-time/late payments, thus

Results

grping	payment_nbr	paid_on_time_flg
1	1006	'Y'
1	1005	'Y'
2	1004	'N'
3	1003	'Y'
3	1002	'Y'
3	1001	'Y'
4	1000	'N'

A solution by Hugo Kornelis depends on the payments always being numbered consecutively. Today we can guarantee this by using a CREATE SEQUENCE statement for each account.

```
SELECT (SELECT COUNT(*)
          FROM Payment_History AS H2,
               Payment_History AS H3
         WHERE H3.payment_nbr = H2.payment_nbr + 1
           AND H3.paid_on_time_flg <> H2.paid_on_time_flg
           AND H2.payment_nbr >= H1.payment_nbr) + 1 AS grping,
     payment_nbr, paid_on_time_flg
 FROM Payment_History AS H1;
```

This can be modified for more types of behavior. This is not a modern SQL idiom and will not perform as well as the ordinal functions. But you need to know it to replace it. Let's assume we have a test that returns 'A' or 'B' and we want to see clusters where the score stayed the same:

```
CREATE TABLE Tests
(sample_time DATE NOT NULL PRIMARY KEY,
  sample_score CHAR(1) NOT NULL);

INSERT INTO Tests
VALUES ('2018-01-01', 'A'),
       ('2018-01-02', 'A'),
       ('2018-01-03', 'A'),
       ('2018-01-04', 'B'),
       ('2018-01-05', 'B'),
       ('2018-01-06', 'A'),
```

```
('2018-01-07', 'A'),
('2018-01-08', 'A'),
('2018-01-09', 'A'),
('2018-01-10', 'B'),
('2018-01-11', 'B'),
('2018-01-12', 'A'),
('2018-01-13', 'A'),
('2018-01-14', 'C'),
('2018-01-15', 'D'),
('2018-01-16', 'A');

SELECT MIN(X.sample_time) AS cluster_start,
       MAX(X.sample_time) AS cluster_end,
       MIN(X.sample_score) AS cluster_score
FROM (SELECT sample_time, sample_score,
             (ROW_NUMBER () OVER (ORDER BY sample_time)
            - ROW_NUMBER() OVER (PARTITION BY sample_score
                                     ORDER BY sample_time))
FROM Tests) AS X(sample_time, sample_score, cluster_nbr)
GROUP BY cluster_nbr;
```

cluster_start	cluster_end	cluster_score
'2014-01-01'	'2014-01-03'	A
'2014-01-04'	'2014-01-05'	B
'2014-01-06'	'2014-01-09'	A
'2014-01-10'	'2014-01-11'	B
'2014-01-12'	'2014-01-13'	A
'2014-01-14'	'2014-01-14'	C
'2014-01-15'	'2014-01-15'	D
'2014-01-16'	'2014-01-16'	A

These groupings are called clusters or islands or "OLAP sorting" in the literature.

32.3 Finding Regions of Maximum Size

A query to find a region, rather than a subregion of a known size, of seats was presented in SQL Forum (Rozenshtein, Abramovich, and Birger, 1997).[2]

[2] Rozenshtein, Abramovich, and Birger (1997). SQL Forum Press. ISBN-13: 978-0964981201.

```
SELECT T1.seat_nbr AS start_seat_nbr, T2.seat_nbr AS end_seat_nbr
  FROM Theater AS T1, Theater AS T2
 WHERE T1.seat_nbr < T2.seat_nbr
   AND NOT EXISTS
       (SELECT *
          FROM Theater AS T3
         WHERE (T3.seat_nbr BETWEEN T1.seat_nbr AND T2.seat_nbr
           AND T3.occupancy_status <> 'A')
            OR (T3.seat_nbr = T2.seat_nbr + 1
                AND T3.occupancy_status = 'A')
            OR (T3.seat_nbr = T1.seat_nbr - 1
                AND T3.occupancy_status = 'A'));
```

The trick here is to look for the starting and ending seats in the region. The starting seat_nbr of a region is to the right of a sold seat_nbr and the ending seat_nbr is to the left of a sold seat. No seat between the start and the end has been sold.

If you only keep the available seat_nbrs in a table, the solution is a bit easier. It is also a more general problem that applies to any table of sequential, possibly noncontiguous, data

```
CREATE TABLE Available_Seating
 (seat_nbr INTEGER NOT NULL
       CONSTRAINT valid_seat_nbr
       CHECK (seat_nbr BETWEEN 001 AND 999));

INSERT INTO Seatings
VALUES (199), (200), (201), (202), (204),
       (210), (211), (212), (214), (218);
```

where you need to create a result which will show the start and finish values of each sequence in the table, thus:

Results

start_seat_nbr	end_seat_nbr
199	202
204	204
210	212
214	214
218	218

This is a common way of finding the missing values in a sequence of tickets sold, unaccounted for invoices and so forth. Imagine a number line with closed dots for the numbers that are in the table and open dots for the numbers that are not. What you see about a sequence? Well, we can start with a fact that anyone who has done inventory knows. The number of elements in a sequence is equal to the ending sequence number minus the starting sequence number plus one. This is a basic property of ordinal numbers:

```
(finish - start + 1) = count of open seats
```

This tells us that we need to have a self-JOIN with two copies of the table, one for the starting value and one for the ending value of each sequence. Once we have those two items, we can compute the length with our formula and see if it is equal to the count of the items between the start and finish.

```
SELECT S1.seat_nbr, MAX(S2.seat_nbr) -- start and rightmost item
  FROM AvailableSeating AS S1
       INNER JOIN
       AvailableSeating AS S2 -- self-join
       ON S1.seat_nbr <= S2.seat_nbr
          AND (S2.seat_nbr - S1.seat_nbr + 1) -- formula for length
              = (SELECT COUNT(*) -- items in the sequence
                   FROM AvailableSeating AS S3
                  WHERE S3.seat_nbr BETWEEN S1.seat_nbr
                                        AND S2.seat_nbr)
                   AND NOT EXISTS (SELECT *
                                     FROM AvailableSeating AS S4
                                    WHERE S1.seat_nbr - 1
                                          = S4.seat_nbr)
 GROUP BY S1.seat_nbr;
```

Finally, we need to be sure that we have the furthest item to the right as the end item. Each sequence of (*n*) items has (*n*) sub-sequences that all start with the same item. So we finally do a GROUP BY on the starting item and use a MAX() to get the rightmost value.

However, there is a faster version with three tables. This solution is based on another property of the longest possible sequences. If you look to the right of the last item, you do not find anything. Likewise, if you look to the left of the first item, you do not find anything either. These missing items that are

"just over the border" define a sequence by framing it. There also cannot be any "gaps"—missing items—inside those borders. That translates into SQL as:

```
SELECT S1.seat_nbr, MIN(S2.seat_nbr) -- start and leftmost border
  FROM AvailableSeating AS S1, AvailableSeating AS S2
 WHERE S1.seat_nbr <= S2.seat_nbr
   AND NOT EXISTS -- border items of the sequence
       (SELECT *
          FROM AvailableSeating AS S3
         WHERE S3.seat_nbr NOT BETWEEN S1.seat_nbr AND S2.seat_nbr
           AND (S3.seat_nbr = S1.seat_nbr - 1
                OR S3.seat_nbr = S2.seat_nbr + 1))
 GROUP BY S1.seat_nbr;
```

The leftmost and rightmost members of the block of seats are found by looking for the status of the seats just over the boundary. Once we have the rightmost seat the block and then we can do a GROUP BY and MIN() to get what we want.

Since the second approach uses only three copies of the original table, it should be a bit faster. Also, the EXISTS() predicates can often take advantage of indexing and thus run faster than subquery expressions which require a table scan.

The new ordinal functions allow you to answer these queries without explicit self-joins or a sequencing column. Since self-joins are expensive, it is better to use ordinal functions that might be optimized. Consider a single column of integers:

```
CREATE TABLE Foobar (data_val INTEGER NOT NULL PRIMARY KEY);
INSERT INTO Foobar
VALUES (1), (2), (5), (6), (7), (8), (9), (11), (12), (22);
```

Here is a query to get the final results:

```
WITH X (data_val, data_seq, absent_data_grp)
AS
(SELECT data_val,
        ROW_NUMBER() OVER (ORDER BY data_val ASC) ,
        (data_val
          - ROW_NUMBER() OVER (ORDER BY data_val ASC))
   FROM Foobar)
```

```
SELECT absent_data_val, COUNT(*), MIN(data_val) AS start_data_val
  FROM X
 GROUP BY absent_data_val;
```

The CTE produces this result. The absent_data_grp tells you how many values are missing from the data values, just not what they are.

data_val	data_seq	absent_data_grp
1	1	0
2	2	0
5	3	2
6	4	2
7	5	2
8	6	2
9	7	2
11	8	3
12	9	3
22	10	12

The final query gives us:

absent_data_grp	COUNT(*)	start_data_val
0	2	1
2	5	5
3	2	11
12	1	22

So, the maximum contiguous sequence is five rows. Since it starts at 5, we know that the contiguous set is {5, 6, 7, 8, 9}.

32.4 Bound Queries

Another form of query asks if there was an overall trend between two points in time bounded by a low value and a high value in the sequence of data. This is easier to show with an example. Let us assume that we have data on the selling prices of a stock in a table. We want to find periods of time when the price was generally increasing. Consider this data:

MyStock

sale_date	stock_price
'2017-12-01'	10
'2017-12-02'	15
'2017-12-03'	13
'2017-12-04'	12
'2017-12-05'	20

The stock was generally increasing in all the periods that began on December 1 or ended on December 5—that is, it finished higher at the ends of those periods, in spite of the slump in the middle. A query for this problem is

```
SELECT S1.sale_date AS start_date, S2.sale_date AS finish_date
  FROM MyStock AS S1, MyStock AS S2
 WHERE S1.sale_date < S2.sale_date
   AND NOT EXISTS
        (SELECT *
           FROM MyStock AS S3
          WHERE S3.sale_date BETWEEN S1.sale_date AND S2.sale_date
            AND S3.stock_price
                NOT BETWEEN S1.stock_price AND S2.stock_price);
```

32.5 Run and Sequence Queries

Runs are informally defined as sequences with gaps. That is, we have a set of unique numbers whose order has some meaning, but the numbers are not all consecutive. Time series information where the samples are taken at irregular intervals is an example of this sort of data. Runs can be constructed in the same manner as the sequences by making a minor change in the search condition. Let's do these queries with an abstract table made up of a sequence number and a value:

```
CREATE TABLE Runs
(list_seq INTEGER NOT NULL PRIMARY KEY,
 list_val INTEGER NOT NULL);
```

Runs

list_seq	list_val
1	6
2	41
3	12
4	51
5	21
6	70
7	79
8	62
9	30
10	31
11	32
12	34
13	35
14	57
15	19
16	84
17	80
18	90
19	63
20	53
21	3
22	59
23	69
24	27
25	33

One of the problems is that we do not want to get back all the runs and sequences of length one. Ideally, the length (*n*) of the run should be adjustable. This query will find runs of length (*n*) or greater; if you want runs of exactly (*n*), change the "greater than" to an equal sign.

```
SELECT R1.list_seq AS start_list_seq,
        R2.list_seq AS end_list_seq_nbr
   FROM Runs AS R1, Runs AS R2
  WHERE R1.list_seq < R2.list_seq -- start and end points
```

```
AND (R2.list_seq - R1.list_seq) > (:n - 1) -- length restrictions
AND NOT EXISTS -- ordering within the end points
    (SELECT *
       FROM Runs AS R3, Runs AS R4
      WHERE R4.list_seq BETWEEN R1.list_seq AND R2.list_seq
        AND R3.list_seq BETWEEN R1.list_seq AND R2.list_seq
        AND R3.list_seq < R4.list_seq
        AND R3.list_val > R4.list_val);
```

What this query does is set up the S1 sequence number as the starting point and the S2 sequence number as the ending point of the run. The monster subquery in the NOT EXISTS() predicate is looking for a row in the middle of the run that violates the ordering of the run. If there is none, the run is valid. The best way to understand what is happening is to draw a linear diagram. This shows that as the ordering, list_seq, increases, so must the corresponding values, list_val.

A sequence has the additional restriction that every value increases by 1 as you scan the run from left to right. This means that in a sequence, the highest value minus the lowest value, plus one, is the length of the sequence.

```
SELECT R1.list_seq AS start_list_seq, R2.list_seq AS end_list_seq_nbr
  FROM Runs AS R1, Runs AS R2
 WHERE R1.list_seq < R2.list_seq
   AND (R2.list_seq - R1.list_seq) = (R2.list_val - R1.list_val) --
order condition
   AND (R2.list_seq - R1.list_seq) > (:n - 1) -- length restrictions
   AND NOT EXISTS
       (SELECT *
          FROM Runs AS R3
         WHERE R3.list_seq BETWEEN R1.list_seq AND R2.list_seq
           AND((R3.list_seq - R1.list_seq)
                 <> (R3.list_val - R1.list_val)
                OR (R2.list_seq - R3.list_seq)
                   <> (R2.list_val - R3.list_val)));
```

The subquery in the NOT EXISTS predicate says that there is no point in between the start and the end of the sequence that violates the ordering condition.

Obviously, any of these queries can be changed from increasing to decreasing, from strictly increasing to simply increasing or simply decreasing, and so on, by

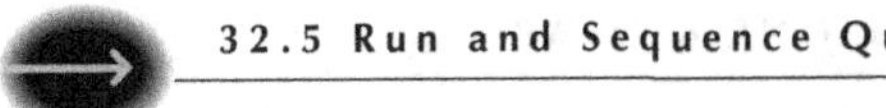

changing the comparison predicates. You can also change the query for finding sequences in a table by altering the size of the step from 1 to *k*, by observing that the difference between the starting position and the ending position should be *k* times the difference between the starting value and the ending value.

32.5.1 Filling in Missing Numbers

A fair number of SQL programmers want to reuse a sequence of numbers for keys. While I do not approve of the practice of generating a meaningless, unverifiable key after the creation of an entity, the problem of inserting missing numbers is interesting. The usual specifications are

1. The sequence starts with 1, if it is missing or the table is empty.
2. We want to reuse the lowest missing number first.
3. Do not exceed some maximum value; if the sequence is full, then give us a warning or a NULL. Another option is to give us (MAX(list_seq)+1) so we can add to the high end of the list.

This answer is a good example of thinking in terms of sets rather than doing row-at-a-time processing.

```
SELECT MIN(new_list_seq)
  FROM (SELECT CASE
               WHEN list_seq + 1 NOT IN (SELECT list_seq FROM List)
               THEN list_seq + 1
               WHEN list_seq - 1 NOT IN (SELECT list_seq FROM List)
               THEN list_seq - 1
               WHEN 1 NOT IN (SELECT list_seq FROM List)
               THEN 1 ELSE NULL END
          FROM List
         WHERE list_seq BETWEEN 1
                   AND (SELECT MAX(list_seq) FROM List)
        AS P(new_list_seq);
```

The idea is to build a table expression of some of the missing values, then pick the minimum one. The starting value, 1, is treated as an exception. Since an aggregate function cannot take a query expression as a parameter, we have to use a derived table.

Along the same lines, we can use aggregate functions in a CASE expression

```
SELECT CASE WHEN MAX(list_seq) = COUNT(*)
            THEN CAST(NULL AS INTEGER)
                -- THEN MAX(list_seq) + 1 as other option
            WHEN MIN(list_seq) > 1
            THEN 1
            WHEN MAX(list_seq) <> COUNT(*)
            THEN (SELECT MIN(list_seq)+1
                    FROM List
                   WHERE (list_seq)+1
            NOT IN (SELECT list_seq FROM List))
            ELSE NULL END
  FROM List;
```

The first WHEN clause sees if the table is already full and returns a NULL; the NULL has to be cast as an INTEGER to become an expression that can then be used in the THEN clause. However, you might want to increment the list by the next value.

The second WHEN clause looks to see if the minimum sequence number is 1 or not. If so, it uses 1 as the next value.

The third WHEN clause handles the situation when there is a gap in the middle of the sequence. It picks the lowest missing number. The ELSE clause is in case of errors and should not be executed.

The order of execution in the CASE expression is important. It is a way of forcing an inspection from front to back of the table's values. Simpler methods based on group characteristics would be:

```
SELECT COALESCE(MIN(L1.list_seq) + 1, 1)
  FROM List AS L1
       LEFT OUTER JOIN
       List AS L2
       ON L1.list_seq = L2.list_seq - 1
 WHERE L2.list_seq IS NULL;
```

or

```
SELECT MIN(list_seq + 1)
  FROM (SELECT list_seq FROM List
       UNION ALL
       SELECT list_seq
```

```
        FROM (VALUES (0)))
      AS X(list_seq)
 WHERE (list_seq +1)
       NOT IN (SELECT list_seq FROM List);
```

Finding entire gaps follows from this pattern and we get this short piece of code.

```
SELECT (s + 1) AS gap_start,
       (e - 1) AS gap_end
  FROM (SELECT L1.list_seq, MIN(L2.list_seq)
          FROM List AS L1, List AS L2
         WHERE L1.list_seq < L2.list_seq
         GROUP BY L1.list_seq)
       AS G(s, e)
 WHERE (e - 1) > s;
```

Or without the derived table:

```
SELECT (L1.list_seq + 1) AS gap_start,
       (MIN(L2.list_seq) - 1) AS gap_end
  FROM List AS L1, List AS L2
 WHERE L1.list_seq < L2.list_seq
 GROUP BY L1.list_seq
HAVING (MIN(L2.list_seq) - L1.list_seq) > 1;
```

32.6 Summation of a Handmade Series

Before we had the ordinal functions, building a running total of the values in a table was a difficult task. Let's build a simple table with a sequencing column and the values we wish to total.

```
CREATE TABLE Handmade_Series
(list_seq INTEGER NOT NULL PRIMARY KEY,
 list_val INTEGER NOT NULL);

SELECT list_seq, list_val,
       SUM (list_val)
          OVER (ORDER BY list_seq
                ROWS BETWEEN UNBOUNDED PRECEDING AND CURRENT ROW)
       AS running_tot
  FROM Handmade_Series;
```

A sample result would look like this:

list_seq	list_val	running_tot
1	6	6
2	41	47
3	12	59
4	51	110
5	21	131
6	70	201
7	79	280
8	62	342
...	...	...

This is the form we can use for most problems of this type with only one level of summation. It is easy to write an UPDATE statement to store the running total in the table, if it does not have to be recomputed each query. But things can be worse. This problem came from Francisco Moreno and on the surface it sounds easy. First create the usual table and populate it.

```
CREATE TABLE Handmade_Series
(list_seq INTEGER NOT NULL,
 list_val REAL NOT NULL,
 running_avg REAL);

INSERT INTO Handmade_Series
VALUES (0, 6.0, NULL),
       (1, 6.0, NULL),
       (2, 10.0, NULL),
       (3, 12.0, NULL),
       (4, 14.0, NULL);
```

The goal is to compute the average of the first two terms, then add the third list_val to the result and average the two of them, and so forth. This is not the same thing as

```
SELECT list_seq, list_val,
       AVG(list_val)
       OVER (ORDER BY list_seq
             ROWS BETWEEN UNBOUNDED PRECEDING AND CURRENT ROW)
```

```
        AS running_avg
    FROM Handmade_Series;
```

In this data, we want this answer:

list_seq	list_val	running_avg
0	6	NULL
1	6	6
2	10	8
3	12	10
4	14	12

list_seq	list_val	running_avg
1	12	NULL
2	10	NULL
3	12	NULL
4	14	NULL

The obvious approach is to do the calculations directly.

```
UPDATE Handmade_Series
   SET running_tot = (Handmade_Series.list_val
                 + (SELECT S1.running_tot
                      FROM Handmade_Series AS S1
                     WHERE S1.list_seq = Handmade_Series.list_seq -
1))/2.0
 WHERE running_tot IS NULL;
```

But there is a problem with this approach. It will only calculate one list_val at a time. The reason is that this series is much more complex than a simple running total.

What we have is actually a double summation, in which the terms are defined by a continued fraction. Let's work out the first four answers by brute force and see if we can find a pattern.

answer1 = (12)/2 = 6

answer2 = ((12)/2 + 10)/2 = 8

answer3 = (((12)/2 + 10)/2 + 12)/2 = 10

answer4 = (((((12)/2 + 10)/2 + 12)/2) + 14)/2 = 12

The real trick is to do some algebra and get rid of the nested parentheses.

answer1 = (12)/2 = 6

answer2 = (12/4) + (10/2) = 8

answer3 = (12/8) + (10/4) + (12/2) = 10

answer4 = (12/16) + (10/8) + (12/4) + (14/2) = 12

When we see powers of 2, we know we can do some algebra:

answer1 = (12)/2^1 = 6

answer2 = (12/(2^2)) + (10/(2^1)) = 8

answer3 = (12/(2^3)) + (10/(2^2)) + (12/(2^1)) = 10

answer4 = (12/2^4) + (10/(2^3)) + (12/(2^2)) + (14/(2^1)) = 12

The problem is that you need to "count backwards" from the current list_val to compute higher powers for the previous terms of the summation. That is simply (current_list_val–previous_list_val+1). Putting it all together, we get this expression.

```
UPDATE Handmade_Series
   SET running_avg
       = (SELECT SUM(list_val
                 * POWER(2,
                         CASE WHEN S1.list_seq > 0
                               THEN Handmade_Series.list_seq - S1.list_
seq + 1
                              ELSE NULL END))
                              FROM Handmade_Series AS S1
           WHERE S1.list_seq < = Handmade_Series.list_seq);
```

The POWER(base, exponent) function is part of SQL:2003, but check your product for implementation defined precision and rounding.

32.7 Swapping and Sliding Values in a List

You will often want to manipulate a list of values, changing their sequence position numbers. The simplest such operation is to swap two values in your table.

```
CREATE PROCEDURE SwapValues
(IN low_list_seq INTEGER, IN high_list_seq INTEGER)
LANGUAGE SQL
BEGIN -- put them in order
SET least_list_seq
    = CASE WHEN low_list_seq <= high_list_seq
           THEN low_list_seq ELSE high_list_seq;
SET greatest_list_seq
    = CASE WHEN low_list_seq <= high_list_seq
           THEN high_list_seq ELSE low_list_seq;
UPDATE Runs -- swap
   SET list_seq = least_list_seq + ABS(list_seq - greatest_list_seq)
 WHERE list_seq IN (least_list_seq, greatest_list_seq);
END;
```

The CASE expressions could be folded into the UPDATE statement, but it makes the code harder to read.

Inserting a new value into the table is easy:

```
CREATE PROCEDURE InsertValue (IN new_value INTEGER)
LANGUAGE SQL
INSERT INTO Runs (list_seq, list_val)
VALUES ((SELECT MAX(list_seq) FROM Runs) + 1, new_value);
```

A bit trickier procedure is moving one value to a new position and sliding the remaining values either up or down. This mimics the way a physical queue would act. Here is a solution from Dave Portas.

```
CREATE PROCEDURE SlideValues
(IN old_list_seq INTEGER, IN new_list_seq INTEGER)
LANGUAGE SQL
UPDATE Runs
   SET list_seq
       = CASE
         WHEN list_seq = old_list_seq THEN new_list_seq
         WHEN list_seq BETWEEN old_list_seq AND new_list_seq THEN
list_seq - 1
         WHEN list_seq BETWEEN new_list_seq AND old_list_seq THEN list_
seq + 1
```

```
        ELSE list_seq END
 WHERE list_seq BETWEEN old_list_seq AND new_list_seq
   OR list_seq BETWEEN new_list_seq AND old_list_seq;
```

This handles moving a value to a higher or to a lower position in the table. You can see how calls or slight changes to these procedures could do other related operations.

One of the most useful tricks is to have calendar table that has a Julianized date column. Instead of trying to manipulate temporal data, convert the dates to a sequence of integers and treat the queries as regions, runs, gaps, and so forth.

The sequence can be made up of calendar days or Julianized business days, which do not include holidays and weekend. There are a lot of possible methods.

32.8 Condensing a List of Numbers

The goal is to take a list of numbers and condense them into contiguous ranges. Show the high and low values for each range; if the range has one number, then the high and low values will be the same. This answer is due to Steve Kass.

```
SELECT MIN(i) AS low, MAX(i) AS high
  FROM (SELECT N1.i, COUNT(N2.i) - N1.i
          FROM Numbers AS N1, Numbers AS N2
         WHERE N2.i <= N1.i
         GROUP BY N1.i)
       AS N(i, gp)
 GROUP BY gp;
```

32.9 Folding a List of Numbers

It is possible to use the Handmade_Series table to give columns in the same row, which are related to each other, values with a little math instead of self-joins.

For example, given the numbers 1-(n), you might want to spread them out across (k) columns. Let ($k = 3$) so we can see the pattern.

```
SELECT list_seq,
       CASE WHEN MOD((list_seq + 1), 3) = 2
                 AND list_seq + 1 <= :n
```

```
            THEN (list_seq + 1)
            ELSE NULL END AS second,
        CASE WHEN MOD((list_seq + 2), 3) = 0
                AND (list_seq + 2) <= :n
            THEN (list_seq + 2)
            ELSE NULL END AS third
  FROM Handmade_Series
 WHERE MOD((list_seq + 3), 3) = 1
  AND list_seq <= :n;
```

Columns which have no value assigned to them will get a NULL. That is, for $(n=8)$ the incomplete row will be (7, 8, NULL) and for $(n=7)$ it would be (7, NULL, NULL). We never get a row with (NULL, NULL, NULL).

The use of math can be fancier. In a golf tournament, the players with the lowest and highest scores are matched together for the next round. Then the players with the second lowest and second highest scores are matched together, and so forth. If there are an odd number of players, the player with the middle score sits out that round. These pairs can be built with a simple query.

```
SELECT list_seq AS low_score,
       CASE WHEN list_seq <= (:n - list_seq)
            THEN (:n - list_seq) + 1
            ELSE NULL END AS high_score
  FROM Handmade_Series AS S1
 WHERE S1.list_seq
       <= CASE WHEN MOD(:n, 2) = 1
               THEN FLOOR(:n/2) + 1
               ELSE (:n/2) END;
```

If you play around with the basic math functions, you can do quite a bit.

32.10 Coverings

Mikito Harakiri proposed the problem of writing the shortest SQL query that would return a minimal cover of a set of intervals. For example, given this table, how do you find the contiguous numbers that are completely covered by the given intervals?

```
CREATE TABLE Intervals
(x INTEGER NOT NULL,
y INTEGER NOT NULL,
CHECK (x <= y),
PRIMARY KEY (x, y));

INSERT INTO Intervals
VALUES (1, 3),(2, 5),(4, 11),
       (10, 12), (20, 21),
       (120, 130), (120, 128), (120, 122),
       (121, 132), (121, 122), (121, 124), (121, 123),
       (126, 127);
```

The query should return

Results

min_x	max_y
1	12
20	21
120	132

Dieter Nöth found an answer with OLAP functions:

```
SELECT min_x, MAX(y) AS max_y
  FROM (SELECT x, y,
               MAX(CASE WHEN x <= MAX_Y THEN NULL ELSE x END)
               OVER (ORDER BY x, y
                     ROWS UNBOUNDED PRECEDING) AS min_x
          FROM (SELECT x, y,
                       MAX(y)
                       OVER(ORDER BY x, y
                       ROWS BETWEEN UNBOUNDED PRECEDING
                       AND 1 PRECEDING) AS max_y
                  FROM Intervals)
               AS DT)
      AS DT
 GROUP BY min_x;
```

Here is a query that uses a self-join and three nested a correlated subquery that uses the same approach.

```
SELECT I1.x, MAX(I2.y) AS y
  FROM Intervals AS I1
       INNER JOIN
       Intervals AS I2
       ON I2.y > I1.x
 WHERE NOT EXISTS
       (SELECT *
          FROM Intervals AS I3
         WHERE I1.x - 1 BETWEEN I3.x AND I3.y)
           AND NOT EXISTS
              (SELECT *
                 FROM Intervals AS I4
                WHERE I4.y > I1.x
                  AND I4.y < I2.y
                  AND NOT EXISTS
                     (SELECT *
                        FROM Intervals AS I5
                       WHERE I4.y + 1 BETWEEN I5.x AND I5.y))
  GROUP BY I1.x;
```

And this is essentially the same format, but converted to use left anti-semi-joins instead of subqueries. I do not think it is shorter, but it might execute better on some platforms and some people prefer this format to subqueries.

```
SELECT I1.x, MAX(I2.y) AS y
  FROM Intervals AS I1
       INNER JOIN
       Intervals AS I2
       ON I2.y > I1.x
         LEFT OUTER JOIN
         Intervals AS I3
         ON I1.x - 1 BETWEEN I3.x AND I3.y
           LEFT OUTER JOIN
           (Intervals AS I4
            LEFT OUTER JOIN
            Intervals AS I5
            ON I4.y + 1 BETWEEN I5.x AND I5.y)
           ON I4.y > I1.x
              AND I4.y < I2.y
```

```
            AND I5.x IS NULL
 WHERE I3.x IS NULL
   AND I4.x IS NULL
 GROUP BY I1.x;
```

If the table is large, the correlated subqueries (version 1) or the quintuple self-join (version 2) will probably make it slow. But we were asked for a short query, not for a quick one.

Tony Andrews came with this answer.

```
SELECT Starts.x, Ends.y
  FROM (SELECT x, ROW_NUMBER() OVER(ORDER BY x) AS rn
          FROM (SELECT x, y,
                       LAG(y) OVER(ORDER BY x) AS prev_y
                  FROM Intervals)
         WHERE prev_y IS NULL
           OR prev_y < x) AS Starts,
       (SELECT y, ROW_NUMBER() OVER(ORDER BY y) AS rn
          FROM (SELECT x, y,
                        LEAD(x) OVER(ORDER BY y) AS next_x
                  FROM Intervals)
                 WHERE next_x IS NULL
                  OR y < next_x) AS Ends
WHERE Starts.rn = Ends.rn;
```

John Gilson decided that using recursion could be used to build coverings:

```
CREATE TABLE Sessions
(user_name VARCHAR(10) NOT NULL,
 start_timestamp TIMESTAMP(0) NOT NULL,
 PRIMARY KEY (user_name, start_timestamp),
 end_timestamp TIMESTAMP(0) NOT NULL,/
 CONSTRAINT End_GE_Start
 CHECK (start_timestamp <= end_timestamp));

 INSERT INTO Sessions
VALUES
('User1', '2017-12-01 08:00:00', '2017-12-01 08:30:00'),
('User1', '2017-12-01 08:30:00', '2017-12-01 09:00:00'),
('User1', '2017-12-01 09:00:00', '2017-12-01 09:30:00'),
```

```
('User1', '2017-12-01 10:00:00', '2017-12-01 11:00:00'),
('User1', '2017-12-01 10:30:00', '2017-12-01 12:00:00'),
('User1', '2017-12-01 11:30:00', '2017-12-01 12:30:00'),
('User2', '2017-12-01 08:00:00', '2017-12-01 10:30:00'),
('User2', '2017-12-01 08:30:00', '2017-12-01 10:00:00'),
('User2', '2017-12-01 09:00:00', '2017-12-01 09:30:00'),
('User2', '2017-12-01 11:00:00', '2017-12-01 11:30:00'),
('User2', '2017-12-01 11:32:00', '2017-12-01 12:00:00'),
('User2', '2017-12-01 12:04:00', '2017-12-01 12:30:00'),
('User3', '2017-12-01 08:00:00', '2017-12-01 09:10:00'),
('User3', '2017-12-01 08:15:00', '2017-12-01 08:30:00'),
('User3', '2017-12-01 08:30:00', '2017-12-01 09:00:00'),
('User3', '2017-12-01 09:30:00', '2017-12-01 09:30:00);

WITH RECURSIVE Sorted_Sessions
AS
(SELECT user_name, start_timestamp, end_timestamp,
        ROW_NUMBER()
        OVER(PARTITION BY user_name
                 ORDER BY start_timestamp, end_timestamp)
        AS session_seq
   FROM Sessions),
Sessions_Groups
AS
(SELECT user_name, start_timestamp, end_timestamp,
        session_seq, 0 AS grp_nbr
   FROM Sorted_Sessions
 WHERE session_seq = 1
 UNION ALL
 SELECT S2.user_name, S2.start_timestamp,
        CASE WHEN S2.end_timestamp > S1.end_timestamp
        THEN S2.end_timestamp ELSE S1.end_timestamp END,
        S2.session_seq,
        S1.grp_nbr +
          CASE WHEN S1.end_timestamp
                 < COALESCE (S2.start_timestamp,
                        CAST('9999-12-31' AS TIMESTAMP(0)))
               THEN 1 ELSE 0 END AS grp_nbr
```

```
    FROM Sessions_Groups AS S1
  INNER JOIN
  Sorted_Sessions AS S2
  ON S1.user_name = S2.user_name
     AND S2.session_seq = S1.session_seq + 1)

SELECT user_name,
       MIN(start_timestamp) AS start_timestamp,
       MAX(end_timestamp) AS end_timestamp
 FROM Sessions_Groups
GROUP BY user_name, grp_nbr;
```

Finally, try this approach. Assume we have the usual Series auxiliary table. Now we find all the holes in the range of the intervals and put them in a VIEW or a WITH clause derived table.

```
CREATE VIEW Holes (hole)
AS
SELECT list_seq
  FROM Series
 WHERE list_seq <= (SELECT MAX(y) FROM Intervals)
   AND NOT EXISTS
       (SELECT *
          FROM Intervals
         WHERE list_seq BETWEEN x AND y)
        UNION (SELECT list_seq FROM (VALUES (0))
              AS L(list_seq)
        UNION SELECT MAX(y) + 1 FROM Intervals
              AS R(list_seq) -- right sentinel value
        );
```

The query picks start and end pairs that are on the edge of a hole and counts the number of holes inside that range. Covering has no holes inside its range.

```
SELECT Starts.x, Ends.y
  FROM Intervals AS Starts,
       Intervals AS Ends,
       Series AS S -- usual auxiliary table
 WHERE S.list_seq BETWEEN Starts.x AND Ends.y -- restrict list_seq
numbers
```

```
   AND S.list_seq < (SELECT MAX(hole) FROM Holes)
   AND S.list_seq NOT IN (SELECT hole FROM Holes) -- not a hole
   AND Starts.x - 1 IN (SELECT hole FROM Holes) -- on a left cusp
   AND Ends.y + 1 IN (SELECT hole FROM Holes) -- on a right cusp
 GROUP BY Starts.x, Ends.y
HAVING COUNT(DISTINCT list_seq) = Ends.y - Starts.x + 1; -- no holes
```

32.11 Equivalence Classes and Cliques

Equivalence classes are probably the most general kind of grouping for a subset. It is based on equivalence relations, which create equivalence classes. These classes are disjoint and we can put an element from a set into one of them with some kind of rule.

Let's use ~ as the notation for an equivalence relation. The definition is that it has three properties:

1. The relation is reflexive: A ~ A. This means the relation applies to itself.
2. The relation is symmetric: (A ~ B) ⇒ (B ~ A). This means when the relation applies to two different elements in the set, it applies both ways.
3. The relation is transitive: (A ~ B) ⇒ (B ~ C) ⇒ (A ~ C). This means we can deduce all elements in a class by applying the relation to any known members of the class.

So, if this is such a basic set operation, why isn't it in SQL? The problem is that it produces *classes*, not a set! A class is a set of sets, but a table is just a set. The notation for each class is a pair of square bracket that contain some representative of each set. Assume we have

$a \in A$

$b \in B$

These expressions are all the same:

$A \sim B$

$[a] = [b]$

$[a] \cap [b] \neq \varnothing$

32.11.1 Definition by Extension and Intention

A common example is the set Z of integers and any MOD() operator will give you equivalence classes. The MOD(n, 2) operation gives you one class consisting of all even numbers and the other consisting of all odd numbers. The nice part is that you can compute the MOD() function with arithmetic. This is a definition by intention; it has a rule that tells us the intent.

An equivalence classes can also be defined by a set of sets. This is an important concept in graph theory and graph database. If you have not seen it, Google "Six Degrees of Kevin Bacon" (http://en.wikipedia.org/wiki/Six_Degrees_of_Kevin_Bacon). The idea is that any individual involved in the Hollywood film industry can be linked through his or her film roles to Kevin Bacon within six steps. This is a definition by extension.

Let's use a sample set of friends, where ~ now means "is a friend of" and that we can use "foaf"—"Friend of a friend"—to build cliches.

{Fred, Jessica, John, Mary}

{Albert, Nancy, Peter}

{Abby}

{Frank, Joe}

A complete graph means that each node is connected to every other node by one edge. If a subgraph is complete, it is actually called a clique in graph theory!

The complete graph K_n of order n is a simple graph with n vertices in which every vertex is adjacent to every other. The complete graph on n vertices has $n(n-1)/2$ edges, which corresponding to all possible choices of pairs of vertices. But *this is not an equivalence relation* because it does not include the reference of each node to itself. Remember A~A? Think about Abby in this set, assuming that she likes herself, in spite of her lack of social skills.

Obviously, if you have a clique with (k) nodes in it, you can have a complete subgraph of any size (j: $j<k$). A maximal clique is a clique that is not a subset of any other clique (some authors reserve the term clique for maximal clique).

SQL *seems* to have two equivalence relations that are major parts of the language. The first is plain old vanilla equal (=) for scalar values in the base data types. SQL is just like any other programming language, but we also have NULLs to consider. Oops! We all know that (NULL = NULL) is not true. So we have to exclude NULLs or work around them.

The other "almost" equivalence relation is GROUP BY in which the class is the grouping columns. A quick example would be "SELECT city_name, state_code FROM Customers GROUP BY state_code;" and this is still not quite right because we have to do some kind of aggregation on the non-grouping columns in the query.

32.11.2 Graphs in SQL

The idiom for graphs in SQL is to use a table with the nodes involved and a second table with pairs of nodes (a, b) to model the edges, which model our ~ relation. This is classic RDBMS; the first table is entities (e.g., cities on a map, electronic components in a device, etc.) and the second table is a relationship (e.g., roads between cities, wiring between components, etc.).

The bad news is that when you use it for equivalence relations, it can get big. A class with one member has one row to show the edge back to itself. A class with two members {a, b} has {(a, a), (b, b), (a, b), (b, a)} to show the ~ properties as edges. Three members give us six rows; { (a, a), (b, b), (c, c), (a, b), (a, c), (b, a), (b, c), (c, a), (c, b)}. The general formula is $(n * (n-1))+n$, which is pretty close to $(n!)$.

First, load the table a few facts we might already know:

```
CREATE TABLE Friends
(lft_member VARCHAR(20) NOT NULL,
 rgt_member VARCHAR(20) NOT NULL,
 PRIMARY KEY (lft_member, rgt_member));

INSERT INTO Friends (lft_member, rgt_member)
VALUES
('John', 'Mary'),
('Mary', 'Jessica'),
('Peter', 'Albert'),
('Peter', 'Nancy'),
('Abby', 'Abby'),
('Jessica', 'Fred'),
('Joe', 'Frank');
```

32.11.3 Reflexive Rows

The first thing we noticed is that only Abby has a reflexive property row. We need to add those rows and can do this with basic set operators. But it is not that easy, as you can see with this insertion statement:

```
INSERT INTO Friends
SELECT X.lft_member, X.rgt_member
 FROM
((SELECT lft_member, lft_member FROM Friends AS F1
UNION
SELECT rgt_member, rgt_member FROM Friends AS F2)
EXCEPT
SELECT lft_member, rgt_member FROM Friends AS F3)
AS X (lft_member, rgt_member);
```

The use of table aliases is tricky. You have to be sure that the SQL engine will construct a table in such a way that you do not get scoping problems. The UNION and EXCEPT operators are used to assure that we do not have primary key violations.

Abby	Abby
Albert	Albert
Frank	Frank
Fred	Fred
Jessica	Jessica
Jessica	Fred
Joe	Joe
Joe	Frank
John	Mary
John	John
Mary	Mary
Mary	Jessica
Nancy	Nancy
Peter	Peter

Peter	Nancy
Peter	Albert

32.11.4 Symmetric Rows

Look at the update table and there are no { (a, b), (b, a)} pairs. We need to add this second property to the relation table. This follows the pattern of set operators we just used:

```
INSERT INTO Friends
SELECT X.lft_member, X.rgt_member
 FROM
(
(SELECT F1.rgt_member, F1.lft_member
  FROM Friends AS F1
 WHERE F1.lft_member <> F1.rgt_member)
EXCEPT
(SELECT F2.lft_member, F2.rgt_member FROM Friends AS F2)
) AS X (lft_member, rgt_member);
```

This will give us:

Abby	Abby
Albert	Peter
Albert	Albert
Frank	Joe
Frank	Frank
Fred	Jessica
Fred	Fred
Jessica	Mary
Jessica	Jessica
Jessica	Fred
Joe	Joe
Joe	Frank

John	Mary
John	John
Mary	Mary
Mary	John
Mary	Jessica
Nancy	Peter
Nancy	Nancy
Peter	Peter
Peter	Nancy
Peter	Albert

If you do quick GROUP BY query, you see that Abby is seriously antisocial with a count of 1, but Mary and Jessica look very social with a count of 3. This is not quite true because the property could be the dreaded "Rock-paper-scissors-lizard-Spock" relationship. But this is what we are using.

32.11.5 Transitive Rows

Transitivity goes on forever. Well, until we have what mathematicians call a closure. This means we have gotten the complete set of elements that can be selected by following the transitive relationship. In some cases, these sets are infinite. But in database, we can only have insanely large tables. Let's pull a subset that is part of a clique of four friends.

Fred	Jessica
Fred	Fred
Jessica	Mary
Jessica	Jessica
Jessica	Fred
John	Mary
John	John
Mary	Mary

Mary	John
Mary	Jessica

Now apply the transitive relation to get some of the missing edges of a graph:

```
INSERT INTO Friends
SELECT X.lft_member, X.rgt_member
 FROM
((SELECT F1.lft_member, F2.rgt_member
  FROM Friends AS F1, Friends AS F2
 WHERE F1.rgt_member = F2.lft_member)
EXCEPT
(SELECT F3.lft_member, F3.rgt_member FROM Friends AS F3)
) AS X (lft_member, rgt_member);
```

This is a simple statement using the definition of transitivity, without a universal quantifier or loop on it. It will add these rows to this subset:

Fred	Mary
Jessica	John
John	Jessica
Mary	Fred

When you look at Mary and Jessica, you have all their friends because they are directly connected. However, Fred and John do not know that they are friends. So we invoke the statement again and get those two rows. If you try it a third time, there are zero rows added.

The first thought is this sounds like a job for a recursive statement. But it is not that easy. If the original graph has a cycle in it, you can hang in an infinite loop if you try to use a recursive CTE. The assumption is that each clique has a spanning graph in the pairs in. Oops! New term: a spanning graph is a subgraph that includes the nodes and some or all of the edges of the graph. A complete graph is the spanning graph that has all the possible edges, so each node is *directly* connected to any other node.

32.11.6 Cliques

Now change your mindset from graphs to sets. Let's look at the size of the cliques:

```
WITH X (member, clique_size)
AS
(SELECT lft_member, COUNT(*) FROM Friends GROUP BY lft_member)
SELECT * FROM X ORDER BY clique_size;
```

Abby	1
Frank	2
Joe	2
Nancy	3
Peter	3
Albert	3
Fred	4
Jessica	4
John	4
Mary	4

What we want to do is assign a number to each clique. This sample data is biased by the fact that the cliques are all different size. You cannot simply use the size to assign a clique_nbr.

Create this table; load it with the names.

```
CREATE TABLE Cliques
(clique_member VARCHAR(20) NOT NULL PRIMARY KEY,
 clique_nbr INTEGER);
```

We can start by assigning everyone their own clique, using whatever your favorite method is

```
INSERT INTO Cliques
 VALUES
('Abby', 1),
('Frank', 2),
```

```
('Joe', 3),
('Nancy', 4),
('Peter', 5),
('Albert', 6),
('Fred', 7),
('Jessica', 8),
('John', 9),
('Mary', 10);
```

Everyone is equally a member of their clique in this model. That means we could start with anyone to get the rest of their clique. The update is very straight forward. Take any clique number; find the member to whom it belongs and use that name to build that clique. But which number do we use? We could use the MIN, MAX, or a random number in the clique; I will use the MAX for no particular reason.

I keep thinking that there is a recursive update statement that will do this in one statement. But I know it will not port (Standard SQL has no recursive update statement right now. We would do it with SQL/PSM or a host language.) and I think it would be expensive. Recursion will happen for each member of the whole set, but if we consolidate a clique for one person, we have removed his friends from consideration.

The worst situation would be a bunch of hermits, so the number of clique would be the cardinality of set. That is not likely or useful in the real world. Let's put the update in the body of a loop.

```
BEGIN
DECLARE in_clique_loop INTEGER;
DECLARE in_mem CHAR(10);
SET in_clique_loop = (SELECT MAX(clique_nbr) FROM Cliques);

WHILE in_clique_loop > 0
DO
SET in_mem = (SELECT clique_member FROM Cliques WHERE clique_nbr = in_
clique_loop);
UPDATE Cliques
   SET clique_nbr
       = (SELECT clique_nbr
            FROM Cliques
           WHERE clique_member = in_mem)
 WHERE clique_member
```

```
        IN (SELECT rgt_member
              FROM Friends
              WHERE lft_member = in_mem);
SET in_clique_loop = in_clique_loop - 1;
END WHILE;
END;
```

As a programming assignment, replace the simple counting loop with one that does not do updates with clique_loop values that were removed in the prior iteration. This can save a lot of work in a larger social network than the sample data used here.

Now that we have a cliques table, we can do a simple insertion if the new guy belongs to one clique. However, we can have someone who knows a people in different cliques. This will merge the two cliques into one.

```
CREATE PROCEDURE Clique_Merge
(IN clique_member_1 CHAR(10),
IN clique_member_2 CHAR(10))
LANGUAGE SQL
BEGIN
UPDATE Cliques
  SET clique_nbr
     =(SELECT MAX(clique_nbr)
         FROM Cliques
        WHERE clique_member
           IN (in_clique_member_1, in_clique_member_2))
 WHERE clique_nbr
      =(SELECT MIN (clique_nbr)
        FROM Cliques
       WHERE clique_member
           IN (in_clique_member_1, in_clique_member_2));
END;
```

Deleting a member or moving him to another clique is trivial.

Auctions

WE LIVE IN the worlds of eBay.com, craigslist.org, stock markets, and bargain shopping via search engines. Yet programmers do not understand how a market works. The first principles of a market are pretty simple.

1. Not everyone values things the same. A lobster dinner looks good to me, but deadly to someone with a shellfish allergy.
2. Personal valuations change over time. I might eat a second lobster dinner immediately after the first one, but a third lobster is too much to eat right now. Call me next week, please. People do not trade unless they feel what they *gain is more valuable than what they lose.* I want that lobster dinner more than I want the $25 in my pocket. But I want $50 in my pocket more than a lobster in my belly.

33.1 General Types of Bidding

Bids have to stop at some point in time, so there is usually a deadline. They can be sealed-bid, where each bidder has a fixed number of bids (usually one) that they traditionally submit in an envelope. Open bid auctions are more lively; the bidders call out their offers until the auctioneer closes the bidding. You can enter and leave the auction at will.

These days, we do it online, so we have "bid snatcher" software that automatically submits a bid that is under your preset limit. The usual strategy is to wait until the last possible minute (second? microsecond?) to get in a bid in so short a time slot that nobody can type fast enough to beat you.

33.2 Types of Auctions

Auctions come in all kinds of flavors, but the basic parts are an offering of something (I have here a first edition of CAPTAIN BILLY'S WHIZBANG, 1919! I start the bidding at $500!) and bids (I'll pay $1000 for it!). The bid can be accepted or rejected. If the bid is accepted, the item changes ownership.

33.2.1 English Auctions

English Auctions are also known as increasing or ascending price auctions. The auctioneer asks for starting price and the bidders increase the price until the item sells or the price offered is not high enough and the auction fails. This is the form that most of us know. It is how eBay works. Sort of eBay is more complicated.

33.2.2 Japanese Auctions

The Japanese auction is an ascending price auction with levels or tiers. Once you drop out, you cannot re-enter the bidding. For example, if the starting bid is $10, every interested bidder agrees to meet it. We then go up a level or $15; anyone who fails to meet the new level is out and cannot re-enter the bidding, even if they are willing to pay a higher price later. You have a lot of information—the number of other bidders at every level and their exit prices. The auction continues until only one bidder remains.

33.2.3 Dutch Auctions

Dutch Auctions are also known as decreasing or descending price auctions. The auctioneer asks for high starting price, and then drops the price lower and lower in steps until the item clears or auction fails. This form of auction used to be popular with small retail stores decades ago. The items would be put in the store window with a flip-chart price tag and an announcement that the price would decrease $\$x$ per day until sold.

Today, the Dutch auction is hidden in online clearance sales. Instead of looking at the store window on Main Street, you get a series of email advertisements at lower and lower prices.

33.2.4 Vickrey Auctions

Obviously, a winner can have "buyer's remorse"—the feeling that they paid too much for the item. If you have seen bidding wars on eBay or real life, you understand how emotions can get mixed up in the heat of the moment.

The solution is Vickrey or second price auctions. The highest bidder wins, but the price paid is between the highest and second highest bids. The winner cannot be unhappy; he paid less than his bid and won. The losers cannot be unhappy; they all bid less than the winner.

The eBay proxy bid system is a form of second price auction. A variant of a Vickrey auction, named generalized second-price auction, is used in Google's and Yahoo!'s online advertisement programs. The computer runs hundreds or thousands of auctions for the on-line adverting slots they sell.

33.2.5 Auction Schema

What would the basic tables be? Let's start with the bidders and a simple skeleton.

```
CREATE TABLE Bidders
(bidder_id INTEGER NOT NULL PRIMARY KEY,
 ..)
```

When we log in an item for an auction, we need to identify the item, get a starting bid amount. The minimum bid is also called the reserve amount. If there is no bid, equal or greater than that amount, the auction is void.

Initially we do not have

```
CREATE TABLE Items
(item_id INTEGER NOT NULL PRIMARY KEY,
 item_name VARCHAR(25) NOT NULL,
 initial_bid_amt DECIMAL (12,2) NOT NULL
   CHECK(initial_bid_amt >= 0.00),
 minimum_bid_amt DECIMAL (12,2) NOT NULL
   CHECK(initial_bid_amt >= 0.00));
```

A bid has to be timestamped and the bid amounts have to increase over time.

```
CREATE TABLE Bids
(item_id INTEGER NOT NULL
  REFERENCES Items (item_id),
 bidder_id INTEGER NOT NULL
  REFERENCES Bidders (bidder_id),
 bid_timestamp TIMESTAMP(0) DEFAULT CURRENT_TIMESTAMP NOT NULL,
 bid_amt DECIMAL (12,2) NOT NULL
   CHECK(bid_amt >= 0.00),
 PRIMARY KEY (item_id, bidder_id, bid_timestamp)
);
```

I recommend using a bid insertion procedure to ensure that bids are always increasing (or decreasing in the case of a Dutch auction) rather than in the DDL. The reason is that a bid can be pulled from the bids table.

33.3 LIFO and FIFO Inventory

Imagine a very simple inventory of one kind of item, Widgets, into which we add stock once a day. This inventory is then used to fill orders that also come in once a day. Here is the table for this toy problem.

```
CREATE TABLE WidgetInventory
(receipt_nbr INTEGER NOT NULL PRIMARY KEY,
 purchase_date TIMESTAMP DEFAULT CURRENT_TIMESTAMP NOT NULL,
 qty_on_hand INTEGER NOT NULL
   CHECK (qty_on_hand >= 0),
 unit_price DECIMAL (12,4) NOT NULL);
```

With the following data:

WidgetInventory

Receipt_nbr	Purchase_date	Qty_on_hand	Unit_price
1	'2017-08-01'	15	10
2	'2017-08-02'	25	12
3	'2017-08-03'	40	13
4	'2017-08-04'	35	12
5	'2017-08-05'	45	10

The business now sells 100 units on 2017-08-05. How do you calculate the value of the stock sold? There is not one right answer, but here are some options:

1. Use the current replacement cost, which is $10.00 per unit as of 2017-08-05. That would mean the sale cost us only $1000.00 because of a recent price break.
2. Use the current average price per unit. We have a total of 160 units, for which we paid a total of $1840.00; that gives us an average cost of $11.50 per unit, or $1150.00 in total inventory costs.
3. Use LIFO, which stands for, "Last In, First Out". We start by looking at the most recent purchases and work backwards through time.

```
2017-08-05: 45 * $10.00 = $450.00 and 45 units
2017-08-04: 35 * $12.00 = $420.00 and 80 units
2017-08-03: 20 * $13.00 = $260.00 and 100 with 20 units left over
```

   For a total of $1130.00 in inventory cost.

4. Use FIFO, which stands for "First In, First Out". We start by looking at the earliest purchases and work forward through time.

```
2017-08-01: 15 * $10.00 = $150.00 and 15 units
2017-08-02: 25 * $12.00 = $300.00 and 40 units
2017-08-03: 40 * $13.00 = $520.00 and 80 units
2017-08-04: 20 * $12.00 = $240.00 with 15 units left over
```

For a total of $1210.00 in inventory costs.

The first two scenarios are trivial to program.

```
CREATE VIEW (current_replacement_cost)
AS
SELECT unit_price
  FROM WidgetInventory
 WHERE purchase_date
       = (SELECT MAX(purchase_date) FROM WidgetInventory);

CREATE VIEW (average_replacement_cost)
AS
```

```
SELECT SUM(unit_price * qty_on_hand)/SUM(qty_on_hand)
  FROM WidgetInventory;
```

The LIFO and FIFO are more interesting because they involve looking at matching the order against the blocks of inventory in a particular order.

33.3.1 LIFO Cost as a VIEW

Consider this VIEW:

```
CREATE VIEW LIFO (stock_date, unit_price, tot_qty_on_hand, tot_cost)
AS
SELECT W1.purchase_date, W1.unit_price, SUM(W2.qty_on_hand), SUM(W2.
qty_on_hand *
W2.unit_price)
  FROM WidgetInventory AS W1,
       WidgetInventory AS W2
 WHERE W2.purchase_date <= W1.purchase_date
 GROUP BY W1.purchase_date, W1.unit_price;
```

A row in this VIEW tells us the total quantity on hand, the total cost of the goods in inventory, and what we were paying for items on each date. The quantity on hand is a running total. We can get the LIFO cost with this query:

```
SELECT (tot_cost - ((tot_qty_on_hand - :order_qty) * unit_price))
       AS cost
  FROM LIFO AS L1
 WHERE stock_date
       = (SELECT MIN(stock_date)
            FROM LIFO AS L2
           WHERE tot_qty_on_hand >= :order_qty);
```

This is straight algebra and a little logic. You need to find the most recent date when we had enough (or more) quantity on hand to meet the order. If, by dumb blind luck, there is a day when the quantity on hand exactly matched the order, return the total cost as the answer. If the order was for more than we have in stock, then return nothing. If we go back to a day when we had more in stock than the order was for, look at the unit price on that day, multiply by the overage, and subtract it.

33.3.2 CASE Expressions

Alternatively, you can use a derived table and a CASE expression. The CASE expression computes the cost of units that have a running total quantity less than the :order_qty and then performs algebra on the final block of inventory, which would put the running total over the limit. The outer query does a sum on these blocks:

```
SELECT SUM(W3.v) AS cost
  FROM (SELECT W1.unit_price
             * CASE WHEN SUM(W2.qty_on_hand) <= :order_qty
                    THEN W1.qty_on_hand
                    ELSE :order_qty
                        - (SUM(W2.qty_on_hand) - W1.qty_on_hand)
                    END
          FROM WidgetInventory AS W1,
               WidgetInventory AS W2
         WHERE W1.purchase_date <= W2.purchase_date
         GROUP BY W1.purchase_date, W1.qty_on_hand, W1.unit_price
        HAVING (SUM(W2.qty_on_hand) - W1.qty_on_hand) <= :order_qty)
       AS W3(v);
```

FIFO can be found with a similar VIEW or derived table:

```
CREATE VIEW FIFO (stock_date, unit_price, tot_qty_on_hand, tot_cost)
AS
SELECT W1.purchase_date, W1.unit_price,
       SUM(W2.qty_on_hand), SUM(W2.qty_on_hand *
W2.unit_price)
 FROM WidgetInventory AS W1,
       WidgetInventory AS W2
 WHERE W2.purchase_date >= W1.purchase_date
 GROUP BY W1.purchase_date, W1.unit_price;
```

With the corresponding query:

```
SELECT (tot_cost - ((tot_qty_on_hand - :order_qty) * unit_price)) AS cost
  FROM FIFO AS F1
 WHERE stock_date
       = (SELECT MAX (stock_date)
```

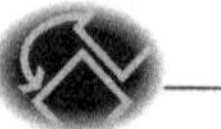

```
          FROM FIFO AS F2
         WHERE tot_qty_on_hand >= :order_qty);
```

These queries and VIEWs only told us the value of the Widget inventory. Notice that we never actually shipped anything from the inventory.

33.3.3 Updating Inventory

How to write the UPDATE statements that let us change this simple inventory.

What we did not do in part 1 was to actually update the inventory when the Widgets were shipped out. Let's build another VIEW that will make life easier.

```
CREATE VIEW StockLevels (purchase_date, previous_qty, current_qty)
AS
SELECT W1.purchase_date,
       SUM(CASE WHEN W2.purchase_date < W1.purchase_date
                THEN W2.qty_on_hand ELSE 0 END),
       SUM(CASE WHEN W2.purchase_date <= W1.purchase_date
                THEN W2.qty_on_hand ELSE 0 END)
  FROM WidgetInventory AS W1,
       WidgetInventory AS W2
 WHERE W2.purchase_date <= W1.purchase_date
 GROUP BY W1.purchase_date, W1.unit_price;
```

StockLevels

Purchase_date	Previous_qty	Current_qty
'2017-08-01'	0	15
'2017-08-02'	15	40
'2017-08-03'	40	80
'2017-08-04'	80	115
'2017-08-05'	115	160

Using CASE expressions will save you a self-join.

```
CREATE PROCEDURE RemoveQty (IN my_order_qty INTEGER)
LANGUAGE SQL
BEGIN
IF my_order_qty > 0
```

```
THEN
UPDATE WidgetInventory
  SET qty_on_hand
      = CASE
        WHEN my_order_qty
             >= (SELECT current_qty
                   FROM StockLevels AS L
                  WHERE L.purchase_date
                        = WidgetInventory.purchase_date)
        THEN 0
        WHEN my_order_qty
             < (SELECT previous_qty
                  FROM StockLevels AS L
                 WHERE L.purchase_date
                       = WidgetInventory.purchase_date)
         THEN WidgetInventory.qty_on_hand
         ELSE (SELECT current_qty
                 FROM StockLevels AS L
                WHERE L.purchase_date = WidgetInventory.purchase_date)
              - my_order_qty END;
END IF;

-- remove empty bins
DELETE FROM WidgetInventory
 WHERE qty_on_hand = 0;
END;
```

Another inventory problem is how to fill an order with the smallest or greatest number of bins. This assumes that the bins are not in order, so you are free to fill the order as you wish. Using the fewest bins would make less work for the order pickers. Using the greatest number of bins would clean out more storage in the warehouse.

For example, with this data, you could fill an order for 80 widgets by shipping out bins (1, 2, 3) or bins (4, 5). These bins happen to be in date and bin number order in the sample data, but that is not required.

Mathematicians call it (logically enough) a bin-packing problem and it belongs to the NP-complete family of problems. This kind of problem is too hard to solve for the general case because the work requires trying all the combinations, and this increases too fast for a computer to do it.

However, there are "greedy algorithms" that are often *nearly* optimal. The idea is to begin by taking the "biggest bite" you can until you have met or passed your goal. In procedural languages, you can back-track when you go over the target amount and try to find an exact match or apply a rule that dictates from which bin to take a partial pick.

33.4 Bin Packing

This is not easy in SQL, because it is a declarative, set-oriented language. A procedural language can stop when it has a solution that is "good enough," while an SQL query tends to find all of the correct answers no matter how long it takes. If you can put a limit on the number of bins you are willing to visit, you can fake an array in a table:

```
CREATE TABLE Picklists
(order_nbr INTEGER NOT NULL PRIMARY KEY,
 goal_qty INTEGER NOT NULL
   CHECK (goal_qty > 0),
 bin_nbr_1 INTEGER NOT NULL UNIQUE,
 qty_on_hand_1 INTEGER DEFAULT 0 NOT NULL
  CHECK (qty_on_hand_1 >= 0),
 bin_nbr_2 INTEGER NOT NULL UNIQUE,
 qty_on_hand_2 INTEGER DEFAULT 0 NOT NULL
  CHECK (qty_on_hand_2 >= 0),
 bin_nbr_3 INTEGER NOT NULL UNIQUE,
 qty_on_hand_3 INTEGER DEFAULT 0 NOT NULL
  CHECK (qty_on_hand_3 >= 0),
 CONSTRAINT not_over_goal
  CHECK (qty_on_hand_1 + qty_on_hand_2 + qty_on_hand_3
         <= goal_qty)
CONSTRAINT bins_sorted
  CHECK (qty_on_hand_1 >= qty_on_hand_2
         AND qty_on_hand_2 >= qty_on_hand_3));
```

Now you can start stuffing bins into the table. This query will give you the ways to fill or almost fill an order with three or fewer bins. The first trick is to load some empty dummy bins into the table. If you want at most (n) picks, then add (n-1) dummy bins:

```
INSERT INTO WidgetInventory
VALUES (-1, '1990-01-01', 0 ,0.00),
       (-2, '1990-01-02', 0 ,0.00);
```

The following code shows how to build a common table expression (CTE) or VIEW with the possible pick lists:

```
CREATE VIEW PickCombos(total_pick, bin_1, qty_on_hand_1,
                 bin_2, qty_on_hand_2,
                 bin_3, qty_on_hand_3)
AS
SELECT DISTINCT
       (W1.qty_on_hand + W2.qty_on_hand + W3.qty_on_hand) AS total_pick,
       CASE WHEN W1.receipt_nbr < 0
            THEN 0 ELSE W1.receipt_nbr END AS bin_1, W1.qty_on_hand,
       CASE WHEN W2.receipt_nbr < 0
            THEN 0 ELSE W2.receipt_nbr END AS bin_2, W2.qty_on_hand,
       CASE WHEN W3.receipt_nbr < 0
            THEN 0 ELSE W3.receipt_nbr END AS bin_3, W3.qty_on_hand
 FROM WidgetInventory AS W1,
      WidgetInventory AS W2,
      WidgetInventory AS W3
WHERE W1.receipt_nbr NOT IN (W2.receipt_nbr, W3.receipt_nbr)
  AND W2.receipt_nbr NOT IN (W1.receipt_nbr, W3.receipt_nbr)
  AND W1.qty_on_hand >= W2.qty_on_hand
  AND W2.qty_on_hand >= W3.qty_on_hand;
```

Now you need a procedure to find the pick combination that meets or comes closest to a certain quantity.

```
CREATE PROCEDURE OverPick (IN goal_qty INTEGER)
LANGUAGE SQL
BEGIN
IF goal_qty > 0
THEN
SELECT goal_qty, total_pick, bin_1, qty_on_hand_1,
     bin_2, qty_on_hand_2,
     bin_3, qty_on_hand_3
  FROM PickCombos
```

```
 WHERE total_pick
        = (SELECT MIN (total_pick)
             FROM PickCombos
            WHERE total_pick >= goal_qty)
END IF;
END;
```

The VIEW could be put into a CTE and produce a query without a VIEW. With the current data and goal of 73 Widgets, you can find two picks that together equal 75, namely {3, 4} and {4, 2, 1}.

I will leave it as an exercise for the reader to find a query that under-picks a target quantity.

Relational Division

RELATIONAL DIVISION IS one of the eight basic operations in Codd's relational algebra. The idea is that a divisor table is used to partition a dividend table and produce a quotient or results table. The quotient table is made up of those values of one column for which a second column had all of the values in the divisor.

This is easier to explain with an example. We have a table of pilots and the planes they can fly (dividend); we have a table of planes in the hangar (divisor); we want the names of the pilots who can fly every plane (quotient) in the hangar. To get this result, we divide the Pilot_Skills table by the planes in the hangar.

```
CREATE TABLE Pilot_Skills
(pilot_name CHAR(15) NOT NULL,
 plane_name CHAR(15) NOT NULL,
 PRIMARY KEY (pilot_name, plane_name));
```

Pilot_Skills

pilot_name	plane_name
'Celko'	'Piper Cub'
'Higgins'	'B-52 Bomber'
'Higgins'	'F-14 Fighter'

pilot_name	plane_name
'Higgins'	'Piper Cub'
'Jones'	'B-52 Bomber'
'Jones'	'F-14 Fighter'
'Smith'	'B-1 Bomber'
'Smith'	'B-52 Bomber'
'Smith'	'F-14 Fighter'
'Wilson'	'B-1 Bomber'
'Wilson'	'B-52 Bomber'
'Wilson'	'F-14 Fighter'
'Wilson'	'F-17 Fighter'

```
CREATE TABLE Hangar
(plane_name CHAR(15) NOT NULL PRIMARY KEY);
```

Hangar

plane_name
'B-1 Bomber'
'B-52 Bomber'
'F-14 Fighter'

Pilot_Skills DIVIDED BY Hangar

pilot_name
'Smith'
'Wilson'

In this example, Smith and Wilson are the two pilots who can fly everything in the hangar. Notice that Higgins and Celko know how to fly a Piper Cub, but we don't have one right now. In Codd's original definition of relational division, having more rows than are called for is not a problem.

The important characteristic of a relational division is that the CROSS JOIN of the divisor and the quotient produces a valid subset of rows from the dividend. This is where the name comes from, since the CROSS JOIN acts like a multiplication operator.

34.1 Division with a Remainder

There are two kinds of relational division. Division with a remainder allows the dividend table to have more values than the divisor, which was Dr. Codd's original definition. For example, if a pilot_name can fly more planes than just those we have in the hangar, this is fine with us. The query can be written as

```
SELECT DISTINCT pilot_name
  FROM Pilot_Skills AS PS1
 WHERE NOT EXISTS
       (SELECT *
          FROM Hangar
         WHERE NOT EXISTS
               (SELECT *
                  FROM Pilot_Skills AS PS2
                 WHERE (PS1.pilot_name = PS2.pilot_name)
                   AND (PS2.plane_name = Hangar.plane_name)));
```

The quickest way to explain what is happening in this query is to imagine a World War II movie where a cocky pilot_name has just walked into the hangar, looked over the fleet, and announced, "There ain't no plane in this hangar that I can't fly!" We want to find the pilots for whom there does not exist a plane in the hangar for which they have no skills. The use of the NOT EXISTS() predicates is for speed. Most SQL implementations will look up a value in an index rather than scan the whole table.

This query for relational division was made popular by Chris Date in his textbooks, but it is neither the only method nor always the fastest. Another version of the division can be written so as to avoid three levels of nesting. While it is not original with me, I have made it popular in my books.

```
SELECT PS1.pilot_name
  FROM Pilot_Skills AS PS1, Hangar AS H1
 WHERE PS1.plane_name = H1.plane_name
 GROUP BY PS1.pilot_name
HAVING COUNT(PS1.plane_name)
       = (SELECT COUNT(plane_name) FROM Hangar);
```

There is a serious difference in the two methods. Burn down the hangar, so that the divisor is empty. Because of the NOT EXISTS() predicates in Date's query,

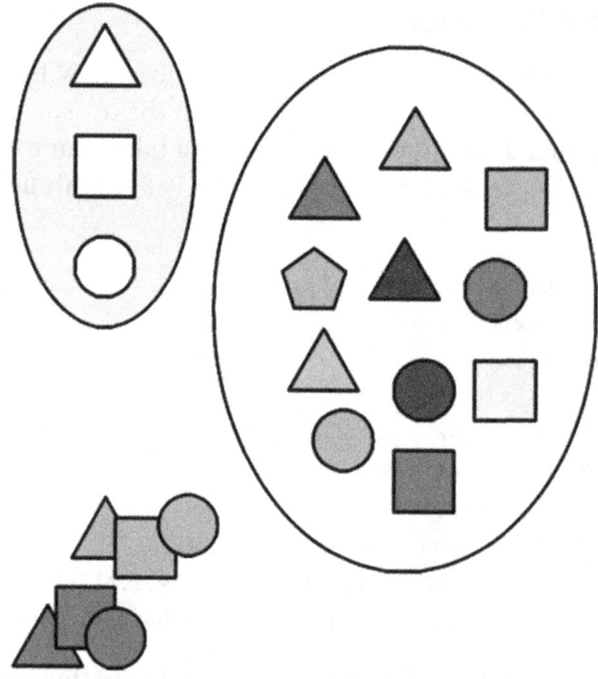

Figure 34.1 Relational Division.

all pilots are returned from a division by an empty set. Because of the COUNT() functions in my query, no pilots are returned from a division by an empty set.

In the sixth edition of his book, INTRODUCTION TO DATABASE SYSTEMS (Addison-Wesley; 1995; ISBN 0-191-82458-2), Chris Date defined another operator (DIVIDEBY ... PER) which produces the same results as my query, but with more complexity (Figure 34.1).

34.2 Exact Division

The second kind of relational division is exact relational division. The dividend table must match exactly with the values of the divisor without any extra values.

```
SELECT PS1.pilot_name
  FROM Pilot_Skills AS PS1
       LEFT OUTER JOIN
       Hangar AS H1
```

```
       ON PS1.plane_name = H1.plane_name
 GROUP BY PS1.pilot_name
HAVING COUNT(PS1.plane_name) = (SELECT COUNT(plane_name) FROM Hangar)
   AND COUNT(H1.plane_name) = (SELECT COUNT(plane_name) FROM Hangar);
```

This says that a pilot must have the same number of certificates as there are planes in the hangar and these certificates all match to a plane in the hangar, not something else. The "something else" is shown by a created NULL from the LEFT OUTER JOIN.

Please do not make the mistake of trying to reduce the HAVING clause with a little algebra to:

```
HAVING COUNT(PS1.plane_name) = COUNT(H1.plane_name)
```

because it does not work; it will tell you that the hangar has (n) planes in it and the pilot_name is certified for (n) planes, but not that those two sets of planes are equal to each other.

34.3 Note on Performance

The nested EXISTS() predicates version of relational division was made popular by Chris Date's textbooks, while the author is associated with popularizing the COUNT(*) version of relational division. The Winter 1996 edition of DB2 ON-LINE MAGAZINE (http://www.db2mag.com/96011ar:htm) had an article entitled "Powerful SQL: Beyond the Basics" by Sheryl Larsen which gave the results of testing both methods. Her conclusion for the then current version of DB2 was that the nested EXISTS() version is better when the quotient has less than 25% of the dividend table's rows and the COUNT(*) version is better when the quotient is more than 25% of the dividend table.

On the other hand, Matthew W. Spaulding at SnapOn Tools reported his test on SQL Server 2000 with the opposite results. He had a table with two million rows for the dividend and around 1,000 rows in the divisor, yielding a quotient of around 1,000 rows as well. The COUNT method completed in well under one second, where as the nested NOT EXISTS query took roughly five seconds to run.

The moral of the story is to test both methods on your particular release of your product.

34.4 Todd's Division

A relational division operator proposed by Stephen Todd is defined on two tables with common columns that are joined together, dropping the JOIN column and retaining only those non-JOIN columns that meet a criterion.

We are given a table, JobParts(job_nbr_nbr, part_nbr), and another table, SupParts(sup_nbr, part_nbr), of suppliers and the parts that they provide. We want to get the supplier-and-job_nbr pairs such that supplier sn supplies all of the parts needed for job_nbr jn. This is not quite the same thing as getting the supplier-and-job_nbr pairs such that job_nbr jn requires all of the parts provided by supplier sn.

You want to divide the JobParts table by the SupParts table. A rule of thumb: The remainder comes from the dividend, but all values in the divisor are present.

JobParts

job_nbr	part_nbr
'j1'	'p1'
'j1'	'p2'
'j2'	'p2'
'j2'	'p4'
'j2'	'p5'
'j3'	'p2'

SupParts

sup_nbr	part_nbr
's1'	'p1'
's1'	'p2'
's1'	'p3'
's1'	'p4'
's1'	'p5'
's1'	'p6'
's2'	'p1'
's2'	'p2'
's3'	'p2'

sup_nbr	part_nbr
's4'	'p2'
's4'	'p4'
's4'	'p5'

Result=JobSups

job_nbr	sup_nbr
'j1'	's1'
'j1'	's2'
'j2'	's1'
'j2'	's4'
'j3'	's1'
'j3'	's2'
'j3'	's3'
'j3'	's4'

Pierre Mullin submitted the following query to carry out the Todd division:

```
SELECT DISTINCT JP1.job_nbr, SP1.supplier
  FROM JobParts AS JP1, SupParts AS SP1
 WHERE NOT EXISTS
        (SELECT *
           FROM JobParts AS JP2
          WHERE JP2.job_nbr = JP1.job_nbr
            AND JP2.part
                NOT IN (SELECT SP2.part
                          FROM SupParts AS SP2
                         WHERE SP2.supplier = SP1.supplier));
```

This is really a modification of the query for Codd's division, extended to use a JOIN on both tables in the outermost SELECT statement. The IN predicate for the second subquery can be replaced with a NOT EXISTS predicate; it might run a bit faster, depending on the optimizer.

Another related query is finding the pairs of suppliers who sell the same parts. In this data, that would be the pairs (s1, p2), (s3, p1), (s4, p1), (s5, p1)

```
SELECT S1.sup, S2.sup
  FROM SupParts AS S1, SupParts AS S2
 WHERE S1.sup < S2.sup -- different suppliers
   AND S1.part = S2.part -- same parts
 GROUP BY S1.sup, S2.sup
HAVING COUNT(*) = (SELECT COUNT (*) -- same count of parts
                     FROM SupParts AS S3
                    WHERE S3.sup = S1.sup)
   AND COUNT(*) = (SELECT COUNT (*)
                     FROM SupParts AS S4
                    WHERE S4.sup = S2.sup);
```

This can be modified into Todd's division easily by adding the restriction that the parts must also belong to a common job.

Steve Kass came up with a specialized version that depends on using a numeric code. Assume we have a table that tells us which players are on which teams.

```
CREATE TABLE Team_Assignments
(player_id INTEGER NOT NULL
     REFERENCES Players(player_id)
     ON DELETE CASCADE
     ON UPDATE CASCADE,
 team_id CHAR(5) NOT NULL
     REFERENCES Teams(team_id)
     ON DELETE CASCADE
     ON UPDATE CASCADE,
 PRIMARY KEY (player_id, team_id));
```

To get pairs of Players on the same team:

```
SELECT P1.player_id, P2.player_id
  FROM Players AS P1, Players AS P2
WHERE P1.player_id < P2.player_id
 GROUP BY P1.player_id, P2.player_id
HAVING P1.player_id + P2.player_id
     = ALL (SELECT SUM(P3.player_id)
```

```
         FROM Team_Assignments AS P3
        WHERE P3.player_id IN (P1.player_id, P2.player_id)
        GROUP BY P3.team_id);
```

34.5 Division with JOINs

Standard SQL has several JOIN operators that can be used to perform a relational division. To find the pilots, who can fly the same planes as Higgins, use this query:

```
SELECT SP1.pilot_name
  FROM (((SELECT plane_name FROM Hangar) AS H1
         INNER JOIN
         (SELECT pilot_name, plane_name FROM Pilot_Skills) AS SP1
         ON H1.plane_name = SP1.plane_name)
        INNER JOIN (SELECT *
                      FROM Pilot_Skills
                     WHERE pilot_name = 'Higgins') AS H2
        ON H2.plane_name = H1.plane_name)
 GROUP BY Pilot
HAVING COUNT(*) >= (SELECT COUNT(*)
                      FROM Pilot_Skills
                     WHERE pilot_name = 'Higgins');
```

The first JOIN finds all of the planes in the hangar for which we have a pilot_name. The next JOIN takes that set and finds which of those match up with (SELECT * FROM Pilot_Skills WHERE pilot_name = 'Higgins') skills. The GROUP BY clause will then see that the intersection we have formed with the joins has at least as many elements as Higgins has planes. The GROUP BY also means that the SELECT DISTINCT can be replaced with a simple SELECT. If the theta operator in the GROUP BY clause is changed from >=to =, the query finds an exact division. If the theta operator in the GROUP BY clause is changed from >=to <= or <, the query finds those pilots whose skills are a superset or a strict superset of the planes that Higgins flies.

It might be a good idea to put the divisor into a VIEW for readability in this query and as a clue to the optimizer to calculate it once. Some products will execute this form of the division query faster than the nested subquery version, because they will use the PRIMARY KEY information to pre-compute the joins between tables.

34.6 Division with Set Operators

The Standard SQL set difference operator, EXCEPT, can be used to write a very compact version of Dr. Codd's relational division. The EXCEPT operator removes the divisor set from the dividend set. If the result is empty, we have a match; if there is anything left over, it has failed. Using the pilots-and-hangar-tables example, we would write

```
SELECT DISTINCT pilot_name
  FROM Pilot_Skills AS P1
 WHERE (SELECT plane_name FROM Hangar
        EXCEPT
        SELECT plane_name
          FROM Pilot_Skills AS P2
         WHERE P1.pilot_name = P2.pilot_name) IS NULL;
```

Again, informally, you can imagine that we got a skill list from each pilot_name, walked over to the hangar, and crossed off each plane_name he could fly. If we marked off all the planes in the hangar, we would keep this guy. Another trick is that an empty subquery expression returns a NULL, which is how we can test for an empty set. The WHERE clause could just as well have used a NOT EXISTS() predicate instead of the IS NULL predicate.

34.7 Romley's Division

This somewhat complicated relational division is due to Richard Romley, a DBA retired from Salomon Smith Barney. The original problem deals with two tables. The first table has a list of managers and the projects they can manage. The second table has a list of Personnel, their departments and the project to which they are assigned. Each employee is assigned to one and only one department and each employee works on one and only one project at a time. But a department can have several different projects at the same time, so a single project can span several departments.

```
CREATE TABLE Mgr_Projects
(mgr_name CHAR(10) NOT NULL,
 project_id CHAR(2) NOT NULL,
 PRIMARY KEY(mgr_name, project_id));
```

```
INSERT INTO Mgr_Project
VALUES ('M1', 'P1'), ('M1', 'P3'),
       ('M2', 'P2'), ('M2', 'P3'),
       ('M3', 'P2'),
       ('M4', 'P1'), ('M4', 'P2'), ('M4', 'P3');

CREATE TABLE Personnel
(emp_id CHAR(10) NOT NULL,
 dept_id CHAR(2) NOT NULL,
 project_id CHAR(2) NOT NULL,
 UNIQUE (emp_id, project_id),
 UNIQUE (emp_id, dept_id),
 PRIMARY KEY (emp_id, dept_id, project_id));

-- load department #1 data
INSERT INTO Personnel
VALUES ('Al', 'D1', 'P1'),
       ('Bob', 'D1', 'P1'),
       ('Carl', 'D1', 'P1'),
       ('Don', 'D1', 'P2'),
       ('Ed', 'D1', 'P2'),
       ('Frank', 'D1', 'P2'),
       ('George', 'D1', 'P2');

-- load department #2 data
INSERT INTO Personnel
VALUES ('Harry', 'D2', 'P2'),
       ('Jack', 'D2', 'P2'),
       ('Larry', 'D2', 'P2'),
       ('Mike', 'D2', 'P2'),
       ('Nat', 'D2', 'P2');

-- load department #3 data
INSERT INTO Personnel
VALUES ('Oscar', 'D3', 'P2'),
       ('Pat', 'D3', 'P2'),
       ('Rich', 'D3', 'P3');
```

The problem is to generate a report showing for each manager each department whether is he qualified to manage none, some or all of the

projects being worked on within the department. To find who can manage some, but not all, of the projects, use a version of relational division.

```
SELECT M1.mgr_name, P1.dept_id_name
  FROM Mgr_Projects AS M1
       CROSS JOIN
       Personnel AS P1
 WHERE M1.project_id = P1.project_id
 GROUP BY M1.mgr_name, P1.dept_id_name
HAVING COUNT(*) <> (SELECT COUNT(emp_id)
                      FROM Personnel AS P2
                     WHERE P2.dept_id_name = P1.dept_id_name);
```

The query is simply a relational division with a <> instead of an = in the HAVING clause. Richard came back with a modification of my answer that uses a characteristic function inside a single aggregate function.

```
SELECT DISTINCT M1.mgr_name, P1.dept_id_name
  FROM (Mgr_Projects AS M1
        INNER JOIN
        Personnel AS P1
        ON M1.project_id = P1.project_id)
         INNER JOIN
         Personnel AS P2
         ON P1.dept_id_name = P2.dept_id_name
 GROUP BY M1.mgr_name, P1.dept_id_name, P2.project_id
HAVING MAX (CASE WHEN M1.project_id = P2.project_id
            THEN 'T' ELSE 'F' END) = 'F';
```

This query uses a characteristic function while my original version compares a count of Personnel under each manager to a count of Personnel under each project_id. The use of "GROUP BY M1.mgr_name, P1.dept_id_name, P2.project_id" with the "SELECT DISTINCT M1.mgr_name, P1.dept_id_name" is really the tricky part in this new query. What we have is a three-dimensional space with the (x, y, z) axis representing (mgr_name, dept_id_name, project_id) and then we reduce it to two dimensions (mgr_name, dept_id) by seeing if Personnel on shared project_ids cover the department or not.

That observation leads to the next changes. We can build a table that shows each combination of manager, department and the level of authority they have over the projects they have in common. That is the derived table T1 in the following query; (authority = 1) means the manager is not on the project and authority = 2 means that he is on the project_id

```
SELECT T1.mgr_name, T1.dept_id_name,
       CASE SUM(T1.authority)
       WHEN 1 THEN 'None'
       WHEN 2 THEN 'All'
       WHEN 3 THEN 'Some'
       ELSE NULL END AS power
  FROM (SELECT DISTINCT M1.mgr_name, P1.dept_id_name,
               MAX (CASE WHEN M1.project_id = P1.project_id
                         THEN 2 ELSE 1 END) AS authority
          FROM Mgr_Projects AS M1
               CROSS JOIN
               Personnel AS P1
         GROUP BY m.mgr_name, P1.dept_id_name, P1.project_id) AS T1
 GROUP BY T1.mgr_name, T1.dept_id_name;
```

Another version, using the airplane hangar example:

```
SELECT PS1.pilot_name,
       CASE WHEN COUNT(PS1.plane_name)
                 > (SELECT COUNT(plane_name) FROM Hanger)
                 AND COUNT(H1.plane_name)
                     = (SELECT COUNT(plane_name) FROM Hanger)
            THEN 'more than all'
            WHEN COUNT(PS1.plane_name)
                 = (SELECT COUNT(plane_name) FROM Hanger)
                 AND COUNT(H1.plane_name)
                     = (SELECT COUNT(plane_name) FROM Hanger)
            THEN 'exactly all '
            WHEN MIN(H1.plane_name) IS NULL
            THEN 'none '
            ELSE 'some ' END AS skill_level
```

```
FROM Pilot_Skills AS PS1
     LEFT OUTER JOIN
     Hanger AS H1
     ON PS1.plane_name = H1.plane_name
GROUP BY PS1.pilot_name;
```

We can now sum the authority numbers for all the projects within a department to determine the power this manager has over the department as a whole. If he had a total of one, he has no authority over Personnel on any project in the department. If he had a total of two, he has power over all Personnel on all projects in the department. If he had a total of three, he has both a 1 and a 2 authority total on some projects within the department. Here is the final answer.

Results

mgr_name	dept_id	power
M1	D1	Some
M1	D2	None
M1	D3	Some
M2	D1	Some
M2	D2	All
M2	D3	All
M3	D1	Some
M3	D2	All
M3	D3	Some
M4	D1	All
M4	D2	All
M4	D3	All

34.8 Boolean Expressions in Relational Division

Given the usual "hangar and pilots" schema, we want to create and store queries that involve Boolean expressions such as "Find the pilots who can fly a Piper Cub and also an F-14 or F-17 Fighter". The trick is to put the expression into the disjunctive canonical form. In English that means a bunch of AND-ed predicates that are then OR-ed together, like this. Any Boolean function can be expressed this way. This form is canonical when each Boolean variable appears exactly once in each term. When all variables are not required to appear in every term, the form is called a disjunctive normal form. The algorithm to convert any Boolean expression into disjunctive canonical form is a bit complicated, but can be found in a good book on circuit design. Our simple example would convert to this predicate.

('Piper Cub' AND 'F-14 Fighter') OR ('Piper Cub' AND 'F-17 Fighter') which we load into this table:

```
CREATE TABLE Boolean_Expressions
(and_grp INTEGER NOT NULL,
 skill CHAR(10) NOT NULL,
 PRIMARY KEY (and_grp, skill));

INSERT INTO BooleanExpressions
VALUES (1, 'Piper Cub'), (1, 'F-14 Fighter'),
       (2, 'Piper Cub'), (2, 'F-17 Fighter');
```

Assume we have a table of job_nbr candidates:

```
CREATE TABLE Candidates
(candidate_name CHAR(15) NOT NULL,
 skill CHAR(10) NOT NULL,
 PRIMARY KEY (candidate_name, skill));

INSERT INTO Candidates
VALUES ('John', 'Piper Cub'), --winner
       ('John', 'B-52 Bomber'),
       ('Mary', 'Piper Cub'), --winner
       ('Mary', 'F-17 Fighter'),
       ('Larry', 'F-14 Fighter'), --winner
       ('Larry', 'F-17 Fighter'),
       ('Moe', 'F-14 Fighter'), --winner
       ('Moe', 'F-17 Fighter'),
       ('Moe', 'Piper Cub'),
       ('Celko', 'Piper Cub'), -- loser
       ('Celko', 'Blimp'),
       ('Smith', 'Kite'), -- loser
       ('Smith', 'Blimp');
```

The query is simple now:

```
SELECT DISTINCT C1.candidate_name
  FROM Candidates AS C1, BooleanExpressions AS Q1
 WHERE C1.skill = Q1.skill
 GROUP BY Q1.and_grp, C1.candidate_name
HAVING COUNT(C1.skill)
       = (SELECT COUNT(*)
            FROM BooleanExpressions AS Q2
           WHERE Q1.and_grp = Q2.and_grp);
```

You can retain the COUNT() information to rank candidates. For example, Moe meets both qualifications, while other candidates meet only one of the two. This means you can do very complex candidate selections in pure SQL, but it does not mean you should do it.

Temporal Queries

TEMPORAL DATA IS the hardest type of data for people to handle conceptually. Perhaps time is difficult because it is dynamic and all other data types are static or perhaps because time allows multiple parallel events. This is an old puzzle that still catches people.

If a hen and a half lays an egg and a half in a day and a half, how many eggs will five hens lay in 6 days? Do not look at the rest of the page and try to answer the question in your head.

Suppose two hens lay four eggs in 3 days. That means that each hen laid two eggs during those 3 days, so each hen lays 2/3 of an egg per day. Now if you had 5 hens and 6 days, they would lay five times as many eggs per day, totaling 10/3 per day; multiply that by 6 days, and there would be 20 eggs.

The algebra in this problem looks like this, where we want to solve for the rate in terms of "eggs per day," a strange but convenient unit of measurement for summarizing the hen house output:

$$1\frac{1}{2} \text{ hens} \times 1\frac{1}{2} \text{ days} \times \text{rate} = 1\frac{1}{2} \text{ eggs}$$

The first urge is to multiply both sides by 2/3 in an attempt to turn ALL of the 1½'s into 1's. But what you actually get is

$$1 \text{ hens} \times 1\frac{1}{2} \text{ days} \times \text{rate} = 1 \text{ egg; multiply by eggs per hen}$$

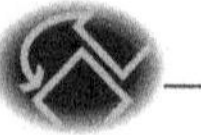

$$1\frac{1}{2}\ \text{days} \times \text{rate} = 1\ \text{egg per hen; divide by the number of hens}$$

$$\text{rate} = \frac{2}{3}\ \text{egg per hen per day}$$

35.1 Temporal Math

SQL has a DATE data type, but the functions available for them vary quite a bit. The most common ones are a constructor that builds a date from integers or strings; extractors to pull out the month, day, or year; and some display options to format output. In Standard SQL, the constructor is CAST (<string expression> AS [DATE | TIME | TIMESTAMP]) for a string expression or you can use literal constructors:

```
<date literal> ::= DATE <date string>
<time literal> ::= TIME <time string>
<timestamp literal> ::= TIMESTAMP <timestamp string>
```

In Standard SQL, *only* ISO-8601 format is allowed for datetime values, that is "yyyy-mm-dd" for dates, "hh:mm:ss.sssss" for times, and "yyyy-mm-dd hh:mm:ss.sssss" for timestamps, with the number of decimal places being implementation defined. However, the FIPS-127 Standards want at least five decimal places in the seconds. You will want to look at a cartoon at http://xkcd.com/1179/to; see why this is important.

The ISO-8601 Standard has many other date and time formats which are not ambiguous and could be added to the strings recognized by SQL. For example, a date without punctuation is legal ("yyyymmdd") and so are strings with embedded letters. We just don't do it to keep things simple. This avoids problems like confusing the British ("dd/mm/yy"), American ("mm/dd/yy"), and other national traditional shorthands.

The extractor is the function EXTRACT(<extract field> FROM <extract source>) defined by:

```
<extract field> ::= <primary datetime field> | <time zone field>
<time zone field> ::= TIMEZONE_HOUR | TIMEZONE_MINUTE
<extract source> ::= <datetime value expression> | <interval value
expression>
```

The extract field options are a little easier to see this in a table

Meaning of <primary datetime field>	Keyword
Year in Common Era calendar (0001-9999)	YEAR
Month within year (01-12)	MONTH
Day within month (01-31)	DAY
Minute within hour (00-59)	MINUTE
Second within minute with decimal fractions (00-59.99...)	SECOND
Hour value of time zone displacement; can be positive or negative (−12 to +14)	TIMEZONE_HOUR
Minute value of time zone displacement; can be positive or negative (−12:59 to +14:00)	TIMEZONE_MINUTE

The obvious ordering is from most significant to least significant: YEAR, MONTH, DAY, HOUR, MINUTE, and SECOND.

The primary datetime fields other than SECOND contain nonnegative integer values, constrained by the natural rules for dates using the Common Era calendar. SECOND, however, can be defined to have a <time fractional seconds precision> that indicates the number of decimal digits maintained following the decimal point in the seconds value, a nonnegative exact numeric value.

There are three classes of datetime data types defined within this part of ISO/IEC 9075 which are defined from the primary datetime fields:

- DATE—contains YEAR, MONTH, and DAY.
- TIME—contains HOUR, MINUTE, and SECOND.
- TIMESTAMP—YEAR, MONTH, DAY, HOUR, MINUTE, and SECOND.

Items of type datetime are comparable only if they have the same primary datetime fields.

You can assume that your SQL implementation has simple date arithmetic functions, although with different syntax from product to product. The basic functions you need are just those that work with dates:

- A date plus or minus an interval of days yields a new date.
- A date minus a second date yields an interval of days.

Here is a table of the valid combinations of <datetime> and <interval> data types in Standard SQL:

```
<datetime> - <datetime> = <interval>

<datetime> + <interval> = <datetime>

<interval> (* or /) <numeric> = <interval>

<interval> + <datetime> = <datetime>

<interval> + <interval> = <interval>

<numeric> * <interval> = <interval>
```

There are other rules, which deal with time zones and the relative precision of the two operands that are intuitively obvious.

There should also be a function that returns the current date from the system clock. This function has a different name with each vendor: TODAY, SYSDATE, NOW(), CURRENT DATE, and getdate() are some examples. There may also be a function to return the day of the week from a date, which is sometimes called DOW() or WEEKDAY(). Standard SQL provides for CURRENT_ DATE, CURRENT_TIME [(<time precision>)], and CURRENT_ TIMESTAMP [(<timestamp precision>)] functions, which are self-explanatory. This is converted into UTC internally so that temporal math will be correct.

INTERVAL data types are either year-month interval or a day-time interval. They can be either single word, such as DAY or HOUR, or a range such as HOUR TO SECOND. This is why strings are used rather than integers—you have to put in punctuation to separate the fields.

```
<interval literal> ::=
INTERVAL [+ | -] <interval string> <interval qualifier>

<interval string> ::=
 <date value string>
  | <time value string> [<time zone interval string>]
  | <timestamp string>

<interval qualifier> ::=

<interval string> ::= [+ | - ] { <year-month literal> | <day-time
literal> }
```

```
<year-month literal> ::= <years value> [<minus sign> <months value>]
| <months value>

<day-time literal> ::= <day-time interval> | <time interval>

<day-time interval> ::=
<days value> [<space> <hours value> [<colon> <minutes value>
[<colon> <seconds value>]]]

<time interval> ::=
<hours value> [<colon> <minutes value> [<colon> <seconds value>]]
| <minutes value> [<colon> <seconds value>] | <seconds value>

<years value> ::= <datetime value>

<months value> ::= <datetime value>

<days value> ::= <datetime value>

<hours value> ::= <datetime value>

<minutes value> ::= <datetime value>

<seconds value> ::= <seconds integer value> [<period> [<seconds
fraction>]]

<seconds integer value> ::= <unsigned integer>

<seconds fraction> ::= <unsigned integer>

<datetime value> ::= <unsigned integer>
```

The <interval qualifier> that describes the precision of the interval data type. A value described by an interval data type descriptor is always signed.

Interval Field and Description	Keyword
Years, constrained by implementation leading field precision	YEAR
Months within years constrained to 0-11	MONTH
Days, constrained by implementation leading field precision	DAY
Hours within days, constrained to 0-23	HOUR
Minutes within hours, constrained to 0-59	MINUTE
Seconds within minutes, constrained to 0-59.999	SECOND

Values in interval fields other than SECOND are integers and have precision 2 when not the first field. SECOND, however, can be defined to have an <interval fractional seconds precision> that indicates the number of decimal digits in the seconds value. When not the first field, SECOND has a precision of 2 places before the decimal point. Fields comprising an item of type interval are also constrained by the definition of the Common Era calendar.

YEAR, MONTH, and YEAR TO MONTH intervals are comparable only with other year-month intervals. If two year-month intervals have different interval precisions, they are, for the purpose of any operations between them, effectively converted to the same precision by appending new <primary datetime field>s to either the most significant end of one interval, the least significant end of one interval, or both. New least significant <primary datetime field>s are assigned a value of 0 (zero). When it is necessary to add new most significant datetime fields, the associated value is effectively converted to the new precision in a manner obeying the natural rules for dates and times associated with the Common Era calendar.

DAY, HOUR, MINUTE, SECOND, DAY TO HOUR, DAY TO MINUTE, DAY TO SECOND, HOUR TO MINUTE, HOUR TO SECOND, and MINUTE TO SECOND intervals are comparable only with other day-time intervals. If two day-time intervals have different interval precisions, they are, for the purpose of any operations between them, effectively converted to the same precision by appending new <primary datetime field>s to either the most significant end of one interval or the least significant end of one interval, or both. New least significant <primary datetime field>s are assigned a value of 0 (zero). When it is necessary to add new most significant datetime fields, the associated value is effectively converted to the new precision in a manner obeying the natural rules for dates and times associated with the Common Era calendar.

In Standard SQL, the interval values are given by strings and not by integers or decimals. However, you can write things like this, assuming it makes sense, to an integer out of them:

```
CAST (CAST (<string expression> AS INTERVAL <interval type>) AS
<exact numeric data type>)
```

Within an <interval literal> that contains a <year-month literal>, the <interval qualifier> shall not specify DAY, HOUR, MINUTE, or SECOND. Within the definition of an <interval literal> that contains a <day-time literal>, the <interval qualifier> shall not specify YEAR or MONTH. Within the definition of a <datetime literal>, the value of the <time zone interval> shall be in the range −12:59 to +14:00. Informally, this says that you need to use sensible values.

35.2 Calendars

Build a calendar table with one column for the calendar data and other columns to show whatever your business needs in the way of temporal information. Do not try to calculate holidays in SQL—Easter alone requires too much math.

```
CREATE TABLE Calendar
(cal_date DATE NOT NULL PRIMARY KEY,
 fiscal_year SMALLINT NOT NULL,
 fiscal_month SMALLINT NOT NULL,
 week_date CHAR(10)NOT NULL
  CHECK (week_date LIKE '[12][0-9][0-9][0-9]W[0-5][0-9]-[1-7]'),
 holiday_type SMALLINT NOT NULL
 CHECK(holiday_type IN ( ..), --
 day_in_year
 SMALLINT NOT NULL,
 ordinal_date CHAR(ordinal_date LIKE '[12][0-9][0-9][0-9]-[0-9][0-9]
[0-9]') NOT NULL,
 julian_date INTEGER NOT NULL,
 julian_business_day INTEGER NOT NULL,
 ...);
```

The Julian business day is a good trick. Number the days from whenever your calendar starts and repeat a number for a weekend or company holiday.

```
CREATE TABLE Calendar
(cal_date DATE NOT NULL PRIMARY KEY,
 julian_business_nbr INTEGER NOT NULL,
 ...);

INSERT INTO Calendar
VALUES ('2007-04-05', 42),
 ('2007-04-06', 43), -- good Friday
 ('2007-04-07', 43),
```

```
('2007-04-08', 43), -- Easter Sunday
('2007-04-09', 44),
('2007-04-10', 45); --Tuesday
```

To compute the business days from Thursday of this week to next Tuesdays:

```
SELECT (C2.julian_business_nbr - C1.julian_business_nbr)
  FROM Calendar AS C1, Calendar AS C2
 WHERE C1.cal_date = '2007-04-05',
   AND C2.cal_date = '2007-04-10';
```

35.2.1 Holidays

Derek Dongray came up with a classification of the public holidays and weekends he needed to work with in multiple countries. Here is his list with more added.

1. Fixed date every year
2. Days relative to Easter
3. Fixed date but will slide to next Monday if on a weekend
4. Fixed date but slides to Monday if Saturday or Tuesday if Sunday (UK Boxing Day is the only one)
5. Specific day of week after a given date (usually first/last Monday in a month but can be other days, e.g. First Thursday after November 22 = Thanksgiving)
6. Days relative to Greek Orthodox Easter (not always the same as Western Easter)
7. Fixed date in Hijri (Muslim) Calendar—this turns out to only be approximate due to the way the calendar works. An Imam has to see a full moon to begin the cycle and declare it
8. Days relative to previous Winter Solstice (Chinese holiday of Qing Ming Ji. Civil holidays set by decree, such as a National Day of Mourning)
9. Fixed date except Saturday slides to Friday, and Sunday slides to Monday

10. Fixed date, but Tuesday slides to Monday, and Thursday to Friday (Argentina celebrates October 12, the day Columbus discovered America is a national holiday in Argentina. Except when it's a Tuesday, they back it one day to Monday.)

As you can see, some of these are getting a bit esoteric and a bit fuzzy. A calendar table for US Secular holidays can be built from the data at this website, so you will get the 3-day weekends:

http://www.smart.net/~mmontes/ushols.html

Time zones with fractional hour displacements:

http://www.timeanddate.com/worldclock/city.html?n=5

http://www.timeanddate.com/worldclock/city.html?n=54

http://www.timeanddate.com/worldclock/city.html?n=176

http://www.timeanddate.com/worldclock/city.html?n=246

But the strange ones are

http://www.timeanddate.com/worldclock/city.html?n=5

http://www.timeanddate.com/worldclock/city.html?n=63

35.2.2 Personal Calendars

One of the most common applications of dates is to build calendars that list upcoming events or actions to be taken by their user. People have no trouble with using a paper calendar to trigger their own actions, but the idea of having an internal calendar, as a table in their database, is somehow strange. Programmers seem to prefer to write a function that calculates the date and matches it to events.

It is easier to a table for cyclic data than people first think. The cycle has to repeat itself every 400 years, so today is on the same day of the week that it was on 400 years ago. This gives us 20,871 weeks or 146,097 days to model in a table. This is not a large table in modern computers.

As an example, consider the rule that a stockbroker must settle a transaction within three business days after a trade. Business days are defined as excluding Saturdays, Sundays, and certain holidays. The holidays are determined at the start of the year by the New York Stock Exchange, but this can be changed by an act of Congress, presidential decree or the Securities

and Exchange Commission can order trading stopped in a single security. The problem is how to write an SQL query that will return the proper settlement date given a trade date.

There are several tricks in this problem. The real trick is to decide what you want and not to be fooled by what you have. You have a list of holidays, but you want a list of settlement days. Let's start with a table of the given holidays and their names:

```
CREATE TABLE Holidays -- Insert holiday list into this table
(holiday_date DATE NOT NULL PRIMARY KEY,
 holiday_name CHAR(20) NOT NULL);
```

The next step is to build a table of trade and settlement dates for the whole year. Building the INSERT INTO statements to load the second table is easily done with a spreadsheet. Spreadsheets always have good date functions and probably already exist in the accounting department of your organization.

Let's start by building a simple list of the dates over the range we want to use and put them into a table called Settlements.

```
CREATE TABLE Settlements
(trade_date DATE NOT NULL PRIMARY KEY,
 settle_date DATE NOT NULL);
```

We know that we cannot trade on a holiday or weekend. You probably could have excluded weekends in the spreadsheet, but if not use this statement.

```
DELETE FROM Settlements
 WHERE trade_date IN (SELECT holiday_date FROM Holidays)
    OR DayOfWeek(trade_date) IN ('Saturday', 'Sunday');
```

This does not handle the holiday settlements, however. The trouble with a holiday is that (1) it can fall on a weekend, in which case we just handled it, (2) it can last 1 day, or (3) it can last any number of days. The table of holidays is built on the assumption that each day of a multi-day holiday has a row in the table.

We now have to update the table so that the regular settlement days are three business days forward of the trade date. But we have all the business days in the trade_date column of the Settlements table now.

```
UPDATE Settlements
   SET settle_date
       = (SELECT trade_date
            FROM Settlements AS S1
           WHERE Settlements.trade_date < S1.trade_date
             AND (SELECT COUNT(*)
                    FROM Settlements AS S2
                   WHERE S2.trade_date
                         BETWEEN Settlements.trade_date
                             AND S1.trade_date) = 3);
```

The final settlement table will be about 250 rows per year and only 2 columns wide. This is quite small; it will fit into main storage easily on any machine. Finding the settlement day is a straight simple query; if you had built just the Holiday table, you would have had to provide procedural code.

35.3 Time Series

One of the major problems in the real world is how to handle a series of events that occur in the same time period or in some particular order. The code is tricky and a bit hard to understand, but the basic idea is that you have a table with start and stop times for events and you want to get information about them as a group.

35.3.1 Gaps in a Time Series

The time line can be partitioned into intervals and a set of intervals can be drawn from that partition for reporting. One of the stock questions on an employment form asks the prospective employee to explain any gaps in his record of employment. Most of the time this gap means that you were unemployed. If you are in data processing, you answer that you were consulting, which is a synonym for unemployed.

Given this table, how would you write an SQL query to display the time periods and their durations for each of the candidates?

```
CREATE TABLE JobApps
(candidate_name CHAR(25) NOT NULL,
 job_title CHAR(15) NOT NULL,
 start_date DATE NOT NULL,
```

```
end_date DATE -- null means still employed
        CONSTRAINT started_before_ended
        CHECK(start_date <= end_date)
...);
```

Notice that the end date of the current job_code is set to NULL because SQL does not support an 'eternity' or 'end of time' value for temporal data types. Using '9999-12-31 23:59:59.999999', which is the highest possible date value that SQL can represent, is not a correct model and can cause problems when you do temporal arithmetic. The NULL can be handled with a COALESCE() function in the code, as I will show later.

It is obvious that this has to be a self-JOIN query, so you have to do some date arithmetic. The first day of each gap is the last day of an employment period plus 1 day and that the last day of each gap is the first day of the next job_code minus 1 day. This start-point and end-point problem is the reason that SQL defined the OVERLAPS predicate this way.

All versions of SQL support temporal data types and arithmetic. But unfortunately, no two implementations look alike and few look like the ANSI Standard. The first attempt at this query is usually something like the following, which will produce the right results, but with a lot of extra rows that are just plain wrong. Assume that if I add a number of days to a date, or subtract a number of days from it, I get a new date.

```
SELECT J1.candidate_name,
      (J1.end_date + INTERVAL '1' DAY) AS gap_start,
      (J2.start_date - INTERVAL '1' DAY) AS gap_end,
      (J2.start_date - J1.end_date) AS gap_length
  FROM JobApps AS J1, JobApps AS J2
 WHERE J1.candidate_name = J2.candidate_name
   AND (J1.end_date + INTERVAL '1' DAY) < J2.start_date;
```

Here is why this does not work. Imagine that we have a table that includes candidate_name name 'Bill Jones' with the following work history:

Result

candidate_name	job_title	start_date	end_date
'John Smith'	'Vice Pres'	'2017-01-10'	'2017-12-31'
'John Smith'	'President'	'2017-01-12'	'2019-12-31'
'Bill Jones'	'Scut Worker'	'2017-02-24'	'2017-04-21'

candidate_name	job_title	start_date	end_date
'Bill Jones'	'Manager'	'2019-01-01'	'2019-01-05'
'Bill Jones'	'Grand Poobah'	'2019-04-04'	'2019-05-15'

We would get this as a result:

Result

candidate_name	gap_start	gap_end	gap_length
'John Smith'	'2017-01-01'	'2017-01-11'	10
'Bill Jones'	'2017-04-22'	'2017-12-31'	253
'Bill Jones'	'2019-01-06'	'2019-04-03'	87
'Bill Jones'	'2011-04-22'	'2019-04-03'	2903 ◄false data

The problem is that the 'John Smith' row looks just fine and can fool you into thinking that you are doing fine. He had two jobs; therefore, there was one gap in between. However, 'Bill Jones' cannot be right because only two gaps can separate three jobs, yet the query shows three gaps.

The query does its JOIN on all possible combinations of start and end dates in the original table. This gives false data in the results by counting the end of one job_code, 'Scut Worker', and the start of another, 'Grand Poobah', as a gap. The idea is to use only the most recently ended job_code for the gap. This can be done with a MIN() function and a correlated subquery. The final result is this:

```
SELECT J1.candidate_name, (J1.end_date + INTERVAL '1' DAY) AS gap_start,
       (J2.start_date - INTERVAL '1' DAY) AS gap_end
  FROM JobApps AS J1, JobApps AS J2
 WHERE J1.candidate_name = J2.candidate_name
   AND J2.start_date
       = (SELECT MIN(J3.start_date)
           FROM JobApps AS J3
          WHERE J3.candidate_name = J1.candidate_name
            AND J3.start_date > J1.end_date)
   AND (J1.end_date + INTERVAL '1' DAY)
        < (J2.start_date - INTERVAL '1' DAY)
UNION ALL
SELECT J1.candidate_name, MAX(J1.end_date) + INTERVAL '1' DAY,
       CURRENT_TIMESTAMP
```

```
  FROM JobApps AS J1
 GROUP BY J1.candidate_name
HAVING COUNT(*) = COUNT(DISTINCT J1.end_date);
```

The length of the gap can be determined with simple temporal arithmetic. The purpose of the UNION ALL is to add the current period of unemployment, if any, to the final answer.

35.3.2 Continuous Time Periods

Given a series of jobs that can start and stop at any time, how can you be sure that an employee doing all these jobs was really working without any gaps? Let's build a table of timesheets for one employee.

```
  TABLE Timesheets
 (job_code CHAR(5) NOT NULL PRIMARY KEY,
  start_date DATE NOT NULL,
  end_date DATE NOT NULL,
  CHECK (start_date <= end_date));

INSERT INTO Timesheets (job_code, start_date, end_date)
VALUES ('j01', '2018-01-01', '2018-01-03');
       ('j02', '2018-01-06', '2018-01-10'),
       ('j03', '2018-01-05', '2018-01-08'),
       ('j04', '2018-01-20', '2018-01-25'),
       ('j05', '2018-01-18', '2018-01-23'),
       ('j06', '2018-02-01', '2018-02-05'),
       ('j07', '2018-02-03', '2018-02-08'),
       ('j08', '2018-02-07', '2018-02-11'),
       ('j09', '2018-02-09', '2018-02-10'),
       ('j10', '2018-02-01', '2018-02-11'),
       ('j11', '2018-03-01', '2018-03-05'),
       ('j12', '2018-03-04', '2018-03-09'),
       ('j13', '2018-03-08', '2018-03-14'),
       ('j14', '2018-03-13', '2018-03-20');
```

The most immediate answer is to build a search condition for all of the characteristics of a continuous time period.

This algorithm is due to Mike Arney, a DBA at BORN Consulting. It uses derived tables to get the extreme start and ending dates of a contiguous run of durations.

```
SELECT Early.start_date, MIN(Latest.end_date)
  FROM (SELECT DISTINCT start_date
          FROM Timesheets AS T1
         WHERE NOT EXISTS
               (SELECT *
                  FROM Timesheets AS T2
                WHERE T2.start_date < T1.start_date
                  AND T2.end_date >= T1.start_date)
       ) AS Early (start_date)
        INNER JOIN
        (SELECT DISTINCT end_date
           FROM Timesheets AS T3
         WHERE NOT EXISTS
              (SELECT *
                 FROM Timesheets AS T4
                WHERE T4.end_date > T3.end_date
                  AND T4.start_date <= T3.end_date)
      ) AS Latest (end_date)
       ON Early.start_date <= Latest.end_dae
GROUP BY Early.start_date;
```

Result

start_date	end_date
'2018-01-01'	'2018-01-03'
'2018-01-05'	'2018-01-10'
'2018-01-18'	'2018-01-25'
'2018-02-01'	'2018-02-11'
'2018-03-01'	'2018-03-20'

However, another way of doing this is a query, which will also tell you which jobs bound the continuous periods.

```
SELECT T2.start_date,
       MAX(T1.end_date) AS finish_date,
       MAX(T1.job_code || ' to ' || T2.job_code) AS job_code_pair
  FROM Timesheets AS T1, Timesheets AS T2
 WHERE T2.job_code <> T1.job_code
   AND T1.start_date BETWEEN T2.start_date AND T2.end_date
   AND T2.end_date BETWEEN T1.start_date AND T1.end_date
 GROUP BY T2.start_date;
```

Result

start_date	finish_date	job_code_pair
'2018-01-05'	'2018-01-10'	'j02 to j03'
'2018-01-18'	'2018-01-25'	'j04 to j05'
'2018-02-01'	'2018-02-08'	'j07 to j06'
'2018-02-03'	'2018-02-11'	'j08 to j07'

```
DELETE FROM Results
 WHERE EXISTS
      (SELECT R1.job_code_list
         FROM Results AS R1
        WHERE POSITION (Results.job_code_list
                        IN R1.job_code_list) > 0);
```

A third solution will handle an isolated job_code like 'j01', as well as three or more overlapping jobs, like 'j06', 'j07', and 'j08'.

```
SELECT T1.start_date,
       MIN(T2.end_date) AS finish_date,
       MIN(T2.end_date + INTERVAL '1' DAY) -
       - MIN(T1.start_date) AS duration -- find any
(T1.start_date)
  FROM Timesheets AS T1, Timesheets AS T2
 WHERE T2.start_date >= T1.start_date
   AND T2.end_date >= T1.end_date
   AND NOT EXISTS
       (SELECT *
          FROM Timesheets AS T3
```

```
        WHERE (T3.start_date <= T2.end_date
               AND T3.end_date > T2.end_date)
          OR (T3.end_date >= T1.start_date
              AND T3.start_date < T1.start_date))
 GROUP BY T1.start_date;
```

You will also want to look at how to consolidate overlapping intervals of integers.

A fourth solution uses the auxiliary Calendar table to find the dates that are and are not covered by any of the durations. The coverage flag and calendar date can then be used directly by other queries that need to look at the status of single days instead of date ranges.

```
SELECT C1.cal_date,
       SUM(DISTINCT
           CASE
           WHEN C1.cal_date BETWEEN T1.start_date AND T1.end_date
           THEN 1 ELSE 0 END) AS covered_date_flag
  FROM Calendar AS C1, Timesheets AS T1
 WHERE C1.cal_date BETWEEN (SELECT MIN(start_date FROM Timesheets)
                        AND (SELECT MAX(end_date FROM Timesheets)
 GROUP BY C1.cal_date;
```

This is reasonably fast because the WHERE clause uses static scalar queries to set the bounds and the Calendar table uses "cal_date" as a primary key, so it will have an index.

A slightly different version of the problem is to group contiguous measurements into durations that have the value on that measurement.

I have the following table:

```
 TABLE Calibrations
(start_time TIMESTAMP DEFAULT CURRENT_TIMESTAMP
            NOT NULL PRIMARY KEY
 end_time TIMESTAMP NOT NULL,
 CHECK (end_time = start_time + INTERVAL '1' MINUTE,
 cal_value INTEGER NOT NULL);
```

with this data:

Calibrations

start_time	end_time	cal_value
'2014-05-11 02:52:00.000'	'2014-05-11 02:53:00.000'	8
'2014-05-11 02:53:00.000'	'2014-05-11 02:54:00.000'	8
'2014-05-11 02:54:00.000'	'2014-05-11 02:55:00.000'	8
'2014-05-11 02:55:00.000'	'2014-05-11 02:56:00.000'	8
'2014-05-11 02:56:00.000'	'2014-05-11 02:57:00.000'	8
'2014-05-11 02:57:00.000'	'2014-05-11 02:58:00.000'	9
'2014-05-11 02:58:00.000'	'2014-05-11 02:59:00.000'	9
'2014-05-11 02:59:00.000'	'2014-05-11 03:00:00.000'	9
'2014-05-11 03:00:00.000'	'2014-05-11 03:01:00.000'	9
'2014-05-11 03:01:00.000'	'2014-05-11 03:02:00.000'	9
'2014-05-11 03:02:00.000'	'2014-05-11 03:03:00.000'	8
'2014-05-11 03:03:00.000'	'2014-05-11 03:04:00.000'	8
'2014-05-11 03:04:00.000'	'2014-05-11 03:05:00.000'	8

I want to be able to group this up so that it looks like this:

start_time	end_time	cal_value
'2014-05-11 02:52:00.000'	'2014-05-11 02:57:00.000'	8
'2014-05-11 02:57:00.000'	'2014-05-11 03:02:00.000'	9
'2014-05-11 03:02:00.000'	'2014-05-11 03:05:00.000'	8

35.3.2.1 Background

The table being selected from is updated every minute with a new calibration value. The calibration value can change from minute to minute. I want a select statement that will sum up the start of the cal_value and the end of the calibration value before it changes.

```
SELECT MIN(start_time) AS start_time,
       MAX(end_time) AS end_time,
```

```
       cal_value
  FROM (SELECT C1.start_time, C1.end_time, C1.cal_value,
               MIN(C2.start_time)
          FROM Calibrations AS C1
               LEFT OUTER JOIN
               Calibrations AS C2
               ON C1.start_time < C2.start_time
                  AND C1.cal_value <> C2.cal_value
         GROUP BY C1.start_time, C1.end_time, C1.cal_value)
       AS T (start_time, end_time, cal_value, x_time))
 GROUP BY cal_value, x_time;
```

35.3.3 Missing Times in Contiguous Events

Consider the following simple table, which we will use to illustrate how to handle missing times in events.

```
CREATE TABLE Events
(event_id CHAR(2) NOT NULL PRIMARY KEY,
start_date DATE,
end_date DATE,
CONSTRAINT Started_Before_Ended
CHECK (start_date < end_date));

INSERT INTO Events
VALUES
('A', '2014-01-01', '2014-12-31'),
('B', '2015-01-01', '2015-01-31'),
('C', '2015-02-01', '2015-02-28'),
('D', '2015-02-01', '2015-02-28');
```

Due to circumstances beyond our control the end_date column may contain a NULL instead of a valid date. Imagine that we had ('B', '2015-01-01', NULL) as a row in the table.

One reasonable solution is to populate the missing end_date with the (start_date -INTERVAL '1' DAY) of the next period. This is easy enough.

```
UPDATE Events
   SET end_date
       = (SELECT MIN(E1.start_date) - INTERVAL '1' DAY)
            FROM Events AS E1
```

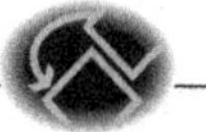

```
          WHERE E1.start_date > Events.start_date)
 WHERE end_date IS NULL;
```

Likewise, if due to circumstances beyond our control the start_date column may contain a NULL instead of a valid date. Imagine that we had ('B', NULL, '2015-01-31') as a row in the table. Using the same logic, we could take the last known ending date and add one to it to give us a guess at the missing starting value.

```
UPDATE Events
   SET start_date
       = (SELECT MIN(E1.end_date) + INTERVAL '1' DAY)
            FROM Events AS E1
           WHERE E1.end_date < Events.end_date)
 WHERE start_date IS NULL;
```

This has a nice symmetry to it, and you can combine them into one update instead of wasting an extra table scan:

```
UPDATE Events
   SET end_date
       = CASE WHEN end_date IS NULL
         THEN (SELECT MIN(E1.start_date) - INTERVAL '1' DAY
                FROM Events AS E1
                WHERE E1.start_date > Events.start_date)
         ELSE end_date END,
       start_date
       = CASE WHEN start_date IS NULL
         THEN (SELECT MIN(E1.end_date) + INTERVAL '1' DAY
                  FROM Events AS E1
                 WHERE E1.end_date < Events.end_date)
         ELSE start_date END
 WHERE start_date IS NULL
    OR end_date IS NULL;

INSERT INTO Events
VALUES
('A', '2014-01-01', '2014-12-31'),
('B', '2015-01-01', NULL),
('C', '2015-02-01', '2015-02-28'),
('D', NULL, '2015-02-28');
```

Results

event_id	start_date	end_date
'A'	'2014-01-01'	'2014-12-31'
'B'	'2015-01-01'	'2015-01-31'
'C'	'2015-02-01'	'2015-02-28'
'D'	'2015-01-01	'2015-02-28'

The real problem is having no boundary dates on contiguous events, like this:

```
INSERT INTO Events
VALUES ('A', '2014-01-01', '2014-12-31'),
       ('B', NULL, NULL),
       ('C', '2015-02-01', '2015-02-28'),
       ('D', '2015-02-01', '2015-02-28');
```

This example does nothing. This example has more problems:

```
INSERT INTO Events
VALUES
('A', '2014-01-01', '2014-12-31'),
('B', '2015-01-01', NULL),
('C', NULL, '2015-02-28'),
('D', '2015-02-01', '2015-02-28');
```

Given the restrictions that each event lasts for at least 1 day, event 'B' could have finished on any day between '2015-01-02' and '2015-02-27' and likewise, event 'C' could have begun on any day between '2015-01-03' and '2015-02-28'; note the two different durations.

When the combined UPDATE was run on SQL Server, the results were

```
Results
event_id start_date end_date
==============================
A    2014-01-01    2014-12-31
B    2015-01-01    2015-01-31
C    2015-01-01    2015-02-28
D    2015-02-01    2015-02-28
```

Any rules we make for resolving the NULLs is going to be arbitrary. For example, we could give event 'B' the benefit of the doubt and assume that it lasted until '2015-02-27' or just as well given event 'C' the same benefit. I might make a random choice of a pair of dates (d, d+1) in the gap between 'B' and 'C' dates. I might pick a middle point.

However, this pairwise approach does not solve the problem of all the possible combinations of NULL dates.

Let me propose these rules and apply them in order

(0) If the start_date is NOT NULL and the end_date is NOT NULL then leave the row alone.

(1) If the table has too many NULLs in a series, then give up. Report too much missing data.

(2) If the start_date IS NULL and the end_date IS NOT NULL then set the start_date to the day before the end_date.

```
UPDATE Events
   SET start_date
       = (SELECT MIN(E1.end_date) + INTERVAL '1' DAY)
            FROM Events AS E1
           WHERE E1.end_date < Events.end_date)
 WHERE start_date IS NULL
   AND end_date IS NOT NULL;
```

(3) If the start_date is NOT NULL and the end_date is NULL then set the end_date to the day before the next known start_date.

```
UPDATE Events
   SET end_date
       = (SELECT MIN(E1.start_date) - INTERVAL '1' DAY)
            FROM Events AS E1
           WHERE E1.start_date > Events.start_date)
 WHERE start_date IS NOT NULL
   AND end_date IS NULL;
```

(4) If the start_date and end_date are both NULL then look at the prior and following events to get the minimal start_date and/or end_date. This will leave a gap in the dates that has to be handled later.

Example:

```
('A', '2014-01-01', '2014-12-31'),
('B', '2015-01-01', NULL),
('C', NULL, '2015-02-28'),
('D', '2015-02-01', '2015-02-28');
```

Becomes:

```
('A', '2014-01-01', '2014-12-31'),
('B', '2015-01-01', NULL),
('C', '2015-02-28', '2015-02-28'), ◄ rule #2
('D', '2015-02-01', '2015-02-28');
```

Becomes:

```
('A', '2014-01-01', '2014-12-31'),
('B', '2015-01-01', '2015-02-27'), ◄ rule #3
('C', '2015-02-28', '2015-02-28'),
('D', '2015-02-01', '2015-02-28');
```

Now consider this data:

```
('A', '2014-01-01', '2014-12-31'),
('B', NULL, NULL),
('C', '2015-02-01', '2015-02-28'),
('D', '2015-02-01', '2015-02-28');
```

Becomes:

```
('A', '2014-01-01', '2014-12-31'),
('B', '2015-01-01', '2015-01-31'), ◄ rule #4
('C', '2015-02-01', '2015-02-28'),
('D', '2015-02-01', '2015-02-28');
```

Consider this example:

```
('A', '2014-01-01', '2014-12-31'),
('B', NULL, NULL),
('C', NULL, '2015-02-28'),
('D', '2015-02-01', '2015-02-28');
```

35.3.4 Locating Dates

This little problem is sneakier than it sounds. I first saw it in EXPLAIN magazine, then met the author, Rudy Limeback, at the Database World conference in Boston years ago. The problem is to print a list of the employees whose birthdays will occur in the next 45 days. The employee files have each date of birth. The answer will depend on what date functions you have in your implementation of SQL, but Rudy was working with DB2.

What makes this problem interesting is the number of possible false starts. Most versions of SQL also have a library function MAKEDATE(year, month, day) or an equivalent, which will construct a date from three numbers representing a year, month, and day and extraction functions to disassemble a date into integers representing the month, day, and year. The SQL Standard would do this with the general function CAST (<string> AS DATE), but there is no provision in the standard for using integers without first converting them to strings, either explicitly or implicitly. For example,

```
-- direct use of strings to build a date
  CAST ('2014-01-01' AS DATE)

-- concatenation causes integer to cast to strings
  CAST (2005 || '-'|| 01 ||'-' || 01 AS DATE)
```

The first "gotcha" in this problem is trying to use the component pieces of the dates in a search condition. If you were looking for birthdays all within the same month, it would be easy:

```
SELECT emp_name, emp_dob,CURRENT_DATE
 FROM Personnel
WHERE EXTRACT(MONTH FROM CURRENT_DATE) = EXTRACT(MONTH FROM dob);
```

Attempts to extend this approach fall apart, however, since a 45-day period could extend across 3 months and possibly into the following year and might fall in a leap year. Very soon, the number of function calls is too high and the logic is too complex.

The second "gotcha" is trying to write a simple search condition with these functions to construct the birthday in the current year from the date of birth (dob) in the Employee table:

```
SELECT emp_name, emp_dob,CURRENT_DATE
  FROM Personnel
 WHERE MAKEDATE(EXTRACT (YEAR FROM CURRENT_DATE),-- birthday this year
               EXTRACT (MONTH FROM dob),
               EXTRACT (DAY FROM dob))
       BETWEEN CURRENT_DATE
           AND (CURRENT_DATE + INTERVAL 45 DAYS);
```

But a leap-year date of birth will cause an exception to be raised on an invalid date if this is not also a leap year. There is also another problem. The third "gotcha" comes when the 45-day period wraps into the next year. For example, if the current month is December 1992, we should include January 1993 birthdays, but they are not constructed by the MAKEDATE() function. At this point, you can build a messy search condition that also goes into the next year when constructing birthdays.

Rory Murchison of the Aetna Institute pointed out that if you are working with DB2 or some other SQL implementations, you will have an AGE(date1 [,date2]) function. This returns the difference in years between date1 and date2. If date2 is missing, it defaults to CURRENT_DATE. The AGE() function can be constructed from other functions in implementations that do not support it. In Standard SQL, the expression would be (date2-date1) YEAR, which would construct an INTERVAL value. That makes the answer quite simple:

```
SELECT emp_name, emp_dob,CURRENT_DATE
  FROM Personnel
 WHERE INTERVAL (CURRENT_DATE - birthday) YEAR
       < INTERVAL (CURRENT_DATE - birthday + INTERVAL 45 DAYS) YEAR;
```

In English, this says that if the employee is a year older 45 days from now, he must have had a birthday in the meantime.

35.3.5 Temporal Starting and Ending Points

Dates can be stored in several different ways in a database. Designers of one product might decide that they want to keep things in a COBOL-like field-oriented format, which has a clear, separate area for the year, month, and day of each date. Another product might want to be more UNIX-like and keep the dates as a displacement in some small unit of time from a starting point, then calculate the display format when it is needed. Standard SQL does not

say how a date should be stored, but the "COBOL approach" is easier to display and the "temporal displacement approach" can do calculations easier.

The result is that there is no best way to calculate either the first day of the month or the last day of the month from a given date. In the COBOL method, you can get the first day of the month easily by using extraction from the date to build the date, with a 1 in the day field.

To return the last day of the previous month, use this expression: CURRENT_TIMESTAMP - INTERVAL (EXTRACT(DAY FROM CURRENT_TIMESTAMP) DAYS).

Obviously, you can get the first day of this month with:

```
CURRENT_TIMESTAMP
 - (EXTRACT (DAY FROM CURRENT_TIMESTAMP)
    + INTERVAL '1' DAY);
```

Another way is with a user-defined function.

```
FUNCTION LastDayOfMonth (IN my_date DATE)
RETURNS INTEGER
LANGUAGE SQL
DETERMINISTIC
RETURN
CAST
CASE
WHEN EXTRACT(MONTH FROM my_date) IN (1, 3, 5, 7, 8, 10, 12) THEN 31
THEN EXTRACT(MONTH FROM my_date) IN (4, 6, 9, 11) THEN 30
ELSE CASE WHEN MOD(EXTRACT (YEAR FROM my_date)/100, 4) <> 0 THEN 28
          WHEN MOD(EXTRACT (YEAR FROM my_date)/100, 400) = 0 THEN 29
          WHEN MOD(EXTRACT (YEAR FROM my_date)/100, 100) = 0 THEN 28
          ELSE 29 END
END AS INTEGER);
```

35.3.5.1 Starting and Ending Times

Another problem that you will find in the real world is that people never read the ISO-8601 Standards for temporal data and they insist upon writing midnight as '24:00:00' and letting it "leak" into the next day. That is, '2014-01-01 24:01:00' probably should have been '2014-01-02 00:01:00' instead. The EXTRACT() function would have a really complicated definition, if this was an acceptable format.

The best bet, if you cannot teach people to use the ISO-8601 Standards, is to correct the string at input time. This can be done with a simple auxiliary time that looks like this:

```
 TABLE FixTheClock
(input_date_string CHAR(6) NOT NULL,
 input_time_pattern CHAR(25) NOT NULL PRIMARY KEY,
 correct_time_string CHAR(25) NOT NULL);

INSERT INTO FixTheClock
VALUES ('2014-01-01', '2014-01-01 24:__:__._____', '2014-01-02 00:');
 ...

Then use a LIKE predicate to replace the pattern with the corrected
time.

SELECT CASE WHEN R1.raw_input_timestamp LIKE F1.input_time_pattern
            THEN F1.correct_time_string
                 || CAST (EXTRACT(TIMEZONE_MINUTE FROM R1.raw_input_
timestamp) AS VARCHAR(10))
            ELSE raw_input_timestamp END, ...
  FROM RawData AS R1, FixTheClock AS F1
 WHERE F1.input_date_string = SUBSTRING (raw_input_timestamp FROM 1 FOR 6);
```

Notice that this is strictly a string function and that the results will have to be cast to a temporal data type before being stored in the database.

35.4 Julian Dates

All SQL implementations support a DATE data type, but there is no standard defining how they should implement it *internally*. Some products represent the year, month, and day as binary fields in a record; others use Julianized dates; some use ISO ordinal dates; and some store dates as character strings. The programmer does not care as long as the dates work correctly.

There is a technical difference between a Julian date and a Julianized date. A Julian date is an astronomer's term that counts the number of days since January 1, 4713 BCE. This count is now well over 2 billion; nobody but astronomers uses it. However, computer companies have corrupted the term to mean a count from some point in time from which they can build a date or time. The fixed point is usually the year 1, or 1900, or the start of the Gregorian calendar.

A Julianized, or ordinal, date is the position of the date within its year, so it falls between 1 and 365 or 366. You will see this number printed on the bottom edges of desk calendar pages. The usual way to find the Julianized day within the current year is to use a simple program that stores the number of days in each month as an array and sums them with the day of the month for the date in question. The only difficult part is remembering to add 1 if the year is a leap year and the month is after February.

Here is a very fast and compact algorithm that computes the Julian date from a Gregorian date and vice versa. These algorithms appeared as Algorithm 199 (ACM 1980) and were first written in ALGOL by Robert Tantzen. Here are SQL translations of the code:

```
CREATE FUNCTION Julianize1
  (greg_day INTEGER, greg_month INTEGER, greg_year INTEGER)
RETURNS INTEGER
LANGUAGE SQL
DETERMINISTIC
BEGIN
DECLARE century INTEGER;
DECLARE yearincentury INTEGER;
IF (greg_month > 2)
THEN SET greg_month = greg_month - 3;
ELSE SET greg_month = greg_month + 9;
     SET greg_year = greg_year - 1;
END IF;
SET century = greg_year/100;
SET yearincentury = greg_year - 100 * century;
RETURN ((146097 * century)/4
      + (1461 * yearincentury)/4
      + (153 * greg_month + 2)/5 + greg_day + 1721119);
END;
```

Remember that the division will be integer division because the variables involved are all integers. Here is a Pascal procedure taken from NUMERICAL RECIPES IN PASCAL (William Press et al.; Cambridge University Press; Revised edition 1990; ISBN 0-52138766-3) for converting a Georgian date to a Julian date. First, you need to know the difference between TRUNCATE() and FLOOR(). The FLOOR() function is also called the greatest integer function; it returns the greatest integer less than its argument. The TRUNCATE() function returns the integer part of a number. Thus, they behave differently with negative decimals.

```
FLOOR(-2.5) = -3
FLOOR(-2) = -2
FLOOR(2.5) = 2
FLOOR(2) = 2
TRUNCATE(-2.5) = -2
TRUNCATE(-2) = -2
TRUNCATE(2.5) = 2
TRUNCATE(2) = 2
```

Here is an SQL/PSM version of the algorithm.

```
CREATE FUNCTION Julianize (IN greg_year INTEGER, IN greg_month INTEGER,
IN greg_day INTEGER)
RETURNS INTEGER
LANGUAGE SQL
DETERMINISTIC
BEGIN
DECLARE gregorian INTEGER;
DECLARE greg_year INTEGER;
DECLARE jul_leap INTEGER;
DECLARE greg_month INTEGER;

SET gregorian = 588829;

IF greg_year = 0 -- error: no greg_year zero
THEN SIGNAL SQLSTATE 'no year zero'; -- not actual SQL state code!
END IF;
IF greg_year < 0
THEN SET greg_year = greg_year + 1;
END IF;

IF greg_month > 2
THEN SET greg_year = greg_year;
     SET greg_month = greg_month + 1;
ELSE SET greg_year = greg_year - 1;
     SET greg_month = greg_month + 13;
```

```
    END IF;
SET greg_day = TRUNCATE(365.2522 * greg_year)
    + TRUNCATE(30.6001 * greg_month)
    + greg_day + 1720995;
IF (greg_day + 31 * (greg_month + 12 * greg_year) >= gregorian)
THEN SET jul_leap = TRUNCATE(greg_year * 0.01);
    SET greg_day = greg_day + 2 - jul_leap + TRUNCATE(0.25 * jul_leap);
END IF;
END;
```

This algorithm to convert a Julian day number into a Gregorian calendar date is due to Peter Meyer. You need to assume that you have FLOOR() and TRUNCATE() functions.

```
CREATE PROCEDURE JulDate (IN julian INTEGER,
                  OUT greg_year INTEGER,
                  OUT greg_month INTEGER,
                  OUT greg_day INTEGER)
LANGUAGE SQL
DETERMINISTIC
BEGIN
DECLARE z INTEGER;
DECLARE r INTEGER;
DECLARE g INTEGER;
DECLARE a INTEGER;
DECLARE b INTEGER;

SET z = FLOOR(julian - 1721118.5);
SET r = julian - 1721118.5 - z;
SET g = z - 0.25;
SET a = FLOOR(g/36524.25);
SET b = a - FLOOR(a/4.0);
SET greg_year = FLOOR((b + g)/365.25);
SET c = b + z - FLOOR(365.25 * greg_year);
SET greg_month = TRUNCATE((5 * c + 456)/153);
SET greg_day = c - TRUNCATE((153 * greg_month - 457)/5) + r;
IF greg_month > 12
THEN SET greg_year = greg_year + 1;
    SET greg_month = greg_month - 12;
```

```
END IF;
END;
```

There are two problems with these algorithms. First, the Julian day the astronomers use starts at noon. If you think about it, it makes sense because they are doing their work at night. The second problem is that the integers involved get large and you cannot use floating-point numbers to replace them because the rounding errors are too great. You need long integers that can go to 2.5 million.

35.5 Other Temporal Functions

Another common set of functions, which are not represented in Standard SQL, deal with weeks. For example, Sybase's SQL Anywhere (nee WATCOM SQL) has a DOW(<date>) that returns a number between 1 and 7 to represent the day of the week (1 = Sunday, 2 = Monday, .., 7 = Saturday, following an ISO Standard convention). You can also find functions that add or subtract weeks from a date given the number of the date within the year and so on. The function for finding the day of the week for a date is called Zeller's algorithm:

```
CREATE FUNCTION Zeller (IN z_year INTEGER, IN z_month INTEGER, IN z_day
INTEGER)
RETURNS INTEGER
LANGUAGE SQL
DETERMINISTIC
BEGIN
DECLARE m INTEGER;
DECLARE d INTEGER;
DECLARE y INTEGER;
SET y = z_year;
SET m = z_month - 2;
IF (m <= 0)
THEN SET m = m + 12;
   SET y = y - 1;
END IF;
RETURN (MOD((z_day + (13 * m - 1)/5
   + 5 * MOD(y, 100)/4 - 7 * y/400), 7) + 1);
END;
```

DB2 and other SQLs have an AGE(<date1>, <date2>) function, which returns the difference in years between <date1> and <date2>.

The OVERLAPS predicate determines whether two chronological periods overlap in time (see Section 13.2 for details). A chronological period is specified either as a pair of <datetimes> (starting and ending) or as a starting <datetime> and an <interval>.

35.6 Multi-day Periods

Calendars often group contiguous dates into multi-day periods. The 7 day week and varying length of months are the obvious examples, but we also have fiscal years. Historically, the current multi-day periods are not the laws of nature. The Romans and parts of Africa used a 10-day week. Chinese and Jewish calendars use lunar months.

35.6.1 Weeks

Weeks are not part of the SQL temporal functions, but they are part of ISO-8601 Standards. While not as common in the United States as it is in Europe, many commercial and industrial applications use the week within a year as a unit of time.

Week 01 of a year is defined as the first week that has the Thursday in that year, which is equivalent to the week that contains the fourth day of January. In other words, the first week of a New Year is the week that has the majority of its days in the New Year. Week 01 might also contain days from the previous year, so it does not align with the years. As an aside, American calendars put Sunday in the leftmost column and split the Friday-Saturday-Sunday weekend. European and other calendars put Sunday in the rightmost column. But Sunday is the last day of the week in ISO Standards.

The standard notation uses the letter 'W' to announce that the following two digits are a week number. The week number component of the vector can be separated with a hyphen or not, as required by space.

1999-W01 or 1999W01

A single digit between 1 and 7 can extend this notation for the day of the week. For example, the day 1996-12-31, which is the Tuesday (day 2) of the first week of 1997, can be shown as

1999-W01-2 or 1999W012

The ISO Standard avoids explicitly stating the possible range of week numbers, but a little thought will show that the range is between 01 and 52 or between 01 and 53, depending on the particular year. There is one exception to the rule that a year has at least 52 weeks; 1753 when the Gregorian calendar was introduced had less than 365 days and therefore less than 52 weeks.

SQL Server programmers have to be very careful because their product does not follow ISO Standards for numbering the weeks in its function library. Furthermore, it is not easy to see how to calculate the weeks between two different dates.

Here is an example from Rudy Limeback (SQL Consultant, r937.com) taken from http://searchdatabase.techtarget.com/ateQuestionNResponse/0,289625,sid13_cid517627_tax285649,00.html

Suppose we have a beginning date of '2014-02-06' and an end date of '2014-02-19'. I would like to see the weeks as two because the 17th is not a Tuesday. There are a number of ways to approach this problem, and the solution depends on what the meaning of the word "week" is. Here is the calendar for that month, just in case you cannot figure it out in your head.

Su	Mo	Tu	We	Th	Fr	Sa
						1
2	3	4	5	6	7	8
9	10	11	12	13	14	15
16	17	18	19	20	21	22
23	24	25	26	27	28	

In this example, we want the number of weeks between February 6 and 19.

First method: one. One week after the 6th is the 13th. Another week is the 20th. Since we are only as far as the 19th, it is not 2 weeks yet.

Second method: two. The number of days is 14 if we count both the 6th and the 19th at the beginning and end of the specified range. Since there are 7 days in a week, 14/7 = 2.

Third method: one. We should not count both the beginning and end days. We do not do it for years, for example. How many years are between 1999 and 2007? Most people would say 8, not 9, and they do this by

subtracting the earlier from the later. So using days, 19 − 6 = 13. Then 13/7 = 1.857142... which truncates to one.

Fourth method: two. We want a whole number of weeks, so it is okay to round 1.857142 up to 2.

Fifth method: one. Did you mean whole weeks? There's only one whole week in that date range, and it is the week from the 9th to the 15th. In fact, if the starting date were the 3rd and the ending date the 21st, that would be 18 (or 19) days, and there's still only one whole week in there.

Sixth method: three. February 6th is in week 6 of 2003. February 19th is in week 8. Between them are several days from each of three different weeks.

Seventh method: two. February 6th is in week 6 of 2003. February 19th is in week 8. Subtract the week numbers to get 2.

This is why Standard SQL prefers to deal with days, a nice unit of time that does not have fractional parts.

This trick is due to Craig S. Mullins. Given a table with a column containing the name of the day of the week, on which an event happened like this:

```
CREATE TABLE Foobar
(..
 day_name CHAR(3) NOT NULL
    CHECK day_name
          IN ('SUN', 'MON', 'TUE', 'WED', 'THU', 'FRI', 'SAT'),
 ..);
```

How do we sort it properly? We'd want Sunday first, followed by Monday, Tuesday, Wednesday, and so on. Well, if we write the first query that comes to mind, the results will obviously be sorted improperly:

```
SELECT day_name, col1, col2, ..
  FROM Foobar
 ORDER BY day_name;
```

The results from this query would be ordered alphabetically; in other words:

FRI

MON

SAT

SUN

THU
TUE
WED

Of course, one solution would be to design the table with a numeric column that uses Zeller's number. There is another solution that is both elegant and does not require any change to the database.

```
SELECT day_name, col1, c12, ...,
       POSITION (day_name IN 'SUNMONTUEWEDTHUFRISAT') AS day_nbr
  FROM Foobar
 ORDER BY day_nbr;
```

Of course, you can go one step further if you'd like. Some queries may need to actually return the day of week. You can use the same technique with a twist to return the day of week value, given only the day's name.

```
CAST (POSITION (day_name IN 'SUNMONTUEWEDTHUFRISAT')/3 AS INTEGER) + 1;
```

Obviously the same trick can be used with the three-letter month abbreviations. This was very handy in the first release of ACCESS that did sort dates alphabetically.

35.6.2 Report Periods

35.6.2.1 Report Period Table

Since SQL is a database language, we prefer to do look ups and not calculations. They can be optimized while temporal math messes up optimization. A useful idiom is a report period calendar that everyone uses, so there is no way to get disagreements in the DML.

The report period table gives a name to a range of dates that is common to the entire enterprise.

```
CREATE TABLE Something_Report_Periods
(something_report_name CHAR(10) NOT NULL PRIMARY KEY
   CHECK (something_report_name LIKE <pattern>),
 something_report_start_date DATE NOT NULL,
 something_report_end_date DATE NOT NULL,
  CONSTRAINT date_ordering
    CHECK (something_report_start_date <= something_report_end_date),
etc);
```

These report periods can overlap or have gaps. Giving a period a name is harder than you might think. I like the MySQL convention of using double zeroes for months and years, That is 'yyyy-mm-00' for a month within a year and 'yyyy-00-00' for the whole year. The advantages are that it will sort with the ISO-8601 data format required by Standard SQL and it is language independent. The pattern for validation is '[12][0-9][0-9][0-9]-00-00' and '[12][0-9][0-9][0-9]-[01][0-9]-00'.

35.7 Modeling Time in Tables

Since the nature of time is a continuum and the ISO model is half-open intervals, the best approach is to have (start_time, end_time) pairs for each event in a history. This is a state transition model of data, where the facts represented by the columns in that row were true for the time period given. For this to work, we need the constraint that the (start_time, end_time) pairs do not overlap.

A NULL ending time is the flag for an "unfinished fact," such as a hotel room stay that is still in progress. A history for an entity can clearly have at most one NULL at a time.

```
CREATE TABLE FoobarHistory
(foo_key INTEGER NOT NULL,
 start_date DATE DEFAULT CURRENT_DATE NOT NULL,
 PRIMARY KEY (foo_key, start_date),
 end_date TIMESTAMP, -- null means current
 foo_status INTEGER NOT NULL,
 ..

CONSTRAINT started_before_ended
CHECK(start_date < end_date),

CONSTRAINT end_time_open_interval
CHECK (end_date = CAST(end_date AS DATE) + INTERVAL ('23:59:59.9999999'
HOUR TO SECOND),

CONSTRAINT no_date_overlaps
CHECK (NOT EXISTS
       (SELECT *
          FROM FoobarHistory AS H1, Calendar AS C1
```

```
          WHERE C1.cal_date BETWEEN H1.start_date
                AND H1.end_date
          GROUP BY foo_key
         HAVING COUNT(*) > 1)),

CONSTRAINT only_one_current_status
 CHECK (NOT EXISTS
        (SELECT *
           FROM FoobarHistory AS H1
          WHERE H1.end_date IS NULL
          GROUP BY foo_key
         HAVING COUNT(*) > 1))
);
```

The real trick here is that the start_date is a DATE data type, so it will start at 00:00:00.00 when it is converted to a TIMESTAMP. The end_time is a TIMESTAMP so we can place it almost but not quite to the next day. This will let us use BETWEEN predicates, as we will see in the next section. You could also do this in a VIEW, make both columns DATE data types and add the extra hours to end_time.

In practice this is going to be highly proprietary code and you might consider using triggers to keep the (start_time, end_time) pairs correct.

35.7.1 Using Duration Pairs

If the table does not have the (start_time, end_time) pairs, then they have to be built with a self-join queries or we have to assume that the status changes are ordered properly. For example, how would you write a SELECT query for returning all Projects whose current project status is 10, given the following schema?

```
CREATE TABLE Projects
(project_id INTEGER NOT NULL PRIMARY KEY,
 project_name CHAR(15) NOT NULL);

CREATE TABLE ProjectStatusHistory
(project_id INTEGER NOT NULL
    REFERENCES Projects(project_id),
```

```
project_date DATE DEFAULT CURRENT_DATE NOT NULL,
project_status INTEGER NOT NULL,
PRIMARY KEY (project_id, project_date));
```

A solution from David Portas, which assumes that the project is still active:

```
SELECT P.project_id, P.project_name
  FROM Projects AS P
 WHERE EXISTS
      (SELECT *
         FROM ProjectStatusHistory AS H
        WHERE H.project_id = P.project_id
       HAVING MAX(CASE WHEN H.project_status = 10
                       THEN project_date END) = MAX(project_date));
```

But now try to answer the question, which projects had a status of 10 on a prior date?

```
SELECT X.project_id
  FROM (SELECT P1.project_id, P1.project_date AS start_date,
               MIN(P2.project_date) AS end_date
          FROM Projects AS P1
               LEFT OUTER JOIN
               Projects AS P2
               ON P1.project_id = P2.project_id
                  AND P1.project_date < P2.project_date
         WHERE project_status = 10
         GROUP BY P1.project_id, P1.project_date)
       AS X(project_id, start_date, end_date)
WHERE :my_date BETWEEN X.start_date
                   AND COALESCE (X.end_date, CURRENT_DATE);
```

The X subquery expression is what Projects would have looked like with (start_time, end_time) pairs.

The COALESCE() handles the use of NULL for an eternity marker. Depending on the circumstances, you might also use this form of the predicate.

```
WHERE :my_date BETWEEN X.start_date
                   AND COALESCE (X.end_date, :my_date)
```

35.8 LEAD() and LAG() Functions

While these functions are not officially part of ANSI/ISO Standard SQL, they are common. And they are most often used with temporal data. Informally, you sort a list of rows, look down this list by an offset of <offset> rows, and return the value on the offset row. If you cannot find such a row, then return the <default> value; if there is no <default>, then return a NULL.

The syntax is

```
[LEAD | LAG] (<scalar expression> [,<offset>], [default])
    OVER (<PARTITION BY <column>] ORDER BY <column> [ASC|DESC])
```

The <scalar expression> is the value, usually a column, we are looking at. This can be any data type but it is most often a timestamp, date, or time column. The offset is always an exact numeric value; if it is not given, then it defaults to one. The direction of the offset is determined by LEAD() to look forward or LAG() to look back in the list. The <default> is a shorthand for an IFNULL() expression.

The OVER ([partition_by_clause] order_by_clause) is the same semantics as we have in the other windowed functions. The PARTITION BY and ORDER BY clauses are the same. The most common idiom is a delta; the change of a value over time. For example, following the trend of a stock portfolio is simple.

```
SELECT trading_date, stock_symbol, closing_price,
       closing_price -
       (LAG(closing_price)
           OVER(PARTITION BY stock_symbol ORDER BY trading_date))
        AS closing_price:delta
  FROM Stock_Portfoilo;
```

35.9 Problems with the Year 2000: A Historical Overview

The special problems with the year 2000 took on a life of their own in the computer community, so they rate a separate section in this book. Yes, I know you thought that the “Y2K Crisis” or “millennium bug” was over by now, but it still shows up and you need to think about it. The four major problems with representations of the year 2000 in computer systems are:

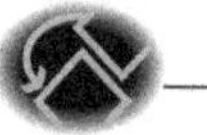

1. The year 2000 has a lot of zeros in it.
2. The year 2000 is a leap year.
3. The year 2000 is the last year of the old millennium.
4. Many date fields are not really dates.

35.9.1 The Zeros

I like to call problem 1—the zeros in 2000—the "odometer problem" because it is in the hardware or system level. This is not the same as the millennium problem, where date arithmetic is invalid. If you are using a year-in-century format, the year 2000 is going to "roll over" like a car odometer that has reached its limit and leave a year that is assumed to be 1900 (or something else other than 2000) by the application program.

This problem lives where you cannot see in hardware and operating systems related to the system clock. Information on such problems is very incomplete, so you will need to keep yourself posted as new releases of your particular products come out.

Another subtle form of "the zero problem" is that some hashing and random number generators use parts of the system date as a parameter. Zero is a perfectly good number until you try to divide by it and your program aborts.

The problem is in mainframes. For example, the Unisys 2200 system was set to fail on the first day of 1996 because the 8th bit of the year field—which is a signed integer—would go to 1. Fortunately, the vendor had some solutions ready. Do you know what other hardware uses this convention? You might want to look.

The real killer will be with older Intel-based PCs. When the odometer wraps around, DOS jumps to 1980 most of the time and sometimes to 1984, depending on your BIOS chip. Windows 3.1 jumps to 1900 most of the time. Since PCs are now common as stand-alone units and as workstations, you can test this for yourself. Set the date and time to 2005-12-31 at 23:59:30h and let the clock run. What happens next depends on your BIOS chip and version of DOS.

The results can be that the clock display shows "12:00 AM" and a date display of "01/01/00," so you think you have no problems. However, you will find that you have newly created files dated 1984 or 1980. Surprise!

This problem is passed along to application programs, but not always the way that you would think. Quicken Version 3 for the IBM PC running on

MS-DOS 6 is one example. As you expect, directly inputting the date 2000-01-01 results in the year resetting to 1980 or 1984 off the system clock. But strangely enough, if you let the date wrap from 2005-12-31 into the year 2000, Quicken Version 3 interprets the change as 1901-01-01 and not as 1900.

It is worth doing a Google search for information on older software when you have to work with.

35.9.2 Leap Year

Problem 2 always seems to shock people. You might remember being told in grade school that there are 365¼ days per year and that the accumulation of the fractional day creates a leap year every 4 years. Once more, your teachers lied to you; there are really 365.2422 days per year. Every 4 years, the extra 0.2400 days accumulate and create an additional day; this gives us a leap year. Every 400 years the extra 0.0022 days accumulate enough to create an additional day and give us this special leap year. Since most of us are not over 400 years old, we did not have to worry about this until the year 2000. However, every 100 years the missing 0.01 days (i.e. 365.25−365.2422 rounded up) balances out and we do not have a leap year.

The correct test for leap years in SQL/PSM is

```
CREATE FUNCTION Test_Leapyear (IN my_year INTEGER)
RETURNS CHAR(3)
LANGUAGE SQL
DETERMINISTIC
RETURN (CASE WHEN MOD(my_year, 400) = 0
        THEN 'Yes'
        WHEN MOD(my_year, 100) = 0
        THEN 'No'
        ELSE CASE WHEN MOD(my_year, 4) = 0
                  THEN 'Yes' ELSE 'No '
             END
        END);
```

Or if you would like a more compact form, you can use this solution from Phil Alexander, which will fit into in-line code as a search expression:

```
(MOD(year, 400) = 0
 OR (MOD(year, 4) = 0 AND NOT (MOD(year, 100) = 0)))
```

People who did not know this algorithm wrote lots of programs. I do not mean COBOL legacy programs in your organization; I mean packaged programs for which you paid good money. The date functions in the first releases of Lotus, Excel, and Quattro Pro did not handle the day 2000-02-29 correctly. Lotus simply made an error and the others followed suit to maintain "Lotus compatibility" in their products. Microsoft Excel for Windows Version 4 shows correctly that the next day after 2000-02-28 is 2000-03-01. However, it thought that the next day after 1900-02-28 is also February 29 instead of March 01. Microsoft Excel for Macintosh did not handle the years 1900-1903.

Have you checked all of your word processors, spreadsheets, desktop databases, appointment calendars, and other off the shelf packages for this problem yet? Just key in the date 2000-02-29, then do some calculations with date arithmetic and see what happens.

With networked systems, this is a real nightmare. All you need is one program on one node in the network to reject leap year day 2000 and the whole network is useless for that day; transactions might not reconcile for some time afterward. How many nodes do you think there are in the ATM banking networks in North America and Europe?

35.9.3 The Millennium

I saved problem 3 for last because it is the one best known in the popular and computer trade press. We programmers have not been keeping TRUE dates in data fields for a few decades. Instead, we have been using one of several year-in-century formats. These will not work in the last year of the previous millennium (the first millennium of the Common Era calendar ends in the year 2000 and the second millennium begins with the year 2001—that is why Arthur C. Clarke used it for the title of his book.

If only we had been good programmers and not tried to save storage space at the expense of accuracy, we would have used ISO Standard formats and would not have to deal with these problems today. Since we did not, programs have been doing arithmetic and comparisons based on the year-in-century and not on the year. A 30-year mortgage taken out in 1992 will be over in the year 2022, but when you subtract the two year-in-centuries, you get

(22−92) = −70 years. This is a very early payoff of a mortgage!

It might be worth mentioning the old COBOL programmer trick of checking to see if the 2-digit year is less than 30 (or some other magical number): if it is, we add 2000 to it, if it isn't then add 1900 to it and come up with a 4-digit year. A lot of old COBOL programs will be exploding 20 or 30 or 40 years from now if they are still chugging along.

Inventory retention programs were throwing away good stock, thinking it is outdated-look at the 10-year retention required in the automobile industry. Lifetime product warranties were dishonored because the services schedule dates and manufacturing dates could not be resolved correctly. One hospital sent a geriatrics patient to the pediatrics ward because it keeps only two digits of the birth year. You can imagine your own horror stories or do a web search for books and articles from that period.

According to Benny Popek of Coopers & Lybrand LLP (Xenakis 1995),[1] "This problem is so big that we will consider these bugs to be out of the scope of our normal software maintenance contracts. For those clients who insist that we should take responsibility, we'll exercise the cancellation clause and terminate the outsourcing contract."

Popek commented, "We've found that a lot of our clients are in denial. We spoke to one CIO who just refused to deal with the problem, since he's going to retire next year."

But the problem is subtler than just looking for date data fields. Timestamps are often buried inside encoding schemes. If the year-in-century is used for the high-order digits of a serial numbering system, then any program that depends on increasing serial numbers will fail. Those of you with magnetic tape libraries might want to look at your tape labels now. The five-digit code is used in many mainframe shops for archives and tape management software also has the convention that if programmers want a tape to be kept indefinitely, they code the label with a retention date of 99365. This method failed at the start of the year 2000 when the retention label has 00001 in it.

35.9.4 Weird Dates in Legacy Data

Some of the problems with dates in legacy data have been discussed in an article by Randall L. Hitchens (Hitchens, 1991)[2] and in one by me on the same subject (Celko, 1981).[3] The problem is subtler than Hitchens implied in his article, which dealt with nonstandard date formats. Dates hide in other

[1] "The Millennium Bug, The Fin De Siecle Computer Virus"; by John Xenakis; CFO: The Magazine for Senior Financial Executives; 1995 July issue.

[2] Hitchens, R. L. (1991, January 28). Viewpoint. *Computerworld*.

[3] Celko, J., & McDonald, J. (1981, February). Father time software secrets allows updating of dates. *Information Systems News*. [This article was later quoted in *Vanity Fair* January 1999 (The Y2K Nightmare by Robert Sam Anson).]

places, not just in date fields. The most common places are serial numbers and computer-generated identifiers.

In the early 1960s, a small insurance company in Atlanta bought out an even smaller company that sold burial insurance policies to poor people in the Deep South. These policies guaranteed the subscriber a funeral in exchange for a weekly or monthly premium of a few dollars and were often sold by local funeral homes; they are now illegal.

The burial insurance company used a policy number format identical to that of the larger company. The numbers began with the two digits of the year-in-century, followed by a dash, followed by an eight-digit sequential number.

The systems analysts decided that the easiest way to do this was to add 20 years to the first two digits. Their logic was that no customer would keep these cheap policies for 20 years—and the analyst who did this would not be working there in 20 years, so who cared? As the years passed, the company moved from a simple file system to a hierarchical database and was using the policy numbers for unique record keys. The system simply generated new policy numbers on demand, using a global counter in a policy library routine and no problems occurred for decades.

There were about 100 burial policies left in the database after 20 years. Nobody had written programs to protect against duplicate keys, since the problem had never occurred. Then, 1 day, they created their first duplicate number. Sometimes the database would crash, but sometimes the child records would get attached to the wrong parent. This second situation was worse, since the company started paying and billing the wrong people.

The company was lucky enough to have someone who recognized the old burial insurance policies when he saw them. It took months to clean up the problem, because they had to search a warehouse to find the original policy documents. If the policies were still valid, there were insurance regulation problems because those policies had been made illegal in the intervening years.

In this case, the date was being used to generate a unique identifier. But consider a situation in which this same scheme is used, starting in the year 1999, for a serial number. Once the company goes into the year 2000, you can no longer select the largest serial number in the database and increment it to get the next one.

35.9.5 The Aftermath

The Y2K crisis is over now and we have some idea of the cost of this conversion. By various estimates, the total expenditure on remediation by governments and businesses ranged from a low of $200 billion to well over half a trillion dollars. As a result of Y2K, many ISO Standards—not just SQL—require that dates be in ISO-8601 format.

The other good side effect was that people actually looked at their data and became aware of their data quality levels. Most companies would not have done such a data audit without the "Y2K Crisis" over their heads.

This was also a major reason that the SQL Standards spent so much time on, well, time.

Implementation and Coding Issues

Procedural Semi-Procedural and Declarative Programming in SQL

A LOT OF THE time, the key to make SQL databases perform well is to take a break from the keyboard and rethink the way of approaching the problem, and rethink in terms of a set-based declarative approach. Joe takes a simple discussion about a problem with a User-Defined Function (UDF) to illustrate the point that ingrained procedural reflexes can often prevent us from seeing simpler set-based techniques.

I have spent many years trying to persuade people to use declarative rather than procedural code in SQL. One of my books is *Thinking in Sets*, with the oversized subtitle *Auxiliary, Temporal, and Virtual Tables in SQL* to explain what topics are covered. Most programmers discover that it is too big a big leap from a procedural mindset to a declarative mindset, and so do not quite make the transition all at once. Instead, they evolve from a procedural paradigm to a variety of semi-procedural programming styles.

This is just the way that we learn; a step at a time, not a leap of insight all at once. The first motion pictures, for example, were shot with a fixed position camera aimed at a stage. That is how people had seen stage plays for several thousand years. W. D. Griffith was to movies as Dr. Codd was to databases. Griffith made the first two-reeler in 1910; nobody had thought about more than one reel before that. Then in 1911 and 1912, he and his cameraman, Billy Bitzer, started moving the camera and lens while filming. He gave us new camera angles such as the close-up and soft focus.

36.1 Words Matter

My wife and I are old. We started listen to audio cassettes years ago when that was the current technology. The term was "books on tape" in those days. But when we play an audio book CD in the car we still call it a tape.

Skeuomorphism refers to a design principle in which design cues are taken from the physical world. Using a paper file holder for a computer filing systems, a letter symbol for email, the sound of a mechanical shutter click on a digital camera, and so forth. Notice that the device does not have to merely mimic the behavior of some physical object. The new tool can add more functions.

People skeuomorph themselves! The new SQL programmer morphs rows into records and screen images, so he expects the rows to be in physical sequence. This means that they use words like "prior" and "next" that do not apply to a set model of data. The most common conceptual errors are:

1. Tables are not spreadsheets. Do not be fooled by the screen image.
2. Tables are not files; they are interrelated into a schema.
3. Rows are not records.
4. Columns are not fields.
5. Do not tibble. This is putting meta-data prefixes on data element names. It comes from the use of "tbl-" on table names.
6. Sets change all at once, not element by element in a sequence of steps.
7. CASE is not a control flow statement.
8. Declarative languages do not use local variables.
9. DDL is where most of the work is done in SQL.
10. Data types are important and you need to get the right. You should not CAST(), EXTRACT(), SUBSTRING(), or do other things too.

These are not the only conceptual errors, but they are the big ones.

36.2 Cleaning Code

In 2010 February, I came across an example in a Newsgroup discussion of programmers making the steps, but not the leap. The code details are not relevant to the point that I am making, so I am going to gloss over them.

The thread starts with a posting about a UDF that is not working. His opening paragraph was:

"I have the code below to take a set of INTEGER values and return a VARCHAR based on the combination of inputs. However, I'm getting an error on line 6, which is the first line where the word CASE pops up. Plenty of CASE statements have passed through my hands before, so I'm lost of why this one is wrong."

What followed was a CASE expression with BETWEENs and ORs and CASE within CASE constructs. It took pairs of (x, y) and produced an answer from a set of three values; call them {'a', 'b', 'c'}. Again, the coding details are not my point. The body of the function could just as well have been a complicated mathematical expression.

Two repliers pointed out that CASE is an expression and not a statement in SQL. They also pointed out that he was returning a VARCHAR(1) instead of a CHAR(1). The CASE function can be confusing to anyone who has been initially trained with a procedural language that has IF-THEN-ELSE statement constructs.

His code looked like this skeleton:

```
CREATE FUNCTION FnFindFoobar (IN x INTEGER, IN y INTEGER)
RETURNS VARCHAR
BEGIN
<< horrible CASE expression with x and y >>;
END;
```

The clean up and quick fix was:

```
CREATE FUNCTION Find_Foobar (in_x INTEGER, in_y INTEGER)
RETURNS CHAR(1)
DETERMINISTIC
BEGIN
RETURN (<< horrible CASE expression with x and y >>);
END;
```

The function name loses the redundant prefix; the body of our function is put in the return, without the need for local variables. The function's data type is made into a CHAR(1) and the compiler gets a hint.

Someone else then asked if he had considered precalculating the CASE expression results and populating a table with them. This was good advice,

since the number of (x, y) pairs involved came to a few thousand cases. There is no point in dismissing this solution when the look-up table is as small as this one. Read-only tables this size tend to be in main storage or cache, so they can be shared among many sessions, and you are not going to save much on memory by choosing a different method.

But the person who made this suggestion went on to add "You can use the table with your UDF or you could use it without the UDF.", but he did not explain what the differences are. They are important. Putting the data in the read-only tables this size will tend to keep it in the main storage or cache. If you are really so tight for primary and/or secondary storage that you cannot fit a ~5KB row table in your hardware, buy some chips and disks. They are so cheap today. Now the data can be shared among many sessions. The table and its indexes can be used by the optimizer. In SQL Server, you can include the single column foobar in the index to get a covering index and performance improvement.

But if you choose to lock the data inside the procedural code of a UDF, can it be shared? Do computations get repeated with each invocation? What about indexes? Ouch! A UDF pretty much locks things inside. Standard SQL/PSM has a DETERMINISTIC option in its procedure declarations. This tells the compiler whether the procedure or function is always going to return the same answer for the same arguments.

Note about Standard SQL terms: a parameter is the formal place holder in the parameter list of a declaration and an argument is the value passed in the invocation of the procedure.

A non-deterministic function has to be computed over and over again, every time the UDF is called; if the query optimizer does not know for certain whether a procedure or function is deterministic, it has to assume it is not and go the long route.

Here is the skeleton of what was posted.

```
-- Create table
CREATE TABLE Foobar
(x INTEGER NOT NULL,
 y INTEGER NOT NULL,
 foobar CHAR(1) NOT NULL,
PRIMARY KEY (x, y));
```

The Series table is a common idiom. It is a table with integers from 1 to (*n*) that can be used to replace iterative loops with declarative set generating code.

```
-- Populate table
INSERT INTO Foobar (x, y, foobar)
SELECT x, y, << horrible CASE expression with x and y >> AS foobar
FROM (SELECT seq FROM Series WHERE seq BETWEEN 1 AND 300) AS x
     CROSS JOIN
     (SELECT seq FROM Series WHERE seq BETWEEN 1 AND 100) AS y
```

This replaced a pair of recursive CTEs that generated the numbers. Recursion, a procedural tool, is expensive. But that is not my point. The first thought was to use a procedural tool and not a data driven approach to get that CROSS JOIN. See what I mean by mindset? This is the semi-procedural guy going back to what he knows. He almost got to a declarative mindset.

Now let's go on with the rest of the skeleton code for the function:

```
CREATE FUNCTION Find_Foobar
(IN in_x INTEGER, IN in_y INTEGER)
RETURNS CHAR(1)
RETURN
COALESCE
((SELECT foobar
    FROM Find_Foobar
   WHERE x = in_x
     AND y = in_y), 'A');
```

The reason for COALESCE() is that 'A' is a default value in the outer CASE expression, but also a valid result in various THEN and ELSE clauses inside inner CASE expressions. The scalar query will return a NULL, if it cannot find an (x, y, foobar) row in the table. If we know that the query covers the entire (x, y) universe, then we did not need the COALESCE() and could have avoided a UDF completely.

Now, let us think about declarative programming. In SQL that means constraints in the table declaration in the DDL. This skeleton has none except the PRIMARY KEY. Aiee! Here is a problem that you find with magazine articles and newsgroup postings; it is so easy to skip over the constraints when you provide a skeleton table. You did not need them when you declared a file, do you? What one can forget is that the three SQL sublanguages (DDL, DML, and DCL) work together. In particular, the DDL constraints are used by the DML optimizer to provide a better execution strategy.

The << horrible CASE expression >> implied expectations for x and y. We were given lower limits (100 and 1), but the upper limits were open after a small range of (x, y) pairs. I think we can assume that the original poster expected the vast majority of cases (or all of them) to fall in that small range and wanted to handle anything else as an error. In the real world, there is usually what Jerry Weinberg called "reasonableness checking" in data. The principle is also known as Zipf's Law or the "look for a horse and not a zebra" principle in medicine.

The simple first shot would be to assume we always know the limits and can simply use:

```
CREATE TABLE FooLookup
(x INTEGER NOT NULL
 CHECK (x BETWEEN 100 AND 300),
 y INTEGER NOT NULL
 CHECK (y BETWEEN 1 AND 100),
 foobar CHAR(1) DEFAULT 'A' NOT NULL
 CHECK (foobar) IN ('A', 'B', 'C'),
PRIMARY KEY (x, y));
```

The DEFAULT 'A' subclause will take care of situation where we did not have an explicit value for foobar. This avoids the COALESCE(). But what if one of the parameters can be anything? That is easy; drop the CHECK() and add a comment. What if one of the parameters is half open or has a huge but sparse space? That is, we know a lower (upper) limit, but not the matching upper (lower) limit. Just use a simple comparison, such as CHECK (y >= 1), instead of a BETWEEN.

A common situation, which was done with nested CASE expression in the original, is that you know a range for a parameter and what the results for the other parameter within that range are. That might be easier to see with code. Here is a CASE expression for some of the possible (x, y) pairs:

```
CASE
WHEN x BETWEEN 100 AND 200
THEN CASE
WHEN y IN (2, 4, 6, 8) THEN 'B'
WHEN y IN (1, 3, 5, 7, 9) THEN 'C'
END
WHEN x BETWEEN 201 AND 300
```

```
THEN CASE
WHEN y IN (2, 4, 6, 8, 99) THEN 'C'
WHEN y IN (3, 5, 7, 9, 100) THEN 'B'
END
ELSE 'A'
END
```

This is the DML version of a constraint. It lives only in the INSERT. UPDATE, INSERT, or SELECT statements where it appears. What we really want is constraints in the DDL so that all statements, present and future, use it. The trick is to create the table with low and high values for each parameter range; a single value is shown with the low and high values that are equal to each other.

```
CREATE TABLE FooLookup
(low_x INTEGER NOT NULL,
high_x INTEGER NOT NULL,
CHECK (low_x <= high_x),
low_y INTEGER NOT NULL,
high_y INTEGER NOT NULL,
CHECK (low_y <= high_y),
foobar CHAR(1) NOT NULL
CHECK (foobar) IN ('A', 'B', 'C'),
PRIMARY KEY (x, y));
```

CASE expression now becomes this table:

low_x	high_x	low_y	high_y	foobar
100	200	2	2	'B'
100	200	6	6	'B'
100	200	8	8	'B'
100	200	1	1	'C'
100	200	3	3	'C'
100	200	5	5	'C'
100	200	7	7	'C'
100	200	9	9	'C'
201	300	2	2	'C'
201	300	4	4	'C'

Continued

low_x	high_x	low_y	high_y	foobar
201	300	6	6	'C'
201	300	8	8	'C'
201	300	99	99	'C'
201	300	3	3	'B'
201	300	5	5	'B'
201	300	7	7	'B'
201	300	9	9	'B'
201	300	100	100	'B'
301	9999	101	9999	'A'
–9999	99	–9999	0	'A'

As a safety device, put the default 'A' in ranges outside the rest of the table. I used –9999 and 9999 for the least and greatest limits, but you get the idea.

The query has to use BETWEENs on the high and low limits:

```
SELECT F.foobar, ..
  FROM FooLookup AS F, ..
 WHERE my_x BETWEEN F.low_x AND F.high_x
   AND my_y BETWEEN F.low_y AND F.high_y
   AND ..;
```

Is this always going to be the best way to do something? Who knows? Test it.

Nesting Levels in SQL

THE ANCESTOR OF SQL was an IBM project named Sequel, which was a shorthand for "Structured English Query Language"; the term "Structured" in the name came from two sources. The first was the "Structured Revolution" at the time. Dijkstra, Youron, DeMacro, and the other early pioneers of modern Software Engineering had just given us "Structured Programming" and "Structured Analysis," so everything had to be Structured. Younger people will remember when everything had to be "Object Oriented," then "Big Data" then "in the Cloud" and whatever the current fad is at this reading.

And for the record, the ANSI/ISO Standard language is called "Ess Que El" and not "SEQUEL" in spite of the fact that we *all* screw up. The informal rules in the Standards world are that an ISO Standard made up of letters is spelled out, but a US Federal standard is pronounced as a word, no matter how weird. This is why a Physician's Standards Review Organization is called a "Piss Row" in Medicate/Medicaid terminology. Another rule is that the French will fight to keep the initials of a standard's name in French order, not English. Did you know that "ISO" is actually named "International Organization for Standardization"?

The second source of the "structured" term was the ability to nest queries inside each other via joins, set operations, and other table-level operations. This is actually a mathematical property called Orthogonality. In English, it is why operations done on numbers produce numbers, so you can use

parentheses to write mathematical expressions. Any place in which you can use a number, you can use a numeric expression. Any place in which you can use a table, you can use a table expression.

In SQL, there is a hierarchy of data in which the outer level is the schema or database. The schema is made up of tables (which can be base or virtual tables) and other schema objects. Each table is made up of a set of rows. These rows have no ordering, but all have the same structure, so it is a proper set. Each row is made up of columns. The columns are scalar values drawn from a domain; a domain is a set of values of one data type that has rules of its own. These rules include the type of scale upon which it is built and reasonable operations with it.

I tell people to use set diagrams (improperly called Venn diagram; Euler invented them) when they want to use a doodle to help them think of a query. But most programmers doodle flow diagrams because they grew up with flowcharts, DFDs, and similar mind tools. Let me show you what I mean.

37.1 Derived Tables

A derived table is a table expression embedded in a containing statement. It has to be placed inside parentheses and it can optionally be given a correlation name and its columns can also optionally be given names.

```
(<table expression>) [[AS] <correlation name> [(<derived column list>)]]
```

The derived table will *act as if* it is materialized during the duration of the statement that uses it. Notice the phrase "act as if" in that last sentence. The optimizer is free to rearrange the statement anyway that it wished so long as the results are the same as the original statement. If there is no (<derived column list>), then the derived table exposes the tables and their columns that created the derived table.

Once the query expression becomes a derived table with a correlation name, the internal structure is hidden. If no (<derived column list>) is given, then it inherits the column names from the component tables. Watch out; if the expression has two or more tables that have common column name, you have to use <table name>.<column name> syntax to avoid ambiguity.

Materialization is not an easy choice. If one statement is using a derived table, it might be better to integrate it into that statement like a text macro. But if many statements are using the same derived table, it might be better to materialize it once, put it in primary or secondary storage and share it. These

are the same decisions the SQL engine had to make with VIEWs. But the derived tables are not in the schema level where the optimizer can find them and keep statistics about them. It takes a pretty smart optimizer to filter them out for materialization.

This is why it is better to put a derived table definition into a VIEW when it is reused often.

37.2 Column Naming Rules

Derived tables should follow the same ISO-11179 Standard naming rules. A table, base or virtual, is a table. The keyword “AS” is not required, but it is a good programming practice and so is naming the columns. If you do not provide names, then the SQL engine will attempt to do it for you. The table name will not be accessible to you since it will be a temporary internal reference in the schema information table. The SQL engine will use scoping rules to qualify the references in the statement—and what you said might not be what you meant. Likewise, columns in a derived table inherit their names from the defining table expression. *But only if the defining table expression creates such names.* For example, the columns in a UNION, EXCEPT, or INTERSECT statement have no names unless you use the AS clause.

When you have multiple copies of the same table expression in a statement, you need to tell them apart with different correlation names. For example, given a table of sports players, we want to show a team captain and team cocaptain.

```
SELECT T1.team_name,
       T1.last_name AS captain,
       T2.last_name AS cocaptain
  FROM Teams AS T1, Teams AS T2
 WHERE T1.team_name = T2.team_name
   AND T1.team_position = 'captain'
   AND T2.team_position = 'cocaptain';
```

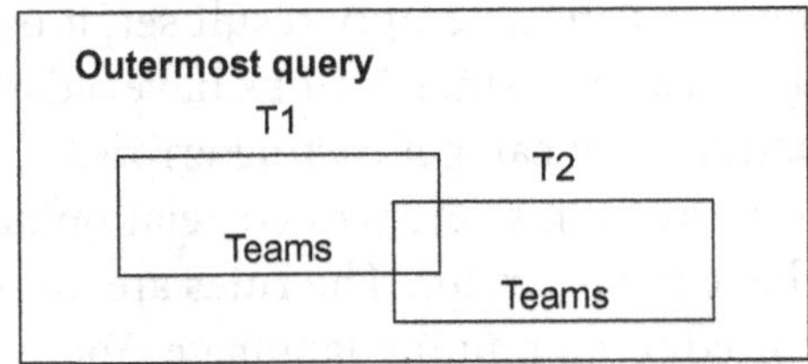

I have found that using a short abbreviation and a sequence of integers for correlation names works very well. This also illustrates another naming rule. The player's last name is used in two different roles in this query, so we need to rename the column to the role name (if it stands by itself without qualification) or use the role name as a prefix (i.e., use "boss_emp_id" and "worker_emp_id" to qualify each employee's role in this table).

37.3 Scoping Rules

A derived table can be complete in itself and without a scoping problem at all. For example, consider this query:

```
SELECT O.order_nbr, B.box_size
 FROM Orders AS O,
   (SELECT box_size, packing_qty)
     FROM Boxes)
     AS B(box_size, packing_qty)
 WHERE O.ship_qty <= B.packing_qty;
```

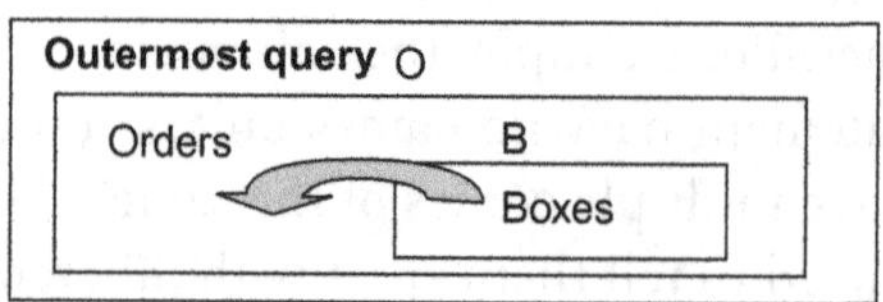

The derived table "B" has no outer references and it can be retrieved immediately while another parallel processor works on the rest of the query. Another form of this kind of derived table is a simple scalar subquery:

```
SELECT O.order_nbr AS over_sized_order
 FROM Orders AS O
 WHERE O.ship_qty > (SELECT MAX(packing_qty) FROM Boxes);
```

The scalar subquery is computed; the one row, one column result table is converted into a unique scalar value and the WHERE clause is tested. If the scalar subquery returns an empty result set, it is converted into a NULL. Watch out for that last case, since NULLs have a data type in SQL and in some weird situations you can get casting errors.

When a table expression references correlation names in which they are contained, you have to be careful. The rules are not that much different from any block-structured programming language. You work your way from the inside out.

This is easier to explain with an example. We have a table of pilots and the planes they can fly (dividend); we have a table of planes in the hangar (divisor); we want the names of the pilots who can fly every plane (quotient) in the hangar. This is Chris Date's version of Relational Division; the idea is that a divisor table is used to partition a dividend table and produce a quotient or results table. The quotient table is made up of those values of one column for which a second column had all of the values in the divisor.

```
SELECT DISTINCT pilot_name
 FROM PilotSkills AS PS1
 WHERE NOT EXISTS
    (SELECT *
     FROM Hangar AS H
     WHERE NOT EXISTS
        (SELECT *
         FROM PilotSkills AS PS2
         WHERE PS1.pilot_name = PS2.pilot_name
          AND PS2.plane_name = H.plane_name));
```

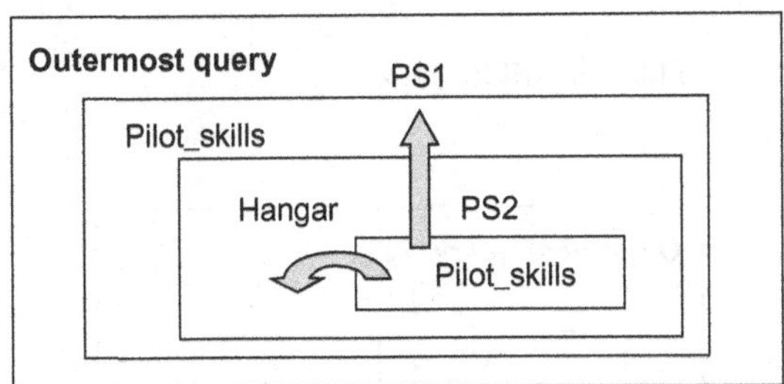

The quickest way to explain what is happening in this query is to imagine a World War II movie where a cocky pilot has just walked into the hangar, looked over the fleet, and announced, "There ain't no plane in this hangar that I can't fly!," which is bad English but good logic.

Notice that PilotSkills appears twice in the query, as PS1 and as PS2. Go to the innermost "SELECT.. FROM.." construct. We have a local copy of PilotSkills as PS2 and outer references to tables H and PS1. We find that H is a copy of the Hangar table one level above us. We find that PS1 is a copy of the PilotSkills table two levels above us.

If we had written "WHERE pilot_name = PS2.pilot_name" in the innermost SELECT, the scoping rules would have looked for a local reference first and found it. The search condition would be the equivalent of

"WHERE PS2.pilot_name = PS2.pilot_name," which is always TRUE since we cannot have a NULL pilot name. Oops, not what we meant!

It is a good idea to always qualify the column references with a correlation name. Hangar did not actually need a correlation name since it appears only once in the statement. But do it anyway. It makes the code a little easier to understand for the people that have to maintain it—consistent style is always good. It protects your code from changes in the tables. Imagine several levels of nesting in which an intermediate table gets a column that had previously been an outer reference.

37.4 Exposed Table Names

The nesting in SQL has the concept of an "exposed name" within a level. An exposed name is a correlation name, a table name that is not followed by a correlation name, or a view name that is not followed by a correlation name. The exposed names must be unique.

Here are some examples to demonstrate scoping rules.

```
SELECT ..
 FROM (SELECT * FROM A WHERE A.x = 1
        INNER JOIN
       SELECT * FROM B WHERE B.x = 2
WHERE ..;
```

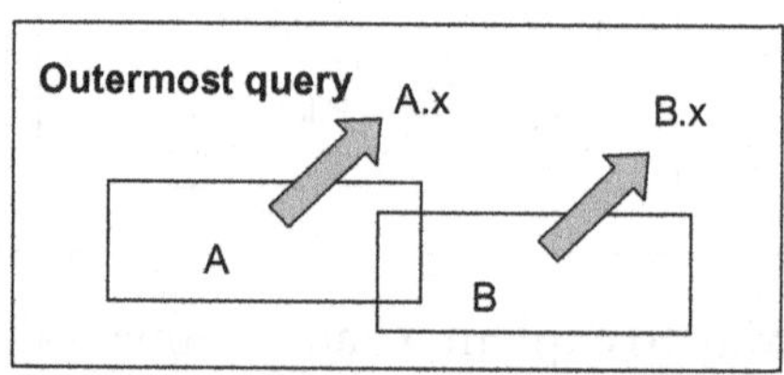

Tables A and B can be referenced in the outer WHERE clause. These are both exposed names. But if you scope them into a new table, X like:

```
SELECT ..
 FROM (SELECT * FROM A WHERE A.x = 1
        INNER JOIN
       SELECT * FROM B WHERE B.x = 2)
     AS X(..)
WHERE ..;
```

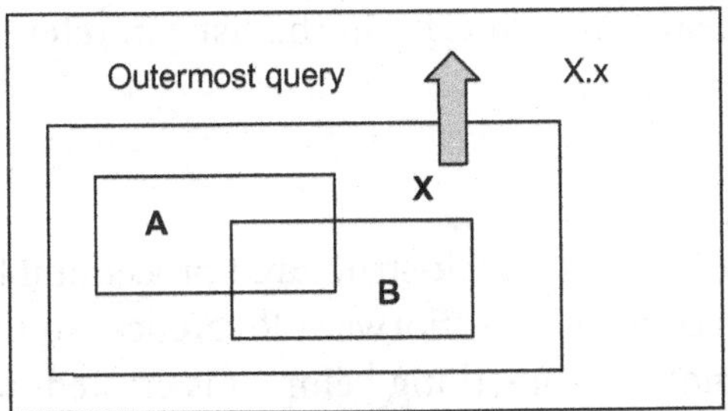

But only Table X can be referenced in the outer WHERE clause. The correlation name X is now an exposed name.

```
SELECT ..
  FROM (SELECT *
          FROM A
         WHERE A.x
            = (SELECT MAX(xx) FROM C))
       INNER JOIN
       SELECT *
         FROM B
        WHERE B.c = 2)
 WHERE ..;
```

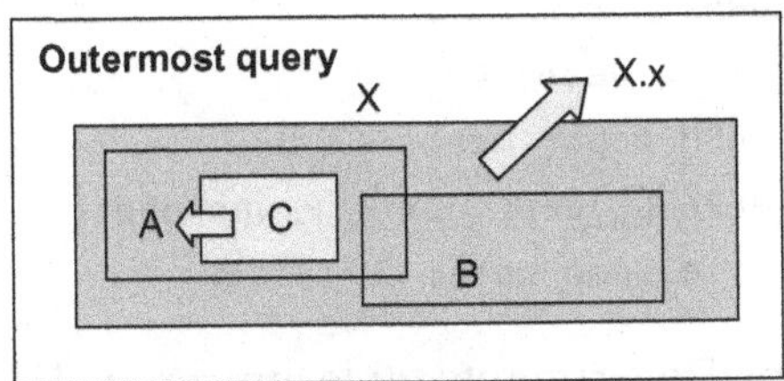

Table C is not exposed to any other SELECT statement.

37.5 Common Table Expressions (CTEs)

ANSI/ISO Standard SQL-99 added the Common Table Expressions or CTEs. It is also a query expression that is given a name, just like a derived table. The difference is that they appear before the SELECT statement in which they are used.

They are just a very useful bit of syntactic sugar. The only thing to remember is that each CTE is exposed in the order it appears in the WITH

clause. That means the *n*th CTE in the list can reference the first through (*n*–1)th CTEs.

37.6 LATERAL Tables

If you have worked with block-structured procedural languages, you will understand the concept of a "Forward Reference" in many of them. The idea is that you cannot use something before it is created in the module unless you signal the compiler. The most common example is a set of co-routines in which Routine A calls Routine B, then Routine B calls Routine A, and so forth. If Routine A is declared first, then calls to B have to have an additional declaration that tells the compiler Routine B will be declared later in the module.

ANSI/ISO Standard SQL has a LATERAL derived table construct which lets one table reference another table as the same level. T-SQL does not have this feature yet, but you can use APPLY to get some of the same results.

This might be easier to demonstrate than to explain. The following example is valid:

```
SELECT D1.dept_nbr, D1.dept_name, E.sal_avg, E.emp_cnt
 FROM Departments AS D1,
     (SELECT AVG(E.salary), COUNT(*)
        FROM Personnel AS P
       WHERE P.dept_nbr
        = (SELECT D2.dept_nbr
             FROM Departments AS D2
            WHERE D2.dept_nbr = P.workdept)
    ) AS E (sal_avg, emp_cnt);
```

Notice that the Departments table appears as **D1** and **D2** at two levels—**D1** is at level one and **D2** is at level three.

The following example is not valid because the reference to **D.dept_nbr** in the **WHERE** clause of the nested table expression references the Personnel table via **P.dept_nbr** that is in the same **FROM** clause.

```
-- Error, Personnel and Departments are on the same level
SELECT D.dept_nbr, D.dept_name, E.sal_avg, E.emp_cnt
  FROM Departments AS D,
  (SELECT AVG(P.salary), COUNT(*)
     FROM Personnel AS P
    WHERE P.dept_nbr = D.dept_nbr) AS E(sal_avg, emp_cnt);
```

To make the query valid, we need to add a LATERAL clause in front of the subquery. Notice the order of Personnel and Departments. This exposes the department number so that a join can be done with it in the derived table labeled E.

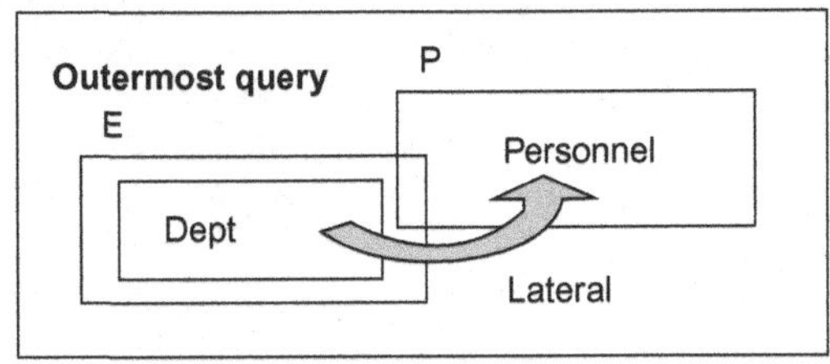


```
-- with a lateral clause
SELECT D.dept_nbr, D.dept_name, E.sal_avg, E.emp_cnt
  FROM Departments AS D,
  LATERAL (SELECT AVG(P.salary), COUNT(*)
     FROM Personnel AS P
     WHERE P.dept_nbr = D.dept_nbr) AS E(sal_avg, emp_cnt);
```

37.7 Programming Tips

Let me finish with some heuristics.

1. Use aliases that tell the guy maintaining this code what tables are referenced. Do not simply use A, B, C,... as names. This comes from the 1950s when files were referenced by the name of the tape drive that held them.
2. "Petty print" the SQL so that the indentation tells the reader what the query structure is. This is a simple task for any of many tools.
3. Never use "SELECT *" in production code; it will eventually bite you when a table changes. You have a text editor and it is easy to cut and paste a list of column names.
4. When you have three or more levels of nesting, think about a CTE. The code will be more readable.
5. When you have two or more references to a query expression, think about a CTE. The code will be more readable, but in many SQLs it will also help the optimizer make a decision about materialization (T-SQL is still behind on this).

Programming Tips

Embedded SQL, CLI Dynamic SQL, and SQL/PSM

ORIGINALLY, SQL STOOD for "Structured Query Language" to differentiate it from the IBM product SEQUEL (short for Structured English Query Language") and then following the pattern for ISO Standards, it became just the letters "Ess-Que-Ell" as the official name. Yes, people still say "Sequel" and nobody seems to care.

The joke in the SQL Standards committee was that "SQL" stands of "Scarcely Qualifies as a Language" because it cannot exist by itself. It is the "middle man" between the database (which is not defined in the standards) and a host language or environment.

There are several ways to do this. This chapter is a very quick overview of the various methods, not a detailed tutorial. In particular, my goal is that an experienced programmer can read the SQL/PSM code in my books.

38.1 Embedded SQL

Embedded SQL is out of favor these days, but it is really useful. You write SQL statements in the host program and use a precompiler to convert it into CLI or other host language calls. This method is usually used with C and COBOL because it precompiles to SQL/CLI or ODBC.

Here is a simple C program that creates two-column table, prompts for values and inserts one row.

```
exec sql include sqlstate;
exec sql whenever sqlerror goto finish;
exec sql begin declare section;
  char host variable1[10];
  char host variable2[10];
exec sql end declare section;
void main()
{
exec sql connect to database;
exec sql whenever sqlerror continue;
exec sql create table foobar (sql_col_1 char(9), sql_col_2 char(9));
exec sql whenever sqlerror goto finish;
printf("input host variable1\n");
gets(host variable1);
printf("input host variable2\n");
gets(host variable2);
exec sql insert into foobar values(:host variable1, :host variable2);
exec sql commit;
finish: printf ("We have a problem;", sqlstate);
}
```

The "exec sql" is the signal to the precompiler. The "exec sql begin declare section" and "exec sql end declare section" create a working storage, which is used to cast C data types to SQL data types. Remember strings in C are terminated with an ASCII nul, so the length have to be included when it is translated into a SQL string.

The sqlstate is where the SQL engines sends error message. The WHENEVER statement catches an error and takes an action. The GOTO jumps control flow to the labeled statement; CONTINUE continues the control flow.

38.2 SQL/CLI

This standard is a set of C and COBOL calls based on Microsoft's ODBC product. The functions always begin with "SQL" and they fall into a few broad groups

1. Handshaking functions: connect or disconnect the host program to the datable.
2. Actions: execute or rollback an SQL statement.

3. Error detection: this uses the SQLSTATE, which is a hierarchical classification (think "Dewey Decimal") of warnings and errors.
4. Host variable functions: they do data transfer.
5. SELECT statement support: this gives you metadata about a query result.

38.3 Dynamic SQL

Dynamic SQL takes a text string of SQL and compiles it at run time, rather than in an SQL tool to get a persistent executable module. *The idea is that you do not know what you want to do until run time.* The PREPARE statement will get you executable module that will persist for your session. This saves the overhead of re-compiling the code every time it is executed in the session.

You then use the EXECUTE statement each time to execute it. If you only wanted to do this once, then you use EXECUTE IMMEDIATE instead. And there is also a REALLOCATE PREPARE to forcibly clear it out the storage. If you need to find out what happened, there is also a DESCRIBE statement that give you metadata.

It gets worse. You can also put question marks as placeholder in the text. The text is changed and re-compiled. This is a problem called "parameter sniffing" in the SQL Server world; when a parameter is a constant or an expression in the first execution, the compiled statement uses that value for its execution plan and never changes it until it is re-compiled.

38.4 SQL/PSM History

SQL/PSM (SQL/Persistent Stored Modules) is an ISO standard mainly defining an extension of SQL with a *procedural language* for use in stored procedures. This was the work of Andrew Eisenberg of DEC (Digital Equipment Corporation), who was impressed with ADA. Younger readers will not remember DEC or the ADA language and the Department of Defense ADA initiative. The first version was published in 1996 as an extension of SQL-92. Later, SQL followed the COBOL Standard model of separate modules for optional facilities to use with the SQL standard.

It is a block structured language that uses the ADA model; a block has the usual scoping rules. Local variables are declared at the start of a block, the

executable cod is in the body and the "condition handling" (error handling) is at the end of the block. The syntax has control flow with the classic if-then-else family, loops, and error signaling. There are also local variables, assignment of expressions to variables and parameters, and (procedural) use of cursors. It also defines an information schema (metadata) for stored procedures.

In practice, you will find SQL venders who have had their own procedural languages which are block structured. Some vendors later added a SQL/PSM dialect, but cannot get rid of their old proprietary languages. This is called the "code museum effect" where the customer base has too much invested in it. Some examples are as follows: MySQL uses only the SQL/PSM procedure headers, but no control flow at all; IBM has a SQL/PSM in DB2; Mimer has a SQL/PSM implementation, and Oracle's PL/SQL is a SQL/PSM dialect. Informix/SPL is more Algol-like and the T-SQL language in MS SQL Server is a mix of Algol and C. A PostgreSQL add-on implements SQL/PSM (alongside its own procedural language), although it is not part of the core product.

38.4.1 SQL Statements

It should be obvious that we can use pretty much any SQL statement in SQL/PSM that makes sense. You cannot generally create schema objects and have to use the existing schema. Declarations are placed at the start of a block, so that variables, conditions, etc. will exist before they are used in the block. They also disappear when the program exits the block.

Variables are easy to understand and use the standard SQL data types. This is like any other programming language. Declaring SQL conditions and handlers is a bit strange. It might be easier to show with an example:

```
DECLARE overflow CONDITION FOR SQLSTATE '22003';
DECLARE EXIT HANDLER FOR overflow;
```

The first declaration gives a name the SQLSTATE code for a mathematical overflow to make the code easier to read. But you will probably use one of these three built-in condition names:

- NOT FOUND

Identifies any condition that results in an SQLCODE of +100 or an SQLSTATE beginning with the characters '02'.

- SQLEXCEPTION

Identifies any condition that results in a negative SQLCODE.

- SQLWARNING

Identifies any condition that results in a warning condition, or that results in a positive SQL return code other than +100. The corresponding SQLSTATE value will begin with the characters '01'. The old SQLCODE is still supported in many SQL products. It is a numeric code that has been replaced by the five-character SQLSTATE. Negative SQLCODE values are fatal errors, zero is normal execution, and positive numbers are warnings.

- CONTINUE

Specifies that after the procedure statement completes, execution continues with the statement after the statement that caused the error.

- EXIT

Specifies that after the procedure statement completes, execution continues at the end of the compound statement that contains the handler.

- UNDO

Specifies that before the procedure statement executes, SQL rolls back any SQL operations that have occurred in the compound statement that contains the handler. After the procedure statement completes, execution continues at the end of the compound statement that contains the handler. *You can only declare UNDO handlers in ATOMIC compound statements.* This is like a ROLLBACK in a transaction.

You should declare separate HANDLER statements to handle specific SQL errors, but declare a generalized HANDLER FOR SQLEXCEPTION and SQLWARNING at the outermost compound statement. Be careful coding CONTINUE HANDLER declarations; you can keep bad data.

You can retrieve diagnostic information using the GET DIAGNOSTICS statement; I am not discussing it here.

38.4.2 Compound Statements

This language uses two versions of the begin-end pair found in other languages. The syntax is

```
[<label>:] BEGIN [NOT [ATOMIC]] <SQL/PSM statements> END <label>;
```

The <label> is an optional name for the block and that name can be used in error messages. The tricky part is the "begin atomic" option. This makes the enclosed statements into a single unit of work, like transaction. ATOMIC blocks cannot have COMMIT or ROLLBACK statements and the only handler allowed is UNDO. While redundant, the NOT ATOMIC option is allowed and it is the default if nothing is given.

38.4.3 SIGNAL and RESIGNAL Statements

You use the SIGNAL and RESIGNAL statements to explicitly raise a specific SQLSTATE. The SET MESSAGE_TEXT clause gives the text displayed with the SQLSTATE. Since we can add custom SQL STATE codes, they can only be signaled this way.

Again, it is easier to show an example:

```
DECLARE EXIT HANDLER FOR SQLSTATE '72822';
BEGIN
IF (silly_flg = 'OK')
THEN RESIGNAL SQLSTATE '72623'
 SET MESSAGE_TEXT = 'signaled SQLSTATE 72822';
ELSE RESIGNAL SQLSTATE '72319'
 SET MESSAGE_TEXT = silly_flg;
END IF;
END;

SIGNAL SQLSTATE '72822';
```

This fragment declares a condition handler for the custom SQLSTATE 72822. When the SQL procedure executes the SIGNAL statement that raises SQLSTATE 72822, SQL invokes the condition handler. The condition handler tests the value of the SQL variable silly_flg with an IF statement. If silly_flg = 'OK', the handler redefines the SQLSTATE value as 72623 and assigns a string literal to the text associated with SQLSTATE 72623. If silly_flg <> 'OK' then the handler redefines the SQLSTATE value as 72319 and assigns the value of the string silly_flg to the text associated with that SQLSTATE.

38.4.4 Assignment Statements

The keyword SET is used in the UPDATE statement to change the values in a column. But it is also used to change schema level parameters like constraints (DEFERRED or IMMEDIATE), time zone, TRANSACTION ISOLATION LEVEL, etc.

Change connection parameters, such as the user name or the time zone or the default schema. In SQL/PSM we will tend to use it for assigning a value for variable.

```
SET <variable name> = <expression>;
```

38.4.5 Conditional Statements

There are two forms of conditional execution statements, the IF and the CASE. The syntax for the simple IF statement is the same as other languages.

```
IF <conditional expression>
THEN <statement list>
[ELSE <statement list>] END IF;
```

If the conditional expression yields TRUE, the statement in the THEN clause is executed. If the conditional expression tests to FALSE or UNKNOWN, then the ELSE clause is executed.

One or more IF statements can be nested, one within the other, by using an ELSEIF clause in place of the ELSE clause in the IF statement containing another.

```
IF <conditional expression>
THEN <statement list>
ELSEIF <conditional expression>
 THEN <statement list>
 ELSE <statement list>
END IF;
```

Once the SQL statements to be executed have been selected, they execute in the same way as any ordinary list of SQL statements. This is important when creating handlers.

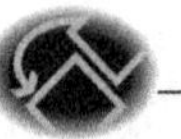

Examples:

```
IF a > 50 THEN
SET a = 50;
SET b = 1;
ELSE
SET b = 0;
END IF;

IF a > 50 THEN
SET a = 50;
SET b = 2;
ELSEIF a > 25
THEN SET b = 1;
ELSE SET b = 0;
END IF;
```

SQL/PSM has a CASE statement, which is not to be confused with the CASE expression in SQL. The simple CASE statement looks like the simple CASE expression with statement lists instead of scalar expressions in the THEN and ELSE clauses. Another difference is that it ends with END CASE, to keep the ADA-style statement terminators

A simple CASE works by evaluating equality between one value expression and one or more alternatives of a second value expression. For example:

```
BEGIN
DECLARE b INTEGER;

CASE b
WHEN 1 THEN UPDATE Foobar SET x =1;
WHEN 2 THEN UPDATE Foobar SET x =2;
WHEN 3 THEN UPDATE Foobar SET x =3;
ELSE UPDATE Foobar SET x =4;
 END CASE;
END;
```

Like wise the searched CASE statement works the same way.

A searched CASE works by evaluating, for truth, a number of alternative search conditions. For example:

```
CASE
 WHEN EXISTS (SELECT * FROM BILL)
```

```
THEN UPDATE Foobar SET x = 1;
 WHEN a > 0 OR b = 1
THEN UPDATE Foobar SET x = a + b;
 ELSE UPDATE Foobar SET x = -99;
END CASE;
```

A list of one or more SQL statements can follow the THEN clause for each of the conditional statements. Each alternative list of SQL statements in a CASE statement is treated in the same way, with respect to the behavior of exception handlers and so forth. They are not considered, in any sense, to be a single statement.

The conditional part of each WHEN clause is evaluated, working from the top of the CASE statement down. The SQL statements that are actually executed are those following the THEN clause of the first WHEN condition to evaluate to TRUE. If none of the WHEN conditions evaluate to TRUE, the SQL statements following the CASE statement ELSE clause are executed.

The presence of an ELSE clause in the CASE statement is optional and if it is not present (and none of the WHEN conditions evaluate to TRUE) an exception condition is raised to indicate that a WHEN or ELSE clause was not found for the CASE statement. If you do not want this exception, use an empty statement—ELSE BEGIN END.

38.4.6 Loops

SQL/PSM went crazy with looping constructs. If you are old enough to remember the Structured Programming Revolution of the 1970s, we started with the simple WHILE or pre-test loop, from, Algol and then added the REPEAT or post-test.

The LOOP statement contains a list of one or more SQL statements that are executed, in order, repeatedly. By itself, it is endless, but you can terminate it with the LEAVE statement, or if an exception condition is raised. You need to put label on the LOOP to use the LEAVE. Again, an example is easier to see.

Example:

```
[<label>:] LOOP
<statement list>
IF <conditional expression> LEAVE <label>;
<statement list>
END LOOP [<label>];
```

Obviously you can write a pre-test or post-test loop with this or a more general loop that exits at any desired point in the execution. SQL/PSM has the classic pre- and post-test loops, while and repeat.

The WHILE loop may be preceded by a label that can be used as an argument to LEAVE in order to terminate the while loop. The WHILE statement can contain a list of one or more SQL statements that are executed, repeatedly until the condition expression is FALSE. This also means that it can be executed zero times if the condition is false at the start.

```
[<label>:] WHILE <conditional expression>
<statement list>
END WHILE [<label>];
```

The REPEAT statement includes an UNTIL clause, which specifies a conditional expression, and iteration continues until this expression evaluates to TRUE. Iteration may also be terminated by executing the LEAVE statement, or if an exception condition is raised.

```
[<label>:] REPEAT
<statement list>;
UNTIL <conditional expression>
END REPEAT [<label>];
```

The ITERATE statement can be used to skip statements. It says go back to the start of the labeled looping statement which contains it. If you have nested labeled statements, control will jump to the label on that statement without regard to the nesting levels.

38.4.7 PRINT Statement

This one explains itself. It is not fancy and does no detailed display formatting. It is used to pass a message to the programmer.

38.4.8 CALL Statements

This keyword is taken from FORTRAN! The argument values given to the parameters in the list are in the same order as the procedure declaration.

```
CALL <procedure name> ([<parameter list>])
```

The argument data type has to be cast to the parameter data type.

38.4.9 CREATE PROCEDURE and CREATE FUNCTION

This is the important stuff. The syntax for the header is partially ADA and features unique to SQL/PSM. The header tells the compiler more information than previous languages.

The SQL/PSM can tell the compiler if the body is in one of the supported ANSI/ISO Standard languages (FORTRAN, COBOL, C, ADA, etc.) with SQL interfaces defined for them. This is part of the ADA heritage in a weird way. I worked with ADA when it was first created and we found it to be unusable for embedded systems. We did "hag fish" programming; this is a horrible technique where you put an ADA wrapper around the real program to meet a legal requirement. For us, this was usually in C, Assembly, or FORTH which are languages suited for designed for embedded systems.

The header tells the compiler if the function or procedure is or is not deterministic. A deterministic code module always produces the same result when invoked with the same parameters. This is important for an optimizer to know in a functional or declarative language. The optimizer can build a look-up table during execution and use it without recomputing the function or procedure over and over.

The header has three different options for the routine access clause (CONTAINS SQL, READS SQL DATA, and MODIFIES SQL DATA), so the optimizer knows how to set up storage and access control.

The parameter list is made of column names that are unique within the scope of the routine body. Each parameter has an optional mode specification (`IN`, `OUT`, or `INOUT`). When the mode is not explicitly specified, `IN` is assumed. This is a solution to how parameters are passed which was a hot topic when Algol-60 was new. The old system had a "call by value" which says that the parameter is evaluated and that value is assigned to a local variable in the scope of the routine. The parameter could be an expression in this model. In contrast, there is "call by name" where the parameter is an expression that is plugged directly into the body of the routine. You can get a good overview at http://en.wikipedia.org/wiki/Evaluation_strategy.

In the SQL/PSM model, each parameter has a local variable in the scope of the procedure. Each parameter of a procedure can have an optional mode specification (IN, OUT, or INOUT). These are defined as:

IN

The parameter is effectively read-only, that is, it cannot be used as the target in an assignment, fetch or select into statement in the procedure.

OUT

The parameter is effectively write-only, that is, it can only be used as the target for an assignment and cannot be used in a value expression in the procedure. This type of parameter must be a variable in the procedure CALL statement.

INOUT

The parameter can be used as both an IN and an OUT parameter; this type of parameter must be a variable in the procedure CALL statement.

If no mode is given then IN is implicit. All the parameters in a function have to be IN mode.

The RETURN statement jumps out of the whole routine and control goes to the containing environment. A function has to use a "RETURN <scalar value>" statement in the body which gives the function its value as it leaves.

There are two major idioms in SQL/PSM.

1. The body of the routine is pure declarative SQL. This is used to encapsulate SQL that might have been submitted via a tool.
2. The body of the routine is a cursor that is used like a sequential file. This is popular with Oracle programmers who tend to use their PL/SQL as an application development language. This is so common; SQL/PSM has a syntax to simplify the usual cursor coding.

FOR-DO Loop

In other languages, a for-loop is a counting construct that increments a local variable whose values are used in a sequence within the scope of the loop body. But in SQL/PSM, a FOR statement iterates through all rows in a result set and performs some operations for each row. This is a vast simplification compared to using a cursor. Again, easier to show an example.

```
FOR SELECT last_name, first_name
      FROM Customers
     WHERE customer_id IN
     (SELECT customer_id
        FROM Orders
       WHERE order_date
             BETWEEN DATE '2018-01-01' AND DATE '2018-06-31')
 DO CALL Classify_Name(last_name, first_name);
END FOR;
```

The FOR clause executes a SELECT statement to create a result set. Within the body of the FOR statement it is possible to reference the columns' values as ordinary variables. This also means that each item in the SELECT list must have a name and that name must be unique within the SELECT list.

The statement in the DO clause has to be an atomic statement. It is possible to use a result procedure in a FOR statement.

```
FOR CALL coming_soon('Blues')
 DO IF producer IN ('Bill Vernon', 'Bill Ham')
    THEN INSERT INTO stats(format, release_date, …)
         VALUES (format, release_date, …);
    END IF;
END FOR;
```

In this case, the correlation names for the result set and its columns in the AS clause can be used as variable names in the body of the FOR statement.

The SELECT or call statement in the FOR statement can be labeled and this label can be used to qualify variable references.

```
L1: BEGIN
    DECLARE first_name CHAR(12);
    SET first_name = 'Joe';
    FOR R1
        AS SELECT C1.last_name
            FROM Customers AS C1
     DO IF L1.first_name <> R1.first_name
        THEN
        ..
        END IF;
    END FOR;
END;
```

The label used cannot be the same as any label of a compound statement enclosing the FOR statement.

38.5 CSV Parameters

The use of the comma-separated list of parameters to a SQL routine, that Phil Factor calls the 'comedy-limited list', is a device that makes seasoned SQL Database developers wince. I am embarrassed that about once a month

someone on an SQL forum will post a request how to pass a CSV (comma separated values) list in a string as a parameter to a stored procedure. For SQL Server programmers the definitive articles are at Erland Sommarskog's website, but the methods will port. The approaches to this problem can be classified as (1) Iterative algorithms, (2) Auxiliary tables, and (3) Non-SQL tools.

The iterative approaches explain themselves. Just imagine that you are back in your freshman C or Assembly language programming class and are working at the lowest level you can. Read the CSV from left to right. When you get to a comma, convert the substring to the left of the comma into the target data type. Drop the comma; repeat the WHILE loop until you have consumed the string. A more recent variation is to use a Recursive CTE, but it is essentially the same thing.

Another classic approach is to use a Series table (a list of numbers from 1 to n). First put a comma on both ends of the input string. All of the substrings we want to cast are bracketed by commas, so we extract them as a set. Here is one version of these procedures.

```
CREATE PROCEDURE ParseList (IN in_csv_string VARCHAR(1000))
LANGUAGE SQL
SELECT S1.i,
       CAST (SUBSTRING (in_csv_string
                        FROM S1.i FOR MIN(S2.i) - S1.i - 1) AS INTEGER)
       AS param
 INTO cvs_list
  FROM Series AS S1, Series AS S2
 WHERE S1.i < S2.i
   AND S1.i <= LEN(in_csv_string) + 2
   AND S2.i <= LEN(in_csv_string) + 2
   AND SUBSTRING(',' || in_csv_string || ',' FROM S1.i FOR 1) = ','
   AND SUBSTRING(',' || in_csv_string || ',' FROM S2.i FOR 1) = ','
 GROUP BY S1.i;
```

To be honest, you would probably want to trim blanks and perhaps do other tests on the string, such as seeing that LOWER(in_csv_string) = UPPER(in_csv_string) to avoid alphabetic characters, and so forth.

The integer substrings are located between the (i)-th and (i+1)-th comma pairs. In effect, the sequence table replaces the loop counter.

Finally, the external methods involve an external, non_SQL function usually XML processing. The most fundamental complaint against them is maintaining code. Your routine will be written in one of the dozens of external languages and you are assuming that the next guy will also be fluent. The same complaint about extra maintenance work can be made against XML. The SQL optimizer is never going to do anything with this external code, and the overhead of passing data via various APIs will never go away.

The long parameter list uses parameters to build a local table inside the procedure body. SQL Server can handle up to 2100 parameters, which should be more than enough for practical purposes. SQL Server is actually a wimp in this regard; DB2 can pass 32 K parameters, and Oracle can have 64 K parameters. Their database engines use those extreme limits for certain system functions that the users will never see. Nobody expects a human being to type in thousands of lines of CSV text with any of these techniques. In practice, I have seen a list of 64 (Chessboard), 81 (Sudoku solver), and 361 (Go board) simple parameters. Most of the time, 100 parameters is a very safe upper limit. If I need to pass more then I want to look at an ETL tool or something else.

The main advantages of the long parameter lists are:

1. The code is highly portable to any Standard SQL. One product bigots need to get over the idea that they are never going to see more than one SQL engine in their careers.

2. The code is pure native SQL and not an external procedural language. The people that maintain it can be SQL programmers. There will be no need to send your C programmer to F classes next year to keep up.

3. The optimizer will treat them like any other parameter. They can be sniffed. You can use a RECOMPILE option and get the best performance possible each time the procedure runs.

4. The compiler will treat them like any other parameter. You get the expected error messages and conversion. Frankly, I have never seen anyone who used one of the other techniques write calls to return the same error messages as the compiler.

5. It is easy to generate the code with a text editor. Think about how hard it is to write in an external language you don't know or to write a loop in T-SQL. I just cut & paste a skeleton with 250 parameters then cut off what I need. I am going to show a list of five parameters in my skeleton code to save space.

6. The simplest example of the long parameter list technique is just to use them: Pass what you need and leave the rest of the list to default to NULLs.

```
CREATE TABLE Zoo
(sku CHAR(11) NOT NULL PRIMARY KEY,
 animal_name VARCHAR(25) NOT NULL);
INSERT INTO Zoo (sku, animal_name)
VALUES ('39634-62349', 'Horse'),
       ('74088-65564', 'Cow'),
       ('16379-19713', 'Pig'),
       ('39153-69459', 'Yak'),
       ('17986-24537', 'Aardvark'),
       ('14595-35050', 'Moose'),
       ('40469-27478', 'Dog'),
       ('44526-67331', 'Cat'),
       ('93365-54526', 'Tiger'),
       ('22356-93208', 'Elephant');

CREATE PROCEDURE Animal_Picker
(in_p1 CHAR(11),
 in_p2 CHAR(11),
 in_p3 CHAR(11),
 in_p4 CHAR(11),
 in_p5 CHAR(11))
SELECT sku, animal_name
INTO Shopping_list
FROM Zoo
     INNER JOIN
     (VALUES(in_p1), (in_p2), (in_p3), (in_p4), (in_p5))
     AS X(sku)
     ON X.sku = Zoo.sku;
CALL Animal_Picker ('39153-69459', '17986-24537', '99999-99999');
```

We need to get the data into a column in a derived table with a VALUES row constructor. NULLs will be left out of the join. The long parameter list is made up of plain old parameters, which means that they can be used for outputs as well as inputs. It is also contained in one statement for the optimizer to use. As an aside, when Erlang tested the long parameter list, he got 19 ms in execution time for 2000 elements which was better than any other method that he tested. But when he ran the procedure from PHP, the total time jumped to over 550 ms, which was horrible. I have no idea what PHP is doing and have had no problems with other host languages.

All but the table-valued parameter approach require that you scrub the input string, if you want data integrity. If the data is already in a table, then you know it is good to go. You can pass local variables with the long parameter list, but not with CSV.

Data scrubbing is hard enough in SQL, but when you have to worry about external language syntax differences, it is a serious problem. Quickly, which languages accept '1E2' versus '1.0E2' versus 'E2.0' for floating point notation? Which ones cast a string like '123abc' to integer 123 and which blow up?

The long parameter code is highly portable to any Standard SQL. It can take advantage of any improvements in the basic SQL engine. The optimizer will treat the members of the long parameter list like any other parameter. They can be sniffed. You can use a RECOMPILE option and get the best performance possible each time the procedure runs. It means that I get the same error messages, testing and logic as any other parameter. *When I use a home-made or external parser, I do not.* Frankly, I have never seen anyone who used one of the other techniques write SIGNAL calls to return the same error messages as the compiler.

A handy example of the technique is to insert a st of children under a parent in a Nested Set model. Let's assume we have a basic Nested Set tree table:

```
CREATE TABLE Tree
(node_name VARCHAR(15) NOT NULL,
 lft INTEGER NOT NULL CHECK (lft > 0) UNIQUE,
 rgt INTEGER NOT NULL CHECK (rgt > 0) UNIQUE,
  CHECK (lft < rgt));

-- Now add the root node to get things started:

INSERT INTO Tree VALUES ('Global', 1, 2);

CREATE PROCEDURE Insert_Children_Into_Tree
(in_root_node VARCHAR(15),
 in_child_01 VARCHAR(15),
```

```
 in_child_02 VARCHAR(15),
 in_child_03 VARCHAR(15),
 in_child_04 VARCHAR(15),
 in_child_05 VARCHAR(15),
 in_child_06 VARCHAR(15),
 in_child_07 VARCHAR(15),
 in_child_08 VARCHAR(15),
 in_child_09 VARCHAR(15),
 in_child_10 VARCHAR(15))
BEGIN

-- Find the parent node of the new subtree

DECLARE local_parent_rgt INTEGER;
SET local_parent_rgt
    = (SELECT rgt
         FROM Tree
        WHERE node_name = in_root_node);

-- Put the children into kindergarten; I just had to be cute.

SELECT node_name,
       (lft + local_parent_rgt -1) AS lft,
       (rgt + local_parent_rgt -1) AS rgt
  INTO Local_Kindergarten
  FROM (VALUES (in_child_01, 1, 2),
               (in_child_02, 3, 4),
               (in_child_03, 5, 6),
               (in_child_04, 7, 8),
               (in_child_05, 9, 10),
               (in_child_06, 11, 12),
               (in_child_07, 13, 14),
               (in_child_08, 15, 16),
               (in_child_09, 17, 18),
               (in_child_10, 19, 20))
       AS Kids (node_name, lft, rgt)
 WHERE node_name IS NOT NULL;
--Use the size of the kindergarten to make a gap in the Tree
```

```
UPDATE Tree
   SET lft = CASE WHEN lft > local_parent_rgt
                  THEN lft + (2 * (SELECT COUNT(*) FROM Local_
Kindergarten))
                  ELSE lft END,
       rgt = CASE WHEN rgt >= local_parent_rgt
                  THEN rgt + (2 * (SELECT COUNT(*) FROM Local_
Kindergarten))
                  ELSE lft END
  WHERE lft > local_parent_rgt
     OR rgt >= local_parent_rgt;

-- Insert kindergarten all at once as a set
INSERT INTO Tree (node_name, lft, rgt)
SELECT node_name, lft, rgt
  FROM Local_Kindergarten;

END;
```

The procedure shown here only does 10 children, but it can be easily extended to 100 or 1000 if needed. The sibling order is the same as the parameter list order. You could also add text edits and other validation and verification code to the statement that built Kindergarten.

```
CALL Insert_Children_Into_Tree
('Global', 'USA', 'Canada', 'Europe', 'Asia');
```

Now that USA is in place, add its substree:

```
CALL Insert_Children_Into_Tree ('USA', 'Texas', 'Georgia', 'Utah',
'New York', 'Maine', 'Alabama');
```

INDEX

Note: Page numbers followed by *f* indicate figures and *t* indicate tables.

A

D

E

F

J

K

Printed in the United States
By Bookmasters